W9-ABE-496

# Valuing Intangible
# Assets

# Valuing Intangible Assets

**ROBERT F. REILLY, CFA, ASA, CPA**
Managing Director
*Willamette Management Associates*

**ROBERT P. SCHWEIHS, ASA**
Managing Director
*Willamette Management Associates*

**McGraw-Hill**

New York   San Francisco   Washington, D.C.   Auckland   Bogotá
Caracas   Lisbon   London   Madrid   Mexico City   Milan
Montreal   New Delhi   San Juan   Singapore
Sydney   Tokyo   Toronto

**Library of Congress Cataloging-in-Publication Data**

Reilly, Robert F.
    Valuing intangible assets   /   Robert F. Reilly, Robert P. Schweihs.
        p.   cm.
    ISBN 0-7863-1065-0
    1. Intangible property—Valuation.   I. Schweihs, Robert P.
II. Title.
    HF5681.I55R45   1998
    657'.7—dc21                                   98-13959
                                                   CIP

## McGraw-Hill

*A Division of The **McGraw·Hill** Companies*

Copyright © 1999 by Robert F. Reilly and Robert P. Schweihs. All rights reserved. Printed in the United States of America. Except as permitted under the United States Copyright Act of 1976, no part of this publication may be reproduced or distributed in any form or by any means, or stored in a database or retrieval system, without the prior written permission of the publisher.

34567890 QWK/QWK 0987654321

ISBN 0-7863-1065-0

*The sponsoring editor for this book was Roger Marsh and the production supervisor was Suzanne W. B. Rapcavage. It was set in Palatino by Inkwell Publishing Services.*

*Printed and bound by R.R. Donnelley & Sons Company.*

This publication is designed to provide accurate and authoritative information in regard to the subject matter covered. It is sold with the understanding that neither the author nor the publisher is engaged in rendering legal, accounting, or other professional service. If legal advice or other expert assistance is required, the services of a competent professional person should be sought.

> —*From a Declaration of Principles jointly adopted by a Committee of the American Bar Association and a Committee of Publishers.*

McGraw-Hill books are available at special quantity discounts to use as premiums and sales promotions, or for use in corporate training programs. For more information, please write to the Director of Special Sales, McGraw-Hill, 11 West 19th Street, New York, NY 10011. Or contact your local bookstore.

This book is printed on acid-free paper.

*To our wives and children.*

# Contents

*Appraisal. The Purpose of the Appraisal.* Selecting the Appropriate Standard of Value. Selecting the Appropriate Premise of Value. *Highest and Best Use Analysis. Alternative Premises of Value.* Describing the Particular Intangible Asset Subject to Appraisal. Describing the Bundle of Legal Rights Subject to Appraisal. Selecting the Appropriate Valuation Date. Communicating the Valuation Assignment in a Client Engagement Letter. Summary.

**PART II**
**INTANGIBLE ASSET VALUATION APPROACHES, METHODS, AND PROCEDURES**

Reconciling an Inconsistency of Results among Valuation
Approaches and Methods. Summary.

# List of Exhibits

# Preface

## Intent of the Book

This book covers a number of related topics, all of which may be generally described as the analysis and appraisal of intangible assets.

The first and principal topic relates to the valuation of intangible assets. This topic involves the estimation of a defined monetary value for a subject intangible.

The second topic relates to the economic analysis of intangible assets. This topic includes the estimation of the effect on an economic unit of the use or ownership of an intangible asset—for example, estimating the incremental value to a business of being awarded a major contract or a new patent. This topic also entails the estimation of the effect on an intangible asset of an exogenous event or influence—for example, estimating the value decrement or other measure of economic damages to a trademark due to an infringement.

The third topic relates to the analysis of the appropriate transfer price for an intangible asset. This topic involves estimating the sale price for an intangible asset—that is the transfer of a fee simple ownership interest in the asset. Sometimes intangible asset transfer price analysis entails estimating a license fee or royalty rate. In this case, the third topic includes the lease, license, or other transfer of certain ownership rights to the intangible for a certain period of time. Finally, this topic covers the estimation of an intercompany transfer price—a fair, market-derived economic rent to pay for the use of an intangible asset, such as proprietary technology or computer software.

It should be noted that throughout all these topics related to the analysis and appraisal of intangible assets, there is a common subtopic that cannot be overlooked. That subtopic may be the most complex—and sometimes the most critical—element of the analysis and appraisal of intangibles: the remaining useful life analysis of intangibles. That element of technical analysis (whether it be implicit or explicit) is one aspect of each of the other topics: valuation, economic event analysis or damage analysis, and transfer pricing.

This book responds to the challenge of documenting a recognizable, systematic approach to valuing intangible assets. Its intent is to clarify and advance the debate on a complex and controversial subject matter. Generally accepted financial valuation techniques regarding intangible assets continue to evolve, just as have the generally accepted valuation techniques regarding tangible real estate and tangible personal property. Future editions of this book will continue the process of explaining and documenting generally accepted intangible asset valuation techniques.

# Content of the Book

This book is presented in six parts. The earlier parts are intended to be more general and fundamental in nature. Later chapters build on the earlier chapters, and they are more specific and more advanced in nature.

Part I presents an introduction and overview to the valuation and economic analysis of intangible assets. Chapter 1 discusses the general methods associated with identifying (or recognizing the legal existence of) intangible assets and with valuing (or recognizing the economic existence of) intangible assets. Chapter 2 also explains many of the more common events that create a reason for conducting a valuation or economic analysis of intangible assets. Chapter 3 discusses professional standards related to intangible asset appraisals. Chapter 4 provides an overview of the basic concepts related to valuing (or recognizing the economic existence of) intangible assets. Chapter 5 introduces the basic procedures related to intangible asset data collection and analysis.

Part II explains the generally accepted intangible asset valuation approaches, methods, and procedures. These approaches, methods, and procedures are presented within the logical context of what is called the appraisal process. Chapters 6 through 10 discuss the proper applications of these analytical procedures and present numerous examples.

Part III discusses the remaining useful life analysis of intangible assets. Various quantitative and qualitative remaining useful life analyses are presented and contrasted. Chapters 11 and 12 discuss the proper applications of these lifing-related analytical procedures and present numerous examples.

Part IV discusses the logical process for reaching an overall analytical conclusion. Chapters 13, 14, and 15 describe the process for synthesizing various alternative analysis methods and quantitative indications and explain the thought process for reaching a final conclusion from among a range of analytical results. As we shall see, this thought process is valid regardless of whether the conclusion is a value estimate, a damage estimate, a royalty rate or transfer price determination, or a remaining useful life or decay rate indication.

Part V describes the analyses associated with various individual categories of intangible assets. Chapters 16 through 24 describe various common categories of intangible assets. Category-specific valuation methods are explained, and category-specific data sources are referenced. An example is provided for each category of intangible asset.

Part VI presents the application of intangible asset valuation and economic analysis procedures to transfer pricing analysis in Chapter 25. Chapter 26 gives detailed examples of intangible asset valuation and economic analysis under several different sets of circumstances and for several different purposes.

## Audience for the Book

This book should be useful to a variety of constituencies who are interested in the valuation and economic analysis of intangible assets, including:

1. Intangible asset owners (individual and institutional) who want to consider strategic alternatives in order to maximize the value of their ownership interests.

2. Intangible asset creators (individual and institutional) who want to implement programs to commercialize, and thereby create value from, their developments.

3. Accountants who want to measure the value of intangible assets for various recording, taxation, or regulatory purposes.

4. Attorneys who want to best represent their clients when those clients are exposed to—or initiate—an event that will affect the historical or prospective economic value of an intangible asset.

5. Market makers who are involved in negotiating and structuring intangible asset license, sale, sale-leaseback, financing, and other commercial exploitation agreements.

6. Appraisers, economists, and financial analysts who are involved in the valuation analysis of intangible assets either as individual economic entities or as contributors to the overall going-concern value of a business enterprise.

Each audience may have different levels of interest in the theoretical concepts, practical applications, and empirical data presented in this book. One word of caution is in order, however. Casual readers of a book like this often read only the first part and convince themselves that they have a rigorous comprehension of this complex subject. The valuation and economic analysis of intangible assets is an evolving discipline. Even the serious reader of the entire book will begin—but not complete—an exploration of this complex topic.

*Robert F. Reilly*
*Robert P. Schweihs*
*Chicago, Illinois*

# Acknowledgments

Many of our colleagues at Willamette Management Associates provided valuable assistance with this book. In particular, we would like to recognize the following individuals.

Charlene M. Blalock, a research associate in the Portland office, served as the project manager for this undertaking. Charlene coordinated all aspects of the writing and publication of this book. She was responsible for obtaining permission to use material reprinted in this book from other sources. Charlene also prepared the index and edited and proofread the manuscript. This book would simply not have been completed without Charlene's dedication and project management.

Manoj Dandekar, a senior associate in the firm's McLean, Virginia, office, prepared Chapter 11, Life Analysis and Remaining Useful Life Estimation. Manoj was also responsible for checking all of the mathematical calculations.

Pamela Garland, a senior associate in the firm's Chicago office, was responsible for drafting two chapters: Chapter 19, Data Processing Intangible Assets, and Chapter 26, Case Studies.

Tom Millon, a principal of the firm and director of the McLean, Virginia office, was responsible for drafting two chapters: Chapter 15, Sample Intangible Asset Valuation Opinion Report, and Chapter 25, Intercompany Transfer Pricing and Royalty Rate Analysis. Tom also reviewed the entire manuscript and provided valuable comments.

James Rabe, a principal of the firm and codirector of the Portland, Oregon office, prepared two chapters: Chapter 21, Human Capital Intangible Assets, and Chapter 23, Marketing Intangible Assets.

Charles Wilhoite, a principal of the firm and codirector of the Portland, Oregon office, prepared two chapters: Chapter 16, Contract Intangible Assets, and Chapter 24, Technology Intangible Assets.

Victoria Platt, a senior associate in the Chicago office and director of information services, and Charlene Blalock, a research associate in the Portland office, prepared the chapter bibliographies. Victoria Platt also prepared the Data Sources sections of several of the chapters. Jan Tudor, a former member of the firm's Portland, Oregon office, drafted Chapter 5, Data Collection and Analysis, and provided information for some of the bibliographies.

The authors have reviewed and edited all of the chapters written by others and take final responsibility for their content.

Mary McCallister, office manager of the Chicago office, was responsible for typing the majority of the manuscript.

We are very grateful for the assistance of all these people.

For permission to use material, we especially wish to thank:

The Appraisal Foundation
Iowa State University Press
McGraw-Hill
Quantitative Software Management, Inc.
Appraisal Institute
John Wiley & Sons
Nolo Press
West Publishing Co.

*Robert F. Reilly*
*Robert P. Schweihs*
*Chicago, Illinois*

Acknowledgments

# Introduction

## Evolution of This Subject

The appraisal and analysis of intangible assets has directly evolved from the academic discipline of economics. The theoretical concepts and quantitative procedures that collectively represent intangible asset valuation are unambiguous applications of applied microeconomics.

Indeed, the collective body of appraisal theory and practice—including the valuation of intangible assets—can ultimately be traced back to the classical economist, Adam Smith, and to his landmark treatise *The Wealth of Nations* that was published in 1776. Of course, the study of economic relationships has been greatly expanded and refined over the centuries. But the theoretical underpinnings of modern appraisal practice can be traced through Adam Smith to the classical economists David Ricardo and Thomas Malthus and, through them, to the neoclassical economists John Stuart Mill, Léon Walras, Alfred Marshall, and Irving Fisher. Of these inspired economists, Alfred Marshall presented the most comprehensive and cogent discussion of "value theory" in his authoritative text, *Principles of Economics,* published in 1890. Economic theory was brought into the modern era—and the foundations of appraisal theory embedded within economic theory became particularly obvious—in *The General Theory of Employment, Interest and Money,* the landmark work published in 1936 by John Meynard Keynes.

Around the time that Keynes published his authoritative text, "value theory" was beginning to be segmented for application to different types of assets, properties, and business interests. A number of land economists focused on the development of real estate appraisal analysis. The work of many of these land economists was ultimately synthesized in the first edition of *The Appraisal of Real Estate,* published in 1951 by the (then) Society of Real Estate Appraisers. A number of financial economists focused on the development of business appraisal and security analysis. The classic example of the development of this discipline segment is Benjamin Graham and David Dodd's *Security Analysis,* first published in 1934.

In 1937, James Bonbright (then a professor of finance at Columbia University) published *The Valuation of Property.* Bonbright attempted to integrate the value theories of the land economists with those of the financial economists. He recognized that the common element in these theories was that the analyst is attempting to value property rights—or the bundle of legal rights and economic benefits related to property ownership (regardless of whether the property is real or personal, tangible or intangible).

The work begun by these economists has continuously evolved and (for better or worse) been further segmented to create the current state of the intangible asset valuation discipline.

## Is the Discipline a Science or an Art?

More than the most esoteric technique or arcane formula used in intangible asset valuation, this question is academic and pedantic and without a purposeful answer. Nonetheless, the question is asked often enough that it should be addressed.

Intangible asset valuation is not a science in the same sense that chemistry and physics are sciences. In those disciplines, there are natural relationships that can be measured with certainty and precision. In chemistry, precise relationships exist between pressure, volume, and temperature. In physics, there are precise relationships between mass, energy, and velocity. These exact and repeatable relationships are based on the laws of nature. There are no corresponding universal laws of nature that relate to intangible asset valuation.

However, intangible asset valuation is a science in the sense that mathematics and economics are sciences. These soft sciences are based on logical relationships, rules of order, consistency, and generally accepted analytical protocols. Based upon such protocols, the various disciplines within mathematics, such as algebra, trigonometry, and calculus, function efficiently. Based upon similar protocols, the various disciplines within economics, such as money and banking, macroeconomics, land economics, and intangible asset valuation, function efficiently.

Some analysts assert that the valuation discipline is purely an art because the application of the discipline requires skill, experience, judgment, knowledge, study, and observation. It is true that the successful application of this discipline does require all these attributes. Of course, the same could be said for the successful application of physical chemistry, astrophysics, or any other recognized hard science.

If the art versus science debate is worth recognizing at all, the answer may be that the valuation discipline incorporates the best elements of both art and science.

## Questions That Intangible Asset Analysis Will Answer

Practitioners involved in the valuation and economic analysis of intangible assets routinely address a variety of legitimate and complicated questions. These questions are often posed by intangible asset owners, by their accounting or legal advisors, by transaction participants, by transaction financing sources, and by lawyers and judges within the context of a controversy. This book is intended to provide a rational framework that will allow the analyst to study and answer questions such as the following:

1. What is an intangible asset? How does one identify an intangible asset? What set of attributes does a property need to have in order to qualify as an intangible asset?

2. What is the worth of an intangible asset? This question invariably leads to the question: Worth to whom? What is the value of the intangible to its current owner? Is that value different from the

value of the intangible to a particular buyer or licensee? Is that value different from the value of the intangible to the commercial marketplace in general?

3. What effect will a certain set of circumstances or events have on the worth of the intangible asset? How will the value of the intangible asset change in response to changes in market conditions, in the competitive environment, in the physical environment in which the intangible asset is commercialized, or in the amount of capital, labor, or coordination dedicated to the intangible asset?

4. How will the intangible asset be damaged—or its value reduced—as a result of a contract, or the breach of a contract, or an infringement, or a disclosure, or a lack of disclosure, or fair or unfair competition, or undercapitalization, or mismanagement, and so on?

5. How will the value of the intangible asset be expected to change over time? Will it increase or decrease? Will it change at a slow and predictable pattern or will it change suddenly, based upon a particular event? What events will cause a change in the value of the intangible asset? What is the expected life of the intangible asset? How is that life measured? What are the consequences of a longer or shorter remaining useful life of the intangible asset?

6. How does the intangible asset affect the worth of other assets, properties, or business entities? How does the intangible affect the value of other intangible assets? Of other tangible assets? Of the overall business enterprise in which the intangible asset is employed? Will the intangible asset affect the value of one business with which it is associated in a different way than it would affect another business with which it could become associated? If so, why?

7. Should the intangible asset be analyzed as an individual, or discrete, economic entity? Should it be analyzed as an integral part of a larger economic entity—for example, as part of an overall going-concern business enterprise? How—and why—will the value of the intangible asset change between these two analytical scenarios? Which analytical scenario is more appropriate?

8. What is the highest and best use of the intangible asset? How is that highest and best use defined? How is it identified? How can the intangible asset owner or licensee achieve the highest and best use? What amounts of labor, capital, and coordination are required? Will there be an adequate economic return (or payback) on the required investments in labor, capital, and coordination?

9. What is a reasonable license fee, royalty rate, lease payment, or other transfer price for the lease of a partial ownership interest—for example, a license to use—in the intangible asset? Is the reasonable fee or rate the same to the licensor and to the licensee? Will the reasonable fee or rate be different for different potential licensees? Will it be different for different potential uses of the intangible?

**10.** What is the best way to structure the license or lease transaction? How will specific terms—such as duration, geography, use limitations, industry limitations, licensor commitments, and so forth—affect the fee or rate associated with the agreement? Is a proposed license or lease structure fair to both parties—or to either party?

Analysts encounter these and many other questions in the normal commercial study of intangible assets.

## Who Is the Appropriate Analyst?

The question as to what type of professional is best qualified to analyze intangible assets has some similarities to the art versus science question discussed earlier. Both questions are frequently asked and forcefully debated. However, the answer to either question, to the extent that there is an answer, will not meaningfully further the discipline of intangible asset analysis.

Accountants, appraisers, economists, engineers, financial analysts, license intermediaries, and other professionals have all made claim that their skills are most relevant to the valuation and analysis of intangible assets. The truth is that all their skills are relevant to this discipline. No one profession has a monopoly on logical thinking and analytical reasoning. The analysis of intangible assets may be considered a multidisciplinary activity. No one set of professional qualifications or academic training grants an individual a monopoly license to practice intangible asset valuation.

Clearly, the qualified analyst will have an understanding of, and grounding in, many academic disciplines, including accounting, appraisal, economics, finance, and so on. While qualitative judgment is essential, intangible asset valuation is fundamentally a quantitative analysis. Therefore, the qualified analyst will need well-defined mathematical skills.

In fact, intangible asset appraisal may require higher-level math skills than either real estate appraisal or business appraisal. In addition to algebra, the intangible asset analyst will need to be proficient in calculus and in intermediate statistics. If necessary, practitioners from other professions should bolster their quantitative skills before performing an intangible asset valuation or economic analysis.

Finally, analysts of every academic background should understand that their role is to interpret, explain, and quantify the actual marketplace for intangible asset transactions. It is not the function of the analyst to second-guess the market. Rather, it is the function of the analyst to emulate the market—to estimate how the appropriate market would actually respond to the subject intangible asset if the subject intangible were actually exposed to the market.

With respect to intangible asset valuation, analysts do not determine the value of intangibles. Analysts do not make the market (although they may study and form opinions on the market). Actual market participants—buyer, sellers, licensors, and licensees—make the market for intangible assets.

The analyst can predict the most likely response of the market to the subject intangible asset. In other words, the market determines value. The analyst estimates value.

# Valuing Intangible Assets

# Introduction to Intangible Asset Valuation

# Identification of
# Intangible Assets

## INTRODUCTION

This chapter focuses on the following introductory topics:

1. The definition of an intangible asset.
2. The distinction between tangible assets and intangible assets.
3. The distinction between real estate and tangible personal property.
4. The distinction between real property interests and intangible personal property.
5. Common categories of intangible assets.
6. The distinction between intangible assets and intellectual properties.

Accordingly, we will establish a framework for answering the question: What is an intangible asset? We will identify attributes or characteristics that should be present in an intangible asset. By corollary, we will attempt to answer the question: What is not an intangible asset? The absence of the necessary attributes or characteristics will indicate that the subject property (if indeed it is a property) is not an intangible asset.

## DEFINITION OF AN INTANGIBLE ASSET

There are numerous legal, accounting, or taxation-related definitions of the term *intangible asset*. However, these definitions are typically purpose-specific. An example is the definition of an intangible asset for purposes of claiming federal income tax amortization deductions under Section 197 of the Internal Revenue Code. Such narrow definitions may be appropriate only for the specific purpose for which they were created. We will attempt to create a more general definition of an intangible asset.

Before defaulting to a general purpose definition, the analyst should perform adequate research to ascertain whether a particular, purpose-specific definition is appropriate to the subject intangible asset analysis, given:

1. the particular purpose and objective of the valuation or economic analysis, and
2. the particular jurisdiction or venue in which the subject intangible assets exist.

Appropriate professional advisors (e.g., lawyers, accountants, etc.) may have to be consulted in this research. The intangible asset analyst may need professional advice to both identify and interpret the appropriate purpose-specific definition.

For purposes of this book, we will focus on the defining questions that are most relevant to the economic analysis and to the valuation of intangible assets. Accordingly, from this economic valuation perspective, there are two defining questions that the analyst should consider:

1. What economic phenomenon or property right qualifies as an intangible asset?
2. What economic phenomenon or property right manifests or is indicative of value in an intangible asset?

## Economic Phenomena That Qualify as Intangible Assets

For an intangible asset to exist from a valuation or economic perspective, typically it should possess a number of characteristics or attributes. Some of the more common characteristics or attributes necessary for qualification as an intangible asset include the following:

1. It should be subject to specific identification and recognizable description.
2. It should be subject to legal existence and protection.
3. It should be subject to the right of private ownership, and the private ownership should be legally transferable.
4. There should be some tangible evidence or manifestation of the existence of the intangible asset (e.g., a contract, a license, a registration document, a computer diskette, a listing of customers, a set of financial statements, etc.)
5. It should have been created or have come into existence at an identifiable time or as the result of an identifiable event.
6. It should be subject to being destroyed or to a termination of existence at an identifiable time or as the result of an identifiable event.

In other words, there should be a specific bundle of legal property rights associated with the existence of any intangible asset. Each of these characteristics or attributes will be described briefly.

To begin with, an intangible asset should be property. Whether an asset is tangible or intangible, it should be subject to the rights of property. For any asset to be subject to property rights, it should be able to be identified. With regard to an intangible asset, there should be a clear and concise description that will identify the particular intangible as a unique property. Of course, intangible assets cannot be easily described by reference to the metes and bounds system that is almost universally used in legal descriptions of real estate. However, an intangible asset should be subject to a fairly straightforward, "25 words or less" description.

If an intangible property cannot be identified and concretely described, then that property may not qualify as an intangible asset. That "property" may be an idea or a concept—but it may be too nebulous to qualify as an intangible asset. Likewise, that "property" may be an attribute, a characteristic, or an element of an asset; but it may not itself qualify as an intangible asset. Characteristics of intangible assets will be discussed later.

For an intangible asset to qualify as property, it should possess the legal rights of property. It should enjoy all of the legal rights, benefits, and privileges of property. Among these rights is the right of the property owner to claim ownership rights and to protect those rights in a court of law. For example, the owner of an intangible asset, like the owner of other types of property, should be able to petition the courts for relief from damages to the asset as a result of the actions of another party. The owner of an intangible asset should also be able to seek protection of the asset from the criminal actions of another party (e.g., from theft by another party).

Likewise, the owner of an intangible asset is subject to the same responsibilities as any other property owner. For example, the owner of an intangible asset may be subject to taxation and to other governmental powers. In addition, the owner of an intangible asset should be legally responsible for damages to another party caused by the intangible asset.

One of the most basic rights of property is that it is subject to private ownership and the private ownership is transferable. These attributes also apply to intangible assets. In order for it to have economic existence, the intangible should be subject to private ownership and that private ownership should be able to be transferred to a new owner. This characteristic does not necessarily mean that the private ownership has to be sold. Rather, it has to be subject to being transferred. The fact that a property can be sold is indicative of its economic value, not of its economic existence.

It is also noteworthy that this condition does not mean that all intangible assets must be transferable separately and independently from all other properties. In fact, some intangible assets are typically transferred separately and independently from other properties and others are typically transferred as an assemblage of properties (e.g., two or more intangible assets transferred collectively or intangible assets transferred with tangible assets). Nonetheless, regardless of the form or structure of the transfer, the legal ownership of the intangible assets is transferable from one property owner to another.

The next characteristic of intangible asset existence is not immediately obvious. That is, there should be some tangible evidence of the existence of an intangible asset. As will be discussed at length in a later section, the economic value of an intangible asset is not derived from or attributable to its tangible element. Nonetheless, there should be some tangible element to the intangible asset both in order for it to have economic existence and in order for it to fulfill some of the other characteristic requisites (e.g., legal protection, transferability, etc.).

Essentially, all property rights are intangible (but that is not to say that all property rights are intangible assets). However, to be enforceable, the property rights should enjoy some tangible documentation. The same concept applies to intangible assets. There should be a file, a list, a drawing, a schematic, a contract, a license, a permit, a document, a letter, a computer diskette, a computer printout, or some other tactile evidence that the intangible asset exists. Again, the intangible's economic value does not accrue from this tactility, but the intangible's economic (and legal) existence does.

For example, the customer relationships intangible may be evidenced by a customer listing, a file of historical purchase orders, a correspondence file, and so on. Franchise, license, and other contract rights are evidenced by a contract or other written agreement. Trademarks, patents, and copyrights are evidenced by written registration documents. The assembled workforce intangible may be evidenced by employee listings, personnel files, employment-related tax returns, and so forth. The proprietary technology intangible (sometimes called simply the "know-how" or "how we do things here" intangible) may be evidenced by drawings, blueprints, flowcharts, diagrams, procedure manuals, notebooks, or memorandums. The goodwill intangible and the going-concern value intangible may be evidenced by historical financial statements, income tax returns, corporate records and documentation, operational and financial budgets, business plans, and so on.

The owners of an intangible asset do not celebrate the intangible's birthday the way parents may celebrate a child's birthday. Nonetheless, an intangible asset should have a birthday. Like any other type of property, an intangible asset comes into existence at a certain point in time. Like many other types of property, an intangible asset may be created or developed over a long gestation period. And, like many other types of property, an intangible asset may evolve or change over time. Nonetheless, and although the date is not necessarily celebrated, all intangible assets that exist had to come into existence at, or by, a particular point in time.

Occasionally, the intangible asset's actual creation date (or birthday) is important to the instant analysis. In that case, one useful method for estimating the intangible's creation date is to measure the creation date of the intangible's tactile manifestation. In other words, the tangible documentation of the intangible asset's existence often provides a useful indication of the creation date of the subject intangible.

If an intangible asset is subject to coming into existence at a particular point in time, then it should be subject to going out of existence at a particular point in time. This is not to say that the intangible asset owner necessarily plans for the demise of the intangible. The intangible owner may hope and plan that the intangible will be in existence indefinitely. Likewise, the owner of an office building may hope and plan that the real estate will be in existence indefinitely. The intangible asset owner may not know in advance when the intangible will demise, and the owner of the office building may not know in advance when the real estate will demise. Nonetheless, both types of property, the intangible and the real estate, will likely cease to exist at a future point in time.

As with other types of property, there may be any number of events that cause or influence the demise of an intangible asset. A nonexhaustive list of illustrative events includes: the expiration of a contract, a franchise, or a trademark or patent registration period; the planned or unplanned replacement of the intangible with a newer intangible; the actions of a government body or of a court; or the cessation of business operations. In any case, all of these causes for the demise of an intangible asset may be associated with an identifiable event.

## Economic Phenomena That Do Not Qualify as Intangible Assets

Economic phenomena that do not meet the specific attribute or characteristic tests described in the previous section do not qualify as identifiable intangible assets. This does not mean that these economic phenomena do not exist. It simply means that these phenomena are not intangible assets.

Many economic phenomena are merely descriptive or expository in nature. These phenomena may describe conditions that contribute to the existence and value of identified intangible assets. These factors or conditions may contribute significantly to the existence of, and to the value of, a going-concern business in which intangible assets do exist. But such phenomena do not possess the requisite elements to distinguish themselves as intangible assets.

This is an important analytical and legal distinction. Unfortunately many analysts have historically confused intangible assets with intangible "factors," "elements," "influences," or "conditions." Likewise, some courts have not distinguished between intangible assets and intangible influences or factors. Indeed, intangible influences or factors do influence intangible asset value. They are just not, in and of themselves, intangible assets.

Such descriptive economic phenomena that do not qualify as identifiable intangible assets—but that may be considered intangible factors or influences—include:

1. Market share.
2. High profitability.
3. Lack of regulation.
4. A regulated (or protected) position.
5. Monopoly position (or barriers to entry).
6. Market potential.
7. Breadth of appeal.
8. Mystique.
9. Heritage or longevity.
10. Competitive edge.
11. Life-cycle status.
12. Uniqueness.
13. Discount prices.
14. Liquidity (or illiquidity).
15. Ownership control (or lack of control).

These intangible factors or influences do not qualify as intangible assets because they lack one or more of the requisite attributes. For example, these intangible factors or influences may not be transferable; or they may not be subject to private ownership; or they may not be legally recognized or legally protected; or there may be no tangible evidence of their existence.

However, while these descriptive conditions or influences do not qualify as intangible assets themselves, they may indicate that the intangible assets that do exist have substantial economic value. For example, these descriptive conditions or influences may indicate the existence of—and greatly contribute to the value of—goodwill.

In any event, intangible factors or influences may be very important contributors to intangible asset value. Likewise, they may enhance the value of tangible assets. Indeed, they may themselves have a value. For example, there is a value to high profitability (compared to low profitability); there is a value to market potential (compared to no market potential); and there is a value to liquidity (compared to illiquidity). However, since these intangible factors or influences are not property of and by themselves, the value accrues to the particular property with which these factors or influences are associated. That property could be an intangible asset, a tangible asset, a business, or the securities of a business.

## Economic Phenomena That Indicate Value in Intangible Assets

It is possible for an intangible asset to have economic existence and not have the requisite attributes in order to have economic value. For an intangible asset to have a quantifiable value from an economic analysis or appraisal perspective, it should possess certain attributes or characteristics in addition to those that indicate the legal existence of the intangible. Some of the additional attributes or characteristics that are indicative of quantifiable economic value are described in the following paragraphs.

First, in order for an intangible to have economic value, it should generate some measurable amount of economic benefit to its owner. The economic benefit to the owner may be in the form of an income increment or of a cost decrement. The economic benefit is sometimes measured by comparing the amount of economic income generated by the subject intangible to the amount of economic income otherwise available to the owner if the subject intangible did not exist. The economic benefit may be quantified using any measure of economic income, including net income (before or after tax), net operating income, gross cash flow, net cash flow, and so on.

Second, in order for an intangible asset to have economic value, it should potentially enhance the value of the other assets with which it is associated. The other assets associated with the subject intangible may include tangible personal property, (tangible) real estate, or other intangible assets. For example, if an intangible asset is added to an assemblage of other assets (tangible or intangible), the combination should result in a value increment.

In other words, the subject intangible should have a positive contributory effect on the value of the assemblage of assets. This is not to say that the measure of the contributory value is an indication of the value of the subject intangible asset. Rather, it is simply indicative of the fact that the subject intangible does add a positive value.

On the other hand, if the addition of an intangible to an assemblage of assets (tangible or intangible) results in a lower collective value for the group of assets, then the subject intangible asset probably does not have a positive economic value, at least for that purpose. This conclusion is true regardless of the standard of value or of the premise of value that is applied to appraise the assemblage of assets. The concepts of standard of value and premise of value are discussed in Chapter 4.

Clearly, there may be a substantial distinction between the economic existence of an intangible asset and the economic value of that intangible asset. An example of this situation is the new registration of a legally binding and enforceable trademark that, upon issuance, is immediately and permanently locked in the corporate vault. For whatever reason, the trademark creator has decided that it will never be used for commercial or any other purposes. If the trademark is never (and will never be) used in the production or protection of income, then it has no economic value, even though it has legal existence. The trademark will continue to have economic existence throughout the life of its legal registration period.

Of course, one way that the trademark may be used is as a defensive measure. If the trademark registration purposefully keeps the trademark (or trade name, or brand name, etc.) out of the reach of a competitor, then that trademark is being "used" in a commercial process. In that case, the defensive use of the trademark may cause the intangible to have economic value as well as economic existence.

# The Distinction between Tangible Assets and Intangible Assets

In order for an analyst to better understand what an intangible asset is, it may be helpful to understand what an intangible asset is not. Obviously, an intangible asset is not tangible. A tangible asset generally possesses all of the attributes previously discussed with regard to an intangible asset. That is, a tangible asset has all of the rights and privileges of property. For example, it is capable of private ownership and legal protection. The ownership of a tangible asset is legally transferable. The rights of a tangible asset may be protected in a court of law.

In addition to these general property attributes, a tangible asset possesses one or more conditions that an intangible asset does not, such as:

1. A tangible asset should have physical existence and substantial form; it should be corporeal.
2. A tangible asset should be capable of being touched and seen.
3. A tangible asset should be perceptible to the touch; it should be tactile.

However, a tangible asset may be either immobile (affixed to the land) or mobile (not affixed to the land). As we will see, these factors distinguish whether the tangible asset is classified as personal property or as real estate.

So far, the distinction between a tangible asset and an intangible asset is not definitive, because one of the conditions for intangible asset existence is some tangible evidence of the intangible. What then is the definitive difference between tangible assets and intangible assets? It certainly isn't this physical difference. Certainly, one can touch and see machinery and equipment, trucks and automobiles, land and buildings, jigs and fixtures, and so on. These are all tangible assets. Certainly, though, one can also touch and see a contract, a license, a franchise agreement, a blueprint, a listing of computer code, a diagram of a computer chip mask (sometimes called a master), a trademark registration, a patent registration, a copyright registration, a laboratory notebook, and so forth. Are these all tangible assets as well?

The latter group is a list of assets that are generally recognized as intangible assets. Clearly, we can all envision the tangible manifestations of these (and other) intangible assets: the documentation, the forms, the files, the drawings, the diskettes, the lists, the agreements, and so on. These manifestations are tactile, corporeal, and visible. These manifestations are essential elements for the creation of intangible asset value because without tangible manifestations, intangible assets do not exist and, as we have seen, a nonexistent asset cannot have value.

The essential difference between tangible assets and intangible assets is this:

1. The value of a tangible asset is created by its tangible nature.
2. The value of an intangible asset is created by its intangible nature.

That is, the tactile, corporeal, and visual elements of tangible assets give them value. The value of a tangible asset flows from its physical features and is entirely dependent upon the physical features. That is not the case at all with regard to intangible assets.

First, the value of intangible assets flows from the property rights associated with the ownership of the intangible asset. These rights include the right to exploit, commercialize, sell, lease, license, use, not use, hypothecate, transfer, and so forth, the intangible asset. As with all legal rights, these property rights are intangible.

Second, the value of intangible assets flows from the intangible factors or influences discussed previously. Such factors or influences as mystique, broad appeal, uniqueness, and competitive edge contribute to the value of the intangible asset. Some of the factors or influences represent the effect of the intangible asset, such as high profitability, high market share, and heritage or longevity.

In summary, the value of the intangible asset does not come from, and does not accrue to, the piece of paper that it is printed on. The piece of paper (or drawing or computer diskette) can be copied and reproduced. Rather, the value of an intangible asset comes from the property rights associated with its intangible value and the intangible factors affecting it and the intangible influences that are affected by it.

## The Relationship between Tangible and Intangible Assets

Tangible assets are often required in order to fully realize the value (or the income-producing capacity) of intangible assets. For example, you must have computer hardware (a tangible asset) in order to effectively exploit the positive attributes of computer software (an intangible asset). Working capital (and other monetary assets) and machinery and equipment are often necessary for the commercialization of intangible assets (such as patents, trademarks, copyrights, goodwill, etc.).

This is not to say that intangible assets have no value separate and distinct from the value of tangible assets. They do. But how can this be the case? How can intangible assets possess a value of and by themselves, and still require the use or using up of tangible assets or financial assets in order to fully realize their value? The answer is that the same party that owns the intangible asset need not own the tangible assets that are used to exploit the intangible's value. In fact, the intangible asset owner need not own any assets at all—except for the intangible asset.

For example, the owner of a plant and equipment can license the use of the subject intangible asset (e.g., trademark, patent, software, etc.). The intangible asset owner receives a royalty income. This situation creates value for the intangible asset owner. Nonetheless, the intangible asset owner does not need to own any tangible assets. Likewise, the owner of tangible assets may exploit the value of (i.e., investment in) those tangible assets through the use (via license) of the subject intangible. In fact, through the combination of tangible assets (e.g., plant and equipment) and intangible assets (e.g., a licensed patent or product formulation), the tangible asset owner could develop a new intangible asset (e.g., customer contracts or relationships, brand value, goodwill, etc.).

Of course, the owner of the intangible asset could realize the value of the subject intangible directly (as opposed to indirectly through a license agreement) without making a substantial investment in tangible assets. For instance, the intangible asset owner could lease the requisite plant and equipment (just as the tangible asset owner could license the requisite intangible). The point is that the intangible asset owner can realize the value of the subject intangible through the *use* of tangible assets, without having to *own* the tangible assets.

Let's consider a final example to illustrate this point. Party A owns an intangible asset (e.g., patent, trademark, franchise, chemical formulation, etc.). Party B owns tangible assets (e.g., a plant and productive machinery and equipment). Party C could license the intangibles from Party A and lease the plant and equipment from Party B. In this case, the intangible asset has value as represented by the stream of license royalty income. The tangible assets have value as represented by the stream of rental income. The owner of the subject intangible (Party A) has realized value without owning any tangible assets. Party C has created a business enterprise (and perhaps created additional intangible assets) without owning either the subject intangible asset or the tangible assets that are used in the commercialization of the subject intangible. In economic terms, Party C has added coordination (i.e., management or entrepreneurial expertise) but not capital (i.e., tangible assets or financial assets) to this hypothetical venture.

In summary, intangible assets have value separate and distinct from tangible assets, even though the intangible asset may (at some point in the commercialization process) require the use of tangible assets in order to realize its full value. Likewise, tangible assets have value separate and distinct from intangible assets and other tangible assets. This is true even though the tangible assets may require the use of intangible assets or of other tangible assets in order to realize their full value. For example, computer hardware (a tangible asset) may need computer software (an intangible asset) in order to fully realize its value. Similarly, a piece of manufacturing equipment such as a hydraulic press (clearly a tangible asset) needs the use of tools, dies, jigs, and fixtures (also clearly tangible assets) in order to fully realize its value.

Intangible assets, which may possess discrete value of and by themselves, may also enhance the value of the tangible assets with which they are associated. This is not to say that the entire value of the intangible asset should accrue to the tangible asset, nor that the entire value of the tangible value should accrue to the intangible asset.

For example, a parcel of land is worth more with a building on it. This does not mean that the entire value of the building should accrue to the land or that the entire value of the land should accrue to the building. Both assets contribute value, in part, to the other. That is, both assets in part enhance the value of the other. The same relationship exists with intangible assets and tangible assets.

As will be discussed in a later section, the incremental value contributed by intangible assets to associated tangible assets is sometimes called the *in-use value* or the *going-concern value* element of tangible asset value. This incremental value is sometimes measured as the difference between the value-in-use of the tangible assets and the value-in-exchange of the tangible assets.

The contributory value of intangible assets that accrues to associated tangible assets is sometimes called enhancement. That is, intangible assets often enhance the value of the tangible assets with which they are associated. Similarly, tangible assets often enhance the value of the intangible assets with which they are associated. The enhancement concept will be explained at greater length in the chapters dealing with valuation approaches and methods (Part II) and in the chapters related to specific types of intangibles (Part V).

## FOUR CATEGORIES OF PROPERTY

For economic analysis and valuation purposes, it is often necessary to distinguish between tangible and intangible assets, as well as between real estate and personal property assets. These distinctions are important for a variety of accounting, taxation, legal, and financial reasons.

For example, it is important to distinguish whether a certain value is tangible or intangible and whether it accrues to real estate or personal property for such purposes as:

1. Financial accounting—The correct classification of values affects financial statement presentation.
2. Income tax accounting—Different depreciation lives and different depreciation rates apply to tangible assets versus intangible assets and to real estate versus personal property.
3. Ad valorem property taxation—Different property tax rates may apply to tangible versus intangible assets and to real estate versus personal property; in fact, some jurisdictions exempt certain property categories (e.g., intangible personal property) entirely from ad valorem property taxation.
4. Collateral value within a secured creditor environment— Different creditors have different claims on the collateral value of a firm's assets (tangible versus intangible, real versus personal); this becomes particularly relevant in matters related to bankruptcy and reorganization, when the value of a secured creditor's collateral interest is relevant to all parties interested in the bankruptcy estate.

In fact, for economic analysis and valuation purposes, all assets or properties may be categorized into one of the following four categories (or types) of property:

1. Tangible real estate.
2. Intangible real property.
3. Tangible personal property.
4. Intangible personal property.

Accordingly, tangible assets can be either real (i.e., their value is derived from the land) or personal (i.e., their value is not derived from the land) in nature. Likewise, intangible assets can either be real (i.e., their value is derived from the land) or personal (i.e., their value is not derived from the land) in nature.

This is an important concept because it means that all of the assets, properties, and business interests that an analyst will encounter may be classified into one of these four distinct property types. Of course, assets within any given property category will have the same fundamental characteristics, at least from a valuation and economic analysis perspective. Assets that fall into different property categories will have fundamentally dissimilar characteristics, at least from a valuation and economic analysis perspective.

However, the proper classification of an asset within its particular property category is more an accounting and legal distinction than a valuation and economic distinction. This is so because the correct property type categorization of an asset affects such accounting and legal applications as negotiating, regulating, and licensing assets; depreciating and amortizing lives and rates for financial accounting and income tax accounting purposes; ad valorem property taxation rates and exemptions; the collateral claims in fraudulent conveyance, bankruptcy, debt default, and other debt-related disputes; and eminent domain, condemnation, and other controversies.

Of course, this book focuses upon intangible assets. As we will see, intangible assets fit into two of the four property types: intangible real property and intangible personal property. That means that the two remaining categories of property are comprised of tangible assets: real estate and tangible personal property. In order to round out the discussion of the four property types, this section briefly describes the real estate and tangible personal property types, and compares and contrasts the attributes of real estate and tangible personal property. In addition, this section compares and contrasts the attributes of those two property types and the attributes of the intangible asset property types.

## Real Estate

Most analysts have an intuitive feel for what type of assets are included in the property category of real estate. Technically, *The Dictionary of Real Estate Appraisal* defines real estate as: "Physical land and appurtenances attached to the land, e.g., structures. An identified parcel or tract of land, including improvements, if any."[1]

An appurtenance is defined as: "Something that has been added or appended to a property and has since become an inherent part of the property; usually passes with the property when title is transferred."[2]

Accordingly, real estate is immobile, because it is land or is permanently affixed to land. Real estate is tangible; in fact, the very definition of the term *real estate* includes the words "physical land."

In addition, the legal definition of real estate includes land and all things that are a natural part of the land (e.g., trees, minerals), as well as all things that are permanently affixed to it by people (e.g., buildings, fences, site improvements). All permanent building attachments (e.g., plumbing, electrical wiring, heating systems) as well as built-in items (e.g., loading docks, elevators) are usually considered part of the real estate. Light fixtures and other fixtures (that may otherwise be considered personal property) are considered part of the real estate only if they are permanently attached to a structure.

Real estate includes all attachments to the land, both below and above the ground. The ownership of real estate typically includes both horizontal interests (the area on the ground) and vertical interests (the area above and below the ground). Owners of real estate may subdivide these vertical interests, as we will see in our discussion of intangible real property interests, although the vertical interests in land accrue to the ownership of the land.

---

1. *The Dictionary of Real Estate Appraisal,* 3rd ed. (Chicago: Appraisal Institute, 1993), p. 252.
2. Ibid., p. 18.

PART 1   Introduction to Intangible Asset Valuation

Vertical interests in real estate fall into two categories: subsurface rights, or the area below the surface of the land; and air rights, or the space above the surface of the land. *The Appraisal of Real Estate* defines subsurface rights and air rights as follows:

> A subsurface right is the right to the use and profits of the underground portion of a designated property. The term usually refers to the right to extract minerals from below the earth's surface and to construct tunnels for railroads, motor vehicles, and public utilities. Air rights are the property rights associated with the use, control, and regulation of air space over a parcel of real estate. Both of these fractional interests represent portions of a fee simple estate, and each embodies the idea of land as a three-dimensional entity.[3]

In summary, the real estate property type is the fee simple estate which includes the surface of the land, any permanent fixtures or structures attached to the surface of the land, the area below the surface of the land (theoretically down to the core of the earth), and the space above the surface of the land (theoretically up to the atmosphere of the earth).

## Tangible Personal Property

Tangible personal property includes those movable property items that are not permanently affixed to, or part of, the real estate. Accordingly, tangible personal property is not endowed with all of the rights of real property ownership.

It is sometimes difficult to determine whether a particular asset should be considered tangible personal property or part of the real estate. For example, a fixture is an article that was once personal property, but if it has since been installed or attached to the land or a building in a permanent manner, it is typically regarded as part of the real estate.

Although such fixtures are generally considered to be a component of real estate, trade fixtures are not. A trade fixture, also called a chattel fixture, is an article that is owned and attached to a rented space or building by a tenant and is used in conducting business.

*Appraising Machinery and Equipment*, sponsored by the American Society of Appraisers, presents the following definition for tangible personal property:

> *Personal property* is defined as those tangible items that are not permanently affixed to real estate and can be moved. A general definition of personal property is anything and everything, excepting intangibles, that is not realty and/or not permanently attached to the realty.[4]

That text presents several examples of tangible personal property and contrasts these examples with the real estate property classification, as follows:

**Examples of Personal Property**
Equipment, for example, could include office furniture and machines, storage shelves, suspended fluorescent lights, manual and powered bench tools, floor-type water coolers, drapes, electric range-sink-refrigerator combinations, wall-mounted cabinets, hoists and monorails, stock storage mezzanines, exterior security lights, and modular office dividers.

---

3. *The Appraisal of Real Estate*, 11th ed. (Chicago: Appraisal Institute, 1997), p. 144.
4. John Alico, ed., *Appraising Machinery and Equipment* (New York: McGraw-Hill Book Company, 1989), p. 10.

It does not include the land, land improvements, or building and heating elements which are attached to and made part of the structure. Specific items considered as real estate by the appraiser could include acoustical ceilings, recessed fluorescent lights, wall paneling, wall-to-wall carpeting, chain link fencing, metal awnings, and stock racks on exterior walls.[5]

*The Dictionary of Real Estate Appraisal* defines personal property, as distinguished from tangible personal property. However, the definition, presented here, is clearly relevant to our discussion of the rights associated with tangible personal property ownership:

> Identifiable, portable, and tangible objects that are considered by the general public to be "personal," e.g., furnishings, artwork, antiques, gems and jewelry, collectibles, machinery and equipment; all property that is not classified as real estate.[6]

Because it is not always easy to distinguish where tangible personal property leaves off and where real estate begins, *The Appraisal of Real Estate* presents the following advice with regard to the distinctions between the tangible personal property and the real estate classifications of property:

> To decide whether an item is personal property or a fixture, and therefore part of the real estate, courts often use the following criteria.
>
> 1. The manner in which the item is affixed. Generally, an item is considered personal property if it can be removed without serious injury to the real estate or to itself. There are exceptions to this rule.
> 2. The character of the item and its adaptation to the real estate. Items that are specifically constructed for use in a particular building or installed to carry out the purpose for which the building was erected are generally considered permanent parts of the building.
> 3. The intention of the party who attached the item. Frequently, the terms of the lease reveal whether the item is permanent or is to be removed at some future time.[7]

In summary, there are several attributes that distinguish tangible personal property from real estate. The most important of these distinguishing features is that tangible personal property is movable and therefore is not permanently affixed to the land. Ownership of tangible personal property, therefore, does not represent the same bundle of legal rights associated with ownership of real estate.

It is noteworthy, though, that tangible personal property and real estate have at least one significant common attribute: Both property types are tangible. That is, the two property classifications share these three features: They are corporeal; they are visible; and they are tactile.

## Intangible Real Property

Intangible real property includes all of the individual interests, benefits, and rights inherent in the ownership of the physical real estate. Real property is different from real estate. Real estate is the name associated with the tangible assets land, land improvements, buildings, and building improvements. Real property represents the individual legal rights associat-

---

5. Ibid.
6. *The Dictionary of Real Estate Appraisal,* 3rd ed., p. 265.
7. *The Appraisal of Real Estate,* 11th ed., p. 9.

ed with ownership of the tangible real estate. Since all legal rights are intangible, real property is intangible. In essence, the classification real property includes all of the intangible rights and benefits associated with the ownership of real estate.

*The Dictionary of Real Estate Appraisal* defines real property as follows:

> All interests, benefits, and rights inherent in the ownership of physical real estate; the bundle of rights with which the ownership of the real estate is endowed.[8]

A right or interest in real estate is also referred to as an estate. For example, an estate in land is the degree, nature, or extent of the ownership interest a person has in the subject land.

Legal interests vary, so real property is said to include the "bundle of rights" that are inherent in the ownership of real estate. For example, real property ownership rights may include, among others:

1. The right to use the real estate.
2. The right to sell the real estate.
3. The right to lease the real estate.
4. The right to control access to the real estate.
5. The right to give the real estate away.
6. The right to choose to exercise all of or none of these rights.

Real property rights, or the bundle of rights associated with real estate, are often compared to a bundle of sticks, with each stick representing a distinct and separate right or interest. Examples of intangible real property include easements, air rights, water rights, mineral rights, development rights, possessory interests, and leasehold interests.

The distinctions between tangible real estate and intangible real property may appear to be subtle and legalistic, especially to the intangible asset analyst. However, these distinctions are very important with regard to real estate appraisals performed for a variety of purposes, including: financing collateralization, financing securitization, ad valorem property taxation, income taxation, financial accounting, bankruptcy, and other purposes. In fact, *The Appraisal of Real Estate* discusses the importance of these distinctions as follows:

> The distinction between real estate, the tangible physical entity, and real property, the intangible bundle of rights, interests, and benefits inherent in the ownership of real estate, is fundamental to appraisal.[9]

The issue of what intangible property rights are included (or excluded) in a real estate appraisal is so fundamental that a discussion of the specific property rights appraised is a standard provision of every real estate appraisal report. Chapter 26 of *The Appraisal of Real Estate* presents the requirements for the appraisal report and includes the following discussion with regard to "property rights appraised":

> In identifying the subject property, the appraiser must state and should define the particular rights or interests being valued. This is particularly important in appraisals of partial interests in property, limited rights such as surface or mineral rights, fee simple estates subject to long-term leases, and

---

8. *The Dictionary of Real Estate Appraisal,* 3rd ed., p. 294.
9. *The Appraisal of Real Estate,* 11th ed., p. 667.

leasehold interests. Other encumbrances such as easements, mortgages, and special occupancy or use requirements should also be identified and explained in relation to the defined value to be estimated.[10]

In summary, real property relates to the rights to use, occupy, develop, exploit, cross over, cross under, encroach upon, buy, sell, and so on, the tangible real estate. These rights are a portion of the entire fee simple interest or bundle of rights associated with the ownership of real estate. These rights are usually articulated in and represented by some sort of contract, such as a license, a lease, an easement, a mineral rights agreement, a development rights agreement, and so forth.

Like all legal rights, these real property rights are intangible. Therefore, intangible real property is one of the four categories of property.

## Intangible Personal Property

The fourth property type is intangible personal property. Technically, the asset category "intangible assets" includes both intangible real property and intangible personal property. But in common language usage, most people mean intangible personal property when they use the words *intangible assets.*

This book covers the category of intangible assets, so we will discuss intangible real property as well as intangible personal property. However, the emphasis of the book is on intangible personal property. This is not meant to reduce the importance of intangible real property. The appraisal and economic analysis of intangible real property is adequately covered in numerous comprehensive real estate appraisal texts. As we will see shortly, there are many more categories of intangible personal property to discuss than there are categories of intangible real property.

The intangible personal property category includes assets with two important attributes: They are intangible and they are personal property.

Because this property category is intangible, the assets do not possess the three attributes of being corporeal, visible, and tactile. That is, intangible personal property assets do not have substantial physical form or substance (at least to the extent that the value of the subject property is not dependent upon its physical form or substance).

Because this property category is personal property, it is not associated with real estate. That is, intangible personal property assets are not physically attached to the land or to other real estate. Accordingly, intangible personal property is mobile.

As with intangible real property, intangible personal property typically encompasses a specific bundle of legal rights, benefits, and interests. Other than real estate–related intangibles (e.g., leases, easements, possessory interests, mineral rights, etc.), most intangible assets generally fall into the category of intangible personal property.

Unfortunately, there exist both contradictory and erroneous definitions of intangible personal property. These definitions sometimes unnecessarily complicate intangible asset analysis. For example, the authoritative *Black's Law Dictionary* defines intangible property as follows:

---

10. Ibid., p. 626.

As used chiefly in the law of taxation, this term means such property as has no intrinsic and marketable value, but is merely the representative or evidence of value, such as certificates of stock, bonds, promissory notes, and franchises.[11]

While the above definition may be appropriate for the term "securities," it is not appropriate for the term "intangible property," at least from an economic perspective. Stock certificates, bonds, notes, and so on, are securities. Their value is truly representative of the underlying issuer of the security (e.g., the corporation that issued the stock certificates). However, this definition does not apply at all to most intangible personal property assets. For example, it doesn't apply to trademarks and trade names, patents, copyrights, contracts, licenses, permits, computer software, and franchise agreements.

As we will see in the remainder of this book, these intangible personal property assets have an intrinsic value. That is, the value is intrinsic to, or internal to, the subject intangible asset. In fact, the value is not intrinsic to the tangible assets with which the intangible assets are associated. Rather, it is intrinsic to the property rights of the intangible asset itself. Most of this book will be devoted to examining the marketable value (either by sale or by license) of intangible personal property.

## COMMON CATEGORIES OF INTANGIBLE ASSETS

Generally, appraisers and economists categorize individual intangible assets into several distinct categories. This categorization of intangible assets is made for general asset identification and classification purposes. The intangible assets are often grouped in the same category when similar valuation methods are particularly applicable to that group of assets.

A common categorization of intangible assets follows:

1. Marketing-related intangible assets (e.g., trademarks, trade names, brand names, logos).
2. Technology-related intangible assets (e.g., process patents, patent applications, technical documentation, such as laboratory notebooks, technical know-how).
3. Artistic-related intangible assets (e.g., literary works and copyrights, musical compositions, copyrights, maps, engravings).
4. Data processing–related intangible assets (e.g., proprietary computer software, software copyrights, automated databases, integrated circuit masks and masters).
5. Engineering-related intangible assets (e.g., industrial design, product patents, trade secrets, engineering drawings and schematics, blueprints, proprietary documentation).
6. Customer-related intangible assets (e.g., customer lists, customer contracts, customer relationships, open purchase orders).
7. Contract-related intangible assets (e.g., favorable supplier contracts, license agreements, franchise agreements, noncompete agreements).

---

11. Henry Campbell Black, *Black's Law Dictionary,* 6th ed. (St. Paul, MN: West Publishing Co., 1990), p. 809.

8. Human capital–related intangible assets (e.g., a trained and assembled workforce, employment agreements, union contracts).

9. Location-related intangible assets (e.g., leasehold interests, mineral exploitation rights, easements, air rights, water rights).

10. Goodwill-related intangible assets (e.g., institutional goodwill, professional practice goodwill, personal goodwill of a professional, celebrity goodwill, general business going-concern value).

The examples given of individual intangible assets that fall into these category types are meant to be illustrative only. Clearly, these examples do not represent a comprehensive listing of intangible assets.

It is also possible for an individual intangible asset to be included in more than one category. For example, one analyst may classify a patent as a technology-related intangible, while another analyst may classify the same patent as an engineering-related intangible assets. Likewise, one analyst may classify an executive's employment agreement as a contract-related intangible asset, while another analyst may classify the same agreement as a human capital–related intangible asset. It is noteworthy that these categories are only general classifications. In the end, the category an individual intangible asset is grouped into will not affect the answers to the important questions we will explore, such as: What is its value? What is its expected remaining useful life? What is an appropriate economic transfer price?

It is also noteworthy that some of the categories of intangible assets may include a special type of intangible asset called an intellectual property. Intellectual properties are discussed next.

## INTELLECTUAL PROPERTIES

There is a specialized classification of intangible assets called intellectual properties. Intellectual properties manifest all of the economic existence and economic value attributes of other intangible assets. However, because of their special status, intellectual properties enjoy special legal recognition and protection. Intangible assets are often created in the normal course of business operations. However, intellectual properties are created by human intellectual or inspirational activity. Such activity (although not always planned) is specific and conscious and the creativity involved can be attributed to identified, specific individuals.

Because of their unique creation process, intellectual properties are generally registered under and protected by specific federal and state statutes. Legal registration provides motivation for intellectual property innovators as well as protection for intellectual property creators. The information content of intellectual properties requires this special protection in order for the intellectual property owners to realize the economic value of these special intangible assets.

As a subset of intangible assets, intellectual properties are often grouped into like categories. The intellectual properties in each category have some general similarities in terms of nature, feature, method of creation, and legal protection. Likewise, similar valuation methods and economic analysis methods often apply to the intellectual properties in each category. A common categorization of intellectual property types is:

1. Creative (e.g., trademarks, copyrights, computer software).
2. Innovative (e.g., patents, industrial designs, trade secrets).

In fact, this categorization in good measure explains the two principal reasons why intellectual properties receive special legal recognition and legal protection. With regard to creative intellectual properties, legislators believe that these property owners need protection. That is, the law was developed to ensure that an owner who spends a great deal of time, effort, and capital to develop a trademark or a musical composition would not be subjected to another party being able to use that development.

With regard to innovative intellectual property, legislators believed that the property owners needed motivation. That is, the law was developed to motivate innovators to spend a great deal of time, effort, and capital to develop a new product or a trade secret. Patent and similar laws ensure that the property owners can commercialize their innovations in an economically friendly (i.e., protected from competition) environment.

It is important to reiterate that intellectual properties are not a different property type from intangible assets. Intellectual properties are not separate and distinct assets from intangible assets. Rather, intellectual properties are a specially recognized subset of intangible assets. In other words, all intellectual properties are intangible assets but not all intangible assets have the special distinction of being intellectual properties.

The next sections identify some of the attributes that distinguish intellectual properties from other intangible assets and explain how some of these distinguishing attributes affect the valuation and economic analysis of intellectual properties.

## Attributes That Distinguish Intellectual Properties

Intellectual properties are intangible assets that enjoy special legal recognition and legal protection. More often than not, this special legal status is the result of a particular statutory authority. That is, a particular federal or state law grants special recognition to intellectual properties. In some cases, the special legal status is the result of judicial precedent. That is, the courts have recognized the special rights and privileges of certain intangible assets often enough that they have become intellectual properties de facto under the law.

We will not discuss the legal attributes of intellectual properties in detail. This is not a legal text; numerous other authoritative texts carefully explore the statutory authority, judicial precedent, and administrative rulings with regard to intellectual properties. Readers are recommended to consult such texts for a rigorous discussion of the legal attributes that distinguish intellectual properties. The economic attributes of the various types of intellectual properties are discussed in greater detail, by asset category, in Part V.

Here we introduce five general types of intellectual properties for purposes of illustrating their unique attributes. These five types of intellectual properties are analogous to the particular categories of intangible assets in which they would be included. These five *types* should not be confused with the two *categories* of intellectual properties—creative and innovative. The two categories are merely descriptive of the intellectual property development process. The five general types of intellectual properties include:

1. Marketing-related, such as trademark and service marks.
2. Technology-related, such as certain types of patents.
3. Artistic-related, such as literary and musical copyrights.
4. Data processing–related, such as computer software copyrights and computer chip masks and masters.
5. Engineering-related, such as industrial designs and trade secrets.

The attributes of each of these five types of intellectual properties are discussed next.[12]

### Marketing-Related Intellectual Properties

Trademarks, trade names, service marks, and logos are protected by the federal Lanham Act and by corresponding state statutes. *The New Role of Intellectual Property in Commercial Transactions* describes the legal attributes of trademarks as follows:

> A trademark is "any word, name, symbol, or device, or any combination thereof—(1) used by a person or (2) which a person has a bona fide intention to use in commerce and applies to register on the principal register established by this [Act], to identify and distinguish his or her goods, including a unique product, from those manufactured or sold by others and to indicate the source of the goods, even if that source is unknown." As explained by the Senate Committee on Patents, the purpose of trademark protection is twofold: "One [purpose] is to protect the public so it may be confident that, in purchasing a product bearing a particular trade-mark which it favorably knows, it will get the product which it asks for and wants to get. Secondly, where the owner of a trade-mark has spent energy, time, and money in presenting to the public the product, he is protected in his investment from its misappropriation by pirates and cheats." The owner of a mark therefore has the right to exclude another from using a symbol so related to his or her own that the ordinary consumer would likely be confused as to the source or sponsorship of the goods or services.
>
> A trademark arises upon use as a source identifier and continues as long as the mark is used to identify the goods or services. Nonuse of a mark for an extended period of time may result in abandonment of trademark rights.[13]

Trademarks do not have to be registered in order to enjoy protection under the Lanham Act. However, commercial trademarks are typically registered with the United States Patent and Trademark Office. Registration provides the trademark owner with several important procedural advantages if a challenge arises regarding the use or ownership of the trademark.

Trademark registrations issued prior to November 16, 1989 were valid for a period of 20 years. Trademark registrations issued on or after November 16, 1989, are valid for a period of 10 years. Registration of a trademark may be renewed for successive 10-year periods.

In addition to federal registration, there is an independent system of trademark registration under most state trademark statutes. Usually, state trademark registrations are applicable to trademarks used within the particular state.

---

12. The attributes are described in greater detail in the legal text, *The New Role of Intellectual Property in Commercial Transactions,* edited by attorneys Melvin Simensky and Lanning Bryer (New York: John Wiley & Sons, 1994). In particular, the reader's attention is directed to Chapter 8 of that book, "The Acquisition and Disposition of Intellectual Property in Commercial Transactions: The U.S. Perspective," written by attorneys Samuel Fifer and Carol Anne Bean.
13. Ibid., p. 290.

*The New Role of Intellectual Property in Commercial Transactions* describes trade names as follows:

> Trade names and fictitious or assumed names identify businesses rather than products or services. Although trade names are not subject to federal trademark registration, they are protected against infringement under Section 43(a) of the federal Lanham Act. Trade name infringement occurs where a business's trade name is used by another as a trade name or trademark so that confusion as to the source of the business, goods, or services is likely to occur.[14]

In addition to protection under the Lanham Act, trade names are also protected under many state statutes through the state trademark registration process.

### Technology-Related Intellectual Properties

Product and process patents are granted by the United States Patent and Trademark Office under the authority of Section 101 of the United States Code. *The New Role of Intellectual Property in Commercial Transactions* describes the legal attributes of patents as follows:

> Patents may be obtained for "any new and useful process, new machine, manufacture or composition of matter, or any new or useful improvement thereof." The claimed invention must also be new, useful, and nonobvious, in relation to the prior art. Patents fall into one of several categories, including utility, process, and design patents. Utility and process patents are valid for a period of 17 years; design patents are valid for 14 years. A patent cannot be obtained for a system of doing business, an arrangement of printed matter, a mental process, or a naturally occurring article, but may cover machines, manufacturing processes, computer applications, and product configurations.[15]

The legal rights of patent protection do not come into existence until the patent is actually granted. For example, the commonly observed "patent pending" notation on many products does not confer any special legal rights or privileges to the product producer. However, once the patent is issued, the owner has the right to exclude others from making, using, or selling the patented product (or process) in the United States during the patent protection period.

### Artistic-Related Intellectual Properties

Copyrights on artistic-related intellectual properties (e.g., literary, musical, dramatic, artistic, and film works) are granted under the authority of the federal Copyright Act of 1976. *The New Role of Intellectual Property in Commercial Transactions* describes the legal attributes of copyrights as follows:

> Copyrights exist in "original works of authorship fixed in any tangible medium of expression, now known or later developed, from which they can be perceived, reproduced, or otherwise communicated, either directly or with the aid of a machine or device." "Works of authorship" include literary works, musical works, dramatic works, pictorial works, and sound recordings. Thus, books, movies, and artwork may be subject to copyright protection, but promotional brochures, training manuals, and computer programs also may be protected by copyright and should not be overlooked. Copy-

---

14. Ibid., p. 290.
15. Ibid., pp. 292–93.

right protection is not available to an idea in the absence of any particular fixed impression, nor to any process, method of operation, or discovery. Copyright protection is also not available to the extent that an item or feature is solely utilitarian or wholly unoriginal (such as a plaid pattern).

A copyright is not a single right, but rather a "bundle" of exclusive rights giving an owner the rights to reproduce a work, to prepare derivative works, to distribute and display copies of the work, and to perform the work in public. A copyright may be infringed if any one of these exclusive rights is violated.[16]

Copyrights are legally valid for the lifetime of the creator of the intellectual property, plus an additional 50 years. An alternative legal protection period is 75 years from the first publication of intellectual properties (e.g., musical compositions, literary works, etc.) that were made for hire.

Although federal registration is not required in order to maintain copyright protection, it is required if the owner decides to initiate infringement litigation. Similarly, federal copyright registration (within 90 days after original publication of an intellectual property) entitles the owner to certain procedural advantages in the case of infringement litigation.

## Data Processing–Related Intellectual Properties

If it meets certain requirements, computer software is subject to copyright registration and copyright protection. The legal attributes of copyrights were introduced above. The second group of intellectual properties included in the data processing type relate to integrated circuit computer chips: masks and masters.

*The New Role of Intellectual Property in Commercial Transactions* describes the legal attributes of these intellectual properties as follows:

> A "mask work" is a series of stencils of integrated circuitry etched onto a semiconductor ship, sometimes called "firm ware." The process of producing mask works can cost millions of dollars and consume thousands of hours of engineering and technician time. However, once a mask work has been produced, the work can be duplicated through photography for a cost of less than $50,000. To guard against piracy of mask works, Congress enacted the Semiconductor Chip Protection Act (SCPA) of 1984.
>
> To qualify for protection under the SCPA, a mask work must be "fixed in a semiconductor chip product, by or under the authority of the owner of the mask work." Fixation occurs where a series of masks or stencils have been employed in stenciling two- and three-dimensional features of shape and configuration onto a chip, thereby creating a "semiconductor chip product." Protection is available only for mask works that are "original," with the same standards of originality as those under the law of copyright.
>
> A mask work is protected under the SCPA if it is either registered in the Copyright Office or "commercially exploited anywhere in the world." Commercial exploitation is defined as distribution "to the public for commercial purposes a semiconductor chip product embodying the mask work." Registration is a prerequisite for filing an infringement action under the SCPA, and statutory protection under the SCPA will be lost if registration is not made within two years after the date on which the mask work was first commercially exploited anywhere in the world.[17]

16. Ibid., p. 291.
17. Ibid., p. 292.

As with copyrights, it is not necessary to publish a notice of ownership of a mask work in order to enjoy protection under the Semiconductor Chip Protection Act of 1984. However, as with copyrights, such a notice of ownership does provide the intellectual property owner with certain procedural advantages in the event that the owner initiates infringement litigation.

### Engineering-Related Intellectual Properties

Trade secrets and related engineering documentation (e.g., designs, drawings, schematics, diagrams, layouts, chemical formulations, etc.) are federally protected by the Uniform Trade Secrets Act. In addition, such intellectual properties may also be protected by various state statutory authority and judicial precedent.

*The New Role of Intellectual Property in Commercial Transactions* describes the legal attributes of this type of intellectual property as follows:

> A trade secret is "information, including a formula, pattern, compilation, program, device, method, technique, or process, that: (1) derives independent economic value, actual or potential, from not being generally known . . . and (2) is the subject of efforts that are reasonable under the circumstances to maintain its secrecy." Trade secrets are not registered by any government office, but are maintained through their owners' precautions to preserve secrecy. A trade secret may be, for example, a formula for a chemical compound; a process of manufacturing, treating, or preserving materials; the design of a machine; or a customer list. The Uniform Trade Secrets Act, variations of which have been adopted in 36 states, greatly standardized the law of trade secrets by defining trade secrets and the protection accorded them. Matters of public knowledge or of general knowledge within an industry cannot be appropriated as trade secrets. Elements to be considered in determining what constitutes a trade secret include the extent to which the information is known outside the business, the extent to which information is known by employees involved in the business, the extent to which the information is guarded, the value of the information to the business and to its competitors, and the ease with which the information can be duplicated.[18]

Under state statutes, protection is usually afforded to engineering-related intellectual properties only if the owner took conscious and active steps to maintain the confidentiality of the intellectual property.

## How Intellectual Property Attributes Affect Value

The various legal attributes of intellectual properties affect the valuation and economic analysis in several ways. This topic will be revisited when individual intellectual properties are discussed in Part V. However, for purposes of this introduction, the analyst should be aware of several factors with respect to the influence of legal attributes on value.

First, most intellectual properties have a specified legal life. As we will see when we explore remaining useful life analysis, this measure of life may not be the most important with regard to the value of the subject intellectual property. Nonetheless, whereas many intangible assets do not have a specified legal (i.e., determined by statute) life, most intellectual properties do.

---

18. Ibid., p. 293.

Second, because of the special legal recognition and protection afforded to intellectual properties, their owners may have more external commercialization opportunities available to them compared to the owners of other intangible assets. For example, intellectual property owners often enter into license, joint venture, or other exploitation and development agreements. These agreements allow them to enjoy the economic benefits of commercializing their intellectual properties external to their current business interests.

External commercialization opportunities could include licensing the use or development rights for the subject intellectual property:

1. through geographic expansion, i.e., in new territories;
2. through industry expansion, i.e., into new industries; or
3. through product expansion, i.e., into new products.

External commercialization opportunities are typically not available to the owners of other intangible assets. For example, the owners of a favorable supplier contract, ongoing customer relationships, or a trained and assembled workforce generally derive the economic benefits from these intangible assets by commercializing them within their current business operations.

Third, more transactional data are available for analysis with respect to intellectual properties, compared with other intangible assets. That is, more data are available with regard to the sale, license, or other external commercialization of intellectual properties, because there are more reported transactions. There are more reported transactions because intellectual property owners are more confident to enter into external commercialization transactions. This is because parties to a transaction are aware that their legal and economic interests are more likely to be protected by the laws associated with their particular intellectual property.

Fourth, intellectual properties generally enjoy higher royalty rates and higher market value pricing multiples than do other intangible assets, all other things being equal. Of course, in the real world, all other things are never equal. Nonetheless, as a general observation, intellectual properties trade (i.e., are licensed or sold) for higher prices than other comparative intangible assets because intellectual property buyers and licensers are willing to pay more due to the protection afforded them by intellectual property laws. Intellectual property laws reduce the risk associated with intellectual property commercial transactions, so intellectual property buyers and licensers may feel that they can afford to pay a bit more to enter into such transactions.

Fifth, substantially more judicial precedent exists regarding intellectual properties than regarding other intangible assets. This factor itself has three implications:

1. There is greater judicially determined definition of certain intellectual properties than of other intangible assets. For example, due to infringement and other litigation, U.S. courts have pretty well defined what is a trade name and what is a trade secret. Analysts can generally rely upon these definitions in the identification and valuation of these intellectual properties. There is much less published precedent with regard to such intangible assets as an optimal distribution system or going-concern value. Therefore, there is somewhat less definition (at least, judicial definition) as to what constitutes those intangible assets.

2. With respect to certain intellectual properties, there have been more judicial decisions in the United States with regard to appropriate (and inappropriate) valuation methodology, with regard to reasonable ranges of royalty rates, and with regard to economic damage analysis methods and amounts. Again, judicial precedent may provide valuable guidance to the intangible asset analyst. This is not to suggest that analysts should naively apply valuation pricing multiples or royalty rates in a specific analysis just because they are published in a judicial decision. Obviously, such pricing multiples and royalty rates are only appropriate given the unique facts and circumstances of the specific court case. Nonetheless, a review of published precedent may provide the analyst with an indication of a reasonable range of pricing multiples, royalty rates, damages-related lost profit margins, and so forth.

3. Participants (i.e., buyers, sellers, licensers, licensees) in the intellectual property secondary market are generally aware of the extent of judicial precedent, and are aware that federal and state laws exist and that the courts recognize and protect various types of intellectual property. This level of judicial awareness and protection may motivate market participants to enter into more market transactions, because market participants may consider the intellectual property market to be relatively safe and protected.

Finally, it is noteworthy that intellectual property attributes can have a positive effect on both the active value and the passive value of intellectual properties. The concepts of active value and passive value will be explored in Chapter 7. For now, let's just say that active value is generated when an intangible asset is used proactively (e.g., to increase prices, market share, or profits). Passive value is generated when an intangible asset is used defensively (e.g., to protect prices, market share, or profits). Both active value and passive value may be positively influenced by the legal attributes of intellectual properties.

## SUMMARY

Chapter 1 introduced the attributes or factors that are relevant for determining what economic phenomena represent intangible assets and what economic phenomena are merely descriptive of intangible influences. It also introduced the economic factors that contribute to a positive value for intangible assets.

This book is devoted to the valuation and economic analysis of intangible assets. However, those economic phenomena that do not qualify as intangible assets may, in fact, still have value. They are simply not intangible assets. For example, there may be a substantial value to a personal or institutional reputation, to high market share, to uniqueness or individuality, but these attributes are not themselves intangible assets.

This is not to say that these attributes cannot be protected or defended in a court of law; they can be. Nor is it to say that these attributes cannot suffer economic damages; they can. The estimation of such damages is itself a legitimate subdiscipline within applied microeconomic analysis. Damages analyses, including lost profits and other analyses, will be mentioned within this book but we will restrict our exploration of that area to its specific application with regard to intangible assets.

This chapter also introduced the concepts of property and of property rights. We reviewed the four types of property:

1. Tangible real estate.
2. Intangible real property.
3. Tangible personal property.
4. Intangible personal property.

Finally, Chapter 1 explored some of the many attributes that distinguish intellectual properties from general commercial intangible assets.

Some individuals who are not trained in intangible asset analysis allege that this discipline has been "invented" within the last few years. They assert that intangible assets are "gimmicks" to allow industrial and commercial firms to achieve certain income taxation, property taxation, bankruptcy protection, or other advantages.

In fact, the study of intangible assets is not a new discipline. The identification, valuation, and remaining useful life analysis of intangible assets was covered in the landmark text, *The Valuation of Property*, by James C. Bonbright, first published in 1937.[19] We will attempt to report some of the theoretical and practical advances that have occurred with regard to the analysis of intangible assets during the last six decades.

---

19. James C. Bonbright, *The Valuation of Property* (Charlottesville, VA: The Michie Company, 1965 [reprint of 1937 edition]).

PART 1   Introduction to Intangible Asset Valuation

# Reasons to Conduct an Appraisal of Intangible Assets

*Intangible assets that make companies click can be a gold mine. Companies increasingly leverage, license, and otherwise capitalize on intellectual property such as trade secrets, client lists, and even sales training programs. Among other things, such properties give companies bargaining rights in the business world.*[1]

## INTRODUCTION

Intangible assets are increasingly being recognized as some of the most important—and hence, some of the most valuable—assets of a business enterprise. Yet a rigorous economic analysis of the value of these important intangible assets is rarely undertaken. Recalling what Mark Twain said about the weather, "Everybody talks about the value of intangible assets, but nobody ever does anything about it."

Some less sophisticated observers simply refer to the economic value of commercial intangible assets collectively as "technology" or "know-how" or "goodwill." Being more discriminating about the characteristics of intangible assets will allow us to uncover many useful reasons to conduct an intangible asset appraisal or economic analysis.

The same intangible asset can exist everywhere at once, as in a famous trade name like Coca-Cola. Intangible assets, by their very nature, are mobile. For example, the Internet moves some intangible assets (e.g., proprietary technology) across the globe in the blink of an eye. The challenge of isolating and protecting the owner's investment in an intangible asset or intellectual property has never been greater.

The practical commercial, legal, and regulatory reasons to conduct an intangible asset appraisal are abundant. As the level of recognition for the economic characteristics of intangible assets increases in the global business community, even more reasons to conduct an intangible asset analysis will become known.

## PURPOSE OF THE APPRAISAL

Intangible asset valuations and economic analyses are performed for transactional purposes as well as for notational purposes. In transactional analyses, clients rely upon the analyst's advice and opinions in order to negotiate, structure, and consummate actual commercial transactions. In other words, at the conclusion of the intangible asset transactional analysis, it is expected that an arm's-length commercial transaction will be consummated. In the vernacular, real money will change hands as the result of the transactional analysis.

Several examples of transactional appraisals are analyses that are performed in order to negotiate the arm's-length purchase or sale of an intangible asset between independent parties; to establish a fair royalty rate associated with the license or other limited-term transfers of a particular intangible asset; or to establish an equity or other ownership exchange rate in the instance where bundles of intangible assets are contributed by two joint venture partners in the formation of a new business enterprise.

Transactional analyses are distinguished from notational analyses. Notational analyses are performed for purely accounting, recording, or in-

---

1. "Business Bulletin: The Intangible Assets That Make Companies Click Can Be a Gold Mine," *Wall Street Journal*, September 12, 1996, p. 1.

formational reasons. At the conclusion of a notational analysis, no commercial transaction will be consummated. That is, no actual cash will change hands as a result of the notational intangible asset valuation conclusion. Several examples of notational analyses are the estimation of the value of an intangible asset for insurance, personal estate planning, corporate strategic planning, or other management information purposes.

This distinction should not be interpreted to mean that notational analyses are any less rigorous than transactional analyses. It would also be inappropriate to conclude that notational analyses are necessarily less accurate or less reliable than transactional analyses. Rather, notational analyses are simply performed for a different set of purposes than transactional analyses are.

Experienced analysts are accustomed to performing intangible asset valuations under a variety of alternative definitions of value and under a variety of alternative premises of value. This occurs because there is such a significant number of alternative situations and varying client motivations regarding the analysis of intangible assets and intellectual properties.

There are numerous individual reasons for conducting an intangible asset appraisal or economic analysis. As discussed in greater detail in Chapter 4, typically all of these individual reasons can be grouped into a few general categories of client motivations:

1. Transaction pricing and structuring, for either the sale, purchase, or license of the intangible asset.
2. Financing securitization and collateralization, for both cash flow–based financing and asset-based financing.
3. Taxation planning and compliance, with regard to intangible asset amortization deductions, abandonment loss deductions, substantiation of charitable contributions, and various other federal income taxation matters, as well as with regard to federal gift and estate tax compliance and estate planning.
4. Management information and planning, including business value enhancement analyses, identification of licensing and other commercialization opportunities, identification of spin-off opportunities, and other long-range strategic issues.
5. Bankruptcy and reorganization analysis, including the value of the estate in bankruptcy, debtor-in-possession financing, traditional refinancing, restructuring, and the assessment of the impact of proposed reorganization plans.
6. Litigation support and dispute resolution, including marital dissolution, infringement, fraud, lender liability, and a wide range of deprivation-related reasons (e.g., breach of contract, expropriation, etc.).

## COMMON REASONS TO APPRAISE AN INTANGIBLE ASSET

Many times, the requirement for an intangible asset or intellectual property valuation and economic analysis is obvious, because the analysis is effectively mandated by statutory provision, administrative ruling, or regulatory authority. An example of this type of obvious statutory reason to conduct an analysis is the intergenerational transfer of an intellectual property, such as a copyright. In this instance, the value of the copyright has to be estimated for federal gift tax return compliance purposes.

Many times, there are opportunities to use the results of an intangible asset valuation and economic analysis for tax planning, business or transaction planning, litigation support, or management information purposes. An example of the discretionary use of an intangible asset valuation is the structuring of a partner or shareholder buy-sell agreement (where the price of the ownership interest being transferred is a function of the value of the entity's intangible assets).

There are many requirements for, and opportunities related to, intangible asset appraisals and economic analyses. The following briefly describes some of the more common reasons for conducting such analyses.

## Allocation of an Overall Business Purchase Price for Financial Accounting Purposes

The allocation of purchase price for financial accounting purposes is a fairly common reason for conducting an appraisal of any type of asset. Accounting Principles Board Opinion Numbers 16 and 17 are the promulgated accounting authority for the recording of the cost of intangible assets purchased as part of a business acquisition. Under APB Opinion Numbers 16 and 17, a company should record as an asset the cost of intangible assets acquired from other enterprises or individuals. The costs of developing, maintaining, or restoring intangible assets that are not specifically identifiable, that have indeterminate useful lives, or that are inherent in a continuing business and are related to an enterprise as a whole (such as goodwill) should be deducted as an expense from income when the costs are incurred. According to the provisions of APB Opinion Number 17, the cost of the intangible asset purchased in a business acquisition should be amortized by systematic charges to income over the period estimated to be benefited by the subject intangible, but not to exceed 40 years.

## Allocation of an Overall Business Purchase Price for Income Tax Accounting Purposes

Internal Revenue Code Section 1060 dictates the income tax accounting provisions for intangible assets that are acquired as part of the lump sum purchase of the assets of a going-concern business. Internal Revenue Code Section 197 allows for the periodic amortization of the cost of most acquired intangible assets. Special income taxation rules apply to the capitalization and cost recovery of certain short-lived purchased intangible assets, such as "in process technology."

## Preacquisition Assessment of Business Value

After the question, "Should we buy this company?" the questions of "How much should we pay?" and "How should we structure the deal?" typically arise as key issues in business acquisition planning and execution. If intangible assets are an important component of either the operations or the strategic development of the acquisition target, then an intangible asset analysis will help to answer each of these questions. The intangible asset valuation results may also be used by the buyers or by the sellers in order to obtain approval for the proposed transaction. The intangible asset valuation results may also be used by the business buyer in order to apply for, negotiate, and finalize the financing related to the proposed business acquisition. An intangible asset valuation may also be used to negotiate the transaction deal price and other transaction structuring parameters.

## The Purchase of Selected Intangible Assets

It may be the case that the acquisition strategy involves only the purchase of particular intangible assets or intellectual properties—such as product designs, patents, special processes, proprietary technology, and so on. In these cases, an intangible asset valuation may be useful as an analytical tool to quantify the expected synergy and other economic benefits involved in the intangible asset purchase. Such an analysis may be useful when estimating different standards of value, such as fair market value versus investment value versus acquisition value. For example, such an analysis could be used in quantifying the maximum purchase price an individual buyer can reasonably pay for the subject intangible asset.

## Capital Formation through Debt Financing

Many financial institutions are willing to consider the particular value of cash flow–generating intangible assets in reaching their lending decisions. These financial institutions typically require an independent appraisal for asset-based financing, for cash flow–based financing, or for intangible assets that are pledged as collateral against loan commitments or lines of credit.

In addition, many financial institutions require appraisals of intangible assets in connection with acquisition financing. These appraisals are obtained in order to refute any possible allegations of "fraudulent conveyance" on the part of the lenders, should the acquisition not prosper and should the financial institution be forced to exercise its secured credit position. One of the tests for fraudulent conveyance related to acquisition financing is to analyze whether all of the borrower's assets—both tangible assets and intangible assets—exceed the amount of the borrower's liabilities.

## Reorganization and Bankruptcy Analysis

An appraisal of the intangible assets of a debtor in possession may be necessary as part of the assessment of the proposed plan of reorganization, in the quantification of a secured creditor collateral position, in the identification of any cancellation of debt income, or for other bankruptcy-related accounting and taxation considerations.

In dividing and distributing the debtors' assets, bankruptcy judges are empowered to authorize the sale of those rights to outside parties as a result of their reorganization. As a result, parties who are involved in intellectual property contracts can sometimes find their licensing agreements radically altered when either the licensor or the licensee files for bankruptcy protection.

## Establishment of Appropriate Royalty Rates for Intangible Asset Licenses

When negotiating arm's-length royalty rates associated with the license of patents, technology, trademarks or trade names, musical or literary creations, to name a few, an intangible asset analysis is helpful in order to understand the projected earnings capacity, cash flow generation ability, and remaining functional, technological, or economic life associated with the subject intangible.

## Establishment of a Fair Intercompany Transfer Price

Internal Revenue Code Section 482, related to the allocation of income and deductions among taxpayers, states: "In the case of any transfer of intangible property, the income with respect to such transfer or license shall be commensurate with the income attributable to the intangible." The purpose of Section 482 is to place a controlled taxpayer (i.e., a business or entity that is part of a controlled group for consolidated federal income tax reporting) on the same playing field as other taxpayers. International conglomerates may otherwise use intangible asset royalty rates so as to shift taxable income into countries with lower income tax rates, for example. Tax parity is achieved by analyzing the true economic income that should be derived from the arm's-length transfer or license of the intangible asset or intellectual property between two or more subsidiaries of the same parent company.

## Income Taxation Planning and Compliance

The analysis of intangible assets may be necessary for substantiating a charitable contribution deduction or an abandonment loss deduction, for establishing the cost basis for intangible asset amortization, for estimating the amount of built-in gain on the conversion from C corporation to S corporation status, and for proving the reasonableness of intangible asset royalty payments between a stockholder and a corporation.

## Ad Valorem Property Taxes

The analysis of commercial intangible assets is often an important aspect of the overall valuation of a taxable entity under the unitary method or under the summation method of property tax assessment. This is because some jurisdictions tax intangible property at different rates than tangible property. In addition, in some jurisdictions, certain intangible assets are exempt from the property taxation of the business enterprise that operates the intangibles. In other jurisdictions, all intangible assets are exempt from ad valorem property taxation. In such instances, the identification and valuation of intangible assets is a particularly important aspect of the property tax administration process.

## Litigation Support and Dispute Resolution

From the perspective of the users and creators of intangible assets, their rights to the subject intangible property should be protected. The intangible asset valuation process will help to identify the expected uses and applications of the subject intangible property. The costs involved in the registration and other legal protection of the intangible property can be better understood and justified when an intangible asset valuation process is conducted.

Other intangible asset analysis services that may be rendered to attorneys and to litigation participants include the identification and quantification of economic damages related to breach of contract, intellectual property infringement, business interruption, and other types of actions. Such controversy-related economic analyses typically include the estimation of the value of the intangible, the estimation of the decrement in the value of the intangible, the amount of lost profits suffered by the owner of the intangible, the appropriate royalty rate or other fee associated with the continued use of the intangible, or some other form of damage estimation.

## Business Formation and Dissolution

When businesses or professional practices merge, the owners' equity allocation is often a function of the relative contribution of intangible assets (e.g., client relationships, patents, know-how) and of tangible assets to the newly formed business enterprise. The appraisal of the contributed assets, both tangible and intangible, is essential for determining the value of the overall merged enterprise, for estimating the value of the shares of stock or of the partnership units issued for tax accounting and financial accounting purposes, for analyzing sale and leaseback opportunities, for developing a joint venture, for setting the rates associated with intangible asset licensing, and for investing in continuing research and development of the intellectual property. When businesses or professional practices dissolve, the settlement payments often relate to the value of the tangible and intangible assets that are transferred from the entity to the equity participants.

## Corporate Planning and Governance

When business owners and managers are responsible for improving a particular business unit's financial performance, it is often the performance of intangible assets that they wish to better leverage. This process of wealth maximization begins with understanding the factors that impact the value of the particular intangible asset (e.g., trade name, brand, customer relationships). The measurement of the change in an intangible asset's value over time is one component of the process of developing strategy and of accurately allocating future resources.

Intangible asset analyses may be useful as a tool for understanding the projected earnings capacity, cash flow generating ability, and remaining functional, technological, or economic life associated with the intangible property. Similarly, the business unit owner or manager may plan for the purchase or divestiture of a portion of an integrated process or product line. An intangible asset analysis can assist both in defining the parameters of that process or product line and in estimating the expected transactional market value of the process or product line.

### CONTRIBUTION OF INTANGIBLE ASSETS TO A BUSINESS ENTITY

Intellectual property developers sometimes contribute their property to a corporation or partnership in exchange for equity ownership interests. It then becomes the responsibility of the corporation or partnership to commercialize the subject intellectual property. The developer realizes an economic benefit associated with the commercialization process through the appreciation of the corporation or partnership ownership interests.

The contribution of intangible assets to a business entity raises two questions. The first question is: How much of the entity's equity ownership is a fair exchange for the subject intangible asset? This is often a three-sided valuation problem. First, the subject intangible asset should be appraised. Second, the subject business entity (and its corresponding equity ownership units) should be appraised. Third, a reasonable value exchange ratio should be estimated.

The second question raised by the contribution of intangible assets to a business entity is: What are the income tax consequences of the transaction? In particular, will economic gain be recognized by the intellectual property developer when the developer receives the equity units?

The Internal Revenue Service's position has been that the granting of rights to intangible property to a corporation will not qualify for non-recognition treatment under Internal Revenue Code Section 351 unless the shareholder transfers "all substantial rights" to the intangible property. The substantial rights test requires the transfer of the right to be: 1) exclusive; 2) for an entire country where the intangible is protected; 3) perpetual or for the entire period during which the intangible is protected; and, 4) for all fields of use.

A similar test applies with regard to the transfer of intangible property to a partnership in exchange for partnership ownership interests. Internal Revenue Code Section 721 provides for nonrecognition of gain to both the partner and the partnership if "all substantial rights" to the subject intangible property have been transferred.

## AUDIENCE FOR THE INTANGIBLE ASSET ANALYSIS

When considering the reasons to conduct an intangible asset analysis, the audience for the analysis is relevant on several levels. Depending on the audience for the analysis, the structure of the analytical work and of the work product could change.

If an intangible asset appraisal or economic analysis is being prepared for internal corporate governance purposes and the audience for the analysis work product is the company management, then the analyst will present the work product in a manner that is expected by the supervisor. A brief memorandum report may be required, for instance, that includes some of the internal company shorthand or jargon.

The manner in which the intangible asset analysis is conducted could also be affected by the audience for the work product. Again, in the case of an analysis that is prepared for management, the analyst may elect to forgo certain approaches to value or may choose to make certain analytical assumptions in order to prepare the analysis in a manner consistent with prior company practice and policies.

On the other hand, let's consider the instance when the very same intangible asset is being analyzed for litigation purposes, and the analysis is going to be presented to a jury as the trier of fact. In that circumstance, both the underlying analysis and the analysis work product will likely be prepared in an entirely different manner.

When intangible asset appraisals are being prepared in accordance with prevailing professional standards, the purpose of the analysis assignment should be clearly stated. Generally, a clear statement of the purpose of the assignment implies who the audience is for the analysis.

Certain audiences expect to see an analysis conducted in a certain manner. For example, for Internal Revenue Code Section 482 transfer pricing purposes, the relevant regulations would lead the analyst to perform certain analytical approaches that might not otherwise be considered. To continue the example, should the analysis ultimately be presented to a United States Tax Court judge, the profit split method, the cost-plus method, the comparable profits method, and other specific transfer pricing methods would be expected to be set forth in the economic analysis report.

Similarly, when an intangible asset appraisal is prepared for consideration by an ad valorem property tax tribunal, the estimated standard of value, the identified categories of intangible assets, and the appraisal procedures performed should comply with the expectations (and the precedent) of the jurisdiction in which the appraisal report will be applied. For example, an intangible asset appraisal report prepared for ad valorem property tax purposes may include a more expansive discussion of the nature of the going-concern value than would an analysis prepared for, say, a bankruptcy court.

These concerns related to the audience of the intangible asset analysis can certainly affect the manner in which the valuation assignment is conducted. They can even affect the intangible asset valuation conclusion.

## ANALYZING AN INTANGIBLE ASSET AS A COMPONENT OF A BUSINESS

Intangible assets often exist as part of an integrated assemblage of other business assets. The assets, some tangible and some intangible, are combined in order to provide economic income to the owners of the assets. It is typical to find intangible assets as part of going-concern businesses. Sometimes the owners of those businesses do not even recognize the individuality of their intangible assets. However, they may recognize that the collective assets of their business are worth more assembled together than they would be worth if they were sold off piecemeal.

In fact, most businesses own intangible assets. This is not a difficult concept to appreciate once you understand that the S&P 500 price index is several times the tangible asset book value of the companies included in the index. Even after adjustments for understated tangible asset values and other factors (such as capital cost recovery, for example), the fact remains that intangible asset value exists on a widespread basis in all sizes of businesses across corporate America.

The value of a business exceeds its tangible asset value because it requires more than capital spending or the addition of labor units to perpetuate business growth. Diminishing returns on those capital asset investments eventually dampen growth. It's the underlying intangible asset value—and the coordination of those assets—that fuels growth.

Rather than simply referring to the business value in excess of tangible asset value as "blue sky" or "goodwill," sophisticated business owners and managers look for a deeper explanation. The intangible assets of a commercial enterprise contribute to the economic income of the business enterprise as much as the buildings and machinery. Earnings from intangible assets may be even less vulnerable to competition than earnings from the more traditional tangible assets.

When appraising an intangible asset component of a going-concern business, the analyst uses procedures that recognize that the value of the business intangible assets depends on those assets' contribution to the overall economic income of the business entity.

## ANALYZING AN INTANGIBLE ASSET AS AN INDEPENDENT ECONOMIC UNIT

While intangible assets typically function as part of a going-concern business enterprise, many intangible assets are bought, sold, and licensed as independent intellectual properties. Intellectual properties such as trade secrets, patents, copyrights, trademarks, and many others are independent economic units. That is, they can generate income (and, therefore, clearly have value) separately and independently from any other assets, tangible or intangible.

In addition, many intangible assets that do not qualify as intellectual properties may qualify as independent economic units. That is, these assets may be sold or licensed separately and independently from other business assets. This is true for many engineering-related, marketing-related, data processing–related, and contract-related intangible assets. To a lesser extent, it is even true with respect to certain customer-related intangible assets. For example, customer lists are routinely rented or licensed.

In the remainder of this text, we will distinguish the various procedures that are applicable to the analysis of an intangible asset as an independent economic unit from those applicable to the analysis of an intangible asset as part of a going-concern business. As we will see, there are many similarities among these procedures, but also some subtle differences.

## SUMMARY

Chapter 2 introduced several of the many common reasons to conduct an appraisal or economic analysis of intangible assets. While there are almost countless client motivations for performing such analyses, these motivations are often grouped into common categories of reasons. These common categories of reasons include: transactional, financing, taxation, informational, bankruptcy, and litigation.

Chapter 2 also introduced the differences between transactional analyses and notational analyses. These differences will be explored in detail in later chapters. Finally, we introduced the differences between analyzing an intangible asset as a component of a business and analyzing it as an independent economic unit. In later chapters, we will distinguish which analytical methods are more appropriate for each of these two premises of analysis.

# Professional Standards Related to Intangible Asset Appraisals

# INTRODUCTION

The need to understand the value of intangible assets has increased dramatically in the last ten years. Transactions encompassing the sale or license of intangible assets as independent economic units are progressively more common in this era of the information superhighway. Disputes involving the rights associated with and the value of intangible assets have become more intense and sophisticated. When a party to either a transaction or a dispute is motivated by the financial consequences of valuing an intangible asset to use one set of valuation standards versus another set of valuation standards, then the dispute may center around which set of professional standards apply.

This chapter provides an overview of intangible asset valuation professional standards, the organizations that promulgate them, and the educational resources available to intangible asset analysts and to the users of intangible asset analyses.

Intangible asset valuation professional standards include the *Uniform Standards of Professional Appraisal Practice* and certain professional standards of the American Society of Appraisers. In addition, some professional guidance is provided by certain pronouncements of the Internal Revenue Service. We will review these standards and pronouncements in the following sections.

# UNIFORM STANDARDS OF PROFESSIONAL APPRAISAL PRACTICE

The *Uniform Standards of Professional Appraisal Practice* (USPAP) may be regarded as an umbrella set of professional standards that are appropriate for many types of appraisal engagements, including appraisals of real estate, personal property, businesses, business interests, or intangible assets.

USPAP is promulgated by the Appraisal Standards Board (ASB) of The Appraisal Foundation. The Appraisal Foundation is a not-for-profit educational organization established in 1987 and funded, in part, by the U.S. government. The goal of The Appraisal Foundation is to foster professionalism in appraising through the establishment and promotion of appraisal standards and appraiser qualifications.

According to the Mission Statement of The Appraisal Foundation, "the Appraisal Standards Board promulgates the generally accepted standards of the appraisal profession." The fact that these standards are, indeed, reaching a position of general acceptance is evidenced by the frequent references to USPAP both in court decisions and in the professional literature.

The USPAP provisions are generally arranged as follows:

1. An introductory section that encompasses ethics provisions, competency provisions, and a statement of definitions.
2. Standards 1 and 2, real property appraisals.
3. Standard 3, review appraisals.
4. Standards 4 and 5, real estate consulting engagements.
5. Standard 6, mass appraisals for ad valorem property taxation purposes.
6. Standards 7 and 8, tangible personal property appraisals.

7. Standards 9 and 10, business appraisals.
8. Statements on professional standards (currently there are nine statements (SMTs)).
9. Advisory opinions (currently there are 17 advisory opinions (AOs)).
10. A comprehensive glossary.

Specifically, USPAP standards 9 and 10 also address the valuation of intangible assets. Standard 9 promulgates guidelines regarding the approaches, methods, and procedures for conducting an intangible asset appraisal. Standard 10 promulgates guidelines with respect to the reporting of the intangible asset appraisal.

The Appraisal Standards Board publishes an updated version of USPAP annually, presently in November. (See the Bibliography at the end of the chapter for ordering information.) An outline of the content of the 1997 edition of USPAP is shown in Exhibit 3-1.

The Appraisal Foundation also has an Appraiser Qualifications Board (AQB). Its mission is to establish educational, experience, and examination criteria for appraisers. At the time of this writing, the AQB has established qualifications for real estate appraisers but has not yet committed to the task of establishing qualifications for intangible asset appraisers.

## AMERICAN SOCIETY OF APPRAISERS

The American Society of Appraisers (ASA) is a multidisciplinary professional society founded in 1952. It awards accreditations in appraisal of real estate, machinery and equipment, personal property, gems and jewelry, business valuation, and appraisal review and management. Within the American Society of Appraisers organizational structure, the general discipline of business valuation encompasses the subdiscipline of intangible asset appraisal.

Through its Business Valuation Committee, the ASA issues the American Society of Appraisers Business Valuation Standards. The ASA standards embrace USPAP and provide some additional professional guidance with respect to the requirements for performing an intangible asset appraisal and for reporting an intangible asset appraisal.

Exhibit 3-2 provides a summary of the ASA business valuation accreditation requirements and educational offerings. (See the Bibliography at the end of the chapter for information on ordering ASA materials.)

## INTERNAL REVENUE SERVICE

The Internal Revenue Service (the "Service") does not promulgate professional standards with respect to intangible asset appraisals. However, the Service issues a number of publications that provide various levels of professional guidance for intangible asset valuations.

The United States Congress directs the U.S. Treasury Department to issue regulations to provide structure for the tax laws Congress passes. These regulations do not have the force of law, but they do present the position of the Service with respect to various tax matters, including the valuation of businesses, business interests, and related intangible assets. Reg-

UNIFORM STANDARDS OF PROFESSIONAL APPRAISAL PRACTICE, TABLE OF CONTENTS

INTRODUCTION

STANDARDS AND STANDARDS RULES

STATEMENTS ON APPRAISAL STANDARDS

ADDENDA

REFERENCE MATERIAL (for guidance only)

ADVISORY OPINIONS

*Source: Uniform Standards of Professional Appraisal Practice* (Washington, DC: The Appraisal Foundation, 1998). Reprinted with permission of The Appraisal Foundation.

American Society of Appraisers (ASA)
P.O. Box 17265, Washington, D.C. 20041, (703) 478-2228

| | | |
|---|---|---|
| Date formed: | 1952      Ownership: | Owned by members |
| Description: | Multidisciplinary professional organization offering courses and exams leading to designations in the appraisal of real estate, machinery and equipment, personal property, gems and jewelry, businesses and business interests (including intangible assets), and certain technical specialties. | |
| Designations offered: | *AM—Accredited Member:* | |
| | Educational requirement: | College degree or equivalent |
| | Courses/exams: | Completion of four courses of three days each, with successful completion of one half-day exam following each of the three courses and a full-day exam following BV204, OR successful completion of one all-day challenge exam. In addition, successful completion of an ethics exam is required. |
| | Reports: | Submission of two actual appraisal reports to satisfaction of Board of Examiners |
| | Experience requirement: | Two years full-time or full-time equivalent (e.g., 5 years of 400 hours business appraisal work per year equals one year full-time equivalent). |
| | Related experience offset: | One full year of the experience requirement is granted to anyone who has any of the following three designations with five years of practice in that respective field: Certified Public Accountant (CPA), Chartered Financial Analyst (CFA), or Certified Business Intermediary (CBI). |
| | *ASA—Accredited Senior Appraiser:* | |
| | | has met all requirements above plus an additional three years of full-time or full-time equivalent experience. |
| | *FASA—Fellow of the American Society of Appraisers:* | |
| | | has met all requirements above plus is voted into the College of Fellows on the basis of technical leadership and contribution to the profession and the Society. |
| Courses: | Each of the core courses (BV201–204) are three days; BV201 through 203 are followed by a half-day exam and BV204 is following by a full-day exam. BV205 and 206 are two days each. | |
| | BV201: | Introduction to business valuation, part one |
| | BV202: | Introduction to business valuation, part two |
| | BV203: | Business valuation case study |
| | BV204: | Business valuation selected advanced topics |
| | BV205: | Appraisal of small businesses and professional practices |
| | BV206: | Employee stock ownership plans: valuing ESOP shares |
| Seminars and Conferences: | Seminars on specialized topics lasting from two hours to two days and sponsored by various groups within the ASA. | |
| | Annual interdisciplinary meeting with two and a half days of technical presentations on each of the Society's appraisal disciplines. | |
| | Annual Advanced Business Valuation Conference with two or two and a half days of advanced business valuation papers, presentations, and discussion. | |
| Publications: | *Business Valuation Review,* quarterly professional journal with articles accepted based on peer review. Published at 2777 South Colorado Boulevard, Suite 200, Denver, Colorado 80222, (303) 758-8818. The other valuation disciplines also have their professional journals, similar to *Business Valuation Review.* *Valuation,* published on an irregular basis, contains articles on all of the disciplines of valuation within the ASA. Published at ASA headquarters (see title of exhibit for address). | |
| Local chapters: | Chapters with regular monthly meetings in 87 cities throughout the United States and Canada | |

*Source:* Shannon P. Pratt, Robert F. Reilly, and Robert P. Schweihs, *Valuing Small Businesses and Professional Practices,* 3rd ed. (New York: McGraw-Hill, 1998).

ulations are actually formulated by the Service, but they are approved by the Secretary of the Treasury or a delegate. As an example, the regulations for Chapter 14 of the estate and gift tax laws require appraisers to use a special valuation methodology in certain circumstances with regard to the appraisal of family-owned businesses.

The Service issues pronouncements representing administrative (as opposed to legislative) tax authority. The pronouncements include: Revenue Rulings, Revenue Procedures, Letter Rulings, Technical Advice

Memorandums, and General Counsel Memorandums. The pronouncements illustrate the treatment of certain issues not clearly addressed in the regulations. Over time, many of the positions espoused by the Service through regulations and revenue rulings come up in court disputes. The resolution of these issues by the courts establishes judicial precedent. Much, but by no means all, of the case law has been supportive of positions taken in the regulations and revenue rulings. The most important revenue ruling that relates to intangible asset valuation is Revenue Ruling 68-609. This ruling discusses the "formula method" for estimating the fair market value of the intangible value in the nature of goodwill of a going-concern business enterprise.

## Section 197

As mentioned in Chapter 2, Internal Revenue Code Section 197 deals with the capitalization and amortization of purchased intangible assets. Accordingly, Section 197 deals with a very specific, income taxation–related area of intangible asset analysis. Nonetheless, Section 197 may provide the most comprehensive discussion of the identification and valuation of intangible assets to be found in the Internal Revenue Code.

According to Section 197, intangible property is personal property that cannot be seen or touched, such as a copyright, franchise, patent, trademark, or trade name. In general, intangible property may be depreciated, usually using the straight-line method over the intangible's useful life, provided that it is used in a trade or business or for the production of income and the useful life can be determined with reasonable accuracy. The depreciation deduction on an intangible asset is commonly referred to as an amortization deduction.

Prior to the enactment of Section 197, the amortization of the costs of acquiring intangible business and income-producing assets had been an area of considerable controversy between the Service and taxpayers. Many types of acquired intangibles could not be amortized in the Service's view, because they were inseparable from goodwill, or because they had no determinable useful life over which to claim deductions. Although it is an intricate provision, Section 197, as enacted by the Revenue Reconciliation Act of 1993 (P.L. 103-66), has eliminated many disputes in this area by providing a uniform 15-year amortization period for the capitalized cost of most intangible assets, including goodwill (which, until this legislation, was not amortizable for tax purposes), acquired for use in a trade or business or in an activity engaged in for the production of income.

This income taxation provision applies to amortizable Section 197 intangibles acquired after August 10, 1993, unless an election was made to apply the new rules to all Section 197 intangibles acquired after July 25, 1991. Amortization under Code Section 197 is claimed ratably over 15 years, beginning in the month that the Section 197 intangible is placed in service, regardless of its actual useful life.

As delineated in Section 197(d), Section 197 intangibles are defined as:

1. Goodwill and going-concern value. (These intangible assets were not amortizable under former law under any circumstance.)
2. Workforce in place, such as the portion of the purchase price of a business attributable to the existence of highly skilled employees.

3. Business books and records, operating systems, or any other information base, including customer lists or other information with respect to current or future customers.
4. Patents, copyrights, formulas, processes, designs, patterns, know-how, formats, or similar items.
5. Customer-based intangibles, such as a business's market composition or market share.
6. Supplier-based intangibles, such as a business's favorable relationships with distributors.
7. Licenses, permits, or other rights granted by a governmental unit or agency, such as a liquor license, a taxi-cab medallion or license, or a television or radio broadcasting license (including issuance and renewal costs).
8. Franchises, trademarks, or trade names.
9. Covenants not to compete entered into in connection with the acquisition of a business.

With the exception of items 7 through 9, a Section 197 intangible that is created through a taxpayer's own efforts is not amortizable unless created in connection with the acquisition of a substantial portion of a trade or business.

In addition to self-created intangibles, these intangibles cannot qualify as Section 197 intangibles under the provisions of Section 197(e):

1. Interests in a corporation, partnership, trust, or estate.
2. Interests under an existing futures contract, foreign currency contract, notional principal contract, or other similar financial contract.
3. Interests in land.
4. Interests under existing leases of tangible property.
5. Interests under existing indebtedness.
6. Sports franchises.
7. Fees paid for professional services and other transaction costs in a tax-free corporate organization or reorganization.

Unless acquired in connection with the acquisition of a trade or business or a substantial portion of a trade or business, and also according to Section 197(e), the exclusion also applies to:

1. An interest in a film, sound recording, videotape, book, or similar property.
2. A right to receive tangible property or services under a contract or granted by a governmental agency.
3. An interest in a patent or copyright.
4. A right under a contract or granted by a governmental agency if the right has a fixed life of less than 15 years or is fixed in amount and (but for the Section 197 intangible provisions) would be recoverable under a method similar to the unit-of-production method.

Computer software acquired after August 10, 1993 is an amortizable Section 197 intangible if it is acquired in connection with a trade or business. However, for federal income tax purposes, computer software is depreciable over 36 months, using the straight-line method beginning in the month of acquisition, provided it is readily available for purchase by the general public, is subject to a nonexclusive license, and has not been substantially modified. The 36-month depreciation period also applies to other computer software not acquired in connection with the purchase of a business, according to the provisions of Section 197(e)(3).

## Section 482

The regulations promulgated under Section 482 include a comprehensive discussion of the methods for estimating an appropriate intercompany transfer price for intangible assets. Technically, these regulations are only applicable with respect to the intercompany transfer of intangible assets between controlled corporations (and, typically, between domestic and foreign controlled corporations). Nonetheless, even in situations where Section 482 does not apply (e.g., for non-income-taxation-related analyses), the analyst may want to reference the regulations because they provide exhaustive technical guidance with respect to this area of economic analysis of intangible assets.

The topic of intercompany transfer pricing is discussed at length in Chapter 25. Accordingly, we will introduce it here only by reference to the voluminous nature of the regulations related to Section 482. Exhibit 3-3 presents Regulation 1.482-0. This regulation presents the outline or table of contents for Regulations 1.482-1 through 1.482-8.

Exhibit 3-4 presents Regulation 1.482-4, Section (b) only. Regulation 1.482-4 deals with the appropriate methods for determining taxable income in connection with the transfer of intangible property between controlled corporations. Section (b) of Regulation 1.482-4 presents the definition of "intangibles" for purposes of Section 482.

## Section 170

Section 170 does not specifically relate to intangible assets. Rather, Section 170 covers the income taxation provisions with respect to a charitable contribution deduction. However, the regulations under Section 170 describe the terms *qualified appraiser* and *qualified appraisal*. While these terms are only directly applicable in connection with the substantiation of charitable contribution deductions (and some other limited income taxation applications), they are noteworthy to intangible asset analysts generally.

In other words, there are surely numerous instances when an analyst wants to be characterized as a qualified appraiser and numerous instances when the analyst would want the analytical work product to be accepted as a qualified appraisal. So, while the regulations under Section 170 certainly do not qualify as promulgated professional standards to intangible asset appraisers, they do reveal the benchmark that the Service uses in recognizing qualified appraisers and qualified appraisals.

Exhibit 3-5 presents Regulation 1.170A-13(c)(3), which describes the Service requirements for a qualified appraisal.

Exhibit 3-6 presents Regulation 1.170A-13(c)(5), which describes the Service requirements for a qualified appraiser.

Treasury Regulations Section 1.482-0

§ 1.482-0. OUTLINE OF REGULATIONS UNDER 482—This section contains major captions for sections 1.482-1 through 1.482-8.

§ 1.482-1 *Allocation of Income and Deductions among Taxpayers.*
- (a) In general.
  - (1) Purpose and scope.
  - (2) Authority to make allocations.
  - (3) Taxpayer's use of section 482.
- (b) Arm's length standard.
  - (1) In general.
  - (2) Arm's length methods.
    - (i) Methods.
    - (ii) Selection of category of method applicable to transaction.
- (c) Best method rule.
  - (1) In general.
  - (2) Determining the best method.
    - (i) Comparability.
    - (ii) Data and assumptions.
      - (A) Completeness and accuracy of data.
      - (B) Reliability of assumptions.
      - (C) Sensitivity of results to deficiencies in data and assumptions.
    - (iii) Confirmation of results by another method.
- (d) Comparability.
  - (1) In general.
  - (2) Standard of comparability.
  - (3) Factors for determining comparability.
    - (i) Functional analysis.
    - (ii) Contractual terms.
      - (A) In general.
      - (B) Identifying contractual terms.
        - (1) Written agreement.
        - (2) No written agreement.
      - (C) Examples.
    - (iii) Risk.
      - (A) Comparability.
      - (B) Identification of party that bears risk.
      - (C) Examples.
    - (iv) Economic conditions.
    - (v) Property or services.
  - (4) Special circumstances.
    - (i) Market share strategy.
    - (ii) Different geographic markets.
      - (A) In general.
      - (B) Example.
      - (C) Location savings.
      - (D) Example.
    - (iii) Transactions ordinarily not accepted as comparables.
      - (A) In general.
      - (B) Examples.
- (e) Arm's length range.
  - (1) In general.
  - (2) Determination of arm's length range.
    - (i) Single method.
    - (ii) Selection of comparables.
    - (iii) Comparables included in arm's length range.

- (A) In general.
- (B) Adjustment of range to increase reliability.
- (C) Interquartile range.
  - (3) Adjustment if taxpayer's results are outside arm's length range.
  - (4) Arm's length range not prerequisite to allocation.
  - (5) Examples.
- (f) Scope of review.
  - (1) In general.
    - (i) Intent to evade or avoid tax not a prerequisite.
    - (ii) Realization of income not a prerequisite.
      - (A) In general.
      - (B) Example.
    - (iii) Nonrecognition provisions may not bar allocation.
      - (A) In general.
      - (B) Example.
    - (iv) Consolidated returns.
  - (2) Rules relating to determination of true taxable income.
    - (i) Aggregation of transactions.
      - (A) In general.
      - (B) Examples.
    - (ii) Allocation based on taxpayer's actual transactions.
      - (A) In general.
      - (B) Example.
    - (iii) Multiple year data.
      - (A) In general.
      - (B) Circumstances warranting consideration of multiple year data.
      - (C) Comparable effect over comparable period.
      - (D) Applications of methods using multiple year averages.
      - (E) Examples.
    - (iv) Product lines and statistical techniques.
    - (v) Allocations apply to results, not methods.
      - (A) In general.
      - (B) Example.
- (g) Collateral adjustments with respect to allocations under section 482.
  - (1) In general.
  - (2) Correlative allocations.
    - (i) In general.
    - (ii) Manner of carrying out correlative allocation.
    - (iii) Events triggering correlative allocation.
    - (iv) Examples.
  - (3) Adjustments to conform accounts to reflect section 482 allocations.
    - (i) In general.
    - (ii) Example.
  - (4) Setoffs.
    - (i) In general.
    - (ii) Requirements.
    - (iii) Examples.
- (h) Special rules.
  - (1) Small taxpayer safe harbor [Reserved].
  - (2) Effect of foreign legal restrictions.
    - (i) In general.
    - (ii) Applicable legal restrictions.

(iii) Requirement for electing the deferred income
  method of accounting
(iv) Deferred income method of accounting.
  (v) Examples.
  (3) Coordination with section 936.
    (i) Cost sharing under section 936.
    (ii) Use of terms.
(i) Definitions.
(j) Effective dates.
§ 1.482-2 *Determination of Taxable Income in Specific Situations.*
(a) Loans or advances.
  (1) Interest on bona fide indebtedness.
    (i) In general.
    (ii) Application of paragraph (a) of this section.
      (A) Interest on bona fide indebtedness.
      (B) Alleged indebtedness.
    (iii) Period for which interest shall be charged.
      (A) General rule.
      (B) Exception for certain intercompany
        transactions in the ordinary course of
        business.
      (C) Exception for trade or business of debtor
        member located outside the United States.
      (D) Exception for regular trade practice of
        creditor member or others in creditor's
        industry.
      (E) Exception for property purchased for resale
        in a foreign country.
        (1) General rule.
        (2) Interest-free period.
        (3) Average collection period.
        (4) Illustration.
    (iv) Payment; book entries.
  (2) Arm's length interest rate.
    (i) In general.
    (ii) Funds obtained at situs of borrower.
    (iii) Safe haven interest rates for certain loans and
      advances made after May 8, 1986.
      (A) Applicability.
        (1) General rule.
        (2) Grandfather rule for existing loans.
      (B) Safe haven interest rate based on
        applicable Federal rate.
      (C) Applicable Federal rate.
      (D) Lender in business of making loans.
      (E) Foreign currency loans.
  (3) Coordination with interest adjustments required
    under certain other Internal Revenue Code
    sections.
  (4) Examples.
(b) Performance of services for another.
  (1) General rule.
  (2) Benefit test.
  (3) Arm's length charge.
  (4) Costs or deductions to be taken into account.
  (5) Costs and deductions not to be taken into account.
  (6) Methods.
  (7) Certain services.
  (8) Services rendered in connection with the transfer of
    property.

(c) Use of tangible property.
  (1) General rule.
  (2) Arm's length charge.
    (i) In general.
    (ii) Safe haven rental charge.
    (iii) Subleases.
(d) Transfer of property.
§ 1.482-3 *Methods to Determine Taxable Income in Connection
with a Transfer of Tangible Property.*
(a) In general.
(b) Comparable uncontrolled price method.
  (1) In general.
  (2) Comparability and reliability considerations.
    (i) In general.
    (ii) Comparability.
      (A) In general.
      (B) Adjustments for differences between
        controlled and uncontrolled transactions.
    (iii) Data and assumptions.
  (3) Arm's length range.
  (4) Examples.
  (5) Indirect evidence of comparable uncontrolled
    transactions.
    (i) In general.
    (ii) Limitations.
    (iii) Examples.
(c) Resale price method.
  (1) In general.
  (2) Determination of arm's length price.
    (i) In general.
    (ii) Applicable resale price.
    (iii) Appropriate gross profit.
    (iv) Arm's length range.
  (3) Comparability and reliability considerations.
    (i) In general.
    (ii) Comparability.
      (A) Functional comparability.
      (B) Other comparability factors.
      (C) Adjustments for differences between
        controlled and uncontrolled transactions.
      (D) Sales agent.
    (iii) Data and assumptions.
      (A) In general.
      (B) Consistency in accounting.
  (4) Examples.
(d) Cost plus method.
  (1) In general.
  (2) Determination of arm's length price.
    (i) In general.
    (ii) Appropriate gross profit.
    (iii) Arm's length range.
  (3) Comparability and reliability considerations.
    (i) In general.
    (ii) Comparability.
      (A) Functional comparability.
      (B) Other comparability factors.
      (C) Adjustments for differences between
        controlled and uncontrolled transactions.
      (D) Purchasing agent.
    (iii) Data and assumptions.
      (A) In general.

(B) Consistency in accounting.
(C) Examples.
(e) Unspecified methods.
(1) In general.
(2) Example.
(f) Coordination with intangible property rules.
§ 1.482-4 *Methods to Determine Taxable Income in Connection with a Transfer of Intangible Property.*
(a) In general.
(b) Definition of intangible.
(c) Comparable uncontrolled transaction method.
(1) In general.
(2) Comparability and reliability considerations.
(i) In general.
(ii) Reliability.
(iii) Comparability.
(A) In general.
(B) Factors to be considered in determining comparability.
(1) Comparable intangible property.
(2) Comparable circumstances.
(iv) Data and assumptions.
(3) Arm's length range.
(4) Examples.
(d) Unspecified methods.
(1) In general.
(2) Example.
(e) Coordination with tangible property rules.
(f) Special rules for transfers of intangible property.
(1) Form of consideration.
(2) Periodic adjustments.
(i) General rule.
(ii) Exceptions.
(A) Transactions involving the same intangible.
(B) Transactions involving comparable intangible.
(C) Methods other than comparable uncontrolled transaction.
(D) Extraordinary events.
(E) Five-year period.
(iii) Examples.
(3) Ownership of intangible property.
(i) In general.
(ii) Identification of the owner.
(A) Legally protected intangible property.
(B) Intangible property that is not legally protected.
(iii) Allocations with respect to assistance provided to the owner.
(iv) Examples.
(4) Consideration not artificially limited.
(5) Lump sum payments.
(i) In general.
(ii) Exceptions.
(iii) Example.
§ 1.482-5 *Comparable Profits Method.*
(a) In general.
(b) Determination of arm's length result.
(1) In general.
(2) Tested party.

(i) In general.
(ii) Adjustments for tested party.
(3) Arm's length range.
(4) Profit level indicators.
(i) Rate of return on capital employed.
(ii) Financial ratios.
(iii) Other profit level indicators.
(c) Comparability and reliability considerations.
(1) In general.
(2) Comparability.
(i) In general.
(ii) Functional, risk and resource comparability.
(iii) Other comparability factors.
(iv) Adjustments for differences between tested party and the uncontrolled taxpayers.
(3) Data and assumptions.
(i) In general.
(ii) Consistency in accounting.
(iii) Allocations between the relevant business activity and other activities.
(d) Definitions.
(e) Examples.
§ 1.482-6 *Profit Split Method.*
(a) In general.
(b) Appropriate share of profits and losses.
(c) Application.
(1) In general.
(2) Comparable profit split.
(i) In general.
(ii) Comparability and reliability considerations.
(A) In general.
(B) Comparability.
(1) In general.
(2) Adjustments for differences between the controlled and uncontrolled taxpayers.
(C) Data and assumptions.
(D) Other factors affecting reliability.
(3) Residual profit split.
(i) In general.
(A) Allocate income to routine contributions.
(B) Allocate residual profit.
(ii) Comparability and reliability considerations.
(A) In general.
(B) Comparability.
(C) Data and assumptions.
(D) Other factors affecting reliability.
(iii) Example.
§ 1.482-7 *Sharing of Costs.*
(a) In general.
(1) Scope and application of the rules in this section.
(2) Limitation on allocations.
(3) Cross references.
(b) Qualified cost sharing arrangement.
(c) Participant.
(1) In general.
(2) Treatment of a controlled taxpayer that is not a controlled participant.
(i) In general.
(ii) Example.

Treasury Regulations Section 1.482-0

(3) Treatment of consolidated group.
(d) Costs.
   (1) Intangible development costs.
   (2) Examples.
(e) Anticipated benefits.
   (1) Benefits.
   (2) Reasonably anticipated benefits.
(f) Cost allocations.
   (1) In general.
   (2) Share of intangible development costs.
      (i) In general.
      (ii) Example.
   (3) Share of reasonably anticipated benefits.
      (i) In general.
      (ii) Measure of benefits.
      (iii) Indirect bases for measuring anticipated benefits.
         (A) Units used, produced or sold.
         (B) Sales.
         (C) Operating profit.
         (D) Other bases for measuring anticipated benefits.
         (E) Examples.
      (iv) Projections used to estimate anticipated benefits.
         (A) In general.
         (B) Unreliable projections.
         (C) Foreign-to-foreign adjustments.
         (D) Examples.
   (4) Timing of allocations.
(g) Allocations of income, deductions or other tax items to reflect transfers of intangibles (buy-in).

(1) In general.
(2) Pre-existing intangibles.
(3) New controlled participant.
(4) Controlled participant relinquishes interests.
(5) Conduct inconsistent with the terms of a cost sharing arrangement.
(6) Failure to assign interests under a qualified cost sharing arrangement.
(7) Form of consideration.
   (i) Lump sum payments.
   (ii) Installment payments.
   (iii) Royalties.
(8) Examples.
(h) Character of payments made pursuant to a qualified cost sharing arrangement.
   (1) In general.
   (2) Examples.
(i) Accounting requirements.
(j) Administrative requirements.
   (1) In general.
   (2) Documentation.
      (i) Requirements.
      (ii) Coordination with penalty regulation.
   (3) Reporting requirements.
(k) Effective date.
(l) Transition rule.
§ 1.482-8 *Examples of the Best Method Rule.*
(a) In general.
(b) Examples.

*Source:* Treas. Reg. §1.482-0 (as amended 1996).

---

**E X H I B I T** 3-4

Treasury Regulations Section 1.482-4(b)

(b) *Definition of Intangible.* For purposes of section 482, an intangible is an asset that comprises any of the following items and has substantial value independent of the services of any individual—

   (1) Patents, inventions, formulae, processes, designs, patterns, or know-how;

   (2) Copyrights and literary, musical, or artistic compositions;

   (3) Trademarks, trade names, or brand names;

   (4) Franchises, licenses, or contracts;

   (5) Methods, programs, systems, procedures, campaigns, surveys, studies, forecasts, estimates, customer lists, or technical data; and

   (6) Other similar items. For purposes of section 482, an item is considered similar to those listed in paragraph (b)(1) through (5) of this section if it derives its value not from its physical attributes but from its intellectual content or other intangible properties.

*Source:* Treas. Reg. §1.482-4(b) (as amended 1994).

EXHIBIT 3-5

Treasury Regulations Section 1.170A-13(c)(3)

---

(3) *Qualified Appraisal*—

(i) *In general.* For purposes of this paragraph (c), the term "qualified appraisal" means an appraisal document that—

(A) Relates to an appraisal that is made not earlier than 60 days prior to the date of contribution of the appraised property nor later than the date specified in paragraph (c) (3)(iv)(B) of this section;

(B) Is prepared, signed, and dated by a qualified appraiser (within the meaning of paragraph (c)(5) of this section);

(C) Includes the information required by paragraph (c)(3)(ii) of this section; and

(D) Does not involve an appraisal fee prohibited by paragraph (c)(6) of this section.

(ii) *Information included in qualified appraisal.* A qualified appraisal shall include the following information:

(A) A description of the property in sufficient detail for a person who is not generally familiar with the type of property to ascertain that the property that was appraised is the property that was (or will be) contributed;

(B) In the case of tangible property, the physical condition of the property;

(C) The date (or expected date) of contribution to the donee;

(D) The terms of any agreement or understanding entered into (or expected to be entered into) by or on behalf of the donor or donee that relates to the use, sale, or other disposition of the property contributed, including, for example, the terms of any agreement or understanding that—

(1) Restricts temporarily or permanently a donee's right to use or dispose of the donated property,

(2) Reserves to, or confers upon, anyone (other than a donee organization or an organization participating with a donee organization in cooperative fundraising) any right to the income from the contributed property or to the possession of the property, including the right to vote donated securities, to acquire the property by purchase or otherwise, or to designate the person having such income, possession, or right to acquire, or

(3) Earmarks donated property for a particular use;

(E) The name, address, and (if a taxpayer identification number is otherwise required by section 6109 and the regulations thereunder) the identifying number of the qualified appraiser; and, if the qualified appraiser is acting in his or her capacity as a partner in a partnership, an employee of any person (whether an individual, corporation, or partnerships), or an independent contractor engaged by a person other than the donor, the name, address, and taxpayer identification number (if a number is otherwise required by section 6109 and the regulations thereunder) of the partnership or the person who employs or engages the qualified appraiser;

(F) The qualifications of the qualified appraiser who signs the appraisal, including the appraiser's background, experience, education, and membership, if any, in professional appraisal associations;

(G) A statement that the appraisal was prepared for income tax purposes;

(H) The date (or dates) on which the property was appraised;

(I) The appraised fair market value (within the meaning of Section 1.170A-1(c)(2)) of the property on the date (or expected date) of contribution;

(J) The method of valuation used to determine the fair market value, such as the income approach, the market-data approach, and the replacement-cost-less-depreciation approach; and

(K) The specific basis for the valuation, such as specific comparable sales transactions or statistical sampling, including a justification for using sampling and an explanation of the sampling procedure employed.

(iii) *Effect of signature of the qualified appraiser.* Any appraiser who falsely or fraudulently overstates the value of the contributed property referred to in a qualified appraisal or appraisal summary (as defined in paragraphs (c)(3) and (4), respectively, of this section) that the appraiser has signed may be subject to a civil penalty under section 6701 for aiding and abetting an understatement of tax liability and, moreover, may have appraisals disregarded pursuant to 31 U.S.C. 330(c).

(iv) *Special rules*—

(A) Number of Qualified Appraisals. For purposes of paragraph (c)(2)(i)(A) of this section, a separate qualified appraisal is required for each item of property that is not included in a group of similar items of property. See paragraph (c)(7)(iii) of this section for the definition of similar items of property. Only one qualified appraisal is required for a group of similar items of property contributed in the same taxable year of the donor, although a donor may obtain separate qualified appraisals for each item of property. A qualified appraisal prepared with respect to a group of similar items of property shall provide all the information required by paragraph (c)(3)(ii) of this section for each item of similar property, except that the appraiser may select any items whose aggregate value is appraised at $100 or less and provide a group description of such items.

(B) Time of Receipt of Qualified Appraisal. The qualified appraisal must be received by the donor before the due date (including extensions) of the return on which a deduction is first claimed (or reported in the case of a donor that is a partnership or S corporation) under section 170 with respect to the donated property, or, in the case of a deduction first claimed (or reported) on an amended return, the date on which the return is filed.

(C) Retention of Qualified Appraisal. The donor must retain the qualified appraisal in the donor's records for so long as it may be relevant in the administration of any internal revenue law.

(D) Appraisal Disregarded Pursuant to 31 U.S.C. 330(c). If an appraisal is disregarded pursuant to 31 U.S.C. 330(c) it shall have no probative effect as to the value of the appraised property. Such appraisal will, however, otherwise constitute a "qualified appraisal" for purposes of this paragraph (c) if the appraisal summary includes the declaration described in paragraph (c)(4)(ii)(L)(2) and the taxpayer had no knowledge that such declaration was false as of the time described in paragraph (c)(4)(i)(B) of this section.

---

*Source:* Treas. Reg. §1.170A-13(c)(3) (as amended 1996).

(5) *Qualified Appraiser—*
  (i) *In general.* The term "qualified appraiser" means an individual (other than a person described in paragraph (c)(5)(iv) of this section) who includes on the appraisal summary (described in paragraph (c)(4) of this section), a declaration that—
    (A) The individual either holds himself or herself out to the public as an appraiser or performs appraisals on a regular basis;
    (B) Because of the appraiser's qualifications as described in the appraisal (pursuant to paragraph (c)(3)(ii)(F) of this section), the appraiser is qualified to make appraisals of the type of property being valued;
    (C) The appraiser is not one of the persons described in paragraph (c)(5)(iv) of this section; and
    (D) The appraiser understands that an intentionally false or fraudulent overstatement of the value of the property described in the qualified appraisal or appraisal summary may subject the appraiser to a civil penalty under section 6701 for aiding and abetting an understatement of tax liability, and, moreover, the appraiser may have appraisals disregarded pursuant to 31 U.S.C. 330(c) (see paragraph (c)(3)(iii) of this section).
  (ii) *Exception.* An individual is not a qualified appraiser with respect to a particular donation, even if the declaration specified in paragraph (c)(5)(i) of this section is provided in the appraisal summary, if the donor had knowledge of facts that would cause a reasonable person to expect the appraiser falsely to overstate the value of the donated property (e.g., the donor and the appraiser make an agreement concerning the amount at which the property will be valued and the donor knows that such amount exceeds the fair market value of the property).
  (iii) *Numbers of appraisers.* More than one appraiser may appraise the donated property. If more than one appraiser appraises the property, the donor does not have to use each appraiser's appraisal for purposes of substantiating the charitable contribution deduction pursuant to this paragraph (c). If the donor uses the appraisal of more than one appraiser, or if two or more appraisers contribute to a single appraisal, each appraiser shall comply with the requirements of this paragraph (c), including signing the qualified appraisal and appraisal summary as required by paragraphs (c)(3)(i)(B) and (c)(4)(i)(C) of this section, respectively.
  (iv) *Qualified appraiser exclusions.* The following persons cannot be qualified appraisers with respect to particular property:
    (A) The donor or the taxpayer who claims or reports a deductions under section 170 for the contribution of the property that is being appraised.
    (B) A party to the transaction in which the donor acquired the property being appraised (i.e., the person who sold, exchanged, or gave the property to the donor, or any person who acted as an agent for the transferor or for the donor with respect to such sale, exchange, or gift), unless the property is donated within 2 months of the date of acquisition and its appraised value does not exceed its acquisition price.
    (C) The donee of the property.
    (D) Any person employed by any of the foregoing persons (e.g., if the donor acquired a painting from an art dealer, neither the art dealer nor persons employed by the dealer can be qualified appraisers with respect to that painting).
    (E) Any person related to any of the foregoing persons under section 267(b), or, with respect to appraisals made after June 6, 1988, married to a person who is in a relationship described in section 267(b) with any of the foregoing persons.
    (F) An appraiser who is regularly used by any person described in paragraph (c)(5)(iv)(A), (B), or (C) of this section and who does not perform a majority of his or her appraisals made during his or her taxable year for other persons.

*Source:* Treas. Reg. §1.170A-13(c)(5) (as amended 1996).

## SUMMARY

Intangible asset appraisal standards have not yet proliferated to the extent of business appraisal standards or real estate appraisal standards. Nonetheless, intangible asset appraisal standards do exist and are becoming increasingly recognized by courts, attorneys, fiduciaries, business brokers and other intermediaries, and business owners.

The *Uniform Standards of Professional Appraisal Practice* and the American Society of Appraisers standards were introduced in this chapter. While it does not issue professional standards, the Internal Revenue Service provides substantial professional guidance with respect to the appraisal and economic analysis of intangible assets for taxation-related purposes. Some of this professional guidance was introduced in this chapter.

Virtually all intangible asset valuations are potentially subject to some sort of challenge. Challenges may come from the Internal Revenue Service, parties to the transaction, spouses or beneficiaries of parties to the transaction, or creditors (in cases of insolvency actions).

It behooves all parties to an intangible asset transaction (and their professional advisors) to ensure that the appraisal or economic analysis work product conforms with the level of professional competence necessary to withstand any potential challenge.

## BIBLIOGRAPHY

### American Society of Appraisers

P.O. Box 17265, Washington, DC 20041, (703) 478-2228

1. Principles of Appraisal Practice and Code of Ethics. Available free from the ASA.
2. American Society of Appraisers Business Valuation Standards. Single copies available free from the publisher of *Business Valuation Review.*
3. *Business Valuation Review,* a quarterly publication of the Business Valuation Committee of the American Society of Appraisers. Subscriptions are available by calling or writing to the publisher: P.O. Box 24222, Denver, CO 80224, (303) 758-6148. Back issues are also available.
4. *Valuation,* published periodically by the ASA, is multidisciplinary.
5. Books recognized as authoritative references by the American Society of Appraisers Business Valuation Committee:
   a. Campbell, Ian R. *The Valuation and Pricing of Privately-Held Business Interests.* Toronto, Canada: The Canadian Institute of Chartered Accountants, 1990.
   b. Fishman, Jay E., et al. *Guide to Business Valuations,* 7th ed. Fort Worth: Practitioners Publishing Company, 1997.
   c. Mercer, Z. Christopher. *Valuing Financial Institutions.* Burr Ridge, IL: Irwin Professional Publishing, 1992.
   d. Pratt, Shannon P., Robert F. Reilly, and Robert P. Schweihs. *Valuing a Business: The Analysis and Appraisal of Closely Held Companies,* 3rd ed. New York: McGraw-Hill, 1996.
   e. Pratt, Shannon P., Robert F. Reilly, and Robert P. Schweihs. *Valuing Small Businesses and Professional Practices,* 3rd ed. New York: McGraw-Hill, 1998.
   f. Smith, Gordon V., and Russell L. Parr. *Valuation of Intellectual Property and Intangible Assets,* 2nd ed. New York: John Wiley & Sons, 1994.
   g. Zukin, James H., ed. *Financial Valuation: Businesses and Business Interests.* New York: Warren, Gorham & Lamont, 1990, updated annually.

### The Appraisal Foundation

1029 Vermont Avenue, NW, Suite 900, Washington, DC 20005, (202) 347-7722

1. *Uniform Standards of Professional Appraisal Practice,* issued annually in November.

2. Information Service. The Information Service is designed to provide summary-oriented information to appraisers, users of appraisal services, and others who have an interest in remaining current on the activities of The Appraisal Foundation, the Appraisal Standards Board (ASB), and the Appraiser Qualifications Board (AQB).

3. Subscription Service. The Subscription Service is the complete source of information for appraisers, users of appraisal services, and others on the activities of The Appraisal Foundation, the Appraisal Standards Board (ASB), and the Appraiser Qualifications Board (AQB).

## Internal Revenue Service

1111 Constitution Avenue, NW, Washington, DC 20224, (202) 566-5000

*Valuation Training for Appeals Officers* (Chicago: Commerce Clearing House, 1998). Available through Commerce Clearing House, (800) 248-3248. This book is also available on *Shannon Pratt's Business Valuation Update Online,* http://www.nvst.com/bvu.

# Basic Valuation Concepts

## INTRODUCTION

The following basic intangible asset valuation and economic analysis of concepts will be presented in this chapter:

1. Defining the objective and the purpose of the intangible asset appraisal.
2. Selecting the appropriate standard of value.
3. Selecting the appropriate premise of value.
4. Describing the particular intangible asset subject to appraisal.
5. Describing the specific bundle of legal rights subject to appraisal.
6. Selecting the appropriate valuation date.
7. Communicating the valuation assignment in a client engagement letter.

These concepts will be discussed principally from the perspective of an intangible asset valuation engagement; that is, an engagement in which the analyst estimates a defined value for a specific intangible asset as of a particular date. These concepts all relate generally to the topic: documenting the appraisal assignment. With minor wording changes, these basic concepts apply equally to an intangible asset economic analysis engagement; that is, an engagement in which the analyst estimates a transfer price or royalty rate for a specific intangible, or estimates a remaining useful life or decay rate for a specific intangible. It is equally important to document an economic analysis engagement and a valuation engagement.

## IMPORTANCE OF DOCUMENTING THE VALUATION ENGAGEMENT

The engagement documentation procedure is an important first step in the intangible asset valuation (or economic analysis) process. This procedure should be performed before any valuation analyses are prepared; before any valuation approaches, methods, or procedures are considered and accepted or rejected; before any data (asset-specific, company-related, industry, or economic) are collected and analyzed; and before the analyst begins any substantive quantitative or qualitative work on the valuation (or on the economic analysis).

The engagement documentation procedure is intended to specify what the analyst is trying to accomplish. Basically, in this procedure, the analyst answers the question: What am I setting out to do?

As introduced in Chapter 6 and explored in detail in Chapter 13, the valuation synthesis and conclusion is the last procedure in the intangible asset valuation process. In the valuation synthesis and conclusion, the analyst performs a procedure often called the valuation reconciliation. As part of the reconciliation, the analyst should answer the following questions:

1. Did I appraise the right thing? (Did I analyze the correct intangible asset?)
2. Did I appraise the right thing the right way? (Did I apply the correct valuation approaches and methods?)
3. Did I reach the right conclusion? (Did I correctly apply the procedures that I performed in order to reach a reasonable value estimate?)

**4.** Did I do what I intended? (Did I accomplish the engagement that I set out to accomplish?)

The analyst cannot answer the last question, and will have difficulty answering any of the questions, unless the valuation engagement was well defined and well documented at the inception of the assignment.

Preferably, engagement documentation procedures should be set down in writing, because a verbal agreement between parties (e.g., between the analyst and the client, or between the analyst and a supervisor) often leads to misunderstandings. Often with respect to verbal agreements, both parties have a clear and precise understanding of the valuation engagement; but the parties often have two different clear and precise understandings of the engagement. The differences between the various understandings (all of which are clear and precise in the minds of each individual) may not become obvious until the valuation is completed. Of course, by then, substantial time and resources may have been invested.

While two parties to the same written agreement may have differing interpretations, the range of differences is not usually as great as is the case with verbal agreements. There are instances in which clients discourage the detailed documentation of the appraisal assignment. For example, attorneys sometimes do not want to enter into detailed engagement letters with valuation experts because such letters may be discoverable during the litigation process. Clients who give out numerous appraisal assignments (e.g., certain financial institutions) may not want to entertain detailed engagement letters because it is time-consuming and expensive to draft, review, and revise such letters. Supervisors within the analyst's organization may not perceive the need for a detailed engagement letter (or an assignment memorandum), because they may perceive this as an unnecessary bureaucratic procedure between a supervisor and a subordinate. Sometimes the intangible asset appraisal assignment is simply not easy to precisely define at the outset. However, one of the best ways to ensure the success of a valuation project is to carefully define the parameters of the engagement.

Obviously, analysts have to deal with their clients' administrative idiosyncrasies as best they can. Nonetheless, we suggest that a certain minimal written documentation should be created as part of every intangible asset valuation or economic analysis assignment.

Several illustrative intangible asset valuation engagement letters are presented at the end of this chapter (Exhibits 4-2 through 4-4). The sample engagement letters illustrate both a typical, complete level of assignment documentation and a more minimal level of assignment documentation.

## DEFINING THE APPRAISAL ASSIGNMENT

There are two components to the definition of an intangible asset valuation engagement: the objective of the appraisal and the purpose of the appraisal. These two components are described here.

## The Objective of the Appraisal

The objective of the appraisal describes what the appraisal is intended to do. The objective of the appraisal should clearly articulate, at least, the following issues:

1. The specific intangible asset being appraised.
2. The ownership interest (or bundle of legal rights) related to the intangible asset being appraised.
3. The standard of value or definition of value being estimated.
4. The "as of" date of the appraisal.

In other words, the objective of the appraisal describes what the valuation analysis is seeking to accomplish. An example of a statement of appraisal objective is: "The objective of this appraisal is to estimate the fair market value of the XYZ computer software, in fee simple ownership interest, as of December 31, 1997." Another example of a statement of appraisal objective is: "The objective of this analysis is to estimate the acquisition value of a ten-year term interest in the XYZ proprietary technology to the ABC Corporation as of December 31, 1997."

## The Purpose of the Appraisal

The purpose of the appraisal describes who the audience (i.e., the expected reader) of the appraisal is and what decisions (if any) will be influenced by the appraisal. The purpose of the appraisal should clearly indicate, at least, the following:

1. Why the appraisal is being performed.
2. The intended use(s) of the appraisal.
3. Who is expected to rely on the appraisal.

In other words, the purpose of the appraisal describes to what use the appraisal analysis is to be put. The purpose statement explains why the appraisal was commissioned. An appraisal conclusion for one purpose may not be applicable or reliable if applied for a different purpose. While there are an infinite number of appraisal purposes (i.e., appraisal uses), most purposes can be grouped into one of the following categories:

1. Transaction pricing and structuring.
2. Financing securitization and collateralization.
3. Taxation planning and compliance.
4. Management information and strategic planning.
5. Bankruptcy and reorganization analyses.
6. Litigation support and dispute resolution.

An example of a statement of appraisal purpose is: "The purpose of this analysis is to recommend an arm's-length transfer price to be incorporated in the proposed license of the ABC trademark and trade name to the Licensee Corporation." Another example of a statement of appraisal purpose is: "The purpose of this valuation analysis is to provide an independent opinion of the damages associated with the infringement of the XYZ copyright to your legal counsel, the law firm of Wheel, Gettum, Buttgood."

To reiterate, we highly recommend that both the purpose of the appraisal and the objective of the appraisal be agreed to in writing between the analyst and the client prior to the commencement of the intangible asset appraisal.

PART 1   Introduction to Intangible Asset Valuation

## SELECTING THE APPROPRIATE STANDARD OF VALUE

One of the essential elements in the statement of the appraisal objective is the identification of the standard of value being estimated. As we will see, the same intangible asset can have many different values. Therefore, it is important for the analyst to explain—and for the readers of the appraisal to understand—exactly what is represented by the particular value that is being quantified.

The term *standard of value* may be considered to be synonymous with the term *definition of value*. The standard or definition of value means: What type of value is being estimated? The alternative standards of value generally answer the question: Value to whom? That question is particularly important because the same intangible asset typically has different values to different parties.

The description of the intangible asset tells what is being appraised. The valuation date tells as of what date the intangible asset is being appraised. The standard of value tells to whom the value estimate applies.

Some of the more common alternative standards of value include:

**1.** *Fair market value:* what a typical (hypothetical) willing buyer will pay to a typical (hypothetical) willing seller with neither being under undue influence to transact. There is no single definition of fair market value. In fact, numerous definitions have come from various statutory authority, judicial precedent, and administrative rulings. Some of these definitions expand the fair market value conditions to include, for example, that both the buyer and the seller are cognizant of all relevant facts and circumstances and that both the buyer and the seller are seeking their maximum economic self-interests. In any event, all of the definitions of fair market value incorporate the concept of typical—but unspecified—willing buyer and typical—but unspecified—willing seller.

While fair market value is often referred to in a regulatory or litigation context, it actually has little empirical relevance in the real world of intangible asset transactions. This is because, in actual intangible asset transactions, the participants don't care what Mr. Hypothetical Seller will accept or what Mr. Hypothetical Buyer will pay. In the real world, a specific buyer consummates a transaction with a particular seller, given their own unique sets of interests and criteria. These sets of transactional circumstances are almost always a departure from fair market value.

**2.** *Fair value:* the amount that will fairly compensate an owner who was involuntarily deprived of the economic enjoyment of an intangible asset where there is neither a willing buyer nor a willing seller. Fair value is primarily a legal concept. Accordingly, there are numerous definitions of fair value that are specific to the particular jurisdictional statutes and judicial precedent.

One general concept common to most definitions is that fair value is intended to estimate a fair or reasonable or equitable amount. It is not necessarily intended to reflect a likely market transaction price for the subject intangible asset, because the owner of the intangible asset did not initiate a market transaction—that is, did not attempt to put the subject intangible asset up for sale in the commercial marketplace. Rather, the instances in which fair value is relevant relate to involuntary transactions. Examples of such involuntary transactions include infringements, eminent domain and condemnations, expropriations, and so forth.

**3.** *Market value:* the most probable (or the most likely) price that an intangible asset would bring in a competitive and open market under all conditions requisite to a fair sale, including the condition that the buyer and seller are each acting prudently and knowledgeably, and assuming the price is not affected by undue stimulus.

While fair value does not always concern itself with the market, market value does not concern itself with fairness. Market prices are not always fair to all parties involved in a transaction (other than through the effect of Adam Smith's "invisible hand"). Nonetheless, market value is often the best estimate of the most likely transaction price for the subject intangible asset.

**4.** *Acquisition value:* the price that a particular, specifically identified buyer would be expected to pay for an intangible asset with consideration given to any and all unique benefits of the intangible asset to the identified buyer. Acquisition value is typically estimated in terms of answering the question: What is the most that an identified buyer can afford to pay for the subject intangible asset, given that buyer's unique set of circumstances?

**5.** *Use value:* the value of an intangible asset in a particular, specified use (which may be different from the intangible asset's current use or from the intangible asset's highest and best use). Use value is typically estimated in terms of answering a question such as: How much would a buyer pay for the subject intangible asset if the buyer could use it in South America only? If the intangible asset's owner expands its current use from the commodity chemicals industry to the consumer packaged goods industry? If the owner discontinues using the subject intangible asset in the data processing services industry, even though that application is clearly the highest and best use for that intangible?

**6.** *Investment value* (or *investor value*): the value of an intangible asset given a particular defined set of individual investment criteria (e.g., given a definite set of internal rate of return or payback period investment criteria). This standard of value does not necessarily contemplate a sale transaction with regard to the subject intangible asset. This standard of value may be relevant to answering questions such as: What is the value of the subject intangible if it is only in commercial use for the next five years? What is the value of the subject intangible asset if its owner requires an 18 percent after-tax, cash-on-cash internal rate of return on his or her investment in that class of intangibles?

**7.** *Owner value:* the value of an intangible asset to its current owner, given that owner's current use of the intangible asset and current resources and capabilities for commercially exploiting the intangible asset. This standard of value also does not necessarily contemplate a sale transaction with regard to the subject intangible asset. Rather, the question that is usually answered through an owner value analysis is: What is the value of this intangible asset, given the owner's abilities (or inabilities), given his or her sources of capital (or lack of sources of capital), given his or her commercialization plans (be they brilliant or incompetent), and so forth?

In this standard of value, the price that the subject intangible would fetch in its appropriate transactional marketplace is not particularly relevant, because the owner may have no intention of selling the subject intangible. Rather, this standard of value is more appropriate for business strategic planning purposes (if the intangible asset owner is a business) or for family wealth management or intergenerational wealth transfer purposes (if the intangible asset owner is an individual).

**8.** *Insurable value:* the amount of insurance proceeds necessary to replace the subject intangible asset with an intangible asset of comparable utility, functionality, and income-producing capacity. Again, this standard of value does not necessarily contemplate a market transaction with respect to the subject intangible. Nonetheless, this standard of value is particularly relevant to answering a very common commercial question: How much insurance is appropriate for the intangible asset? This analysis may be relevant for purposes of business interruption insurance, expropriation insurance, property and casualty insurance, and so on, and is relevant if the subject intangible is directly an income-producing asset or if it is indirectly income-producing—through its use in a production, distribution, or other commercial process.

**9.** *Collateral value:* the amount that a creditor would be willing to loan with the subject intangible asset serving as security for the loan. In other words, this standard of value answers the common commercial question: How much can be borrowed against this intangible asset?

The collateral value of an intangible asset is often (but not always) a percentage of its fair market value or its market value on a stand-alone basis. This is reasonable because the lender is really interested in how much the intangible asset could actually be sold for if the borrower does not meet the loan obligations and the lender has to foreclose on the intangible asset collateral.

**10.** *Ad valorem value:* the value of an intangible asset for property taxation purposes, given the statutory standards of the particular taxing jurisdiction. Ad valorem value is sometimes (but not always) a function of fair market value. Note that some intangible assets that have a measurable market value may not be recognized for ad valorem taxation purposes. This nonrecognition is due to statutory standards of the jurisdictional property taxation code.

The selection of the appropriate standard of value is greatly influenced by the purpose (i.e., by the intended use) of the appraisal. More often than not, the analyst is directed to estimate a specific standard of value by the client in order to accomplish the stated purpose of the appraisal. Sometimes, the analyst must decide what the appropriate standard of value is, given the known purpose of the appraisal and given the known facts and circumstances regarding the subject intangible.

The selection of the appropriate standard of value will obviously have a direct impact on the value estimate. Clearly, the same intangible asset may have different values depending upon the standard of value that is estimated. At this point, it is important to reiterate that the analyst only estimates value. Only the market determines value. This is true regardless of which standard of value is being sought.

## SELECTING THE APPROPRIATE PREMISE OF VALUE

The standard of value answered the question, Value to whom? While the standard of value explains the *who* in the transactional analysis, it does not explain the *how*. It does not explain the conditions under which the parties will consummate the intangible asset transaction. That question is answered by the premise of value.

The premise of value is the assumed set of intangible asset transactional circumstances under which the subject intangible asset will be analyzed. For example, when the fair market value standard considers a willing buyer and a willing seller, in what marketplace are they meeting? How will the subject intangible asset be sold between the willing buyer and willing seller? Under what set of circumstances will they enter into their fair market value transaction?

Certainly, the transactional marketplace affects the transaction price. Is the market a wholesale market, retail market, auction market, dealer market, broker market, or some other type of market? The question implies that there can be a range of values within the same standard of value. In other words, there can be different fair market values, given the assumed market in which the willing buyer and willing seller meet and transact. There can be different fair market value conclusions, given different premises of value.

The selection of the appropriate premise of value may be dictated by the highest and best use of the subject intangible asset. The highest and best use of an intangible asset is typically defined as the reasonably probable and legal use of the intangible asset that is physically possible, appropriately supported, financially feasible, and results in the highest value.

## Highest and Best Use Analysis

The highest and best use for an intangible asset may be analyzed under and selected using the following four criteria:

**1.** *Legal permissibility*—The highest and best use should be a lawful use for that particular intangible asset or intellectual property. It must comply with regulatory, licensing, fair trade, truth in advertising, and other legal requirements.

**2.** *Physical possibility*—The highest and best use should be physically possible, given the physical, functional, and technological attributes of the subject intangible asset or intellectual property.

**3.** *Financial feasibility*—The highest and best use generates a positive rate of return on the investment in the subject intangible asset or intellectual property. Even though a particular use can be the "best" use among several unprofitable uses (i.e., it is the least unprofitable use), it still may not be the highest and best use. The highest and best use generates a positive economic return to the intangible asset owner. (Even a bankrupt company can have intangible assets.) Otherwise, the intangible asset will not be used at all.

**4.** *Maximum profitability*—Of all the remaining alternative uses for the subject intangible asset that are legally permissible, physically possible, and financially feasible, the one use that results in the greatest value for the subject intangible asset is its highest and best use.

Among all reasonable, alternative uses, the use of the intangible asset that yields the highest present value after payments are made for all economic costs—that is, for labor, capital, and coordination—typically represents the highest and best use of the subject intangible asset. Unless otherwise constrained, the subject intangible asset should be appraised at its highest and best use. This is true regardless of what standard of value is being estimated.

The assessment of the highest and best use of the subject intangible asset will determine which of the four alternative fundamental premises of value should be applied in the subject appraisal. These alternative premises of value or alternative sets of market conditions may apply to virtually every standard of value. They certainly apply to every standard of value that contemplates a sale transaction, such as fair market value and market value.

## Alternative Premises of Value

Virtually any type of intangible asset may be appraised under each of the following four alternative premises of value:

**1.** *Value in continued use, as part of a going-concern business enterprise.* Under this premise, the subject individual intangible asset is analyzed as part of a mass assemblage of assets, some of which may be tangible and some of which may be intangible. This premise of value contemplates the contributory value of the subject intangible asset both to the other assets (both tangible and intangible) of a business enterprise, and from the other assets (both tangible and intangible) of a business enterprise. This premise of value assumes that the subject intangible will transact in the marketplace that encompasses the sale of operating going-concern businesses.

**2.** *Value in place, but not in current use in the production of income.* Under this premise, the subject individual intangible asset is also analyzed as part of a mass assemblage of assets and as part of a going-concern business enterprise.

This premise of value assumes that the subject intangible will transact in the marketplace that encompasses the sale of nonoperating going-concern businesses. A nonoperating going-concern business is a business that is functional but not currently functioning. Examples of this apparent contradiction include: a business that is temporarily shut down because of a labor strike or the death of the business owner; a business that is fully assembled but that has not yet opened for business (e.g., a regional shopping mall that is fully leased out and awaiting its grand opening); and a business that is temporarily shut down pending a sale (e.g., a chain hotel that is put up for sale after the chain opened a newer, competing property in the same city).

**3.** *Value in exchange, as part of an orderly disposition.* This premise of value contemplates that the subject intangible asset will enjoy a normal period of exposure to its appropriate secondary market.

Under this premise of value, the individual intangible asset is not sold as part of a going-concern business enterprise, but is sold on a piecemeal basis. That is, this premise of value assumes that the subject intangible asset will transact in the marketplace that encompasses the sale or license of discrete, individual intangible assets.

**4.** *Value in exchange, as part of a forced liquidation.* This premise contemplates that the subject intangible asset will experience less than a normal period of exposure to its appropriate secondary market.

Under this premise of value, the individual intangible asset is not sold as part of a going-concern business enterprise. It is sold on a piecemeal basis. It is also assumed that the intangible will transact in the marketplace that encompasses the auction or other rapid sale of discrete, individual intangible assets.

Virtually any intangible asset may be appraised under each of these four alternative fundamental premises of value. Of course, the value conclusions reached under each premise for the same intangible asset may be dramatically different. For example, there may be four different estimates of fair market value for the same intangible asset, depending upon which market is analyzed (i.e., depending upon which premise of value is assumed).

As mentioned earlier, the client often instructs the analyst as to the appropriate standard of value. Sometimes, the appropriate standard of value is dictated by statutory, judicial, or regulatory requirements. However, the selection of the appropriate premise of value is typically left to the judgment of the analyst. The analyst selects the appropriate premise of value based upon:

1. The purpose and objective of the appraisal; that is, what premise of value makes the most sense, given the stated purpose and objective of the appraisal?
2. The actual functional and economic status of the subject intangible asset; that is, under what premise of value is the subject intangible asset actually operating?
3. The highest and best use of the subject intangible asset; that is, what premise of value (or what marketplace) would conclude the greatest estimated value for the subject if and when the intangible asset was actually put up for sale?

## DESCRIBING THE PARTICULAR INTANGIBLE ASSET SUBJECT TO APPRAISAL

The description of the subject intangible asset should be complete enough to clearly identify the particular intangible asset to the reader of the appraisal. The description may include reference to the common categories of intangible assets and intellectual properties that were discussed in Chapter 1 (e.g., marketing-related intangible assets). The description may identify the physical, functional, technical, or economic parameters of the subject intangible asset. In other words, the description should be adequate in order to ensure that the reader of the appraisal clearly understands what intangible asset is included in the analysis and what intangible asset(s) is (are) not included in the analysis.

The description of the subject intangible asset in an intangible asset appraisal provides the same kind of information as the legal description of the subject property provides in a real estate appraisal. Unfortunately, in the discipline of intangible asset analysis, we do not have the precise systems of metes and bounds that real estate appraisers use in describing a property subject to appraisal. Usually, there is no formal, legal description of the subject intangible asset. Nonetheless, it is the analyst's responsibility to create a description that is as complete and unambiguous as possible. Obviously, even the most comprehensive and rigorous intangible asset analysis is essentially useless if the reader cannot discern exactly what intangible asset (or what intangible asset bundle of rights) is the subject of the appraisal or economic analysis.

Exhibit 4-1 presents an illustrative listing of many of the intangible assets and intellectual properties that are commonly subject to economic analysis and appraisal. This listing is not intended to be comprehensive, and it presents only the most summarized identification of each intangible asset. The listing does not purport to present complete descriptions of each intangible asset.

Illustrative Listing of Intangible Assets and Intellectual Properties Commonly Subject to Appraisal and Economic Analysis

| | |
|---|---|
| Advertising campaigns and programs | Leasehold estates |
| Agreements | Leasehold interests |
| Airport gates and landing slots | Licenses—professional, business, etc. |
| Appraisal plants (files and records) | Literary works |
| Awards and judgments (legal) | Litigation awards and damage claims |
| Bank customers—deposit, loan, trust, credit card, etc. | Loan portfolios |
| Blueprints and drawings | Location value |
| Book and other publication libraries | Management contracts |
| Brand names and logos | Manual (versus automated) databases |
| Broadcast licenses (radio, television, etc.) | Manuscripts |
| Buy-sell agreements | Marketing and promotional materials |
| Certificates of need for healthcare institutions | Masks and masters (for integrated circuits) |
| Chemical formulations | Medical (and other professional) charts and records |
| Claims (against insurers, etc.) | Mineral rights |
| Computer software (both internally developed and externally purchased) | Musical compositions |
| | Natural resources |
| Computerized databases | Newspaper morgue files |
| Contracts | Noncompete covenants |
| Cooperative agreements | Nondiversion agreements |
| Copyrights | Open to ship customer orders |
| Credit information files | Options, warrants, grants, rights—related to securities |
| Customer contracts | Ore deposits |
| Customer lists | Patent applications |
| Customer relationships | Patents—both product and process |
| Designs, patterns, diagrams, schematics, technical drawings | Permits |
| Development rights | Personality contracts |
| Distribution networks | Possessory interest |
| Distribution rights | Prescription drug files |
| Drilling rights | Prizes and awards (related to professional recognition) |
| Easements | Procedural ("how we do things here") manuals and related documentation |
| Employment contracts | |
| Engineering drawings and related documentation | Production backlogs |
| Environmental rights (and exemptions) | Product designs |
| FCC licenses related to radio bands (cellular telephone, paging, etc.) | Property use rights |
| | Proposals outstanding, related to contracts, customers, etc. |
| Favorable financing | Proprietary processes—and related technical documentation |
| Favorable leases | Proprietary products—and related technical documentation |
| Film libraries | Proprietary technology—and related technical documentation |
| Food flavorings and recipes | Regulatory approvals (or exemptions from regulatory requirements) |
| Franchise agreements (commercial) | |
| Franchise ordinances (governmental) | Retail shelf space |
| Going-concern value (and immediate use value) | Royalty agreements |
| Goodwill—institutional | Shareholder agreements |
| Goodwill—personal | Solicitation rights |
| Goodwill—professional | Subscription lists (for magazines, services, etc.) |
| Government contracts | Supplier contracts |
| Government programs | Technical and specialty libraries (books, records, drawings, etc.) |
| Governmental registrations (and exemptions) | Technical documentation |
| Historical documents | Technology sharing agreements |
| HMO enrollment lists | Title plants |
| Insurance expirations | Trade secrets |
| Insurance in force | Trained and assembled workforce |
| Joint ventures | Trademarks and trade names |
| Know-how and associated procedural documentation | Training manuals and related educational materials, courses, and programs |
| Laboratory notebooks | |
| Landing rights (for airlines) | Use rights—air, water, land |

## DESCRIBING THE BUNDLE OF LEGAL RIGHTS SUBJECT TO APPRAISAL

An important step in the intangible asset valuation process is the identification of the specific bundle of legal rights that is subject to appraisal. According to the bundle of rights theory of valuation, complete intangible asset ownership, or title in fee, consists of a group of distinct legal rights. Each of these rights can be separated from the bundle and can be conveyed by the fee owner to other parties, either in perpetuity or for a limited time period. When an individual legal right is separated from the entire bundle of rights and is transferred to another party, then a partial or fractional property interest is created.

Property ownership interests may be examined from many perspectives because the ownership, legal, economic, and financial aspects of intangible assets overlap. The ownership of intangible property interests can be divided in various ways. Separate economic and legal interests derived from the total bundle of rights are involved in many kinds of income-producing intangible assets and intellectual properties. Each of these separate economic and legal interests is distinct in its form and content. Licensee, licenser, and sublicensee estates are created when licenses or franchises to certain intangible asset ownership (or use) rights are conveyed in accordance with established legal procedures.

There are often specific legal definitions related to property ownership interests, including intangible property. The following definitions are presented from an economic and appraisal perspective, not from a legal perspective. Obtaining the advice of competent legal counsel is recommended in cases where a specific legal definition associated with certain rights is needed.

Some of the more common legal rights related to intangible assets and intellectual properties include the following:

**1.** *Fee simple interest*—The owner has the total bundle of legal rights related to the intangible property. The owner has absolute ownership of the subject intangible asset.

**2.** *Life interest or estate*—The duration of ownership of the intangible property is limited to the life of the owner (or to the life of a specified other party). In a life estate, the life tenant (i.e., the beneficiary) is entitled to the income generated by the subject intangible during the tenant's lifetime.

**3.** *Term interest or estate*—The duration of the term of ownership of the intangible property is specified as a term or number of years, for example, for ten years. After the specified term, the ownership of the subject intangible transfers to someone else.

**4.** *Licenser or franchiser interests*—Specific rights and privileges are retained by a licenser or a franchiser in the license or franchise agreements. Alternatively, this bundle of rights may be construed as all of the remaining ownership privileges related to the intangible property that were not specifically transferred to the licensee or the franchisee.

**5.** *Licensee or franchisee interests*—Specific rights and privileges are granted to the licensee or franchisee, by contrast, in the license or franchise agreement. These rights may be limited as to term, use, geography, etc.

**6.** *Sub-licensee or sub-franchisee interests*—Specific rights and privileges are transferred by contract from the licensee to the sub-licensee or from the franchisee to the sub-franchisee. These rights themselves cannot exceed the licensee or franchisee legal interests.

**7.** *Reversionary interests*—These are the rights to the future ownership and economic enjoyment of an intangible property, where such rights are currently enjoyed by another. This bundle of rights usually includes all of the ownership rights of an intangible asset after the conclusion of a term interest or an income interest. These ownership rights revert back to the intangible asset owner after the conclusion of a contract, license, franchise, term interest, etc.

**8.** *Development rights*—These rights are transferred by contract and allow the transferee to develop and commercialize the subject intangible property for the transferee's own benefit.

**9.** *Exploitation rights*—These rights are transferred by contract and allow the transferee to make use of the subject intangible property. Exploitation rights often relate to the using or using up of natural resources, such as mining or forest properties.

**10.** *Use rights*—The rights to enjoy, hold, occupy, or derive some manner of benefit from the subject intangible property, they are usually transferred or granted by contract. Like development rights and exploitation rights, use rights are usually granted for a specific term, in a specific geography, and related to certain specified industries, products, or services.

**11.** *Other fractional ownership interests*—This category includes any other limited interest, estate, or portion of a bundle of rights related to intangible property.

Obviously, the selection of the bundle of legal rights to be appraised has a direct impact on the intangible asset value estimate. Normally, the client instructs the analyst as to what bundle of legal rights should be included in (or excluded from) the appraisal.

## SELECTING THE APPROPRIATE VALUATION DATE

The intangible asset and intellectual property value estimate should be made and stated "as of" a specified valuation date because the value of an intangible asset changes over time, due to both endogenous and exogenous factors. Accordingly, the value conclusion may only be relevant as to a certain specified date.

Intangible asset valuation dates may be:

1. Historical, that is, as of a date previous to the performance of the actual appraisal or economic analyses;
2. Contemporaneous, that is, as of a current date, or as of the date of performance of the actual appraisal or economic analyses; or
3. Prospective, that is, as of a future date or a date that is chronologically after the performance of the actual appraisal or economic analyses.

Prospective valuation dates always result in hypothetical appraisals. The appraisals are hypothetical because they relate to conditions that have not yet come to pass. According to the professional standards of the American Society of Appraisers, hypothetical appraisals are professionally permitted, but they should be clearly identified as such.

The selection of the appropriate valuation date is typically a function of the purpose of the appraisal assignment. The "as of" valuation date is disclosed in the statement of the appraisal objective. Nonetheless, the appropriate valuation date is most often determined by the purpose of the appraisal, that is, the use to which the intangible asset appraisal will be put.

As with all the components of the purpose and objective of the intangible asset appraisal, the selection of the appropriate valuation date should be agreed to between the analyst and the client. Most often, the client selects the appropriate valuation date because the client needs the value estimate to be "as of" a certain date to make it relevant to the client's decision-making or other informational needs. Sometimes, the appropriate valuation date is dictated by statutory authority or regulatory ruling. For example, certain appraisals may have to be performed "as of" the date of death, the date of transfer, the date of marriage, the date of merger, the lien date, and so forth.

## COMMUNICATING THE VALUATION ASSIGNMENT IN A CLIENT ENGAGEMENT LETTER

We recommend that the engagement letter or assignment memorandum contains as thorough an understanding as possible of the intangible asset analysis. Proper documentation will help to prevent misunderstandings between parties to the engagement both during and after the analysis.

There is no single preferred format or ideal engagement letter for communicating the intangible asset appraisal or economic analysis assignment. Exhibits 4-2 through 4-4 present examples of typical client engagement letters.

Exhibit 4-2 presents an illustrative client engagement letter with regard to the economic analysis (specifically transfer pricing for licensing purposes) of a typical intangible asset (specifically proprietary technology).

Exhibit 4-3 presents an illustrative client engagement letter with regard to the appraisal of an intangible asset. In this case, the assignment relates to the fair market valuation of an FCC license for a cellular telephone company.

Exhibit 4-4 presents an illustrative client engagement letter with regard to the appraisal of a common intellectual property. In this case, the engagement relates to the fair market valuation of internally developed computer software.

## SUMMARY

Chapter 4 presented the various concepts related to documenting the intangible asset valuation assignment. While these concepts are presented from the perspective of an intangible asset or intellectual property appraisal, they are equally applicable to the economic analysis of these intangible assets.

In particular, this chapter discussed: defining the purpose and objective of the analysis, describing the intangible asset subject to analysis, selecting the appropriate valuation date, selecting the appropriate standard of value, selecting the appropriate premise of value, and describing the specific bundle of legal rights subject to analysis. The chapter also presented several examples of client engagement letters.

The engagement documentation procedure is an important first step in the intangible asset valuation or economic analysis process. The engagement documentation procedure allows the analyst and the client to understand what the analysis is intended to accomplish. As one result of such documentation, the analyst can look back at the procedures and conclusions and determine whether the analysis, in fact, accomplished what it set out to accomplish.

**EXHIBIT 4-2**

Illustrative Engagement Letter
Economic Analysis of Intangible Asset

---

June 30, 1998

Mr. Paymore Taxes
Vice President, Tax Planning
Taxpayer Corporation
1000 Client Street
Suite 100
Client City, Florida 33333

Dear Mr. Taxes:

We are pleased to submit this engagement letter for valuation consulting and economic analysis services.

This letter describes the intangible assets subject to economic analysis, the objective and purpose of the economic analysis, the proposed analytical procedures, the analysis work product, engagement staffing, engagement timing and fees, and our standard engagement terms and conditions.

### Intangible Assets Subject to Economic Analysis

Stop-Um Company (hereinafter "S-U"), a division of Taxpayer Corporation, is the leading maker of anti-lock braking systems (hereinafter "ABS") for light trucks in North America and an important supplier for both cars and trucks worldwide. S-U is benefiting from the gradual shift to ABS in automotive markets and the increasing shift from two-wheel to the more effective and costly four-wheel type.

We understand that S-U has entered into a licensing agreement with its subsidiary Stop ABS Manufacturing, CV (hereinafter "CV"), a Netherlands corporation. CV has entered into consignment manufacturing, purchase and service agreements with its 100 percent owned subsidiary Stop BV (hereinafter "BV"). CV has also entered into distribution and service agreements with Stop, GmbH (hereinafter "GmbH"), a 100 percent owned subsidiary of BV.

CV and its wholly owned subsidiaries are engaged in the manufacture, distribution, and service of ABS units to original equipment manufacturers (OEM) in Europe.

### Objective and Purpose of the Economic Analysis

The objective of the analysis is to estimate the appropriate arm's-length transfer price royalty rate for the license of the subject proprietary technology to CV.

The estimation of the arm's-length royalty rate will be consistent with the provisions and methodology promulgated in Internal Revenue Code Section 482 and the relating Treasury Regulations.

The purpose of the analysis is to provide to you an independent economic opinion of the fair, arm's-length royalty rate that you will use for the structuring of the contemplated license agreement.

### Proposed Analytical Procedures

Any valuation performed as part of our analysis will be prepared in accordance with the *Uniform Standards of Professional Appraisal Practice* (USPAP) as promulgated by The Appraisal Foundation.

We will use the applicable transfer pricing methods that are appropriate to technology-related intangible assets, namely the comparable uncontrolled transaction method, the comparable profits method, and several profit split methods.

We will select the approaches that, in our experience and judgment, provide the best estimation of an arm's-length royalty rate. In selecting the appropriate transfer price (i.e., royalty rate) methodology, we will consider the quality and quantity of available data, the utility and functionality of the subject proprietary technology, as well as the purpose and objective of this analysis.

We propose to perform our economic analysis in two phases.

In Phase I, we will assess the data available at S-U and from various public sources. We will select the royalty rate approaches upon which we will ultimately rely. We will also perform a preliminary transfer pricing economic analysis to establish reasonable ranges of the fair market value of the proprietary technology and of the arm's-length royalty rates.

In Phase II, we will perform a more intensive and thorough economic analysis of the arm's-length royalty rate and the fair market value of the subject proprietary technology. We will conclude a point estimate of both the arm's-length royalty rate and the fair market value of the subject intangible asset.

### Appraisal Work Product

The work product of Phase I will be a meeting with you to present the results of our preliminary economic analysis. We will present draft schedules and exhibits at this meeting.

Illustrative Engagement Letter
Economic Analysis of Intangible Asset

The work product of Phase II will be a narrative economic analysis opinion report. This opinion report will describe our economic analyses, procedures, and conclusions. It will include exhibits and tables summarizing our quantitative and qualitative analyses.

Each report will be personally signed by the principal analyst and by the concurring analyst assigned to the engagement.

We will first issue our report as an unsigned draft. At that time, we will solicit your questions, comments, and suggestions. We will not issue our final, signed report until you have reviewed our draft report.

### Engagement Staffing

Thomas J. Appraiser Jr., CFA, ASA, will be the principal analyst for this assignment. Tom is a principal of our firm. Mary F. Analyst, CFA, ASA, CPA will be the concurring appraiser. Mary is a managing director of our firm. Mark Economist, Ph.D., will perform the professional standards review. Mark is a principal of our firm. The professional qualifications of these three analysts are appended to this proposal.

### Engagement Timing and Fees

We are prepared to begin our analysis immediately upon receipt of your written authorization to proceed. We will complete Phase I within 60 days of our receipt of your written authorization and of receipt of certain required financial and operational data. We will complete Phase II within 30 days of your authorization to proceed to Phase II.

Our professional fee for this economic analysis will be based upon the time required by our professional staff to perform the required procedures, at our standard billing rates. Given the information currently available to us, we commit that professional fees will not exceed $XX,XXX for Phase I and an additional $XX,XXX for Phase II.

In addition to our professional fees, you will be responsible for out-of-pocket expenses related to this assignment. These expenses include travel, lodging, purchased data, data processing, clerical support, telephone, express delivery, and report production and reproduction charges. Out-of-pocket expenses will be indicated as a separate line item on our invoices. We recommend that you budget out-of-pocket expenses at approximately 15 to 20 percent of professional fees.

You will be invoiced semi-monthly for professional fees and out-of-pocket expenses incurred to date. Invoices are due within 15 days of date of invoice. Invoices outstanding for more than thirty (30) days accrue interest at the rate of one and one-half percent (1.5%) per month (18% annual percentage rate).

To protect our independence, and as a matter of company policy, we cannot issue our final, signed report until all outstanding invoices have been paid.

### Engagement Terms and Conditions

Our work product is valid only for the purpose stated herein. You agree not to reference our name or our report, in whole or in part, in any document distributed to third parties without our written consent. We will maintain the confidentiality of all data provided to us by you. We will provide independent valuation and economic analysis assistance only. Our work product is not intended to provide legal, accounting, or taxation advice.

We will rely upon any data provided to us by you without independent verification or confirmation. You will warrant that all information provided to us is complete and accurate to the best of your knowledge. We will rely on your involvement in the development of required data and certain planning activities.

You agree to indemnify and hold us harmless against any and all liability, claim, loss, cost, and expense, whatever kind or nature, which we may incur, or be subject to, as a party, expert witness, witness or participant in connection with any dispute or litigation involving you unless such liability, claim, loss, cost, and expense, whatever kind or nature, is due to our wrongdoing and such wrongdoing is not caused by, related to, or the result of information provided to us by you.

This indemnity includes all out-of-pocket expenses (including travel costs and attorney fees) and payment for all our staff members' time at standard hourly rates in effect at the time rendered to the extent we attend, prepare for, or participate in meetings, hearings, depositions, trials, and all other proceedings, including travel time. If we must bring legal action to enforce this indemnity, you agree to pay all costs of such action, including any sum the court may fix as reasonable attorney fees.

If this agreement, or any moneys due under the terms hereof, is placed in the hands of an attorney for collection of the account, you promise and agree to pay our attorney fees and collection costs, plus interest at the then legal rate, whether or not any legal action is filed. If any suit or action is brought to enforce, interpret, or collect damages for the breach of this agreement, you agree to pay our reasonable attorney fees and costs of such suit or action, including any appeal as fixed by the applicable court or courts.

### Summary and Conclusion

We are eminently qualified to perform this valuation and economic analysis. Our firm is one of the leading independent valuation consulting, economic analysis, and financial advisory firms in the nation.

We understand the purpose and objective of this economic analysis. We also understand the importance of your obtaining an opinion from an independent firm.

Illustrative Engagement Letter
Economic Analysis of Intangible Asset

If this proposal correctly reflects your understanding of our engagement and acceptance of its terms, please sign below and return a signed copy to us along with a retainer check in the amount of $XX,XXX. This retainer will be applied against the final outstanding invoice related to this assignment.

If you have any questions regarding this proposal, please contact the undersigned.

Very truly yours,

**Realgood Economic Analysts**

Thomas J. Appraiser Jr., CFA, ASA

**Accepted by:**

Company:       Stop-Um Company
By:            _____
Name:          _____
Title:         _____
Date:          _____

Illustrative Engagement Letter
Appraisal of Intangible Asset

September 29, 1998

Ms. Payless Taxes
Tax Manager
Yourstate Cellular Corporation
3333 Client Street, Suite 350
Client City, Client State 60606

Dear Ms. Taxes:

We are pleased to submit this proposal for valuation consulting and litigation support services.

This proposal will describe the objective and purpose of our analysis, the proposed analytical procedures, the appraisal work product, engagement staffing, engagement timing and fees, and our standard engagement terms and conditions.

### Objective and Purpose of the Valuation Analysis

We understand that you have retained the law firm of Wee, Always, Winn to represent you in an ad valorem property tax appeal brought by Yourstate Cellular Corporation (hereinafter "Yourstate") in Client State. We understand that Yourstate is contesting the valuation of its intangible asset in the nature of the Federal Communication Commission (FCC) cellular license.

The objective of the analysis is to estimate the fair market value of the FCC cellular license as of January 1, 1997.

The purpose of the analysis is to provide an independent valuation opinion to assist Wee, Always, Winn in their representation of Yourstate in your ad valorem property tax appeal with regard to the valuation of the intangible asset FCC license.

### Proposed Analytical Procedures

This analysis, and the resulting work product, will be prepared in accordance with the *Uniform Standards of Professional Appraisal Practice* (USPAP) as promulgated by The Appraisal Foundation.

**Phase I**

First, we will review and critique Client State's valuation analyses and valuation conclusion. We will identify the strengths and weaknesses of the assessment, both from a qualitative and a quantitative perspective.

Second, we will prepare our own independent valuation analysis of the subject FCC license. We will consider all generally accepted intangible asset valuation approaches.

The procedures will encompass both an analysis of all of the transactional activity regarding FCC cellular licenses and an economic analysis of the subject industry.

**Phase II**

In Phase II, we will provide expert witness testimony. This phase includes pretrial preparation and assistance to legal counsel, deposition preparation and testimony, and trial preparation and testimony.

### Appraisal Work Product

**Phase I**

The work product for the first procedure of Phase I will be a series of oral presentations. At your counsel's request, we may also prepare a set of confidential schedules and exhibits.

The work product for the second procedure will be a narrative valuation report. This report will be personally signed by both the principal analyst and the concurring analyst responsible for this engagement.

The report will include the following:

1. a valuation opinion
2. a description of the subject FCC license
3. a description of the economics of the subject industry
4. summaries of our quantitative and qualitative valuation analyses
5. a listing of the data and facts on which we relied in our appraisal
6. an appraisal certification
7. a statement of contingent and limiting conditions
8. the professional qualification of the responsible analysts

We will first issue this report as an unsigned draft. At that time, we will solicit your questions, comments, and suggestions.

**Phase II**

The work product for this phase will be a set of schedules and exhibits that will be prepared for litigation purposes only. We will also prepare such additional documents and analyses that your counsel may specifically request. The main work product will be the oral testimony.

Illustrative Engagement Letter
Appraisal of Intangible Asset

### Engagement Staffing

Manoj P. Engineer, Ph.D., will be the principal analyst for this assignment. Manoj is a senior associate in our firm. Mary F. Analyst, CFA, ASA, CPA will be the concurring analyst. Mary is a managing director of our firm. The professional qualifications of these two analysts are appended to this proposal.

### Engagement Timing and Fees

We will perform this analysis consistent with a timetable to which we will mutually agree.

Our professional fee for this engagement will be based upon the time required by our professional staff to perform the required procedures, at our standard billing rates. Our standard hourly billing rates range from $XXX to $YYY. The standard hourly billing rate for Dr. Engineer is $XXX; the standard hourly billing rate for Ms. Analyst is $YYY. Based upon the information currently available to us, our professional fees are estimated at $XX,XXX for Phase I. Our professional fees for Phase II will be based upon the actual time required by us to perform the requisite litigation support services at our standard hourly billing rates.

In addition to our professional fees, you will be responsible for out-of-pocket expenses related to this assignment. These expenses include travel, lodging, purchased data, data processing, clerical support, telephone, express delivery, and report production and reproduction charges. Out-of-pocket expenses will be indicated as a separate line item on our invoices.

You will be invoiced semi-monthly for professional fees and out-of-pocket expenses incurred to date. Invoices are due within 15 days of date of invoice. Invoices outstanding for more than thirty (30) days accrue interest at the rate of one and one-half percent (1.5%) per month (18% annual percentage rate).

To protect our independence, and as a matter of company policy, we cannot issue our final, signed report or offer expert testimony until all outstanding invoices have been paid.

### Engagement Terms and Conditions

Our work product is valid only for the purpose stated herein. You agree not to reference our name or our report, in whole or in part, in any document distributed to third parties without our written consent. We will maintain the confidentiality of all data provided to us by you. We will provide independent valuation and economic analysis assistance only. Our work product is not intended to provide legal, accounting, or taxation advice.

We will rely upon any data provided to us by you without independent verification or confirmation. You will warrant that all information provided to us is complete and accurate to the best of your knowledge. We will rely on your involvement in the development of required data and certain planning activities.

We are ready, willing, and able to attend conferences with the parties in interest or with the other independent appraisers and consultants associated with this matter after the completion of the valuation opinion report. However, these services are not included in the above fee estimate. These additional services will be performed at our standard hourly billing rates, plus out-of-pocket expenses.

### Summary and Conclusion

We are eminently qualified to perform this valuation analysis. We have substantial experience in taxation-related litigation with respect to the valuation of intangible assets.

We understand the purpose and objective of this analysis, and we will work with you to achieve that purpose and objective. We also understand the time and other pressures related to litigation and controversy engagements.

If this engagement letter correctly describes our assignment, please sign below and return a signed copy to us along with a retainer check in the amount of $XX,XXX. This retainer will be applied against the final outstanding invoice related to this assignment.

If you have any questions regarding this proposal, please contact the undersigned.

Very truly yours,

### Competent Analysts

Manoj P. Engineer, Ph.D.

### Accepted by:

Company:    Yourstate Cellular Corporation

By:        _____

Name:      _____

Title:      _____

Date:      _____

**EXHIBIT 4-4**

Illustrative Engagement Letter
Appraisal of Intellectual Property

February 27, 1998
**Counsel**

**Confidential to Legal**

**Prepared in Anticipation of**

**Litigation**

Aggressive Attorney, Esq.
Tax Counsel
Client Corporation
4242 Client Street, Suite 4200
Client City, Client State 24242

Dear Mr. Attorney:

We are pleased to submit this proposal for valuation consulting services.

This proposal will describe the property subject to appraisal, the purpose and objective of the appraisal, the proposed analytical procedures, the appraisal work product, engagement staffing, engagement timing and fees, and our standard engagement terms and conditions.

### Property Subject to Appraisal

The property subject to appraisal is the internally developed application computer software owned and operated by Client Corporation (hereinafter the "subject software").

Due to the way that descriptive measurement data are available, we will categorize (and analyze) the subject software in two groups:

1. Distribution applications, coded principally in COBOL, for which function point and/or executable lines of code metrics are available by application; we understand that there are approximately 20 million executable lines of code in this group.
2. Administrative applications, coded principally in COBOL and Assembler, for which measurement metric data are not readily available—except in the aggregate; we understand that there are approximately 10 million executable lines of code in this group.

### Objective and Purpose of the Appraisal

The objective of the appraisal is to estimate the fair market value of the subject software as of January 1, 1998.

The purpose of the appraisal is to provide an independent valuation opinion to assist you in negotiating and/or appealing the ad valorem property tax assessment for Client Corporation.

### Proposed Analytical Procedures

This appraisal will be prepared in accordance with the *Uniform Standards of Professional Appraisal Practice* (USPAP) as promulgated by The Appraisal Foundation.

We will consider all generally accepted approaches to the appraisal of computer software.

Based upon the information currently available to us, we plan to use one or more software engineering cost estimation models. These models generally estimate the number of person-months required to recreate the subject software.

In addition to this estimate of person-months, we will perform an analysis of the Client Corporation compensation and benefit levels. The objective of this analysis is to conclude the fully loaded cost per person-month of Client Corporation software development personnel.

The product of the cost estimation model's person-month estimate and our conclusion of the cost per person-month is our estimate of the fair market value of the subject software.

In addition to factual data, we will need access to Client Corporation data processing personnel. First, we will need to document the Client Corporation software development environment. Second, we will need adequate descriptions of the software subject to appraisal. Third, we will need to review a representative sample of the system documentation with regard to the subject software. And, fourth, we will need to see a representative sample of the subject software in actual operation (particularly system inputs and outputs).

### Appraisal Work Product

The work product of this appraisal will be a written valuation opinion report, prepared in accordance with the professional standards of USPAP and of the American Society of Appraisers.

We will first issue this report as an unsigned draft. At that time, we will solicit your questions, comments, and suggestions. We will not issue our final, signed report until you have reviewed our draft report.

### Engagement Staffing

Mary F. Analyst, CFA, ASA, CPA will be the principal analyst for this engagement. Mary is a managing director of our firm.

Mary will be assisted by Manoj Engineer, Ph.D., and Pamela Programmer. Manoj and Pamela are senior associates of our firm who specialize in software analysis, appraisal, and licensing.

The professional qualifications of these three analysts are appended to this proposal.

Illustrative Engagement Letter
Appraisal of Intellectual Property

---

#### *Engagement Timing and Fees*

We will begin this engagement immediately upon receipt of your written authorization to proceed and our retainer. We will issue the first draft of our report within 30 days of our receipt of your written authorization to proceed and of certain required technical data. We will issue our final report promptly after your review of our draft report.

Our professional fee for this appraisal will be based upon the actual time required by our professional staff to perform the required procedures, at our standard billing rates. Based upon the information currently available to us, we recommend that you budget $XX,XXX for professional fees.

Of course, the actual fees will be a function of (1) how much time is required in order to obtain the required data from Client Corporation, and (2) the extent that there is more software included in the appraisal subject than we have defined herein.

In addition to our professional fees, you will be responsible for out-of-pocket expenses related to this assignment. These expenses include travel, lodging, purchased data, data processing, clerical support, telephone, express delivery, and report production and reproduction charges. Out-of-pocket expenses will be indicated as a separate line item on our invoices.

You will be invoiced semi-monthly for professional fees and out-of-pocket expenses incurred to date. Invoices are due within 15 days of date of invoice. Invoices outstanding for more than thirty (30) days accrue interest at the rate of one and one-half percent (1.5%) per month (18% annual percentage rate).

To protect our independence, and as a matter of company policy, we can not issue our final, signed report until all outstanding invoices have been paid.

#### *Engagement Terms and Conditions*

Our work product is valid only for the purpose stated herein. You agree not to reference our name or our report, in whole or in part, in any document distributed to third parties without our written consent. However, we understand that you will use this report in order to negotiate, appeal, or litigate state ad valorem property tax assessments.

We will maintain the confidentiality of all data provided to us by you. We will provide independent valuation and economic analysis assistance only. Our work product is not intended to provide legal, accounting, or taxation advice.

We will rely upon any data provided to us by you without independent verification or confirmation. You will warrant that all information provided to us is complete and accurate to the best of your knowledge. We will rely on your involvement in the development of required data and certain planning activities.

We would be pleased to work with you in a valuation consulting and litigation support capacity—to attend conferences subsequent to the issuance of our report, to confer with your independent legal counsel, to meet with assessors to explain our analysis, or to prepare for and offer expert witness testimony. However, these services are not included in the above fee estimate. At your request, these additional services will be performed at our standard hourly billing rates, plus out-of-pocket expenses.

#### *Summary and Conclusion*

We are eminently qualified to perform this appraisal analysis.

We understand the purpose and objective of this analysis, and we will work with you to achieve that objective.

If this engagement letter correctly describes our assignment, please sign below and return a signed copy to us along with a retainer check in the amount of $XX,XXX. This retainer will be applied against the final outstanding invoice related to this assignment.

If you have any questions regarding this proposal, please contact the undersigned. We look forward to working with you again.

Very truly yours,

#### *Computer Software Appraisers*

Mary F. Analyst, CPA, CFA, ASA

#### *Accepted by:*

Company:      Client Corporation
By:            _____
Name:          _____
Title:         _____
Date:          _____

---

# Data Collection and Analysis

## INTRODUCTION

After carefully defining the intangible asset appraisal or economic analysis assignment, the next step is gathering the data necessary to conduct the assignment.

One of the greatest challenges in conducting an intangible asset analysis is generating the appropriate information required to complete the assignment. This step is challenging because it is sometimes difficult even to know the right questions to ask, let alone how to understand and interpret the answers.

This chapter presents some of the information that should be investigated during the course of conducting an intangible asset analysis. The specific data necessary to conduct an intangible asset appraisal or economic analysis can be categorized into three groups: general industry and economic environment data, company-specific data, and specific intangible asset market data.

## GENERALIZED INTANGIBLE ASSET INFORMATION CHECKLIST

Exhibit 5-1 presents a generalized checklist of documents and information commonly used in intangible asset analyses. Not every item on the list is necessarily required for every analysis. In many instances, special circumstances require the analyst to request and review certain documents not included on this checklist.

Having requested whatever documents are relevant and likely available, the analyst should be flexible enough to work within the limits of the documentation that the client is able to provide. It would be unusual to find every item on the checklist readily available. Therefore, the analyst usually needs to obtain some of the information through interviews with the client or with other parties. As the analysis progresses, the analyst can review the written information and supplement it, when necessary, by requesting more documents through interviews with management and by reference to written information obtained from outside of the business currently using the subject intangible asset.

## RELEVANT TIME PERIOD

The most common period of relevant history is five years. However, conceptually, the relevant period covers the most recent time period immediately before the valuation date that represents the general developmental or commercial operations of the intangible asset. If the operations involving the intangible asset changed significantly a few years before the valuation date, then the relevant period may include only the previous three or four years. On the other hand, if the intangible has a long commercial history, and some or all recent years were abnormal in some way, then financial statements for a period longer than five years may constitute a relevant period for analytical purposes.

## DATA SOURCES INTERNAL TO THE INTANGIBLE ASSET OWNER

If the intangible asset is operating as part of a going-concern company, then a typical business valuation information request list is a good place to

EXHIBIT 5-1

Valuing Intangible Assets
Preliminary Information Request

1. Copies of all current **patents** and patent applications, including descriptions of the products and processes encompassed in the patents and patent applications, date of each patent award and patent expiration, date of each patent application, and current status of application.

2. A detailed listing of all technical **drawings,** blueprints, and specifications related to each product in the current product line. Each description should include a drawing size, a drawing identification number, a description of the part of process encompassed by the drawing, the date that the drawing was first produced, the date that the drawing was last materially revised, and the date that the drawing is anticipated to become obsolete (i.e., the product or process will either be substantially revised or dropped from the current product line).

3. A detailed listing of all **customers** on the current customer list, including customer identification number, a customer name and description, the date on which the customer first placed an order with the company, total revenues from each customer for the last three fiscal years, and anticipated revenues from each customer for the current fiscal year.

4. Copies of all open **contracts** with customers or clients, including the inception date and termination date of the contract, revenues from each contract since its inception to date, and anticipated revenues from each contract until its expected termination.

5. A synopsis of all current customer **proposals** and quotations outstanding, including the date the proposal was issued, the term of the contract if the proposal is accepted by the customer, the anticipated revenue over the life of the contract if the proposal is accepted by the customer, the date on which the proposal or quotation will expire (if any), and the anticipated probability of customer acceptance (i.e., award of the contract).

6. A detailed listing of the current backlog of confirmed customer **purchase orders,** purchase releases, or other purchase commitments in-house that have not yet been produced and/or shipped to customers. This listing should include the name of each customer, the date the order was received, the date the order is to be shipped, and the total anticipated revenue to be generated from each open order.

7. A detailed description and listing of all in-house **libraries** including purchased volumes and internally generated documentation. These libraries could be technical or general laboratory notebooks, analysis of market conditions including firm's and competitor's market share, other internally generated notes and materials, trade publications, suppliers and equipment manuals and brochures, sets of governmental regulations, etc. The listing should include the name and description of each publication, the date that it was acquired, and the original cost (if any).

8. A detailed listing of all externally purchased and internally prepared **computer software,** including proprietary and general operating systems software, firmware and utilities programs, and applications programs and systems. This listing should include the name and description of each system, the date that it was acquired or developed, the original cost (if externally purchased), the operating platform on which each system operates, the level of system documentation related to each system, and the level and frequency of current usage of each system.

9. A detailed listing of all internally generated or externally purchased **training materials,** including manuals, courses, workbooks, films, cassettes, etc. This includes training materials for management personnel, operations personnel, sales and marketing personnel, etc. This listing should include the name of each material, a description of its contents, the date of acquisition or development, and the original cost (if externally purchased).

10. A detailed listing of all externally developed or externally purchased promotional and **marketing materials,** including sales brochures, displays, advertising programs and formats, promotional films and cassettes, technical marketing manuals and literature, etc. This listing should include the name of each material, a description of its content, the date of acquisition or development, and the original cost (if externally purchased).

11. A detailed listing of all current **employees** who are subject to current employment contracts with the company and current or past employees who have signed currently enforceable covenants not to compete with the company. This listing should include the name of each employee, the date on which the employment agreement or noncompete agreement was signed, and the date on which the employment agreement or noncompete agreement expires. Copies of each employment contract and covenant not to compete are required.

12. A synopsis of all current supplier and **vendor contracts,** including the name and address of each supplier, the inception date of the contract, the termination date of the contract, the products/supply/materials sourced to that supplier, and a synopsis description of the purchase price, purchase quantity, credit terms, and delivery terms of each contract.

13. A summary listing of all current **trademarks,** trade names, and registrations. This listing should include the registration number of each trademark, a description of each trademark, and a date of registration of each trademark.

14. A listing of current **licenses,** rights, contracts, or agreements that allow the company to use another party's products, processes, technology, brand name, registration, etc. This listing should include the name of the license granter, the inception date of the license, the termination date of the license, a description of the right or privilege being licensed, and a description of the royalties, fees, or other payments made for the use of the license.

15. A synopsis of all **leases.** This synopsis should include the name of the lesser, the inception date of the lease, the termination date of the lease, a description and location of the property being leased (including size, condition, and special features), the periodic lease payments, and any special terms relating to the lease (e.g., escalator clauses, operating cost pass-throughs).

start the investigation of general information. The history of the company and its legal structure, its brochures and catalogs, key personnel, customer and supplier base, contractual obligations, and budgets and forecasts are all general issues to investigate.

The analyst should gather data about the subject intangible asset's historical operating performance and its future prospects. Data are also gathered so that the analyst is in a position to perform the traditional approaches to value for each subject intangible asset. Generally, then, the analyst inquires about all of the costs incurred to get the intangible asset into its current condition (as of the valuation date), about transactions involving the subject intangible asset and similar intangible assets, about the future application and utilization of the intangible asset as part of the current business operations, and about how it might fit into the commercial use or licensing marketplace at large.

The expected remaining useful life of the intangible asset is an important component of an appraisal or economic analysis. An intangible asset's expected remaining useful life may be influenced by legal, contractual, judicial, physical, functional, technological, economic, or analytical determinants.

Exhibit 5-1 provides a general list of data elements that are helpful when analyzing the value of an intangible asset. Starting with this list will help the analyst develop a subject engagement-specific information request list. It may also be useful to the intangible asset owner (and to related professional advisers) in the planning stages of the appraisal or economic analysis engagement.

## PRIOR TRANSACTIONS OR OFFERS

Verifying prior sale or license transactions or offers is a good analytical practice. Overlooking or overemphasizing prior transactions is a common area of controversy in intangible asset valuation. Whether there were strings attached, whether it was at arm's length, or whether contingent payments were involved all become typical points of contention when prior transactions are relied upon in reaching a valuation opinion.

Intangible asset sale or license offers that were never consummated may still provide valuable analytical information. If there was a bona fide arm's-length offer, even a rejected offer may provide useful evidence of value. Written documentation of any such offers should be requested and investigated.

## DATA SOURCES EXTERNAL TO THE INTANGIBLE ASSET OWNER

Numerous sources of external information are available and applicable with respect to an analysis of intangible assets. This external information may include industry data, technological trends, economic and demographic data, empirical transactional pricing data (related both to sales and licenses), and intangible asset–specific or industry-specific methodological information.

The general sources for these external data fall into the following categories:

1. Scholarly and legal publications.
2. Trade publications.

3. News sources.
4. Court cases.
5. Published books.

Sources specific to certain types of intangibles will be discussed in Part V.

## Scholarly and Legal Publications

Published articles regarding the appraisal and economic analysis of intangible assets can be found in standard indexes such as the *Business Periodicals Index*, published by H.W. Wilson. These standard indexes may be found at most public and academic libraries. The ABI/Inform database, produced by UMI and found on-line via Lexis/Nexis, Dialog Information Services, and ProQuest Direct, is another source of scholarly and trade publication articles. Examples of journals indexed in ABI/Inform include *Managing Intellectual Property* and *Dispute Resolution Journal*. Journals not indexed by either print or electronic source but that contain useful articles include the *Business Valuation Review* and the *Licensing Economics Review*.

For articles written from a legal point of view, a noteworthy source is the *Legal Resource Index*, published by Information Access Co., or the *Index to Legal Periodicals*, published by H.W. Wilson. Both indexes can be found at most academic and county law libraries, as well as on-line via Lexis/Nexis, Westlaw, and Dialog Information Services. These indexes provide citations to general and specialized law reviews, as well as to bar association publications.

## Trade Publications

Specialized newsletters often provide the best statistical data regarding intangible asset licensing agreements and royalty rates. One of the best sources of royalty rates is *Licensing Economics Review*, published by AUS Consultants. The *Review* provides data on recent transactions, alliances, and litigation, as well as editorials. *Licensing Journal*, published monthly by EPM Communications, Inc., provides statistics, research, and descriptions of licensers, licensing accounts, and licensees. For example, the February 1, 1997, issue published a detailed "Special Report on Character and Entertainment Licensing." *Licensing Law and Business Report*, published by Clark Boardman Callaghan, provides legal analyses of court cases and recent developments relating to technology management, tax considerations, and antitrust law.

## News Sources

Newswires and newspapers often provide details on particular intangible asset licensing agreements and on the actual royalties paid. For example, *Business Wire*, available on most on-line information services, recently published a press release that detailed the royalty rate paid by Designer Holdings, Inc., to CK/Calvin Klein for certain rights pertaining to Calvin Klein Outlet Stores. The *Los Angeles Times* frequently publishes articles that mention the royalties paid for musical recordings. For worldwide data, the analyst may consult on-line international news sources such as Reuters and Textline.

## Court Cases

Published decisions from the U.S. Tax Court, the U.S. District Courts, and the U.S. Circuit Courts of Appeal may provide pertinent data on intangible asset royalty rates, transfer pricing arrangements, and methods for estimating damages from litigated infringement cases. Researchers will find reasonable royalty rates for patent licenses, as discussed in the classic case *Georgia-Pacific Corporation v. United States Plywood Corporation.*[1] In cases such as *Sundstrand Corp., et al. v. Commissioner,*[2] the U.S. Tax Court determined the appropriate royalty rate for Section 482 transfer pricing purposes. Many of these cases provide examples of the valuation and economic analysis methodology provided by various expert witnesses. Court cases can be searched by keywords on-line from Lexis/Nexis and Westlaw, or by consulting digests and law reviews in law libraries. Tax court cases may also be searched by keywords on Kleinrocks Tax Library, available on CD-ROM.

## Published Books

Kent Press publishes *An Insider's Guide to Royalty Rates.* This book provides a compilation of empirical transactional data with respect to the licensing of the intangible property rights related to products from action toys to frozen yogurt. The authors provide a range of royalty rates for each product by types of licensed product: art, celebrity, character, collegiate, corporate, designer, event, and sports.

### INTERVIEWING THE INTANGIBLE ASSET OWNER

The need for the analyst to inspect the business facilities and to have personal contact with business management and other related people varies greatly from one analytical situation to another. The extent of the necessary fieldwork depends on many things, including the purpose of the analysis, the nature of the industry, and the size and complexity of the case. Another factor is how extensively the written materials referenced here cover the many subjects that the analyst needs to investigate.

The objectives of the analyst's fieldwork range from gaining a broad, general perspective on the subject industry and its operations to filling in necessary minutiae. Generally, a visit to the business in which the intangible asset exists or will exist, in order to observe daily operations, may provide substantial insight beyond what is gleaned solely from financial statements and other written material. Seeing the business operate firsthand and participating in face-to-face interviews with management typically makes the industry come alive for an analyst. The analyst can fill in many details more easily and productively through a direct conversation than through written material.

The analyst can get the most out of the field trip and interview process by thinking and planning in terms of accomplishing three objectives:

---

1. *Georgia-Pacific Corporation v. United States Plywood Corporation,* 318 F.Supp. 1116 (S.D.N.Y., May 28, 1970).
2. *Sundstrand Corp., et al. v. Commissioner,* 96 T.C. 226 (February 19, 1991).

1. To gain a better overall understanding of the subject industry;
2. To better understand the implications of the business's financial statements, operating statistics, and other written information for the intangible asset analysis;
3. To identify current or potential changes that may cause the future of the subject intangible asset—or the future of the particular company or industry—to differ from what is indicated by a mere extrapolation of historical financial and operational data.

## SCHEDULING THE SEQUENCE OF DUE DILIGENCE STEPS

The sequence of reading and analyzing various aspects of the written material, visiting the business facilities, and conducting interviews must be scheduled to suit each appraisal or economic analysis assignment. Scheduling the various due diligence steps should be a priority at the beginning of the analysis, along with precisely defining and documenting the analytical assignment. The schedule should be reviewed and changed as necessary throughout the process.

Generally, it is advisable to prepare in advance a thorough list of questions to ask during the analysis fieldwork. While the specific issues pertinent to the intangible asset analysis vary from case to case, it is often useful to review a standard list of questions in preparing a specific list for a particular intangible asset analysis to ensure that an important question is not overlooked.

The analysis fieldwork also helps to identify other analytical and research steps to take. Among the myriad of written materials discussed already, the analysis field trip can indicate whether the analyst needs certain additional documentation. Some items can be dismissed as irrelevant, and some items can be examined on-site without making copies for the analyst's files. In other cases, the analysis fieldwork may turn up circumstances suggesting the need for additional documentation.

For these reasons, it is usually best to conduct the fieldwork and interview management fairly early in the analysis process, after obtaining and reviewing enough preliminary information to get a general overview of the intangible asset. The analyst can then conduct follow-up interviews, if needed, either in person or by telephone.

When valuing an intangible asset as one component of the valuation of an overall business, it is important to analyze and make appropriate adjustments to the financial statements. The valuation of an intangible asset differs from the valuation of a typical business, however, because the types of expenses required to support the value of an intangible asset may be very different from those required to support the value of the entire business. Perhaps the most important difference is that intangible asset value may depend on only a few critical factors, whereas overall business value depends upon the coordinated operation of all the assets of the company.

The completeness and accuracy of the data affect the ability to identify and quantify those factors that would affect the result under any particular analytical method. An analysis is relatively more reliable as the completeness and accuracy of the data increase. Deficiencies in the data used may have a greater effect on some analytical methods than others.

## SUMMARY

Chapter 5 introduced the general categories of data that are available for and applicable to the appraisal or economic analysis of intangible assets. Data may be gathered from sources that are internal or external to the current intangible asset owner.

This chapter is intended to be general in nature. Data sources specific to each type of intangible asset are introduced in Part V, Analysis of Specific Types of Intangible Assets.

# PART TWO

# Intangible Asset Valuation Approaches, Methods, and Procedures

# The Appraisal Process

## INTRODUCTION

The appraisal process is a systematic approach to answering a client's specific question about property value. The appraisal process begins with the identification of the specific question to be answered, and it ends when an answer is reported to all interested parties.

Each intangible asset appraisal assignment is unique, and many different types of value can be estimated for a particular intangible asset. Even under unique circumstances, the appraisal process provides the analytical framework for estimating the value of an intangible asset.

The appraisal process provides a pattern that can be used in any appraisal assignment to perform market research and data analysis, to apply appraisal methods and procedures, and to integrate the results of these analyses into an estimate of a specifically defined value.

## THE NATURE OF THE APPRAISAL PROCESS

The appraisal of intangible assets is an evolving discipline. The intangible asset appraisal process provides a structure for the analysis of the value of intangible assets so that the analytical discipline can continue to develop and improve over time.

As with most property, the value of an intangible asset is a reflection of the present value of the future economic income that the intangible asset is expected to generate. One immediate purpose of an intangible asset appraisal assignment is to make reasonable projections of future events.

The predictable economic performance of an intangible asset adds greatly to the understanding and acceptance of its estimated valuation. In many ways, the appraisal of intangible assets is the culmination of exploratory research into the predictable economic performance of an intangible asset.

Any type of exploratory research follows these consecutive steps:

1. Question.
2. Analyze.
3. Test.
4. Conclude.

The intangible asset appraisal process expands on this pattern. Analysts follow four similar steps:

1. Identification of the intangible asset appraisal problem.
2. Data collection and analysis.
3. Application of the three approaches to value.
4. Estimation of the value conclusion.

When results of the process are unexpected, a new cycle begins. As with any exploratory research, the new postulates associated with each intangible asset appraisal assignment are subject to testing, sometimes leading to dozens of subsequent investigations.

If the intangible asset appraisal process were perfect, then it would always determine at one stroke which model or theory is correct. This determination would be made by simply comparing the values observed with those predicted. The "perfect" appraisal process could also precisely detect the slightest flaw in the agreement between the predicted value and the actual value. Thus, the "perfect" appraisal process would itself point the way to a refinement of the model.

But the intangible asset appraisal process is not perfect. Since the estimate of the value of any property is sensitive to prevailing economic conditions during the time period in question, actual economic events that have taken place subsequent to the valuation date are only relevant to the extent that they were predictable as of the valuation date. The analyst is asked to estimate value without the benefit of knowing with certainty about future events. In fact, the analyst performs the appraisal by only considering the events one could reasonably expect to occur after the valuation date. In many intangible asset appraisal assignments, this perspective becomes most important.

The main purpose of the intangible asset appraisal process, then, is to make reliable predictions. If the predictions are reasonably accurate, the appraisal is successful. If the predictions are not reasonably accurate, the appraisal model is replaced or adjusted until accurate predictions result. Analysts do not expect a model to be permanently successful, because more extensive or more accurate experimental measurements are likely to be made.

The purpose of the intangible asset appraisal process is to postulate a conceptual valuation model from which the observable behavior of the marketplace may be predicted with reasonable accuracy. The validation of the valuation model follows the appraisal method:

1. Postulate a model based upon existing experimental observations or measurements.
2. Check the predictions of this model against further observations or measurements.
3. Adjust or replace the model as required by the new observations or measurements.

The third step leads back to the first step, and the process continues without end. No claim can be made about the reality of the model; the sole criterion for assessing the quality of the model is the reasonable prediction of economic performance from the simplest, most convenient, or most satisfying model.

No prediction of the future behavior of the marketplace is either perfectly accurate or perfectly certain. Analysts should always be prepared to observe experimental results that will necessitate the adjustment or replacement of the model. Models should not only predict with reasonable accuracy, but they should also conform to the prevailing analytical standards of the times.

The construction of a valuation model for a particular intangible asset appraisal assignment is a creative act that somewhat defies the standardization of analytical procedures. However, the validation of the model follows a regular process called the appraisal process. Models are never certain and are always subject to revision, but each new model includes the successful parts of older models. Thus, appraisal knowledge is cumulative.

Valuation models are not proved, they are validated. The process of being *validated* means that the model has made reasonably accurate predictions. In considering the continued application of an already validated model, it is expected that the model will continue to predict as accurately in the future as it has in the past. However, there is no guarantee of any model's continued predictive ability.

The appraisal process is merely a formalization of learning by experience. Analysts who learn by experience are implicitly using the appraisal process. The basic postulate of value analysis and estimation is that the marketplace is predictable. The critical analysis of the intangible asset appraisal process has a lofty final objective: to evoke new thinking or to reveal new approaches to old problems. Critical analysis presents the analyst with an unending task. Analysts rarely achieve a final, perfect valuation model. Rather, they begin with the question, "How do we estimate value?" and they conclude with the question, "How can we estimate value more accurately?"

## IDENTIFICATION OF THE APPRAISAL PROBLEM

Posing the right question is sometimes more difficult than finding the correct answer. When presented with an intangible asset appraisal assignment, the analyst first identifies the central issues to be addressed and plans a strategy for completing the assignment. The inability to complete an intangible asset appraisal assignment is usually the result of poor communication between the analyst and the client about the objectives of the appraisal. Clients who are unfamiliar with the appraisal process may not understand how the implementation of the valuation methods may affect the valuation conclusion. Different property types, ownership interests, legal rights and privileges, and uses of the appraisal conclusion can significantly affect the appraisal process and the appraisal conclusion.

The client and the analyst should fully understand and reach agreement on the assignment, preferably in writing, before the valuation analysis begins.

In Part I, we introduced various terms that should be useful in clearly identifying the appraisal problem. Many ownership interests and potential value conclusions exist for an intangible asset.

Any change in the applicable standard of value, premise of value, or valuation date can radically change the value conclusion for the very same intangible asset.

The statement of the intangible asset appraisal problem should include:

- Identification of the subject intangible asset.
- Identification of the subject intangible asset property rights to be valued.
- Objective of the intangible asset appraisal assignment.
- Purpose of the intangible asset appraisal assignment.
- Definition of the appropriate standard of value.
- Date of the value estimate.
- A listing of limiting conditions, if any.

The intangible asset property rights to be valued include the rights that are legally held, or may be held, by the owner of the intangible asset. An analyst may estimate the fee simple interest or partial ownership interests created by the severance or division of ownership rights. Information regarding the specific rights to be valued and the financing involved may be critical at the start of the assignment, because the complexity of these rights and terms may affect the procedures, skills, and time required to complete the assignment.

Also, the sum of the partial interests in a particular intangible asset may not equal its fee simple value. To estimate the value of a partial interest in a particular intangible asset, direct evidence of the attitude of the market to such a partial interest is usually preferred by analysts. A clear identification of the intangible asset appraisal assignment will help direct the analyst toward the essential information and help the analyst to avoid unnecessary and expensive tangential analysis.

## HIGHEST AND BEST USE

Through highest and best use analysis, the analyst interprets the market forces that influence the subject property and identifies the use upon which the final value estimate is based. The highest and best use analysis helps the analyst to identify comparable properties and to identify obsolescence factors that may affect the value or the life of the subject intangible asset.

Critical valuation factors are identified during the highest and best use analysis including: systematic and nonsystematic risk, economic income estimates, and economic income capitalization rates. During the course of the appraisal, the analyst may test the sensitivity of the valuation. In this manner, a reasonable range of values for the intangible asset may be established.

The identification of various operating scenarios may be uncovered during a highest and best use analysis. Interrelationships between several of the critical valuation factors—and their probability of occurrence in the future—may be analyzed. Again, this helps establish a reasonable range of values for the subject intangible asset.

## DATA COLLECTION

After defining the appraisal problem, the next step is a preliminary data analysis. During this step, the analyst develops the analytical work plan. The analyst gathers, analyzes, and adjusts data, as appropriate, when performing the appraisal assignment. Such data and information include:

1. Characteristics of the intangible asset: ownership interest to be valued, rights, privileges, conditions, and factors affecting ownership or operational control.
2. Nature, history, and outlook of the business and industry in which the intangible asset operates.
3. Historical financial information for the intangible asset.
4. Related assets and liabilities required for economic operation of the subject intangible asset.
5. The nature and conditions of the relevant industries that have an impact on the intangible asset.
6. Local, national, and international economic factors affecting the intangible asset.
7. Available rates of return on alternative investments and a description of relevant market transactions.
8. Prior transactions involving the subject intangible asset.
9. Other relevant information.

The work plan includes an analysis of the market for the intangible asset and its supply and demand relationships. To complete an intangible asset appraisal assignment quickly and efficiently, the primary steps in the appraisal process are planned and scheduled. Time and personnel requirements vary with the complexity of the appraisal objective and with the complexity of the available data. Some assignments can be completed in a few days and others require months to gather and analyze the appropriate data.

On some assignments, the assistance of specialists with expertise in other fields is needed. For example, the valuation of the contract rights associated with the distribution of a particular entertainer's work product may benefit from the opinion of a professional agent.

The analyst is responsible for the work product and should, therefore, have a clear understanding of the responsibilities of each of the appraisal assignment team members. Taking a comprehensive view, the assignment's primary analyst recognizes the type, volume, and sequence of work to be done.

The amount and type of data collected for an appraisal depend on how the assignment has been defined. For example, the appraisal problem may require that one valuation approach be given greater emphasis in the final value estimate. Ultimately, the analyst's expertise and professional judgment and the quality and quantity of available data will determine the applicability of the valuation approach or approaches. The data collected and analyzed affect the judgments made in the valuation analysis, so the appraisal report usually includes a description of the information considered by the analyst.

## THREE APPROACHES TO VALUE

The appraisal process is applied to develop a well-supported estimate of a defined value based on consideration of all pertinent data. The intangible asset property value is estimated after considering three distinct approaches to value: cost, market, and income. One or more of these approaches are used in all estimations of value. Which of the three approaches is most applicable in the particular analysis depends upon the type of property, the use of the appraisal, and the quality and quantity of data available for analysis.

All three approaches are applicable to many appraisal problems. Depending on the specific assignment, one or more of the approaches may have greater significance. Where possible, the analyst should apply more than one approach. Alternative value indications can serve as useful comparisons for assessing the reasonableness of the results of the principal approach.

## CONTINGENT AND LIMITING CONDITIONS

It is important to realize that it is necessary for the analyst to make general assumptions in order to carry out an appraisal assignment in an efficient manner. General assumptions deal with issues such as legal and title considerations, liens and encumbrances, information furnished by others (e.g., engineering studies, market studies), hidden conditions and environmental hazards, and compliance with laws and regulations.

The analyst should make it clear that possession and use of the report is limited to the specific purpose and to the specific audience for which it was prepared. Typically, no updating of the report or further consultation or expert testimony is required as part of a particular appraisal assignment.

The report is based upon all the information available to the analyst as of the date of the report. The analyst typically assumes the information to be accurate without auditing the information for accuracy. Projections used as part of the analysis are based on information current as of the valuation date and are subject to change with changes in future economic and market conditions.

Independent appraisals certify that the analyst has personally conducted the appraisal and has no present or prospective interest in the property that is the subject of the appraisal report. The analyst admits no personal interest or bias with respect to the parties involved. With regard to independent appraisals, the fee for performing the analysis is not contingent upon the value reported or the attainment of a stipulated event. Also with regard to independent appraisals, many analysts are required to conduct their professional appraisal activities in compliance with the *Uniform Standards of Professional Appraisal Practice.*

## VALUATION CONCLUSION

From an overall engagement perspective, the analyst should consider the question: "Did I accomplish what I set out to accomplish?"

A review of the intangible asset appraisal assignment should consider:

1. Identification of the subject intangible asset (including the ownership characteristics subject to appraisal).
2. The objective of the appraisal.
3. The purpose of the appraisal.
4. The intangible asset ownership interest (including the bundle of legal rights) subject to appraisal.
5. The date of the value estimate.
6. Definition of the appropriate standard of value to be estimated.
7. The premise of value to be used (that is, based upon the conclusion of the highest and best use of the subject intangible asset).

The intangible asset appraisal assignment is performed to answer a question about the value of an intangible asset. Even within the same valuation approach, different methods will typically result in different indications of value. For example, it is likely that different indicated values would result from two different income approach methods (e.g., from the capitalized economic income method versus the discounted economic income method).

The process of reconciliation involves the analysis of the alternative valuation conclusions in order to arrive at a final value estimate for the subject intangible asset. Before reaching a final value estimate, the analyst should review the entire intangible asset appraisal for appropriateness and for accuracy. It is noteworthy that the definition of value estimated, and its relationship to each step in the valuation process, should be carefully considered throughout the reconciliation process.

## REPORTING THE VALUATION CONCLUSION

The results of the intangible asset appraisal process are presented in an appraisal report. Appraisal reports may be oral (e.g., expert testimony) or written.

If the report is being prepared in a manner consistent with the *Uniform Standards of Professional Appraisal Practice,* it should clearly and accurately set forth the appraisal in a manner that is not misleading. It should contain sufficient information to enable the audience to understand it properly, and it should clearly disclose any extraordinary contingent or limiting condition that impacts the appraisal.

The analyst's professional qualifications and experience are included in an independent appraisal report as evidence of the analyst's competence to perform the assignment.

## SUMMARY

Understanding the basic steps in the appraisal process—and the reasons for the basic steps—is essential to the successful conduct of an intangible asset valuation or economic analysis. The appraisal process provides a general analytical structure that assists the analyst in the collection, assessment, manipulation, and interpretation of market-derived valuation evidence. These steps provide a logical framework that allows the analyst to synthesize and conclude a reasonable estimate of value. They also assist the analyst in communicating the results of the appraisal in a well-reasoned and adequately documented report.

Exhibit 6-1 summarizes the basic steps in the appraisal process.

The most complex appraisal problem can be more easily understood and more effectively solved if the analyst perceives it in terms of the appraisal process.

**EXHIBIT 6-1**

The Intangible Asset Appraisal Process

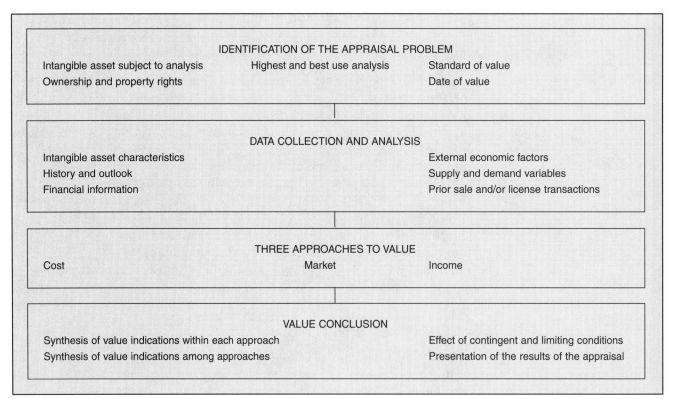

# Basic Valuation Approaches

## INTRODUCTION

The fundamental intangible asset valuation topics are presented in this chapter. First, we present a general introduction to the three approaches to intangible asset valuation. Second, we summarize the general theoretical concepts and practical applications of the three fundamental approaches to intangible asset valuation. Third, we outline the general procedures regarding the preparation of the valuation synthesis and conclusion. Last, we present a general introduction to the process of reporting the conclusion of the value estimate.

As mentioned previously, there are numerous methods and procedures that may be appropriate to the economic analysis and appraisal of intangible assets and intellectual properties. However, when analysts consider the fundamental similarities and differences among these numerous methods and procedures, they all logically group together into the three general categories of valuation analysis. These three fundamental ways of analyzing the economics of intangible assets are often called the cost approach, the market approach, and the income approach.

Each of these three valuation approaches has the same basic analytical objective: to arrive at a reasonable indication of a defined value for the subject intangible asset as of a certain date. Accordingly, methods and procedures that are premised upon the same fundamental economic principles are grouped together into these valuation approaches. The three approaches to intangible asset value, collectively, encompass a broad spectrum of economic theory and property investment concepts.

The basic concepts of the three approaches to value have been an integral part of the property valuation literature since the nineteenth century. However, there is no law of nature or other scientific reason to group all valuation methods into three categories, as opposed to, say, two or four categories. Rather, the only justification for the three approaches is that it is a logical classification system. All of the numerous methods can be logically grouped into three categories where: (1) all of the methods in each category share one or more fundamental economic principal underpinnings, and (2) the methods in each approach have some basic analytical differences from the methods in each other approach. The number *three* just happens to be the smallest number of categories that meet both of these conditions.

This is not to say that there are no similarities among the three approaches. In fact this is to be expected since they all have the same basic analytical objective. For example, to a greater or lesser extent, the analytical methods in each of the three approaches rely upon market-derived empirical data and are influenced by the same general economic, industry, and investment conditions.

There are also discrete technical differences between the analytical methods within a given valuation approach. This also is to be expected since if there were no technical differences between two different analytical methods, then they wouldn't be two different methods after all. They would, in fact, be the same method, using perhaps two slightly different definitions of the relevant valuation variables.

## GENERAL INTRODUCTION TO THE COST APPROACH

The cost approach to intangible asset analysis is based upon the economic principles of substitution and price equilibrium (often called the competitive equilibrium price). These basic economic principles assert that an investor will pay no more for an investment than the cost to obtain (i.e., either by purchase or by construction) an investment of equal utility. In other words, a willing buyer for an intangible asset will pay no more for the subject intangible asset than the price of an intangible property of comparable utility. Accordingly, an efficient market adjusts the prices of all properties (including intangible assets) in equilibrium so that the price the market will pay is a function of the comparative utility of each property.

Utility is an economic concept. Functionality is an engineering concept. Some analysts mistakenly believe that the cost approach to intangible asset valuation is based upon the functionality of the subject intangible. This is not conceptually correct (except to the extent that the intangible's functionality indirectly influences its utility). The differences between utility and functionality are described in greater detail in Chapter 8.

The availability (and, therefore, the cost) of substitute properties is directly affected by shifts in the supply and demand functions with regard to the universe of substitute properties. As the supply of substitute properties increases, ceteris paribus, market influences tend to drive down the cost of the substitute. As the supply of substitute properties decreases, market influences tend to drive up the cost of the substitute. Likewise, as the demand for substitute properties increases, market influences tend to drive up the cost of the substitute, and as the demand for substitute properties decreases, market influences tend to drive down the cost of properties.

The relevant components of cost are introduced in the next section and explained in greater detail in Chapter 8. However, the basic supply-and-demand price equilibrium principles illustrate what is meant by the term cost. In the cost approach to intangible asset analysis, cost is influenced by the marketplace. That is, the relevant cost is the greatest amount that the marketplace is willing to pay for the subject intangible asset. It is not necessarily the actual historical cost of creating the subject intangible and it is not necessarily the sum of the costs for which the willing seller would like to be compensated.

In other words, value is not necessarily equal to cost, at least not to cost as measured in the historical accounting sense. Rather, value is equal to cost measured in the economic sense. The economic measure of cost is usually equal to an accounting measure of cost that has been adjusted by either (or both) incremental and decremental influences caused by market conditions.

There is one application limitation with regard to the use of the cost approach to valuing intangible assets. Unlike fungible tangible assets, often there are no reasonable substitute properties to compare to many intangible assets and intellectual properties. Accordingly, with regard to the valuation of intangible assets with unique qualities, the cost approach may have application limitations.

## Cost Approach Methods—Theoretical Concepts

Within the cost approach to intangible asset valuation, there are several related analytical methods. Each group of analytical methods uses a similar definition of the type of cost that is relevant to the valuation. The most common types or definitions of cost are the following:

1. Reproduction cost.
2. Replacement cost.

There are subtle but important differences in the definitions of these two types of cost.

Reproduction cost contemplates the construction (or purchase) of an exact replica of the subject intangible asset. Before appropriate adjustments are made for the purposes of deriving an indication of value, reproduction cost does not consider either the market demand for or the market acceptance of the subject intangible. In other words, before the requisite valuation adjustments, the reproduction cost estimate does not answer (or even consider) the question of whether anyone would even want an exact replica of the subject intangible asset.

Replacement cost contemplates the cost to recreate the utility of the subject intangible asset, but in a form or appearance that may be quite different from an exact replica of the actual intangible property subject to appraisal. Utility is an economic concept that refers to the ability of the replacement intangible asset to provide an equivalent amount of satisfaction as the subject intangible.

It is noteworthy that while the replacement intangible asset performs the same task as the subject intangible, the replacement asset may be "better" (in some way) than the subject. In that case, the replacement intangible may yield more satisfaction (i.e., generate more utility) than the subject intangible. If this is the case, the analyst should be careful to adjust for this factor in the obsolescence estimation procedure of the replacement cost analysis.

Unlike the reproduction cost concept, the replacement cost concept does consider the market demand and the market acceptance for the subject intangible asset, at least in part. That is, if there are elements or components of the subject intangible asset that generate little or no market demand, they are not included in the replacement intangible. Since these undesirable elements or components add no value to the subject intangible, they are not designed into the replacement intangible.

Particularly with regard to the analysis of intellectual properties, it may also be useful to analyze costs from the perspective of creation cost versus recreation cost.

Creation cost considers the cost to originally create the subject intangible asset from its conceptual inception, with no guideline (such as a previous version of the subject intangible) for the current creator to use as a point of reference.

Recreation cost considers the cost to duplicate the subject asset, assuming that the current recreator possesses the knowledge, experience, and expertise already developed during the (actual) original creation process. For example, the recreation cost concept would assume that a guideline (such as a previous version of the subject intangible) does exist as a point of reference during the intangible asset recreation process.

There are several other definitions of cost that may be encompassed by the cost approach to intangible asset valuation. For example, some analysts consider a measure of cost avoidance as a cost approach methodology. This method quantifies some measure of either historical or prospective costs that are avoided (i.e., not incurred) by the intangible asset owner due to his or her ownership of the subject intangible property. Some analysts also consider trended historical costs as a beginning procedure in a cost approach analysis to estimate an indication of value. In this methodology, actual historical intangible asset development costs are identified and quantified, then trended to the valuation date by an appropriate inflation-based index factor.

Of course, all of these (and any other) definitions of cost merely represent the first procedure in the cost approach analysis. That is, they provide the baseline of the valuation analysis. As with the traditional reproduction and replacement definitions of cost, the alternative definitions of cost are subject to several additional procedures before they represent an indication of value.

All cost approach valuation methods typically involve a comprehensive or all-inclusive analysis of the relevant cost components. That is, all of the definitions of cost (i.e., reproduction, replacement, etc.) typically include consideration of the cost components of all:

1. Materials.
2. Labor.
3. Overhead.
4. Intangible asset developer's profit (i.e., an adequate profit margin on the incurred material, labor, and overhead costs).
5. Entrepreneurial incentive (i.e., an adequate return on the intangible asset developer's capital, coordination, and labor during the development period sufficient to induce the intangible asset development process).

All these components or elements of cost should be encompassed within each particular type of cost estimated in each individual intangible asset valuation method.

## The Concept of Obsolescence within the Cost Approach

Basic economic theory indicates that cost alone typically does not provide a reasonable indication of value. This is true regardless of the type of cost quantified (e.g., historical cost, trended historical cost, replacement cost, reproduction cost, etc.). It is noteworthy that the cost approach analysis begins with some measure of cost, but concludes with some measure of value. In order to get from a cost indication to a value indication, all relevant measures of obsolescence have to be identified and quantified; that is, all the relevant forms of obsolescence have to be identified, quantified, and subtracted from the *cost* of the intangible asset in order to estimate the *value* of the intangible asset. The common forms of obsolescence that are considered in a cost approach analysis of intangible assets include the following:

1. Physical deterioration.
2. Functional obsolescence.
3. Technological obsolescence.
4. Economic obsolescence.

It is unusual for intangible assets to suffer from physical deterioration. Physical deterioration represents the physical wear and tear of an asset. Since intangible assets rarely suffer from the wear and tear of being used or used up, physical deterioration usually does not apply.

Functional obsolescence relates to the fact that the subject intangible asset may be less than the perfect replacement for itself. When it was originally developed, the subject intangible asset was created to perform a certain function. Depending on the type of intangible asset, that function may have been to attract customers, allow for the exclusive production of a certain type of product, process a certain number of transactions per period or cycle, and so forth.

Over time, the subject intangible asset may be less able to accomplish the specific functions for which it was originally developed. This may be due to factors internal or external to the intangible asset. Whether the causes of the functional obsolescence are internal or external may have an impact on the quantification of the obsolescence. For the current discussion, however, it is only important to recognize that the subject intangible asset has experienced some degree of functional obsolescence.

Some analysts consider technological obsolescence to be a subset (or a special case) of functional obsolescence. Remember that functional obsolescence occurs when the subject intangible asset can no longer perform (at least, to intended specifications) the function for which it was developed. Technological obsolescence occurs when the intended function itself is no longer desirable, due to changes in the state of the art of the subject type of intangible asset. There are instances in the economic analysis of technology-related intangible assets when it may be worthwhile to identify and quantify the specific components of technological obsolescence. However, technological obsolescence does not relate only to technology-related or engineering-related intangible assets. Likewise, it does not relate only to innovative types of intellectual properties. Rather, to varying degrees, technological obsolescence could apply to any intangible asset.

Some of the appraisal literature refers to external obsolescence instead of economic obsolescence. External obsolescence relates to reasons for decrements in the value of the subject asset that are external to the asset itself. This is a relevant distinction with regard to the appraisal of tangible assets. However, it is not particularly relevant to the appraisal of most intangible assets because most of the reasons for all forms of obsolescence are external to intangible assets.

External obsolescence is generally considered to have two components: location-related obsolescence and economic-related obsolescence. Locational factors typically do not have a great influence on the value of most intangible assets. Because of this, and because most forms of obsolescence are external to intangible assets, we will refer to this value influence as economic obsolescence throughout this book.

Each form of obsolescence indicates a decrease in value of the subject intangible asset due to a very specific reason. Clearly, not every intangible asset suffers from each form of obsolescence. However, the consideration, identification, and quantification of the various forms of obsolescence (to the extent that they exist) is an important and necessary procedure in the cost approach valuation process.

The measure of cost (as defined by the individual cost approach method) adjusted by the measure of all relevant forms of obsolescence (which may be greatly influenced by the type of cost approach method selected) provides an indication of the defined value of the subject intangible asset.

## GENERAL INTRODUCTION TO THE MARKET APPROACH

The market approach to intangible asset valuation is based upon the related economic principles of competition and equilibrium. These economic principles conclude that, in a free and unrestricted market, supply and demand factors will drive the price of any good (such as an investment instrument or an intangible asset) to a point of equilibrium.

The economic principle of substitution also provides conceptual support for the market approach, because the identification and analysis of equilibrium prices or substitute goods provides empirical evidence for the analyst to consider with regard to the indicated value for the subject good (e.g., the subject intangible asset).

Value is often defined as *expected price*. Value is the price that a property would expect to fetch in its appropriate marketplace.

Value is not cost. For the reasons previously discussed, cost (or, at least, unadjusted cost) measures an historical price, not an expected price. Unless the current marketplace accepts some measure of cost as a reasonable price, no transactions (e.g., purchase, sale, license, etc.) will be expected to take place at the intangible asset's historical cost.

Value is not price. Price represents what one particular buyer or licensee actually paid to one particular seller or licensor for one particular intangible asset. In any particular single transaction, either participant may have been influenced by nonmarket, participant-specific influences. If such influences did occur, and if such influences are not general to the marketplace, then a particular transactional price may not be indicative of the expected market price.

In addition, a particular transaction price is representative of the condition of, the supply of, and the demand for the particular intangible asset that was sold or licensed. If the condition of the subject intangible asset is not sufficiently similar to the transactional intangible asset, then the historical transactional price may not be indicative of the expected price for the subject intangible asset. Likewise, if market-influenced supply and demand conditions have changed between the time of the transactional price and the date of analysis of the subject intangible asset, then the transactional price may not necessarily be indicative of the expected price for the subject intangible asset.

Even if the subject intangible asset was itself bought or licensed, that subject transactional price should not be naively relied upon to indicate an expected future price. The transactional price may have been influenced by nonmarket, participant-specific influences. So, the subject transaction should be analyzed to ensure that it was an uninfluenced, market-controlled transaction. In addition, the timing of the subject transaction should be considered in order to assess whether market supply and demand conditions have changed between the date of the subject transaction and the date of the analysis.

In all cases, market conditions influence what the expected sale or license price will be for an intangible asset, so market conditions influence what the value of an intangible asset is. Market conditions are influenced by the degree of competition in the marketplace (that is, the demand side of the equation) and the availability of substitute goods in the marketplace (that is, the supply side of the equation).

Assuming an unrestricted and (at least somewhat) efficient marketplace, the intersection of the supply and demand influences creates an equilibrium price for the intangible asset. The equilibrium price is the expected price (not the cost and not the last price) of the intangible asset. It is the expected price measure for the next transaction (not the last transaction or some original transaction) of the intangible asset. That is, it is the value of the intangible asset.

Accordingly, market influences directly affect the value—that is, the expected price—of an intangible asset.

## Market Approach Methods—Theoretical Concepts

The market approach uses two categories of analytical procedures to indicate value:

1. The collection and analysis of market-derived empirical transactional data; that is, data regarding the sale or licensing of the subject intangible asset itself and of comparative intangible assets.
2. An assessment of the current market conditions (i.e., the economic conditions that influence price) and of the changes in market conditions between the dates of the empirical transactional data and the date of the analysis.

There are somewhat fewer analytical methods within the market approach as compared to the cost or income approaches to intangible asset valuation. Nonetheless, the practical application of a market approach method is a very complex and rigorous analytical process.

With regard to the cost and income approaches, some of the valuation variable data are market-derived and some are intrinsic to (or derived from an analysis of) the subject intangible asset. Of course, all of the valuation variable data used in both cost approach and income approach analyses (whether externally-derived or internally-derived) should be consistent with market conditions extant as of the valuation date.

With regard to the market approach, essentially all of the valuation variable data are extracted from market-derived, empirical data sources. It is often more difficult to collect and verify these external data as compared to the internal data that are sometimes applicable to the cost and income approaches. More importantly, however, it is often more difficult to apply these external data to the analysis of the subject intangible, because the data usually have to be arranged, analyzed, selected, reanalyzed, and adjusted before they can be applied to the valuation of the subject intangible asset.

## Application of the Market Approach

There is a general systematic process or framework to the application of market approach methods with regard to the valuation of intangible assets. The eight basic steps of this general systematic process are summarized as follows:

1. Data collection and selection.
2. Classification of selected data.

3. Verification of selected data.
4. Selection of units of comparison.
5. Quantification of pricing multiples.
6. Adjustment of pricing multiples.
7. Application of pricing multiples.
8. Reconciliation of value indications.

The eight basic steps in the market approach analysis are described below.

## Data Collection and Selection

In this step, the analyst researches the appropriate exchange market in order to obtain information on: 1) the sale transactions, listings, and offers to purchase or sell comparative intangible assets, and 2) the license transactions, listings, and offers to license, lease, franchise, or otherwise contract for the use of comparative intangible assets.

Several factors should be considered in assessing whether the exchange market that is being researched is, indeed, an appropriate marketplace. Some of the factors include:

1. The efficiency of the market—Are there adequate market participants? Is the information about previous transactions quickly and accurately communicated to potential market participants? Are there recognized and effective transactional intermediaries? Is the cost of consummating a transaction reasonable (and predictable) in comparison to the total transaction price?

2. The timeliness of the market—Are market participants effectively informed when new participants wish to enter the market? Is the amount of the elapsed time required to consummate a transaction (the intangible asset's market exposure period) reasonable (and predictable) in comparison to the value of the transaction?

3. The applicability of the market—Are the properties exchanged in this market sufficiently comparative to the subject intangible asset in order to provide relevant pricing guidance? Are the properties exchanged in this market sufficiently comparative to each other in order to qualify as one homogenous market (instead of several heterogeneous markets)? Are the transactional data from this marketplace available in a format that they may be applied to the subject intangible asset? In other words, can prices, rates, multiples, and so on, be extracted from this market based on some relevant means of comparison so that they can provide relevant pricing evidence?

4. The relevance of the market—If the intangible asset subject to analysis were to be sold, licensed, or otherwise transferred, is this the marketplace in which such a transaction would be likely to occur?

Once the analyst is convinced that the marketplace being researched is an appropriate exchange market, several additional factors should be considered in order to assess whether the actual transactional data elements will provide useful pricing guidance with respect to the subject analysis. The analyst has to decide, of all the transactions that are available for study in this exchange market, which transactions are relevant to the subject analysis. The analyst first selects what data elements: (1) are possibly relevant and should be included in the analysis and (2) are clearly irrelevant and should be excluded from the analysis.

Some of the factors the analyst should consider in this initial data screening and selection process include:

1. Intangible asset type—Do the transactions selected for further analysis represent intangibles in the same general descriptive category as the subject, such as data processing–related, contract-related, engineering-related, and so on?

2. Intangible asset use—Do the transactions selected for further analysis involve an asset use that is sufficiently comparative to the subject asset's actual use? Do the selected transactions represent defensive or offensive uses of the comparative intangible assets? Do the selected transactions represent an asset use that appears to be the highest and best use?

3. Industry in which the intangible asset functions—Do the transactions selected for further analysis include assets that are used in an industry that is sufficiently comparative (in terms of risk and expected return economic characteristics) to the industry in which the subject intangible asset operates?

4. Date of the transactional data—Do the transactions selected for further analysis include sales, licensing, or other transfers that are sufficiently contemporaneous to the date of the analysis so as to provide meaningful pricing guidance? If market conditions have changed between the date of the transactional data and the date of the analysis, can the transactional data be adjusted in order to retain their relevance with regard to proving meaningful pricing evidence?

Ideally, the analyst assesses the available market-derived data with respect to all of the above (and any other) factors and concludes that the selected data are perfectly applicable to the subject intangible asset. Unfortunately, that scenario never occurs. Rather, even the most relevant market-derived data have strengths and weaknesses with regard to their applicability to the subject intangible asset.

Market-derived transactional data should not necessarily be discarded if they do not score favorably on each of the above factors. If the market-derived data are appropriate to the subject intangible asset based on several of these factors, they may still provide relevant pricing evidence. Ultimately, it is the professional judgment of the experienced analyst that concludes which market-derived transactional data are sufficiently relevant for further analysis and what adjustments are required to make the selected data more applicable to the subject analysis.

Ultimately, the consideration of how comparative the selected empirical data are to the subject intangible asset determines whether the selected data function as either *comparable transactions* or *guideline transactions*. This important distinction—that is, the quality of the comparative market-derived transactional data—influences whether the analyst will apply comparable analytical methods or guideline analytical methods. This may appear to be a subtle and almost pedantic distinction. However, it is an important conceptual and practical issue in the use of market approach valuation methods.

## Classification of Selected Data

After the appropriate market and the relevant market-derived transactional data have been selected, it is time to classify the selection data as either comparable transactional data or as guideline transactional data.

Comparable transactions are directly comparative to the subject intangible asset. Each individual comparable transaction can meet relevant comparability criteria with respect to the subject intangible asset. For example, transactions that are classified as comparable may relate to assets of the same type, employed in the same industry, functioning within the same general use, and approximately the same age as the subject intangible asset.

While not necessarily identical to the subject, comparable intangible assets are very similar to the subject intangible asset. Based upon either a superficial or a substantive examination, they would "look like" the subject intangible asset in many ways. It is difficult, but not impossible, to identify comparable intangible assets.

Each comparable intangible asset should individually qualify as being very similar to the subject asset. Of course, some comparable intangible assets are more similar to the subject asset than other comparable intangible assets. For that reason, the more comparable intangible assets may provide better pricing evidence than the less comparable intangible assets. Not all comparable intangible assets are equally comparative to the subject. Therefore, the pricing evidence of each comparable intangible asset should not necessarily be weighted equally in the valuation process. Rather, each comparable intangible asset can meet a reasonable comparability threshold with respect to the subject.

It may be necessary to make adjustments to pricing data (e.g., prices, rates, multiples, etc.) extracted from comparable intangible assets in order to make the selected comparable intangible transactions more comparative to the subject intangible asset.

Likewise, the analyst should not assume that simple statistical measures of pricing data (such as means and medians) are automatically applicable to the subject analysis just because those data were extracted from comparable transactions. On the contrary, even if all the data used to derive mean and median pricing multiples were derived from comparable transactions, pricing multiples above or below the mean and median may be more appropriate, because all comparable transactions are not equally comparable. In fact, sometimes it is appropriate to select the pricing multiples that are closest to those indicated by the most comparable of the selected groups of comparable transactions.

Guideline transactions are indirectly comparative to the subject intangible asset. Individual guideline transactions may not meet strict comparability criteria with respect to the subject intangible asset. For example, the guideline intangible assets may not be of the same type, operate in the same industry, function in the same use, or be of the same age as the subject asset.

Nonetheless, guideline intangible assets can still provide very useful pricing evidence with regard to the subject intangible asset. How can that be? There are three significant factors to consider with respect to the selection of, application of, and reliance upon guideline intangible assets. The three factors are: economic comparability, portfolio effect, and judgment in selection of pricing variables.

First, guideline intangible assets may not be very similar to the subject in terms of physical, functional, or technological attributes. On a superficial level, they may not "look like" the subject intangible asset. However, on a more substantive level, the guideline intangible assets may "look like" the subject intangible asset from the perspective of risk and expected return investment characteristics. That is, the guideline intangible assets should be subject to similar levels of economic risk, even though they may be used for different purposes in different industries.

The guideline intangible assets should also be expected to generate similar levels of investment return to their owners (given their specific levels of risks) as the subject intangible asset. So, from a financial perspective, investors would perceive that the guideline intangible assets were similar to the subject asset. This is true even if the intangible asset creators—such as marketers, personnel officers, programmers, engineers, and so on—would perceive the guideline intangible assets to be poor substitutes for the subject asset from their purely technical perspectives.

Second, with regard to comparable intangible assets, each individual asset has a greater or lesser degree of direct comparability to the subject. With regard to guideline intangible assets, we are not so much interested in the similarity (or dissimilarity) of each individual intangible asset. Rather, we are interested in the group of guideline intangible assets as a whole. The selected group is often referred to as a portfolio of guideline intangible assets. We are interested in the comparability of the portfolio of guideline intangible assets to the subject asset on a risk and expected return criteria basis.

In fact, it is possible that one particular guideline intangible asset may, superficially, appear quite dissimilar to the subject asset. However, the dissimilar intangible asset may be the most important guideline in the portfolio of intangible assets because the apparently dissimilar intangible asset was specifically added to the group in order to ensure that the collective portfolio has the same risk and expected return characteristics as the subject. For example, the apparently dissimilar guideline intangible asset may add a very important dimension to the portfolio (e.g., heavy government regulation, risk of technological obsolescence) that makes the collection more comparable, in the aggregate, to the subject intangible asset.

Third, professional judgment is certainly involved in the ultimate selection of pricing variables derived from comparable intangible assets. Professional judgment is even more important with respect to the ultimate selection of pricing variables derived from guideline intangible assets.

As their name implies, guideline transactions provide relevant pricing guidance to the analyst for use in the estimation of the value of the subject asset. It is important to reiterate this point: The guideline transactions provide guidance to the analyst. They do not provide a single solution to a simple algorithm. They do not provide an unambiguous and irrefutable answer to the valuation question. They provide guidance. The analyst should take the guidance provided by this market evidence and then extract, extrapolate, and interpret. Ultimately, the analyst should apply informed judgment to the empirical market evidence in order to conclude the appropriate pricing variable.

Adjustments to the pricing multiples implied by guideline transactions are not uncommon. In fact, they are quite common. Based upon informed judgment, the experienced analyst may select a valuation variable that is near some statistical midpoint of the guideline evidence, either at the low end or the high end of the range of guideline evidence or even outside of the actual range of the guideline evidence. In all cases, the market-derived empirical evidence (albeit imperfect) provides guidance to the analyst in the selection of a valuation variable that is appropriate to the subject intangible asset.

## Verification of Selected Data

The data verification step is one series of procedures in the market approach analysis that many analysts fail to perform, or fail to perform adequately. There are three important and interrelated objectives to the data verification step:

1. To verify that the market-derived transactional data are factually accurate.
2. To verify that the empirical transactions relied upon to derive pricing multiples reflect arm's-length market considerations.
3. To verify that the transactional pricing data relate only to (or are adjusted so as to only reflect) sales, licenses, or other transfers of intangible assets.

In order to achieve the first objective (i.e., accuracy), the analyst has to verify that the transactional data are obtained from a reliable source. However, even information obtained from a recognized service may not be factually accurate. The unintentional use of inaccurate transactional data can seriously distort and invalidate the results of an otherwise rigorous valuation or economic analysis.

First, it is preferable if the analyst has primary source data with regard to the comparative transactions. The best evidence regarding a sale, license, or other transfer is gathered by inspecting the transactional documents. Ideally, the analyst should review the actual sale contract, license agreement, franchise agreement or ordinance, or other relevant document. However, such documentation is rarely available to analysts because such documents are extremely confidential.

Second, the analyst may become aware of comparative transactions through primary or secondary research. If information regarding the transaction is not obviously confirmed by the service that is reporting the data, then it is the responsibility of the analyst to confirm the transactional data. The best way to confirm reported (but unverified) transactional data is to actually contact one or more of the parties to the transaction and to request verification that the reported transaction actually occurred and that the reported terms of the transaction are correct as stated.

Another way to confirm reported (but unverified) transactional data is to compare descriptions of the transaction in several independent sources. For example, the analyst may discover that a given transaction was reported in a newspaper, an industry trade publication, and one of the several commercial sources that report on intellectual property sales and licenses. If the reported terms of the transaction are essentially identical in all of these sources, the analyst may have some degree of confidence with regard to the use of these data in the subject analysis. However, if the reported terms of the transaction vary between different sources, then the analyst may have little confidence with regard to these transactional data. In such a case, the analyst may either attempt to independently confirm the transactional data or eliminate that particular reported transaction from further consideration.

Third, the analyst may have confidence in the use of transactional data obtained from professionally recognized sources. For example, if a transaction is reported in a publication with recognized integrity, it may be assumed that the data are accurately stated. It is reasonable to believe that the reporters at a publication such as, say, the *Wall Street Journal* have verified the reported data through several sources.

Transactional data that are disclosed to public investors or to securities regulators are generally accepted without independent verification or confirmation. For example, it is assumed that the reported data are accurate when one party to a transaction discloses the details of that transaction to the investment community in a public press release. Likewise, it is assumed that transactional information disclosed in a public registrant's annual report to shareholders or reports to the Securities and Exchange Commission are reliable. Similarly, information reported by a transaction participant to a governmental agency (many regulated industries have governmental agency reporting requirements) are considered reliable. Transactional data reported by governmental agencies are considered reliable, although these government reports may not disclose enough detail about individual transactions to be useful to the analyst.

In order to achieve the second objective of data verification, the analyst needs to know enough or learn enough about the comparative transaction to assess whether it meets the arm's-length test. In other words, the analyst should assess whether the comparative transaction reflects market conditions. If the transaction does not reflect market conditions, then it is probably not useful with regard to either a valuation or an economic analysis.

The analyst should verify that each comparative transaction analyzed represents arm's-length pricing and arm's-length terms. If the participants to the comparative transaction are independent of each other and if they clearly negotiated in an arm's-length fashion so as to achieve their own economic self-interests, then the transaction can be assumed to represent market conditions.

Even when there is no current evidence that the comparative transaction was independently bargained for, there are certain instances when analysts typically assume that a reported transaction represents arm's-length market conditions. Examples of such transfers include transactions in which one or more participants has a duty of fairness to minority investors, when one or more participants has a fiduciary duty such as in the case of a trust, when the transaction has to be approved by a governmental or regulatory agency, or when the transaction has to be approved by a court or other judicial authority.

However, there are numerous instances when reported intangible asset sale or license transactions may not necessarily be at arm's-length. Examples of such transactions include:

1. A transaction between parties who have the appearance of a conflict of interest, such as between a parent corporation and a subsidiary corporation, between a brother and sister corporation, or between similarly related or commonly controlled entities.

2. A transaction in which one participant is under financial duress.

3. A transaction in which one participant has to enter into some transaction due to a regulatory or judicial order (e.g., a Federal Trade Commission order to divest a certain line of business).

4. A transaction in which the seller or licensor provides below-market or otherwise unusual financing.

5. A transaction that involves a joint venture between the participants and in which there is a disproportionate ownership of the joint venture.

6. A step transaction in which the comparative intangible asset transfer is one small part of a larger transaction.

7. A complex cross-transaction that is based on terms other than cash (e.g., I'll sell my product patent to you for one dollar if you'll sell your manufactured finished products to me at half their normal price).

Unless the analyst has reason to believe otherwise, these types of transactions may not represent arm's-length market conditions. Accordingly, they may not be useful in a market approach comparative transaction analysis.

With regard to the third objective of data verification (intangible assets only), the analyst should know enough or learn enough about each comparative transaction to ensure that the only property being transferred is the comparative intangible asset. Ideally, the comparative transaction involves the sale, license, or other transfer of a single intangible asset.

Also ideally, all the terms and conditions of the transaction are known to the analyst. In that event, the analyst can adjust the reported transaction pricing parameters to their cash equivalency value, if necessary. For example, a sale price of $2 million that will be paid in one lump-sum payment at the end of five years may have a cash equivalency value of only $1 million.

Sometimes, the comparative transactions are complex transactions; that is, they involve the transfer of many intangible assets or of both intangible and tangible assets. In those cases, the analyst needs to have enough detailed information regarding the transaction in order to perform a sale price or license payment allocation. In other words, the comparative transaction sale price or royalty rate should be reasonably allocated among the various bundles of assets in the complex transaction.

If the analyst does not have adequate information to perform such an allocation, then the complex comparative transaction may not be useful to the subject analysis because the complex transaction does not provide meaningful pricing guidance for the single subject intangible asset.

Clearly, the data verification procedure involves some degree of research and investigation. Regardless of the magnitude of any adjustments that are made during the data verification, the research and investigation itself may provide useful information regarding current market conditions related to the comparative intangible assets (and, indirectly, the subject intangible asset).

## Selection of Units of Comparison

The next step in the market approach valuation process is to distill the selected and verified transactional data into common units of value. This distillation procedure is necessary for two reasons:

1. To make all of the comparable or guideline transactional data comparative to themselves.
2. To make any meaningful statistical compilation of the comparable or guideline transactional data applicable to the subject analysis.

The selected units of comparison vary depending upon the category of intangible asset subject to analysis. They may also vary depending upon the individual intangible asset within each category. The selection of the most appropriate unit of comparison is a matter of professional judgment. Frequently, the most appropriate units of comparison are easy to recognize. The likely appropriate units of comparison are those typically referred to by participants in the subject industry or often discussed in the professional literature related to the subject intangible asset. Also, the likely appropriate units of comparison are those for which the analyst has adequate evidence to measure both the comparable or guideline transactional data and the subject intangible asset.

The following list includes some of the more common units of comparison for typical intangible assets:

1. Customer-related intangible assets—price per customer, per contract, per renewal, per subscriber, per enrollee, per thousand (or million) of population.
2. Data processing–related intangible assets—price per line of code, per function point, per decision node, per deliverable source instruction.
3. Marketing-related intangible assets—price per name, per mark, per advertisement, per impression, per exposure, per territory.
4. Human capital–related intangible assets—price per employee, per department, per organization level.
5. Technology-related intangible assets—price per patent, per drawing, per design, per schematic, per plate, per formula, per compound, per recipe.

In real estate appraisal, it is also necessary to designate relevant units of comparison when using the sales comparison approach. In a real estate appraisal analysis, typical units of comparison may include price per square foot, per acre, per room, per floor, per cubic foot, and so on. As is the case with real estate appraisals, there are no absolutely right or wrong units of comparison to use with regard to intangible asset analysis. Rather, there are only more or less relevant units of comparison, based on the quantity and quality of available data.

## Quantification of Pricing Multiples

The selection of units of comparison procedure allows the analyst to designate a common denominator or yardstick to apply both to the market-derived transactional data and to the subject intangible asset. In this phase of the analysis, that common denominator or yardstick is actually applied to the market-derived transactional data.

In this procedure, all the verified and (if necessary) purified empirical data are measured and restated in terms of the selected units of comparison. In other words, total transaction prices are divided by the selected units of comparison in order to conclude a "price per" unit of comparison. These pricing multiples may be expressed in terms of physical units, financial units, or both. Physical units may be price per customer, price per drawing, price per line of code, and so forth. Financial units may be price per dollar of revenue generated, price per dollar of income earned, price per dollar of original investment, and so on. It is not uncommon to apply several physical unit and several financial unit common denominators to the subject set of transactional data.

At this step in the process, it is often useful (but not necessary) to array the transactional data that are now expressed as pricing multiples. The transactional data could be arrayed from highest multiple to lowest multiple or from lowest multiple to highest multiple. Such arrays often allow the analyst to quickly discern certain trends that may not be as obvious from an inspection of the pure data. For example, arrays may help the analyst to quickly assess the degree of dispersion of the pricing multiples, whether the dispersion is normally distributed around a mean point or not, and whether there are any modes (or clumps) of pricing multiples within the data set.

Data arrays of pricing multiples may also facilitate performing basic statistical analyses of the market-derived transactional data. Such basic statistical analyses could include calculating means, medians, modes, standard deviations, quartiles, deciles, and so on.

## Adjustment of Pricing Multiples

Conversion of the transactional data into common denominator pricing multiples may help to identify adjustments that need to be made in the individual transactional data. Likewise, arranging standard unit of comparison pricing multiples from highest to lowest (or vice versa) may help to identify adjustments that need to be made in the individual transactional data. The transactional data that may require adjustment often stand out or appear abberational compared with the rest of the transactional data set.

There is no single list of all of the adjustments that may ever be appropriate in a market approach analysis. Some of the more common pricing multiple adjustments include:

1. Adjustments for transactional elements not involving the subject intangible asset type.
2. Adjustments for differences in market conditions.
3. Adjustments for systematic changes in market dynamics.

If a particular pricing multiple relates to a complex transaction (i.e., a transaction involving an intangible asset and some other type of property), that pricing multiple should be adjusted so as to only reflect the value influence of the comparable intangible asset. If such an adjustment cannot be made, that particular pricing multiple may not be useful to the subject analysis.

Market conditions related to some types of intangible assets change systematically over time. For example, the price per customer in some industries may systematically increase (or decrease) as the industry becomes more (or less) prosperous. In these instances, the transactional pricing multiples may be arranged by the age of the transaction, for example, from oldest to newest. The pricing multiples of different age groups (or vintages) may be adjusted by an index factor. This index or trend factor may relate to an index of prices of publicly traded securities in the subject industry, or to any other relevant trend. Nonetheless, the purpose of applying these index factors is to trend all of the transactional pricing multiples upward or downward to reflect the current market conditions experienced by the subject intangible asset.

Some systematic (or systemwide) changes in pricing multiples may be due to stochastic or one-time changes in market dynamics. When such changes in market dynamics occur during the transactional data observation period, some of the pricing multiples may need to be adjusted. For example, all market multiples related to transactions occurring prior to the change in market dynamics may need to be adjusted in order to reflect the current market conditions experienced by the subject intangible asset.

If such adjustments cannot be made, then the pre-event pricing multiples may have to be eliminated from consideration in the subject analysis. Some examples of events that may cause such changes in market dynamics include changes in income taxation regulations (e.g., allowing for the amortization of certain types of intangible assets), changes in the regulatory environment of the subject industry, changes in the legal environment regarding protection for intellectual properties, and so forth.

## Application of Pricing Multiples

The estimation of value indications occurs in this step of the market approach analysis. In this phase of the analysis, the analyst selects the appropriate market-derived pricing multiple for each relevant unit of comparison and multiplies the selected pricing multiples by the subject intangible asset's unit measurement in order to reach a value indication.

Considerable professional judgment is associated with the selection of the appropriate pricing multiple. The analyst studies the entire range of pricing multiples derived from the transactional data and considers the statistical analyses of these market-derived pricing multiple data, including means, medians, modes, quartiles, deciles, and so on.

Ultimately, the analyst selects the pricing multiple that is most appropriate to the subject intangible asset, based upon a comparison of the subject intangible asset to the transactional intangible assets. The selected pricing multiple should represent how the market would respond to the subject intangible asset given how the market has already responded to the transactional intangible assets.

Finally, the analyst applies the selected pricing multiple to the same unit of comparison for the subject intangible. If the data are available, the analyst attempts to use several different units of comparison. For example, the analyst may use the same transactional data to apply a price per customer multiple, a price per point of market share multiple, and a price per dollar of income earned multiple to the subject intangible asset. As another example, the analyst may apply a price per line of code multiple, a price per function point multiple, and a price per dollar of revenue multiple to the subject intangible asset. This use of several pricing multiples results in a range of indicated values for the subject intangible asset.

## Reconciliation of Value Indications

If only one pricing multiple is available to or selected by the analyst, the market approach analysis concludes only one indicated value. If several pricing multiples are used, the market approach analysis results in a range of indicated values. Sometimes, a range of indicated values is perfectly appropriate given the appraisal assignment. However, when a single point estimate is necessary, the analyst must reconcile the various value indications.

The reconciliation phase of the market approach analysis involves assessing the relative strengths and weaknesses of each pricing multiple. The analyst assesses the quality and quantity of transactional data related to each pricing multiple, and considers the quantity and magnitude of adjustments made to the transactional data related to each pricing multiple. Then the analyst evaluates which pricing multiples are more or less relied upon by industry participants as measures of intangible asset value.

Based upon these and other factors, the analyst assigns a weighting to the value indications concluded by each pricing multiple. This weighting procedure may be implicit or explicit to the reconciliation process. Ultimately, the analyst's conclusion of value is based on a synthesis of the various value indicators suggested by each pricing multiple analysis.

## GENERAL INTRODUCTION TO THE INCOME APPROACH

The income approach is based upon the economic principle of anticipation (sometimes also called the principle of expectation). In this approach, the value of the subject intangible asset is the present value of the expected economic income to be earned from the ownership of that intangible asset. As the name of the principle implies, the investor *anticipates* the *expected* economic income to be earned from the investment in the subject intangible asset. This expectation of prospective economic income is converted to a present worth—that is, the indicated value of the subject intangible asset.

Numerous alternative definitions of economic income are appropriate to an intangible asset valuation or economic analysis. Many different definitions of economic income can be analyzed to provide a reasonable indication of value for the subject intangible asset. This valuation approach requires the analyst to estimate the investor's required rate of return on the investment generating the prospective economic income. The required rate of return is a function of many economic variables, including the risk or uncertainty of the expected economic income associated with the subject intangible asset.

Perhaps the most important consideration in an income approach analysis is that the measure of economic income (however defined) used in the valuation should represent only the income that relates to the subject intangible asset. In other words, the income stream should not include income earned by (or otherwise associated with): 1) intangible assets other than the subject intangible asset; 2) the overall business enterprise in which the subject intangible asset functions (unless an appropriate charge is made against the business enterprise income stream for the assets that are used or used up in the production of the subject intangible's income); or 3) tangible assets that are used or used up in the production of the subject intangible asset's income (unless an appropriate capital charge is provided for in the income stream projection to allow for a fair allocation of the income (and the value) between the subject intangible asset and the associated tangible assets).

## Income Approach Methods—Theoretical Concepts

Numerous measures of economic income may be relevant to the various intangible asset income approach methods. Some of the alternative measures of economic income include: gross or net revenues, gross income, net operating income, net income before tax, net income after tax, operating cash flow, net cash flow, and several others.

There are at least as many intangible asset income approach valuation methods as there are measures of economic income. However, most of the methods may be grouped into several categories that have similar conceptual underpinnings and similar practical applications. Several categories of income approach methods are:

1. Methods that quantify incremental levels of economic income (i.e., the intangible asset owner will enjoy a greater level of economic income by owning the subject asset as compared to not owning the subject asset).

2. Methods that quantify decremental levels of economic costs (i.e., the intangible asset owner will suffer a lower level of economic costs—such as otherwise required investments in capital assets or decreased levels of operating expenses—by owning the subject asset as compared to not owning the subject asset).

3. Methods that estimate a relief from a hypothetical royalty or license payment (i.e., the amount of a royalty or license payment that the intangible asset owner would be willing to pay to an independent third party of the subject asset in order to obtain the use of and the legal rights to the intangible asset).

4. Methods that quantify the difference in the value of the overall business enterprise or of a similar economic unit as the result of owning the subject intangible asset (and using it in the business enterprise) as compared to not owning the subject intangible asset (and not using it in the business enterprise).

5. Methods that estimate the value of the intangible asset as a residual from the value of an overall business enterprise value (or from the value of a similar economic unit), or as a residual from the value of an overall estimation of total intangible value of a business enterprise (or of the total intangible value of a similar economic unit).

All of these intangible asset income approach methods may be grouped into two other analytical categories: methods that rely upon a direct capitalization analysis and methods that rely upon a yield capitalization analysis.

## Application of the Income Approach

In a direct capitalization analysis, the analyst first estimates the appropriate measure of economic income for a normalized or stabilized period (i.e., one period future to the valuation date) and then divides that measure of one period economic income by an appropriate investment rate of return. The appropriate investment rate of return is called the direct capitalization rate. The direct capitalization rate may be a rate appropriate for an indefinite period of time or for a specified, finite period of time. The conclusion of the term or the duration of the appropriate direct capitalization rate depends upon the analyst's expectation of the duration of the intangible asset's economic income stream.

In a yield capitalization analysis, the analyst projects the appropriate measure of economic income for several discrete time periods into the future. The projection of prospective economic income is converted into a present value by the use of a present value discount rate. The discount rate is the investor's required annual rate of return over the expected term of the intangible asset's economic income projection.

The length (or duration) of the discrete income projection period is a very important consideration in the yield capitalization analysis. It is noteworthy that the duration of the discrete projection period—and whether or not a residual or terminal value should be considered at the conclusion of the discrete projection period—depends upon the analyst's expectation of the duration of the subject intangible asset's economic income stream.

In any event, the result of either the direct capitalization analysis or the yield capitalization analysis provides an indication of the value of the subject intangible asset. Some intangible assets lend themselves more to direct capitalization analyses and others to yield capitalization analyses. Some intangible assets may be analyzed using both methods of income approach analysis. When both yield capitalization and direct capitalization analyses are performed, a range of value indications results. The analyst may then have to reconcile the alternative value indications in one income approach value conclusion.

## INTRODUCTION TO VALUATION SYNTHESIS AND CONCLUSION

Analysts attempt to appraise intangible assets using methods from all three of the generally accepted valuation approaches in order to obtain a multidimensional perspective on the subject intangible asset. The final value estimate conclusion is typically based upon a synthesis of the value indications derived from the results of the various alternative valuation methods.

The valuation synthesis is the analysis of alternative value indications in order to arrive at a final value estimate. A valuation synthesis is required because different value indications result both from the use of multiple valuation approaches and from the application of various analytical methods within a single valuation approach.

To perform the valuation synthesis, the analyst reviews the entire appraisal in order to ascertain that the data, techniques, and logic used are valid and consistent. Inconsistencies among the various valuation approaches used in the analysis should be reconciled before reaching a final value estimate.

The analyst should make sure that the methods used relate to the same bundle of intangible asset legal rights being appraised, the same definition of value under consideration, the same purpose and objective of the analysis, and so on. Of course, a final, independent check of all mathematical calculations should be performed at this stage of the analysis.

The final intangible asset value estimate conclusion is not derived simply by applying the technical and quantitative valuation procedures. Rather, it involves the application of the analyst's professional judgment and experience to the intangible asset valuation process.

## INTRODUCTION TO REPORTING VALUATION CONCLUSIONS

Regardless of the specific form or format of the report, the basic intangible asset valuation report generally should:

1. Conform to the *Uniform Standards of Professional Appraisal Practice* (USPAP) adopted by the Appraisal Standards Board of The Appraisal Foundation.

2. Be presented in a format or form that is sufficiently descriptive in order to enable the reader to ascertain the estimated defined value and the rationale for the estimate, and to provide detail and depth of analysis that reflect the complexity of the intangible asset subject to analysis.

3. Analyze and report on the current market conditions and trends that will affect the projected income or marketability of the subject intangible asset.

4. Contain sufficient supporting documentation so as to adequately describe to the reader the analyst's logic, reasoned judgment, and analysis in arriving at the defined value reported.

5. Follow a valuation methodology that includes active consideration of the cost, market, and income approaches; reconciles the valuation indications produced by the application of the three valuation approaches; and explains the reason for the elimination of any of the three approaches that were not used in the valuation analysis.

Regardless of the purpose of the analysis, the following practices should be considered unacceptable in an intangible asset valuation report:

1. The inclusion of inaccurate or incomplete data about the subject intangible asset.

2. The failure to report and consider any apparent factor that has an adverse effect on the value or the marketability of the subject intangible asset.

3. The reliance in the valuation analysis on either comparable or guideline market transactional data that were not verified by the analyst.

4. The reliance on any valuation analyses of inappropriate comparable or guideline sales or license transactions, or the failure to use comparable or guideline sales or license transactions that are more appropriate to the subject intangible asset, without adequate explanation.

5. The development of value or marketability conclusions with regard to the subject intangible asset that are not supported by reliable market-derived empirical pricing data.

6. The failure to provide in the valuation opinion report a signed certification or similar valuation opinion, statement of contingent and limiting conditions, and the professional qualifications of the analyst or analysts principally responsible for the valuation analyses and conclusions.

## SUMMARY

The valuation of intangible assets has become an increasingly more integral and more complex part of the corporate and institutional commercial environment. Economic analyses and appraisals of intangible assets have numerous information and strategic benefits to the parties-in-interest to many commercial transactions.

Numerous generally accepted methods may be appropriate to the analysis and appraisal of intangible assets within the general commercial context. Each of these methods may be grouped into the three basic intangible asset valuation approaches.

Analysts typically use more than one valuation approach (and more than one method within each approach) to analyze the subject intangible asset. A synthesis of the value indications derived from the several approaches or methods, based upon the analyst's professional judgment and experience, results in the conclusion of an overall value estimate for the subject intangible asset.

Chapter 7 introduced the basic factors associated with the identification and valuation of intangible assets. In addition, this chapter presented an introduction to the process of reaching the intangible asset valuation synthesis and conclusion.

# Cost Approach Methods

## INTRODUCTION

This chapter discusses the application of various cost approach methods to intangible asset analysis. In this chapter, we discuss the indirect relationship between cost and value and we identify that specific point in the cost approach analysis when cost provides an indication of value. We further explain the various types of costs and the various related cost approach methods. We explore the various components of cost that are integral to a cost approach analysis. At this point in our discussion, analysts may realize that there are many more components to a rigorous cost approach analysis than they would have imagined.

We consider the applications and limitations of data sources. These data sources include the inventory of the intangible assets subject to analysis, the collection of historical cost data regarding the subject intangible asset, and the application of cost trend factors (and other indicia of current costs). We explore the identification and quantification of the various forms of obsolescence that are integral to a cost approach analysis. That topic involves an introduction to remaining useful life analysis.

We present several examples of intangible asset cost approach analyses. The examples are not intended to be comprehensive with regard to the illustration of all possible cost approach methods. Rather, they illustrate the application and limitations of several common analyses. Finally, we consider how to assess the weight to be assigned to a cost approach analysis in an overall valuation or other economic analysis of an intangible asset.

Cost approach methods are an appropriate component of many types of economic analyses related to intangible assets. Of course, cost approach methods are an integral part of intangible asset valuation. Cost approach methods may also play a role in transfer pricing and royalty rate analyses because transfer prices or royalty rates for some intangible assets may be set as a fair rate of return on the cost-based value of the intangible. The product of a rate of return times a value produces the total dollar amount of a royalty that the asset licensor would require during a time period, such as a year. The dollar amount can then be divided by the projected sales volume of the licensee in order to estimate a royalty rate, expressed either as a percent of sales or as a dollar amount per unit of sales volume.

Cost approach methods may also be applicable when estimating the amount of damages suffered by the intangible asset owner in an infringement, expropriation, breach of contract, or similar type of litigation. In these cases, the analyst may estimate the amount of damages as the amount of benefit gained by the defendant associated with the unlawful act; for example, the cost of creating the intangible asset that the defendants avoided due to their actions. Or, the analyst could estimate the cost-based value of the intangible asset to the owner, that is, the value before the defendants' actions. Since the intangible has been somehow damaged, its current value is less than its (pre-damage) cost-based value. Accordingly, the difference between these two value indications is one measure of economic damages.

Cost approach methods are obviously appropriate when the objective of the analysis is to estimate the cost of an intangible asset (whether or not that cost is equal to value). For example, this could be a consideration when the asset owner is purchasing property insurance to protect the subject intangible asset. Finally, cost approach methods are applicable when the objective of the analysis is to estimate the remaining useful life—or projected rate of diminution of asset value—of the intangible asset. Remaining useful life and value decay rate analyses are integral procedures in quantifying obsolescence in a cost approach analysis.

Before we discuss cost approach procedures further, it is appropriate to consider under what circumstances the cost approach is more applicable (or less applicable) to an intangible asset analysis. Generally, cost approach methods may be more applicable when the subject intangible asset is newer and when it is a fungible property. Here, the term *fungible* means that the subject intangible asset could be exchanged or substituted for another intangible. For example, certain computer software compiled code may be unique. However, another software program written with different code could perform the same data processing function. Therefore, the subject software could be considered somewhat fungible.

In addition, cost approach methods may be more applicable when the analyst is estimating the value of the intangible asset to its current owner. These methods may also be more applicable when estimating the value of an intangible asset under the premise of value in continued use. This makes sense because if the current owner did not have the subject in-use intangible, he or she would have to create a substitute intangible asset and incur the cost of that creation process.

Cost approach methods may be less applicable when the subject intangible asset is older or is unique. This may be particularly true if the subject intangible is an intellectual property that benefits from certain legal rights, such as trademark or copyright protection. For example, there is only one trade name Coca-Cola. The cost to create a substitute name for a cola beverage may not be the best indication of the value of the name Coca-Cola. Also, if a manuscript or a film master is protected by a legally binding copyright, cost may not be the best indication of value because, other than the copyright holder, no one has the legal right to create (certainly) a reproduction or (arguably) a replacement of the copyrighted materials.

In addition, cost approach methods may be less applicable (but certainly not totally inapplicable) when the analyst is estimating the value of the intangible asset to the marketplace (and not to the current owner). These methods may be less applicable when estimating the value of an intangible asset under the premise of value in exchange because the typical willing buyer may be more interested in the expected future economic benefits associated with intangible asset ownership than in the most likely cost to create a substitute for the subject intangible asset.

## COST, PRICE, AND VALUE

It is worth reiterating that cost, price, and value are three separate and distinct valuation concepts. It is naïve and usually incorrect to assume that "cost equals price equals value." In fact, the reverse is often more likely to be true; that is, "cost does not equal price does not equal value." Analysts should not make the assumption regarding the equality of cost, price, and value in any particular assignment unless they have performed an adequate investigation to confirm that assumption.

This is not to say that there is no relationship between cost, price, and value. In fact, there is usually a direct relationship between them. However, that relationship is not necessarily one of equality. Analysts often need to make adjustments to cost and price in order to estimate value. At the very least, analysts need to rigorously examine and investigate cost and price data before the data can be used to estimate value.

With regard to intangible assets, cost relates to the production process and not to the marketplace exchange process. Cost can be either a historical fact or a current estimate. The historical fact relates to the actual cost to create or develop an intangible asset. In this instance, perhaps the word *fact* should be in quotations because the historical cost is a "fact" based on how the intangible asset owner or developer interpreted and recorded the cost elements of the intangible asset production process. The current estimate relates to the cost to replace or reproduce the intangible asset as of a particular date (i.e., the valuation date). Again, there is some uncertainty and subjectivity regarding such current cost estimates, particularly with regard to how much of the entire intangible asset development process should be included in the estimate.

In any event, none of these cost concepts assumes a marketplace (efficient or otherwise) or a transaction involving the intangible asset per se. Costs describe what the intangible asset owner spent in the original production process, or what the owner would have to spend as of a certain date to recreate that production process. Cost, by itself, does not tell us how much a buyer would pay to acquire the intangible asset, or how much a seller would seek to motivate the sale of the intangible asset.

With regard to intangible assets, price is always a historical fact. The concept of price, by its very nature, involves a marketplace and a transaction. However, price is not necessarily the same as value. *The Appraisal of Real Estate* includes the following noteworthy comment regarding price: "A price, once finalized, represents the amount a particular purchaser agrees to pay and a particular seller agrees to accept under the circumstances surrounding their transaction."[1]

There are at least five factors that analysts should consider before they conclude that a price is indicative of value. The five factors are:

1. Market conditions.
2. Marketplace.
3. Buyer and seller motivations.
4. Payment terms.
5. Elements of the transaction.

Each of the five factors could distinguish a price from a value.

A historical price does not indicate whether the buyer and seller would accept the same amount again on the valuation date. What if market conditions have changed between the date of the actual transaction and the valuation date? Would the same intangible asset command a higher price or a lower price on the valuation date? Even if the historical price represented the value on the transaction date, does it still indicate a value six months later? A year later? Two years later?

The existence of a historical price indicates that there once was a marketplace. There had to be at least one buyer and one seller for a transaction to have occurred. However, it does not inform the analyst as to whether there was an efficient market at the time of the transaction. The existence

---

1. *The Appraisal of Real Estate,* 11th ed. (Chicago: Appraisal Institute, 1996), p. 19.

of a historical price, of and by itself, does not tell us whether it was a buyer's market or a seller's market; whether there was a great deal of competitive bidding or no bidding for the intangible asset; or whether the intangible asset was exposed to the market (i.e., held out for sale) for days, weeks, months, or years.

The existence of a historical price does not indicate whether either the buyer or the seller (or both) were willing participants to the transaction. A historical price does not indicate whether either party was particularly motivated to transact or had greater negotiating clout, or whether both parties were attempting to maximize their economic self-interests.

A historical price usually discloses no information regarding payment terms. Was the payment made in cash, or was it an exchange for securities, other intangible assets, or something else? Was the price paid at the time of the sale or were there extended terms? Were the extended payment terms typical or atypical for that type of transaction?

A historical price usually does not inform us as to all of the elements of the transaction. Was it a simple sale of a single intangible asset or were there other tangible or intangible assets involved in the transaction? Were there guarantees related to the sale? Noncompetition agreements? Future development or exploitation sharing agreements? Were there provisions regarding the tax treatment of the transaction?

Obviously, each of the factors mentioned could indicate that a price agreed to between a particular buyer and a particular seller may not be indicative of a value to the marketplace.

With regard to intangible assets, value relates to an expected price. Since value involves the expectation of a price, it incorporates consideration of a marketplace and of a transaction. Value is usually expressed in monetary terms and anticipates the price a buyer and a seller will agree to when they are exposed to the market conditions that exist as of the valuation date.

## TYPE OF COST

There are two fundamental types of cost quantified in cost approach valuation analyses. The types of cost relate to the two fundamental cost approach valuation methods: reproduction cost and replacement cost. At the inception of the cost approach analysis, the analyst should decide which type of cost will be estimated and which cost approach method will be used. If these decisions are not made at the outset, confusion and inconsistencies will arise when the cost approach analysis is underway.

Reproduction cost is the estimated cost to construct, at current prices as of the date of the analysis, an exact duplicate or replica of the subject intangible asset, using the same materials, production standards, design, layout, and quality of workmanship as the subject intangible asset. The reproduction intangible asset will include the same inadequacies, superadequacies, and obsolescence as the subject intangible asset.

Replacement cost is the estimated cost to construct, at current prices as of the date of the analysis, an intangible asset with equivalent utility to the subject intangible, using modern materials, production standards, design, layout, and quality of workmanship. The replacement intangible asset will exclude all curable inadequacies, superadequacies, and obsolescence that are present in the subject intangible asset.

Some analysts prefer to use the terms *reproduction cost new* and *replacement cost new*. For our purposes, we will treat these terms as synonyms for *reproduction cost* and *replacement cost*.

As these definitions imply, there are important conceptual differences between reproduction cost and replacement cost. However, the ultimate valuation indications derived from these two methods should not be materially different. In fact, other than for some necessary rounding differences, they should be the same.

Of course, the reproduction cost and the replacement cost are likely to be materially different for the same intangible asset. Then how can the value indications not be materially different? The answer is that the allowances for obsolescence should also be different, depending upon the base from which the obsolescence is measured—that is, reproduction cost or replacement cost. In other words, the selection of the reproduction cost method versus the replacement cost method should not materially influence the final value estimate. Therefore, the analyst should select the cost approach method to use based upon which method has the better quantity and quality of available pricing data.

Additional classifications of cost are relevant to intangible asset analysis that may not be relevant to tangible personal property or real estate valuation. These classifications are more along the lines of distinctions of cost as opposed to types of cost. Nonetheless, they do represent an important consideration with regard to intangible asset analysis. The additional classifications of cost are *creation cost* and *recreation cost*.

These two classifications of cost distinguish themselves by measuring how far back in the intangible asset production process costs should be measured. Therefore, both reproduction cost and replacement cost can be measured on either a creation cost basis or a recreation cost basis.

Distinguishing between these two classifications of cost is not relevant in the analysis of tangible assets. For example, there is no uncertainty in the appraisal of productive machinery or of commercial real estate as to how far back in the asset production process costs should be measured. In the case of both the machine and the building, costs are measured from the time just before a set of blueprints, production schematics, or engineering drawings are prepared. In other words, the machine or the building have already been conceptually designed and engineered. They need only to be structurally designed and engineered and then built.

The engineer's time to design a particular machine—for example a steam engine—is included in the cost approach to equipment appraisal. Likewise, the architect's time to design a steel-framed, brick veneer office building is included in the cost approach to real estate appraisal. However, the engineering time required to originally develop the concept of a steam engine and the architectural time required to originally conceive of the first multistory steel-framed office building structure are not included in the analyses. In the appraisal of equipment and real estate, we assume that engineers and architects don't have to create original technology. We assume that there is little original intellectual content to the designs and drawings because engineers already know the basics of steam engines and architects already know the basics of steel frame designs.

In every steam engine, there is at least one wheel (often with sprockets). What if our engineer had to design the first wheel? In other words, what if our engineer had to invent the wheel before he or she could build the steam engine? In that case, there would be a great deal of original intellectual content in the designs and drawings. But isn't that true of many intangible assets? They contain a great deal of original intellectual content. Many intangible assets, regardless of type, are unique, innovative, and proprietary. In their own ways, they are somewhat analogous to the newly invented wheel.

In a tangible asset analysis, we are usually concerned with *recreation cost*. We assume that the engineer or the architect does not have to reinvent the wheel. We assume that the original intellectual content is well known to the creator of the machine or the building. While our valuation can focus on either the reproduction cost or the replacement cost of all of the structural components of the machine or building, they are both indications of recreation cost. In other words, we don't include the time, effort, and expense of inventing the wheel.

With regard to intangible assets, the analyst should consciously decide whether to consider creation cost or recreation cost in the valuation. Recreation cost assumes that the original intellectual content is already known. Creation cost assumes that the original intellectual content has to be created or invented as part of the intangible asset.

Determining which classification of cost is relevant in each analysis is a function of the type of intangible asset; the purpose and objective of the analysis; and most importantly, the degree of uniqueness or propriety of the original intellectual content component of the subject intangible asset. Before beginning the valuation, the analyst should decide whether to estimate creation cost or recreation cost. That decision should be adequately documented in the cost approach analysis and communicated in the reporting of the valuation results.


## COMPONENTS OF COST

The analyst has some latitude in the selection of the appropriate type of cost to estimate. The same cannot be said for the selection of the components of cost to be included in the analysis.

Regardless of the type of cost being estimated (e.g., reproduction, replacement, or other) five components of cost are generally included in the analysis. The five components of cost are:

1. Material.
2. Labor.
3. Overhead.
4. Developer's profit.
5. Entrepreneurial incentive.

The components of cost are sometimes referred to as elements of cost. Regardless of which term is used, analysts have little latitude in the selection of which factors to consider.

Material costs include expenditures and accruals related to the tangible elements of the intangible asset development process. Typically, material costs do not represent a significant percentage of the overall cost of intangible asset development, of course, because there are typically few tangible manifestations of an intangible asset.

Nonetheless, material costs should not be ignored in the cost approach analysis. Such costs may include computer diskettes, integrated circuit masks, film or audio tape masters, engineering drawing supplies, copyrighted models or prototypes, a printed copy of a manual or manuscript, and so forth. The material costs should include all such costs incurred between the conceptualization stage and the current (e.g., commercialization) stage of the intangible asset life cycle. Material costs should be estimated at (or trended to) current costs as of the valuation date.

Labor costs often represent a significant percentage of the overall cost of the intangible asset development process. Labor costs include expenditures and accruals related to the human capital efforts associated with intangible asset development. As with the labor costs associated with the construction of a tangible asset, intangible asset labor costs can be either direct or indirect. Direct labor costs relate to the individuals who participated hands-on in the development process.

Labor costs typically include all salaries and wages to employees and all monetary compensation to contractors. Obviously, these costs should be estimated only for the amount of time that the employees or contractors were involved in the intangible asset development process. Of course, labor costs should be estimated at (or trended to) current costs as of the valuation date.

The overhead cost component itself has several subcomponents. The categories of overhead cost typically include employment-related taxes, employment-related perquisites and fringe benefits, management and supervisory efforts, support and secretarial efforts, and utility and operating expenses.

Employment-related taxes include payroll taxes such as FICA (employer portion), FUTA, SUTA, worker's compensation, and so on. Fringe benefits include such employer-paid benefits as pension contributions, health insurance, life insurance, and other benefits for employees. Management includes the time, efforts, and contributions of any individuals involved in the direct supervision or review of the intangible asset development personnel. Generally, this is the group of management personnel who give assignments to and review the work of, the employees or contractors who are directly involved in the intangible asset development process. Support includes the time, efforts, and contributions of any individuals involved in the direct support of the intangible asset development personnel. Generally, this group could include secretaries, word processors, computer operators, technicians, laboratory assistants, researchers, and so forth. Operating expenses include the costs of heat, electricity, telephone, and other utilities related to the development workplace; the costs of rent, insurance, and maintenance of the development workplace; and the costs of tools and supplies used or used up in the development workplace.

The developer's profit is a cost component that is frequently overlooked. From the perspective of the developer of any intangible asset, first, the developer expects a return *of* all of the material, labor, and overhead costs related to the development process; and second, the developer expects a return *on* all of the material, labor, and overhead costs related to the development process. A building contractor expects to earn a reasonable profit on the construction of any residential or commercial building. Likewise, an intangible asset developer expects to earn a reasonable profit on the development of the intangible.

The developer's profit can be estimated in several ways. It can be estimated as a percentage return on the developer's investment in material, labor, and overhead. It can be estimated as a percentage markup or as a fixed dollar markup to the amount of time involved in the development process. It can simply be estimated as a fixed dollar amount.

Analysts sometimes disaggregate the developer's investment into two subcomponents: the amount financed by external financing sources (e.g., banks and other financial institutions) and the amount financed by the intangible asset owner directly. The developer's profit associated with the costs financed by external sources is analogous to construction period interest accrued in tangible asset production. Some analysts include this construction period interest in the developer's profit cost category and some analysts include it in the overhead cost category. Usually, a higher rate of return is assigned to the cost amount financed by the intangible asset owner directly, as compared to the cost amount financed by external financing sources.

Entrepreneurial incentive is another cost component that is frequently overlooked. Nonetheless, entrepreneurial incentive is an integral component of the cost approach analysis. The entrepreneurial incentive is the amount of economic benefit required to motivate the intangible asset owner to enter into the development process. From the perspective of the intangible asset owner, entrepreneurial incentive is often perceived as an opportunity cost.

With regard to the application of the cost approach analysis, intangible asset developers are sometimes compared to building contractors. However, that is not a perfect analogy. Perhaps a better analogy is to compare the intangible asset developer to a real estate developer (e.g., the developer of a shopping mall or a residential apartment complex). There is an opportunity cost associated with the development process for both the intangible asset developer and the real estate developer. The time (and resources) they devote to the project is time (and resources) they are diverting from another project.

Likewise, both the intangible asset developer and the real estate developer expect and deserve to be compensated for the conceptual, planning, and administrative efforts associated with putting the entire project together. They want to be compensated for the period of time between when they initially begin production of the project and when they realize the full commercial potential of the project. Perhaps this "cost" is easier to understand with regard to the real estate developer. From the time the developer first begins to construct the shopping mall until the time all of the stores are leased and occupied, the developer is likely to experience negative cash flow. Suppose this time period is two years. A developer who had purchased an already leased shopping mall two years earlier would likely have experienced positive cash flow during that same two-year period. The foregone cash flow during the two-year development period is one indication of the entrepreneurial incentive required to motivate the real estate developer to build a new mall (instead of buying an existing mall).

The same type of entrepreneurial incentive is necessary to motivate the intangible asset developer to produce a new patent, trademark, computer program, chemical formulation, food recipe, or other intangible. The intangible asset owner should be compensated for the risk of the new development process compared to the relatively low risk of using the last generation of technology, consumer brands, computer software, and so on.

All five components of cost—material, labor, overhead, developer's profit, and entrepreneurial incentive—should be considered as part of a comprehensive cost approach analysis to intangible asset value.

## WHEN DOES COST INDICATE VALUE?

As we have said, cost does not necessarily equal value. Nonetheless, the cost approach is one of the three fundamental approaches to intangible asset valuation. At what point does the cost approach provide a reasonable indication of value? The answer is when two conditions are met: The first condition is that the measure of cost included in the analysis considers all of the cost components discussed in the previous section. The second condition is that the measure of cost included in the analysis is reduced for all forms of obsolescence.

Simply put, if all components of cost, including entrepreneurial incentive, are included in the analysis and if all forms of obsolescence are subtracted from the analysis, then the cost approach analysis provides a meaningful indication of value. Although the concept of cost (of and by itself) is not the same as the concept of value, the cost approach, when properly applied, provides one of the foundational indications of value. Essentially, the mistakes that many analysts make are defining the components of cost too narrowly and ignoring one or more of the forms of obsolescence. In either of those cases the cost approach analysis is simply incomplete, and an incomplete analysis leads to an incorrect indication of value.

When estimating the cost of a new intangible asset, the analyst should adjust the cost estimate for all appropriate forms of obsolescence, whether the cost new that is estimated is reproduction cost, replacement cost, or some other measure of current cost. This is done because the intangible asset subject to analysis is not new; it is a seasoned intangible asset. The new intangible asset (however defined) will likely be superior in some way to the subject intangible. Therefore, the analyst has to adjust the new intangible asset in order to make it more like the subject intangible asset. This adjustment process requires the quantification of obsolescence.

Of course, if the subject intangible asset is, in fact, brand new, then it is not necessary to recognize any obsolescence in the cost approach analysis. Likewise, if the subject intangible asset is in like-new condition, albeit in fact a seasoned intangible asset, then it may be appropriate to recognize little or no obsolescence in the cost approach analysis.

The forms of obsolescence that are generally considered in the cost approach analysis of intangible assets are: physical deterioration, functional obsolescence, technological obsolescence, and external obsolescence.

Physical deterioration is the reduction in the value of an intangible asset due to physical wear and tear resulting from continued use. It is unlikely (but not impossible) for most intangible assets to experience any appreciable effects of physical deterioration.

Functional obsolescence is the reduction in the value of an intangible asset due to its inability to perform the function (or yield the economic utility) for which it was originally designed. This can occur even when the intended function of the intangible asset is still a valid functional objective. This simply means that, over time, most intangible assets (but not all intangible assets) do not perform as well as they used to (however "well" is measured). Functional obsolescence may be one reason why the subject intangible asset typically becomes less than the ideal replacement for itself.

Technological obsolescence is a decrease in the value of an intangible asset due to improvements in technology. Technological obsolescence is another reason why the subject intangible asset typically becomes less than the ideal replacement for itself. Technological obsolescence occurs when, due to improvements in design or engineering technology, a new replacement intangible asset produces a greater standardized measure of utility production than the subject intangible asset.

External obsolescence is a reduction in the value of the subject intangible asset due to the effects, events, or conditions, that are external to, and not controlled by, the current use or condition of the intangible asset. The impact of external obsolescence is typically beyond the control of the intangible asset's owner. There are two subcategories of external obsolescence: locational obsolescence and economic obsolescence. Except for real estate–related intangible assets (e.g., easements, development rights, building permits), locational obsolescence does not typically affect intangible assets. Therefore, we will focus our discussion of external obsolescence on the identification and quantification of economic obsolescence.

When identifying and quantifying the amounts of physical deterioration (if any), functional obsolescence, technological obsolescence, and economic obsolescence related to the subject intangible asset, consideration of the subject asset's actual age and its expected remaining useful life is essential to the proper application of the cost approach analysis.

Using the cost approach analysis, a typical formula for estimating an intangible asset's replacement cost is:

Reproduction cost new − Curable functional and technological obsolescence = Replacement cost new

In order to estimate the intangible asset value based on the estimate of cost new (i.e., either reproduction cost or replacement cost), the following formula is typically used:

Replacement cost new − Physical deterioration − Economic obsolescence − Incurable functional and technological obsolescence = Value

Most forms of obsolescence can be categorized as either curable or incurable. An intangible asset's deficiencies are considered curable when the prospective economic benefit of enhancing or modifying the intangible asset exceeds the current cost (in terms of material, labor, and time) to change the intangible asset. An intangible asset's deficiencies are considered incurable when the current cost of enhancing or modifying the intangible (in terms of material, labor, and time) exceeds the expected future economic benefits of improving the intangible asset.

Since the causes of economic obsolescence are often external to the subject intangible asset itself, economic obsolescence is often considered to be incurable. Even if the cost–benefit relationship were such that the intangible asset owner would be motivated to cure the deficiency, it is not within the control of the intangible asset owner to do so.

## DATA VERIFICATION WITH REGARD TO
## COST APPROACH ANALYSIS

In addition to including all components of costs and recognizing all forms of obsolescence, the analyst must start with a correct factual description of the subject intangible asset. This may be a fairly simple procedure when the cost approach analysis is applied to a single intangible asset. A single intangible asset could be an individual patent, trademark, copyright, and so on. However, it becomes a slightly more difficult procedure and an exponentially more important procedure when the cost approach analysis is applied to a group or collection of intangible assets. A group of intangible assets could include a listing of customers or subscribers, a portfolio of credit card or other bank accounts, a collection of chemical formulations or food recipes, a system containing numerous computer programs, or some other grouping.

When the analysis involves groups of intangible assets, the analyst is often presented with a listing of the intangible assets prepared by the asset owner (or by a client, if the client is not the asset owner). It is important for the analyst to verify the data included on the listing (or otherwise represented by the owner or client) before continuing with the cost approach analysis.

Often the owner or client represents the following data with regard to the subject group of intangible assets:

1. General description (e.g., registration numbers, terms of an agreement).
2. Quantity (i.e., the number of individual intangible assets in the group).
3. Size metrics (e.g., number of lines of software code).
4. Age (e.g., date developed, date placed in service, etc.).
5. Original cost (e.g., cost of development and enhancements).
6. Retirement data (e.g., remaining terms, historical renewal rates, and expiration rates).

The analyst should perform adequate verification and confirmation procedures before relying upon these data in the cost approach analysis. In other words, the analyst has to perform reasonable procedures to verify the existence and condition of the intangible assets subject to analysis. Presumably, a personal property or real estate appraiser would not appraise an owner or client's listing of properties without some property inspection procedures. Likewise, the intangible asset analyst should perform adequate property inspection procedures.

Two methods that may be used to verify intangible asset data prior to the application of cost approach analysis procedures are the inventory method and the audit method. As with all analytical tools, each method has both advantages and disadvantages. If applied properly, either method should assure analysts that the data they are using are reasonably reliable for purposes of performing a cost approach analysis.

Using the inventory method, the analyst essentially starts with a blank clipboard. The analyst independently verifies the existence of each individual intangible asset and independently records a description and identification (e.g., serial or registration) number. If owner or client data are relied upon at all in the appraisal, the analyst independently searches through historical accounting or operational records. This search produces independent evidence of age, development cost, renewal or attrition rates, and so forth. As a result of these procedures, the analyst knows exactly what cost components are included (and excluded) in the development cost data.

Presumably, the inventory method produces a detailed listing of the group of intangible assets subject to analysis. This listing can be considered accurate from the perspective of the analyst who created the listing. However, this method is time-consuming and expensive. The procedure is not necessarily perfect, because it allows the analyst to make recording errors—errors in the count of the intangible assets, in the descriptive identification of the intangible assets, in the interpretation of historical cost data, and other errors. Accordingly, the inventory method is typically not used unless no owner or client records exist or the owner or client records are proved to be unreliable.

Using the audit method, the analyst starts with the data listing provided by the intangible asset owner or client. The analyst then performs audit procedures in order to gain assurance that the data on the listing are accurate enough and complete enough to use in the valuation analysis. The audit procedures typically include the following:

1. Tests of inclusion (to ensure that all of the intangible assets included on the listing are, in fact, in existence).
2. Tests of exclusion (to ensure that all of the intangible assets that are in existence are, in fact, on the list).
3. Tests of data accuracy (vouching for data items back to original source documents to ensure that data were recorded and summarized correctly).
4. Tests of data completeness (reconstruction and reconciliation of certain data fields to ensure that appropriate information was not left out).
5. Documentation of data (understanding what elements—e.g., cost components—are included and what elements are excluded in each account or data field).

The audit procedures should give the analyst confidence that he or she can rely upon the data supplied by the owner or client. If there are minor errors in the data, the procedures provide the analyst with the opportunity to correct the data—that is, to purify an otherwise imperfect data set so that it becomes usable for analytical purposes. Of course, if the audit procedures reveal that there are material errors in the owner or client's data listing, the analyst may not be able to rely upon the data in the cost approach analysis. In that case the analyst will have to perform the inventory method instead of the audit method in order to assemble the data set that will serve as the starting point in the cost approach analysis.

## CURRENT COST TREND FACTORS

In tangible personal property and real estate appraisal, there are recognized publications that appraisers consult with regard to the development of cost trend factors. The trend factors (or indexes) are applied to the historical construction cost of a machine or a building in order to estimate a current (typically reproduction) cost. There are various sets of trend factors for different types of personal property and for different types of building construction, and sets of trend factors (or at least adjustments to national trend factors) to account for geographic regional differences with regard to cost indexes. Published trend factors generally do not exist with regard to intangible assets and intellectual properties.

For this reason (and for other reasons), analysts typically do not trend historical development costs in order to estimate the current development cost of an intangible asset. More often than not, reproduction cost and replacement cost estimates are made based upon the analyst's estimate of development time and effort rather than upon a trend index applied to a historical cost number. This is not to imply that a trending procedure is absolutely incorrect or is never performed. Rather, it simply implies that the procedure is less common because reliable historical development cost data and recognized and published cost trend factors (or indexes) are generally not available with regard to intangible assets.

If the analyst elects to perform a trended historical cost analysis, the analyst should:

1. Confirm that the historical cost base represents complete, accurate, and reliable data.
2. Apply a cost trend factor or index that is as applicable as possible to the subject type of intangible, the industry that the intangible asset functions in, and the relevant time period between when the intangible asset was developed and the current valuation date.

Also, an analyst who elects to perform a trended historical cost analysis should specifically identify what type of cost measure the trend factor will estimate, for example, reproduction cost versus replacement cost.

## IDENTIFICATION AND QUANTIFICATION OF OBSOLESCENCE

Regardless of whether the current cost estimate is derived de novo or by reference to historical development costs, the current cost estimate should be adjusted for all forms of obsolescence that relate to the subject intangible assets. The estimation of remaining useful life is an important—and often necessary—procedure with regard to the identification and quantification of obsolescence in a cost approach analysis. The topic of remaining useful life analysis is discussed in Chapter 11.

One method of remaining useful life analysis detailed in Chapter 11 is the analytical method. The analytical method estimates life characteristics, including expected remaining useful life, based upon a quantitative attrition analysis of the historical placements and retirements of the subject intangible asset. This method is particularly applicable in the analysis of a single intangible asset that is part of a group of intangible assets (e.g., one customer from a customer list, one drawing from a collection of drawings, one airport landing slot from a group of landing slots, etc.).

The analytical method is particularly useful in the recognition of the total amount of obsolescence associated with an intangible asset because the analytical method analyzes the fact pattern of historical intangible asset placements and retirements. The analytical method does not necessarily analyze the reasons for or the causes of the intangible asset placements and retirements. Rather, it acknowledges that such historical attrition activity occurred and then interprets and extrapolates that historical attrition activity.

For example, the analytical method may indicate that the actual age of the subject intangible asset is 6 years and the expected remaining life of that intangible asset is 12 years. Accordingly, the analyst could imply that the subject intangible asset is 33 percent obsolete. The 33 percent estimate is based on the relationship of the total life to date (6 years) divided by the total expected life of 18 years (6 years age plus 12 years expected remaining life). The analytical method does not necessarily tell the analyst what forms of obsolescence have affected the subject intangible asset to date or what forms of obsolescence will affect the subject intangible asset in the future. That is why this method is adequate for estimating the total amount of obsolescence related to a subject intangible asset. It is not adequate for identifying (or quantifying) the components of the obsolescence related to a subject intangible asset.

If it is necessary to quantify the components of the subject intangible asset obsolescence (or if data are not available to perform the analytical method), then analysts should identify and consider each form of obsolescence separately. Accordingly, there should be a separate value decrement for each form of obsolescence that relates to the subject intangible asset. The value decrement may be expressed in the form of a dollar amount or a percentage of the current cost estimate.

With regard to physical deterioration, there is no particular formula or equation to quantify this form of obsolescence for intangible assets. The analyst has to physically inspect the intangible asset to perceive if there is any manifestation of physical deterioration. The most common procedure related to quantifying physical deterioration is to estimate the cost to cure the obsolescence (if it is, in fact, curable). Very few types of intangible assets experience any value decrement due to physical deterioration. For the few types of intangible assets that do experience wear and tear, physical deterioration is usually not a big component of the total obsolescence related to them.

With regard to functional obsolescence, there are two principal factors that the analyst should consider:

1. Excess development costs (more relevant to the reproduction cost method).
2. Excess operating costs (relevant to both the reproduction cost and the replacement cost methods).

Consideration of excess development costs compares the cost to develop the intangible asset today versus the historical cost to develop the subject intangible. In both cases, the costs should relate to the function for which the subject intangible asset was developed. In other words, if it would cost less to develop the asset today than it did when the subject intangible was created, that difference is one measure of functional obsolescence.

Consideration of excess operating costs compares the current cost of maintaining or using the intangible asset versus the cost of maintaining or using the intangible asset when it was first developed or put into service. The increase in maintenance or use costs is then projected out over the remaining useful life of the subject intangible. The present value of the excess operating costs (i.e., maintenance or use costs) over the remaining life of the subject intangible asset is another measure of functional obsolescence.

With regard to technological obsolescence, the same two principal factors should be considered:

1. Excess development costs (more relevant to the reproduction cost method).
2. Excess operating costs (relevant to both the reproduction cost and the replacement cost methods).

Remember that functional obsolescence signifies that the subject intangible can no longer perform the function for which it was developed. Technological obsolescence indicates that the function has become obsolete; the intangible asset still performs the job that it was created to perform. A new intangible asset would perform the job in an entirely different way. It is important to distinguish between these two related forms of obsolescence. In particular, the analyst should make an effort not to double-count (i.e., penalize the intangible twice for) these two forms of obsolescence.

If it costs less to develop a new (technologically superior) intangible than it costs to develop the subject intangible asset, then the excess development cost is one measure of technological obsolescence. One example of technological obsolescence is the cost associated with the development of a computer software system in a new, high generation programming language compared to the cost associated with the development of the actual system in a second- or third-generation programming language.

The excess operating cost relates to the cost of maintaining or using the new (technologically superior) intangible compared to the cost of maintaining or using the subject intangible asset. Excess operating costs are often expressed on a unitary basis, such as cost per unit of production, cost per dollar of sales, cost per cycle, cost per operation, and so forth. Excess operating costs are often multiplied by the production, sales, and other factors associated with the subject intangible asset in order to estimate annual excess operating costs. The excess operating costs are projected over the remaining useful life of the subject intangible asset. The present value of the excess operating costs is a measure of technological obsolescence.

With regard to economic obsolescence, there are several procedures for measuring whether the intangible asset is suffering from economic obsolescence. The existence of economic obsolescence is identified by the answer to the following question: Can the intangible asset generate a fair rate of return to its owner based upon the value indication? Keep in mind that, at this point in the cost approach analysis, the value indication is represented by the following formula:

| | Reproduction cost |
|---|---|
| Less: | Curable functional and technological obsolescence |
| Equals: | Replacement cost |
| Less: | Physical deterioration |
| Equals: | Value indication before economic obsolescence |

If the subject intangible asset can generate an adequate rate of return over its expected remaining life based on this indication of value, then no economic obsolescence is evident. If the subject intangible asset cannot generate an adequate rate of return based on this value indication, then economic obsolescence is evident.

Whether or not economic obsolescence is present, it is noteworthy that the cost approach analysis includes an additional step after the identification and quantification of economic obsolescence. After subtracting economic obsolescence (if any exists), it is necessary to subtract incurable functional and technological obsolescence (if any) in order to conclude the final indication of value.

While there are several procedures related to the quantification of economic obsolescence, they all generally relate to identifying an economic shortfall. An economic shortfall occurs in the following instances:

1. Actual return on investment (i.e., value) on the intangible is less than the owner's required return on investment.
2. Actual return on investment (i.e., value) on the intangible is less than the owner's historical return on investment (i.e., historical cost) at the time of the intangible's development.
3. Actual profit margin (return on sales) is less than the owner's required (or budgeted) profit margin.
4. Actual profit margin (return on sales) is less than the owner's historical profit margin at the time that the intangible was developed.

Economic shortfalls (measured as either returns or margins) are projected over the remaining useful life of the subject intangible asset. The present value of the projected economic shortfall is a measure of economic obsolescence.

As a reasonableness check, the analyst should note that if economic obsolescence is quantified directly, then the intangible asset will be able to generate an adequate rate of return to the intangible asset owner. That is, the economic obsolescence will reduce the cost approach value indication by an amount whereby the intangible asset will just earn an adequate rate of return on this new value indication.

## COST APPROACH ANALYSIS—EXAMPLE

For this example, we have been asked to appraise certain proprietary documentation and records and certain proprietary policy and procedural manuals (the subject intellectual property materials) of Community Hospital. We performed this appraisal as of December 31, 1997.

The subject intellectual property materials include documents, records, manuals, policies, and procedures. Most of the intellectual property materials were developed by Community Hospital during the normal course of its hospital operation business. The intellectual property materials are proprietary in nature.

We have appraised the subject intellectual property materials of Community Hospital under the premise of value in continued use, as a part of an ongoing business enterprise. The premise assumes that the subject intellectual property will continue to be used as part of the income-producing business of operating a hospital, that management of the business will act rationally, and that the subject intellectual property will continue to enjoy the contributory value of the other assets of the ongoing hospital business.

Based upon our analysis, and in our opinion, this premise of value represents the highest and best use of the subject intellectual property materials.

For the subject intellectual property materials, we considered all of the generally accepted intangible asset valuation approaches and methods. We relied principally on a cost approach valuation analysis. In our opinion, a cost approach valuation analysis is an appropriate valuation approach with respect to the appraisal of the subject intellectual property.

A healthcare organization such as Community Hospital cannot function unless the employees know what to do and how to do it in an organized and efficient manner. Intellectual property materials such as documents, records, manuals, policies, and procedures encompass an unglamorous but important aspect of a healthcare organization because the materials document "how things are done" at Community Hospital. Exhibit 8-1 presents a listing of the various intellectual property materials of Community Hospital.

The application of the cost approach aggregates all the costs that are required to develop all the intellectual property components of the subject materials. The development costs are based on:

1. The amount of unique documentation in the intellectual property materials.

2. The fully loaded salaries (i.e., employee salaries plus employment-benefits, employment related taxes, and other employee-related costs) of the type of individuals who would be involved in the recreation of the subject materials.

3. The estimated amount of time that would be devoted to the process of recreating the subject materials.

In addition to the time required by Community Hospital employees to actually write the subject documents, records, manuals, policies, and procedures, there would be a time cost associated with the conceptualization and development of the proposed materials. The time cost would involve various relevant parties within the Community Hospital organization and would include the time cost required to obtain the appropriate approvals of Community Hospital.

As a part of our analysis, we have included only those documents, policies, procedures, or records that can be considered unique. For example, each of the 115 departments in Community Hospital could have its own administrative manual. The administrative manual contains 250 to 500 policies, depending on the department to which it applies. If these 115 administrative manuals were arranged end to end and the number of policies counted, there would be 28,750 policies, assuming 250 policies in each of the 115 manuals (i.e., $115 \times 250 = 28,750$).

However, we have considered that there may be 250 policies that are standard and applicable to all the departments. We also considered that there may be, on an average, at least 10 policies applicable only to those specific departments. The total number of unique, individual policies would be 250 standard policies plus 10 times 115 (i.e., 10 policies for each of the 115 departments), which equals 1,400 individual policies. In our analysis, we have considered the recreation of 1,400 individual policies for the administrative manual. Accordingly, our analysis considers only the unique polices and procedures in the various intellectual property materials.

EXHIBIT 8-1

Community Hospital Intellectual Property Materials Including Documents, Reports, Manuals, Policies, and Procedures—
Partial Listing

| Documents/Manuals | General Description |
| --- | --- |
| Administrative Manual Volume I and II | This manual maintains/provides guidelines for ongoing operations of the facility. Most policies required are for compliance with federal, state, local, and regulatory laws, and JCAHO compliance. The manual provides a description of operational guidelines. |
| Personnel Policy and Managerial Manuals | These manuals provide managers and personnel with general rules and regulations on issues of rights and privileges of each and their responsibility to the others. |
| Safety Manual | This manual is required by accreditation and OSHA standards. This manual includes standards for safety, overall safety policies, housewide safety plan, and departmental specific safety policies. |
| Infection Control Manual | This manual contains standards, policies, and procedures related to managing the facility's infection control practices. These are required by accrediting and regulatory agencies. This manual contains approximately 60 to 100 policies and procedures and standards. |
| Hazardous Waste Manual | This manual presents the required policies and procedures on handling of hazardous wastes and required area-specific materials safety data sheets (MSDA) that are required per OSHA and regulatory agencies. |
| Lab Specimen Collection Manual | This manual is required for identifying types of specimens that can be processed by the laboratory, and the types of tubes, containers, and collection ports to be used to obtain and store specimens after collection and to transport to the laboratory. |
| Department Policy Manual | Each department, patient, and nonpatient areas must have departmental policies specific for their area. The number of policies can range from 30 to 50 policies per area. |
| Critical Care Policies/Manual | These were policies developed specifically for critical care areas, SICU, CCU, MICU, TCU, burn unit, bone marrow transplant, PACU. The same manual is used for all areas. Has adopted policies from the AACN who provides standards for caring for the critically ill patient. Approximate number of policies 300-400. |
| Hospital Formulary | This manual contains those medications that are approved for use by the hospital and its medical staff. |
| Nursing Policies & Procedures | This manual describes how to perform patient care procedures for nursing, such as inserting a tube, catheter, etc. It consists of two volumes and has approximately 1,500-2,000 individual policies and procedures. |
| Manual of Nutrition Case Management | Guidelines on nutritional care for the patient are presented in this manual. This manual is required information per accreditation and regulatory standards. Includes standards, guidelines, diets, nutrition and disease/disorders, nutritional assessments, meal planning guidelines, etc. |
| Case Cart/Physician Profiles | Each case cart/physician profile includes physician preferences for apparatus, instrument layout, and supplies for different types of procedures. |
| Diagnostic Testing Guidelines | This manual describes the lab tests, x-ray tests, etc. This manual provides instruction on the amount of blood to be drawn, how to order the test, what kind of preparations need to be done for the patient prior to the test, etc. |
| Quality Assurance Manual | This manual contains hospital and medical staff quality plans and departmental specific quality data. This manual is kept by each department. |
| Job Descriptions Manual | Each job classification requires a job description which includes ADA requirements as well as clear physical and psychological requirements of the job. The job description manual also includes performance appraisals which define the criteria and expectations of how an individual's job performance is evaluated. |
| Bylaws | The hospital governing body or authority has adopted bylaws addressing its legal accountabilities and responsibility to the patient population served. These bylaws are required for the medical staff and for the board of trustees per accreditation standards. |
| Medical Staff Records | Records pertinent to credentialing and peer review of medical staff. |
| Community Hospital Employee Handbook | The handbook contains pertinent information relating to employees/polices/information regarding parking, recording time worked, information about the hospital in general, grievance procedures, etc. |
| Education Manual | Education manual contains education-specific policies, competencies, and unit-specific education grids. |

EXHIBIT 8-1 *(continued)*

Community Hospital Intellectual Property Materials Including Documents, Reports, Manuals, Policies, and Procedures—
Partial Listing

| Documents/Manuals | General Description |
|---|---|
| *Patient Education Manual* | This manual contains guidelines/policies and procedures regarding strategies for patient family education. Information required per JCAHO. This manual contains listings for patient education materials available for use in instruction, contains samples of materials, contains forms for documentation of assessment of the learner and evaluation of teaching. |
| *Supply Catalog* | This manual provides information on how to order supplies, order number, quantity of item, price, where ordered from, etc. |
| *Equipment Manual* | This manual is required for all departments who have equipment in use whether business or patient care related. Includes standard policies for equipment safety but can include how to operate specific equipment, safety guidelines, etc. The average number of policies is 50-100. |
| *Seldom Used Forms Notebook* | The notebook contains low volume use forms, i.e., one-of-a-kind types of forms that are seldom used. |
| *Patient Business Systems Manual & Accounting Manual* | These manuals contain policy and procedures related to how to process all business and patient accounting information. These manuals include 200-300 policies on processes, forms and how to handle patient billing. |
| *Operating Room Course/Critical Care Course* | Courses that are designed to teach specific competencies and skills to registered nurses who are entering those specialty areas to practice. |

We obtained from Community Hospital management an estimate of average overall salary ranges for employees in the various job categories that would be responsible for such intellectual property development. The salary ranges are presented in Exhibit 8-2.

Due to a lack of actual employee tenure data, we could not directly quantify the employee experience and expertise component of the intellectual property recreation process. However, in our opinion, it is reasonable to project that such responsibilities would fall on those Community Hospital personnel who have ten years or more of hospital or related healthcare experience. This assumed level of healthcare industry experience is necessary in order for the Community Hospital employees to make reasonable contributions of their accumulated experience and expertise in the process of recreating the subject materials.

Accordingly, for each Community Hospital employee job category considered in our analysis, we included an hourly salary estimate that was prorated above the mean of the actual minimum and maximum salary range provided to us.

In addition to actual personnel salaries, Community Hospital management provided us with an overhead factor of 25 percent. Based upon our analysis, the 25 percent overhead factor appears to be conservative. The overhead factor includes items such as employee perquisites, employee benefits (including life, health, disability and dental insurance, and pension and retirement plans), and employment-related payroll taxes. However, it does not include an allocation of such overhead expense items as office space, equipment usage, office utilities, and development personnel management. Accordingly, the personnel costs that we used to estimate the recreation cost of the subject materials are conservative in that they do not represent a fully loaded personnel cost.

Community Hospital management provided us with an estimate of the amount of time required to develop, review, approve, and promulgate the subject intellectual property materials. The recreation time estimate is presented in Exhibit 8-3.

EXHIBIT 8-2

Community Hospital Intellectual Property Materials Including Documents, Reports, Manuals, Policies, and Procedures—Personnel Loaded Hourly Rates, as of December 31, 1997

| | Position | Per Hour Salary | | |
|---|---|---|---|---|
| | | Minimum Loaded[1] | Maximum | |
| 1 | Ancillary Dept. Manager | $ 20.00 | $ 34.00 | $ 35.50 |
| 2 | Chief Executive Officer | $ 85.00 | $ 85.00 | $106.25 |
| 3 | Chief Financial Officer | $ 32.00 | $ 56.00 | $ 58.00 |
| 4 | Chief Nursing Officer | $ 54.00 | $ 54.00 | $ 67.50 |
| 5 | Clinical Coordinator—RN | $ 18.00 | $ 30.00 | $ 31.50 |
| 6 | Clinical Educator | $ 16.00 | $ 25.00 | $ 26.75 |
| 7 | Clinical Pharmacist | $ 20.00 | $ 34.00 | $ 35.50 |
| 8 | Credentialling Coordinator | $ 10.00 | $ 16.00 | $ 17.00 |
| 9 | Data Entry Clerk | $ 7.00 | $ 12.00 | $ 12.50 |
| 10 | Diagnostic Imaging Technician | $ 10.00 | $ 14.00 | $ 15.50 |
| 11 | Dietitian | $ 12.00 | $ 20.00 | $ 21.00 |
| 12 | Director of Pharmacy | $ 21.00 | $ 36.00 | $ 37.50 |
| 13 | Director of Bio-Med | $ 14.00 | $ 25.00 | $ 25.75 |
| 14 | Director of Education | $ 18.00 | $ 30.00 | $ 31.50 |
| 15 | Director of Engineering | $ 15.00 | $ 25.00 | $ 26.25 |
| 16 | Director of Infection Control | $ 18.00 | $ 30.00 | $ 31.50 |
| 17 | Director of Lab | $ 20.00 | $ 32.00 | $ 34.00 |
| 18 | Director of Quality Management | $ 18.00 | $ 30.00 | $ 31.50 |
| 19 | Director of Respiratory Care | $ 18.00 | $ 30.00 | $ 31.50 |
| 20 | Employee Health Nurse | $ 16.00 | $ 26.00 | $ 27.50 |
| 21 | Fileroom Clerk | $ 6.00 | $ 8.00 | $ 9.00 |
| 22 | Financial Analyst | $ 15.00 | $ 24.00 | $ 25.50 |
| 23 | Human Resource Director | $ 20.00 | $ 35.00 | $ 36.25 |
| 24 | Lab Technologist | $ 8.00 | $ 12.00 | $ 13.00 |
| 25 | Materials Management Director | $ 16.00 | $ 26.00 | $ 27.50 |
| 26 | MD Advisor | $120.00 | $120.00 | $150.00 |
| 27 | Medical Records Abstractor | $ 7.00 | $ 10.00 | $ 11.00 |
| 28 | Medical Staff Coordinator | $ 11.00 | $ 17.00 | $ 18.25 |
| 29 | Medical Staff Secretary | $ 8.00 | $ 14.00 | $ 14.50 |
| 30 | Medical Technologist | $ 12.00 | $ 17.00 | $ 18.75 |
| 31 | Nurse LPN | $ 9.00 | $ 14.00 | $ 15.00 |
| 32 | Nurse RN | $ 14.00 | $ 21.00 | $ 22.75 |
| 33 | Nursing Clinical Coordinator | $ 18.00 | $ 30.00 | $ 31.50 |
| 34 | Pathology Assistant | $ 12.00 | $ 18.00 | $ 19.50 |
| 35 | Physician | $105.00 | $115.00 | $138.75 |
| 36 | Radiology Technician | $ 10.00 | $ 16.00 | $ 17.00 |
| 37 | Registered Dietitian | $ 12.00 | $ 20.00 | $ 21.00 |
| 38 | Risk Manager | $ 18.00 | $ 30.00 | $ 31.50 |
| 39 | RN—Transplant | $ 14.00 | $ 22.00 | $ 23.50 |
| 40 | Safety Officer | $ 16.00 | $ 26.00 | $ 27.50 |
| 41 | Secretary | $ 7.00 | $ 10.00 | $ 11.00 |
| 42 | Security | $ 8.00 | $ 12.00 | $ 13.00 |

Community Hospital Intellectual Property Materials Including Documents, Reports, Manuals, Policies, and Procedures—Personnel Loaded Hourly Rates, as of December 31, 1997

| Committee | Loaded | Number[2] | Loaded |
|---|---|---|---|
| *Safety Committee* | | | $302.80 |
| Director of Education | $ 31.50 | 1 | |
| Director of Engineering | $ 26.25 | 1 | |
| Ancillary Dept. Manager | $ 35.50 | 1 | |
| Director of Quality Management | $ 31.50 | 1 | |
| Security | $ 13.00 | 1 | |
| MD Advisor | $150.00 | 1 | |
| Nurse LPN | $ 15.00 | 1 | |
| *Education Committee* | | | $210.60 |
| Director of Education | $ 31.50 | 1 | |
| Clinical Educator | $ 26.75 | 1 | |
| Clinical Coordinator—RN | $ 31.50 | 2 | |
| Ancillary Dept. Manager | $ 35.50 | 1 | |
| Safety Officer | $ 27.50 | 1 | |
| Director of Engineering | $ 26.25 | 1 | |
| *Medical Executive Committee* | | | $928.30 |
| Ancillary Dept. Manager | $ 35.50 | 5 | |
| Chief Financial Officer | $ 58.00 | 1 | |
| Chief Nursing Officer | $ 67.50 | 1 | |
| Chief Executive Officer | $106.25 | 1 | |
| Director of Quality Management | $ 31.50 | 1 | |
| MD Advisory | $150.00 | 3 | |
| Director of Pharmacy | $ 37.50 | 1 | |
| *Pharmacy Committee* | | | $666.50 |
| Clinical Pharmacist | $ 35.50 | 1 | |
| MD Advisor | $150.00 | 3 | |
| Director of Quality Management | $ 31.50 | 1 | |
| Dietitian | $ 21.00 | 1 | |
| Director of Infection Control | $ 31.50 | 1 | |
| Clinical Coordinator—RN | $ 31.50 | 1 | |
| Nursing Clinical Coordinator | $ 31.50 | 1 | |
| Director of Lab | $ 34.00 | 1 | |
| *Infection Control Committee* | | | $510.00 |
| MD Advisor | $150.00 | 2 | |
| Director of Lab | $ 34.00 | 1 | |
| Director of Quality Management | $ 31.50 | 1 | |
| Clinical Coordinator—RN | $ 31.50 | 3 | |
| Clinical Pharmacist | $ 35.50 | 1 | |
| Medical Staff Secretary | $ 14.50 | 1 | |
| *Nutrition Support Committee* | | | $563.00 |
| MD Advisor | $150.00 | 3 | |
| Director of Quality Management | $ 31.50 | 1 | |
| Clinical Pharmacist | $ 35.50 | 1 | |
| Clinical Coordinator—RN | $ 31.50 | 1 | |
| Medical Staff Secretary | $ 14.50 | 1 | |
| *Hazardous Waste Committee* | | | $133.80 |
| Director of Engineering | $ 26.25 | 1 | |
| Risk Manager | $ 31.50 | 1 | |
| Director of Quality Management | $ 31.50 | 1 | |
| Director of Infection Control | $ 31.50 | 1 | |
| Security | $ 13.00 | 1 | |
| *Bylaw Committee* | | | $677.80 |
| Physicians | $ 90.00 | 6 | |
| Chief Executive Officer | $106.25 | 1 | |
| Director of Quality Management | $ 31.50 | 1 | |

Note that numbers may not total due to rounding.

1. Includes an hourly salary interpolated at 60% between minimum and maximum, and a 21% overhead factor.

2. Represents number of such personnel in a typical committee

EXHIBIT 8-3

Community Hospital Intellectual Property Materials Including Documents, Reports, Manuals, Policies, and Procedures—Fair Market Value Indication, as of December 31, 1997

| Item | Intellectual Property Materials | Number of Unique Policies, Procedures, or Items (Unit) | Personnel | Loaded Hourly Rate | Recreation Time | | Cost to Recreate | | |
|---|---|---|---|---|---|---|---|---|---|
| | | | | | Per Unit (hours) | Total Time | Recreation Cost | Total Cost | Value Indication |
| 1 | Administrative Manual (115 depts., 200-400 policies in each department @250 common, 10 department-specific) | 1,400 | Risk Manager | $ 31.50 | 0.14 | 200.00 | $ 6,300 | | |
| | | 1,400 | Director of Quality Management | $ 31.50 | 0.14 | 200.00 | $ 6,300 | | |
| | | 1,400 | Materials Management Director | $ 27.50 | 0.14 | 200.00 | $ 5,500 | | |
| | | 1,400 | Chief Nursing Officer | $ 67.50 | 0.14 | 200.00 | $ 13,500 | | |
| | | 1,400 | Chief Financial Officer | $ 58.00 | 0.14 | 200.00 | $ 11,600 | | |
| | | 1,400 | Chief Executive Officer | $106.25 | 0.14 | 200.00 | $ 21,250 | | |
| | | 1,400 | Human Resource Director | $ 36.25 | 0.14 | 200.00 | $ 7,250 | | |
| | | 1,400 | Secretary | $ 11.00 | 0.25 | 350.00 | $ 3,850 | | |
| | | 1,400 | Safety Committee[1] | $302.80 | 0.25 | 350.00 | $105,980 | | |
| | | 1,400 | Medical Executive Committee[1] | $923.30 | 0.25 | 350.00 | $324,905 | 506,435 | $ 506,400 |
| 2 | Personnel Policy and Managerial Manuals (50-150 policies) | 100 | Human Resource Director | $ 36.25 | 0.50 | 50.00 | $ 1,813 | | |
| | | 100 | Chief Executive Officer | $106.25 | 0.25 | 25.00 | $ 2,656 | | |
| | | 100 | Secretary | $ 11.00 | 0.25 | 25.00 | $ 275 | | |
| | | 100 | Safety Committee | $302.80 | 0.25 | 25.00 | $ 7,570 | | |
| | | 100 | Medical Executive Committee | $928.30 | 0.25 | 25.00 | $ 23,208 | 35,521 | $ 35,500 |
| 3 | Safety Manual (500-1000 policies, 4-6 week total) | 1 | Safety Officer | $ 27.50 | 160.00 | 160.00 | $ 4,400 | | |
| | | 1 | Director of Quality Management | $ 31.50 | 80.00 | 80.00 | $ 2,520 | | |
| | | 1 | Secretary | $ 11.00 | 100.00 | 100.00 | $ 1,100 | | |
| | | 750 | Safety Committee | $302.80 | 0.50 | 375.00 | $113,550 | 121,570 | $ 121,600 |
| 4 | Infection Control (I.C.) Manual (115 departments, 60-100 policies in each department @50 common, 25 department-specific) | 2,925 | Director of Infection Control | $ 31.50 | 1.00 | 2,925.00 | $ 92,138 | | |
| | | 2,925 | Director of Quality Management | $ 31.50 | 1.00 | 2,925.00 | $ 92,138 | | |
| | | 2,925 | MD Advisor | $150.00 | 0.25 | 731.25 | $109,688 | | |
| | | 2,925 | Secretary | $ 11.00 | 0.25 | 731.25 | $ 8,044 | | |
| | | 2,925 | I.C. Committee | $510.00 | 0.25 | 731.25 | $372,938 | 674,944 | $ 674,900 |
| 5 | Hazardous Waste Manual (30-50 policies @ 1-2 hr., 2000-3500 MSDS sheets @ 1-3 hr.) (MSDS Materials Safety Data Sheets) | 40 | Safety Officer | $ 27.50 | 1.00 | 40.00 | $ 1,100 | | |
| | | 40 | Director of Quality Management | $ 31.50 | 0.50 | 20.00 | $ 630 | | |
| | | 2,500 | Safety Officer | $ 27.50 | 1.50 | 3,750.00 | $103,125 | | |
| | | 2,500 | Director of Quality Management | $ 31.50 | 0.50 | 1,250.00 | $ 39,375 | | |
| | | 2,500 | Secretary | $ 11.00 | 0.25 | 625.00 | $ 6,875 | | |
| | | 1 | Hazardous Waste Committee | $133.80 | 40.00 | 40.00 | $ 5,352 | | |
| | | 1 | Safety Committee | $302.80 | 20.00 | 20.00 | $ 6,056 | | |
| | | 1 | Medical Executive Committee | $928.30 | 10.00 | 10.00 | $ 9,283 | 171,796 | $ 171,800 |
| 6 | Lab Specimen Collection Manual (500-1000 specimens, 4-6 weeks total) | 1 | Director of Lab | $ 34.00 | 160.00 | 160.00 | $ 5,440 | | |
| | | 1 | MD Advisor | $150.00 | 40.00 | 40.00 | $ 6,000 | | |
| | | 1 | Secretary | $ 11.00 | 100.00 | 100.00 | $ 1,100 | 12,540 | $ 12,500 |

Community Hospital Intellectual Property Materials Including Documents, Reports, Manuals, Policies, and Procedures—Fair Market Value Indication, as of December 31, 1997

| | | | | | Recreation Time | | | Cost to Recreate | |
|---|---|---|---|---|---|---|---|---|---|
| Item | Intellectual Property Materials | Number of Unique Policies, Procedures, or Items (Unit) | Personnel | Loaded Hourly Rate | Per Unit (hours) | Total Time | Recreation Cost | Total Cost | Value Indication |
| 7 | Departmental Policy Manual (115 departments, 30-50 policies each department) | 2,875 | Risk Manager | $ 31.50 | 0.50 | 1,437.50 | $ 45,281 | | |
| | | 2,875 | Director of Quality Management | $ 31.50 | 0.50 | 1,437.50 | $ 45,281 | | |
| | | 2,875 | Department Heads | $ 22.00 | 0.50 | 1,437.50 | $ 31,625 | | |
| | | 2,875 | Secretary | $ 11.00 | 0.25 | 718.75 | $ 7,906 | 130,094 | $ 130,100 |
| 8 | Critical Care Policies/Manual | 350 | Director of Education | $ 31.50 | 0.25 | 87.50 | $ 2,756 | | |
| | | 350 | Clinical Coordinator—RN | $ 31.50 | 1.00 | 350.00 | $ 11,025 | | |
| | | 350 | Clinical Coordinator—RN | $ 31.50 | 1.00 | 350.00 | $ 11,025 | | |
| | | 350 | Chief Nursing Officer | $ 67.50 | 0.25 | 87.50 | $ 5,906 | | |
| | | 350 | Secretary | $ 11.00 | 0.25 | 87.50 | $ 963 | 31,675 | $ 31,700 |
| 9 | Hospital Formulary (500-600 drugs) | 500 | Director of Pharmacy | $ 37.50 | 0.50 | 250.00 | $ 9,375 | | |
| | | 500 | Clinical Pharmacist | $ 35.50 | 1.00 | 500.00 | $ 17,750 | | |
| | | 500 | Secretary | $ 11.00 | 0.25 | 125.00 | $ 1,375 | | |
| | | 500 | Pharmacy Committee | $666.50 | 0.17 | 83.33 | $ 55,542 | 84,042 | $ 84,000 |
| 10 | Nursing Procedures (1,500 to 2,000 policies & procedures in 2 volumes) | 1,500 | Clinical Coordinator—RN | $ 31.50 | 0.40 | 600.00 | $ 18,900 | | |
| | | 1,500 | Clinical Coordinator—RN | $ 31.50 | 0.40 | 600.00 | $ 18,900 | | |
| | | 1,500 | Clinical Coordinator—RN | $ 31.50 | 0.40 | 600.00 | $ 18,900 | | |
| | | 1,500 | Clinical Educator | $ 26.75 | 0.30 | 450.00 | $ 12,038 | | |
| | | 1,500 | Director of Education | $ 31.50 | 0.25 | 375.00 | $ 11,813 | | |
| | | 1,500 | Chief Nursing Officer | $ 67.50 | 0.25 | 375.00 | $ 25,313 | | |
| | | 1,500 | Secretary | $ 11.00 | 0.25 | 375.00 | $ 4,125 | 109,988 | $ 110,000 |
| 11 | Nutrition Case Management Manual (@ 225 policies) | 200 | Registered Dietitian | $ 21.00 | 1.00 | 200.00 | $ 4,200 | | |
| | | 200 | Director, Dietary Services | $ 25.00 | 0.50 | 100.00 | $ 2,500 | | |
| | | 200 | Secretary | $ 11.00 | 0.25 | 50.00 | $ 550 | | |
| | | 200 | Nutrition Support Committee | $563.00 | 0.25 | 50.00 | $ 28,150 | 35,400 | $ 35,400 |
| 12 | Case Cart/Physician Profiles (OR 1500, day surgery 500-750, Endoscopy 300) | 2,400 | Sterile Processing Director | $ 25.00 | 1.50 | 3,600.00 | $ 90,000 | | |
| | | 2,400 | OR Director | $ 31.00 | 1.50 | 3,600.00 | $111,600 | | |
| | | 2,400 | MD Advisor | $150.00 | 0.25 | 600.00 | $ 90,000 | | |
| | | 2,400 | Secretary | $ 11.00 | 0.25 | 600.00 | $ 6,600 | 298,200 | $ 298,200 |
| 13 | Diagnostic Testing Guidelines (500-600 tests) | 500 | Director of Lab | $ 34.00 | 0.17 | 83.33 | $ 2,833 | | |
| | | 500 | Director of Respiratory Care | $ 31.50 | 0.17 | 83.33 | $ 2,625 | | |
| | | 500 | Secretary | $ 11.00 | 0.25 | 125.00 | $ 1,375 | 4,208 | $ 4,200 |
| 14 | Quality Assurance Manual | 115 | Director of Quality Management | $ 31.50 | 1.00 | 115.00 | $ 3,623 | 3,623 | $ 3,600 |

EXHIBIT 8-3 (continued)

Community Hospital Intellectual Property Materials Including Documents, Reports, Manuals, Policies, and Procedures—Fair Market Value Indication, As of December 31, 1997

| Item | Intellectual Property Materials | Number of Unique Policies, Procedures, or Items (Unit) | Personnel | Recreation Time | | | Cost to Recreate | | |
|---|---|---|---|---|---|---|---|---|---|
| | | | | Loaded Hourly Rate | Per Unit (hours) | Total Time | Recreation Cost | Total Cost | Value Indication |
| 15 | Job Descriptions Manual (Nursing 110; others 350) | 450 | Human Resource Director | $ 36.25 | 0.25 | 112.50 | $ 4,078 | | |
| | | 450 | Human Resource Assistant | $ 23.56 | 0.50 | 225.00 | $ 5,302 | | |
| | | 450 | Employee Health Nurse | $ 27.50 | 0.25 | 112.50 | $ 3,094 | | |
| | | 450 | Occupational Health Nurse | $ 27.50 | 0.25 | 112.50 | $ 3,094 | | |
| | | 450 | Director of Infection Control | $ 31.50 | 0.25 | 112.50 | $ 3,544 | | |
| | | 450 | Director of Quality Management | $ 31.50 | 0.25 | 112.50 | $ 3,544 | | |
| | | 450 | Risk Manager | $ 31.50 | 0.25 | 112.50 | $ 3,544 | | |
| | | 450 | Safety Officer | $ 27.50 | 0.25 | 112.50 | $ 3,094 | | |
| | | 450 | Secretary | $ 11.00 | 0.25 | 112.50 | $ 1,238 | 30,530 | $ 30,500 |
| 16 | By-laws (10-12 meetings 3-4 hours; legal 20-50 hours) | 60 | Medical Records Abstractor | $ 11.00 | 1.00 | 60.00 | $ 660 | | |
| | | 60 | Medical Staff Coordinator | $ 18.25 | 1.00 | 60.00 | $ 1,095 | | |
| | | 60 | Secretary | $ 11.00 | 0.25 | 15.00 | $ 165 | | |
| | | 60 | Bylaw Committee | $677.80 | 1.00 | 60.00 | $40,668 | | |
| | | 80 | Legal Personnel | $250.00 | 1.00 | 80.00 | $20,000 | 62,588 | $ 62,600 |
| 17 | Medical Staff Records (@ 1,500 staff) | 1,500 | Medical Staff Coordinator | $ 18.25 | 6.00 | 9,000.00 | $164,250 | | |
| | | 1,500 | Credentialing Coordinator | $ 17.00 | 4.00 | 6,000.00 | $102,000 | | |
| | | 1,500 | Secretary | $ 11.00 | 0.25 | 375.00 | $ 4,125 | 168,375 | $ 168,400 |
| 18 | Community Hospital Employee Handbook | 1 | Human Resource Director | $ 36.25 | 60.00 | 60.00 | $ 2,175 | | |
| | | 1 | Secretary | $ 11.00 | 20.00 | 20.00 | $ 220 | 2,395 | $ 2,400 |
| 19 | Education Manual | | | | | | | | |
| | a. Programs (@ 14 programs minimum) | 14 | Director of Education | $ 31.50 | 0.50 | 7.00 | $ 221 | | |
| | | 14 | Clinical Educator | $ 26.75 | 1.50 | 21.00 | $ 562 | | |
| | | 14 | Secretary | $ 11.00 | 0.50 | 7.00 | $ 77 | | |
| | | 14 | Education Committee | $210.60 | 0.50 | 7.00 | $ 1,474 | 2,333 | $ 2,300 |
| | b. Competencies (115 departments, 3 self-learning packages) | 345 | Director of Education | $ 31.50 | 1.00 | 345.00 | $10,868 | | |
| | | 345 | Clinical Educator | $ 26.75 | 3.00 | 1,035.00 | $27,686 | | |
| | | 345 | Secretary | $ 11.00 | 0.50 | 172.50 | $ 1,898 | | |
| | | 345 | Education Committee | $210.60 | 0.75 | 258.75 | $54,493 | 94,944 | $ 94,900 |
| | c. Policies (115 departments, 10-20 policies) | 1,150 | Director of Education | $ 31.50 | 0.50 | 575.00 | $18,113 | | |
| | | 1,150 | Clinical Educator | $ 26.75 | 1.50 | 1,725.00 | $46,144 | | |
| | | 1,150 | Secretary | $ 11.00 | 0.25 | 287.50 | $ 3,163 | | |
| | | 1,150 | Education Committee | $210.60 | 0.08 | 95.83 | $20,183 | 87,601 | $ 87,600 |
| 20 | Patient Education Manual (15-20 policies; documentation guidelines; 2,500-3,000 patient education materials) | 1 | Director of Education | $ 31.50 | 30.00 | 30.00 | $ 945 | | |
| | | 2,500 | Clinical Educator | $ 26.75 | 1.00 | 2,500.00 | $66,875 | | |
| | | 1 | Chief Nursing Officer | $ 67.50 | 30.00 | 30.00 | $ 2,025 | | |

Community Hospital Intellectual Property Materials Including Documents, Reports, Manuals, Policies, and Procedures—Fair Market Value Indication, As of December 31, 1997

| Item | Intellectual Property Materials | Number of Unique Policies, Procedures, or Items (Unit) | Personnel | Loaded Hourly Rate | Recreation Time | | Cost to Recreate | | |
|------|----------------------------------|-----|-----------|--------|--------|--------|-----------|-------|-------|
| | | | | | Per Unit (hours) | Total Time | Recreation Cost | Total Cost | Value Indication |
| | | 2,500 | Secretary | $ 11.00 | 0.25 | 625.00 | $ 6,875 | | |
| | | 2,500 | Patient Education Committee | $210.60 | 0.17 | 416.67 | $ 87,750 | | |
| | | 2,500 | Medical Executive Committee | $928.30 | 0.08 | 208.33 | $193,396 | 357,866 | $ 357,900 |
| 21 | Supply Catalog | 300 | Materials Management Director | $ 27.50 | 1.00 | 300.00 | $ 8,250 | | |
| | (3-4 months, 5-8 hours/day) | 200 | Secretary | $ 11.00 | 1.00 | 200.00 | $ 2,200 | | |
| | | 100 | Data Entry Clerk | $ 12.50 | 1.00 | 100.00 | $ 1,250 | | |
| | | 25 | Chief Financial Officer | $ 58.00 | 1.00 | 25.00 | $ 1,450 | 13,150 | $ 13,200 |
| 22 | Equipment Manual | 75 | Director of Engineering | $ 26.25 | 1.00 | 75.00 | $ 1,969 | | |
| | (@ 50-100 policies) | 75 | Safety Officer | $ 27.50 | 0.50 | 37.50 | $ 1,031 | | |
| | | 75 | Secretary | $ 11.00 | 0.25 | 18.75 | $ 206 | | |
| | | 75 | Safety Committee | $302.80 | 0.17 | 12.50 | $ 3,785 | 6,991 | $ 7,000 |
| 23 | Seldom Used Forms Notebook | 100 | Secretary | $ 11.00 | 1.00 | 100.00 | $ 1,100 | | |
| | (project 100 forms) | 100 | Ancillary Department Manager | $ 35.50 | 0.50 | 50.00 | $ 1,775 | 2,875 | $ 2,900 |
| 24 | Patient Business Systems Manual & | 200 | Chief Financial Officer | $ 58.00 | 0.50 | 100.00 | $ 5,800 | | |
| | Accounting Manual | 200 | Financial Analyst | $ 25.50 | 1.00 | 200.00 | $ 5,100 | | |
| | (@ 200-300 policies) | 200 | Secretary | $ 11.00 | 0.25 | 50.00 | $ 550 | 5,650 | $ 5,700 |
| 25 | OR Course | 1 | Director of Education | $ 31.50 | 80.00 | 80.00 | $ 2,520 | | |
| | | 1 | Clinical Educator | $ 26.75 | 200.00 | 200.00 | $ 5,350 | | |
| | | 1 | Chief Nursing Officer | $ 67.50 | 20.00 | 20.00 | $ 1,350 | | |
| | | 1 | Secretary | $ 11.00 | 20.00 | 20.00 | $ 220 | 9,440 | $ 9,400 |
| 26 | Critical Care Course | 1 | Director of Education | $ 31.50 | 80.00 | 80.00 | $ 2,520 | | |
| | | 1 | Clinical Educator | $ 26.75 | 200.00 | 200.00 | $ 5,350 | | |
| | | 1 | Chief Nursing Officer | $ 67.50 | 20.00 | 20.00 | $ 1,350 | | |
| | | 1 | Secretary | $ 11.00 | 20.00 | 20.00 | $ 220 | 9,440 | $ 9,400 |
| | | | | | | | Total | | $3,074,100 |

Fair Market Value Indication (rounded)  $3,070,000

Note that numbers may not total due to rounding.

Notes: 1. All committees involved in this and other manuals are required for the approval of the various policies and procedures developed by the individual personnel listed.

Exhibit 8-3 also summarizes our cost analyses. It estimates the recreation costs for the subject intellectual property materials and the resulting value indication. We have not considered in our analysis the cost of typesetting, printing, and binding the actual number of manuals required in the hospital's 115 departments.

We considered all forms of obsolescence in our cost approach analysis.

We inspected the subject materials, and we found no evidence of physical deterioration.

We interviewed hospital personnel in various departments. We found no evidence of functional obsolescence with regard to the subject materials because the materials are constantly reviewed and updated so they are in compliance with regulatory changes.

Likewise, we observed no evidence of technological obsolescence. The subject materials document the most current systems and procedures used in the hospital.

Finally, we observed no evidence of economic obsolescence. Historically, Community Hospital has been a profitable healthcare institution. In fact, its rate of return on assets is higher than the industry average for hospitals. Therefore, we observed no evidence that Community Hospital was not earning a fair rate of return on the subject intellectual property materials.

Based on our cost approach valuation analysis, the indicated fair market value of the subject intellectual property materials, as of December 31, 1997, is **$3,070,000.**

## SUMMARY

The cost approach is one fundamental way of estimating the value of intangible assets and intellectual properties. There are several cost approach valuation methods, the most common being the reproduction cost method and the replacement cost method. If properly applied (and except for rounding), each cost approach method should eventually result in a similar indication of value.

It is noteworthy that there are elements of market analyses and of income analyses in the cost approach. For example, supply and demand factors in the marketplace determine the current cost of the materials, labor, and overhead associated with the development of the subject intangible asset. The analyst should consider lost income (in the form of an opportunity cost) when estimating the amount of developer's profit and entrepreneurial incentive associated with the intangible asset development project. All of these components of cost should be considered in a rigorous cost approach analysis.

Cost is not necessarily equal to price, and price is not necessarily equal to value. However, the cost approach analysis can provide a reasonable indication of value if all forms of obsolescence are properly identified, quantified, and subtracted from the current cost estimate. Note, however, that the obsolescence that is subtracted from the current cost estimate should relate to the subject intangible asset only. In other words, it is not appropriate (but it is sometimes easy to do) to import obsolescence from any tangible assets that are used with the subject intangible asset and to assign that imported obsolescence to the subject intangible asset. Experienced analysts are careful to assign the obsolescence related to tangible assets to those assets and to assign only the obsolescence related to intangible assets to those assets.

## BIBLIOGRAPHY

Ford, David J. "Intellectual Property Valuation—Part II: Cost and Income Approaches." *CPA Litigation Service Counselor,* March 1998, pp. 3–4

Paulsen, Jon. "Measuring Rods for Intangible Assets." *Mergers & Acquisitions,* Spring 1984, pp. 45–49.

————. "Tax Effect and the Cost Approach." *ASA Valuation,* June 1986, pp. 30–49.

Rabe, James G., and Robert F. Reilly. "Valuation of Intangible Assets for Property Tax Purposes." *National Public Accountant,* April 1994, pp. 26–28+.

————. "Valuing Intangible Assets as Part of a Unitary Assessment." *Journal of Property Tax Management,* Winter 1994, pp. 12–20.

Reilly, Robert F. "Valuing Intangible Assets" (Parts 1 and 2). *CPA Expert,* Winter 1996, pp. 4–6, and Spring 1996, pp. 9–11.

————. "Valuing Intangible Assets—A Case Study." *CPA Expert,* Summer 1996, pp. 11–14.

Reilly, Robert F., and Bruce L. Richman. "Identification and Valuation of Individual Intangible Assets" (Chapter 5). In Bruce L. Richman, ed., *Tax and Financial Planning Strategies in Divorce,* 2d ed. New York: John Wiley & Sons, 1996, pp. 5-1–5-53.

Reilly, Robert F., and Robert P. Schweihs. "Issues in Unit Valuation for Ad Valorem Purposes." *Journal of Property Tax Management,* Fall 1997, pp. 55–67.

# Market Approach Methods

## INTRODUCTION

The market approach to valuing intangible assets is the process by which a market value estimate is derived by analyzing similar intangible assets that have recently been sold or licensed, and then comparing these transactional intangible assets to the subject intangible asset.

While the income approach is the core of valuation theory, actual market transaction data can provide compelling empirical evidence of value. Analysts who habitually revert to the discounted net cash flow method to estimate the value of an intangible asset without researching the market approach are neglecting important valuation information. The market approach is applicable to all types of intangible assets when there are reliable transactions to indicate value patterns or trends in the market. When reliable transactional data are available, the market approach is considered the most direct and systematic approach to value estimation.

When it comes to various licenses granted by the Federal Communication Commission (FCC), such as television or radio broadcast licenses, market transactions can provide meaningful valuation information. Similarly with franchise operations, credit card portfolios, trademarks, insurance expirations, and even professional sports player contracts, market-derived valuation information is often essential.

There is no single marketplace where intangible assets change hands (or are licensed) between buyers and sellers who are well informed and have no special motivations or compulsions to buy or to sell. Nonetheless, transactions involving intangible assets do take place between willing buyers and willing sellers and, after careful research and analysis, they can provide meaningful valuation information.

Market conditions influence what the expected sale or license price will be for an intangible asset and, hence, its value. The analyst should consider factors surrounding historical transactions, especially the timing and the participant-specific influences of those transactions.

Market-derived, empirical data usually have to be arranged, analyzed, selected, reanalyzed, adjusted, and reanalyzed before they can be applied to the valuation of the subject intangible asset. So while applying the market approach may represent an imposing research project, it is an approach that should not be rejected from consideration out of hand.

When applying the market approach to valuing intangible assets, a systematic process is followed. This chapter discusses the quantitative and qualitative application of the basic steps of the general systematic process to the market approach methods. Also in this chapter we discuss individual market approach methods and some of the common errors that are made by analysts when applying those methods.

## COLLECTING, CLASSIFYING, AND VERIFYING DATA

One reason many analysts are reluctant to perform the market approach is because of the challenge of collecting and selecting relevant data. Thoroughly analyzing transactions involving income-producing intangible assets is difficult because information on the economic factors influencing buyers' decisions is not readily available from public records or interviews with buyers and sellers.

In some transactions, the intangible asset may represent only one component of a transaction in which the total price reflects real estate, machinery, and an assembled workforce. Rapidly changing economic conditions and legislation may also limit the applicability of the market approach.

To apply the market approach, an analyst gathers data on sales, licences, contracts, offers, refusals, options, and listings of intangible assets considered competitive with, and comparative to, the subject intangible asset. Data on completed transactions are, of course, considered the most reliable value indicators.

The analyst should identify the property rights being conveyed in each comparative transaction as precisely as possible. The transaction price is dependent upon the bundle of rights being conveyed. With sufficient information, the analyst can make adjustments as necessary to reflect the difference between intangible assets licensed at market rates and those licensed below or above market levels. The duration of a license and other terms of the license agreement influence the income generated and the value of the licensed asset.

The transaction price of one intangible asset may differ from that of an identical intangible asset due to different financing arrangements. For example, the licensor of a comparable or guideline intangible asset may have committed to providing advertising or technical expertise to further develop the income-producing capacity of a trademark. In another case, the licensee may have specifically accepted financial responsibility for those activities.

Often it is difficult to obtain third-party royalty rate data, which may constitute proprietary trade secret information. Sometimes, however, the owner or potential buyer may know about previous licensing transactions involving the same intangible asset or another in the family of intangible assets, and these transactions can provide compelling data.

The definition of market value generally involves cash equivalent terms (provided the relevant market operates on cash equivalent terms). In cash equivalency analysis, the analyst investigates the market transactions of comparable or guideline intangible assets that appear to have been transferred with nonmarket financing to determine whether adjustments to reflect typical market terms are warranted. Conditions of sale may reveal other noneconomic interests on the part of buyers and sellers.

Comparable or guideline sales that occurred under different market conditions from those applicable to the intangible subject on the valuation date require adjustment for any differences that affect values. An adjustment for market conditions might be necessary if, since the time the comparable sales were transacted, intangible asset values have increased or decreased because investors' perceptions of the market have changed.

Adjustments for the conditions surrounding the sale might be appropriate in order to properly reflect the motivations of the buyer and the seller. A buyer may pay more than market value for an intangible asset needed in order for the buyer to capitalize on a unique market condition. A sale may be transacted at a below-market price if the seller needs cash in a hurry. Affiliated corporate entities may record a sale at a nonmarket price in order to serve unique business purposes. Family members may transact at nonmarket levels in order to protect a legacy.

Circumstances surrounding a transaction should be thoroughly researched before the transaction is used in comparative analyses.

## ESTABLISHING AND APPLYING PRICING MULTIPLES

The elements of comparison include all attributes of the intangible asset.

At least ten basic elements of comparison have been identified as requiring careful consideration when selecting and analyzing guideline sales or license transactions:

1. The bundle of legal rights of intangible asset ownership conveyed in the guideline transaction.
2. The existence of any special financing terms or arrangements (e.g., between the buyer and the seller).
3. The existence, or absence, of arm's-length sale conditions.
4. The economic conditions existing in the appropriate secondary market at the time of the guideline sale or license transactions.
5. The industry in which the intangible asset will be used.
6. The geographic or territorial characteristics of the guideline sale or license transactions compared to the subject intangible asset.
7. The term or duration characteristics of the guideline sale or license transactions compared to the subject intangible asset.
8. The use, exploitation, or obsolescence characteristics of the guideline sale or license transactions compared to the subject intangible asset.
9. The economic characteristics of the guideline sale or license transactions compared to the subject intangible asset (i.e., who is responsible for continued development, commercialization, or legal protection of the intangible asset.)
10. The inclusion of other assets in the guideline sale or license transactions. (This may include the sale of a bundle or a portfolio of assets that could include marketing assistance, trademarks, product development, or other contractual rights).

Comparative analysis focuses on similarities and differences among intangible assets and transactions that may affect value. These may include differences in property rights appraised, the motivations of buyers and sellers, financing terms, market conditions at the time of sale (the comparative numbers of buyers, sellers, and lenders), size, attributes, and economic characteristics. Elements of comparison may need to be tested against market evidence in order to estimate which elements are sensitive to change and how they affect value.

A "value measure" is usually a multiple computed by dividing the price of the guideline transaction as of the valuation date by some relevant economic variable observed or calculated from the guideline transaction's financial statements. Other value measures are based upon projections of next year's earnings, or market potential (e.g., cable TV operations are sometimes measured on the basis of price per subscriber).

Income statement variables are measured over one or more periods of time. The income statement variables most often used to develop intangible asset value measures from guideline transactions are the following:

- Average selling price.
- Average unit volume.
- Net sales.

- Net income before or after tax.
- Gross cash flow (net income plus noncash charges).
- Net cash flow.

All the performance variables and time periods may have various other permutations, depending on the availability and relevance of data.

Occasionally, balance sheet data can be used to develop intangible asset value measures. These kinds of value measures are developed by dividing the price as of the valuation date by the balance sheet variables as of a date as close as possible preceding the valuation date for which both guideline transaction and subject company data are available. Balance sheet variables typically used include:

- Depreciated original cost.
- Book value.
- Adjusted book value.

Unlike income statement variables, asset value variables normally are measured only at the latest practical point in time.

Other ways of developing value measures that can be applied to the subject intangible in the market approach are frequency of use, market potential, and units of production.

## Frequency of Use

The value of an intangible asset can be dependent upon the fact that the asset is an inherent part of a process, and the process could not be completed without the intangible asset. Sometimes one particular engineering drawing is used repetitively in designing or operating a manufacturing process. The value of the drawing may depend more on its frequency of use than its cost to create. In this case, the drawing's value might be measured in terms of its price per use.

## Market Potential

Cable television franchise transactions or cellular telephone franchise transactions are sometimes described in terms of their price per subscriber, price per home passed, or price per population. In these situations, the price of a guideline transaction is expressed in terms of the existing customer base, the number of potential customers who could subscribe to cable TV without additional wiring to reach those customers, and the number of potential customers living within the franchise territory.

The number of patients within a reasonable geographic area of a hospital or other health facility might provide a value measure related to market potential.

These value measures indicate that the price of the guideline transaction is a function of the seller's experience in penetrating the available market and the buyer's potential for market share growth.

## Units of Production

The price of some intangible asset transactions is described as being based more on units of production than on the intangible's ability to generate income. The value of a proprietary engineering process technology might be expressed in terms of its ability to increase output by 50 units per hour over a competing process, for example. The analyst may be able to use this information as a valid measure of value. The intangible asset analyst may use this information by extrapolating the superior yield over the subject company's various production facilities as a cost savings estimate or in valuing the proprietary technology as part of a collection of services in a licensing scenario.

Comparative analysis includes the consideration of both quantitative and qualitative factors, and identifies which elements of comparison affect intangible asset values in the relevant market. When quantitative analytical techniques are applied, mathematical processes are used to identify which elements of comparison require adjustment and to measure the amount of these adjustments.

Relative qualitative analysis studies the relationships indicated by market data without recourse to quantification. In carrying out the qualitative adjustment process, the analyst compares transaction data to determine whether the comparable or guideline transaction's characteristics are inferior, superior, or equal to those of the subject intangible asset. The analyst might rank the transaction data in descending or ascending order. Specific value trends can sometimes be recognized. The analyst determines the relative position of the subject intangible asset in the array and selects the pricing multiple.

In the absence of a compelling reason to do otherwise, the time period most commonly used for analysis of operating data is five years. This conventional time period should not, however, be blindly and mechanistically adopted as the relevant time period.

For a cyclical industry, a complete economic cycle for that industry is widely considered to be a good choice of time period from which to develop average operating results to be used as the basis for value measures. On occasion, averages of data for as long as ten years might be relevant.

Sometimes the relevant time period is constrained by major changes that affect either the subject intangible asset or the industry as a whole. Such events may render comparative financial data before such changes irrelevant for valuation purposes. In these cases, it may only be relevant to use one or a few years' comparative data.

Also, if the historical data include an aberration that is so clearly extraordinary or nonrecurring for either the intangible asset's relevant market or the industry, one option is to omit those data when computing the value measures, unless one can clearly isolate and adjust for the aberrant event. In such cases, however, the data normally are tabulated and presented and the reason for omitting that year from the value measure calculations is explained.

In the sales transaction method, guideline transaction dates are whenever they occurred and not necessarily on the selected valuation date. This creates the additional problem of adjusting for differences in conditions between the guideline transaction dates and the subject effective valuation date. If enough transactions are available, the analyst may wish to omit those that occurred when economic conditions were significantly different rather than try to make drastic adjustments to account for the differences. A common way to adjust for time differences is through either industry average stock price differences or industry average differences in valuation multiples, such as price–earnings multiples. Generally, adjusting for industry valuation multiples is more effective than adjusting for industry price indexes if the subject and guideline intangible assets are similar in terms of profitability and other operating characteristics. However, it should be recognized that the relation between market multiples and acquisition multiples varies over time.

Typically, whatever time period is used for gathering and presenting data is also used for both income statement and balance sheet data. Value measures based on income statement data are typically computed by dividing the valuation date price by the income variables or averages of variables for one or a number of prior periods, usually (but not necessarily) years. Value measures based on balance sheet variables (e.g., price–book value) are typically computed by dividing the valuation date price by the most recent balance sheet variable. The reason for collecting and presenting several years of balance sheet information is to identify and interpret comparative trends among the guideline and subject intangible assets, although the earlier years' balance sheet data usually are not used directly in the computation of value measures.

## ALTERNATIVE MARKET APPROACH METHODS

### Sales Transaction Method

This method estimates the value of the subject intangible asset based upon actual market transactions—that is, the sale of comparable or guideline intangible assets to independent third parties in arm's-length transactions. When data are available, this is considered the most direct and systematic approach to value estimation.

The first step in the analysis is an assessment of the relative economic strengths and weaknesses of each individual market observation and of the subject intangible asset.

The second step is the identification and quantification of adjustment factors related to the differences between the market observations (i.e., comparable or guideline transactions) and the subject intangible asset.

In the third step in the analysis, valuation multiples are estimated and applied to the appropriate subject intangible asset financial parameter (e.g., sales operating profit, cost, subscribers) in order to estimate the value indication via the sales transaction method.

### Relief from Royalty Method

This method is sometimes considered an income approach valuation method, because the estimated royalty income is capitalized to reach an indication of value. This method is also sometimes referred to as a cost approach method, because the value of the subject intangible asset is estimated by reference to the royalty cost the owner is relieved from having to pay had the intangible asset been licensed from a third party.

In the relief from royalty method, the subject intangible asset is valued by reference to the amount of royalty income it would generate if the intangible asset was instead licensed in an arm's-length transaction. In using this method, arm's-length royalty or license agreements are analyzed. The licensing transactions selected should reflect similar risk and return investment characteristics that make them comparative to the subject intangible asset.

The net revenues expected to be generated by the subject intangible asset from all sources during its expected remaining life are then multiplied by the selected benchmark royalty rate. The product is an estimate of the royalty income that could hypothetically be generated by licensing the subject intangible asset.

The estimated royalty stream, which the owner is relieved from paying since the intangible asset is already owned, is capitalized. This results in an indication of the value of owning the intangible asset.

The relief from royalty method requires the subject intangible asset to generate some identifiable stream of economic income so the analyst can apply the royalty compensation formula (e.g., a percent of revenue, a percent of gross profits, etc.) derived from the guideline license agreements.

In the valuation analysis related to the relief from royalty method, the following procedures are typically performed:

1. Assess the terms of each guideline license agreement with special consideration of the following terms:
   a. The description of the bundle of legal rights for the guideline licensed property.
   b. The description of any maintenance required for the guideline intangible property (e.g., product advertising, product enhancements, quality controls).
   c. The effective date of the guideline license agreement.
   d. The termination date of the guideline license agreement.
   e. The degree of exclusivity of the guideline license agreement.
2. Assess the current status of the industry and the associated relevant markets and prospective trends.
3. Estimate an appropriate market-derived capitalization rate.
4. Apply the market-derived capitalization rate to the appropriate economic income measure with respect to the subject intangible asset in order to arrive at an indication of value.

## Comparative Income Differential Method

In some circumstances, information gathered from the market may permit the analyst to compare the income generated by two similar operations—one that operates with an intangible asset and one without. When these two operations consistently generate significantly different income, the value of the intangible asset can be estimated using the comparative income differential method.

This method may be applicable to intangibles such as franchise agreements, proprietary technology, trade names, and patents, to name a few.

The following represent typical comparative income differential method procedures:

1. Estimate the projected normalized economic income differential associated with the use of the subject intangible asset.
2. Apply the market-derived capitalization rate to the estimate of prospective economic income differential in order to conclude an indication of the value of the subject intangible asset.

## Rules of Thumb

Some industries have rules of thumb (sometimes given an aura of credibility by being referred to as industry valuation formulas) about how intangible assets in their industry are valued for transfer purposes. On the one hand, if such rules of thumb are widely disseminated and referenced in the industry, the analyst probably should not ignore them. On the other hand, there usually is no credible evidence of how such rules were developed or how well they actually comport to actual transaction data.

Rules of thumb are usually quite simplistic. As such they obscure many important details. They fail to account for how differences in either operating characteristics or assets from one company to another affect the valuation. They also fail to differentiate changes in conditions for companies in various industries from one time period to another.

Furthermore, it is common for intangible assets employed in many industries to sell or be licensed on terms other than cash, so the "prices" generated by the rules of thumb often are not cash equivalent values. The terms may vary considerably from one transaction to another. Consequently, rules of thumb should rarely, if ever, be used without considering other, more reliable valuation methods.

## Market Replacement Cost Method

This method contemplates the replacement cost of the intangible asset in the open market. While the traditional replacement cost method begins with the internal records of the intangible asset's owner, this method considers estimates of the replacement cost of the intangible asset by knowledgeable outsiders. If objective arm's-length estimates can be obtained, they may lead to a reliable market-derived estimate of the intangible asset's replacement cost. From the point of determining the replacement cost estimate, the subsequent procedures described in the cost approach (i.e., analyzing obsolescence factors that differentiate the subject intangible asset's characteristics from its replacement cost) should be followed.

## APPLICATIONS AND LIMITATIONS OF THE MARKET APPROACH
## Standard of Value

While the market approach can be used in conjunction with any standard of value, it is generally most applicable when the standard of value is fair market value. By definition, the method is based on making comparisons between the subject intangible asset and reliable sales transactions. Fair market value is the standard of value in most taxation-related valuation assignments.

Investment value is the standard of value that could depart the most from the value developed by a strict application of the sales transaction method. The sales transaction method is expected to develop a value based on a consensus of market participants, as evidenced by their intangible asset transactions. Investment value, by definition, is the value to a particular buyer or seller. Therefore, the income approach gives more opportunity for a specific party to project economic income flows and use discount and capitalization rates that are appropriate to his or her individual investment criteria.

Even a party primarily interested in investment value of an intangible asset, however, generally wants to have some notion of what a consensus value would be. Furthermore, the analyst interested in investment value can always adjust the financial variables on a pro forma basis reflecting anticipated changes in the subject intangible asset financial performance and then use the sales transaction method to see the sensitivity of market value to various possible changes in the financial variables.

In almost all cases, the market prices intangible assets in accordance with their anticipated contribution to the value of a going-concern business. Unless there is evidence to the contrary, the market approach methods are expected to produce a value on the premise that the subject intangible is expected to be used as part of a going concern.

## Marketability

Marketability of individual intangible assets, or the lack of marketability, is often an issue that is not totally black or white. The full value of most intangible asset ownership positions depends upon the intangible's fit as part of a collection of other assets and capital components.

When intangible assets are to be valued separately from the other assets necessary for the full exploitation of the intangible, a valuation adjustment to reflect marketability may be appropriate. When analyzing market data, the analyst should remember that the guideline transactions represent the results of a successful effort to transfer the intangible. If there is no intention to transfer the subject intangible, a lack of marketability adjustment may be warranted.

## Control versus Fractional Interests

Unlike shares of stock, the valuation of fractional ownership interests in intangible assets is a less common and therefore a more cumbersome problem.

When valuing fractional ownership interests in intangible assets, it may be preferred to apply the market approach by using only guideline fractional interest transactions. However, the practical reality is that there are far more reliable guideline controlling sales transaction data available than there are data on minority interests.

It is sometimes useful to use the guideline sales transaction method even when valuing fractional interests. This usually requires some adjustment from the sales transaction method equivalent to account for the lack of control.

Generally, owners of a fractional interest in an intangible asset enjoy fewer rights if they are dissatisfied with the management of the intangible asset than do fractional interest owners in corporations or partnerships. As a consequence, discounts from a pro rata portion of the value of 100 percent ownership of the property taken as a whole are generally greater for fractional ownership interests in intangible assets than for minority ownership interests in corporations or partnerships.

## Deal Structure

It is common for the deal price used to develop a value measure to be expressed as a cash or cash equivalent price. In many transactions, the consideration paid is (all or partly) something other than cash, such as equity, notes, services, joint venture interests, and so on. The cash value of such consideration is often less than its face value. When using a guideline transaction in which the consideration was not paid entirely in cash, the analyst should make the best possible effort to convert the noncash components of the consideration paid to their cash equivalent value.

When intangible assets are sold, the deal is sometimes structured as a sale of a collection of assets. In such circumstances, it is important to know exactly what assets were sold and what liabilities were assumed. In addition to the fact that off-balance-sheet assets or liabilities may have been included in the transaction, the income tax ramifications of an asset sale are usually considerably different from those for a stock sale. Differences in the deal structure between the guideline transactions and the contemplated subject transaction should be noted and adjusted (or otherwise accounted for) appropriately in developing value measures.

## Reconciliation of Value Indications

If two or more market approach methods are used, the analyst should reconcile at least two value indications. In the sales transaction method, for example, the analysis of each transaction produces an adjusted price that provides an indication of value for each relevant statistic. When the sales transactions are considered together, the various units of comparison may also produce different value indications (e.g., price to gross revenue, price to net revenue, price to cost savings). The analyst often resolves multiple value indications derived from various market approach methods as part of the application of the market approach. This may be done as the market approach value indication is determined, or the analyst may do it after reviewing the entire appraisal, including the results of the cost approach and the income approach.

Reconciling the results from various market approach methods requires recognizing differences in data, techniques, judgment, and the intended use of the analysis.

While the market approach to valuing intangible assets may not be of primary importance in arriving at a value conclusion in every intangible asset appraisal assignment, the results of the research of the market may nevertheless be useful in the value reconciliation process.

### DATA SOURCES

Sources of price and underlying financial data on privately arranged intangible asset transactions are more expensive and less consistent in content and reliability than public market disclosures. Data on intangible asset transactions vary tremendously in scope and format. When publicly held companies are involved in material transactions, the participants submit disclosure documents. Data on acquisitions involving asset transactions (whether considered material or not) are not subject to the consistent reporting requirements of the SEC and the accounting profession.

Nevertheless, some reliable information about intangible asset transactions may be obtained from disclosure filings, the news media, and business intermediaries (e.g., business brokers and investment bankers).

An amazing variety of reporting services, newsletters, and on-line databases utilize information from disclosure filings, company announcements, the media, and business intermediaries to provide extensive, organized analyses of transactions as they unfold. General business indexes and news databases can be useful in conducting research, but errors and inconsistencies may occur. Viewing original source documents is the only guarantee of absolute accuracy.

The quantity and quality of relevant data available to implement an approach will have an important bearing on its usefulness. As noted earlier, there are more transaction data sources than most people realize and it is important to search them out. Chapter 5 listed some general reference sources. The chapters on specific types of intangible assets (Part V) list data sources for those types of intangibles assets. Licensing periodicals, such as *Licensing Economics Review,* provide data on licensing transactions involving intangible assets. In addition, the following sources often provide useful information for selecting guideline intangible assets:

1. Company data of industry participants using guideline intangible assets:
   a. SEC reports from EDGAR (Electronic Data Gathering and Retrieval), including 10Ks and 10Qs.
   b. Standard & Poor's Corporation publicly traded security database.
   c. Disclosure Compact D/SEC publicly traded security database.
   d. Dialog Information Services.
   e. Moody's *Corporate Profiles.*
   f. *Company Intelligence.*
2. Economic income data with respect to the industry in which the guideline and subject intangible assets operate:
   a. *Industrial Outlook.*
   b. Industry trade journals and publications.
   c. *Standard & Poor's Industry Reports.*
   d. Financial periodicals.

Court case decisions concerning similar intangibles (e.g., U.S. Tax Court cases, patent and trademark infringement cases, and international and interstate transfer pricing cases) often provide useful information as well.

We usually would not reject the market approach just because we were not completely satisfied with either the number or the degree of comparability of available guideline transactions. In the final analysis, the quantity and quality of the guideline transaction data compared to the quantity and quality of data available for other methods influences the weight accorded the method in correlating the results of various methods and reaching a value conclusion.

## SUMMARY

The market approach to valuing intangible assets is the process by which a market value estimate is derived by analyzing similar intangible assets that have recently been sold or licensed, and then comparing those intangible assets to the subject intangible asset. This chapter discussed the quantitative and qualitative application of the basic steps of the general systematic process to the market approach methods.

Accurately applying the market approach to valuing intangible assets can often provide a compelling estimate of value.

In practice, analysts sometimes ignore the market approach because of the amount of research required in its application. Guideline sales and license transactions need to be identified and analyzed in order to measure the following factors related to the subject intangible asset:

- Economic income (or costs), without double-counting.
- Risk associated with achieving the economic income.
- Expected remaining useful life (or contract life).

Several methods for generating an indication of the value of an intangible asset by relying on the market approach were discussed, including the sales transaction method, the relief from royalty method, the comparative income differential method, and the market replacement cost method.

## BIBLIOGRAPHY

Battersby, Gregory J., and Charles W. Grimes. *An Insider's Guide to Royalty Rates: A Comprehensive Survey of Royalty Rates and Licensed Products.* Stamford, CN: Kent Press, 1996.

Ford, David J. "Intellectual Property Valuation—Part I: Market Approach." *CPA Litigation Service Counselor,* February 1998, pp. 1–3.

Mullen, Maggie. "How to Value Intangibles." *Accountancy,* November 1993, pp. 92–94.

Paulsen, Jon. "Measuring Rods for Intangible Assets." *Mergers & Acquisitions,* Spring 1984, pp. 45–49.

Rabe, James G., and Robert F. Reilly. "Valuation of Intangible Assets for Property Tax Purposes." *National Public Accountant,* April 1994, pp. 26–28+.

———. "Valuing Intangible Assets as Part of a Unitary Assessment." *Journal of Property Tax Management,* Winter 1994, pp. 12–20.

Reilly, Robert F. "Valuing Intangible Assets" (Parts 1 and 2). *CPA Expert,* Winter 1996, pp. 4–6, and Spring 1996, pp. 9–11.

———. "Valuing Intangible Assets—A Case Study." *CPA Expert,* Summer 1996, pp. 11–14.

Reilly, Robert F., and Bruce L. Richman. "Identification and Valuation of Individual Intangible Assets" (Chapter 5). In Bruce L. Richman, ed., *Tax and Financial Planning Strategies in Divorce,* 2d ed. New York: John Wiley & Sons, 1996, pp. 5-1–5-53.

Reilly, Robert F., and Robert P. Schweihs. "Issues in Unit Valuation for Ad Valorem Purposes." *Journal of Property Tax Management,* Fall 1997, pp. 55–67.

Smith, Gordon. *Valuation of Intellectual Property and Intangible Assets.* New York: John Wiley & Sons, 1994, supplemented annually.

# Income Approach Methods

## INTRODUCTION

This chapter discusses the components and the mechanics of the income approach to the valuation and economic analysis of intangible assets. Most of this chapter focuses on the three principal components of the income approach:

1. The estimation of economic income.
2. The estimation of the projection period.
3. The estimation of the appropriate income capitalization rate.

A number of analytical procedures are applicable to each of these three components of the income approach.

In addition to the practical application of the income approach, we include considerable discussion with regard to the theoretical development and the conceptual underpinnings of the income approach methods. Arguably, the income approach methods are the most frequently used methods in the valuation and economic analysis of intangible assets. We specifically discuss the particular pros and cons of the income approach methods.

With regard to general applicability, the analyst should be aware that income approach methods are adaptable to virtually any type of intangible asset analysis, including:

1. Appraisal of various defined values (e.g., market value, use value, investment value, etc.).
2. Estimation of the appropriate transfer price or royalty rate (e.g., intercompany, intracompany, license agreement, etc.).
3. Analysis of damages (e.g., effects of various actions or inactions on the value, market share, pricing, etc. of an intangible asset).
4. Analysis of intangible asset value increment—or decrement—due to alternative strategic plans (e.g., alternative levels of investment, commercialization, pricing, operational synergies, etc.).
5. Assessment of the fairness of an intangible asset transaction (sale or license) structure, terms, pricing, and so on.

Also with regard to general applicability, the analyst should be aware that income approach methods are adaptable to most categories or types of intangible assets. While market approach and cost approach methods have particular applicability with regard to certain categories of intangibles, the income approach methods have general applicability to virtually all categories of intangible assets and intellectual properties.

In particular, we discuss and illustrate the applicability of income approach methods to mass intangible assets (sometimes called group or collective intangible assets). These situations involve the collective analysis of hundreds or even thousands of customers, contracts, brands, licenses, franchises, and so on. In the analysis of, say, a thousand customers (or patients, subscribers, members, etc.), we compare and contrast the procedures for valuing each customer relationship individually versus valuing the group of customer relationships collectively.

We also compare and contrast the income approach methods for the valuation of intangible assets to the income approach methods for the valuation of businesses and securities. As we will see, there are numerous conceptual similarities between these two sets of income approach methods. However, it is more important for analysts to understand the conceptual and procedural differences—both obvious and subtle—between intangible asset analysis and business enterprise valuation.

Finally, we present several examples of the application of income approach methods. The examples help to illustrate the impact of several of the conceptual issues regarding intangible asset analysis, such as: How do we isolate one portion of an enterprise's income and associate it with a single intangible? Should the analysis be performed on a before-tax basis or an after-tax basis? What measure of income and what projection period are most relevant to a particular intangible asset?

## INCOME APPROACH METHODS

As we will see, there are numerous analytical procedures within the income approach. Likewise, there are numerous ways to measure the amount of economic income associated with a particular intangible asset. Nonetheless, all of the analytical procedures and all of the alternative measures of income can be grouped into two categories of income approach methods:

1. Yield capitalization method.
2. Direct capitalization method.

We consider the procedural differences between these two categories of methods. However, the conceptual similarities between these two categories of methods may be more noteworthy than the procedural differences between them.

Both the yield capitalization method and the direct capitalization method share a common conceptual basis: The value of an intangible asset is the present value of the expected economic income associated with the ownership, use, or forbearance of that intangible asset. The two methods employ different mechanical procedures in order to quantify that present value. Nonetheless, both methods strive to quantify the present value of expected economic income. Accordingly, both the yield capitalization method and the direct capitalization method can be applied to the valuation and economic analysis of the same intangible asset. If they are both applied correctly, both analytical methods will reach approximately the same valuation conclusion (after consideration for rounding) for the same intangible asset.

## Yield Capitalization Method

The definition of the yield capitalization method of intangible asset valuation is: *The present value of a nonconstant stream of projected economic income flows over a discrete time period.*

The first step in the yield capitalization method is the estimation of an appropriate measurement of economic income to be used in the valuation analysis. Numerous alternative measures of economic income can be used in the yield capitalization method.

The second step in the yield capitalization method is the estimation of the remaining expected term of the economic income projection. In other words, this step encompasses the estimation of the expected remaining useful life of the subject intangible asset. The expected remaining useful life becomes the discrete period of time over which the economic income is projected.

The third step in the yield capitalization method is the estimation of a discrete economic income projection. In this projection, a specific flow of economic income is estimated for each particular period in the term of the projection. The selected term for the time period could be monthly, quarterly, or annually; however, the selection of an annual time period is the most common. In the yield capitalization method, the economic income projections may be *nonconstant*—that is, there is a different amount of economic income projected in the different periods. If the economic income projections are constant (or change at a constant rate) over the projection period, then the yield capitalization method becomes mathematically identical to the direct capitalization method.

The fourth step in the yield capitalization method is the estimation of the appropriate present value discount rate—also called the yield capitalization rate—that is used to convert the series of projected economic income to a present value. The selected present value discount rate has to be consistent with:

1. The risk of the subject intangible asset actually generating the projected level of economic income; the greater the probability that the subject intangible will generate a level of economic income different (i.e., higher or lower) from the specific projection, the greater the appropriate present value discount rate.

2. The measure of economic income included in the projection; for example: a before-tax measure of income requires a before-tax discount rate; a measure of income to the equity component of the intangible asset requires an equity-derived present value discount rate; and so forth.

The fifth step in the yield capitalization method is to reach an indication of the value of the subject intangible asset. The value indication is reached by calculating the present value of the projected economic income stream over the expected term of the economic income, at the selected present value discount rate.

## Simplified Yield Capitalization Method Example

The following example illustrates a simplified application of the yield capitalization method. The individual procedures in this method are described later in the chapter.

The objective of this illustrative analysis is to estimate the value of a customer list intangible asset.

| Item | Projection Variable Component | Projection Variable Estimate |
|---|---|---|
| 1 | Projected next year revenue specifically related to the subject customer list | $3,000,000 |
| 2 | Gross profit margin and operating expenses related to sales from the subject customer list | Based on management projections |
| 3 | Projected revenue growth rate | 5% |
| 4 | Present value discount rate | 18% |
| 5 | Effective income tax rate | 36% |

| 6 | Average remaining useful life of the subject customer list | 4 years |
|---|---|---|
| 7 | Depreciation expense (the amount that is included in the cost of sales and/or operating expenses), capital expenditures, and additional net working capital investments | Based on management projections |
| 8 | Capital charge on the associated assets (equals the market-derived rate of return times the value of all tangible and intangible assets used or used up in the production of the economic income generated from the subject customer list) | Based on a function analysis of the associated assets |

The yield capitalization method valuation analysis is illustrated as follows:

| | (in $000s) | | | |
|---|---|---|---|---|
| Projection Variable | Year 1 | Year 2 | Year 3 | Year 4 |
| Revenue | 3,000 | 3,150 | 3,308 | 3,473 |
| − Cost of sales | 1,732 | 1,780 | 1,856 | 1,963 |
| = Gross profit margin | 1,268 | 1,370 | 1,452 | 1,510 |
| − Operating expenses | 1,056 | 1,141 | 1,209 | 1,258 |
| = Earnings before interest and taxes | 212 | 229 | 243 | 252 |
| − Income tax expense | 76 | 82 | 87 | 91 |
| = Predebt net income | 136 | 147 | 156 | 161 |
| + Annual depreciation expense | 40 | 42 | 44 | 46 |
| − Projected capital expenditures | 44 | 46 | 48 | 50 |
| − Additional net working capital investments | 32 | 34 | 36 | 38 |
| − Capital charge on the associated tangible and intangible assets | 60 | 56 | 52 | 48 |
| = Economic income—that is, net cash flow | 40 | 53 | 64 | 71 |
| × Present value discount factor (based on 18% present value discount rate assuming midyear compounding convention) | 0.917 | 0.777 | 0.659 | 0.558 |
| = Discounted net cash flow | 37 | 41 | 42 | 40 |
| **Indicated value of the subject customer list** | | | | **$ 160** |

## Direct Capitalization Method

The definition of the direct capitalization method of intangible asset valuation is: *The capitalization (meaning the division by an appropriate rate of return) of a constant or a constantly changing stream of economic income flows over a specific time period.*

The first step in the direct capitalization method is the estimation of an appropriate measurement of economic income to be used in the valuation or economic analysis. As with the yield capitalization method, numerous alternative measures of economic income can be used in a direct capitalization analysis.

The second step in the direct capitalization method is the estimation of the remaining expected term of the economic income projection. In other words, this step encompasses the estimation of the expected remaining useful life of the subject intangible asset. Some inexperienced analysts believe that it is not necessary to consider remaining useful life when using the direct capitalization method. This is simply not correct.

Some inexperienced analysts also believe that direct capitalization can only be used when the economic income stream can be projected in perpetuity. In other words, direct capitalization can only be used when the expected remaining useful life of the subject intangible asset equals infinity. This is not correct either.

However, it is true that the direct capitalization method can only be used when the projected income stream represents either an annuity or a perpetuity. An annuity is an income stream that is constant (or changing at a constant rate) over a finite period of time. A perpetuity is an income stream that is constant (or changing at a constant rate) over an infinite period of time. Direct capitalization certainly works when the projected income stream is a perpetuity—that is, when the expected remaining useful life of the subject intangible is infinity. Direct capitalization also works when the projected income stream is an annuity—that is, when the expected remaining useful life of the subject intangible is finite (i.e., less than infinity).

Therefore, the direct capitalization method does require an analysis and estimation of remaining useful life. If the analyst uses a perpetuity capitalization rate in the direct capitalization method, then the analyst is implicitly (and perhaps incorrectly) assuming an infinite remaining useful life for the subject intangible. Remaining useful life analysis is discussed in detail in Chapters 11 and 12.

The third step in the direct capitalization method is the estimation of the economic income projection. In order to use direct capitalization, the economic income projection should be either:

1. Constant (i.e., the same in either period) either for a finite number of periods or for an infinite number of periods.
2. Constantly changing (i.e., changing by a constant rate each period), either for a finite number of periods or for an infinite number of periods.

If the change in the income projection is not a constant rate of change, then the direct capitalization method cannot be used. For example, if the income projection changes by a different percentage each period, then direct capitalization does not apply. Also, if the income projection changes by a constant dollar amount—but not by a constant percentage—then direct capitalization cannot be used. In those instances, the yield capitalization method should be used.

The fourth step in the direct capitalization method is the estimation of the appropriate direct capitalization rate. The direct capitalization rate is used to convert the projected economic income to a present value. As we will see, the direct capitalization rate includes a growth rate factor. The growth rate factor allows the rate of change of the economic income projection to be positive, negative, or zero.

The fifth step in the direct capitalization method is to reach an indication of the value of the subject intangible asset. The indication of value is reached by calculating the present value of the projected economic income stream over the expected term of the economic income, at the selected direct capitalization rate.

## Simplified Direct Capitalization Method Example

The following example illustrates a simplified application of the direct capitalization method. The individual procedures in this method are described later in this chapter.

The objective of this illustrative analysis is to estimate the value of a customer list intangible asset.

| Item | Projection Variable Component | Projection Variable Estimate |
|------|------------------------------|------------------------------|
| 1 | Projected next year revenue specifically related to the subject customer list | $3,000,000 |
| 2 | Gross profit margin and operating expenses related to sales from the subject customer list | Based on management projections |
| 3 | Projected economic income (i.e., net cash flow) growth rate | 10% |
| 4 | Present value discount rate | 18% |
| 5 | Effective income tax rate | 36% |
| 6 | Depreciation expense, capital expenditures and additional net working capital investments | Based on management projections |
| 7 | Capital charge on the associated assets (equals the market-derived rate of return times the value of all of the tangible and intangible assets used or used up in the production of the economic income generated from the subject customer list) | Based on a functional analysis of the associated assets |
| 8 | Average remaining life of customers | 4 years |
| 9 | Direct capitalization factor— the present value of an annuity factor for 8%—that is, the 18% discount rate less the 10% projected growth rate—for 4 years using mid-year convention (from Exhibit 10-1) | 6.733 times |

The direct capitalization method valuation analysis is illustrated as follows:

| Projection Variable | Next Period Projection ($000s) |
|---|---|
| Revenue | 3,000 |
| − Cost of sales | 1,732 |
| = Gross profit margin | 1,268 |
| − Operating expenses | 1,056 |
| = Earnings before interest and taxes | 212 |
| − Income tax expense | 76 |
| = Pre-debt net income | 136 |
| + Annual depreciation expense | 40 |
| − Capital expenditures | 44 |
| − Additional net working capital investments | 32 |
| − Average (or normalized) capital charge on the associated tangible and intangible assets | 54 |
| = Economic income—that is, net cash flow | 46 |
| ÷ Half for midyear convention | 2 |
| = Net cash flow each midyear period | 23 |
| × Capitalization factor (based on 8% direct capitalization rate for 4 years assuming mid-year compounding convention) | 6.733 |
| Indicated value of the subject customer list | $ 155 |
| **Indicated value of the subject customer list (rounded)** | **$ 160** |

## Components of the Income Approach

There are three fundamental components to every income approach valuation analysis. The three fundamental components are: 1) projection of economic income subject to capitalization, 2) estimation of the time period over which to project the economic income, and 3) selection of the appropriate risk-adjusted capitalization rate. The mechanics of the application of the three components varies somewhat between the yield capitalization method and the direct capitalization method. However, the same three fundamental components relate to both categories of income approach methods.

### Income Component

As we will discuss shortly, numerous alternative measures of economic income may be used in income approach analyses. In fact, the most salient difference among the various income approach applications is the specific measure of economic income that is used in each application. All of the alternative measures of economic income can generally be grouped into the following categories:

1. Income derived from increases in revenues related to the subject intangible.
2. Income derived from decreases in expenses related to the subject intangible.
3. Income derived from decreases in investments related to the subject intangible.

Before selecting the appropriate measure of economic income to quantify, the analyst should consider how the subject intangible asset will generate that income. An intangible asset can generate income in the following ways:

1. The use of the intangible.
2. The ownership of the intangible.
3. The forbearance of use of the intangible.

How the subject intangible asset generates income may influence the selection of the measure of economic income to use in the analysis.

The concept of an intangible asset generating income through its use is easy to understand. For example, the use of a license or permit or franchise allows for the operation of a going-concern business. The business could not produce income without the required contract-related intangible asset. The use of a marketing-related intangible allows a manufacturer of a trademarked product to sell more product (or to sell a product at a higher price) than the manufacturer of a generic brand product. The use of a patent allows a processor to process a formulation faster, more efficiently, at a lower cost, and so forth, than a processor that does not use the technology-related intangible asset.

In each of the examples given, the use of the intangible asset created some form of comparative economic advantage—comparative with respect to performance of the same activity without the benefit of the subject intangible. It is this specific comparative economic advantage that generates income with regard to the use of the intangible asset.

However, the owner of an intangible asset can generate substantial economic income without ever having to use the subject intangible. This concept may be less understandable to analysts who are not familiar with the licensing of intangible assets and intellectual properties. Individuals who are familiar with intangible asset licensing understand the concept of how income can be generated from the ownership of an intangible asset, separately and distinctly from the income that is generated from the use of the intangible.

The leasing of tangible personal property and real estate is very common in commercial business transactions. Similarly, the licensing of intangible assets and intellectual properties is very common in commercial business transactions. In such transactions, Entity A owns the subject intangible asset. Entity B licenses the subject intangible asset from Entity A. The license transfers limited rights regarding the intangible asset from Entity A to Entity B. Frequently, the transferred right is the permission to use (or exploit or commercialize) the subject intangible.

The license agreement separates the right of ownership of the subject intangible (that is retained by Entity A) from the right of use of the subject intangible (that is transferred to Entity B). The limitations on the use rights are typically delineated in the license agreement. For example, Entity B may only have the right to use the subject intangible for a stated period of time; within a certain geographic territory; in association with a specific product or service; within a specified industry; and under the quality control requirements of Entity A.

In this example, the license of the subject intangible asset is an outbound license to Entity A (the licenser). That is, Entity A has entered into an agreement to license *out* its intangible to Entity B (the licensee). The license of the subject intangible asset is an inbound license to Entity B. That is, Entity B has entered into an agreement to license *in* the intangible from Entity A.

Under this arrangement, Entity B will pay a fee to Entity A for the license of the subject intangible asset. The license fee may be structured in any number of ways. For example, intangible asset license fees are often structured under one of the following arrangements:

1. A fixed dollar amount per period (i.e., per month, quarter, or year).
2. A fixed dollar amount per unit of production or service (e.g., $X per unit produced or $Y dollars per unit sold or $Z per customer signed up, etc.).
3. A percentage of the revenues generated by the licensee from the sale of goods or services related to the subject intangible asset (e.g., 6 percent of all wholesale-level revenues associated with the use of the subject intangible).
4. A percentage of the profits generated by the licensee from the sale of goods or services related to the subject intangible asset (e.g., 33 percent of all profits, as strictly defined in the license agreement, associated with the use of the subject intangible).

The percentage of revenues licensee fee arrangement is probably the most common license structure because it is relatively easy to identify and quantify the components of the formula. The percentage of profits license fee arrangement is also quite common. This license structure shifts some of the risk of the successful commercialization of the subject intangible from the licensee to the licensor. This license arrangement is the conceptual and empirical genesis of the profit split intangible asset valuation method. As the name of the analytical method implies, the profits associated with the use of the subject intangible asset are split—by contractual formula—between the licensor and the licensee.

In addition, an almost limitless number of permutations of the basic license fee arrangements is possible. For example, for each category of license fee arrangements:

1. There may or may not be an up-front payment—that is, a fixed dollar amount paid at the inception of the license term.
2. There may or may not be guaranteed minimum or maximum license payments—either per period or over the entire term of the agreement.
3. The stated dollar payments per unit or percentage payments per unit may change with volume (e.g., the license fee royalty rate may be 10 percent of the first $1 million of sales volume, 8 percent of sales volume between $2 million and $10 million, and 6 percent of sales volume over $10 million).
4. The stated dollar payments per unit or percentage payments per unit may change over time (e.g., the license fee royalty rate is $10 per unit for the first year of the license period, $15 per unit for years 2 through 10 of the license period, and $20 per unit after the tenth year of the license period).

Nonetheless, no matter how straightforward or complex the license fee arrangement, the license fees represent economic income to the licensor. That is, the owner of the subject intangible asset receives income merely from the ownership (and the associated right to partially transfer or license out some of the ownership rights) of the intangible. The income from ownership may be called license income or royalty income or lease income. In all cases, it is economic income generated from the ownership of the subject intangible.

The economic income generated from the ownership of the intangible is clearly separated from the economic income generated from the use of the intangible. In the common license arrangements, the ownership income accrues to the licensor—that is, the owner of the intangible asset—and the use income accrues to the licensee—that is, the user of the intangible asset.

It is also possible for an intangible asset to generate income through the forbearance of its use. This is a less common scenario in commercial business transactions. In that case, the intangible asset is typically used (or not used, as the case may be) for defensive purposes.

In some instances, the ownership—but forbearance of use—of an intangible asset may prevent a competitor from using that asset. This may protect the competitive position, market share, revenues and profits, and so on, of the intangible asset owner. For example, the ownership but forbearance of use of a trademark or patent may mean that the intangible owner's competitors cannot use that trademark or patent. Therefore, the competitor cannot obtain the competitive advantage that may accrue to the use of the subject trademark or patent. While conservative, the strategy of forbearance of use of an intangible (combined with the unavailability of the intangible to competitors) may preserve the competitive status quo in a given industry. That may be exactly the strategic objective that the intangible asset owner desires to achieve.

In other cases, the owner of the subject intangible asset elects not to commercialize the intangible in order to protect the value of other intangible assets. For example, the owner of the next generation of computer software or of proprietary technology may elect not to commercialize these state-of-the-art intangible assets. In this way, the subject intangible asset owner may be protecting the competitive position and the value of the previous generation of computer software or proprietary technology. The owners of the next generation of intangible assets may pursue this strategy because they have a vested interest in protecting the last generation of intangible assets.

In both of these forbearance examples, the economic income is not generated directly by the subject intangibles. Rather, a stream of economic income is protected by the subject intangible, or rather, by the forbearance of use of the subject intangible. In these cases, the economic income associated with the subject intangible asset is the measure of income that would have been lost if the intangible asset owner did not own the intangible.

The hypothetical lost income could be related to the market share that would be lost to a competitor if the intangible had not been protected from the competitor. Or, the lost income could be related to the revenues and profits that the owner would lose if the subject intangible replaced the previous generation of intangible. In either case, there is a forbearance of use of the subject intangible asset for defensive purposes and a stream of economic income that can be associated with the forbearance of use of the subject intangible asset.

In all cases, the income approach analysis of the subject intangible asset involves a projection and assessment of the income-producing capacity of the intangible. It is noteworthy that the income-producing capacity of the subject intangible may differ from the actual income that was historically generated by that intangible. Regardless of the definition of value being estimated, the analysis of income-generating capacity is always appropriate. That is, whether the value is being analyzed from the perspective of the typical willing buyer, of the current owner, or of a particular acquiror, all investors are interested in the income-generating capacity of the subject intangible.

This is not to say that analysts should not examine and interpret the actual historical income generation of the subject intangible. Certainly, intangible asset transaction participants consider actual historical income generation in their transaction pricing and structuring, for intangible asset license transactions as well as sale transactions. However, the historical income generation of the subject intangible asset only informs the analyst to the extent that it is a reasonable predictor of future income-generating capacity. In all intangible asset license, sale, or other transfer transactions, the investor is buying the future, not the past.

To conclude this topic, we consider how the analyst decides which of the three measures of income (or analytical framework) is most relevant to the income approach analysis of a subject intangible asset:

1. Income from the use of the intangible.
2. Income from the ownership of the intangible.
3. Income from the forbearance of use of the intangible.

Two related factors may be considered with respect to the selection of the appropriate analytical framework. The first factor is the highest and best use of the subject intangible. That is, the analyst may consider which of the three analytical frameworks is consistent with the highest and best use of the subject intangible. The second factor is the actual use of the subject intangible. That is, the analyst may be cognizant of the way in which the subject intangible is actually generating income at the time of the valuation. It is noteworthy that the intangible's actual income-generating use may not be consistent with its highest and best use. The consideration of these two factors should provide valuable guidance to the analyst with respect to which analytical framework to apply in the income approach analysis of the subject intangible.

### Time Period Component

The second component in the application of the income approach is the estimation of the time period over which to project the economic income generated by the subject intangible. There are two issues with regard to this component. The first issue is how long a projection period is relevant. In other words: How long is the subject intangible expected to generate the measure of economic income? The answer to this question is based upon the remaining useful life analysis of the subject intangible. The topic of remaining useful life analysis is discussed in depth in Chapters 11 and 12.

This component is obviously very important to the intangible asset income approach analysis. Obviously, all other things being equal, an intangible asset with a 20-year expected remaining life will have greater value than an otherwise identical intangible with a 10-year expected remaining life, because we project a 20-year stream of income in the first case and a 10-year stream of income in the second case. For any present value discount rate (except infinity), the present value of a 20-year stream of income will be greater than the present value of a 10-year stream of income.

With regard to the application of income approach methods, we discuss the difference between business valuation and intangible asset valuation later in this chapter. As an introduction to this discussion, one of the significant differences is the selection of the projection period. The selection of the appropriate projection period has a direct impact on the valuation of an intangible asset. In all intangible asset income approach analyses, there is an explicit conclusion with regard to the life of the intangible. This is true even when the conclusion is that the subject intangible enjoys an infinite life.

In several business valuation income approach methods, there is no need whatsoever to conclude the period of the economic income projection, because the subject going-concern business enterprise is usually assumed to have a perpetual remaining useful life. That is, the business is assumed to continue in existence indefinitely.

Even as part of an income approach analysis that requires a specific projection period (such as the yield capitalization method), the selection of the projection period is not critically important, because the business enterprise has residual value (also called a terminal value) at the end of the discrete income projection period. Of course, many intangible assets do not have a residual value at the end of the discrete income projection period. Therefore, in the case of a business valuation, it is not mathematically significant whether the analyst projects income for 5 years and then adds a residual value, projects income for 10 years and then adds a residual value, or projects income for 20 years and then adds a residual value. If there is internal consistency with respect to the variables in the yield capitalization model, the selection of the discrete projection period should not affect the value conclusion.

The second issue with regard to the time period component is periodicity. This issue relates to the question of how large each time period should be. In other words, should the projection period be monthly, quarterly, semiannual, annual, or some other duration? The answer to this question relates to the facts and circumstances of the particular analysis. That is, the selection of the projection period relates to the actual expected flow of economic income related to the subject intangible asset.

If the subject intangible asset is expected to generate income that will vary significantly over time, then shorter projection periods are usually preferred. For example, let's assume that the subject intangible will generate levels of income that are substantially disparate from month to month. In this case, the use of monthly periods in the discrete projection period will more accurately model the expected flow of economic income.

On the other hand, if the subject intangible asset is expected to generate income that will not vary significantly over time, then longer time periods are usually preferred. For example, let's assume that the subject intangible will generate income that is fairly constant over the period of a year. In that case, the use of an annual period in the discrete projection period will more than adequately model the expected flow of economic income.

## Capitalization Rate Component

The third component in the application of the income approach is the selection of the appropriate capitalization rate. The capitalization rate, of course, is used to convert the projection of economic income generated by the subject intangible into a value estimate.

There are two specific types of capitalization rates: yield capitalization rates and direct capitalization rates. The term *yield capitalization rate* is synonymous with the term *present value discount rate.*

The yield capitalization rate, or discount rate, is used to convert a stream of uneven income flows to a present value. The discount rate is the expected rate of return on an investment in an intangible asset (or on any other investment, for that matter) over the expected term of the investment. For economic analysis purposes, the expected term of the investment is typically considered to be the expected remaining useful life of the subject intangible.

The direct capitalization rate is used to convert a stream of constant (or constantly changing) income flows to a present value. Direct capitalization rates are often used to convert a perpetual stream of income flows to a present value. However, they may also be used to convert a multiperiod stream of income flows to a present value. A multiperiod stream of constant (or of constantly changing) income flows is called an *annuity*. A perpetual stream of constant (or of constantly changing) income flows is called a *perpetuity.*

Mathematically, the difference between a yield capitalization (or discount) rate and a direct capitalization rate is the expected growth rate in the income stream over the term of the investment. In other words, the discount rate minus the expected growth rate equals the capitalization rate. The expected growth rate can be positive, negative, or zero. When the expected growth rate is zero, then the discount rate equals the capitalization rate.

Note that the difference between the discount rate and the capitalization rate is the expected growth rate. Therefore, growth has to be expressed as a rate (i.e., a percentage) and not as an amount. So, if the prospective income stream to be generated by an intangible asset is expected to increase (or decrease) by 10 percent per year (i.e., a constant percentage, or rate, of change), then a direct capitalization analysis—and a direct capitalization rate—is appropriate. In contrast, if the prospective income stream to be generated by an intangible asset is expected to increase (or decrease) by $1,000 per year (i.e., a constant amount of change), then a direct capitalization analysis—and a direct capitalization rate—is inappropriate. Rather, a yield capitalization analysis and a present value discount rate is more appropriate.

The topic of capitalization rates is discussed in greater detail later in this chapter. For now, it is sufficient to reiterate several caveats regarding the selection of the appropriate capitalization rate (whether yield or direct):

1. To the extent possible, the data used to derive the capitalization rate should be market-derived.
2. The capitalization rate should be derived in order to reflect the risk associated with the intangible asset investment; the capitalization rate should reflect the risk associated with the income-generating capacity of the subject intangible asset.

3. The capitalization rate should be derived so as to be consistent with the measure of economic income projected in the intangible asset analysis.

4. The capitalization rate should be forward-looking. It is not an historical rate of return, unless the analyst concludes that history is the best indication of the future.

5. The capitalization rate should be consistent with the expected term of the intangible asset income stream. For example, if the intangible asset is expected to generate economic income for a 10-year period, then the capitalization rate (either yield or direct) should be consistent with a 10-year projection period.

This section introduced the mechanical components of the income approach to intangible asset analysis. The next section discusses the strengths and weaknesses of the application of the income approach (vis-à-vis the market approach or the cost approach) to intangible asset analysis.

## PROS AND CONS OF THE INCOME APPROACH

As with any structured set of analytical methods, there are both pros and cons associated with the application of the income approach to intangible asset valuation and economic analysis. For purposes of this discussion, application pros and cons may be construed as the analytical strengths and weaknesses of the income approach. First, we summarize several of the more significant analytical strengths of this approach. Then we summarize several of the more significant analytical weaknesses of this approach.

The following list presents several of the positive attributes associated with the use of the income approach to analyze intangible assets:

1. Income approach methods are adaptable and flexible. That is, they can easily be adapted in order to analyze numerous standards of value within numerous premises of value. Income approach methods can also be used for transfer pricing and royalty rate analysis, damages analysis, event analysis, and numerous other types of economic analysis.

2. Income approach methods are well known and widely recognized. Intangible asset analysts are familiar with these methods through training and experience. However, even the parties who review the work of or rely upon intangible asset analysts (such as nonfinancial executives, bankers, lawyers, and judges) are generally familiar with basic income approach methods.

3. Income approach methods translate well across the various valuation and appraisal disciplines. That is, there is a general similarity of income approach methods between intangible asset analysis and security analysis, business valuation, and real estate appraisal.

4. Income approach methods closely emulate the actual decision-making processes of intangible asset market participants. Intangible asset creators, owners, buyers, sellers, licensors, and licensees all analyze possible transactions, implicitly or explicitly, from an income approach analysis perspective.

5. Income approach methods are arguably the most rigorous and structured intangible asset analysis tools. Income approach methods require the analyst to explicitly consider all the critical economic variables associated with the subject intangible asset, including income-generating capacity, allocation of income between the intangible asset and associated assets, the expected remaining life of the intangible, and the risk associated with an investment in the intangible. Other valuation approaches, of course, require the analyst to implicitly consider all of these variables. However, the income approach requires that these variables be addressed explicitly and individually.

As with all analytical approaches, there are also weaknesses associated with the use of the income approach. The following list presents several of the negative attributes associated with the use of the income approach to analyze intangible assets:

1. Income approach methods are subject to the introduction of a bias. Because some of the methods are fairly complicated, it is possible for a goal-oriented analyst to subtly influence the particularly sensitive economic variables in such a way as to manipulate or otherwise bias the analysis.

2. Income approach methods are subject to honest mistakes as well as to unscrupulous manipulation. Again, this is true because these methods are often analytically complex. It is relatively easy for an analyst to make an honest mistake, yet a mistake that can have a material impact on the indicated valuation conclusion.

3. Income approach methods are subject to double-counting (i.e., overestimating) the value of intangible assets. This weakness is easily overcome by the correct assessment of a capital charge in the analysis. However, some analysts sometimes make the mistake of underestimating (or even ignoring) the requisite capital charge.

4. Income approach methods are sometimes not subject to market confirmation. Because these methods appear analytically sophisticated, some analysts do not always confirm the economic variable inputs with market-derived empirical data. Of course, the use of projection variables that are inconsistent with actual market dynamics will result in dubious analytical conclusions, regardless of how rigorous and structured the analysis is.

5. Income approach methods for intangible assets are sometimes confused with income approach methods for other appraisal disciplines. As mentioned earlier, intangible asset income approach methods have numerous similarities to security analysis, business valuation, and real estate appraisal methods. However, because of this, some analysts fail to recognize the subtle but important differences in income approach analyses among various disciplines. Some analysts incorrectly attempt to apply to intangible asset analysis methods that are only appropriate to other valuation disciplines.

All structured analytical methods have application strengths and weaknesses. With regard to the income approach methods, many of the analytical strengths, when misapplied, turn around to become analytical weaknesses.

## MEASURES OF ECONOMIC INCOME

Of the several issues related to the selection of the appropriate measure of economic income, the first issue relates to the question: Income to whom? In other words, from whose perspective should the analyst assess, project, and (ultimately) value the intangible asset economic income stream?

## Income to Whom?

Practically, the following parties to an intangible asset transaction could each have a different perspective with regard to the value of the economic income-generating capacity: the owner who will operate the intangible, the owner who will sell the intangible, the owner who will license the intangible, the average buyer of the intangible, the most strategic buyer of the intangible, the average licensee of the intangible, the most strategic licensee of the intangible, the party that caused the damages associated with the intangible, the party that suffered the damages, the party that committed an infringement, the party that suffered the infringement, and so on. Each of these parties could perceive:

1. A different periodic amount of expected future income from the intangible.
2. A different remaining useful life for the income stream from the intangible.
3. A different degree of risk associated with the expectation of the future income stream from the intangible.

Accordingly, each potential transaction participant could perceive a different value for the same intangible. Again, the question is relevant: With respect to the measure of economic income expected to be generated by the intangible, whose perspective should the analyst adopt?

The answer to this question is based on two of the fundamental elements related to the analysis: the standard of value sought and the premise of value sought. With regard to a valuation, an economic analysis, a damages analysis, or other similar analysis, the standard of value answers the question: From whose perspective (actual or hypothetical) should the economic income stream be analyzed? The premise of value answers the question: Under what set of transactional circumstances (actual or hypothetical) will the subject intangible generate the expected income stream?

## Alternative Measures of Economic Income

The list of actual measures or levels of economic income that are appropriate for analysis is fairly extensive. The income approach to intangible asset analysis may be based on any of the following alternative measures of economic income:

1. Gross or net revenues (or gross or net sales).
2. Gross profit (net revenues less cost of goods sold).
3. Net operating profit (gross profit less selling, general, and administrative expenses).
4. Profit before interest and taxes (net operating profit plus nonoperating income less nonoperating expense).

5. Profit before tax (profit before interest and taxes less interest expense).

6. Profit after tax (profit before tax less income tax expense).

7. Gross cash flow before tax (profit before interest, taxes, and depreciation).

8. Gross cash flow after tax (profit before interest and deprecation but after income taxes).

9. Net cash flow before tax (gross cash flow before tax less capital expenditures and less changes in net working capital).

10. Net cash flow after tax (gross cash flow after tax less capital expenditures and less changes in net working capital).

Note that this "top ten" list of alternative economic income measures is not an exhaustive list. However, it includes the most common measures of economic income that are considered in intangible asset analysis.

Each of these measures of income may be considered accounting-oriented measures of income. Most of these measures of income, as defined, do not appear on traditional accounting-based financial statements. However, the data elements needed to calculate the measures of income are all presented in traditional accounting-based financial statements.

Depending upon the particular type of intangible asset analysis (e.g., valuation, damages, transfer price, etc.), several important adjustments may need to be made to the accounting-oriented measures of income in order to arrive at the level of economic income associated with a particular intangible asset. While there are numerous potential adjustments, they can generally be grouped into three categories of adjustments. The three categories are:

1. Funnel of enterprise income adjustments.
2. Capital charge adjustments.
3. Portion of income adjustments.

The funnel of enterprise income adjustments recognize the fact that not all of the income generated by a business enterprise is generated by a particular intangible asset. This conclusion is valid regardless of how economic income is measured, as long as economic income is measured on an enterprise basis.

Many of the projections of intangible asset income start with projections of enterprise income. The enterprise income is the economic income (however measured) generated by the entire business operations that include the subject intangible asset. Typically, the business enterprise also includes tangible real and personal property assets, net working capital assets, and a variety of intangible assets other than the specific intangible asset subject to analysis. Accordingly, in order to analyze only the subject intangible asset, it is often necessary to separate the total enterprise income and to isolate that portion of the total enterprise income that can be directly associated with the subject intangible.

There are two reasons why funnel of enterprise income adjustments are often necessary. First, the historical income available for analysis is typically on an enterprise basis. That is, if the analyst has obtained historical financial statements related to the business that employs the subject intangible, those financial statements are on an enterprise basis—they relate to the entire going-concern business enterprise. Second, except for intangible assets that are licensed separately from an operating business, the income contributed by the subject intangible is just one part of the overall income generated by the business enterprise in which it functions.

The adjustment, therefore, relates to an allocation of the overall enterprise income to the constituent components of the business enterprise, including all tangible and intangible assets. The adjustment is referred to as a funnel of income adjustment because all of the income that is generated by a business enterprise can be analogized to the top (or wide) end of a funnel. For analytical purposes, we are only interested in that portion of the total enterprise income that gets down to the bottom (or narrow) end of the funnel—that is, that relates directly to the subject intangible asset. The adjustment is often necessary in order to avoid double-counting or overestimating intangible asset values.

Usually, 100 percent of the enterprise income should not be assigned to an individual intangible asset. After all, tangible assets and net working capital assets are also needed in order to generate that level of enterprise income. Furthermore, the analyst should be cognizant of situations in which a business enterprise enjoys the benefit of more than one intangible asset. If a business owns more than one intangible asset (e.g., a recognized trademark, a proprietary patented process, and loyal recurring customer relationships), then the funnel of income may have to be allocated among the various intangible assets.

If all of the funnel of income is assigned to each of the intangible assets owned by the enterprise, then the value of the intangibles will most likely be overstated because, without a proper allocation, more than 100 percent of the total enterprise income will be included in the various intangible asset analyses.

One way to think about the funnel of income adjustment is to recognize that any income approach analysis should provide a return of the investment in all of the assets of the business enterprise. If the measure of economic income considered in the analysis does not provide for a return of all of the enterprise assets other than the subject intangible, then a specific income allocation should be made. This would be the case if the selected economic income measure is on a gross level of income, such as revenues or gross profits. Such an allocation may not be necessary if the selected measure of economic income is on a net level of income, such as net income or net cash flow. In net measures of economic income, provisions for a return of tangible assets, net working capital, and some intangible assets through deductions for cost of materials and labor, depreciation expense, selling and administrative expenses, and so forth, need to be made.

The capital charge adjustment is a common component of most intangible asset income approach analyses. However, it is a component that many analysts fail to make. The funnel of income adjustment is intended to ensure that, when economic income is analyzed on an enterprise level, there is a fair return *of* the investment of all the assets that are used or used up in the production of the income associated with the subject intangible. The capital charge adjustment is intended to ensure that, when economic income is analyzed on an enterprise level, there is a fair return *on* the investment of all the assets that are used or used up in the production of the income associated with the subject intangible.

The first step in the adjustment is to identify all the assets that are used or used up in the production of the enterprise income associated with the subject intangible. The assets may include real estate and tangible personal property, net working capital, and other intangible assets (meaning intangibles used by the enterprise other than the subject intangible).

The second step is to estimate a value for all the assets to which a capital charge will be applied. Ideally, the value estimate represents the market value of the capital charge assets. When it is not practical or possible to estimate the market value of the capital charge assets, some analysts apply the capital charge rate to the accounting book value of the assets. The use of accounting book values is not the preferred procedure; however, it is preferable to not making any attempt to calculate a capital charge.

The third step is to estimate a fair rate of return on each of the asset categories subject to the capital charge. The fair rate of return should reflect the risk associated with an investment in the various asset categories. Typically, investments in net working capital are liquid and have little risk associated with them. Investments in land, buildings, and equipment are somewhat riskier. Investments in other intangible assets are considered riskier than investments in tangible assets. Many analysts apply discrete rates of return to each asset category, based upon the risk complexion of the asset group. Some analysts apply a weighted average rate of return to all the asset categories. The weighted average rate of return is based on an assessment of the blended risk of the total assets subject to the capital charge.

The fourth step is to multiply the asset values by the fair rate of return in order to calculate the amount of the capital charge. The capital charge is subtracted from the measure of economic income associated with the subject intangible (assuming such income was derived at the enterprise level). Subtracting the capital charge allocates part of the economic income in order to provide for a fair return on the assets (tangible and intangible) that are used or used up in the production of the income associated with the subject intangible.

Note that some of the asset categories may have an expected remaining useful life that is shorter than the remaining life of the subject intangible. In that case, the short-lived asset will be totally used up during the period of income generation of the subject intangible. Clearly, it is not necessary to provide a capital charge for (or a return on) an asset that is already used up. Therefore, in multiperiod economic income analyses, the capital charge may decrease over time as the assets upon which the capital charge is calculated have reached the ends of their remaining useful lives.

The portion of income adjustment relates to the question of how much of the economic income generated by the subject intangible should be included in a particular analysis. This issue is considered after any appropriate funnel of income adjustment is made and after any appropriate capital charges are subtracted from the economic income projection. The portion of income adjustment, when it is necessary, is a function of the type of analysis that is being performed.

Typically, there are three portions of income that are relevant to most intangible asset analyses:

1. All of the income (i.e., 100 percent of the income "coming out" of the funnel after appropriate capital charge allowances).

2. Differential income (i.e., the difference between the income actually generated by the intangible and some other real or hypothetical level of income).

3. Incremental income (i.e., the additional amount of income generated by an enterprise related to the use of the subject intangible, compared to the amount of income that would be generated without the subject intangible).

In most valuation analyses, all of the income associated with the subject intangible should be considered. However, in certain pricing analyses, the portion of income that is relevant to a buyer or to a licensor is differential income. For example, when deciding how much to pay to buy or license an intangible, an investor may consider the question: How much more income can I generate with the new intangible compared to what I could generate with the old (or with no) intangible?

In some valuation analyses, incremental income may be a relevant consideration. For example, one way to value a covenant not to compete is to analyze the incremental income that would be earned by the covenant grantee without competition (i.e., with the covenant in place) versus with competition (i.e., without the covenant in place). Incremental income is also a relevant consideration in many types of damages analyses, including infringement analysis. In such cases, a relevant consideration is: How much more income did the infringing party earn by using the intangible as compared to not using the intangible?

Finally, with regard to measures of income, many analysts vehemently debate whether intangible asset income approach analyses should be performed on a before-tax basis or an after-tax basis. The simple resolution to this debate is: It simply doesn't matter. If the analysis is performed correctly and with consistent variables, there should be no material difference in the conclusion between a before-tax analysis and an after-tax analysis. Obviously, for this assertion to be true, there should always be consistency between the measure of income analyzed and the capitalization rate.

## ECONOMIC INCOME PROJECTION PERIOD

The conclusion of the appropriate projection period is a necessary procedure in all income approach methods. Even methods that involve direct capitalization as an annuity in perpetuity have an implicit projection period. In the case of a perpetuity, the implicit projection period is infinity. Clearly, the analyst should consciously conclude that an infinite projection period is appropriate before using a perpetuity valuation method. In our other income approach methods, the selection of the projection period is even more important. That is, the analyst has to estimate a discrete projection period over which to assess the intangible asset's expected economic income generation.

The appropriate projection period is the period of time during which the subject intangible asset is expected to generate economic income. Most commonly, the projection period is measured in years. However, the projection period can be measured in whatever intervals are most relevant to the subject analysis, including days, weeks, months, quarters, and so forth. There are two, sometimes contradictory factors that should be considered with respect to the selection of the projection period:

1. **Intrinsic factor**—The projection period represents the best estimate of how much time in the future the subject intangible is capable of generating any measurable amount of economic income.
2. **Extrinsic factor**—The projection period represents how far into the future the analyst can project economic income with a reasonable degree of certainty.

The projection period that is intrinsic to the intangible asset is a function of the remaining useful life of the subject intangible. Every intangible asset (and every tangible asset, for that matter) is subject to a number of alternative remaining useful life estimates, because life can be measured as economic life, functional life, technological life, legal or statutory life, contractual life, actuarial life, and so on.

Typically, of the various life estimates associated with an intangible, the shortest is appropriate for most valuation and economic analyses. For example, it is not particularly relevant to the analysis if a patent has a 17-year legal life when the associated proprietary process is expected to become technologically obsolete in 5 years. If the patent can only generate economic income over its 5-year technological life (through production cost reductions, associated product sales, direct license fees, etc.), then the 5-year period is relevant for analysis. The 17-year period, while noteworthy, is irrelevant for purposes of the analysis.

There are a few instances when the longer of alternative useful life measures is appropriate for analysis. In these instances, however, the character of the subject intangible asset sometimes changes after the conclusion of the shorter useful life period. The analyst should be cognizant of such a change in character, albeit subtle.

For example, let's assume that ABC Company provides contract data processing services for Big Bank. The current relationship is documented in a five-year professional services agreement, which has three years remaining as of the valuation date. Big Bank has a history of successively renewing its five-year data processing contracts each time one expires. We have performed an analysis of the Big Bank account relationship and the ABC Company historical experience with similar data processing clients. Based upon that analysis, we believe that Big Bank is expected to renew the current contract when it expires. In fact, we expect two more 5-year renewal contracts. Now, what is the appropriate life over which to value the Big Bank contract relationship: 3 years, the remaining term of the current contract? Or 13 years, the remaining term of the current contract plus two expected 5-year renewal periods?

The correct answer to this question may be: Both. What do we mean by that? The current contract clearly has a three-year remaining term. If we are valuing the contract only, we would project and find the present value of the economic income generated by this contract to ABC Company over the next three-year period. If we are valuing the contract relationship, we would also project and find the present value of the expected economic income to ABC Company associated with two contract renewals—that is, for the period of years 4 through 13. But the character of the intangible asset changed after the expiration of the current contract. The intangible asset changed from a contract to a contract relationship (otherwise called an expected contract renewal or a customer relationship). In fact, some analysts would say that there are really two related intangible assets here: the contract and the expected contract relationship beyond the expiration of the current contract.

If our analysis is limited to the current contract only, clearly we will have understated the value of the Big Bank relationship to ABC Company. On the other hand, we have to analyze the change in the character of this intangible asset after the expiration of the current contract. For example, the level of income earned by ABC Company could be lower during the contract renewal period; this could occur if ABC Company had to lower its rates in order to retain the Big Bank data processing business. There is certainly some probability that Big Bank may not renew the contract; or if Big Bank renews the contract one time, it may not renew the contract the second time. There are several ways that the analyst could consider these character changes in the analysis of the Big Bank contract. The analyst could project a lower level of economic income during the contract renewal term of the projection period. Alternatively, the analyst could use a higher present value discount rate during the contract renewal term of the projection period. The higher discount rate could reflect the risk of the contract not being renewed.

It is easy to construct a similar example involving patented proprietary technology. Let's assume that the patent owner uses the proprietary technology to manufacture a product. Due to the superior nature of the technology, the patent owner enjoys a comparative economic advantage. The owner can manufacture the products faster or at a lower cost or can sell more products or sell them at a higher price. One way or another, the patent owner enjoys a higher level of economic income than would be the case without the proprietary technology.

Now, let's assume that the remaining legal registration period of the patent expires in three years. However, even without the patent, the manufacturer enjoys a proprietary technological advantage over its competitors. Based on an assessment of the industry, the analyst concludes that it will be at least five years before competitors can develop a substitute technology. It will take a substitute technology for the competitors to bridge the technological gap and offer a seriously competitive product.

The analyst is asked to value the patented proprietary technology. Of course, the analyst will have to estimate the remaining useful life of the subject intangible asset. As with the customer contract versus customer relationship example, there appear to be two intangible assets here. First, the patent itself has a remaining useful life of three years. Second, the proprietary technology has a remaining useful life of another two years beyond the expiration of the patent protection.

A reasonable valuation would include the estimation and present value of the incremental income earned by the manufacturer over the three-year life of the patent. The valuation could also include an analysis of the second intangible asset: the proprietary technology that will still exist beyond the patent expiration date. That valuation would include the estimation and present value of the incremental income expected to be earned by the manufacturer in years four and five.

Again, the analyst should recognize the change in character of the subject intangible asset after year three. Accordingly, the incremental income projections for years four and five may be lower than for the first three years, to represent the costs of competing in a competitive market without patent protection. The present value discount rate may be higher in years four and five, to reflect the additional business risk associated with new competition.

Of course, all income approach analyses are based on the premise that the analyst can project economic income with a reasonable degree of certainty. There is no strict definition of what constitutes a reasonable degree of certainty. The measure of a reasonable degree of certainty can certainly vary among analysts. That is, two equally qualified analysts can review the same data regarding the same intangible asset. Analyst A may conclude that he or she can prepare a 10-year projection with a reasonable degree of certainty. However, Analyst B may conclude that he or she can prepare only a 5-year projection with a reasonable degree of certainty, concluding that a projection beyond a 5-year period would be unreasonably speculative.

There is no absolute answer to this dilemma. The term *reasonable degree of certainty* is, by its very nature, subjective. Often, differences over how long a projection period is reasonable become moot. For example, if the expected remaining useful life of the subject intangible asset is four years, the debate between Analyst A and Analyst B becomes academic. Neither analyst has to project income for more than a four-year period. This projection period falls into the reasonable degree of certainty comfort zone for both analysts.

What happens, though, if both analysts agree that the remaining useful life of the subject intangible asset is eight years? In that case, Analyst A would be professionally comfortable in performing an eight-year income projection. However, Analyst B would not be professionally comfortable in projecting economic income beyond year five. Yet, Analyst B would admit that if he or she terminates the income projection after year five, then that income approach analysis would understate the correct value of the subject intangible, because such an analysis would exclude three years of (unpredictable, according to Analyst B) income.

One solution to this problem for Analyst B is not to perform an income approach analysis. Rather, Analyst B could attempt to value the subject intangible using other approaches and methods. Another solution for Analyst B is to prepare a conservative income projection for years six, seven, and eight, and then discount those years at a present value discount rate adjusted to reflect the uncertainty of the projection. A less acceptable alternative for Analyst B is to simply ignore the value of the subject intangible asset income-generation potential in years six, seven, and eight. There is always some degree of uncertainty in any income projection. The last alternative (truncating the projection after year five) adds some degree of certainty to the conclusion—the certainty that the conclusion will be incorrect.

The topic of income projection variability may appear to be more related to measures of income than to estimating the projection period. However, the uncertainty regarding the topic on the part of practitioners seems to show itself when it comes to dealing with the term of the remaining useful life estimate. Economic income projections can vary materially over the term of an income projection. This is consistent with the typical life cycle of many intangible assets. Economic income projections can vary by different percentages and by different amounts in each period during the remaining useful life of the intangible. Furthermore, economic income can turn from positive to negative (and back again) during the analysis projection period.

Sometimes, the economic income projection changes by a constant amount or by a constant percentage during the remaining useful life of the intangible. An example of this is a projection that indicates that income will increase at ten percent per year or decrease at five percent per year. While such constant change scenarios do occur, it is also entirely likely that the income generated by the subject intangible may vary by different amounts and percentages, and in different directions, during the term of the projection period.

Many intangible assets require periodic investment in research and development, function maintenance, marketing and promotion, legal, and other expenses in order for the intangible to maintain its income-generating capacity. Some intangible assets require small amounts of such maintenance expenditures on a regular basis. Some intangible assets require large amounts of such maintenance expenditures on an infrequent, periodic basis. Depending upon the nature of the intangible asset and its position in its life cycle as of the date of analysis, the effect of these maintenance expenditures on projected income could be negligible or could be very material.

In addition to maintenance expenditures, analysts should consider exogenous factors that affect the income-generating capacity of the intangible. Such factors could include the effects of expected competition in the industry and the effects of an expected replacement for the subject intangible. The replacement intangible asset could be developed by the owner of the subject intangible asset or by a competitor. In either case, periodic competitive factors have an effect on the projected income-generating capacity of the subject intangible.

The term of the income projection period should be estimated independently of the variability in the projected measure of economic income. However, if there is a great deal of expected variability in the income measure, the analyst may not feel comfortable in projecting income over the entire remaining useful life of the subject intangible. If there is so much variability in the income stream that the analyst cannot project income with a reasonable degree of certainty, the analyst may decide to truncate the income projection period.

## INCOME CAPITALIZATION RATES

The appropriate income capitalization rate to use in the income approach analysis is the cost of capital appropriate for an investment in the subject intangible. The cost of capital is a function of the risk of the investment in the subject intangible. While these statements are conceptually correct, they represent practical problems associated with selecting the appropriate income capitalization rate:

1. What is the cost of capital appropriate for an investment in the subject intangible?
2. What is the degree of risk associated with an investment in the subject intangible?

Before applying the mechanics of income capitalization rate analysis, the analyst must consider whether the rate being estimated will be used:

1. to value the intangible asset as one component of a going-concern business enterprise; or

2. to value the intangible asset as an individual economic entity, independent of the contributor effects of a going-concern business enterprise.

If the subject intangible is to be analyzed as one part of a going-concern business, many analysts believe that it is relevant to use a capitalization rate that is relevant to the overall business enterprise. That rate would be a function of the costs of the capital components of the subject business enterprise. The use of the overall business capitalization rate should conclude the value of the intangible to the business, meaning as a contributory part of that business enterprise. The value conclusion would be consistent with the premise of value in continued use (as part of a going-concern business).

If the subject intangible is to be analyzed on a stand-alone basis, many analysts believe that it is appropriate to use a capitalization rate that is specific to the individual intangible. That rate would be a function of the specific risks associated with the individual intangible. Since individual intangible assets generally have greater risk attributes than going-concern businesses, one would expect an asset-specific capitalization rate to be greater than an overall business enterprise capitalization rate. The use of the asset-specific capitalization rate should conclude the value of the intangible as an independent economic unit. The value conclusion would be consistent with the premise of value in exchange.

There are three factors that analysts may consider in the determination of which of these two alternative capitalization rate scenarios is appropriate to the subject analysis:

1. What is the objective of the valuation or economic analysis? The statement of the assignment should indicate whether the subject intangible should be analyzed as part of a business enterprise or as an individual, independent asset.
2. What is the highest and best use of the subject intangible? Absent an instruction to the contrary in the assignment statement, the analyst should value the subject intangible based on the valuation premise that will conclude the highest and best use of the asset.
3. How is the intangible actually being used? Or, how will the intangible be used if the intended use is different from the current use? If the intangible is actually used as one contributory component of an overall business, that condition would be meaningful evidence to the analyst. If the intangible is not currently being used, or if it is used only passively to generate license or royalty income, that condition would also be meaningful evidence to the analyst.

The next question that should be addressed in the capitalization rate process is: Does the analysis call for a yield capitalization rate or a direct capitalization rate? The answer to this question is based upon what valuation method or methods will be used.

The yield capitalization rate is often called the present value discount rate. It represents the total cost of capital associated with an investment in the subject asset. The total cost of capital—or the total yield on the investment—has two components: an income yield and an appreciation yield.

The income yield relates to the periodic income that is earned due to the ownership of the asset. The appreciation yield relates to the increase in the value of the asset during the investment holding period. (If the asset decreases in value during the investment holding period, then the appreciation yield is negative.) The sum of these two yields represents the total yield rate, or the total rate of return on the asset during the investment holding period.

The direct capitalization rate represents a rate that is less than the total cost of capital associated with an investment, because it does not include consideration of an appreciation yield. The appreciation yield is often called the expected growth rate in the value of the investment. The expected growth rate is specifically excluded from the direct capitalization rate. Therefore, in instances when an asset is expected to appreciate in value (i.e., have a positive expected growth rate), the direct capitalization rate is always less than the yield capitalization rate. This also means that in instances when an asset is expected to depreciate in value (i.e., have a negative expected growth rate), the direct capitalization rate will be greater than the yield capitalization rate.

The use of the yield capitalization rate, or discount rate, is appropriate in valuation methods that involve a discrete projection of income over the entire remaining useful life of the intangible. The use of the direct capitalization rate is appropriate in valuation methods that convert a single-period estimate of income into a value. Direct capitalization methods can be used when the income generated by the intangible will increase or decrease at a constant rate. (That constant rate of change can be zero.) When the income generated by the intangible will change at varying rates (or amounts) over the life of the asset, then yield capitalization methods are more appropriate.

The mathematical relationship between the discount rate and the direct capitalization rate is simple:

Discount rate − Expected growth rate = Direct capitalization rate

While this mathematical relationship is true, it is only true over the expected remaining useful life of the intangible. The direct capitalization rate should be a rate that is consistent with the remaining useful life of the intangible. That is, the direct capitalization rate should be converted to a present value of annuity factor over the life of the intangible.

For example, let's assume that the appropriate discount rate for our analysis is 20 percent and the income stream from the intangible is expected to grow at 8 percent per year. This fact set implies a direct capitalization rate of 12 percent (20 percent discount rate minus 8 percent growth rate). However, let's also assume that the expected remaining useful life of this intangible is 5 years. In that case, simply capitalizing (i.e., dividing) the annual income by 12 percent will greatly overstate the value of the intangible, because the simple capitalization process assumes a perpetual life.

Rather, the appropriate procedure is to calculate the present value of an annuity factor for the 12 percent rate and a 5-year period. When the present value annuity factor is multiplied by the annual income, the value of the intangible will be correctly estimated. This procedure is still a direct capitalization method. However, it is direct capitalization over the appropriate period of the intangible asset income annuity stream, and not over the inappropriate period of an income perpetuity stream.

It is also noteworthy that the growth rate of the income stream generated by an intangible asset can be positive, negative, or zero. In the valuation of businesses or securities, the analyst normally expects to project positive (at the least, zero) growth rates. However, it is certainly possible that the income generated by an intangible could decrease each period during its remaining life. For example, this may be expected from technology intangibles that experience increasing obsolescence during the later years of their life cycle.

Direct capitalization methods may still be used in the analysis of intangibles that experience negative income growth. However, the analyst should be careful to include the negative growth rate in the estimation of the direct capitalization rate. Let's return to our previous example. However, this time, let's assume a 20 percent discount rate and a negative 8 percent growth rate. That is, our analysis indicates that the income generated by the intangible will decrease by 8 percent per year over its remaining 5-year life.

In this case, the appropriate direct capitalization rate is 28 percent. That rate is derived as follows: 20 percent discount rate minus a negative 8 percent growth rate equals 28 percent. To perform the valuation, the analyst multiplies the annual income from the intangible asset by the present value of an annuity factor for 28 percent over 5 years.

Another issue that has to be decided before the income capitalization procedure can be performed is the issue of the periodicity of the income flow. The first periodicity question is: What compounding convention should be used in the income approach analysis? The most common compounding conventions are annual and semiannual. However, quarterly and monthly compounding conventions are also used when appropriate.

The selection of the compounding periods can have a material impact on the results of an analysis. Of course, the more frequent the compounding, the greater the value of an income stream. Let's consider a simple example. We are analyzing an intangible asset that we expect will generate a fixed amount of $1,200 in royalty income per year for each of the next 10 years. Based upon our analysis, we have concluded that 12 percent is the appropriate present value discount rate. We will value the subject intangible using a simple yield capitalization method.

If we assume annual compounding (at year-end), the value of the intangible asset is the present value of $1,200 every 12 months for 10 periods at a 12 percent discount rate, or $6,780.

If we assume semiannual compounding, the value of the intangible is the present value of $600 every 6 months for 20 periods at a 6 percent discount rate, or $6,882.

If we assume quarterly compounding, the value of the intangible is the present value of $300 every quarter for 40 periods at a 3 percent discount rate, or $6,934.

If we assume monthly compounding, the value of the intangible is the present value of $100 every month for 120 periods at a 1 percent discount rate, or $6,970.

Exhibit 10-1 presents the algebraic adjustments necessary to convert present value analyses and present value annuity analyses from an annual compounding convention to a periodic compounding convention.

Adjusting Present Value Formulas for Periodic Compounding

Present value interest factor formula for annual compounding:

$$\text{PVIF} = \frac{1}{(1 + k)^t}$$

Present value annuity factor formula for annual compounding:

$$\text{PVAF} = \sum_{t=1}^{n} \frac{1}{(1 + k)^t}$$

Present value interest factor formula for periodic compounding:

$$\text{PVIF} = \frac{1}{(1 + k/m)^{n^*m}}$$

Present value annuity factor formula for periodic compounding:

$$\text{PVAF} = \sum_{t=1}^{n^*m} \frac{1}{(1 + k/m)^t}$$

where:

PVIF = present value interest factor
PVAF = present value annuity factor
$k$ = present value discount rate
$t$ = total number of periods
$n$ = total number of years in the income projection period
$m$ = number of compound periods per year

How does the analyst decide the appropriate compounding period? The selection criterion is fairly straightforward: The analyst selects the compounding period that is most representative of the timing of the actual (or projected) income flow. In the example of the $1,200 royalty income, the analyst would consider the actual royalty agreement. Does the royalty agreement call for annual, quarterly, or monthly payments? If the intangible is not subject to a license, contract, or other agreement, the analyst considers what periodicity best represents when the subject income is expected to be generated.

The second periodicity question is: When is the income expected to be generated within the period? Will all of the income be generated at the end of the period, or will the income be generated evenly throughout the period? As we have discussed, there are several compounding conventions available. However, the most common compounding period is the annual convention. This question relates to whether the intangible will generate the annual income at the beginning of the year, at the end of the year, or throughout the year.

This issue is often referred to as the alternative between the year-end convention and the midyear convention. The year-end convention assumes that all of the subject income is received at the end of the year. Therefore, the present value calculation is performed at the end of each year in the projection period. This convention is often appropriate with regard to the analysis of license agreements when royalty payments are made at (and only at) the end of each year.

The midyear convention assumes that all of the subject income is received at the middle of the year. Therefore, the present value calculation is performed at the midpoint of each year in the projection period. It is rather unusual for an intangible asset to generate all of its annual income right at the middle of a year. However, this convention is very commonly used in intangible asset analyses. The midyear convention is commonly used when income is generated evenly throughout the year or when income is generated randomly or sporadically throughout the year. In this regard, the midyear convention is used to approximate the condition whereby half of the intangible income is generated in the first half of the year and half of the intangible income is generated in the second half of the year.

The midyear convention is a simplifying assumption for analytical purposes, because the intangible income is not all generated at exactly the middle of the year. However, the midyear convention may be more reasonable than the year-end convention in approximating the conditions of even, random, or sporadic generation of income.

The question of when income is generated within a period is applicable to semiannual, quarterly, or monthly compounding as well as to annual compounding. However, the mathematical difference between midperiod convention and period-end convention becomes less significant as the number of compounding periods increases. Therefore, the issue is considered much more seriously when the income approach analysis involves annual compounding.

As with compounding, determining when income is to be discounted within the period can have a material effect on the results of the analysis. Let's return to the previous example of the intangible that will generate $1,200 per year in royalty income for the next 10 years. Assuming annual compounding, we recall that the value of the intangible was $6,780, using a 12 percent discount rate. That analysis was performed using the year-end convention.

Let's leave all of the variables the same (i.e., $1,200 income per year, 12 percent discount rate) and estimate the value of the intangible using the midyear convention. The value of the same intangible assuming the midyear convention is $6,882.

Since the amount of income, periodicity of income, and discount rate remained unchanged, the difference between the $6,780 value and the $6,882 value represents the effect of the intangible asset generating the annual income at the middle of each year instead of at the end of each year.

The formulas shown in Exhibit 10-2 are used to convert present value analyses and present value annuity analyses from the year-end discounting convention to the midyear discounting convention.

After considering all of the issues described so far, the analyst can calculate the appropriate yield or direct capitalization rate for the subject intangible asset. The mathematics of deriving present value discount rates and direct capitalization rates are beyond the scope of this book. Readers who want a refresher course on estimating present values and the opportunity cost of capital are referred to any recognized introductory corporate finance textbook, such as the latest edition of *Principles of Corporate Finance* by Richard A. Brealey and Stewart C. Myers.[1] Other recognized corporate finance texts are listed in the bibliography at the end of this chapter.

Likewise, the procedures for analyzing investment risks and corresponding rates of return are beyond the scope of this book. Readers who want a refresher course on risk and expected return investment analysis

---

1. Richard A. Brealey and Stewart C. Myers, *Principles of Corporate Finance*, 5th ed. (New York: McGraw-Hill, 1996).

Adjusting Present Value Formulas for MidYear Discounting Convention

Present value interest factor formula for year-end discounting convention:

$$PVIF = \frac{1}{(1 + k)^t}$$

Present value annuity factor formula for year-end discounting convention:

$$PVAF = \sum_{t=1}^{n} \frac{1}{(1 + k)^t}$$

Present value interest factor formula for midyear discounting convention:

$$PVIF = \frac{1}{(1 + k)^{t-0.5}}$$

Present value annuity factor formula for midyear discounting convention:

$$PVAF = \sum_{t=1}^{n} \frac{1}{(1 + k)^{t-0.5}}$$

where:

PVIF = present value interest factor

PVAF = present value annuity factor

$k$ = present value discount rate

$t$ = time period in years

$n$ = total number of years in the income projection period

are referred to any recognized security analysis and portfolio management textbook, such as the latest edition of *Investments* by Zvi Bodie, Alex Kane, and Alan J. Marcus.[2] Other recognized security analysis texts are listed in the bibliography at the end of this chapter.

Finally, readers who are particularly interested in estimating discount rates, direct capitalization rates, and risk-adjusted rates of return for purposes of valuing businesses and business interests are referred to the latest edition of *Valuing a Business: The Analysis and Appraisal of Closely Held Companies*, by Shannon P. Pratt, Robert F. Reilly, and Robert P. Schweihs,[3] and *Cost of Capital: Estimation and Application*, by Shannon P. Pratt.[4]

## DISCRETE VALUATION VERSUS COLLECTIVE VALUATION OF INTANGIBLE ASSETS

If performed correctly, income approach methods are equally applicable to the individual valuation of discrete intangible assets and to the collective valuation of a group of intangible assets. Many intangible assets are analyzed individually. Examples of these intangibles include individual franchise agreements, contracts (such as sports player contracts or advantageous supplier contracts), patents, copyrights, and trademarks. However, other intangible assets are often analyzed en masse. Examples of these intangibles

2. Zvi Bodie, Alex Kane, and Alan J. Marcus, *Investments* (New York: McGraw-Hill, 1997).

3. Shannon P. Pratt, Robert F. Reilly, and Robert P. Schweihs, *Valuing a Business: The Analysis and Appraisal of Closely Held Companies,* 3d ed. (New York: McGraw-Hill, 1996).

4. Shannon P. Pratt, *Cost of Capital: Estimation and Application* (New York: John Wiley & Sons, 1998).

include customer relationships, medical patient charts and records, bank depositors, credit card portfolios, and mortgage servicing rights.

All the intangibles mentioned are subject to analysis by income approach methods. Procedurally, it may be somewhat easier to analyze a discrete intangible using the income approach. Typically, there is only one income stream to analyze and one remaining useful life to estimate. Also, the valuation model is limited to one present value calculation: the present value of one economic income projection over a single, finite period.

Procedurally, it is somewhat more complex to analyze a group of intangible assets using the income approach. For example, different types of customers may generate different profit margins, have different expected revenue growth rates, and exhibit different remaining useful life characteristics. If the valuation variables related to heterogeneous groups of the same intangible are different enough, the analyst may choose to disaggregate the intangible into several more homogeneous groups.

Even within homogeneous groups of intangibles, income approach analyses have certain complexities. When analyzing customer intangibles, for example, some analysts project income over the average remaining life of the entire group of customers. On the other hand, some analysts project an income stream that decays annually in relationship to the pattern of expected customer retirements. While the second procedure more accurately reflects how customers interact with a business (i.e., some customers turn over every year; they usually don't all leave at once), neither method is necessarily wrong.

More importantly, as long as there is consistency in all of the valuation variables (e.g., growth rates, profit margins, life estimates, discount rates, etc.), collective income approach analyses will yield virtually the same results as individual income approach analyses. That is, the conclusion of the collective analysis will equal the sum of all of the individual analyses (if the valuation variables are treated consistently). So, let's assume the analysis is to estimate the value of a credit card portfolio that includes 10,000 customer accounts. One procedure is to perform 10,000 individual discounted cash flow analyses, based on individual account balances, account expected remaining lives, and so on. An alternative is to perform one analysis based upon total account balances, average account expected remaining life, and similar aggregate valuation variables. If performed consistently and correctly, both procedures should conclude virtually the same valuation estimate.

## DIFFERENCES BETWEEN INTANGIBLE ASSET AND BUSINESS VALUATION

There are three principal differences in the application of the income approach to intangible asset valuation as compared to business enterprise valuation. First, most intangible assets have a finite remaining useful life. Generally, businesses and business securities are assumed to have a perpetual life. Therefore, the income approach analysis of an intangible asset involves a finite, discrete projection period. The income approach analysis of a business enterprise involves an indefinite, perpetual projection period. The analytical difference between intangible asset and business enterprise valuation will be discussed in greater detail in Chapter 12.

Second, there is usually greater risk associated with an investment in an intangible asset as compared to an investment in a business enterprise, ceteris paribus. Within the context of the income approach analysis, this additional risk generally translates into a higher present value discount rate applicable to the intangible asset. Of course, this statement is only correct assuming all other things are equal. Some intangible assets may involve considerably less risk than many business entities. For example, a valuable franchise agreement (e.g., sports franchise, FCC license, cable television franchise) may involve considerably less investment risk than a nonmarketable, noncontrolling equity ownership interest in a development phase business.

Another consideration regarding risk is whether the intangible is being valued as part of a going-concern business enterprise or as an independent economic unit (to be sold or exchanged separately from other business assets). As mentioned in the discount rate section of this chapter, it is common to use an overall business enterprise discount rate when estimating the contributory value of the intangible as part of a going-concern business. Likewise, it is common to use a higher discount rate (reflecting the additional investment risk) when estimating the independent value of a stand-alone intangible. Some analysts use the cost of equity capital of the typical business that would buy or license the stand-alone intangible as an indication of the appropriate present value discount rate.

Third, in intangible asset valuation, only the income that is directly attributable to the subject intangible is considered in the income approach analysis. In the business enterprise valuation, all of the income generated by the subject business (regardless of what assets generate that income) is included in the income approach analysis. In the intangible asset analysis, we are only interested in the value associated with the individual intangible. In the business enterprise analysis, we are interested in the collective value of all of the assets that comprise the subject business. In the business enterprise analysis, there is generally no reason to allocate or assign value to the individual component assets of the subject business, tangible or intangible.

In order to capture only that income directly attributable to the subject intangible in the income approach analysis, analysts consider the following three types of income:

1. Residual income is the total income generated by the economic unit that uses (or will use) the subject intangible less a specific capital charge. The capital charge represents a fair economic return on the tangible and other intangible assets associated with the subject intangible asset.

2. Profit split income is the total income generated by the economic unit that uses (or will use) the subject intangible, split between the subject intangible and all of the other tangible and intangible assets that are used by the economic unit. The profit split percentage should be a market-derived allocation percentage between intangible asset owners (licensors) and intangible asset users (licensees). The allocation percentage is intended to provide for a fair economic return on the tangible and other intangible assets that are used in the production of the total economic unit income.

3. Royalty income is the payment the licensee pays the licensor (however structured) for the use of a discrete individual

intangible. Typically, the licensee has to provide for all of the tangible and other intangible assets that will be used with the subject intangible in order to generate operating income for the licensee. Therefore, 100 percent of the royalty income (or of the hypothetical relief from not having to pay a royalty income) is directly associated with the subject intangible.

Intangible asset and business enterprise valuation both use the income approach as a basic analytical tool. In both types of valuation analyses, the yield capitalization method and the direct capitalization method are fundamental income approach analyses. However, as described earlier, there are several fundamental differences in the income approach analyses as they relate to intangible asset versus business enterprise valuation. Those differences are illustrated in the next section.

## VALUATION METHODS AND ILLUSTRATIVE EXAMPLES

All intangible asset income approach methods can be grouped into three categories of analyses:

1. Methods that analyze incremental income.
2. Methods that analyze a split of total income.
3. Methods that analyze actual or hypothetical royalty income.

### Incremental Income Analyses

There are numerous incremental income analyses, presented in the yield capitalization, or discounted economic income, format and some in the direct capitalization format. Although there are numerous versions, cash flow is the most common measure of economic income used in these analyses.

All incremental income analyses attempt to quantify the following economic phenomena:

1. Increased revenues associated with the subject intangible.
2. Decreased costs associated with the subject intangible.
3. The combined effects of both increased revenues and decreased costs.

With regard to increased revenues, any of the following conditions may be attributed to the subject intangible:

1. Increased dollar revenues.
2. Increased unit revenues.
3. Increased selling price per unit.
4. Increased market share.
5. Increased number of customers (or contracts, patients, clients, etc.).
6. Increased time period of revenue recognition.

All of the analyses are incremental because, directly or indirectly, they compare the expected revenues with the intangible to the expected revenues without the intangible. Some individual methods describe the nature of the incremental analysis in their names, such as the *selling price differential method.* However, all the methods are based on some form of differential analysis.

With regard to decreased costs, any of the following conditions may be attributed to the subject intangible:

1. Decreased bad debt expense.
2. Decreased cost of goods sold.
3. Decreased material cost.
4. Decreased material scrap expense.
5. Increased operating efficiency.
6. Increased production levels.
7. Decreased utilities expense.
8. Decreased labor-related expense.
9. Decreased administrative expense.
10. Decreased rent expense.
11. Decreased advertising, selling, or promotion expense.
12. Decreased or deferred capital expenditures.
13. Decreased asset maintenance expense.
14. Decreased investments in receivables or inventory.
15. Decreased cost of capital components (e.g., interest expense).
16. Decreased overall cost of capital (e.g., discount rate).

Again, all the analyses are incremental because, directly or indirectly, they compare the expected costs with the intangible to the expected costs without the intangible. Again, some of the names of the individual methods make the comparative form of analysis obvious, such as the *advertising cost savings method.* Nonetheless, all the methods rely upon some form of differential income analysis.

Some analysts classify several (if not all) of the cost savings analyses as cost approach methods. The classification of analyses as either income approach methods or cost approach methods is really semantic. Neither classification affects the objective—or the mechanical procedures—of the analysis.

Of course, methods that consider both revenue increases (however defined) and cost decreases (however defined) are incremental analyses that attribute two or more economic benefits to the use or ownership of the subject intangible.

## Profit Split Analyses

Profit split analyses attempt to "split" or allocate some measure of economic income and assign it directly to the subject intangible. Some profit split analyses allocate gross measures of economic income, such as total revenues. Most profit split analyses allocate net measures of economic income, such as operating income, operating cash flow, or net cash flow.

All profit split analyses start with the total income (however defined) of the economic unit that uses (or will use) the intangible and split the total income between the subject intangible and all of the other tangible and intangible assets that contribute to generating the total income of the economic unit.

The actual profit split percentages (e.g., 20 percent, 33 percent, 50 percent) vary based on:

1. The specific type of intangible asset and intellectual property;
2. The type of operations of the subject economic unit; or
3. The industry in which the subject economic unit operates.

When selecting the profit split percentage to use in any particular analysis, analysts consider these factors:

1. Market-derived profit split percentages stated in, or implied from, actual arm's-length royalty or other intangible transfer agreements.
2. A functional analysis of how the subject intangible actually operates within the subject economic unit.
3. A relative analysis of the contributory importance to income generation of the subject intangible vis-à-vis all other assets of the subject economic unit.
4. The extent to which the measure of economic income selected for analysis already provides for a fair economic return for the other tangible and intangible assets of the subject economic unit.

In the typical profit split analysis, the split to the intangible (e.g., 25 percent) provides an allocation of total enterprise income to the subject intangible, and the residual split (e.g., 75 percent) provides an allocation of total enterprise income to all other assets of the subject economic unit.

## Royalty Rate Analyses

There are relatively few royalty rate analyses. They all relate to one of two analytical scenarios:

1. Royalty income that is actually earned—or could hypothetically be earned—by the intangible owner by licensing the intangible to an independent party.
2. Hypothetical royalty expense that is not paid to an independent party because the owner in fact owns the subject intangible and does not have to license it from anyone else. This analytical scenario is the basis for the *royalty cost savings* or *relief from royalty* method.

The royalty income measures in these analyses may take many forms:

1. Total royalty dollar payments per period.
2. Royalty rate as a percentage of revenues.
3. Royalty rate as a percentage of profits.
4. Royalty dollar amount per unit sold.
5. Royalty dollar amount per unit produced.

In any event, actual or hypothetical royalty payments are intended to be market-derived estimates. For that reason, many analysts classify royalty rate analyses as market approach methods. Indeed, these analyses are described in Chapter 9, Market Approach Methods. Chapter 9 describes the procedures for finding, selecting or rejecting, and adjusting market-derived royalty rate data to use in these analyses. In any event, the classification of these analyses as either income approach methods or market approach methods is really a semantic issue.

# Illustrative Examples

Example I uses an incremental income method to value a proprietary technology (and the related FDA regulatory approval).

Example II uses a profit split method to value a consumer-oriented trademark and associated trade name.

Example III uses a royalty income method to value the same consumer-oriented trademark and trade name.

### Example I—Incremental Income Analysis

Big Dog pet food company has developed a drug that prevents fleas in cats and dogs. Based upon years of research, Big Dog developed a way to include the drug in their pet food. After testing the drug, called Fleabegone, and the new dog food on thousands of animals over the past decade, Big Dog went to the U.S. Food and Drug Administration (FDA) for approval to produce and sell the medicated pet food.

As of January 1, 1999, the FDA approved the sale of the pet food containing the Fleabegone medication. Big Dog has already built a pilot plant and is ready to produce and sell the medicated pet food. Our assignment is to estimate the value of the medicated pet food proprietary technology (and the related FDA approval) as of January 1, 1999, for management information purposes.

We have concluded that the income approach, using an incremental income method, is the most appropriate form of analysis.

Big Dog marketing management has created unit selling price, unit volume, and market share projections for the 10 years after the introduction of the new medicated pet food product. Big Dog manufacturing and engineering management has projected cost of goods sold data and capital expenditures data for the next 10 years. Big Dog financial management has projected all the various selling, general, and administrative expenses related to this new product over the next 10 years. After thorough reviews and comprehensive interviews, we have concluded that all of these projections are reasonable.

The projected results of operations for the flea repellent medicated pet food are presented in Exhibit 10-3.

Based upon the data available to us, we have selected net cash flow as the appropriate measure of economic income in our analysis.

Based upon the actual experience of Big Dog, and based upon our research of the FDA approval process, it would take a competitor nine years to obtain FDA approval for their own version of a flea repellent medicated pet food. Big Dog management knows that no other competitor has been experimenting in this area of research. However, once the competition sees the Fleabegone product on the market, they are expected to quickly reverse-engineer a competing product. So, it is reasonable to assume that Big Dog will enjoy a monopolistic competitive advantage for nine years. Therefore, we have selected nine years as the remaining useful life of the economic advantages associated with the subject intangible.

Based upon the speculative nature of this new product, in a new product category, created by a new proprietary technology, we have selected 40 percent as the appropriate present value discount rate.

Exhibit 10-3 presents a summary of the incremental income analysis related to the Fleabegone medicated pet food proprietary technology. Note that Exhibit 10-3 presents an incremental analysis, even though it includes all the projected income of the subject product line (after subtracting an appropriate capital charge), because Big Dog does not already produce a medicated pet food using a previous technology. All the projected income is incremental when compared to the zero income associated with not producing a medicated pet food product.

**E X H I B I T  10-3**

Big Dog Pet Food Company Proprietary Technology Valuation, Fleabegone Pet Food, as of January 1, 1999 (in 000s)

| Valuation Variables | 1999 | 2000 | 2001 | 2002 | 2003 | 2004 | 2005 | 2006 | 2007 |
|---|---|---|---|---|---|---|---|---|---|
| Net sales | $48,269 | $64,358 | $80,448 | $84,470 | $88,694 | $93,129 | $97,785 | $102,674 | $107,808 |
| Net sales annual growth rate | | 33.33% | 25.00% | 5.00% | 5.00% | 5.00% | 5.00% | 5.00% | 5.00% |
| Cost of sales (including depreciation expense) | 24,135 | 32,179 | 40,224 | 42,235 | 44,347 | 46,564 | 48,892 | 51,337 | 53,904 |
| Gross profit | 24,134 | 32,179 | 40,224 | 42,235 | 44,347 | 46,564 | 48,893 | 51,337 | 53,904 |
| Selling expense: | | | | | | | | | |
| Advertising expense | 8,688 | 11,584 | 14,481 | 7,602 | 7,982 | 8,381 | 8,801 | 9,241 | 9,703 |
| Deals expense | 6,758 | 9,010 | 11,263 | 5,913 | 6,209 | 6,519 | 6,845 | 7,187 | 7,547 |
| Other expense | 2,896 | 3,861 | 4,827 | 5,068 | 5,322 | 5,588 | 5,867 | 6,160 | 6,468 |
| Total selling expense | 18,342 | 24,455 | 30,571 | 18,583 | 19,513 | 20,488 | 21,513 | 22,588 | 23,718 |
| General expense | 2,365 | 3,154 | 3,942 | 4,139 | 4,345 | 4,563 | 4,791 | 5,031 | 5,283 |
| Amortization expense | 1,403 | 1,403 | 1,403 | 1,403 | 1,403 | 1,403 | 1,403 | 1,403 | 1,403 |
| Total selling, general, and amortization expenses | 22,110 | 29,012 | 35,916 | 24,125 | 25,261 | 26,454 | 27,707 | 29,022 | 30,404 |
| Pretax income | 2,024 | 3,167 | 4,308 | 18,110 | 19,086 | 20,110 | 21,186 | 22,315 | 23,500 |
| Income tax expense | 1,012 | 1,584 | 2,153 | 9,055 | 9,543 | 10,055 | 10,593 | 11,157 | 11,750 |
| After-tax income | 1,012 | 1,583 | 2,155 | 9,055 | 9,543 | 10,055 | 10,593 | 11,158 | 11,750 |
| Plus: depreciation expense | 820 | 1,094 | 1,368 | 1,436 | 1,508 | 1,583 | 1,662 | 1,745 | 1,833 |
| Plus: amortization expense | 1,403 | 1,403 | 1,403 | 1,403 | 1,403 | 1,403 | 1,403 | 1,403 | 1,403 |
| Less: capital expenditures | (1,000) | (644) | (804) | (845) | (887) | (931) | (978) | (1,027) | (1,078) |
| Less: capital charge on associated tangible and intangible assets | (1,148) | (1,465) | (1,753) | (1,741) | (1,750) | (1,759) | (1,768) | (1,777) | (1,786) |
| Net cash flow | 1,087 | 1,971 | 2,369 | 9,308 | 9,817 | 10,351 | 10,912 | 11,502 | 12,122 |
| Present value discount factors @40% discount rate | 0.8452 | 0.6037 | 0.4312 | 0.3080 | 0.2200 | 0.1571 | 0.1122 | 0.0802 | 0.0573 |
| Discounted net cash flow | 919 | 1,190 | 1,022 | 2,867 | 2,160 | 1,626 | 1,224 | 922 | 695 |
| Sum of discounted net cash flow | $12,624 | | | | | | | | |
| Indicated value of proprietary technology (rounded) | $12,600 | | | | | | | | |

Based upon the incremental income analysis summarized in Exhibit 10-3, the value of the subject proprietary technology, as of January 1, 1999, is $12,600,000.

### Example II—Profit Split Analysis

Friendly Foods Company manufactures and distributes the number one brand of artificial beverage sweetener in the country. The brand is called SweetStuff. The trade name SweetStuff became a registered trade name in the United States, and the stylized trademark associated with SweetStuff was also registered, in 1994.

The SweetStuff product is somewhat technologically superior to other artificial beverage sweeteners. In addition, due to creative advertising and promotion and to extraordinary consumer brand loyalty, SweetStuff quickly became the top-selling brand in its product category.

During the years 1995 through 1998, SweetStuff enjoyed average net sales in excess of $97 million per year. It has the leading consumer franchise in its product category. It enjoys a 43 percent price premium at the wholesale (or manufacturer's) level over the average of the other leading brand artificial beverage sweeteners.

For the period 1995 through 1998, the average annual profit associated with the SweetStuff product line was 36 percent of net sales.

Our assignment is to estimate the value of the SweetStuff trademark and trade name as of January 1, 1999, for management information purposes.

Based upon the data available to us, we have concluded that a profit split analysis is the most appropriate income approach valuation method. In fact, based on the available data, we have concluded that we can perform two discrete profit split analyses: a split of net operating income and a split of the selling price differential.

The split of net operating income method is based on the split of the after-tax operating margin that a hypothetical licensee would be willing to pay to a hypothetical licensor for the use of the subject trademark and trade name. Through the payment of a royalty, the licensee is willing to pay a split of its after-tax profits to the licensor, because the use of the trademark or trade name enhances the licensee's operating profits.

Let's begin with the Friendly Foods Company 1999 budgeted operating profit. The operating profit is then tax affected using the combined effective federal and state income tax rate of 50 percent in order to determine the after-tax operating profit. Once the after-tax operating profit is determined, a capital charge is applied to take into consideration a return on all the other Friendly Foods Company tangible and intangible assets that are used or used up in producing the sales associated with the subject trademarks and trade names. Let's assume that in the instant case, we should apply a capital charge for proprietary technology associated with the SweetStuff product.

Next, let's estimate the allocation or split of the adjusted after-tax operating profit that the licensee would be willing to pay to the licensor for the use of the subject trademark and trade name.

The after-tax required rate of return on the Friendly Foods Company equity capital is estimated by analyzing an average equity return for guideline publicly traded companies. In our opinion, based on our analysis of the instant case, the after-tax required rate of return is the appropriate discount rate to use in our valuation of the subject trademark and trade name.

The appropriate direct capitalization rate for the subject trademark and trade name is calculated using the following formula:

$$1 \div (k - g)$$

where:

$k$ = the appropriate present value discount rate

$g$ = the long-term expected growth rate for the subject brand

Exhibit 10-4 summarizes the net operating income profit split analysis associated with the SweetStuff trademark and trade name.

Based upon this analysis, the indicated value of the subject trademark and trade name, as of January 1, 1999, is $64,000,000.

The selling price differential profit split method begins by analyzing the wholesale selling prices for each of the competitive brands in the same product category as SweetStuff—that is, artificial beverage sweeteners. The selling price information is collected by Nielsen and by SAMI.

By comparing the subject branded product's wholesale selling price with the competitive branded products' average selling prices, we can understand the price advantage (and, therefore, value increment) that the subject trademark and trade name brings to the SweetStuff product.

The estimated wholesale selling price differential percentage is applied to the budgeted 1999 net sales for the subject brand in order to determine the total budgeted 1999 selling price differential. The selling price differential is tax affected by the effective combined federal and state income tax rates in order to derive an after-tax selling price differential.

Once the after-tax selling price differential is determined, a capital charge is applied to take into consideration a return on any Friendly Foods Company assets that are used or used up in producing the sales associated with the subject trademark and trade names. The capital charge includes a fair return on the associated proprietary technology intangible asset and the associated retail shelf space intangible asset.

After we estimate the after-tax adjusted selling price differential, we must estimate the share or split of the selling price differential that a hypothetical licensee would be willing to pay to a hypothetical licensor for the use of the subject trademark and trade name. The licensee is willing to pay this share of the selling price differential to the licensor because the use of the subject trademark or trade name is expected to enhance the licensee's business.

Based on our analysis, the appropriate profit split percentage in this case is 50 percent. The split percentage is applied to the (after-tax) selling price

**EXHIBIT 10-4**

Friendly Foods Company Trademark and Trade Name Valuation of Sweetstuff, Net Operating Income Analysis, As of January 1, 1999 (in 000's)

| Valuation Variables | | Trademark and Trade Name Valuation | |
| --- | --- | --- | --- |
| Expected long-term growth rate (g) | 0.5% | Projected 1999 brand net sales | $105,485 |
| Present value discount rate (k) | 15.0% | Projected 1999 net operating profit | 40,344 |
| Effective income tax rate | 50.0% | Less: income taxes | (20,172) |
| Direct capitalization rate | 14.5% | Projected 1999 net operating profit (after taxes) | 20,172 |
| Proprietary technology capital charge | 1.4% | Less: associated proprietary technology capital charge | (1,477) |
| (as % of net sales) | | Projected 1999 economic income | $ 18,695 |
| | | Projected 1999 economic income | $ 18,695 |
| | | Multiplied by: appropriate profit split percent | 50.0% |
| | | Indicated profit "split" | 9,348 |
| | | Divided by: direct capitalization rate | 14.5% |
| | | Indicated trademark and trade name capitalized profit split | $ 64,469 |
| | | Trademark and trade name value (rounded) | $ 64,000 |

EXHIBIT 10-5

Friendly Foods Company Trademark and Trade Name Valuation of Sweetstuff, Selling Price Differential Profit Split Method, as of January 1, 1999 (in 000s)

| Valuation Variables | | Trademark and Trade Name Valuation | |
|---|---|---|---|
| Expected long-term growth rate (g) | 0.5% | Projected 1999 brand net sales | $105,485 |
| Present value discount rate (k) | 15.0% | Multiplied by: wholesale selling price differential percentage | 43.0% |
| Effective income tax rate | 50.0% | Projected 1999 selling price differential amount | 43,359 |
| Direct capitalization rate | 14.5% | Less: income taxes | (22,680) |
| Subject brand wholesale selling price differential | 43.0% | Projected 1999 selling price differential amount—after tax | 22,679 |
| Shelf space intangible asset capital charge | 72.0% | Less: | |
| (as % of net sales) | | Shelf space intangible asst capital charge | (759) |
| Proprietary technology intangible asset capital | 1.4% | Proprietary technology intangible asset capital charge | (1,477) |
| charge (as % of net sales) | | Total capital charge | (2,236) |
| | | Projected 1999 selling price differential economic income | $ 20,443 |
| | | Projected 1999 selling price differential economic income | $ 20,443 |
| | | Multiplied by: selling price differential split percentage | 50.0% |
| | | Selling price differential "split" | 10,221 |
| | | Divided by: direct capitalization rate | 14.5% |
| | | Indicated trademark and trade name capitalized selling pricing differential split | $ 70,490 |
| | | Trademark and trade name value (rounded) | $ 70,000 |

differential. The after-tax selling price differential split is then capitalized to estimate the value for the subject trademark and trade name.

Exhibit 10-5 presents a summary of the selling price differential profit split analysis.

Based on this analysis, the indicated value of the subject trademark and trade name, as of January 1, 1999, is $70,000,000.

Exhibit 10-6 presents a summary of the historical operating results of the SweetStuff product line. Exhibit 10-6 also presents our trademark and trade name valuation synthesis and conclusion based upon the results of these two income profit split analyses.

### Example III—Royalty Rate Analysis

This example relates to the same SweetStuff trademark and trade name as in Example II. Again, the objective of this analysis is to estimate the value of the Friendly Foods Company trademark and trade name as of January 1, 1999, for management information purposes.

The royalty rate analysis begins with the search for guideline trademark license transactions. Frequently, a trademark or trade name that has been purchased or developed by a company is licensed or rented to other companies, in an arm's-length transaction, for a license fee or royalty rate fee. The users are willing to pay this fee or royalty payment because the use of the trademark or trade name enhances the value of the licensee's business.

We researched various public databases and marketing and licensing publications and contacted various food industry executives concerning licensing fees for similar products. We researched licensing agreements entered into by the Friendly Foods Company and by other food companies. All such licenses were for food products and all were for the trademark or trade name alone (i.e., none included the transfers of proprietary technology or other intangible assets).

Friendly Foods Company Trademark and Trade Name Valuation for Sweetstuff, Valuation Synthesis and Conclusion, As of January 1, 1999

**Date of Registration: January 1, 1994**

| Quantitative Brand Attributes | 1995 | 1996 | 1997 | 1998 | Weighted Average |
|---|---|---|---|---|---|
| Historical product net sales (000s) | $ 93,639 | $ 93,673 | $ 97,531 | $100,572 | $ 97,587 |
| Historical product net sales growth (%) | | 0% | 4% | 3% | 2% |
| Operating profit (000s) | $ 31,596 | $ 31,201 | $ 34,509 | $ 38,668 | $ 35,220 |
| Operating profit (as a % of net sales) | 34% | 33% | 35% | 38% | 36% |
| Absolute size of market (000s) | $217,425 | $218,891 | $222,066 | $223,710 | $221,625 |
| Absolute market share (%) | 12% | 12% | 11% | 11% | 11% |
| Wholesale brand selling price differential ($) at 43% | $   0.68 | $   0.75 | $   0.86 | $   0.94 | $   0.85 |

| Valuation Variables | | | | | |
|---|---|---|---|---|---|
| Operating income profit split percentage | | | 50% | | |
| Wholesale selling price differential (as a % of sales price) | | | 43% | | |
| Wholesale selling price differential profit "split" percentage | | | 50% | | |

| Valuation Analysis (000s) | | | | | |
|---|---|---|---|---|---|
| Operating income profit split value | | | $64,000 | | |
| Selling price differential profit split value | | | $70,000 | | |
| Valuation synthesis and conclusion | | | $67,000 | | |

We used these market-derived license royalty rates for our valuation of the subject trademark and trade name. Based upon our analysis of empirical data, the appropriate royalty rate associated with the license of the Sweet-Stuff trademark and trade name is 18 percent of net sales.

Exhibit 10-7 presents the key valuation variables and projections for our royalty rate analysis of the subject trademark and trade name.

Exhibit 10-7 also summarizes the capitalized royalty income valuation analysis. Based upon this analysis, the indicated value of the subject trademark and trade name, as of January 1, 1999, is $65,000,000.

## SUMMARY

The income approach is applicable to the valuation and economic analysis of many types of intangible assets and intellectual properties. It is often

Friendly Foods Company Trademark and Trade Name Valuation Royalty Rate Analysis, As of January 1, 1999 (in 000s)

| Valuation Variables | | Trademark and Trade Name Valuation | |
|---|---|---|---|
| Expected long-term growth rate (g) | 0.5% | Projected 1999 brand net sales | $105,485 |
| Present value discount rate (k) | 15.0% | Multiplied by: market-derived royalty rate | 18.0% |
| Effective income tax rate | 50.0% | Projected 1999 brand royalty income | 18,987 |
| Direct capitalization rate | 14.5% | Less: income taxes | (9,493) |
| | | Forecasted 1999 royalties—after-tax | 9,494 |
| | | Divided by: direct capitalization rate | 14.5% |
| | | Indicated trademark and trade name capitalized royalty income | $ 65,476 |
| | | Trademark and trade name value (rounded) | $ 65,000 |

considered the most conceptually elegant valuation approach because the value of any property (e.g., intangible asset, business debt and equity instruments, real estate, etc.) is the present value of the expected income that can be generated through the ownership of that property. The income approach is eminently applicable to many types of economic analyses. As examples, damages analyses, lost income analyses, event analyses, royalty rate estimation, and transfer pricing typically all rely greatly on income approach methods.

However, as with all valuation methods, there are pros and cons to the application of the income approach. For example, it is relatively easy to undervalue or to overvalue intangible assets; this is particularly true for analysts who do not fully comprehend the analytical differences (both subtle and gross) between intangible asset valuation and business enterprise valuation. In particular, both experienced and inexperienced analysts should focus on the estimation of, and the documentation of, the following three essential components of all income approach analyses:

1. The appropriate, specifically defined measure of economic income (including consideration of capital charges and profit splits, when appropriate).

2. The appropriate income projection period for either a yield capitalization or a direct capitalization analysis (resulting from the rigorous estimation of the remaining useful life of the subject intangible).

3. The appropriate capitalization rate (either yield or direct) that is consistent with: the measure of economic income selected for analysis, the remaining useful life of the subject intangible, and the highest and best use of the subject intangible.

## BIBLIOGRAPHY

## Articles

Annin, Michael E., and Dominic A. Falaschetti. "Equity Risk Premium Still Produces Debate." *Valuation Strategies,* January/February 1998, pp. 17–23, 44.

Baumann, Barbara, and Marjorie Oxaal. "Estimating the Value of Group Medical Practices: A Primer." *Healthcare Financial Management,* December 1993, pp. 58–62+.

Black, Fischer. "A Simple Discounting Rule." *Financial Management,* Summer 1988, pp. 7–11.

Brooks, Robin C. "The Valuation of Trademarks and Trade Names Using an Income Approach." Willamette Management Associates *Insights,* Winter 1992, pp. 1–3.

Burton, James H. *Evolution of the Income Approach.* Chicago: Appraisal Institute, 1982.

Evans, Frank C. "Recognizing the Key Factors in the Income Approach to Business Valuation." *Business Valuation Review,* June 1996, pp. 80–86.

Ford, David J. "Intellectual Property Valuation—Part II: Cost and Income Approaches." *CPA Litigation Service Counselor,* March 1998, pp. 3–4.

Fowler, Bradley A. "Venture Capital Rates of Return Revisited." *Business Valuation Review,* March 1996, pp. 13–16.

Hartl, Robert J. "DCF Analysis: The Special Case of Risky Cash Outflows." *Real Estate Appraiser & Analyst,* Summer 1990, pp. 67–72.

Kaltman, Todd A. "Capitalization Using a Mid-Year Convention." *Business Valuation Review,* December 1995, pp. 178–82.

Lippitt, Jeffrey W., and Nicholas J. Mastrachhio Jr. "Developing Capitalization Rates for Valuing a Business." *CPA Journal,* November 1995, pp. 24–28.

Mellen, Chris. "Valuing a Long-Term Care Facility." *Healthcare Financial Management,* October 1992, pp. 20–25.

Mullen, Maggie. "How to Value Intangibles." *Accountancy,* November 1993, pp. 92–94.

Paulsen, Jon. "CAPM Issues." *Business Valuation Review,* December 1991, pp. 175–76.
———. "Measuring Rods for Intangible Assets." *Mergers & Acquisitions,* Spring 1984, pp. 45–49.
Raabe, William A., and Gerald E. Whittenburg. "Is the Capital Asset Pricing Model Appropriate in Tax Litigation?" *Valuation Strategies,* January/February 1998, pp. 10–15, 36–37.
Rabe, James G., and Robert F. Reilly. "Valuation of Intangible Assets for Property Tax Purposes." *National Public Accountant,* April 1994, pp. 26–28+.
———. "Valuing Intangible Assets as Part of a Unitary Assessment." *Journal of Property Tax Management,* Winter 1994, pp. 12–20.
Reilly, Robert F. "The Valuation of Intangible Assets and Intellectual Properties." *Buyouts & Acquisitions,* January/February 1988, pp. 24–30.
———. "Valuing Intangible Assets" (Parts 1 and 2). *CPA Expert,* Winter 1996, pp. 4–6, and Spring 1996, pp. 9–11.
———. "Valuing Intangible Assets—A Case Study." *CPA Expert,* Summer 1996, pp. 11–14.
Reilly, Robert F., and Bruce L. Richman. "Identification and Valuation of Individual Intangible Assets" (Chapter 5). In Bruce L. Richman, ed., *Tax and Financial Planning Strategies in Divorce,* 2d ed. New York: John Wiley & Sons, 1996, pp. 5-1–5-53.
Reilly, Robert F., and Robert P. Schweihs. "Issues in Unit Valuation for Ad Valorem Purposes." *Journal of Property Tax Management,* Fall 1997, pp. 55–67.
Rushmore, Stephen. *The Computerized Income Approach to Hotel-Motel Valuations & Market Studies.* Chicago: Appraisal Institute, 1990.
Simonds, Richard R. "Issues Involving the Use of Direct and Yield Capitalization in the Income Approach to Valuation." *Proceedings of the 1996 Wichita Public Utilities Workshop on Appraisal for Ad Valorem Taxation of Communications, Energy and Transportation Properties.* Wichita: Kansas State University, 1996.
Wacker, Raymond F. "Treasury's Proposed Regulations Allow Profit Split Method on Self-Developed Intangibles." *International Tax Journal,* Fall 1993, pp. 12–29.

# Books

Bierman, Harold Jr., and Seymour Smidt. *The Capital Budgeting Decision: Economic Analysis of Investment Projects,* 8th ed. New York: Macmillan Publishing Company, 1993.
Bodie, Zvi, Alex Kane, and Alan J. Marcus. *Investments.* New York: McGraw-Hill, 1997.
Bonbright, James C. *The Valuation of Property.* Charlottesville, VA: The Michie Company, 1965 (reprint of 1937 edition).
Brealey, Richard A., and Stewart C. Myers. *Principles of Corporate Finance,* 5th ed. New York: McGraw-Hill, 1996.
Cohen, Jerome B., Edward D. Zinbarg, and Arthur Zeikel. *Investment Analysis and Portfolio Management,* 5th ed. New York: McGraw-Hill, 1987.
Copeland, Tom, Tim Koller, and Jack Murrin. *Valuation: Measuring and Managing the Value of Companies.* New York: John Wiley & Sons, 1990.
Cottle, Sidney, et al. *Graham and Dodd's Security Analysis,* 5th ed. New York: McGraw-Hill, 1988.
Damodaran, Aswath. *Damodaran on Valuation: Security Analysis for Investment and Corporate Finance.* New York: John Wiley & Sons, 1993.
Harrington, Diana R. *Modern Portfolio Theory, the Capital Asset Pricing Model & Arbitrage Pricing Theory: A User's Guide,* 2d ed. Englewood Cliffs, NJ: Prentice Hall, 1987.
Pratt, Shannon P. *Cost of Capital: Estimation and Applications.* New York: John Wiley & Sons, 1998.
Pratt, Shannon P., Robert F. Reilly, and Robert P. Schweihs. *Valuing a Business: The Analysis and Appraisal of Closely Held Companies,* 3d ed. New York: McGraw-Hill, 1996.
Reilly, Frank K. *Investment Analysis and Portfolio Management,* 2d ed. Chicago: The Dryden Press, 1985.
Sharpe, William F. *Investments,* 2nd ed. Englewood Cliffs, NJ: Prentice Hall, 1981.

# PART THREE

# Intangible Asset Remaining Useful Life Analysis

# CHAPTER 11

# Life Analysis and Remaining Useful Life Estimation

## INTRODUCTION

This chapter presents the reasons why the expected remaining life of an intangible asset is important to understand during the valuation of the intangible. Various methods of estimating the expected remaining life of intangible assets are described, including a rigorous analytical method called *survivor curve analysis*.

## LIFE AND RETIREMENTS ANALYSIS

Life analysis is the study of the placements of (or investment in) similar assets—and of their subsequent retirements—in order to develop their life characteristics. In particular, the relevant life characteristics are average life and retirement pattern (sometimes referred to as decay rate). Based upon an evaluation of these life characteristics, and with informed judgment of the current and probable future operating environment, the analyst can estimate the remaining useful lives of the surviving assets.

Tangible assets tend to possess an *economic life* separate from a *service life*. The economic life of an asset is the period over which it may be profitably utilized or "over which improvements to real property contribute to property value."[1] The service life of an asset is the period of time (or other measurement of service) from the time of its installation to the time of its retirement from service.

There also exists a third category of life—*physical life.* The physical life of an asset extends from the date of the asset's manufacture to the date of its final destruction. For instance, a piece of machinery possesses one economic life while in the production line. After its retirement from the production line, it may continue its service either in another operation or for another owner. Finally, the machine comes to an end of its physical life due to wear and tear, stress, or calamity, when it is finally carted away as scrap.

For intangible assets and intellectual properties, on the other hand, economic life is usually the same as service life. However, some intangible assets may display separate economic and service lives, similar to those of tangible assets. For example, an engineering drawing remains in service as long as the subassembly part that it diagrams continues to be in production or is otherwise not obsolete. Even when the machine or model is discontinued, it may still be economical to maintain the engineering drawing as long as that subassembly part is produced, as spare parts may be needed for the existing models that are still in use. In this example, the economic life of the engineering drawing is longer than its service life.

An asset is retired when it is removed from useful service or operation. Except in the case of calamities or accidents, the owner of a tangible asset usually decides when the asset is retired. Whereas similar situations may exist for intangible assets and intellectual properties, forces beyond the control of the intangible asset owner typically influence the retirement or expiration of intangible assets. For example, in the case of the engineering drawing, if the part is no longer produced for whatever reason, the manufacturer loses the value of that intangible asset, even though the capacity and capability to manufacture the part diagrammed in the drawing still exist.

---

1. *The Dictionary of Real Estate Appraisal,* 3d ed. (Chicago: Appraisal Institute, 1993), p. 112.

## CAUSES OF RETIREMENT, ATTRITION, AND EXPIRATION IN INTANGIBLE ASSETS

The conditions that lead to the retirement, attrition, or withdrawal of an intangible asset or intellectual property include the following:

1. Physical:
   a. Accident.
   b. Catastrophe.
   c. Deterioration.
   d. Physical wear and tear.
2. Functional:
   a. Inadequacy.
   b. Obsolescence.
   c. Interrelated assets.
   d. Evolution—technology.
3. Operational:
   a. Accounting policy.
   b. Management policy.
   c. Regulatory policy.
4. Economic:
   a. Lack of demand.
   b. Interest rates.
   c. Inflation.
   d. Financing.
   e. Inadequacy of return on investment.

### Physical Characteristics

While deterioration from time, wear, and tear may be the main cause of retirement of tangible assets, intangible assets and intellectual properties—because of their intrinsic characteristic of lack of form—seldom retire from this cause. Similarly, accidents and catastrophe may eliminate the physical manifestation of an intangible asset such as the plant designed and built using proprietary technology, but the intellectual property content of the intangible asset still remains. However, certain intangible assets, such as a trained and assembled workforce, could be lost due to accidents, calamities, or acts of war.

### Functional Characteristics

Intangible assets usually tend to retire or expire due to functional inefficiencies. The inadequacy of an efficient, proprietary plant process layout—due to changes in a component in the production line, for example—is a cause of retirement of that proprietary process.

Obsolescence is a major cause of retirement, especially of technology-related intangible assets. While a patent or copyright may provide legal defense against infringement, the value of an intellectual property may decline rapidly if a new development renders it obsolete. The development of 3.5-inch diskettes and CD-ROMs, which have replaced the 5.25-inch floppy diskettes and the increasing number of compact disk (CD) musical recordings as opposed to vinyl records, are examples of retirements due to functional obsolescence.

In certain cases, the evolution of a product renders the existing intangible asset obsolete. The "new and improved" version causes the intangible asset owner to consider the new asset, even though the current asset satisfies his or her needs. The recent (as of 1997) nonavailability of lower frequency (less than 100 MHz) microchip processors is an example of the obsolescence of a data processing–related proprietary technology.

## Operational Characteristics

Changes in operating policies and procedures may cause the discontinuance of a process or product and, thereby, the retirement of all related intangible assets. Such changes in policies and procedures may be caused by influences from within the company (for example, due to management restructuring) or from without the company (for example, due to regulatory requirements). The abandonment of promising new proprietary technology that would improve the efficiency of cigarette production (because of government restrictions on tobacco products) is an example of this kind of obsolescence.

## Economic Characteristics

External factors, such as changes in demand or changes in interest rates, may render an operating process or the production of a certain product uneconomical. Economic characteristics may also cause the retirement of the associated intangible assets. For example, while a proprietary technology may allow the continued extraction of a mineral, either a lack of demand or the discovery of an abundant supply elsewhere may cause a change in the existing intangible asset owner's attitude regarding ownership of the proprietary technology.

While the causes of historical intangible asset retirement patterns may not seem important to the analyst, knowledge regarding the causes of the retirement may be helpful to the analyst in projecting the useful life characteristics of the intangible asset.

### VALUE AND REMAINING USEFUL LIFE

Intangible asset value is sometimes defined as the present worth of future economic income expected to be derived from the ownership or use of an intangible asset during the remaining economic life of the intangible asset. At the end of its economic life, the intangible asset owner perceives that it is no longer profitable to use the intangible asset. At the time of its retirement, the intangible asset portrays minimal value to its owner.

Accordingly, intangible asset value is a function of potential economic life. An intangible asset that has been used may not be worth as much as an otherwise identical, new intangible asset because the used (or seasoned) intangible asset gave up some of its potential economic usefulness during its life to date. Projection of the remaining useful life of a seasoned intangible asset is usually necessary in the estimation of value of that intangible asset.

The three generally accepted approaches to valuing an intangible asset all require the estimation of remaining useful life, albeit with varying degrees of priority and necessity. The outcome of the remaining useful life estimation also influences the quantitative results of the three approaches to value in a direct, predictable manner.

## The Cost Approach

In the cost approach, life analysis and remaining useful life estimation assist in the identification and quantification of value depreciation and obsolescence. As stated earlier, an intangible asset currently used in the generation of economic income has given up some of its value potential. Accordingly, the ratio of the effective age of that intangible asset to its total expected life represents one measure of obsolescence—or of value depreciation—for that particular intangible asset.

The complement of this ratio—that is, one minus the ratio of effective age to total expected life—is the expectancy life factor, sometimes called the percent good factor. This factor provides one measure for comparing the expected remaining life of a seasoned intangible asset to that of a new intangible asset at the beginning of its service life.

Mathematically:

$$Value\ depreciation\ or\ obsolescence = f\ \frac{Effective\ age}{Total\ expected\ life}$$

and its complement:

$$Expectancy\ life\ factor\ or\ percent\ good\ factor = f\left\{1 - \frac{Effective\ age}{Total\ expected\ life}\right\}$$

$$= f\ \frac{Expectancy\ or\ expected\ remaining\ life}{Total\ expected\ life}$$

where:

$f$ = a function of

Since the expectancy life factor multiplied by *cost new* represents one indication of the value of an existing intangible asset, the expected remaining life estimate clearly and directly has an influence on the indicated value of that intangible asset using an application of the cost approach. For example, all other characteristics of the intangible asset being the same, a longer remaining life implies a higher value indication and a short remaining life implies a lower value indication.

## The Market Approach

In the market approach, life analysis and remaining life estimation primarily provide a basis both to select and to adjust the comparable or guideline intangible asset sale or license transactional data. Based upon the comparability of the remaining life estimate of the subject intangible asset versus the comparative transaction intangible assets, remaining life analysis often serves as a basis for the acceptance or rejection of the market approach itself—or of any particular guideline transaction.

Conducting a life analysis and remaining useful life estimation of the subject intangible asset and comparing the results to those of a comparative intangible asset also provides an adjustment factor in the market approach. Comparative intangible asset transactions that have extreme life outcomes—life estimates that are either too short or too long—may not be suitable for inclusion in the market approach analysis. Likewise, if the adjustments to the comparative transactional data (i.e., adjustments to make the comparative intangible assets more comparable to the subject intangible asset) are too great, then the comparative intangible assets may not be suitable for further analysis.

An extremely short remaining useful life estimation (e.g., less than a year on an absolute basis) for the intangible asset, in comparison to longer remaining useful life estimates for the comparative intangible assets, results in an adjustment factor of significant magnitude. Other things remaining the same, the magnitude of adjustment to the comparative transactional data would indicate a fairly small value for the subject intangible asset—that is, considerably lower than that indicated for the comparative intangible assets. In fact, some analysts would doubt that any significant market exists for an intangible asset with an extremely short remaining useful life estimate.

On the other hand, an extremely long remaining useful life estimate for the subject intangible asset in comparison to that of the comparative intangible assets indicates a very valuable subject intangible asset. However, extremely long life estimates raise questions regarding the life analyses both of the subject and of the comparative intangible assets, including the following:

- Why is the remaining useful life of the subject intangible asset so long?
- What are the causes of the short life of the comparative intangible asset(s)?
- Are there any extraordinary terms in the comparative intangible asset transaction(s)?
- Would the market (i.e., the buyer) be able to finance the indicated high value of the subject intangible asset?
- Would the market be able to sustain the subject intangible asset over the long period of its remaining life?
- Are there any exogenous factors that should be considered in establishing the remaining useful life of the subject intangible asset?

Among intangible asset categories, internally generated intangible assets, such as customer lists, are sometimes prone to exhibit such extreme remaining useful life characteristics. In addition, certain intellectual properties, such as trademarks and copyrights, inherently tend to have longer remaining useful lives.

From a remaining useful life perspective, some analysts may assert that "one customer list is the same as any other customer list." However, this is analytically incorrect. In fact, from a remaining useful life perspective, no two customer lists are exactly alike. For that matter, from a remaining useful life perspective, no two intangible assets within the same category are exactly alike. Customer lists embody relationships developed by a company and a group of product or service consumers. Clearly, customer relationships vary based on the business of the company. Additionally, there are many factors—socioeconomical and geographical among them—that define the characteristics of the customer list. So, even within a fairly narrowly defined category of customer relationships, such as bank depositor customer relationships, one would still expect to find a high degree of variation in the estimated remaining lives of the intangible assets.

## The Income Approach

In the income approach, life analysis and remaining useful life estimation are prerequisite steps in the valuation analysis. This is especially true when applying yield capitalization methods, but it is also true when applying direct capitalization methods. The yield capitalization methods of the income approach project some measure of economic income over a finite discrete time period. In order to confirm the length of the time period, or the number of economic income flows to be projected, remaining useful life must be estimated.

Accordingly, estimation of a longer remaining useful life means a greater number of periodic economic income flows to be projected. This implies a higher value for the subject intangible asset compared to another intangible asset with a shorter remaining useful life, all other factors remaining constant. Analysts observe that value indications are very sensitive to variations in remaining useful life when the life estimate is under 10 years and are generally insensitive to remaining useful life variations when the life estimate is above 20 years. For example, the difference between a three-year and a four-year remaining useful life has a material effect on the conclusion of an income approach valuation analysis. On the other hand, the difference between a 23-year and a 24-year remaining useful life has a relatively immaterial effect on the conclusion of the income approach analysis.

### REASONS TO ESTIMATE USEFUL LIFE OF AN INTANGIBLE ASSET OR INTELLECTUAL PROPERTY

Prior to the inclusion of Section 197 in the Internal Revenue Code (which occurred in 1993), a major reason to estimate remaining useful life was to determine the amortization period for a purchased intangible asset. However, since the enactment of Section 197, all purchased intangible assets, including goodwill (with certain exceptions such as computer software), can be amortized over a 15-year period.

In addition to establishing an amortization period (wherever required) for income tax accounting or financial accounting purposes, the following are some of the more common reasons to estimate the remaining useful life of intangible assets:

1. Valuation of an intangible asset for sale transaction pricing, license structuring, or transfer pricing.
2. Cost recovery for financial accounting or regulatory accounting purposes.

3. Cost accounting for capital recovery purposes in normal business operations, either as a product expense or a period expense.
4. "Percent good" studies for financing purposes and for ad valorem tax assessment purposes.
5. Controversy and litigation support purposes; for example, for estimating damages (such as damages due to a breach of contract and damages due to an expropriation), or for estimating or substantiating insurance claims.
6. Other—for miscellaneous owner or creditor information, financial planning, and other strategic information purposes.

## DETERMINANTS TO ESTIMATE REMAINING USEFUL LIFE

There are several *determinants,* or factors, that can be analyzed in order to estimate the remaining useful life of most intangible assets. The following list presents some common life determinants, along with examples, that can provide some basis for estimating remaining useful life:

1. Legal determinants—patents, copyrights, certificates of need.
2. Contractual determinants—contracts, licenses, loans, employment agreements.
3. Judicial determinants—computer software.
4. Physical determinants—engineering drawings.
5. Technological determinants—proprietary technology, technical documentation, know-how.
6. Functional determinants—procedural manual, patented or unpatented technology, computer software.
7. Economic determinants—proprietary technology, trademarks, trade names.
8. Analytical determinants—customer relationships, contract renewals, credit card portfolios.

Usually the type or category of the intangible asset influences the selection of the appropriate life estimation determinant. The type of data and information required, the amount and detail of analysis to be conducted, and the nature of the final remaining useful life conclusion are all influenced by the selection of the appropriate life determinant. Several of the factors that are influenced by the selection of the life determinant are indicated in the following table:

| Type of Life Determinant | Type of Information or Data Required | Nature of Analysis and Life Estimate |
|---|---|---|
| Legal | Document | Definite |
| Contractual | Document | Definite |
| Judicial | Document | Definite |
| Physical | Engineering/Experience | Qualitative |
| Technological | Engineering/Technical | Qualitative |
| Functional | Engineering/Professional | Qualitative |
| Economic | Engineering/Economic | Quantitative |
| Analytical | Age (asset placement and retirement) data | Quantitative |

## Definite Analysis

For the types of intangible assets that lend themselves to the application of the first three types of life determinants, it is relatively easy to estimate the remaining term (once the analyst ascertains the date of the intangible asset's creation or generation) and their actual age as of the valuation date. However, even in these instances, analysts should consider whether or not external developments exist that would cause the subject intangible to lose its economic potential prior to its remaining term.

For instance, a patent registered 2 years prior to the valuation date would have a remaining legal term of 15 years. However, the legal protection of the patent over the next 15-year period does not guarantee the sustained economic benefit of the patent for the same period of time. For example, a new technological development may render the patent technologically (and therefore economically) obsolete long before the conclusion of the remaining 15-year patent protection period.

Some considerable amount of engineering expertise and asset retirement experience is necessary in order to evaluate the remaining useful life of an intangible asset using the physical life determinant. However, since physical wear and tear are seldom found in intangible assets, the use of the physical life determinant in intangible asset lifing analysis is rare.

## Qualitative Analysis

Life cycle analysis is one of the most commonly used qualitative methods for the estimation of the remaining useful life of intangible assets. Life cycle analysis incorporates qualitative considerations of future technological and marketplace conditions with quantitative considerations of existing and historical environments. This type of analysis allows for changes in the future with a logically derived estimate of when these changes may occur. The analysis examines technological trends and relationships and projects the timing and amount of anticipated changes.

The life cycle process, with its origins in the biological sciences, has evolved from the theory of marketing and marketing management. Graphically, a typical life cycle curve is depicted by an introduction stage, a rapidly increasing growth stage, a decreasing growth stage leading to maturity, a decline stage when substitution occurs, and finally a demise or a residual use stage. The characteristics of these life cycle process stages are:

- *Introduction*—technological leader or innovator, small production capacity, minor technical problems, customer reluctance.
- *Increasing growth*—product or technology acceptance, demand, price.
- *Maturity*—increased demand, competition, imitations.
- *Decline*—substitutive technology or product, loss of economical or functional superiority.
- *Residual/demise*—small numbers of assets still in service for maintenance purposes, small number of product or service providers.

The shape or contour of the life cycle is defined with a unit measure—such as revenues generated from a proprietary technology or the number of patented products currently in service—along the *y* axis; and a measure of time—such as months or years—along the $x$ axis. A life cycle measured in terms of revenues from up-front royalties for a proprietary technology or a registered patent may have a different shape—and probably a shorter expected life span—than a life cycle for the same asset when the measurement is in terms of annual unit sales or production volume.

In some instances, the life cycle of an intellectual property may not display a typical bell shape. Sometimes, the life cycle of an intangible asset may be defined by just two points of demarcation—the first for the intangible asset's introduction and the second for the intangible asset's demise. The demise of the intangible asset often coincides with the introduction of a new intangible asset.

A life cycle usually provides a functional relationship between service from a product or technology or other intangible asset (i.e., the dependent variable) and time (i.e., the independent variable). While time is the principal variable measuring the stages of the life cycle, several factors within and without the intangible asset owner's business may significantly influence its life cycle, and very few of these factors are measurable. The contour of the life cycle—and the length of its stages—are functions of technological change, rate of market acceptance, the ease of competitive entry, and other factors. The concepts of diffusion and adoption of innovation are the basis for the theoretical underpinnings of the life cycle analysis.

From historical life cycles, certain parameters such as growth rates, infusion rates, life span, and retirement patterns during the various stages can be estimated. Using technology substitution models (such as the Fisher-Pry model[2]), conducting discussions with industry experts, and using historically developed parameters, it is possible to estimate the life cycle for an existing intangible asset.

A key to projecting service life is not the chronological age of the subject intangible asset, but rather its age in relation to the stage of the life cycle that it is currently in. By locating the valuation date along the life cycle timeline, it is possible to estimate a remaining useful life for that intangible asset.

The remaining useful life of most intangible assets is longer in the growth phase of the asset's life cycle, decreases gradually as it moves from the rapid growth stage to the maturity stage, and deteriorates rapidly in the decline phase of the life cycle.

## Quantitative Analysis

Through the observation and classification of ages at death of millions of people, actuaries have developed mortality tables used to estimate the average life of humans and their life expectancy at any age. Similarly, engineers and statisticians have assembled retirement histories of assets that enable them to project probable lives of similar assets remaining in service.

For certain types of intangible assets (such as customer-related intangible assets), if age data are available on customer or contract renewals, it is possible to perform quantitative analysis using actuarial techniques to estimate the life characteristics of the subject assets. Intangible asset age data should include the following three items of information:

---

[2] J.C. Fisher and R.H. Pry, "A Simple Substitution Model of Technology Change," Report No. 70-C-215 (Schenectady, NY: General Electric Co., R&D Center, 1970). See also: *Technological Forecasting and Social Change*, Vol. 3, 1971, p. 77.

1. The age of all of the active intangible asset units as of the valuation date.

2. The age (at retirement) of all the retired intangible asset units.

3. The dates of the placements of all the retired intangible asset units.


## SURVIVOR CURVES

### Definition of Terms

The following terminology is commonly used in survivor curve analysis:

1. An intangible asset category or group (such as a credit card portfolio, a listing of customer relationships, a group of bank core depositors) is a group of like individual units (such as credit card holders, customers, individual checking account holders) regardless of the ages of the individual intangible asset units within the group.

2. The age of an active intangible asset unit is the lapsed time from the date of its placement in the business or operation (e.g., the opening of the bank account) up to the valuation date.

3. The service life of an intangible asset unit is the period of time extending from the date of the asset's placement into the system (such as opening an account, buying a subscription, a customer starting to do business with a supplier) to the date of the unit's retirement from the system.

4. The average service life (ASL) of a group of intangible assets is the quotient obtained by dividing the sum of the service life of each of the units (individual intangible assets) by the number of units (individual intangible assets). Using a survivor curve, the average service life of a group of intangible assets is defined as follows:

$$ASL = \frac{Area\ under\ the\ Complete\ Survivor\ Curve}{Total\ Number\ of\ Units\ at\ Age\ Zero}$$

5. The life expectancy or the remaining useful life of a unit is that period of time from the valuation date to the projected date when the unit will probably be retired from service (e.g., when an individual bank customer will close his or her account). The actual age of the intangible asset plus the life expectancy of the intangible equals the probable life of the intangible asset. The probable life of the intangible asset is the period from the intangible unit's first business operation (e.g., opening a bank account) to its final retirement (e.g., closing a bank account).

6. The average remaining life (ARL) of an intangible asset is similar to the ASL of an intangible asset, except that it is defined as of an age other than age zero. Age zero is the age of a brand new intangible asset (e.g., the date of opening of a new account, hiring a new employee, or registering a new patent). However, most intangible assets subject to analysis are used (i.e., seasoned) intangible assets—that is, they are not brand new. For this reason, the estimation of the average remaining life of a seasoned intangible asset is a much more common procedure than the estimation of the average service life of a brand new intangible asset. The average remaining life of a group of intangible assets is defined as follows:

$$ARL = \frac{Area\ under\ the\ Survivor\ Curve\ to\ the\ Right\ of\ an\ Age}{Number\ of\ Units\ Surviving\ at\ That\ Age}$$

**7.** The maximum life of a group of intangible assets (e.g., customers, drawings, patents) is the age of the last unit in a given group to be retired from service. It is the age at which a survivor curve representing the expected retirements of the intangible asset group has a zero ordinate or zero percent surviving. Note that the *maximum* life of a group of intangible assets should not be confused with the *average* life of the group of intangible assets.

**8.** Survivor curves are downward sloped (or reverse S) graphs presenting the number of units from the given group of intangible assets that are still surviving (or functioning) in service at various ages. The ordinates, or the $y$ axis measurements, of the curve at any given age, measured along the $x$ axis, give either the percentage or the actual number of the original group of intangible assets that are still surviving (i.e., still in service) at that age.

Exhibit 11-1 presents a survivor curve indicating the percent of the intangible assets that survive in service at various ages from age zero to the maximum life. This exhibit also presents other age and life parameters that both define and are defined by the survivor curve. On the survivor curve, the intangible assets can be presented as either physical units (such as subscribers, engineering drawings, etc.) or dollar balances (such as outstanding balances, revenues, etc.).

Survivor curves are often referred to as mortality curves in the human actuarial literature. However, since mortality suggests the expected rate of death of human beings, and since we are interested more in the expected rate of survival of intangible asset units, the term *survivor curve* is used in the valuation literature.

**9.** A stub survivor curve is an incomplete survivor curve that does not extend all the way to either the zero percent surviving point or the zero number surviving point, because the stub survivor curve includes intangible assets that are still in active service. That is, all of the intangible assets depicted on the stub curve have not yet retired, so the percent surviving has not yet reached zero.

**10.** Analytical-type survivor curves are theoretical curves, meaning that they are physical representations of mathematical functions. Analytical-type survivor curves are derived by various quantitative methods from the study and analysis of actual retirements. Analytical-type survivor curves are presented on a normalized basis, giving them the versatility to adapt to different classes or groups of intangible assets.

**11.** The experience band is the period of one or more consecutive time periods (e.g., calendar years, fiscal quarters, etc.) at or prior to the valuation date over which life analysis is performed. The experience band provides important information regarding the influences of external factors, such as management policies or economic conditions, on the service life of the intangible asset subject to analysis. To average out any extremities, a "wider" experience band is preferred. A wider experience band means that the historical placements and retirements are analyzed over a longer (as opposed to a shorter) period of time. However, the experience band should not be so wide as to include influences of events that are (chronologically) far removed from the valuation date. In many cases, the width of the experience band (i.e., the number of years of placement and retirement data subject to analysis) is limited by the quantity and quality of the historical retirement data available.

**12.** The placement band is a period of one or more consecutive time periods (e.g., calendar years, fiscal quarters, etc.) from the date at which certain units from the intangible asset group were placed into service. The placement band reflects the impact of management decisions and economic conditions from the time of the first placement (i.e., first functioning) of the subject intangible asset up to the valuation date. Practically, the lack of historical intangible asset retirement data often precludes the placement band analysis of the earlier vintages of the group of intangible assets.

## Survivor Curve Analysis

In order to conduct an analytical-type of remaining useful life analysis, an analyst examines the following data:

1. Active units (e.g., existing customers, credit card holders, contracts, etc.):
   a. Unique unit identification (name, account number, etc.).
   b. Start date (date of first conducting business, opening account, etc.).
   c. Measurement of economic income associated with the intangible asset (e.g., average revenues generated by the customers, average outstanding account balance of credit card holder, etc.).

**EXHIBIT 11-1**

Analytical Methods to Remaining Useful Life Estimation Survivor Curve Analysis

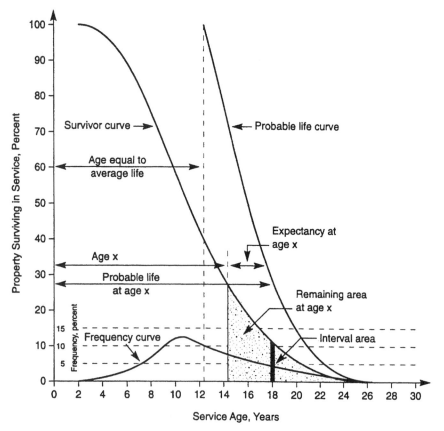

*Source:* Anson Marston, Robley Winfrey, and Jean C. Hempstead, *Engineering Valuation and Depreciation* (Ames, IA: Iowa State University Press, 1953), p. 147.

2. Retired units:
   a. Unique unit identification.
   b. Start date.
   c. End date (date when business relationship was terminated, closing of account, etc.).

In many instances, the ages of the individual retired intangible asset units are not available. In these cases, the data available are usually limited to the following, and only for a few time periods (years) prior to the valuation date:

1. Number of units in service at beginning of each time period.
2. Number of units that retired from service during each time period (where the actual ages of individual retired units are not known).

This is a special case of remaining useful life analysis, in which the semiactuarial type of life analysis methods may be applied. We discuss the application of semiactuarial life analysis methods later in this chapter.

Exhibit 11-2 presents an illustrative set of intangible asset life analysis data. Exhibit 11-2 presents the age and life data of the customer list of a securities brokerage business. In this example, we have the history of all surviving customer relationships for each vintage—or customer account placements—for the period from 1985 to 1996. For example, of the 29 customer accounts that were opened in 1987—that is, the 1987 vintage group or account placements—21 customers continued their account relationships into 1988. Of the same vintage group, 12 customers continued their account relationships into 1989, 6 customers maintained their account relationships into 1990, and 4 customers continued their account relationships into 1991.

The bottom row of Exhibit 11-2 sums up the total number of surviving customers from each vintage group as well as the total number of retired customers (i.e., those customers that stopped doing business with the subject broker) from each vintage group. As mentioned earlier, this bottom row of age or life data may be the only amount of intangible asset life information available for examination in many intangible asset analyses.

To construct the survivor curve used in the analytical life method, we first start with an experience band of a certain width, say for the three-year period from 1993 to 1995 (i.e., with 1996 being the valuation year). The experience band width may subsequently change:

1. After we have performed a preliminary analysis of the age or life data and considered such factors as retirement patterns, trends, and deviations due to management and economic conditions.
2. After we have performed a sensitivity analysis in order to assess the "fitness of fit" of the various analytical curves that will be matched against the subject intangible asset's actual survivor curve.

It should be noted that the experience band corresponds to the specific years prior to the valuation date for which the lifing data will be subject to rigorous analysis. In Exhibit 11-2, we selected the most recent three-year experience band prior to the valuation date—that is, the years 1993, 1994, and 1995. This experience band is represented by the shaded columns corresponding to years 1993, 1994, and 1995.

**EXHIBIT 11-2**

Analytical Method Life Analysis Illustrative Survivor Curve Construction
Historical Customer Account Age and Life Data, Customer Account Placements and Retirements

| Placements | | Experience | | | | | | | | | | | (b.o.y. '96) |
|---|---|---|---|---|---|---|---|---|---|---|---|---|---|
| | | 1985 | 1986 | 1987 | 1988 | 1989 | 1990 | 1991 | 1992 | 1993 | 1994 | 1995 | 1996 |
| 1985 | 95 | 95 / 0 | 95 / 9 | 86 / 19 | 67 / 6 | 61 / 16 | 45 / 4 | 41 / 3 | 38 / 1 | 37 / 9 | 28 / 0 | 28 / 3 | 25 |
| 1986 | 21 | | 21 / 6 | 15 / 5 | 10 / 2 | 8 / 1 | 7 / 1 | 6 / 1 | 5 / 0 | 5 / 1 | 4 / 0 | 4 / 1 | 3 |
| 1987 | 29 | | | 29 / 8 | 21 / 9 | 12 / 6 | 6 / 2 | 4 / 0 | 4 / 0 | 4 / 2 | 2 / 0 | 2 / 0 | 2 |
| 1988 | 23 | | | | 23 / 3 | 20 / 10 | 10 / 1 | 9 / 2 | 7 / 1 | 6 / 1 | 5 / 0 | 5 / 2 | 3 |
| 1989 | 14 | | | | | 14 / 7 | 7 / 1 | 6 / 1 | 5 / 1 | 4 / 2 | 2 / 0 | 2 / 0 | 2 |
| 1990 | 41 | | | | | | 41 / 10 | 31 / 2 | 29 / 3 | 26 / 12 | 14 / 0 | 14 / 2 | 12 |
| 1991 | 63 | | | | | | | 63 / 17 | 46 / 9 | 37 / 15 | 22 / 3 | 19 / 3 | 16 |
| 1992 | 39 | | | | | | | | 39 / 15 | 24 / 17 | 7 / 0 | 7 / 1 | 6 |
| 1993 | 23 | | | | | | | | | 23 / 17 | 6 / 0 | 6 / 0 | 6 |
| 1994 | 27 | | | | | | | | | | 27 / 2 | 25 / 1 | 24 |
| 1995 | 35 | | | | | | | | | | | 35 / 6 | 29 |
| 1996 | 60 | | | | | | | | | | | | 60 |
| Total | 470 | | | | | | | | | | | | |
| Balance | | 95 | 116 | 130 | 121 | 115 | 116 | 160 | 173 | 166 | 117 | 147 | 188 |
| Retired | | 0 | 15 | 32 | 20 | 40 | 19 | 26 | 30 | 76 | 5 | 19 | |

*Notes:*

1. In each cell, top number represents "EXPOSED TO RETIREMENTS" at beginning of year and bottom number represents "RETIREMENTS" during the year.

2. For each age-interval, Retirement Ratio = Retirements/Exposed to Retirements.

3. Horizontal rows correspond to Placement Band.

4. Vertical columns correspond to Experience Band.

As a point of comparison, the placement bands correspond to the analysis of the historical account placements. In comparison to experience bands (which are represented in the *columns* of age or life data), placement bands are represented by the data in the *rows* contained by the vintage groups under investigation, as presented in Exhibit 11-2.

After we have selected the appropriate width of the experience band subject to analysis, we next sort and group the active customer account data and the retired customer account data by like age groups (also called age intervals). From the exhibit, we can see that 4 customers from the 1989 account placements, 14 customers from the 1990 account placements, and 19 customers from the 1991 account placements are four years old in 1993, 1994, and 1995, respectively. This is relevant because the period of 1993 to

1995 is the experience band that we have selected for detailed analysis. Similarly, we can see that 2, 0, and 3 customers from the 1989 to 1991 age vintages retired during the four- to five-year age interval. Again, the four- to five-year age interval is 1993 for 1989 account placements, 1994 for 1990 account placements, and 1995 for 1991 account placements.

Adding the number of customer account placements from 1989, 1990, and 1991, we have 37 (4 + 14 + 19 = 37) four-year-old customer accounts in the 1993 to 1995 experience band. Of the 37 accounts that lasted to be four years old, 5 (2 + 0 + 3 = 5) customer accounts were retired (i.e., closed) during their fourth year of service. The total number (37) of customer accounts that were still open at the beginning of their fourth year—or the number of customer accounts that were "exposed to retirement" during their fourth year of services—is shown in column [2] and the row for age interval 4–5 in Exhibit 11-3. Similarly, the number of customer accounts that actually retired (i.e., closed) in the age interval 4–5 (i.e., the 5 accounts that were four years old and that closed during their fourth year of service) is shown in column [3] of Exhibit 11-3.

**EXHIBIT 11-3**

Illustrative Survivor Curve Construction, Calculation of the Survivor Curve
Selected Experience Band of 1993–1995 Using the Retirement Rate Method

| Age Interval | Number of Accounts Exposed to to Retirement | Number of Accounts Retired During Age Interval | Retirement Ratio | Survivor Ratio | Survivor Curve |
|---|---|---|---|---|---|
| [1] | [2] | [3] | [4] | [5] | [6] |
| 10–11 | 28 | 3 | 10.71% | 89.29% | 7.39% |
| 9–10 | 32 | 1 | 3.13% | 96.88% | 8.28% |
| 8–9 | 43 | 9 | 20.93% | 79.07% | 8.54% |
| 7–8 | 12 | 3 | 25.00% | 75.00% | 10.80% |
| 6–7 | 11 | 2 | 18.18% | 81.82% | 14.40% |
| 5–6 | 22 | 3 | 13.64% | 86.36% | 17.61% |
| 4–5 | 37 | 5 | 13.51% | 86.49% | 20.39% |
| 3–4 | 55 | 16 | 29.09% | 70.91% | 23.57% |
| 2–3 | 50 | 15 | 30.00% | 70.00% | 33.24% |
| 1–2 | 55 | 18 | 32.73% | 67.27% | 47.49% |
| 0–1 | 85 | 25 | 29.41% | 70.59% | 70.59% |
| 0 | 85 | | | | 100.00% |

Notes:

Column [4] = column [3]/column [2]

Column 5 = 1 − column [4]

Column 6 = column [6] (from row beneath) * column [5]

In Exhibit 11-3, we have developed a table such that the number of accounts retired during an age interval corresponds to the number of accounts exposed to retirement at the beginning of that age interval.

By comparing the number of accounts retired during an age interval to the number of accounts exposed to retirement (in other words, to the number of active accounts at the beginning of the age interval), we can compute the retirement ratio. The retirement ratio is sometimes called the force of mortality. The proportion of intangible asset units—or customer account relationships, in this example—remaining active is one minus the retirement ratio. Therefore, the annual retirement ratio is defined as follows:

$$Retirement\ Ratio = \frac{Number\ of\ Units\ Retired\ during\ a\ Period}{Number\ of\ Units\ Exposed\ to\ Retirement\ (i.e.,\ Active)\ at\ Beginning\ of\ Period}$$

From the annual retirement ratio, we can easily calculate the annual survivor ratio. The annual survivor ratio is defined as follows:

$$Survivor\ ratio = 1 - Retirement\ Ratio$$

Accordingly, for the four–to–five-year-old age interval of customer accounts in the selected 1993 to 1995 experience band, we have:

1. A retirement ratio = $5 \div 37 = 0.1351$, or 13.51 percent.
2. A survivor ratio = $1 - 0.1351 = 0.8649$, or 86.49 percent.

Columns [4] and [5] of Exhibit 11-3 present the retirement ratios and survivor ratios, respectively, for the various age intervals of the customer accounts in the selected 1993 to 1995 experience band.

The survivor curve is the cumulative proportion of the intangible asset units remaining active through the previous age interval. For example, for the age interval of four to five years, from the last column in Exhibit 11-3, we see that 23.57 percent of the customer accounts are "exposed to retirements." The 23.57 percent number corresponds to the percentage of the customer account relationships surviving (or still active) at the end of the age interval of three to four years. Of these account "exposures," 13.51 percent retire, or 86.49 percent survive, during the next (i.e., four- to five-year) age interval. Based on this, we have 20.39 percent (i.e., $23.57 \times 0.8649 = 20.39$) of the customer account relationships surviving at the end of the age interval of four to five years.

The constructed survivor curve starts at 100 percent surviving at the age of zero and goes to $y$ percent surviving at age $x$. In Exhibit 11-3, the constructed survivor curve goes to 7.39 percent surviving at the age interval of 10 to 11 years. By definition, this is the stub survivor curve. By necessity (since all of the accounts have not yet closed), the stub survivor curve does not get to the point of zero percent of accounts surviving.

Exhibit 11-4 is a graphical representation of the constructed stub curve.

## Methods of Calculating Survivor Curves

The method used in the example to construct the stub survivor curve is called the *annual rate*, or *retirement rate*, method. Because this method uses information and data regarding intangible assets in service as well as in-

**EXHIBIT 11-4**

Illustrative Survivor Curve Construction
Stub Curve: 1993–1995 Experience Band

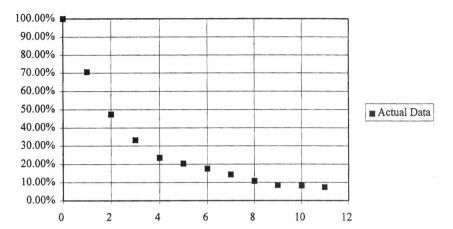

tangible assets that have retired, it is considered to be the most rigorous of the three systematic analytical methods for calculating survivor curves. The other two methods are called the *original group* method and the *individual unit* method.

The original group method uses only age and life data associated with one vintage installation. The individual unit method, considered by some analysts to be a last resort method, uses only the age and life data related to retired intangible assets (i.e., the age of the retired intangible asset units must be available).

## ASL from Survivor Curves

It is not possible to directly estimate an unbiased average life or a remaining useful life from a stub survivor curve because the stub curve does not reach the level of zero percent surviving. Based on the quantity of age and life data analyzed, the stub curve can stop at any point between 99 percent and 1 percent surviving. Therefore, the stub survivor curve does not allow for the calculation of the total service rendered by the intangible asset group under investigation.

However, the discrete observations of the stub curve can be used to project a complete curve by comparing the constructed stub curve to a set of standard survivor curve functions. The selection of the standard survivor curve function that is most appropriate for the extrapolation of the actual stub curve is often based on two methods: "eyeballing" the stub curve or using the *least square* method of statistical curve fitting process. In eyeballing a stub curve, the stub curve is physically compared against a set of standard type curves for various average service lives, as presented in Exhibit 11-5.

In the least squared method (sometimes called the least squared error method) of curve fitting, the vertical difference between the standard survivor curve and the actual stub curve at the discrete points is first calculated, and then squared—that is, multiplied by itself. The squared differences between all of the standard survivor curve observation points and the actual stub observation points are then summed. The standard sur-

**EXHIBIT 11-5**

Eyeballing the Stub Curve

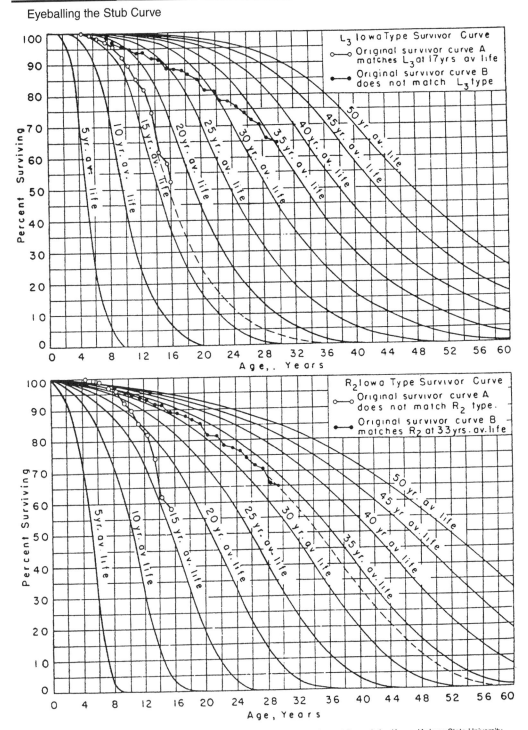

*Source:* Anson Marston, Robley Winfrey, and Jean C. Hempstead, *Engineering Valuation and Depreciation* (Ames, IA: Iowa State University Press, 1953), p. 166.

vivor curve that has the lowest or least squared difference is considered to be the curve that is most representative of the life characteristics of the intangible asset under consideration.

Since the standard survivor curve reaches the level of zero percent surviving, it is possible to calculate the area under the curve and, therefore, to reliably estimate the ASL of the subject intangible asset group.

With a reliable estimate of the actual average age of the subject intangible asset group, the ARL can be computed from the selected standard survivor curve.

## Standard Survivor Curve Functions

The following are some of the most common types of standard survivor curve functions used in the analytical method of intangible asset remaining life analysis:

1. Iowa-type curves.
2. Weibull distribution (the Iowa-type curves themselves can be a special case of this type of survivor curve).
3. Gompertz-Makeham curves.
4. Polynomial functions.

## Iowa-Type Curves

The original Iowa-type survivor curves resulted from studies of empirical data with respect to the survivor characteristics of many different types of industrial and public utility property. The data included empirical observations with respect to: railroad ties, railroad boxcars, telephone poles, central office equipment (e.g., telephone equipment), electric transformers and conductors, motor cars, commercial trucks, and so on.

Exhibit 11-6 is a graphical representation of an exponential curve fitted to the constructed stub curve. The exponential curve with a three-year average life (exp. 3.0) provides a better fit than the exp. 3.5 on the basis of the sum of squared differences. The exhibit indicates the exponential curves reaching zero percent surviving.

From the 176 standard survivor curves generated from such empirical data, the following *original* three families or *types* of Iowa curves evolved: left modal, symmetrical, and right modal. Subsequent research led to the development of a family of J-shaped or near origin modal curves. This classifica-

**EXHIBIT 11-6**

Illustrative Survivor Curve Construction
Curve Fitting: Exponential Curve

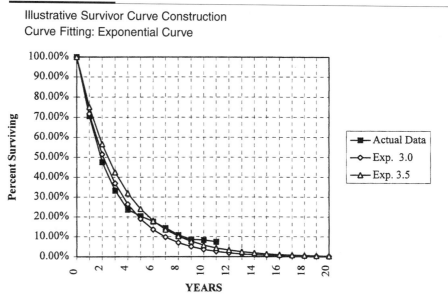

tion of Iowa-type survivor curves was made according to whether the mode of the frequency distribution in the curve was to the origin (O), to the left (L), symmetrical (S), or to the right (R) of the average life. Exhibits 11-7 to 11-10 present the four classifications of Iowa-type standard survivor curves.

The O-, L-, S-, and R-type survivor curves make it relatively easy to communicate the retirement or survivor life characteristics of a group of intangible assets:

- The modal frequency of the O-type curves occurs at or very close to the origin, indicating a high degree of "infant mortality" retirement rate. The O-type survivor curves tend to represent relationship-type intangible assets generally. This type of relationship implies that the intangible asset may last longer if it does not turn over or retire during an early (or trial) period. Typical types of relationship-type intangible assets include the category of customer-type intangible assets, such as newspaper subscribers, credit card customers, bank core depositors, and so on.

**E X H I B I T  11-7**

Illustrative Original Modal Type Curves

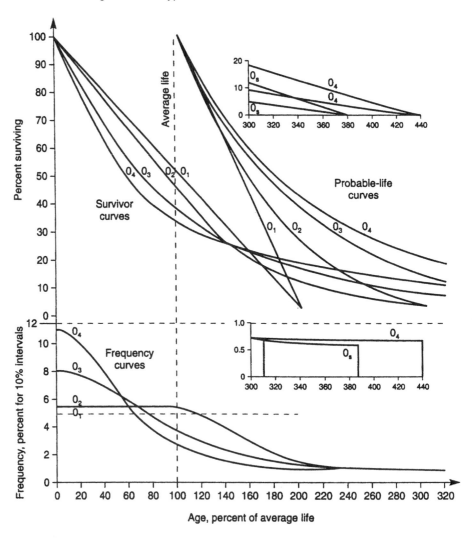

*Source:* Robley Winfrey, *Statistical Analyses of Industrial Property Retirements* (Ames, IA: Engineering Research Institute, Iowa State University, 1953). Revised April 1967 by Harold A. Cowles, p. 179.

EXHIBIT 11-8

Illustrative Left Modal Type Curves

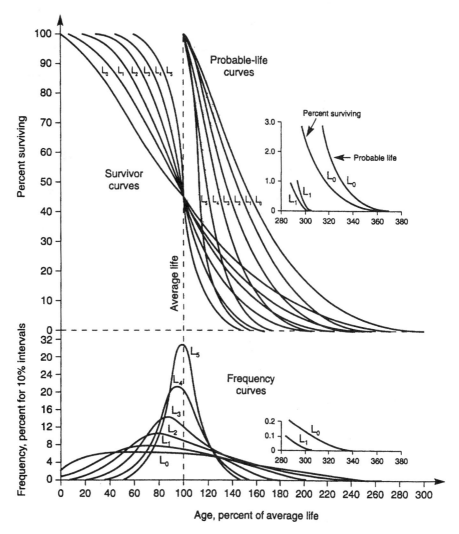

Source: Robley Winfrey, *Statistical Analyses of Industrial Property Retirements* (Ames, IA: Engineering Research Institute, Iowa State University, 1953). Revised April 1967 by Harold A. Cowles, p. 70.

- A left modal curve (L-type) is representative of a group of intangible assets that retires at a faster rate before its average life. An interpretation of this type of observation is that the intangible asset group's older members are more loyal (meaning here, less subject to turnover or retirement) than the group's younger members.

- A symmetrical curve (S-type) predicts that a group of intangible assets will retire at a similar rate at any given age, on either side of the group's average life. A symmetrical survivor curve implies that this group of intangible assets is probably exposed to a typical competitive environment.

- A right modal curve (R-type) shows its retirements to be higher after its average life. Tangible personal property and real estate assets usually display the right modal tendency—that is, minimal retirement initially, but a higher turnover or retirement rate after the average life.

**EXHIBIT 11-9**

Illustrative Right Modal Type Curves

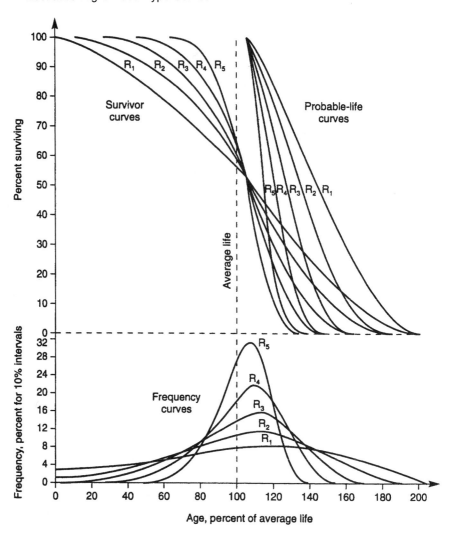

*Source:* Robley Winfrey, *Statistical Analyses of Industrial Property Retirements* (Ames, IA: Engineering Research Institute, Iowa State University, 1953). Revised April 1967 by Harold A. Cowles, p. 71.

The original Iowa-type survivor curves were mathematically derived from a variety of tangible personal property asset types, with each type of property subject to a different combination of the forces that cause retirements. Different methods of construction were used in the development of the survivor curves in order to capture the various forces that cause retirements in different ways. A general process of retirement for each type is the result. For purposes of the subject analysis, the Iowa-type survivor curves generalization process disassociates the various retirement forces from the specific type of property subject to analysis, thereby allowing their application to various forms of property types—that is, to either tangible or intangible assets.

While the conceptual support for Iowa-type survivor curves originates from human mortality studies, their initial application was in the remaining useful life estimation of property used in various utilities, including electric, gas, water, railroads, and telephone. Their extended application has been found in the remaining useful life analysis of various

EXHIBIT 11-10

Illustrative Symmetrical-Type Curves

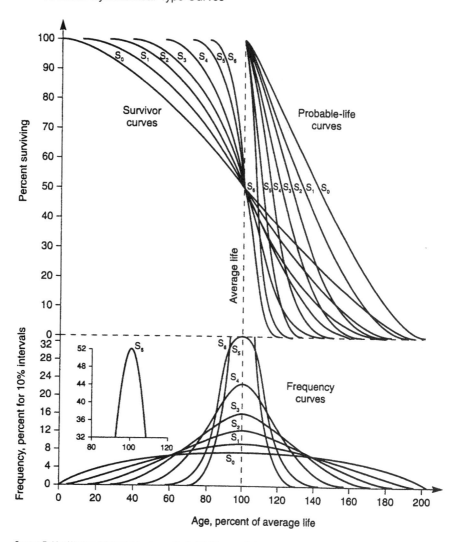

Source: Robley Winfrey, *Statistical Analyses of Industrial Property Retirements* (Ames, IA: Engineering Research Institute, Iowa State University, 1953). Revised April 1967 by Harold A. Cowles, p. 72.

types of intangible assets, including customer-related, marketing-related, engineering-related, technology-related, and other categories of intangible assets.

## Weibull Function

When Professor Waladdi Weibull presented his landmark paper in 1951, he made no claims for his formula on the basis of any theory. He stated:

> Furthermore, it is utterly hopeless to expect a theoretical basis for distribution functions of random variables such as strength properties of materials or of machine parts, . . . or even adult males born in the British Isles.
>
> It is believed that in such cases the only practicable way of progressing is to choose a simple function, test it empirically, and stick to it as long as none better has been found.

The Weibull distribution is useful in a great variety of economic analysis, engineering, and valuation applications, particularly as a model for estimating product or process life. Its versatility arises from the fact that the Weibull distribution can take a great variety of shapes. It is extremely flexible in fitting empirical life and retirement data, particularly because it fits many different kinds of empirical age and life data. However, flexibility in fitting empirical age and life data may give the Weibull distribution certain unexpected and undesirable attributes, especially with regard to the remaining useful life analysis of intangible assets.

Mathematically, the Weibull distribution survivor function is presented as follows:

$$S(t) = exp\ (-\ (t/a)\ \wedge\ B),\ t > 0$$

where:

$S(t)$ = the survivor percentage at age $t$

$exp$ = exponential function

$t$ = time period (such as months, quarters, or years)

$a$ = the distribution scale parameter; it is positive and determines the spread of the function; it has the same units as $t$

$B$ = the distribution shape parameter, a dimensionless number greater than zero; it determines the shape of the distribution

A noteworthy special case of the Weibull distribution occurs when $B = 1$. In that case, the Weibull distribution takes the form of a simple exponential distribution.

While the Weibull distribution is extremely flexible and useful in many situations involving the remaining useful life analysis of both tangible properties and intangible assets, there are several analytical caveats associated with the use of the Weibull distribution for life characteristic estimation purposes.

As mentioned earlier, the versatility of the Weibull distribution arises from its ability to fit virtually any kind of empirical age and life data. At certain shape and scale parameters, the Weibull function approximates the Iowa-type survivor curves. It has been observed that for $B < 1$, the Weibull function approximates the Iowa O-type curves. Other Iowa-type survivor curves (i.e., the L-, S-, and R-type curves) are represented by a Weibull function with $B > 1$.

Even though the two distribution description parameters, $a$ and $B$, generate the versatility of the Weibull distribution, the exponential nature of the function makes it difficult to estimate these two parameters. Moreover, in certain instances, because of the apparent precise fit of the Weibull distribution, the calculated remaining property lives at different age intervals tend to "run away"—that is, they continue to increase with age.

## Parameter Estimation

Not only does the Weibull distribution contain two unknown parameters, it also takes the form of an exponential function. The estimation of the two parameters—the $a$ scale parameter and the $B$ shape parameter—is a difficult task, requiring more than a simple working familiarity with statistical theories. The two parameters can only be estimated by the use of procedures developed by the application of the *theory of extreme values*.

However, the Weibull distribution can fairly easily be transposed into a linear relation in a logarithmic form. Since the Weibull distribution is an exponential function of the second order, it requires a double logarithmic (or *ln*) transformation.

Consider the Weibull distribution survivor function:

$$S(t) = exp\ (-\ (t/a) \wedge B),\ t > 0$$

Next, taking logarithms on both sides of the mathematical expression, we have:

$$ln\ S(t) = -\ (t/a) \wedge B = (-1/a) \wedge B * t \wedge B$$

$$ln\ (1/S\ (t)) = (1/a) \wedge B * t \wedge B$$

or:

$$ln\ (1/(S(t)) = exp(c) * t \wedge B$$

where:

$$exp(c) = (1/a) \wedge B$$

Next, taking logarithms again on both sides of the mathematical expression, we have:

$$ln\ ln\ (1/S(t)) = c + B\ ln(t)$$

This is similar to the following linear mathematical expression:

$$Y = c + mX$$

This is the equation of a straight line (i.e., of the slope and intercept form). A Weibull distribution *probability graph paper* that has an "*ln ln* to *ln*" scale is available. On such Weibull distribution probability graph paper, the *Y*s and *X*s can be plotted in order to estimate a straight line through the plot, and then the parameters can be estimated. Alternately, the equation can be solved in a convenient way by using the linear regression function in any of the more commonly available spreadsheet computer software packages.

## Remaining Life Estimation

In certain instances of survivor curves completed using the Weibull distribution, it has been observed that the average remaining lives keep on increasing with age, or tend to "run away." Also, while the average life is quite small, the remaining lives of the older intangible assets become unrealistically large.

This analytical problem arises because the Weibull distribution has fit the data points quite precisely, as can be observed from the R-square for the regression analysis. Because of this particular analytical problem, the naïve application of the estimated Weibull distribution parameters could be detrimental to the validity of the intangible asset valuation analysis.

A solution to this analytical problem is to force the constructed Weibull survivor curve to zero percent surviving at some foreseeable future, say at 40 or 50 years from the beginning time period. Arguably, the least controversial way to accomplish this adjustment would be to assume a straight-line decline after the actual survivor curve. Of course, any other justifiable decay pattern could also be applied.

Once the new survivor curve is constructed with the last survivor forced to zero, then the remaining lives can be calculated as described earlier. It can be observed that the average remaining lives will increase up to a certain age, and then start declining. The tendency for remaining lives to increase with age for a certain period is also found in the O-type Iowa survivor curves, especially in the O3- and O4-type Iowa survivor curves.

Thus, naively fitting intangible asset actuarial data to the Weibull distribution is not analytically sufficient to generate meaningful remaining life estimates. While the Weibull distribution will fit the data very well, it may not always converge to the analytically necessary point of zero percent surviving.

## CALCULATION OF AVERAGE SERVICE LIFE

The following processes summarize the analysis performed in order to estimate the average service life of an intangible asset:

1. Calculation of the area under the complete survivor curve:
   a. Using integral calculus, estimate the mathematical function that defines the survivor curve and integrate between the point of age equal to zero and the maximum age.
   b. Using ordinate approximation, the area under the survivor curve can be approximately calculated by adding the height (i.e., the percent surviving) of the survivor curve at each age (e.g., 0, 1, 2, . . . years).
   (Exhibits 11-11 and 11-12 present illustrations of average ordinate approximation when there are retirements in the 0 to $\frac{1}{2}$ age interval and no retirements in the 0 to $\frac{1}{2}$ age interval, respectively.)

2. Calculation of the expectancy of the remaining life (RL):

$$RL = \frac{\textit{Area to the Right of a Particular Age}}{\textit{Proportion Surviving at That Age}}$$

Note that, from the actuarial data, a fitted standard survivor curve (e.g., Iowa-type curve, Weibull distribution, etc.) is representative of a new intangible asset (i.e., an intangible asset at age equal to zero), while the existing or seasoned intangible asset is probably several years old. Therefore, remaining useful life (and not just average service life) computations are required in order to estimate the remaining useful life of a seasoned (or already in service) intangible asset from the fitted standard survivor curve.

## REMAINING LIFE ESTIMATION WHEN ACTUARIAL DATA ARE NOT AVAILABLE

In many cases, detailed intangible asset age records—such as the date when the customer first did business with the company, or the age or length of subscription of a subscriber discontinuing the service—are not maintained or are not available. Again, using customer relationships as an illustrative intangible asset, sometimes the only available information may be the following:

EXHIBIT 11-11

Calculation of the Area under a Survivor Curve

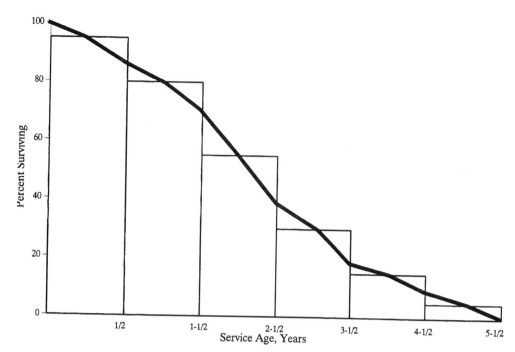

| Age Interval | Average Ordinate for Age Interval | Interval Area | Cumulative Area, % - Years |
|---|---|---|---|
| 0 - 1/2 | 95 | 47.5 | 47.5 |
| 1/2 - 1-1/2 | 80 | 80.0 | 127.5 |
| 1-1/2 - 2-1/2 | 55 | 55.0 | 182.5 |
| 2-1/2 - 3-1/2 | 30 | 30.0 | 212.5 |
| 3-1/2 - 4-1/2 | 15 | 15.0 | 227.5 |
| 4-1/2 - 5-1/2 | 5 | 5.0 | 232.5 |

- The number of customers doing business with the subject company (i.e., the active customers) at the beginning of each year for, say, three to five years prior to the valuation date.
- The number of customers who stopped doing business with the subject company (i.e., the retired customers) in each of those years.

Such a situation is identical to having data as presented in the last row of Exhibit 11-2 only. From this last row of data, we have the number of accounts exposed to retirement at the beginning of the year of 166, 117, and 147 in years 1993, 1994, and 1995, respectively. We have the corresponding number of retirements during the years of 76, 5, and 19, respectively.

In cases when the ages of the active and retired customers are not known—that is, when historical actuarial age and life data are not available—a turnover approximation method is applicable. In this method, we first calculate the retirement ratio for each year of age and life data available:

EXHIBIT 11-12

Calculation of the Area under a Survivor Curve

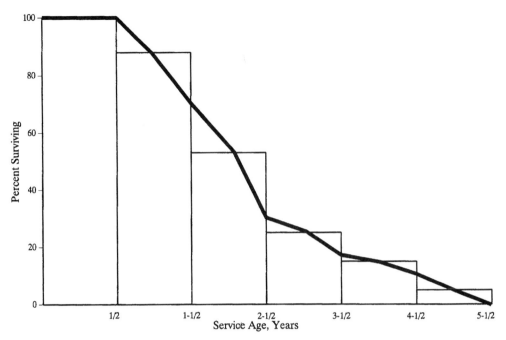

| Age Interval | Average Ordinate for Age Interval | Interval Area | Cumulative Area, % - Years |
|---|---|---|---|
| 0 - 1/2 | 100.00 | 50.00 | 50.00 |
| 1/2 - 1-1/2 | 87.50 | 87.50 | 137.50 |
| 1-1/2 - 2-1/2 | 52.50 | 52.50 | 190.00 |
| 2-1/2 - 3-1/2 | 23.75 | 23.75 | 213.75 |
| 3-1/2 - 4-1/2 | 13.75 | 13.75 | 227.50 |
| 4-1/2 - 5-1/2 | 5.00 | 5.00 | 232.50 |

Retirement ratio (RR) calculation:

1. Estimate the number of units—that is, accounts—surviving at beginning of a given year.
2. Determine the number of units—that is, accounts—retired during that year.
3. Calculate the retirement ratio (RR) as follows:

$$RR = \frac{Number\ of\ Accounts\ Retired\ during\ Year}{Number\ of\ Accounts\ Surviving\ at\ the\ Beginning\ of\ Year}$$

From the data above, we calculate the retirement ratio for 1993 (RR93) to be 76 ÷ 166 = 45.8 percent. Similarly, we have:

RR94 = 4.3 percent, and

RR95 = 12.9 percent.

Conducting discussions with management regarding the business operations during each of these years, marketing policies, customer retention strategies, and so on, would be helpful to the analyst in the process of weighting these retirement ratios. Based on this analysis, we can estimate a weighted average retirement ratio that may be applicable to the number of active customer accounts existing as of the valuation date.

Under this scenario, the projections of the surviving customer accounts in the subsequent year are made by applying the same retirement ratio to the number of customer accounts surviving in the previous year.

In the above example, from the average of the three retirement ratios of approximately 21 percent, we project the retirement ratio to be 20 percent. From Exhibit 11-2, we know that the number of active customer accounts at the beginning of 1996 is 188. We apply the 20 percent retirement ratio to the number of customer account survivors each year in order to estimate the number of surviving customer accounts in the subsequent years, as presented in Exhibit 11-13.

Since the retirement ratio is projected to be constant, we can estimate the remaining life to be the reciprocal of the retirement ratio as follows:

$$Remaining\ Life = 1/RR$$

Therefore, the 20 percent retirement ratio in the above example would indicate an average life of 5 years $(1 \div 0.2 = 5)$ for the remaining active customer accounts.

Exhibit 11-13 stops in year 2015, because the remaining customer accounts surviving beyond that point would probably not have a significant impact on the intangible asset valuation analysis. However, it would be around year 2044 that the number surviving at the beginning of the year (column [2]) would reach the level of absolute zero. Adding the number surviving for each year would present an amount of 940 (which is representative of service rendered from the customer accounts). Dividing this number by the number of active customer accounts at the beginning (i.e., 188), the average customer account service life of 5 years $(940 \div 188 = 5)$ is estimated.

## THE USE OF SURVIVOR CURVE ANALYSIS FOR DCF CALCULATIONS

The following points are particularly noteworthy with regard to the use of survivor curve analysis in income approach methods (e.g., discounted cash flow or yield capitalization) to intangible asset valuation:

1. The maximum life of the survivor curve is required for the purpose of estimating the number of discrete expected economic income flows from an intangible asset.
2. The percent surviving of the survivor curve is a basis for estimating the levels of future economic income from the wasting, or decaying, intangible asset:
   a. From actuarial data—The fitted standard survivor curve (Iowa-type curve, Weibull distribution, etc.) is representative of a new intangible asset (i.e., at age equal to zero), while the existing intangible asset is a few years old. Therefore, adjustments are required to recognize the fact that the subject intangible asset is a seasoned intangible asset.

Illustrative Survivor Curve Construction, Calculation of Surviving Customer Relationships
Semiactuarial Data Using Turnover Rate Approximation Method

| Year [1] | Customer Relationship Survivors at the Beginning of Year [2] | Retirement Ratio [3] | Customer Accounts Retirements During the Year [4] | Customer Relationship Survivors at the End of Year [5] | Survivor Curve (Midyear) [6] |
|---|---|---|---|---|---|
| 1996 | 188 | 20% | 38 | 150 | 169 |
| 1997 | 150 | 20% | 30 | 120 | 135 |
| 1998 | 120 | 20% | 24 | 96 | 108 |
| 1999 | 96 | 20% | 19 | 77 | 87 |
| 2000 | 77 | 20% | 15 | 62 | 69 |
| 2001 | 62 | 20% | 12 | 49 | 55 |
| 2002 | 49 | 20% | 10 | 39 | 44 |
| 2003 | 39 | 20% | 8 | 32 | 35 |
| 2004 | 32 | 20% | 6 | 25 | 28 |
| 2005 | 25 | 20% | 5 | 20 | 23 |
| 2006 | 20 | 20% | 4 | 16 | 18 |
| 2007 | 16 | 20% | 3 | 13 | 15 |
| 2008 | 13 | 20% | 3 | 10 | 12 |
| 2009 | 10 | 20% | 2 | 8 | 9 |
| 2010 | 8 | 20% | 2 | 7 | 7 |
| 2011 | 7 | 20% | 1 | 5 | 6 |
| 2012 | 5 | 20% | 1 | 4 | 5 |
| 2013 | 4 | 20% | 1 | 3 | 4 |
| 2014 | 3 | 20% | 1 | 3 | 3 |
| 2015 | 3 | 20% | 1 | 2 | 2 |

Notes:

a. Column [2] from 1997 onward = column [5] from previous year. The 188 for beginning of year 1996 is from Exhibit 11-2.

b. Column [3], estimated retirement ratio projected to be constant in the subsequent years.

c. Column [4] = column [2] * column [3]

d. Column [5] = column [2] – column [4]

e. Column [6] = average of column [2] and column [5]

b. From semiactuarial data—Apply the calculated retirement rate to the number of each year's intangible asset survivors in order to estimate the number of year-end intangible asset survivors until we reach the level of zero percent surviving.

## SUMMARY

This chapter summarized the importance of—and the application of—remaining useful life analysis to the valuation of intangible assets. Remaining useful life analysis is an integral component of the valuation process, regardless of which valuation approach or approaches (cost, income, and market) are used.

While methods of remaining useful life estimation range from totally qualitative to rigorously quantitative, remaining useful life estimation involves a consideration of many factors, including:

1. Life analysis.
2. Technological progress.

3. Economic trends.

4. Management policy decisions.

5. Government and regulatory policies.

6. Present condition of the asset.

7. Character and amount of service historically rendered by the asset.

8. Character and amount of service expected from the asset.

9. Other pertinent information.

10. Professional judgment on the part of the experienced analyst.

## BIBLIOGRAPHY

Boehm, Ted. "'Hoskold's Formula' for the Valuation of Intangibles." *Capital University Law Review,* Winter 1980, pp. 293–307.

Clark, Stanley J., and Charles E. Jordan. "Seeking Guidance: How and When to Group Old Assets for New Write-Downs." *National Public Accountant,* December 1994, pp. 17–19+.

Dandekar, Manoj P., and Harold A. Cowles. *Capital Recovery and Investment Life Cycles.* Ames, IA: Engineering Research Institute, Iowa State University, February 1987.

Ellsworth, Richard K. "Amortization of Core Deposit Intangibles: A Matter of Proof." *Journal of Bank Taxation,* Spring 1992, pp. 11–13.

———. "Supporting Cable Television Subscriber Amortization." *ASA Valuation,* January 1992, pp. 42–47.

———. "The Weibull Distribution: Descriptor of Industrial Property Retirement." *ASA Valuation,* August 1994, pp. 68–75.

Falk, Charles Edward. "Amortizing Insurance Expirations: The Meaning of Decker." *TAXES,* June 1989, p. 391+.

Fuller, David N. "Amortizing Intangibles—A Break-Even Analysis." *Journal of Accountancy,* June 1994, pp. 31–34.

Garbarino, Lloyd N., and Charles A. Smith. "An Alternative Method of Measuring External Obsolescence (Where Supply Exceeds Demand)." *ASA Valuation,* July 1993, pp. 54–58.

Gehan, Raymond F. "How to Establish a Limited Useful Life in Order to Amortize Purchased Intangibles." *Taxation for Accountants,* June 1986, pp. 356–59.

Marston, Anson, Robley Winfrey, and Jean C. Hempstead. *Engineering Valuation and Depreciation.* Ames, IA: Iowa State University Press, 1953.

Nelson, Wayne. *Applied Life Data Analysis.* New York: John Wiley & Sons, 1982.

Parmar, Mahesh K.B., and David Machin. *Survival Analysis: A Practical Approach.* Chicester, UK: John Wiley & Sons, 1995.

Paschall, Robert H. "Measuring Functional Obsolescence at Manufacturing Plants." *ASA Valuation,* March 1994, pp. 56–62.

Reilly, Robert F. "How to Determine the Value and Useful Life of Core Deposit Intangibles." *Journal of Bank Taxation,* Winter 1991, pp. 10–18.

Winfrey, Robley (revised by Harold A. Cowles). *Statistical Analyses of Industrial Property Retirements.* Ames, IA: Engineering Research Institute, Iowa State University, 1967.

# CHAPTER 12

# Concluding Remaining Useful Life

INTRODUCTION

DIFFERENCES BETWEEN BUSINESS ENTERPRISE
  VALUATION AND INTANGIBLE ASSET VALUATION

DETERMINANTS OF REMAINING USEFUL LIFE

SELECTING A REMAINING USEFUL LIFE ESTIMATE

SUMMARY

## INTRODUCTION

The remaining useful life estimation is one of the most overlooked procedures related to intangible asset analysis. This is true whether the analysis relates to transfer pricing, royalty rate estimation, damages estimation, licensing assessment, or valuation. However, in all of these intangible asset analyses, there is at least an implicit—if not an explicit—remaining useful life estimation being made. Ideally, the remaining useful life estimation should be a conscious conclusion reached by the analyst and based upon the rigorous application of life estimation procedures. Often, however, the remaining useful life estimation is an afterthought or a default conclusion based upon the mathematics of the particular valuation or other analytical method used.

In the days prior to the passage of Internal Revenue Code Section 197, analysts may have been more cognizant of the need to estimate the remaining useful life of intangible assets. This is because the estimation of a remaining useful life was an important component of the federal income tax accounting related to the purchase of intangible assets. Taxpayers could claim a cost recovery deduction associated with the amortization of the purchased intangible asset. However, the amortization deduction could only be claimed over the remaining useful life of the purchased intangible asset (and only if the purchased intangible asset indeed had a determinable expected remaining useful life).

Internal Revenue Code Section 197 now allows for the cost recovery of most purchased intangible assets over a statutorily determined 15-year amortization period. Accordingly, the issue of the expected remaining useful life of purchased intangible assets is no longer as significant a federal taxation issue for taxpayers. Even with this simplification of the Internal Revenue Code with regard to purchased intangible asset cost recovery, there are still numerous reasons why a buyer, seller, or owner would need to know the remaining useful life of an intangible asset or intellectual property.

Regardless of federal income tax accounting, owners still need to know the remaining useful life of intangible assets for various cost recovery purposes, including financial accounting cost recovery (amortization) purposes and internal product or service cost accounting purposes (e.g., charging the periodic cost of an intangible that is used or used up against the product or service in order to properly match costs and to measure product line or business unit profitability).

Remaining useful life estimation is an important component of license agreement negotiation and royalty rate determination. Obviously, neither a licensor nor a licensee wants to enter into a license agreement in which the contractual term is longer than the expected remaining life of the subject intangible. The same consideration is true with regard to concluding a fair intercompany or intracompany transfer price related to the subject intangible. The transfer price should provide a fair return to the transferor over the term of the transfer agreement, and that term should not ignore the expected remaining life of the subject intangible. This subject is discussed in Chapter 25, Intercompany Transfer Pricing and Royalty Rate Analysis.

Intangible asset remaining useful life estimation is just as important a consideration in the sale of an intangible as in the licensing of an intangible. Certainly, the buyer is interested in whether the transactional intangible is expected to have a 5-year remaining life or a 25-year remaining life. It is reasonable to conclude that the estimation of the remaining life of the transactional intangible (e.g., whether it is 5 years or 25 years) will affect the negotiated purchase price.

The estimation of an intangible asset's remaining useful life is an integral component of damages analysis. Let's assume that causation and liability related to a claimed wrongdoing have already been established. Now we have to estimate the damages suffered by the aggrieved party and the penalty due from the wrongdoer. Whatever caused the damage to the aggrieved party (e.g., expropriation, breach of contract, infringement), the amount of the damage liability will likely be different depending on whether the subject intangible has a 5-year or a 25-year remaining life.

As has been discussed in previous chapters, the valuation of intangible assets and intellectual properties is directly affected by issues of remaining useful life. This is true regardless of the purpose of the valuation and regardless of whether cost approach, income approach, or market approach valuation methods are used.

In this chapter, we briefly review the differences between business enterprise valuation and intangible asset valuation, particularly with regard to remaining useful life analysis. We summarize the various measures of remaining useful life for an intangible asset and discuss the factors to consider with regard to selecting among various remaining useful life estimates for the subject intangible. In other words, we answer the question: Of various estimates of useful life, how does the analyst select the estimate that is most relevant to the instant analysis?

## DIFFERENCES BETWEEN BUSINESS ENTERPRISE VALUATION AND INTANGIBLE ASSET VALUATION

Of course, there are numerous procedural differences in the valuation of a business enterprise compared to the valuation of an intangible asset or intellectual property. For purposes of this comparison, we will define business enterprise valuation to include the valuation of an entire business (i.e., a 100 percent ownership interest); a business ownership interest (i.e., both controlling and noncontrolling, but less than 100 percent); and a particular class of security (e.g., a block of common stock, preferred stock, etc., whether controlling or noncontrolling).

All of the procedural differences between business enterprise valuation and intangible asset valuation relate to four factors:

1. *Increment of income.* In a business valuation, all of the income (however measured) of the operating enterprise is included in the analysis. In an intangible asset valuation, only the portion of the income (however measured) of the operating enterprise that is attributable to the intangible asset is typically included in the analysis. The increment of the total enterprise income may be in the form of a royalty payment, a profit split, or some other form. Increments of expected income attributable to the intangible asset that are from sources outside of the operating enterprise should be carefully justified.

2. *Allocation of income.* In a business valuation, income (however measured) is not typically allocated between the tangible and intangible assets of the overall enterprise. An allocation is not needed because all assets con-

tribute to the overall enterprise value. In an intangible asset valuation, income (however measured) is typically allocated between tangible and intangible assets. The procedure is performed so that only the marginal income attributable to the intangible is included in the valuation. The allocation of income may be in the form of a capital charge, in order to recognize the income attributable to any tangible assets that are used or used up in the production of the income associated with the intangible asset.

**3.** *Risk.* A business enterprise typically includes lower-risk tangible assets and higher-risk intangible assets. Therefore, the risk of an investment in a business enterprise is typically lower than the risk of an investment in a discrete intangible asset. For that reason, present value discount rates and direct capitalization rates (however derived) are typically lower in a business enterprise valuation than in a discrete intangible asset valuation.

**4.** *Lifing.* A business enterprise valuation typically assumes an unlimited life with respect to the subject income stream. That is, business valuation and security analysis procedures usually assume that the subject business will last forever. An intangible asset valuation typically assumes a limited life with respect to the subject income stream. That is, intangible asset analysis procedures assume that the discrete intangible will have a finite remaining useful life.

Of the four factors that distinguish business enterprise valuation and intangible asset valuation, the last factor (lifing) typically has the greatest effect on the valuation analysis and on the valuation conclusion. This is why an entire chapter (Chapter 11) is devoted to intangible asset life analysis and remaining useful life estimation.

## DETERMINANTS OF REMAINING USEFUL LIFE

As described in Chapter 11, there are eight determinants of the useful life of an intangible asset. In other words, there are eight different ways to measure the useful life of an intangible asset. Not all of the eight different measures apply to each and every intangible. Usually, however, there are at least several different ways to measure the useful life of a particular intangible. Therefore, the analyst is typically faced with the question: From among the various different measures of useful life that are relevant to the subject intangible, which measure should I use in the valuation or economic analysis?

The eight determinants, or ways to measure, intangible asset useful life are:

1. Legal life.
2. Contractual life.
3. Judicial life.
4. Physical life.
5. Technological life.
6. Functional life.
7. Economic life.
8. Analytical life.

A legal life is set by a law, statute, ordinance, or administrative ruling. For instance, many intellectual properties have specific legal lives. This is typically the period of time over which the intellectual property is granted special legal recognition and protection. For many intellectual properties, the initial legal life can be extended if specific renewal and reregistration procedures are followed.

A contractual life is set by a contract, agreement, license, or franchise. The term of the intangible asset existence is specified in the contract. The contract indicates the performance rights and obligations of the parties. These rights and obligations create the existence of—and the value of—the subject intangible asset. The contract life may be subject to extension or renewal if such a provision is made in the agreement, license, or franchise.

A judicial life is set by the decree or order of a judge or similar authority (such as an arbitrator or tribunal member). The judicial order may grant certain protection or may require that a certain event occur (such as the transfer of property or of a series of payments).

A physical life is set by the amount of wear and tear on the subject intangible asset. All intangible assets have some tangible manifestation of their existence. However, the economic value of an intangible asset is rarely related to that tangible manifestation. Relatively few intangible assets actually wear out due to physical use or to the passing of time. However, some intangible assets do. Therefore, a physical life should still be considered.

A technological life is influenced by changes in technology. The subject intangible asset can still perform the function for which it was intended. However, due to technological improvements, a replacement intangible asset can perform the same function better, cheaper, faster, and so on, than the subject intangible. When a user would no longer use the subject intangible asset, but would always use the more technologically advanced intangible asset, then the subject has reached the end of its technological life.

A functional life is influenced by the intangible asset's ability to continue to perform the function for which it was intended. When the intangible asset becomes dysfunctional, when it can no longer perform the task that it was intended to perform, then it has reached the end of its functional life. Also, when the task itself is no longer desired by the user of the intangible, the intangible asset has also reached the end of its functional life.

An economic life is influenced by the ability of the subject intangible asset to provide a fair rate of return to the owner or user of the intangible asset. If an intangible asset can no longer generate an adequate amount of economic income (either through operation or through license) to justify its continued use, it has reached the end of its economic life.

An analytical life is the expected period of utility of the subject intangible asset based upon a study of the historical mortality characteristics of similar intangible assets. An analytical life is determined in a way that is very similar to the way actuaries estimate human mortality patterns for insurance and other purposes. The mechanics and mathematics of analytical life analysis are described in detail in Chapter 11.

The analytical life may be seen as somewhat of a composite of all the other types of life determinants. For each of the other seven life determinants, there is a specific reason why the subject intangible asset reaches the end of its period of utility. The analyst (or the intangible asset owner) knows why the intangible asset becomes obsolete and, ultimately, reaches the end of its life.

With regard to the analytical life, the reason for intangible asset mortality is not particularly relevant. What is relevant is that, historically, intangible assets similar to the subject "lived" for a measurable period of time and then stopped "living." They could have stopped living because they had reached the end of their legal, contractual, judicial, or other lives. It doesn't really matter. From an analytical perspective, they stopped living.

In this regard, analytical lifing methods are particularly analogous to human actuarial methods. When estimating human life characteristics, actuaries measure when their subjects stopped living. Actuaries are not particularly concerned about whether the subjects stopped living because of accidents, disease, suicide, or old age. All of these reasons contribute to human actuarial life estimates. Likewise, all of the life determinant reasons contribute to intangible asset analytical life estimates.

Many intangible asset analysts favor the analytical determinant for that reason—that it takes into account all of the other determinants of (or reasons for) intangible asset mortality. Many analysts favor the analytical determinant because it is less subjective than most intangible asset useful life estimates. Finally, many analysts favor the analytical determinant because all of the life characteristics (i.e., total useful life, average useful life, and remaining useful life) can be calculated with substantial mathematical precision. However, this should not imply that the analytical determinant always provides the best (i.e., most accurate) remaining useful life estimate.

## SELECTING A REMAINING USEFUL LIFE ESTIMATE

Often, the shortest useful life estimate of the various life determinants relevant to the subject intangible asset is the life conclusion to be used in the valuation or economic analysis. For example, if a particular patent has a legal life of 17 years, a contractual life of 10 years, and an analytical life of 6 years, then the 6-year useful life estimate would be appropriate for most analyses.

Of course, as with most general rules, this rule should not be applied without the consideration of professional judgment and common sense. The shortest life determinant is usually the appropriate useful life conclusion. However, that is not always the case. The reasonableness of each life determinant should be considered.

Let's reconsider the patent life analysis. The shortest useful life estimate was 6 years, based on the analytical determinant. That life estimate would have been based on a study of the historical placements and retirements of similar patents (e.g., in the same industry, used by the same owner, related to the same product or process, etc.). However, those similar patents all retired for various reasons: Their legal protection period expired, they were replaced by new technology, the related product or process was no longer commercially successful, and so forth.

For the subject patent, though, the example indicates that there is a contract with a 10-year remaining life. Let's assume that the contract is a license agreement whereby the licensee guarantees to pay the licensor (i.e., the patent owner) a minimum of $1,000,000 per year for the next 10 years for the use of the subject patented technology. The licensee is solvent and has always honored its agreements and the license agreement is legally enforceable. In that case, a strong argument can be made for using the 10-year legal life instead of the 6-year analytical life in a valuation or economic analysis of the subject patent.

## SUMMARY

Remaining useful life analysis is one of the most important, yet one of the most overlooked, procedures with regard to intangible asset analysis. Remaining useful life analysis is relevant to intangible asset valuation and economic analyses performed for virtually any purpose. Likewise, remaining useful life analysis is an integral component of all intangible asset valuation approaches.

There are eight determinants, or measures, of intangible asset useful life. The eight determinants were discussed in Chapter 11 and were summarized in this chapter. Many analysts favor the analytical method of measuring intangible asset useful life. However, for all of its quantitative precision, this determinant is not always the best method for estimating useful life.

With regard to a particular intangible asset, analysts should generally consider all relevant life determinants. The general rule is that the shortest life determinant is appropriate for most valuation and economic analysis purposes. However, as with all general rules, there are exceptions. Analysts should apply professional judgment and common sense in selecting among the various remaining useful life estimates. The appropriate remaining useful life conclusion is the life estimate that is most relevant to the purpose and objective of the particular intangible asset analysis.

# PART FOUR

# Intangible Asset Valuation Synthesis and Reporting

# Valuation Synthesis

## INTRODUCTION

In this chapter, we discuss the final step in the intangible asset appraisal process: performing the valuation synthesis and reaching the valuation conclusion. Therefore, this chapter is effectively a review of all the techniques, data, work, and appraiser inputs needed to reach the final value estimate.

In the valuation synthesis and conclusion, the analyst performs a set of procedures that are often called the valuation reconciliation. As part of the reconciliation, the analyst should answer the following questions:

1. Did I appraise the right thing (i.e., did I analyze the correct intangible asset)?
2. Did I appraise the right thing the right way (i.e., did I apply the correct valuation approaches and methods)?
3. Did I reach the right conclusion (i.e., did I correctly apply the procedures that I performed in order to reach a reasonable value estimate)?
4. Did I do what I intended (i.e., did I accomplish the engagement that I set out to accomplish)?

In this chapter, we discuss:

1. How to conduct a thorough and effective review of the appraisal work.
2. How to reconcile different value estimates developed from the different methods into a single estimate of the most probable price the subject intangible asset will bring under the market conditions at the time of the appraisal and in conformance with a client's instructions, legal considerations, and the limiting conditions and assumptions used by the appraiser.

To prepare for the final valuation conclusion process, the analyst reviews the definition of the appraisal assignment and the data available in order to judge whether the analytical techniques and logic have been applied consistently. The value definition, the identified property rights, and the prescribed qualifying conditions are reconsidered to find out whether the approaches and methods utilized address these components.

During the reconciliation process, all of the steps of the intangible asset appraisal process are reviewed. To begin with, the review should consider the following:

1. Identification of the subject intangible asset (including the ownership characteristics subject to appraisal).
2. The objective of the appraisal.
3. The purpose of the appraisal.
4. The intangible ownership interest (including the bundle of legal rights) subject to appraisal.
5. The date of the value estimate.
6. Definition of the appropriate standard of value to be estimated.
7. The premise of value to be used (that is, based upon the highest and best use of the subject intangible asset).

The intangible asset valuation engagement is performed to answer a question about the value of an intangible asset. Even within the same valuation approach, different methods typically result in different indications of value. For example, it is likely that different indicated values would result from two different income approach methods.

The process of reconciliation involves the analysis of the alternative valuation indications in order to arrive at a final value estimate for the subject intangible asset. Before reaching a final value estimate, the analyst should review all the intangible asset valuation project material for appropriateness and accuracy. Of course, the analyst should carefully consider throughout the reconciliation process the definition of value sought and its relationship to each step in the valuation process.

## CRITERIA FOR THE SELECTION OF VALUATION APPROACHES AND METHODS

Of the generally accepted intangible asset valuation approaches, there are no absolutely right or wrong approaches for any particular valuation engagement. There is also no precise guideline or quantitative formula for selecting which approach (or approaches) is most applicable in a given intangible asset valuation situation. However, the following list presents the most common and most important factors to be considered by the analyst when selecting the appropriate valuation approaches and methods to apply in a particular analysis:

1. Quantity and quality of available data.
2. Access to available data.
3. Supply of relevant transactional data.
4. Type and nature of the subject intangible, and industry conditions in which the subject intangible is expected to operate.
5. The particular bundle of rights represented in the intangible asset subject to appraisal.
6. Statutory, judicial, contractual, and administrative requirements and considerations.
7. Informational needs of the particular appraisal audience.
8. Purpose and objective of the appraisal.
9. Compliance with promulgated professional standards.
10. Professional judgment and technical expertise of the analyst.

## Quantity and Quality of Available Data

Practically, this may be the most important methodological selection criterion. An analyst simply cannot perform a valuation approach or method (no matter how conceptually robust it is) if the requisite financial, operational, or market-derived data are not available.

The analyst should keep in mind that the audience for the appraisal will want to know the basis for the value opinion. The final value estimate represents the application of judgment to the data that market participants would consider appropriate to solve the appraisal problem as defined.

## Access to Available Data

If an intangible asset valuation is performed for litigation support, dispute resolution, or other controversy purposes, the analyst may not have unrestricted access to intangible asset data, to company management, to company facilities, and so forth. In these cases, not all of the desired historical and prospective data may exist, or the analyst may not be granted reasonable access to the existing data. Accordingly, in selecting among valuation approaches and methods, the analyst may have to consider not only what data exist, but also what data are readily available to the analyst.

Having said that, we should point out that if an attorney pursues the issue vigorously with the judge, many courts will order access to the appropriate data.

## Supply of Industry Transactional Data

In some industries, there is a large quantity of publicly available data regarding intangible asset sale or purchase transactions. When the supply of reliable industry transactional data is substantial, the analyst will more likely select and rely upon market-based intangible asset valuation approaches.

Approaches to value that are not of primary importance in a specific intangible asset appraisal project may nevertheless be important in the reconciliation process. In some cases, the analyst may not include a market approach analysis but, in reconciliation, will consider the difference between the high pricing indicated in transactions involving intangible assets with less favorable characteristics and the relatively low final opinion of value reached for the subject intangible asset.

## Type and Nature of the Subject Intangible, and Industry Conditions in Which the Subject Intangible Is Expected to Operate

Certain industries have rules of thumb that may be used as quick, preliminary estimates regarding the value of intangible assets in the industry. While industry rules of thumb, guidelines, or conventions should not be relied upon exclusively in a rigorous intangible asset valuation, they need not be totally ignored either. Depending upon the nature of the valuation assignment (e.g., whether it is subject to intensive scrutiny and cross-examination or is for management estimation purposes only), different valuation approaches may be more or less applicable.

## The Particular Bundle of Rights Represented in the Intangible Asset Subject to Appraisal

Property ownership interests may be examined from many perspectives because the ownership, legal, economic, and financial aspects of intangible assets overlap. The ownership of intangible property interests can be divided in various ways. Separate economic and legal interests derived from the total bundle of rights are involved in many kinds of income-producing intangible assets and intellectual properties. Each of the separate economic and legal interests is distinct in its form and content. There are often specific legal definitions related to property ownership interests, including intangible property. Some examples of fractional interests in intangible assets are: fee simple interest, life interest or estate, licenser or franchiser interests, licensee or franchisee interests, sublicensee or subfranchisee interests, reversionary interests, development rights, exploitation rights, and use rights.

## Statutory, Judicial, Contractual, and Administrative Considerations

For intangible asset valuations that are performed for certain taxation and litigation purposes, the analyst should research whether certain valuation approaches and methods are required and whether other valuation approaches and methods are prohibited. Certainly, the Internal Revenue Service has published valuation procedures and guidelines for appraisals performed for federal transfer pricing purposes.

Prevailing case decisions, rather than statutory law, generally provide the guidance on state-by-state issues. The analyst should be aware of whatever specific statutory requirements, administrative guidance, or judicial precedents affect the subject intangible asset valuation. The analyst should also consider whether there are any applicable contractual requirements or restrictions relating to the operation and ownership of the intangible asset.

## Informational Needs of the Particular Appraisal Audience

The ultimate audience for the appraisal may affect the selection of intangible asset valuation approaches and methods. These considerations include the level of sophistication of the particular appraisal audience and the degree of familiarity of the particular appraisal audience with the subject intangible asset. The ultimate purpose of the appraisal—as either a notational or a transactional appraisal—may also affect which valuation approaches and methods will be selected.

## Purpose and Objective of the Appraisal

Overall, the purpose and objective of the intangible asset valuation may influence the selection of the valuation approaches. The various components of the appraisal objective include: the description of the intangible asset subject to appraisal; the definition (or standard) of value applied; the premise of value applied; and the valuation date. The various components of the appraisal purpose include: the audience for the appraisal; and the decision (or decisions) that will be influenced by the appraisal.

## Compliance with Promulgated Professional Standards

Obviously, analysts who are members of professional societies and institutes should comply with the promulgated professional pronouncements of those organizations. To varying degrees, The Appraisal Foundation, the American Society of Appraisers, the Institute of Business Appraisers, the National Association of Certified Valuation Analysts, and the American Institute of Certified Public Accountants have prepared standards or other professional guidance with respect to intangible asset valuation approaches and methods. These professional organizations and their related professional guidance were introduced earlier in this book.

# Professional Judgment and Technical Expertise
## of the Analyst

When all is said and done, subject to applicable legal requirements, the most important factor affecting the selection of the appropriate intangible asset valuation approaches and methods is the professional judgment, technical expertise, and practiced common sense of a competent and experienced analyst.

## CRITERIA FOR THE SYNTHESIS OF MULTIPLE VALUATION INDICATIONS

As with the selection of valuation approaches and methods, there are no scientific formulas or specific rules to use with regard to the synthesis or weighting of the results of two or more intangible asset valuation methods. In fact, the same factors or guidelines that affect the selection of valuation methods will influence the appraiser with regard to the synthesis of the indications of the valuation methods.

Some analysts use an implicit weighting scheme in their final valuation synthesis and conclusion. That is, they present the valuation indications for each method performed. Then they directly arrive at a valuation conclusion. They do not quantitatively document or qualitatively justify the valuation synthesis process.

An example of this implicit weighting scheme follows:

Intangible Asset Subject to Appraisal, Intangible Asset Valuation Approaches and Methods, Valuation Synthesis and Conclusion, as of December 31, 1999

| Valuation Approach | Valuation Method Indication | Valu |
|---|---|---|
| Income approach | Direct capitalization method | $1,800,000 |
| Income approach | Yield capitalization method | $2,000,000 |
| Cost approach | Inventory method | $2,400,000 |
| Valuation synthesis and conclusion | | $2,200,000 |

This valuation synthesis, of course, presents the final valuation conclusion. While that valuation conclusion may be perfectly reasonable, the analyst has not explained (either quantitatively or qualitatively) the implicit weighting—that is, the intrinsic thought process that led to the $2,200,000 valuation conclusion.

An alternative valuation synthesis procedure is to explicitly present the weighting of the several valuation methods employed in the analysis. The explicit weighting scheme allows the analyst to communicate the degree of confidence in each of the several intangible asset valuation methods selected and in the reasonableness of the several intangible asset value indications. In fact, a narrative description of the rationale behind the analyst's explicit weighting scheme is often included in the narrative valuation opinion report.

An example of an explicit weighting scheme follows:

Intangible Asset Subject to Appraisal, Intangible Asset Valuation Approaches and Methods, Valuation Synthesis and Conclusion, as of December 31, 1999

| Valuation Approach | Valuation Method | Value Indication | Value Reconciliation Weighting | Weighted Value |
|---|---|---|---|---|
| Income approach | Direct capitalization method | $1,800,000 | 25% | $ 450,000 |
| Income approach | Yield capitalization method | $2,000,000 | 25% | 500,000 |
| Cost approach | Inventory method | $2,400,000 | 50% | 1,200,000 |
| Total weighted value | | | | $2,150,000 |
| Valuation synthesis and conclusion (rounded) | | | | $2,200,000 |

Even if a narrative discussion of the weighting scheme is not included in the valuation opinion report, the explicit weighting provides important information as to the analyst's thought process regarding and degree of confidence in the alternative valuation methods and the alternative valuation indications. The explicit weighting allows the appraisal reader to follow—and to reconstruct, if necessary—the analyst's entire quantitative (if not qualitative) analyses.

There is no generally accepted formula or model used to quantify the weighting factors. The implicit or explicit weighting will vary for each appraisal. The weighting assigned to each individual valuation method in each individual appraisal engagement is ultimately based upon the experience and judgment of the analyst. When using explicit weights, the analyst might acknowledge in the written report that there are no empirical bases by which to assign weights to various methods, and that the purpose of the quantitative weighting is to aid the reader in understanding the analyst's thought process.

## Income Approach Methods

The following sections discuss some of the factors that influence the weighting of the income approach methods in valuation synthesis and conclusion.

### Yield Capitalization Method

The primary criterion for heavy weighting of the yield capitalization valuation method is the existence of a credible business plan or projection of the intangible asset's expected financial results. This valuation method also becomes relatively more important when it is expected that future operating results of the subject intangible asset will differ significantly enough from past operating results. Relying solely on historical results is likely to lead to a misleading indication of value.

The yield capitalization valuation method is most commonly used when the owner of the intangible asset has discretion to take those actions needed to actually realize the projected economic income. When the projected financial results for the intangible asset are not under the control of the intangible asset owner, or when the future financial performance is dubious, the veracity of this method is less reliable.

## Direct Capitalization Method

The validity of the direct capitalization method depends on the ability to estimate some reasonably credible level of normalized economic income (however measured) for the intangible asset that can be considered sustainable. As with the yield capitalization method, this method is based on the premise that future economic income capacity is important in the intangible asset valuation. Sometimes it is easier (or more reliable) to develop a "normalized" level of economic income than it is to estimate the timing of that economic income (as is necessary in the yield capitalization method).

The direct capitalization of economic income method can also work well if there is a modest and fairly sustainable expected long-term growth rate related to the intangible asset's economic income.

## Cost Approach Methods

The cost approach methods are most applicable (and most practical) when detailed data are available with regard to the costs to create the intangible assets that are subject to appraisal. Generally, cost approach methods may be more applicable when the subject intangible is newer and when it is a fungible property. More weight is given to the cost approach methods when the analyst is estimating the value of the intangible to its current owner. These methods may also be more applicable when estimating the value of an intangible under the premise of value in continued use. This makes sense because if the current owner did not have the subject in-use intangible, he or she would have to create a substitute intangible and incur the cost of that creation process.

Cost approach methods may be less applicable when the subject intangible is older or is unique. This may be particularly true if the subject intangible is an intellectual property that benefits from certain legal rights, such as trademark or copyright protection. Cost approach methods may be less applicable (but certainly not inapplicable) when the analyst is estimating the value of the intangible to the marketplace (and not to the current owner). These methods may also be less applicable when estimating the value of an intangible under the premise of value in exchange, because the typical willing buyer may be more interested in the expected future economic benefits associated with the intangible asset ownership than in the most likely cost to create a substitute for the subject intangible.

## Market Approach Methods

The market approach to valuing intangible assets is the process in which a market value estimate is derived by analyzing similar intangible assets that have recently been sold or licensed, and then comparing those intangible assets to the subject intangible asset. The market approach is applicable to all types of intangible assets when there are reliable transactions to indicate value patterns or trends in the market. When data are available, this is considered the most direct and systematic approach to value estimation.

The following sections discuss some of the factors that influence the weighting of the market approach methods in valuation synthesis and conclusion.

### Sales Transaction Method

The primary criterion for using the sales transaction method is the existence of reasonably comparative transactions involving the arm's-length sale of an intangible asset. This method can be especially useful for appraising seasoned or mature intangible assets because most of the reported guideline transactions represent interests in mature intangible assets. The application of this valuation method is expected when appraising intangible assets for certain income tax purposes, given existing regulatory authority and judicial precedent.

An experienced analyst can deal with appropriate valuation adjustments for alternative terms and conditions and the other risk and expected return differences that need to be considered when using this method. If enough good sales transaction data are available, this method can provide compelling evidence of value.

### Relief from Royalty Method

Using this method, arm's-length royalty or license agreements are analyzed. The transactions selected should reflect similar risk and return investment characteristics to make them comparable to the subject intangible asset. This method is most reliable when each guideline license agreement involves a similar bundle of legal rights, required maintenance (e.g., product advertising, product enhancements, quality controls), effective date, termination date, and degree of exclusivity.

Again, an experienced analyst can apply valuation adjustments to less than perfect guideline transaction data in order to derive a reliable indication of value using this method.

### Comparative Income Differential Method

When the analyst has information gathered from the market that allows a comparison between the income generated by two similar operations—one that operates with an intangible asset and one that operates without a similar intangible asset—this method may be most applicable. It is well-suited to valuing intangibles such as franchise agreements, proprietary technology, trade names, and patents, to name a few.

## RECONCILING AN INCONSISTENCY OF RESULTS AMONG VALUATION APPROACHES AND METHODS

Ideally, the analyst uses several approaches and methods in the subject intangible asset valuation and the several methods used all yield identical value indications. Practically, this rarely happens.

Experienced analysts expect to conclude a range of value indications when several alternative valuation methods are used. Preferably, the several valuation methods all conclude a reasonably narrow dispersion of value indications. The alternative value indications, then, indicate the reasonable range of values for the subject intangible asset. They also provide mutually supportive evidence as to the final valuation synthesis and conclusion.

Occasionally, a situation occurs when two or more valuation methods produce value indications within a reasonable range and one valuation method produces a value indication outlier.

An example of the value indication outlier phenomenon follows:

Intangible Asset Subject to Appraisal, Intangible Asset Valuation Approaches and Methods, Valuation Synthesis and Conclusion, as of December 31, 1999

| Valuation Approach | Valuation Method Indication | Valu |
|---|---|---|
| Income approach | Direct capitalization method | $1,800,000 |
| Income approach | Yield capitalization method | $2,000,000 |
| Cost approach | Audit method | $2,200,000 |
| Cost approach | Inventory method | $1,000,000 |
| Valuation synthesis and conclusion | | $2,0500,000 |

In the example, the value indication of the inventory method is an obvious outlier compared to the three other value indications. Accordingly, the appraisal requires further analysis and consideration before a valuation conclusion can be reached. The question raised is: What is the analyst to do regarding such an outlier value indication? There are three alternatives.

First, the analyst could disregard the valuation method that yields the outlier value indication. This decision is based upon the rationale that the outlier valuation method simply does not provide reliable valuation information given the subject set of facts and circumstances.

Second, the analyst could keep the outlier valuation method but assign it a very low weight. This procedure is based upon the rationale that if the valuation method is fundamentally sound, even an unreasonable value indication should be given some weight in the final valuation conclusion.

Third, the analyst could thoroughly investigate why one particular method is producing outlier value indications. The analyst could attempt to reconcile all of the value indications and search for an answer, or at least an explanation, to this apparent anomaly. As part of this investigation and reconcilement, the analyst should recheck all of the quantitative analyses and rethink all of the qualitative conclusions. After the analytical or data error is discovered, it can be corrected. Then the outlier method may produce a more reasonable, and more consistent, value indication.

The third alternative is typically preferable for handling the phenomenon of an outlier value indication. Of course, this alternative involves additional analyses and reconciliation procedures. Only through such analysis can such a discrepancy be adequately explained and reconciled with the other indications of value.

## SUMMARY

Numerous factors affect the analyst's decision as to which intangible asset valuation approaches and methods to select. Of the numerous factors, the professional judgment and technical expertise of the individual analyst is the most important.

Numerous factors also affect the analyst's selection of a weighting scheme regarding the value indications generated by the alternative valuation methods used. The weighting scheme selected indicates the degree of confidence that the analyst has in the selected valuation method and in the derived value indications. Clearly, the weighting scheme used should be appropriate, given the purpose and objective of the intangible asset valuation. Typically, an explicit weighting scheme should be presented and explained (either quantitatively or qualitatively) in the final intangible asset valuation synthesis and conclusion, along with a careful explanation of the analyst's thought process leading to the weightings.

Finally, alternative valuation methods often yield value indications in a reasonably tight range. The value indications, then, provide mutually supportive evidence regarding the valuation synthesis and conclusion. When an intangible asset valuation method derives an outlier value indication, the analyst should thoroughly research and reconcile the outlier value indication in an attempt to explain and correct the apparent anomaly.

# CHAPTER 14

# Reporting of Intangible Asset Appraisals

## INTRODUCTION

This chapter presents an overview of the process for reporting the results of an intangible asset valuation and economic analysis. We discuss promulgated professional standards, with emphasis on the *Uniform Standards of Professional Appraisal Practice* (USPAP). While focusing on the USPAP appraisal reporting standards, we also introduce other related USPAP standards, such as documentation and record retention requirements. We also consider non-USPAP guidelines related to the presentation of the results of an intangible asset valuation and economic analysis. These guidelines include such report writing issues as completeness, consistency, clarity, and quantitative and qualitative correctness.

Many experienced analysts believe that reporting, and particularly report writing, is the most important part of the appraisal process. However, in practice, reporting the results of the valuation or economic analysis is often afforded precious little time and attention. Many analysts focus most of their time and attention on comprehensive research regarding industry and transactional data and on the rigor and sophistication of their applied microeconomics procedures. This statement does not imply that such time and attention are not important to the quality of the analysis. Rather, it reflects the reality that many analysts do not adequately consider the reporting of the results of their research and analysis until they have already exhausted their time or other resource budgets.

As a practical shibboleth, reporting the results of the analysis is as important as performing the analysis. This assertion is true regardless of the form or format of the report. That is, the assertion applies equally to a verbal report (including expert witness testimony) and to a written report, to a limited report and to a comprehensive report.

If the report is confusing, misleading, or incomplete, then the analysis has failed regardless of the rigor, sophistication, or elegance of the analytical models used and regardless of the relative or absolute correctness of the analysis. If the report audience (i.e., reader or listener) is confused, cannot follow the logic of the presentation, or does not understand the presented results, then the analysis is deficient. The results of the analysis may be one hundred percent "right." However, that "rightness" doesn't matter if the report fails to effectively communicate the results of the analysis to the intended audience.

## OVERVIEW OF THE APPRAISAL REPORT

There is no specific statutory, judicial, or regulatory requirement that a valuation analysis must be consummated in a report. Practically, of course, the analyst cannot communicate the results of the analysis to the intended audience without some type of report.

Likewise, there is no single, specific statutory, judicial, or regulatory requirement with regard to the form or format of an appraisal report. As we will see shortly, even USPAP provides for a number of different report formats. Therefore, even under USPAP, the analyst may select the reporting format that is the most appropriate to the particular assignment. However, it is noteworthy that USPAP does issue certain minimum disclosure requirements even under the most abbreviated reporting format.

A fundamental question is: What constitutes an appraisal report? One definition of an appraisal report is any communication, written or oral, of a value estimate. This definition encompasses any document that reports the results of an appraisal. An appraisal report should lead the audience—that is, reader or listener—from the definition of the appraisal problem through the analysis and relevant descriptive data to a specific value conclusion.

The length, type, format, and content of an intangible asset appraisal report may be influenced by:

1. The informational needs of a client.

2. The informational needs of an intended third party that will rely upon the results of the analysis (e.g., a banker).

3. Any particular regulatory requirements related to the specific purpose of the appraisal (e.g., particular regulatory requirements related to income taxation, ad valorem property taxation, etc.).

4. Federal or other rules of evidence related to expert opinions and reports before certain courts or tribunals.

5. The type of intangible asset subject to analysis (i.e., the more esoteric the subject intangible asset, the more elaborate the intangible asset appraisal report, ceteris paribus).

6. The nature of the subject appraisal problem (i.e., the more complex the appraisal problem to be solved by the subject analysis, the more complex the intangible asset appraisal report, ceteris paribus).

## USPAP REPORTING STANDARDS

The *Uniform Standards of Professional Appraisal Practice* dictate minimum standards to be applied in all types of appraisal reports. However, these standards are somewhat specific to the type of property subject to appraisal. That is, there are slightly different reporting requirements related to real property appraisals, personal property appraisals, and business and intangible asset appraisals. In addition, there are certain standards that apply across the board to all types of appraisal reports.

USPAP defines the term *report* broadly, as follows: "any communication, written or oral, of an appraisal, review, or consulting service that is communicated to the client upon completion of an assignment."[1] USPAP Standard 9 relates to the performance of a business or intangible asset appraisal. USPAP Standard 10 relates to the reporting of a business or intangible asset appraisal. Analysts are strongly encouraged to subscribe to the current edition of USPAP. USPAP subscriptions are available through The Appraisal Foundation. Needless to say, analysts are also strongly encouraged to comply with the current editions of USPAP. The following paragraphs briefly summarize the more salient provisions related to the current (as of this writing) USPAP intangible asset reporting requirements.

USPAP Standards Rule 10-1 presents three requirements with regard to the reporting of an intangible asset appraisal:

---

1. *Uniform Standards of Professional Appraisal Practice,* 1998 ed., Washington, DC: The Appraisal Foundation, 1998, p. 10. USPAP is published annually in November and is available by calling or writing to The Appraisal Foundation, 1029 Vermont Avenue, NW, Suite 900, Washington, DC 20005-3517, (202) 347-7722.

1. An intangible asset appraisal report must clearly and accurately set forth the appraisal in a manner that will not be misleading.

2. An intangible asset appraisal report must contain sufficient information to enable the intended audience to understand it.

3. An intangible asset appraisal report must clearly and accurately disclose any extraordinary assumption that will directly affect the appraisal; the report must also disclose the impact on value of any extraordinary assumption.[2]

It is noteworthy that these reporting rules are binding requirements of USPAP. As such, departures from these reporting requirements are not permitted.

USPAP Standards Rule 10-2 presents several specific minimum disclosures with regard to every intangible asset appraisal report. Under Standards Rule 10-2, each intangible asset appraisal report (oral or written) must:

1. Identify and describe the intangible asset subject to appraisal.

2. State the purpose and intended use of the appraisal.

3. Define the standard of value to be estimated.

4. Specify the "as of" effective date of the value estimate and the date of issuance of the appraisal report.

5. Describe the extent of the appraisal process employed.

6. List all contingent and limiting conditions that may affect the intangible asset appraisal analyses, opinions, and conclusions.

7. Set forth the information considered, the intangible asset appraisal procedures used, and the reasoning that supports the appraisal analyses, opinions, and conclusions.

8. Describe any additional information that may be appropriate to document compliance with or clearly identify and explain permitted departures from the requirements of USPAP Standard 9 (USPAP Standard 9 presents the requirements for the conduct of the intangible asset appraisal).

9. Explain the rationale for the intangible asset valuation methods and procedures that were considered and those that were ultimately used.

10. Include a signed certification statement in compliance with USPAP Standards Rule 10-3.

Whether or not a particular intangible asset valuation or economic analysis is required to be in technical compliance with USPAP, Standards Rule 10-2 presents a concise checklist of minimum reporting disclosures. In other words, the disclosure provisions of USPAP Standards Rule 10-2 would logically be applicable to most intangible asset analyses regardless of whether the strict provisions of USPAP would be legally required.

USPAP Standards Rule 10-3 presents several representations that the analyst should assert with regard to an intangible asset appraisal. This Rule indicates that the analyst should personally certify (by means of signature) that:

---

2. Ibid., pp. 59–61, USPAP Standard 10 and Standards Rules 10-1 through 10-5.

1. The statements of fact included in the intangible asset appraisal report are true and correct.
2. The reported appraisal analyses, opinions, and conclusions are limited only by the specifically disclosed contingent and limiting conditions.
3. The reported appraisal analyses, opinions, and conclusions are unbiased and are the professional work product of the signatory analyst.
4. The analyst has no financial interest in the intangible asset subject to appraisal.
5. The analyst has no financial interest or other bias with regard to any parties involved with the appraisal.
6. The analyst's compensation for the appraisal is not contingent upon a predetermined value conclusion or other action or event.
7. The intangible asset analysis was conducted in compliance with USPAP.
8. No individuals other than the signatory analyst and any analysts specifically named provided significant professional assistance related to the appraisal.

Note that USPAP does not permit departure from the binding disclosure requirements of Standards Rule 10-3 and that these disclosure requirements would be of interest to any audience to the appraisal report (whether the report be oral or written). In other words, even when legal compliance with USPAP is not required, these representations on the part of the analyst would appear to be useful within most intangible asset appraisal contexts.

USPAP Standards Rule 10-4 states that oral intangible asset appraisal reports—including expert witness testimony—should comply with the representation provisions of Standards Rule 10-3. Standards Rule 10-4 also states that, in an oral report, the analyst must declare his or her compliance with Standards Rule 10-3.

USPAP Standards Rule 10-5 states that any analyst who signs an intangible asset appraisal report accepts complete professional responsibility for that report. This is true even when he or she signed the intangible asset appraisal report under the label of a "review appraiser." Paraphrasing this Standards Rule, each analyst who signs an intangible asset appraisal report (in any capacity) is professionally responsible for the content and conclusions of that report.

USPAP does not specify the particular form or format of an intangible asset appraisal report. For instance, USPAP does not specify a minimum number of pages or a minimum number of exhibits for a written report. Likewise, USPAP does not indicate that a written intangible asset appraisal report must be in the form of a narrative report as opposed to a memorandum or letter form. Of course, given the disclosure and representation requirements of Standards Rules 10-2 and 10-3, any memorandum or letter report would likely be several pages in length, at a minimum.

USPAP does provide for several alternative formats of written reports with regard to real property appraisals. These specific report format types are not mentioned at all in the sections of USPAP related to intangible asset appraisals. Therefore, they are not binding with regard to intangible asset appraisal reports (including reports prepared in compliance with USPAP). Nonetheless, the three types or formats of real estate appraisal reports described in USPAP are informative to intangible asset appraisers because they can easily be adapted to intangible asset appraisal reports.

USPAP defines the following three types or formats of real estate appraisal reports:

1. *Self-contained appraisal report.* A written report prepared under Standards Rule 2-2(a) of a complete or limited real estate appraisal.

2. *Summary appraisal report.* A written report prepared under Standards Rule 2-2(b) of a complete or limited real estate appraisal.

3. *Restricted appraisal report.* A written report prepared under Standards Rule 2-2(c) of a complete or limited real estate appraisal.[3]

USPAP Standards Rules 2-2(a), (b), and (c) each list twelve disclosure and representation requirements related to each of the three types of real estate appraisal reports. Essentially all of the twelve disclosure and representation requirements correspond to the intangible asset reporting requirements under USPAP Standard 10. The principal difference between the self-contained appraisal report and the summary appraisal report relates to the level of detail in the presentation of the disclosure provisions. The principal difference between the restricted appraisal report and either the self-contained or the summary appraisal reports is the inclusion of a use restriction that limits the reliance on the appraisal report to the named client. The restricted appraisal report considers anyone else using the report (other than the named client) to be an unintended user.

Intangible asset analysts should be familiar with the three types of formats of real estate appraisal reports described in Standards Rule 2. Even though these report types are not described in USPAP Standard 10, they do appear to have general applicability to the reporting of intangible asset appraisals.

## INTANGIBLE ASSET APPRAISAL REPORTING GUIDANCE

The following paragraphs present general guidelines to assist the analyst in the preparation of clear, cogent, and convincing intangible asset valuation or economic analysis reports. These guidelines do not correspond specifically to USPAP, to American Society of Appraisers promulgated standards, or to any other authoritative professional requirements. Rather, they are common-sense rules based upon years of practical experience related to communicating (and, in some cases, miscommunicating) the results of intangible asset analyses.

The first general reporting guidelines are arguably of biblical significance. While it may seem unambiguously obvious once they are articulated, all analysts should remember these two simple rules related to reporting the results of their analyses:

1. Do what you said.
2. Say what you did.

---

3. Ibid., p. 10.

Obviously, all statements made in a written or oral report should be true, to the best of the analyst's understanding. Each statement or assertion in the report should be associated with a documented research or analytical procedure. The report should not state (or even imply) that a document was reviewed, some research was conducted, a method was considered, a variable was estimated, a transaction was analyzed, a number was calculated, and so on, if that statement (or implication) is not true.

Analysts tend to bend (if not break) this rule most often when it comes to the support for the various input variables used in the analysis (e.g., growth rates, prospective price–volume–cost relationships, profit split allocations, etc.). Some analysts attempt to justify such variables with unidentified (and unperformed) research or with years of experience (unsupported by any empirical evidence). However, in truth, those variables may have been suggested by the client, projected in a company document, or merely assumed. If that is the case, the analyst should simply state the actual source of the variable and not imply support that does not exist.

Likewise, the analyst who faithfully describes each procedure that was performed will generally produce a complete and comprehensive report. It is disconcerting to the report audience when the analyst performed procedures that are not described. The typical reaction of the report reader is, "How did the analyst get here from there?" When procedures appear to be missing (even if they were actually performed), the credibility of the report and the reported conclusion may suffer.

The following specific reporting guidelines are not inscribed in stone. However, they are useful guidelines with regard to the preparation of the report of the intangible asset valuation or economic analysis. These guidelines should be equally useful to experienced as well as to neophyte analysts.

First, analysts should avoid the use of "mystery" variables. These are variables that mysteriously appear in the report text or in the analytical exhibits. No empirical evidence or analytical procedures are presented to support mystery variables. The report reader is left to wonder: Where did that variable come from? The use of unsupported mystery variables often undermines the credibility of an otherwise sound analysis.

Second, analysts should avoid the use of "mystery" data. These are significant data for which the report presents no citation or other data source. Clearly, the source of significant data elements (e.g., inflation rates, risk-free rate of return, capital market performance indices, etc.) should be referenced. The references should be specific enough so that the reader can verify the subject data. For example, the phrase, "economists' consensus of the near-term inflation rate is three percent" would not typically qualify as an adequately supported data source reference.

Third, analysts should avoid the use of vague or ambiguous statements. If the report reader has to ask, "What does the analyst mean by this statement?" then the report has failed to adequately communicate the analysis. Often, a vague statement in a report can be more misleading than a factually incorrect statement, because the reader can check and correct an incorrect fact. However, the reader may never know if he or she has simply misinterpreted a vague or ambiguous statement.

Fourth, analysts should avoid the use of superfluous narrative. This sometimes occurs when the report includes generically prepared boilerplate descriptions of data sources or analytical procedures. It also occurs when the analyst has attempted to cut and paste narrative sections of previous reports for insertion in the subject report. All statements should have a purpose in the report and it should be fairly obvious where and how each statement or data element is used in the analysis. If the reader has to wonder, "Where (or how) does the analyst use this statement (or data element) in the analysis?" then the report is not clear, convincing, and cogent.

Fifth, analysts should include an analysis of the historical results of financial performance related to the subject intangible asset. Such an analysis is clearly appropriate if the subject intangible is, itself, an income-producing asset, as would be the case with an intangible that generates license, royalty, or other income. Such an analysis is also appropriate if the subject intangible is directly associated with an income stream, such as historical revenues (e.g., for a trademark), historical production volume (e.g., for a product patent), or historical cost savings (e.g., for a proprietary process technology). It is informative for the report reader to understand the historical results of financial performance of the subject intangible, specifically if some version of an income approach method is used in the subject analysis.

Sixth, analysts should include an explanation for any adjustments that are made to the historical financial statements or to the historical operational data subject to analysis. It may be entirely appropriate for the analyst to make adjustments to historical financial and operational data. The adjustments may relate to the effects of discontinued operations, excess or nonoperating tangible or intangible assets, or extraordinary items (including nonrecurring revenue, expense, or investment items). Adjustments may also be appropriate to allocate revenues, expenses, and profits between or among tangible and intangible assets. However, it is appropriate for the analyst to list and explain any such adjustments in the report. When adjustments to historical detail are either aggregated or not adequately explained, the report does not allow the reader to recreate all of the appraisal analysis. The use of "mystery" adjustments represents a report deficiency, even if all of the adjustments are appropriate and correctly made.

Seventh, analysts should ensure that there are no inconsistent valuation variables used in alternative analyses or presented in different pages of the report. For example, without a very convincing explanation, it would be inappropriate to use different present value discount rates or different expected growth rates in alternative analyses of the same intangible asset. It is also inappropriate to use related valuation variables that are internally inconsistent with each other. For example, without a very convincing explanation, it would be inappropriate to derive a yield capitalization (present value discount) rate of 18 percent and an expected long-term growth rate of 5 percent and then use a direct capitalization rate of 10 percent. Assuming they all apply to the same measure of economic income, a yield capitalization rate of 18 percent less an expected growth rate of 5 percent mathematically indicates a direct capitalization rate of 13 percent. Such inconsistencies (especially if unexplained) cause the report reader to doubt the credibility of the analysis.

Eighth, analysts should ensure that there are no inconsistent valuation variables presented between the analysis and the report. This reporting guideline means that if a certain variable is derived in the report narrative, it should be used in the quantitative analysis, and vice versa. For example, if a 30 percent profit split allocation is derived in the report narrative, then a 30 percent profit split (and not a 25 percent or a 35 percent profit split) should be used in the analysis. It is particularly confusing to the report reader if, for example, one figure for a valuation variable is derived on page 18 of the report and a different figure of the same valuation variable is used in the analysis presented in Exhibit III of the report.

Ninth, analysts should avoid using undefined terms in the report. Also, analysts should avoid using different terms with the same meaning or definition or defining the same term two different ways in different sections of the report. The jargon of intangible asset valuation and economic analysis is confusing enough for most report readers. The analyst should avoid making the report more confusing by inconsistent or imprecise language. Finally, analysts should avoid creating their own glossaries. There is a fairly well accepted lexicon with regard to intangible asset terminology. It is usually unnecessary (and generally confusing to the report reader) for the analyst to create a new vocabulary of terminology.

Tenth, the most common report writing error is to present the analytical conclusions without any supporting logic. Analysts should avoid the use of such "leap of faith" conclusions. Leap of faith conclusions are usually preceded by the word "therefore": ". . . therefore, the royalty rate is . . ."; ". . . therefore, the remaining useful life is . . ."; ". . . therefore, the amount of the damage estimate is. . . ." Ideally, the analytical conclusion should be presented with the logical rigor and inescapable certainty of a mathematical proof. Of course, this is not always the case. There is a fair amount of professional judgment involved in most intangible asset analyses. However, if the report reader cannot follow the analysis from point A to point B to conclusion C, then the conclusion is not adequately supported.

These ten guidelines should help the analyst communicate the analyses related to and the conclusions of the intangible asset valuation or economic analysis efficiently and effectively. The guidelines are intended to help make the report presentation clear, convincing, and cogent.

## OTHER RELATED USPAP STANDARDS

Intangible asset analysts should be familiar with several other USPAP standards. These standards do not relate to either the conduct or the reporting of the intangible asset appraisal. However, recognition of these standards is mandatory for any intangible asset appraisal performed in compliance with USPAP. Furthermore, these standards describe sound professional practices for any intangible asset analyst.

## Retention of Appraisal Reports and Workpaper Files

The recordkeeping section of the Ethics Provision of USPAP states: "An appraiser must prepare written records of appraisal, review, and consulting assignments—including oral testimony and reports—and retain such records for a period of at least five (5) years after preparation or at least two (2) years after final disposition of any judicial proceeding in which testimony was given, whichever period expires last. The written records are the workfile."[4]

The written records of the intangible asset appraisal include true copies of written reports, written summaries of oral testimony and reports,

---

4. Ibid., p. 3.

and all data required by the USPAP professional standards. The analyst's written records also include information stored on electronic or magnetic files. According to the USPAP recordkeeping requirements, all supporting notes, documentation, and file memorandums related to the intangible asset appraisal should also be retained.

## USPAP Confidentiality Provisions

The confidentiality section of the Ethics Provision of USPAP addresses the confidential nature of the appraiser–client relationship. These confidentiality provisions apply to intangible asset appraisals (as well as to appraisals of other types of properties).

The USPAP confidentiality requirement states: "An appraiser must protect the confidential nature of the appraiser–client relationship."[5] This means that the analyst should not disclose confidential factual data obtained from a client or the results of an appraisal assignment prepared for a client or for anyone other than:

1. The subject client and those persons specifically authorized by the subject client.
2. Such third parties as are authorized by the due process of law.
3. A duly authorized professional peer review committee (e.g., a peer review committee of the American Society of Appraisers).

### SUMMARY

It is the objective of the professional report to communicate as efficiently and effectively as possible: 1) the data sources used, 2) analyses performed, and 3) conclusions reached. This is true whether the report is a written or an oral report. It is also the objective of the professional report to be clear, convincing, and cogent. However, analysts should be aware that there is sometimes a fine line between being convincing and being an advocate. Analysts should consider that if the analyses are rigorously prepared and thoroughly documented, the conclusions will be convincing without the report being an advocacy document.

This chapter reviewed the USPAP professional standards related to reporting the results of intangible asset appraisals. It also introduced several other USPAP professional standards not specifically related to report preparation and presented general and specific guidelines for the preparation of effective reports related to intangible asset valuation and economic analysis.

---

5. Ibid.

# CHAPTER 15

# Sample Intangible Asset Valuation Opinion Report

## INTRODUCTION

This chapter presents an illustrative valuation opinion report. The valuation includes the appraisal and analysis of several discrete intangible assets.

The valuation opinion report is intended to comply with the *Uniform Standards of Professional Appraisal Practice* (USPAP) and with all relevant professional standards. However, due to space constraints the report is illustrative in nature. It is not intended to present an ideal report format and it should not be used as a template for all intangible assets valuation reports.

The valuation opinion report format that is used in each analysis is a function of the purpose and objective of the analysis. Based upon the facts and circumstances of an individual analysis, alternative reporting formats may be accepted or, in fact, preferred.

The Best Appraisal Company (BAC) was engaged to perform a valuation with respect to a business and several business interests. The following sections summarize the BAC analysis and present the BAC valuation opinion report.

**Best Appraisal Company**
**8600 West Bryn Mawr Avenue**
**Chicago, Illinois 60631**

November 30, 1997

Board of Directors
All Directions Supply, Inc.
1234 N.E. Southwest Street
McLean, Virginia 22102

Dear Sirs:

At your request, we have performed a valuation with regard to the business and certain tangible and intangible assets of North-South Supply Company, Inc.

The objective of this analysis is twofold: (1) to estimate the fair market value of the North-South Supply Company, Inc. (NSSC) business enterprise and (2) to estimate the fair market value of certain specified tangible and intangible assets of NSSC. The date of the analysis is as of November 30, 1997.

The management of All Directions Supply, Inc., is contemplating an offer to purchase the net assets of NSSC. It is the intention of All Directions' management to consummate this acquisitive transaction by December 31, 1997. The purpose of this valuation is to assist the management of All Directions Supply, Inc., with the pricing and structuring of the proposed acquisitive transaction. No other purpose is intended or should be inferred.

### SUMMARY DESCRIPTION OF THE COMPANY

NSSC is a division of World Wide Supply, Inc. NSSC was organized in October 1993 as an S corporation for federal income tax purposes. NSSC designs and manufactures pay telephone components and subassemblies. These products are marketed to the regional Bell and independent telephone operating companies. In addition, NSSC is a reseller of cellular telephone services, a distributor of imported Western Electric parts, and a contract manufacturer of various telephone components.

For the 11 months ended November 30, 1997, the company generated $14.6 million in revenues and had $6.3 million in total assets (on a historical cost basis).

### DEFINITION OF VALUE

For purposes of this appraisal, we define *fair market value* as "the price at which a property would change hands between a willing buyer and a willing seller, with neither being under compulsion to transact, with both reasonably cognizant of all relevant facts and circumstances, and both seeking their maximum economic self-interest."

### HIGHEST AND BEST USE

We have appraised the subject business and subject tangible and intangible assets under the premise of value in continued use, as part of a going-concern business enterprise.

Based upon our analysis, and in our opinion, this valuation premise represents the highest and best use of the properties subject to appraisal.

### VALUATION REPORT OUTLINE

The report sections that follow provide descriptions of the economy, industry, business operations, and financial history of NSSC. Following these sections, we discuss the general valuation methodology and the valuation procedures and analyses related to the individual assets subject to appraisal.

As part of this appraisal, we valued all of the tangible personal property of NSSC. In addition, valued certain intangible personal property of NSSC, specifically patents, customer contracts, a customer list, and noncompete agreements. We also valued the overall business enterprise of NSSC.

## U.S. ECONOMIC INDICATORS

Before estimating the fair market value of an intangible asset or business interest, it is important to examine the key economic factors that impact the subject property. These analyses aid in the development of the appropriate valuation variables.

At the end of the second quarter of 1997, the nation's economic expansion is well into its seventh year. Economists believe the economy will rebound in the second half of 1997 from its sluggish performance in the second quarter of 1997. Gross domestic product increased 2.2 percent in the second quarter, less than half the gain recorded in the first quarter of 1997.

The federal government's fiscal 1997 budget deficit is less than estimated earlier, and tax receipts from individuals and corporations are up substantially. The Federal Reserve Board left short-term interest rates unchanged during the second quarter of 1997. Interest rates are fairly low, and inflation is barely present. Global competition, a strong dollar, and a capacity glut in Asia and Europe are discouraging many companies from raising prices.

Unemployment is near the 24-year low reached in May 1997. Wages and salaries are beginning to increase at a more rapid pace, but economists think temporary faster pay growth would correct a trend in which labor's share of national income has declined in recent years.

Consumers appear to be exuberant about the condition of the economy but did not increase their spending in 1997's second quarter, although incomes were up strongly. The consumer confidence index was at a 28-year high in June 1997. With incomes rising, the growth in spending probably will pick up in 1997's second half.

Construction spending in the second quarter of 1997 increased very slightly. Privately owned housing starts increased in June 1997, but were down for the year ending June 30, 1997. Sales of new single-family homes increased briskly, while sales of existing homes dropped slightly. The supply of new homes on the market is the lowest in 26 years. The average rate for a 30-year mortgage fell slightly in June 1997.

Thus far, 1997 has been an outstanding year for investors. The stock market is booming and mutual funds are thriving. Americans continue to plow huge amounts of cash into mutual funds, mostly stock funds, creating demand for stocks.

Although industrial production increased moderately in June 1997, capacity utilization was unchanged from May 1997. Companies are investing in new equipment to expand capacity or to use their old factories more efficiently. Industrial capacity is increasing moderately in the United States.

Orders for manufactured durable goods were up modestly in June 1997 and for the second quarter of 1997. Orders for nondurable goods declined slightly in June 1997. The National Association of Purchasing Management index of industrial activity decreased in June 1997, but is still well above the 50.0 percent mark that determines expansion in industrial activity.

The producer price index for finished goods fell in June 1997, the sixth consecutive decline. The six consecutive declines are the longest streak of producer price deflation since the government started measuring such figures 50 years ago. Business inventories increased at a modest rate in May 1997, while total business sales decreased moderately.

Business investment spending surged ahead during the three months ended June 30, 1997. The economy is expected to continue expanding at a moderate rate during the last half of 1997.

Sources consulted regarding the current economic conditions include: the *Wall Street Journal*, *Trends & Projections* (Standard & Poor's Corporation), *U.S. Financial Data*, *Fortune*, *Barron's*, *The New York Times*, *Business Week*, Lycos, MSNBC, and Reuters Limited.

## HISTORY AND DESCRIPTION OF THE COMPANY

North-South Supply Company, Inc. (NSSC) is a division of World Wide Supply, Inc. The company was organized in October 1993, when the current management and investors purchased the assets of a previously bankrupt NSSC operation. Headquartered in Reno, Nevada, the company is a nonunion shop that employs approximately 180 full-time employees. In addition, NSSC has entered into a labor supply contract with an independent personnel company to provide temporary labor in times of peak production.

The company's business activities can be divided into five basic segments: Manufactured Products; Distribution Products; OEM Customer Services; Baby Bell Cellular Service Reselling; and Telecommunication Consulting. The principal line of business of NSSC is designing, manufacturing, and marketing pay telephone components and subassemblies to telephone operating companies. These proprietary components include: electronic modular dials, modular microswitch and coinless switchhooks, vandal resistant handsets and armored cable assemblies, handset lanyard anchors, directory binders, keypad assemblies, rate selectors, and coin slot blockers. In addition, the company provides contract manufacturing to original equipment manufacturer (OEM) customers and salvages and refurbishes Western Electric parts. Through its Distribution Products segment, NSSC is the sole importer of many parts from the Far East.

As a cellular service reseller, the company resells Baby Bell cellular service to approximately 1,800 customers on a rebilling basis. The cellular service resell revenues are approximately 9 percent of NSSC's total revenues. In addition, NSSC provides specialized telecommunication consulting services to its customers as required.

NSSC's clients, who purchase pay telephone components and subassemblies, include Baby Bell, Western Bell, Eastern Bell, Northern Bell, Southern Bell and over 100 independent operating companies across the United States. The company also provides services to several telephone companies in Canada.

## FINANCIAL STATEMENT ANALYSIS

An essential component of the appraisal process is assessing a company's performance over time. Past sales and earnings, while not a guarantee of future performance, can provide an indication of future growth potential and can put the company's current performance into a historical context. Other things being equal, a company with steadily rising sales and earnings is worth more than one with little or no growth. This section examines the historical trends of selected line items in the balance sheets and income statements.

## FINANCIAL OVERVIEW

NSSC experienced rapid growth from December 1994 through November 1997 due primarily to the company management obtaining patents and designs for some unique components used in pay phone systems. Through the utilization of this technology, management has positioned the company as a leader in the pay phone industry.

While revenues increased materially, overall operating expenses declined and direct costs remained relatively flat, resulting in a shift from the negative earnings in 1994 to positive net income for the last three years.

The earnings growth also impacted the balance sheet as stockholders' equity increased from its deficit levels in 1993 and 1994 to $2.9 million as of November 30, 1997. The capitalization of NSSC consists wholly of equity, as the company repaid all of its long-term debt in 1995.

Exhibits 15-1 through 15-3 present summaries of the NSSC unaudited financial statements and financial ratios.

### Balance Sheets

Exhibit 15-1 presents the balance sheets of NSSC for the fiscal years ended December 31, 1993 through 1996, and as of November 30, 1997.

An important aspect of the NSSC balance sheet is the change in capital structure since 1993. Stockholders' equity increased to positive $2,931,000 as of November 30, 1997, marking a significant increase from the negative levels of 1993 and 1994. One reason for the increase was the repayment of the company's long-term debt and the addition of $1,474,000 of paid-in capital in 1995. However, the remainder of the increase was the result of retained earnings.

On the asset side of the balance sheet, current assets increased materially, resulting in a total asset increase of over 250 percent from 1993 to 1997. Current liabilities decreased as a percent of total assets during that same time, resulting in working capital of $2.5 million in 1997.

### Statement of Earnings

Important elements of the statements of earnings can be revealed not only by looking at aggregate levels, but also by looking at the common-size statements. The common-size statements are constructed by dividing each line item in the statement of earnings by the total revenues. These statements illustrate the percentage of sales represented by each line item. Exhibit 15-2 presents the NSSC audited statements of operations for the periods ended December 31, 1993 through 1996, actual results for the 11 months ended November 30, 1997, and 12-month annualized 1997 results.

NSSC experienced considerable revenue growth over the last four years with an average compound growth rate of almost 50 percent through annualized 1997. A significant portion of the growth occurred in 1997 as revenues increased over 200 percent from $5.2 million in 1996 to almost $15.9 million in annualized 1997. The increase in revenues developed primarily from the company's pay phone manufacturing business. The cellular service revenue level has remained relatively flat.

During the three-year period between 1994 and 1997, gross margins as a percent of revenues declined steadily from 36.1 percent in 1994 to 24.1 percent in 1997. NSSC also managed to reduce its operating expenses, both absolutely and on a common-size basis, from 55.2 percent of revenues to less than 9.0 percent. A significant portion of the reduction came from officers' salaries, which were reduced over 70 percent on an overall basis, and decreased from 39.7 percent of revenues in 1994 to less than 4.0 percent in annualized 1997.

### Financial and Operational Ratios

Exhibit 15-3 presents the financial and operating ratios for the fiscal years ended 1993 to 1996 and the 12-month annualized figures for 1997.

The *current ratio* was 1.75, the highest level since 1993. The increase was due mainly to increases in current assets without a proportionate increase in current liabilities.

The NSSC *activity ratios* showed an overall increase. *Sales to receivables* reached its highest level in the four-year period, as did *cost of sales to inventory, working capital turnover, fixed asset turnover,* and *total asset turnover. Days in inventory* decreased to 64 and *days in receivables* decreased to 32.

EXHIBIT 15-1

North-South Supply Company, Inc. Balance Sheets and Common-Size Analysis, as of November 30, 1997

| | As of Nov. 30 1997 | As of December 31: | | | | As of Nov. 30 1997 | As of December 31: | | | |
|---|---|---|---|---|---|---|---|---|---|---|
| | | 1996 | 1995 | 1994 | 1993 | | 1996 | 1995 | 1994 | 1993 |
| | $ | $ | $ | $ | $ | % | % | % | % | % |
| **Assets** | | | | | | | | | | |
| Current assets: | | | | | | | | | | |
| Cash | 164,340 | 314,124 | 1,518 | 5,292 | 39,570 | 2.6 | 10.7 | 0.1 | 0.2 | 2.2 |
| Accounts receivable | 2,306,724 | 514,008 | 560,700 | 557,724 | 443,838 | 36.6 | 17.6 | 20.9 | 23.6 | 24.8 |
| Accounts receivable—cellular | 329,190 | 218,670 | — | — | — | 5.2 | 7.5 | — | — | — |
| Inventory | 2,880,450 | 1,371,102 | 1,340,646 | 1,048,554 | 666,078 | 45.7 | 46.9 | 49.9 | 44.4 | 37.2 |
| Letters of credit | 221,196 | — | — | — | — | 3.5 | — | — | — | — |
| Other receivables and prepaids | — | — | 162,138 | 7,332 | 1,800 | — | — | 6.0 | 0.3 | 0.1 |
| Total current assets | 5,901,900 | 2,417,904 | 2,065,002 | 1,618,902 | 1,151,286 | 93.6 | 82.6 | 76.8 | 68.6 | 64.3 |
| Property and equipment: | | | | | | | | | | |
| Warehouse equipment & tooling | 674,904 | 642,924 | 623,634 | 521,616 | 531,774 | 10.7 | 22.0 | 23.2 | 22.1 | 29.7 |
| Office equipment | 96,288 | 96,288 | 356,928 | 325,044 | 71,622 | 1.5 | 3.3 | 13.3 | 13.8 | 4.0 |
| Computer equipment | 82,986 | 82,986 | — | — | — | 1.3 | 2.8 | — | — | — |
| Furniture & fixtures | 230,520 | 230,520 | — | — | — | 3.7 | 7.9 | — | — | — |
| Leasehold improvements | 112,272 | 102,786 | 102,786 | 102,786 | — | 1.8 | 3.5 | 3.8 | 4.4 | — |
| Total property & equipment | 1,196,970 | 1,155,504 | 1,083,348 | 949,446 | 603,396 | 19.01 | 39.5 | 40.3 | 40.2 | 33.7 |
| Less accumulated depreciation | (849,750) | (697,950) | (519,774) | (291,492) | (29,580) | (13.5) | (23.9) | (19.3) | (12.3) | (1.7) |
| Net property & equipment | 347,220 | 457,554 | 563,574 | 657,954 | 573,816 | 5.5 | 15.6 | 21.0 | 27.9 | 32.1 |
| Other assets: | | | | | | | | | | |
| Deposits | 40,194 | 34,494 | 34,494 | 49,494 | 20,610 | 0.6 | 1.2 | 1.3 | 2.1 | 1.2 |
| Organization cost | 16,320 | 16,320 | 25,680 | 35,040 | 44,400 | 0.3 | 0.6 | 1.0 | 1.5 | 2.5 |
| Total other assets | 56,514 | 50,814 | 60,174 | 84,534 | 65,010 | 0.9 | 1.7 | 2.2 | 3.6 | 3.6 |
| TOTAL ASSETS | 6,305,634 | 2,926,272 | 2,688,750 | 2,361,390 | 1,790,112 | 100.0 | 100.0 | 100.0 | 100.0 | 100.0 |
| **LIABILITIES & EQUITY** | | | | | | | | | | |
| Liabilities: | | | | | | | | | | |
| Current liabilities: | | | | | | | | | | |
| Notes payable to shareholder | 1,854,000 | 1,854,000 | 1,854,000 | 1,158,000 | 174,00 | 29.4 | 63.4 | 69.0 | 49.0 | 9.7 |
| Compensation payable to shareholder | — | — | — | 687,498 | — | — | — | — | 29.1 | — |
| Current portion of long-term debt | — | — | — | 115,728 | 94,854 | — | — | — | 4.9 | 5.3 |
| Accounts payable | 1,152,642 | 221,034 | 259,362 | 135,774 | 188,916 | 18.3 | 7.6 | 9.6 | 5.7 | 10.6 |
| Accounts payable—cellular | 225,030 | 232,014 | — | — | — | 3.6 | 7.9 | — | — | — |
| Accrued federal unemployment taxes | — | 2,130 | — | — | — | — | 0.1 | — | — | — |
| Accrued industrial insurance | 4,488 | 2,328 | — | — | — | 0.1 | 0.1 | — | — | — |
| Accrued sales taxes | 11,838 | 9,498 | — | — | — | 0.2 | 0.3 | — | — | — |
| Accrued interest payable | 126,636 | 91,674 | — | — | — | 2.0 | 3.1 | 00 | 00 | 00 |
| Accrued taxes & expenses | — | — | 463,404 | 355,128 | 196,728 | — | — | 17.2 | 15.0 | 11.0 |
| Total current liabilities | 3,374,634 | 2,412,678 | 2,576,766 | 2,452,128 | 654,498 | 53.5 | 82.4 | 95.8 | 103.8 | 36.6 |
| Long-term debt | — | — | — | 1,453,878 | 1,510,266 | — | — | — | 61.6 | 84.4 |
| Total liabilities | 3,374,634 | 2,412,678 | 2,576,766 | 3,906,006 | 2,164,764 | 53.5 | 82.4 | 95.8 | 165.4 | 120.9 |
| Stockholders' equity | | | | | | | | | | |
| Common stock, $1 par | 120,000 | 120,000 | 120,000 | 24,000 | 24,000 | 1.9 | 4.1 | 4.5 | 1.0 | 1.3 |
| Additional paid-in capital | 1,473,606 | 1,473,606 | 1,473,606 | — | — | 23.4 | 50.4 | 54.8 | — | — |
| Retained earnings | 1,337,394 | (1,080,012) | (1,481,622) | (1,568,616) | (398,652) | 21.2 | (36.9) | (55.1) | (66.4) | (22.3) |
| Total stockholders' equity | 2,931,000 | 513,594 | 111,984 | (1,544,616) | (374,652) | 46.5 | 17.6 | 4.2 | (65.4) | (20.9) |
| TOTAL LIABILITIES & EQUITY | 6,305,634 | 2,926,272 | 2,688,750 | 2,361,390 | 1,790,112 | 100.0 | 100.0 | 100.0 | 100.0 | 100.0 |
| Common shares outstanding | 120,000 | 120,000 | 120,000 | 24,000 | 24,000 | | | | | |
| Per share book value | 24 | 4 | 1 | (64) | (16) | | | | | |

Source: Debit & Credit, Certified Public Accountants, and company financial statements.

Note: Numbers may not total due to rounding.

With respect to the NSSC coverage ratios, the company has no long-term debt. As a result, NSSC maintained adequate earnings capacity to cover interest expenses.

The company's profitability ratios all exhibited marked increases, with the exception of *debt-free income to total capital, cash flow to equity,* and *debt-free cash flow to total capital,* which showed slight declines due primarily to the large increase in equity. All of the exceptional profitability measures remained well above the 1994–1995 levels.

## North-South Supply Company, Inc., Statements of Operations and Common-Size Analysis, as of November 30, 1997

| | 12 Mos. Annualized 1997 | 11 Mos. Ended Nov. 30, 1997 | Fiscal Years Ended December 31: 1996 | Ended 1995 | 1994 | For 3 Mos. Ended 1993 | 12 Mos. Annualized 1997 | 11 Mos. Ended Nov. 30 1997 | Fiscal Years Ended December 31: 1996 | 1995 | 1994 | For 3 Mos. 1993 |
|---|---|---|---|---|---|---|---|---|---|---|---|---|
| | $ | $ | $ | $ | $ | $ | % | % | % | % | % | % |
| Sales | 15,900,192 | 14,575,176 | 5,196,768 | 4,800,518 | 4,759,236 | 852,522 | 100.0 | 100.0 | 100.0 | 100.0 | 100.0 | 100.0 |
| Cost of sales: | | | | | | | | | | | | |
| Materials | 8,648,025 | 7,927,356 | 2,068,620 | 1,515,780 | 2,158,752 | 490,398 | 54.5 | 54.4 | 39.8 | 37.9 | 45.4 | 57.5 |
| Freight | 631,852 | 579,198 | 113,820 | — | — | — | 4.0 | 4.0 | 2.2 | — | — | — |
| Direct labor | 1,083,868 | 993,546 | 471,924 | 489,858 | 292,392 | 45,030 | 6.8 | 6.8 | 9.1 | 12.2 | 6.1 | 5.3 |
| Payroll taxes | 170,038 | 155,868 | 68,868 | 89,220 | 45,402 | 8,166 | 1.1 | 1.1 | 1.3 | 2.2 | 1.0 | 1.0 |
| Contract labor | 482,734 | 442,506 | 119,742 | — | — | — | 3.0 | 3.0 | 2.3 | — | — | — |
| Medical insurance | 49,948 | 45,786 | 78,918 | — | — | — | 0.3 | 0.3 | 1.5 | — | — | — |
| Personal prop. tax | 10,787 | 9,888 | 9,768 | — | — | — | 0.1 | 0.1 | 0.2 | — | — | — |
| Rent | 455,289 | 417,348 | 347,460 | 391,500 | 239,946 | 55,932 | 2.9 | 2.9 | 6.7 | 9.8 | 5.0 | 6.6 |
| Utilities | 72,026 | 66,024 | 54,588 | 43,116 | 21,870 | 2,502 | 0.5 | 0.5 | 1.1 | 1.1 | 0.5 | 0.3 |
| Equipment rental | 13,012 | 11,928 | 21,166 | — | — | — | 0.1 | 0.1 | 0.4 | — | — | — |
| Packaging | 116,771 | 107,040 | 6,012 | — | — | — | 0.7 | 0.7 | 0.1 | — | — | — |
| Depreciation | 165,600 | 151,800 | 178,176 | 142,158 | 192,678 | 29,580 | 1.0 | 1.0 | 3.4 | 3.6 | 4.0 | 3.5 |
| Shop supplies | 158,151 | 144,972 | 60,042 | 30,264 | 35,502 | 7,224 | 1.0 | 1.0 | 1.2 | 0.8 | 0.7 | 0.8 |
| Repairs, maint. & other | 9,943 | 9,114 | 11,154 | 44,724 | 52,686 | 2,490 | 0.1 | 0.1 | 0.2 | 1.1 | 1.1 | 0.3 |
| Total cost of sales | 12,068,044 | 11,062,374 | 3,612,258 | 2,746,620 | 3,039,228 | 641,322 | 75.9 | 75.9 | 69.5 | 68.7 | 63.9 | 75.2 |
| Gross margin | 3,832,148 | 3,512,802 | 1,584,510 | 1,253,898 | 1,720,008 | 211,200 | 24.1 | 24.1 | 30.5 | 31.3 | 36.1 | 24.8 |
| Gen'l & admin. expenses: | | | | | | | | | | | | |
| Officers' salaries | 599,904 | 549,912 | 661,362 | 993,438 | 1,887,306 | 343,746 | 3.8 | 3.8 | 12.7 | 24.8 | 39.7 | 40.3 |
| Office salaries | 312,873 | 286,800 | 210,978 | 102,150 | 58,386 | 20,400 | 2.0 | 2.0 | 4.1 | 2.6 | 1.2 | 2.4 |
| Payroll taxes | 49,955 | 45,792 | 49,698 | 163,926 | 157,014 | 39,264 | 0.3 | 0.3 | 1.0 | 4.1 | 3.3 | 4.6 |
| Medical insurance | 39,391 | 36,108 | 4,392 | — | — | — | 0.2 | 0.2 | 0.1 | — | — | — |
| Professional fees | 55,715 | 51,072 | 51,156 | 202,602 | 172,020 | 54,594 | 0.4 | 0.4 | 1.0 | 5.1 | 3.6 | 6.4 |
| ADP payroll services | 5,407 | 4,956 | 2,472 | — | — | — | 0.0 | 0.0 | 0.0 | — | — | — |
| Deprec. & amort. | — | — | 9,360 | 96,348 | 79,032 | 2,340 | — | — | 0.2 | 2.4 | 1.7 | 0.3 |
| Office expenses | 96,951 | 88,872 | 113,166 | 67,140 | 81,486 | 17,874 | 0.6 | 0.6 | 2.2 | 1.7 | 1.7 | 2.1 |
| Discounts & freight out | 105 | 96 | — | 54,414 | 24,660 | 28,812 | 0.0 | 0.0 | — | 1.4 | 0.5 | 3.4 |
| Telephone | 59,780 | 54,798 | 64,248 | 65,034 | 65,118 | 15,924 | 0.4 | 0.4 | 1.2 | 1.6 | 1.4 | 1.9 |
| Research & develop. | 1,388 | 1,272 | 11,514 | — | — | — | 0.0 | 0.0 | 0.2 | — | — | — |
| Bad debts expense | 47,023 | 43,104 | 7,038 | — | — | — | 0.3 | 0.3 | 0.1 | — | — | — |
| Travel & meals | 18,982 | 17,400 | 27,666 | 79,482 | 70,164 | 4,968 | 0.1 | 0.1 | 0.5 | 2.0 | 1.5 | 0.6 |
| Liability insurance | 19,774 | 18,126 | 10,116 | — | — | — | 0.1 | 0.1 | 0.2 | — | — | — |
| Licenses & filing fees | 713 | 654 | — | 53,082 | 18,156 | 4,674 | 0.0 | 0.0 | — | 1.3 | 0.4 | 0.5 |
| Professional education | 2,330 | 2,136 | — | — | — | — | 0.0 | 0.0 | — | — | — | — |
| Business taxes | 82,335 | 75,474 | 41,076 | — | — | — | 0.5 | 0.5 | 0.8 | — | — | — |
| Trade ad. & trade shows | 4,732 | 4,338 | 8,442 | 11,430 | — | — | 0.0 | 0.0 | 0.2 | 0.3 | — | — |
| Donations & other | 733 | 672 | — | 7,986 | 15,624 | — | 0.0 | 0.0 | — | 0.2 | 0.3 | — |
| Total operating exp. | 1,398,089 | 1,281,582 | 1,272,684 | 1,897,032 | 2,628,966 | 532,596 | 8.8 | 8.8 | 24.5 | 47.4 | 55.2 | 62.5 |
| Operating income | 2,434,058 | 2,231,220 | 311,826 | (643,134) | (908,958) | (321,396) | 15.3 | 15.3 | 6.0 | (16.1) | (19.1) | (37.7) |
| Other recur. inc. (exp.): | | | | | | | | | | | | |
| Cellular air sales | 1,549,944 | 1,420,782 | 1,579,854 | — | — | — | 9.7 | 9.7 | 30.4 | — | — | — |
| Cellular airtime exp. | (1,204,213) | (1,103,862) | (1,351,296) | — | — | — | (7.6) | (7.6) | (26.0) | — | — | — |
| Interest expense | (142,828) | (130,926) | (138,774) | — | (260,112) | (77,256) | (0.9) | (0.9) | (2.7) | — | (5.5) | (9.1) |
| Total other recurring | 202,903 | 185,994 | 89,784 | — | (260,112) | (77,256) | 1.3 | 1.3 | 1.7 | — | (5.5) | (9.1) |
| Pretax income | 2,636,961 | 2,417,214 | 401,610 | (643,134) | (1,169,070) | (398,652) | 16.6 | 16.6 | 7.7 | (16.1) | (24.6) | (46.8) |
| Other nonrecurring (exp.): | | | | | | | | | | | | |
| Forgive. of prior indebt. | — | — | — | 731,058 | — | — | — | — | — | 18.3 | — | — |
| Loss on sale of equip. | — | — | — | (930) | (894) | — | — | — | — | (0.0) | (0.0) | — |
| Total other nonrecurr. | — | — | — | 730,128 | (894) | — | — | — | — | 18.3 | (0.0) | — |
| Net income | 2,636,961 | 2,417,214 | 401,610 | 86,994 | (1,169,964) | (398,652) | 16.6 | 16.6 | 7.7 | 2.2 | (24.6) | (46.8) |
| Pretax cash flow | 2,802,561 | 2,569,014 | 589,146 | (404,628) | (897,360) | (366,732) | 17.6 | 17.6 | 11.3 | (10.1) | (18.9) | (43.0) |
| Avg. shares outstanding | 120,000 | 120,000 | 120,000 | 120,000 | 72,000 | 24,000 | | | | | | |
| Per-share pretax income | 22 | 20 | 3 | (5) | (16) | (17) | | | | | | |

Source: Debit & Credit, Certified Public Accountants, and company financial statements.

Note: Numbers may not total due to rounding.

**EXHIBIT 15-3**

North-South Supply Company, Inc., Financial and Operational Ratios, as of November 30, 1997

| | 12 Months Annualized 1997 | For Fiscal Years Ended December 31: | | |
| --- | --- | --- | --- | --- |
| | | 1996 | 1995 | 1994 |
| **LIQUIDITY RATIOS** | | | | |
| Current ratio | 1.75 | 1.00 | 0.80 | 0.66 |
| Quick ratio | 0.73 | 0.34 | 0.22 | 0.23 |
| Working capital ($000) | 2,527 | 5 | (512) | (833) |
| **ACTIVITY RATIOS** | | | | |
| Sales/receivables | 11.27 | 9.67 | 7.15 | 9.50 |
| Days in receivables | 32 | 38 | 51 | 38 |
| Cost of sales/inventory | 5.68 | 2.66 | 5.24 | 3.55 |
| Days in inventory | 64 | 137 | 70 | 103 |
| Working capital turnover | 12.56 | (20.52) | (5.95) | (28.29) |
| Fixed asset turnover | 39.51 | 10.18 | 6.55 | 7.73 |
| Asset turnover | 3.44 | 1.85 | 1.58 | 2.29 |
| **COVERAGE/LEVERAGE RATIOS** | | | | |
| Interest expense coverage: | | | | |
| EBIT | 19.46 | 3.89 | NM | (3.49) |
| EBDIT | 20.62 | 5.25 | NM | (2.45) |
| Cash flow/current maturity long-term debt | NM | NM | (3.50) | (9.46) |
| Fixed assets/equity | 0.12 | 0.89 | 5.03 | (0.43) |
| Equity/total capital (%) | 100.0 | 100.0 | 100.0 | NM |
| **PROFITABILITY RATIOS (%)** | | | | |
| Net income/average equity | 153.1 | 128.4 | 89.8 | 121.8 |
| Net income/average assets | 57.1 | 14.3 | (25.5) | (56.3) |
| Net income/sales | 16.6 | 7.7 | (16.1) | (24.6) |
| Cash flow/average equity | 162.7 | 188.4 | 56.5 | 93.5 |
| Cash flow/assets | 60.7 | 21.0 | (16.0) | (43.2) |
| Cash flow/sales | 17.6 | 11.3 | (10.1) | (18.9) |

EBIT = Earnings before interest and taxes.

EBDIT = Earnings before depreciation, interest, and taxes.

Cash flow = Net income plus depreciation expense.

Debt-free income = Income plus interest expense.

NM = Not meaningful.

Total capital = Long-term debt plus stockholders' equity.

*Source:* Exhibits 15-1 and 15-2 and Best Appraisal Company calculations.

## VALUATION METHODOLOGY

### Asset Valuation Approaches

As recognized by the *Uniform Standards of Professional Appraisal Practice* (USPAP), there are three generally accepted approaches to estimating the value of all assets. These three generally accepted approaches apply to intangible assets and intellectual properties, as well as to real estate and to tangible personal property. The three generally accepted asset valuation approaches are: the market approach, the income approach, and the cost approach.

The three generally accepted asset valuation approaches are intended to reflect the respective comparative (market), economic (income), and utility (cost) characteristics of the subject property.

Because each valuation approach emphasizes a different attribute of the subject property, a level of confidence in the value conclusions is increased by using all applicable approaches, presuming that each is well documented and reflects the proper use of logic.

However, it is better to avoid the use of a poorly supported valuation approach than to naively satisfy a strategy of using all three generally accepted asset valuation approaches.

The market approach stresses the comparative characteristics of reasonably competitive properties. This approach is appropriately used when there are sufficient market-derived transactional data from which to abstract units of comparison and to support market adjustments for items of dissimilarity between the subject and comparative properties. The market approach is weakened if the selected comparable properties are not comparative (at least from an economic perspective) to the subject property on or about the valuation date.

The income approach attempts to simulate the economies of a particular property. This approach can be most useful if the valuation subject is or has the potential to become an income-producing property. The approach is weakened if there are not sufficient data to adequately support estimates of economic income, capital charges (if any), and the selection of the appropriate direct capitalization rate or yield capitalization rate.

The cost approach stresses the utility characteristics of the property. This approach is most useful as a value indicator when the components of the property are relatively new and reasonably reflect the highest and best use of the subject property. This approach is often used to estimate the value of special-purpose property, where there may be little potential for sale or lease in the marketplace.

It should be noted that each of these three valuation approaches produces an indication of value, but the final market value estimate is concluded from the correlation, or reconciliation, of the various valuation indications derived from each approach used in the analysis.

In most appraisals, one or two of the approaches are more applicable or appropriate as an indicator of value. The more appropriate approaches are afforded a greater weighting in the valuation synthesis and conclusion. Accordingly, the appraisal should recognize the strengths and weaknesses of the market data and the relative reliability of the processes used in deriving a synthesis and conclusion of value.

### Intangible Asset Valuation Methods

Intangible assets and intellectual properties often have little guideline transactional data available. This is because these assets and properties are created over time and are designed to service the needs of a particular organization. In this appraisal, the appropriate valuation for valuing the subject intangible assets and intellectual properties are the cost and income approaches.

Under the cost approach, the concept of the cost to replace the subject intangible asset is relied upon as an indicator of value. For fungible intangible assets, a prudent investor would pay no more than the cost to reconstruct or replace the subject intangible with another of like utility.

Accordingly, for fungible intangible assets, the highest price an investor would pay is the replacement cost new. To the extent that the subject intangible asset provides less utility than the new one, the value of the subject intangible is less than its replacement cost new.

Adjustments are made for curable and incurable losses in value due to physical deterioration and to all forms of obsolescence. These forms of obsolescence are described below:

1. *Physical deterioration* refers to the loss in value brought about by wear and tear, disintegration, use in service, and all physical factors that reduce the life and serviceability of the property.

2. *Functional obsolescence* refers to the loss in value caused by factors internal to the property itself that limit the ability of the subject property to perform the function for which it was intended.

3. *Technological obsolescence* is a form of functional obsolescence that is caused by the constantly improving technological environment and its impact on the value of the subject property.

4. *Economic obsolescence* refers to the loss in value caused by factors external to the property such as legislative enactments, changes in supply–demand relationships, and changes in the optimum use of the property.

Under the relief from royalty method, either the net operating income, net income, net cash flow, or a similar measure of economic income attributable to the subject property is capitalized in order to estimate value. For licensed intellectual property, for example, net operating license royalty payments from future years are discounted to their present value.

A related income approach method involves the use of a discounted net cash flow analysis. This method involves a rigorous and comprehensive analysis of historical financial and operational data in order to develop a projection of the net cash flow generation capacity of the subject intangible asset.

## TANGIBLE PERSONAL PROPERTY

In reviewing the various approaches that are appropriate for the appraisal of tangible personal property, several factors are taken into consideration. These factors include, but are not limited to, the following:

1. Appropriate premise of value.
2. Availability of empirical pricing data.
3. Various current and potential uses of the subject tangible personal property.
4. The size of the set of tangible assets subject to appraisal.
5. Age of the tangible personal property assets.

Based upon our analysis of these factors, we concluded that the most appropriate valuation approach for the subject tangible personal property is the cost approach. Within this valuation approach, we will use the depreciated replacement cost method.

### Valuation Analysis

In using the depreciated replacement cost method, there are two primary factors that should be quantified in order to ensure the appropriate application of this method. The first factor is the determination of the inflation or deflation factor; this factor relates the original asset cost to its current replacement cost. The second factor is the determination of the appropriate depreciation and obsolescence factors, which account for the influences of obsolescence from all sources.

The inflation or deflation factor is an estimate of the trend in pricing for the replacement of a particular asset or piece of equipment. The appropriate inflation or deflation factor is selected and applied to all classes of tangible personal property. For this appraisal, we have selected these factors from the data published in the *Marshall Valuation Service*.[1]

The critical factor in determining the obsolescence adjustment that should be applied to the replacement cost new is the estimate of the remaining life of the tangible personal property assets. This can be accomplished by examining the subject tangible assets with an emphasis upon the causes of attrition, retirement, and obsolescence. In the subject appraisal, we have applied a depreciation factor corresponding to a 10-year average service life.

---

1. *Marshall Valuation Service* (Los Angeles: Marshall & Swift, 1998, updated periodically).

Exhibit 15-4 lists NSSC's tangible personal property and their corresponding fair market values as of November 30, 1997.

### Valuation Conclusion

Based upon the analysis presented herein, and in our opinion, the fair market value of the tangible personal property assets of NSSC, as of November 30, 1997, is $544,000.

### PATENT LICENSE AGREEMENTS

A patent is a grant by the U.S. government, administered by the U.S. Patent and Trademark Office, to an inventor or the inventor's assignee for a stated period of time. A patent confers the exclusive right to make, use, license, or vend an invention or process.

The scope of protection provided under a patent is determined by the depth and breadth of the invention identified in the claims. Patent protection may be enforced legally from infringements during the patent term. The patent term is usually 17 years for technical inventions or innovations and 14 years for design patents. The degree of protection afforded worldwide varies depending upon the foreign countries in which a patent is registered.

The value of a patent is influenced by numerous factors, including those listed below:

1. Is the patent a basic patent?
2. Does the patent constitute a major improvement?
3. Can the patent be used in other industries?
4. Are substitutes available?

#### General Theory of Patent Valuation

Patented or unpatented technology may be valued using all three generally accepted approaches to valuation: market, cost, and income. The market approach is a particularly valid approach to patent valuation when there are market-derived empirical pricing data available. However, the market approach is not particularly applicable when there is a paucity of market-derived empirical pricing data (i.e., data regarding intellectual properties that were sold, licensed, or otherwise exchanged apart from a business enterprise).

In the instant case, to value the patent licenses of NSSC, we concluded that the market and income approach methods are the most appropriate. Specifically, based on the quantity and quality of available data, we used the relief from royalty method to estimate the fair market value of the NSSC patent licenses.

#### Relief from Royalty Method

This market approach method is based on the premise that the intangible asset owner would be willing to pay a reasonable royalty rate to inbound license the subject patented technology. Inbound licensing royalty rates can be estimated from an analysis of market-derived data with respect to empirical licenses of comparative patented technology. In addition, inbound licensing royalty rates can be approximated based on the profit split method—that is, based on a split (between the licensor and the licensee) of the percentage of expected profit margin associated with the commercialization of the subject patented technology.

In *Ciba-Geigy Corp. v. Commissioner,* the U.S. Tax Court found that "a standard widely recognized in the licensing literature is that the licensor and licensee share

EXHIBIT 15-4

North-South Supply Company, Inc., Tangible Personal Property, Fair Market Value, as of November 30, 1997

| Asset Number | Asset Description | Year of Purchase | Indicated Fair Market Value |
|---|---|---|---|
| 1 | Datsun forklift | 1993 | $  8,062 |
| 2 | Humphery J hook crimper | 1993 | 151 |
| 3 | Humphery cable crimper | 1993 | 202 |
| 4 | Drill press | 1993 | 202 |
| 5 | Pitney Bowes letter scale | 1993 | 81 |
| 6 | Compressor 5 hp | 1993 | 705 |
| 8 | 2 propane tanks | 1993 | 141 |
| 9 | Hand truck | 1993 | 50 |
| 10 | Weller EC 200 soldering | 1993 | 71 |
| 11 | Scope PVM 638 | 1993 | 50 |
| 12 | Global spec | 1993 | 71 |
| 13 | Global spec PB-503 | 1993 | 50 |
| 14 | Metal racks | 1993 | 1,008 |
| 15 | Tectronix oscilloscope | 1993 | 806 |
| 16 | Proctor test equipment | 1993 | 2,419 |
| 17 | Permax placement system | 1993 | 78,606 |
| 18 | Reflow systems (Vitonix) | 1993 | 33,861 |
| 19 | Screen printer (circuit) | 1993 | 13,303 |
| 20 | Marshall Ind. production equipment | 1993 | 403 |
| 21 | Scale ek-12A | 1993 | 252 |
| 22 | Permax tape feeder | 1993 | 403 |
| 23 | Twin power sup TW5005 | 1993 | 302 |
| 24 | Tracking generator | 1993 | 1,814 |
| 25 | Spectrum analyzer | 1993 | 8,062 |
| 26 | Tooling inspection molds | 1993 | 504 |
| 27 | Tooling tools | 1993 | 4,031 |
| 28 | Pin applicator conn. set | 1993 | 806 |
| 29 | EX 2001 station soldering | 1993 | 71 |
| 30 | C&D coin set-test equip. | 1994 | 2,279 |
| 31 | Tape feeder | 1994 | 4,170 |
| 32 | Pallet jack | 1994 | 1,686 |
| 33 | Surface mount Technique | 1994 | 1,347 |
| 34 | Permateck feeder | 1994 | 6,406 |
| 35 | Mod rubber key pads | 1995 | 5,496 |
| 36 | Hydraulic swage unit | 1995 | 8,794 |
| 37 | Tooling change dial bracket | 1995 | 971 |
| 38 | Micro switch bracket | 1995 | 21,407 |
| 39 | Dispenser kit | 1995 | 2,953 |
| 40 | Lanyard anchor | 1995 | 13,521 |
| 41 | Toolin La Croix | 1996 | 13,731 |
|  |  |  | 239,248 |
| 1 | Letter & paper cutter | 1993 | 121 |
| 2 | Phone system (Merlin) | 1993 | 1,612 |
| 3 | IBM copier Model 610 | 1993 | 1,209 |
| 4 | Phones AT&T/Merlin | 1993 | 7,054 |
| 5 | Facit 2261 Calculator | 1993 | 71 |
| 8 | 2 refrigerators | 1993 | 403 |
| 9 | 2 microwaves | 1993 | 202 |
| 10 | Sharp fax machine | 1993 | 2,736 |
| 11 | Vacuum cleaner | 1993 | 391 |
| 12 | Answering machine | 1993 | 171 |
| 13 | Audiovox cellular phone | 1993 | 403 |
| 14 | Audiovox cellular phone | 1993 | 403 |
| 16 | Calculator | 1994 | 454 |
| 17 | PT Motorola cellular phone | 1994 | 2,316 |
| 18 | Calculator | 1994 | 324 |
| 19 | IBM Wheelwriter typewriter | 1994 | 4,108 |

EXHIBIT 15-4 *(continued)*

North-South Supply Company, Inc., Tangible Personal Property, Fair Market Value, as of November 30, 1997

| Asset Number | Asset Description | Year of Purchase | Indicated Fair Market Value |
|---|---|---|---|
| 20 | 3 Merlin sets | 1995 | 4,295 |
| 21 | 2 phones | 1995 | 436 |
| 22 | Cellular telephone | 1995 | 1,228 |
| 23 | Copier | 1996 | 26,586 |
| | | | 54,524 |
| 1 | Compac Deskpro/mouse | 1993 | 4,800 |
| 2 | JDL printer/plotter | 1993 | 1,713 |
| 3 | Laser printer Series II | 1993 | 2,519 |
| 4 | Bullet printer | 1993 | 1,612 |
| 7 | Computer equipment | 1994 | 5,794 |
| 8 | Microage-computer equipment | 1994 | 500 |
| 12 | Burgundy chair | 1995 | 300 |
| 13 | 5 chairs, secretary | 1995 | 1,191 |
| 14 | 2 lateral file cabinets | 1995 | 1,521 |
| 15 | Visual board | 1995 | 3,386 |
| 16 | Time clock | 1995 | 3,155 |
| 17 | Shelving unit lancer | 1995 | 1,598 |
| 18 | Brian's chair | 1995 | 3,826 |
| 19 | Computer | 1996 | 8,400 |
| | | | 40,316 |
| 1 | Conference table w/ 6 chairs | 1993 | 504 |
| 2 | 4 oak desks | 1993 | 746 |
| 3 | 6 chairs | 1993 | 363 |
| 4 | Office chairs | 1993 | 363 |
| 5 | Gray modular furniture | 1993 | 10,078 |
| 6 | Cubicle walls | 1993 | 5,122 |
| 7 | Lunch table 2, chairs 8 | 1994 | 828 |
| 8 | 2 chairs, typewriter pedestal, 2 tables | 1994 | 686 |
| 9 | Lobby chairs, secretarial chair | 1994 | 6,001 |
| 10 | Office furniture—Brian, Tony, Heather | 1994 | 89,428 |
| 11 | Table, 2 chairs | 1994 | 667 |
| | | | 114,784 |
| 1 | Leasehold improvements | 1994 | 95,240 |
| | Grand total | | $544,112 |
| | Fair market value (rounded) | | $544,000 |

*Source:* Company records.

*Note:* Numbers may not total due to rounding.

the net profits in ratio of 25 percent and 75 percent, respectively."[2] As a practical matter, as stated in *W.I. Gore & Associates v. Carlile Corp.*, in which a royalty rate based upon a 30 percent profit split was considered to be reasonable, ". . . [a] patent empowers the owner to exact royalties as high as he can negotiate with the leverage of that monopoly."[3]

A remaining useful life analysis is a critical area of inquiry to the subject patent valuation because the remaining useful life analysis estimates the economic term over which the licensee can expect to pay, and the licensor can expect to receive, the royalty payments. With a determination of the projected royalty payment stream over the specific term, the value of the subject patent can be reasonably estimated.

---

2. 85 TC 172 (Aug. 1, 1985), *acg.* 1987-2 CB 1.
3. 183 USPQ 459 (D. Del. 1974).

**Valuation Analysis**

The Pay Telephone Hook Switch Assembly and the Deformable Membrane Keypad Assembly for Public Telephones were patented in May 1992 and August 1993, respectively. By an agreement, the patent owners licensed these two patents to NSSC until the expiration date of the subject patents.

NSSC has been granted a perpetual license, with full and unrestricted rights to make, use, or sell, within the United States and throughout the world, products using the subject licensed technology. In the event of an infringement, with successful settlement, the patent owners shall receive 25 percent of any recoveries remaining after all due expenses have been considered.

Priced at $67.50 and $204.00 per unit of the Kit (i.e., the pay phone switchhook assembly) and Dial (i.e., keypad assembly), NSSC projects its 1998 sales volume to be $11,394,000. Gross profits are projected to be 63.4 percent of total sales, and operating expenses are projected to be 11 percent. Based upon our analysis of the infringement recovery clause, we project that NSSC would have to pay a royalty of 25 percent of operating income—that is, about $1,492,000—in 1998 with regard to the inbound license of the subject patented technology. This is an indication of the relief from royalty savings for NSSC with regard to the subject patent agreement.

Based on our assessment of management plans and forecasts, we projected a 20 percent growth rate in net sales for the next year (i.e., for 1999). Based on our assessment of industry market concentration and of technological advances, we projected the annual net sales growth rate to decline by 5 percent in the following three years, and we projected a 3 percent annual decline thereafter for the remainder of the patent license term. The inbound license royalty payment savings from each patent license are projected for a period of 17 years after the issue of each patent.

We applied a 17 percent present value discount rate to the projected inbound license royalty payment savings stream in order to estimate the present worth of the future royalty stream.

Internal Revenue Code Section 197 allows for the amortization of purchased intangible assets over a period of 15 years. Using the 15-year period and the company's effective federal income tax rate, we quantified the value associated with the asset owner's ability to amortize the subject intangible asset. We quantified this increment in value by deriving a factor related to the income tax amortization effect. We applied this factor to the projection of the royalty stream.

Exhibit 15-5 presents our analysis for the subject patent license valuation as of November 30, 1997.

**Valuation Conclusion**

Based on the analysis presented herein, and in our opinion, the fair market value of the subject patent license, as of November 30, 1997, is $8,060,000.

## CUSTOMER CONTRACT VALUATION

Customer contracts represent a significant portion of the total NSSC business enterprise value. Based upon our analysis of the subject customer contract relationships, these contracts have a separate and distinct value apart from both the tangible assets and the goodwill of NSSC.

As discussed previously, there are three generally accepted approaches (market, income, and cost) to intangible asset valuation. Due to the paucity of market-derived empirical data in the instant case, the appraisal of the subject contracts was limited to the cost and income valuation approaches.

**Valuation Analysis**

While NSSC had several customer contracts as of November 30, 1997, its contracts with Baby Bell and Eastern Bell generated relatively large revenues. The current

**E X H I B I T  15-5**

North-South Supply Company, Inc., Patent License Agreement, Fair Market Value, as of November 30, 1997 ($ in 000s)

| | 1998 | 1999 | 2000 | 2001 | 2002 | 2003 | 2004 | 2005 | 2006 | 2007 | 2008 | 2009 | 2010 |
|---|---|---|---|---|---|---|---|---|---|---|---|---|---|
| Growth rate | | 20% | 15% | 10% | 5% | 2% | -1% | -4% | -7% | -10% | -13% | -16% | -19% |
| Net sales (kit @ $67.50) (2005) | $ 4,050.0 | $ 4,860.0 | $ 5,589.0 | $ 6,147.9 | $ 6,455.4 | $ 6,584.4 | $ 6,518.6 | $ 6,257.8 | $ 5,819.8 | $ 5,237.8 | $ 4,556.9 | $ 3,827.8 | |
| Net sales (dial @ $204.00) (2006) | 7,344.0 | 8,812.8 | 10,134.7 | 11,148.2 | 11,705.6 | 11,939.7 | 11,820.3 | 11,347.5 | 10,553.2 | 9,497.9 | 8,263.1 | 6,941.0 | $5,622.2 |
| Total net sales (kit & dial) | 11,394.0 | 13,672.8 | 15,723.7 | 17,296.1 | 18,160.9 | 18,524.1 | 18,338.9 | 17,605.3 | 16,372.9 | 14,735.7 | 12,820.0 | 10,768.8 | 5,622.2 |
| Dir. mat. & lab (kit @ $20.00) | 1,198.8 | 1,438.6 | 1,654.3 | 1,819.8 | 1,910.8 | 1,949.0 | 1,929.5 | 1,852.3 | 1,722.7 | 1,550.4 | 1,348.8 | 1,133.0 | |
| Dir. mat. & lab (dial @ $36.06) | 1,298.2 | 1,557.8 | 1,791.5 | 1,970.6 | 2,069.1 | 2,110.5 | 2,089.4 | 2,005.8 | 1,865.4 | 1,678.9 | 1,460.6 | 1,226.9 | 993.8 |
| Cost of goods sold | 1,674.9 | 2,009.9 | 2,311.4 | 2,542.5 | 2,669.7 | 2,723.0 | 2,695.8 | 2,588.0 | 2,406.8 | 2,166.1 | 1,884.5 | 1,583.0 | 826.5 |
| Gross profit | 7,222.1 | 8,666.5 | 9,966.5 | 10,963.2 | 11,511.3 | 11,741.6 | 11,624.2 | 11,159.2 | 10,378.0 | 9,340.2 | 8,126.0 | 6,825.8 | 3,801.9 |
| Total operating expenses | 1,253.3 | 1,504.0 | 1,729.6 | 1,902.6 | 1,997.7 | 2,037.7 | 2,017.3 | 1,936.6 | 1,801.0 | 1,620.9 | 1,410.2 | 1,184.6 | 618.4 |
| Operating income | 5,968.8 | 7,162.5 | 8,236.9 | 9,060.6 | 9,513.6 | 9,703.9 | 9,606.9 | 9,222.6 | 8,577.0 | 7,719.3 | 6,715.8 | 5,641.3 | 3,183.5 |
| Royalty payment @ 25% royalty rate | 1,492.2 | 1,790.6 | 2,059.2 | 2,265.2 | 2,378.4 | 2,426.0 | 2,401.7 | 2,305.7 | 2,144.3 | 1,929.8 | 1,679.0 | 1,410.3 | 795.9 |
| Income taxes | 552.1 | 662.5 | 761.9 | 838.1 | 880.0 | 897.6 | 888.6 | 853.1 | 793.4 | 714.0 | 621.2 | 521.8 | 294.5 |
| After-tax royalty payment | $ 940.1 | $ 1,128.1 | $ 1,297.3 | $ 1,427.0 | $ 1,498.4 | $ 1,528.4 | $ 1,513.1 | $ 1,452.6 | $ 1,350.9 | $ 1,215.8 | $ 1,057.7 | $ 888.5 | $ 501.4 |
| Discount period | 0.5 | 1.5 | 2.5 | 3.5 | 4.5 | 5.5 | 6.5 | 7.5 | 8.5 | 9.5 | 10.5 | 11.5 | 12.5 |
| Present value discount factor | 0.9245 | 0.7902 | 0.6754 | 0.5772 | 0.4934 | 0.4217 | 0.3604 | 0.3080 | 0.2633 | 0.2250 | 0.1923 | 0.1644 | 0.1405 |
| Discounted royalty payment | $ 869.1 | $ 891.4 | $ 876.2 | $ 823.7 | $ 739.2 | $ 644.5 | $ 545.3 | $ 447.4 | $ 355.7 | $ 273.6 | $ 203.4 | $ 146.1 | $ 70.4 |
| Sum of discounted royalty payments | $ 6,886 | | | | | | | | | | | | |
| Income tax amortization effect factor | 1.17 | | | | | | | | | | | | |
| Indicated fair market value (rounded) | 8,060 | | | | | | | | | | | | |

Note: Numbers may not total due to rounding.

Eastern Bell contract term of three years ends in June 2000. Based upon our analysis of historical NSSC contract renewal patterns, we projected a renewal for another three-year term. The current Baby Bell contract of two years ends in January 1999. Based upon our analysis of historical NSSC contract renewal patterns, we projected a renewal for another two-year term.

We used the income approach, and specifically the discounted cash flow method, to value the NSSC contracts with Eastern Bell and Baby Bell. The discounted net cash flow method is an appropriate valuation method when the intangible asset subject to appraisal represents the principal income-generating asset of the subject business enterprise. The discounted net cash flow method values the intangible asset as the present value of the economic income, measured as net cash flow, attributed to the contracts.

To arrive at after-tax net cash flow, the revenue stream for the contract is projected over the remaining useful life of the intangible asset. Based upon our assessment of management expectations and on the limited availability of quality parts from competitors, the Eastern Bell and Baby Bell contracts have a high potential for renewal. Accordingly, in our opinion, the remaining useful life of the subject intangible asset (i.e., the customer contract) is the current remaining term plus a renewal of one term.

The 1998 expected revenues from Eastern Bell and Baby Bell are $6 million and $10.2 million, respectively. We estimated a revenue growth rate of 20 percent in the following year (i.e., the year 1999), with revenue growth rates of 15 percent, 10 percent, and 5 percent thereafter, for each future net cash flow projection period.

Next, the costs associated with supporting the contract work are subtracted from projected contract revenues. Based on our financial analysis of historical contract profitability, the cost of goods sold is estimated to be 74 percent of net sales. Operating expenses are estimated to be 11 percent of net sales. This pretax income stream projection is then tax-affected at the company's effective combined federal and state income tax rates.

This net income projection is then adjusted by an economic capital charge. The capital charge includes a return on the assets (i.e., the patent license in this case) that are used or used up in the generation of the subject intangible asset's income projection.

The projected net cash flow is then discounted at an appropriate weighted average cost of capital. Based on our analysis, we have concluded that the appropriate present value discount rate is 17 percent.

The sum of the discounted net cash flows is then adjusted for the income tax amortization effect factor associated with this intangible asset in order to estimate the fair market value of the subject contracts.

Exhibit 15-6 presents our discounted cash flow analysis for the subject contract valuation.

### Valuation Conclusion

Based on the valuation analysis performed herein, and in our opinion, the fair market value of the Eastern Bell and Baby Bell contracts with NSSC, as of November 30, 1997, is $1,420,000.

### CELLULAR SERVICE CUSTOMER LIST VALUATION

Customer relationships sometimes represent a major component of value of a purchased going-concern business enterprise. Quite commonly, this value is left buried in the total purchase price paid for tangible assets, identifiable intangible assets, and associated goodwill. Nevertheless, these customer relationships represent a key intangible asset that has a separate and distinct value apart from both the purchased tangible assets and the purchased goodwill.

EXHIBIT 15-6

North-South Supply Company, Inc., Customer Contracts, Fair Market Value, as of November 31, 1997 ($ in 000s)

| | 1998 | 1999 | 2000 | 2001 | 2002 | 2003 |
|---|---|---|---|---|---|---|
| Revenue growth rate [a] | | 20% | 15% | 10% | 5% | 5% |
| Eastern Bell [b] | $ 6,000 | $ 7,200 | $ 8,280 | $ 9,108 | $ 9,563 | $ 5,021 |
| Baby Bell [c] | 10,200 | 12,240 | 14,076 | 1,290 | | |
| Total revenues | 16,200 | 19,440 | 22,356 | 10,398 | 9,563 | 5,021 |
| Cost of goods sold | 11,988 | 14,386 | 16,543 | 7,694 | 7,077 | 3,716 |
| Gross profits | 4,212 | 5,054 | 5,813 | 2,704 | 2,486 | 1,305 |
| Operating expenses | 1,782 | 2,138 | 2,459 | 1,144 | 1,052 | 552 |
| Operating income | 2,430 | 2,916 | 3,354 | 1,560 | 1,435 | 753 |
| Income tax expense | 899 | 1,079 | 1,241 | 577 | 531 | 279 |
| Net income | 1,531 | 1,837 | 2,113 | 983 | 904 | 474 |
| Economic capital charge (patents) | 1,194 | 1,433 | 1,648 | 767 | 705 | 370 |
| Net cash flow | $ 337 | $ 404 | $ 465 | $ 216 | $ 199 | $ 104 |
| | | | | | | |
| Discount periods | 0.5 | 1.5 | 2.5 | 3.5 | 4.5 | 5.5 |
| Present value discount factor | 0.9245 | 0.7902 | 0.6754 | 0.5772 | 0.4934 | 0.4217 |
| Discounted cash flow | $ 311 | $ 319 | $ 314 | $ 125 | $ 98 | $ 44 |
| Sum of discounted cash flow | $ 1,211 | | | | | |
| | | | | | | |
| Income tax amortization effect factor | 1.17 | | | | | |
| Indicated fair market value (rounded) | $ 1,420 | | | | | |

a. 1998 revenue projections by management; growth rates are Best Appraisal Company estimates.

b. Current contract ends June 2000, estimate renewal of one 3-year term.

c. Current contract ends January 1999, estimate renewal of one 2-year term.

Note: Numbers may not total due to rounding.

We performed an appraisal analysis of the cellular service customers of NSSC. The nature of these customers will be discussed in more detail below. We used the discounted net cash flow method of the income approach to value the subject customers. In order to use this method to value the subject customer relationships intangible asset, we performed two important procedures:

1. The stimation of a remaining useful life for the customer group.

2. The projection of an economic income (e.g., net cash flow) stream for the customers for the period of those customers' remaining useful lives.

First, we will briefly present the methodology for estimating the customer remaining useful life. Then, we will present the methodology for estimating the value of each customer and the key valuation projection variables for projecting a net cash flow stream associated with each customer. Finally, we will present the conclusions of our valuation analysis.

### Customer List—Remaining Useful Life Analysis

The first step in the valuation of a customer list and customer relationships is to establish a remaining useful life for the subject customer population. Statistical life analysis of the group of customers on the list would provide the estimates of the average life and the expected remaining useful life.

Statistical life analysis requires the availability of aged data for the subject customers. By aged data, we mean that we would have information regarding the age of all current customers, as well as the durations (or lives) of the past customers. Using the aged data, a survivor curve is constructed and matched to standard survivor functions such as Iowa-type curves, the Weibull function, the Gompertz-

Makeham function, or any other predictable mortality function, through a statistical curve fitting procedure. Based on an analysis of these standard mortality curves, the remaining useful life of the subject customers is then estimated.

In the case of the NSSC cellular service customer list, no aged data for the customers were available. This is because NSSC has only been providing the service for a short time.

Based upon our discussions with NSSC management and our assessment of the subject industry, we considered it appropriate to assume an exponential decay function as to the appropriate survivor characteristics of the NSSC cellular service customer base. Exponential decay functions portray attrition at a constant rate—that is, the attrition rate is independent of the age of the subject. We estimated that the cellular customers' attrition rate is 10 percent each year. Based upon this estimation, we assumed an average life—and average remaining life—of the cellular service customer to be 10 years.

### Customer Relationships—Valuation Analysis

The fair market value of the subject customer list is estimated by calculating the present value of the after-tax net cash flow attributed to the customers over their expected remaining useful lives.

While this process is easy to describe, its execution is a complex matter. There are several key valuation input variables encompassed in our valuation model for the the subject customer list intangible asset.

The overall valuation model is described algebraically below. Following this, each term or key input variable of the model is described separately.

#### Customer List Valuation Model

*Step one:*

This year's actual customer revenues

× Growth (shrinkage) rate in revenues

= Next year's expected customer revenues

*Step two:*

Expected customer revenues

× Survivor curve decay rate

= Surviving customer revenues

*Step three:*

Surviving customer revenues

− Customer servicing costs

= Profit before income tax from each customer

× 1 − Effective income tax rate for the subject customer

= Profit after tax from the subject customer

*Step four:*

Profit after income tax from the subject customer

− Economic capital charge due to a fair return on tangible and intangible assets

= Net cash flow from the subject customer

*Step five:*

Net cash flow from the subject customer

× Present value interest factor

= Present value of net cash flow from the subject customer

*Step six:*

Sum of present value of net cash flow for each year in expected
   remaining useful life of the subject customer base

= Indicated fair market value

### Description of Valuation Model Key Input Variables

As described algebraically above, there are six principal steps in our valuation
model of the the subject customer list intangible asset. Each step includes several
key valuation input variables.

These valuation variables are described briefly below.

1. *Actual Customer Revenues* (i.e., cellular air sales). NSSC provides cellular
   service to 1,800 clients. We concluded that the base year revenues are
   approximately $1,740,000.

2. *Customer Revenue Growth Rate.* This is the expected average growth rate (or
   shrinkage rate) of the subject customer account balance over its expected
   remaining useful life. For this analysis, we project an inflationary growth
   rate of 4 percent.

3. *Customer Servicing Costs.* These are the direct and indirect costs associated
   with servicing the customer accounts. These costs include operating
   expenses and general and administrative expenses. Operating expenses are
   mainly cellular airtime expenses. We projected the base year expenses to be
   approximately $1,352,300. We projected these expenses to increase at a rate
   of 4.5 percent. We have applied general, administrative, and miscellaneous
   expenses at 10 percent of cellular air sales.

4. *Customer-Specific Effective Income Tax Rate.* In the instant case, we used a
   typical acquiring company's overall combined federal and state effective
   income tax rate to arrive at the preliminary value conclusions, based on the
   sum of discounted net cash flows. We used a combined effective income
   tax rate of 37 percent in our analysis.

5. *Economic Capital Charge Due to Return on Tangible and Intangible Assets.* The
   model uses an economic capital charge to represent a proportional return
   of and on associated tangible and intangible assets. Since this service is
   independent of other businesses of NSSC, we have applied a 1 percent
   economic capital charge in our analysis.

6. *Present Value Discount Rate.* The present value interest factor is a function of
   the present value discount rate. We concluded that a 17 percent discount
   factor is appropriate in this case.

Exhibit 15-7 presents the discounted cash flow analysis for a cellular service
customer list valuation with an average remaining useful life of 10 years. As explained earlier, we applied an income tax amortization effect factor in order to estimate the fair market value of the asset.

### Valuation Conclusion

Based on the analysis performed herein, and in our opinion, the fair market value
of the subject cellular service customer list of NSSC, as of November 30, 1997, is
$520,200.

### VALUATION OF THE NONCOMPETE AGREEMENT

An agreement by a seller to refrain from competing with the purchaser of a business is a valuable intangible asset. The noncompete agreement restricts the seller
from continuing in the same line of business for a certain period of time. There are

North-South Supply Company, Inc., Cellular Service Customer List, Fair Market Value, as of November 30, 1997

| | 1998 | 1999 | 2000 | 2001 | 2002 | 2003 | 2004 | 2005 | 2006 | 2007 | 2008 | 2009 | 2010 | 2011 | 2012 | 2013 |
|---|---|---|---|---|---|---|---|---|---|---|---|---|---|---|---|---|
| Number of customers [a] | 1,712 | 1,549 | 1,402 | 1,268 | 1,148 | 1,039 | 940 | 850 | 769 | 696 | 630 | 570 | 516 | 467 | 422 | 382 |
| Cellular air sales | $1,688,439 | $1,588,873 | $1,495,179 | $1,407,010 | $1,324,040 | $1,245,962 | $1,172,489 | $1,103,348 | $1,038,285 | $ 977,058 | $ 919,442 | $ 865,223 | $ 814,202 | $ 766,189 | $ 721,008 | $ 678,491 |
| Cellular airtime expense | 1,314,965 | 1,243,372 | 1,175,677 | 1,111,667 | 1,051,143 | 993,913 | 939,800 | 888,632 | 840,251 | 794,503 | 751,247 | 710,345 | 671,671 | 635,102 | 600,524 | 567,829 |
| General & administrative | 168,844 | 158,887 | 149,518 | 140,701 | 132,404 | 124,596 | 117,249 | 110,335 | 103,828 | 97,706 | 91,944 | 86,522 | 81,420 | 76,619 | 72,101 | 67,849 |
| Operating income | 204,630 | 186,614 | 169,984 | 154,642 | 140,493 | 127,453 | 115,440 | 104,381 | 94,206 | 84,849 | 76,251 | 68,356 | 61,111 | 54,469 | 48,383 | 42,812 |
| Income taxes | 75,713 | 69,047 | 62,894 | 57,217 | 51,982 | 47,158 | 42,713 | 38,621 | 34,856 | 31,394 | 28,213 | 25,292 | 22,611 | 20,153 | 17,902 | 15,841 |
| Net income | 128,917 | 117,567 | 107,090 | 97,424 | 88,511 | 80,295 | 72,727 | 65,760 | 59,350 | 53,455 | 48,038 | 43,064 | 38,500 | 34,315 | 30,482 | 26,972 |
| Economic capital charge | 16,884 | 15,889 | 14,952 | 14,070 | 13,240 | 12,460 | 11,725 | 11,033 | 10,383 | 9,771 | 9,194 | 8,652 | 8,142 | 7,662 | 7,210 | 6,785 |
| Net cash flow | $ 112,033 | $ 101,678 | $ 92,138 | $ 83,354 | $ 75,270 | $ 67,836 | $ 61,003 | $ 54,727 | $ 48,967 | $ 43,685 | $ 38,844 | $ 34,412 | $ 30,358 | $ 26,653 | $ 23,271 | $ 20,187 |
| | | | | | | | | | | | | | | | | |
| Discount period | 0.5 | 1.5 | 2.5 | 3.5 | 4.5 | 5.5 | 6.5 | 7.5 | 8.5 | 9.5 | 10.5 | 11.5 | 12.5 | 13.5 | 14.5 | 15.5 |
| Present value discount factor | 0.9245 | 0.7902 | 0.6754 | 0.5772 | 0.4934 | 0.4217 | 0.3604 | 0.3080 | 0.2633 | 0.2250 | 0.1923 | 0.1644 | 0.1405 | 0.1201 | 0.1026 | 0.0877 |
| Discounted cash flow | $ 103,574 | $ 80,346 | $ 62,230 | $ 48,112 | $ 37,136 | $ 28,606 | $ 21,985 | $ 16,856 | $ 12,893 | $ 9,829 | $ 7,470 | $ 5,657 | $ 4,265 | $ 3,201 | $ 2,388 | $ 1,770 |
| Sum of discounted cash flow | $ 446,320 | | | | | | | | | | | | | | | |
| | | | | | | | | | | | | | | | | |
| Income tax amortization effect factor | 1.17 | | | | | | | | | | | | | | | |
| Indicated fair market value (rounded) | $ 520,200 | | | | | | | | | | | | | | | |

a. Attrition rate based on exponential function with average life of 10 years, Best Appraisal Company estimate.

*Note:* Numbers may not total due to rounding.

several generally accepted methods for the valuation of noncompete agreements. Based upon the quantity and quality of available data, we have selected the comparative business valuation method for the subject analysis.

In the comparative business valuation method, we first project the prospective cash flows of the subject business with the subject noncompete agreement in place (see Scenario I below). Next, we project the prospective cash flows of the subject business without the subject noncompete agreement in place—that is, under the most likely competitive environment (see Scenario II below). The value of the subject noncompete agreement is based on the difference between the values of the subject business under these two alternative cash flow projection scenarios.

The incremental difference in the two cash flow projections is one measure of the most likely level of economic damage that the business seller could cause if allowed to compete against the business buyer.

The comparative business enterprise valuation method involves comparing the economic earnings capacity of the subject company both without and with the most likely level of competition from the grantor of the noncompete covenant. Economic earnings capacity represents the net economic income that is available for distribution to the owners of the business after consideration of a required level of reinvestment for continued operations and growth. This available earnings capacity is sometimes measured as net cash flow.

Algebraically, net cash flow may be defined as follows:

Net sales
− Cost of sales
− Operating expenses
= Net income before taxes
− Income taxes
+ Depreciation and amortization expense
− Capital expenditures
− Additions to net working capital
= Available net cash flow

The available cash flow is then projected over a discrete period of time and discounted at an appropriate rate in order to conclude a present value. The residual value of the company at the end of the discrete projection period is also discounted to indicate a present value.

The sum of these two present values (i.e., the discrete projection period cash flow plus the residual value) represents what a prudent investor would pay for the subject overall business entity.

### Scenario I: Business Value with Noncompete Agreement in Place

In the instant case, we selected five years as the discrete projection period for the discounted cash flow analysis because five years equals the contractual term of the noncompete agreement.

Based on the annualized 1997 net sales, we projected base period net sales of $22,500,000 for 1998.

From our analysis of the historical trends and management projections of NSSC, we projected annual increases in net sales to be 20 percent in year one (i.e., 1999). Based on our industry analysis, we projected the net sales growth rate to decrease by 5 percent each subsequent year, until a 5 percent growth rate is reflected in year five. The net sales growth rate from then on is projected at 5 percent per annum.

Based on our analysis of the historical results of operations of the subject company, we projected the gross profits to be 26.0 percent of the net sales. Other operating expenses are projected to be 11.1 percent of net sales. We used a combined effective federal and state income tax rate of 36.0 percent in our projection.

The NSSC depreciation expense is equal to 1.0 percent of net sales. We used this percentage in our analysis, and we projected an equal amount of net capital expenditures for each year to be equal to the company's annual depreciation expense. We projected the company's net working capital requirements to be 12.9 percent of net sales.

To determine the present value of the projected net cash flows, we used a 17 percent present value discount rate. We estimated the residual value based on the present value of the adjusted net cash flow in year six as an annuity in perpetuity. This residual value is calculated based on the Gordon direct capitalization model. In the Gordon direct capitalization model, the residual multiple equals one divided by $(k - g)$, where $k$ is the risk-adjusted present value discount rate and $g$ is the expected long-term growth rate after the discrete projection period. We used the 17 percent present value discount rate for $k$ and an expected long-term growth rate of 5 percent for $g$.

The detailed calculation of the prospective net cash flow, assuming a level of protection from competition afforded by the subject noncompete agreement, is presented in Exhibit 15-8.

### Scenario II: Business Value Without the Noncompete Agreement in Place

The analytical premise used in Scenario II is that NSSC will face the most likely level of competition from the current three shareholders—that is, competition that it would be protected from (due to the noncompete agreement) in Scenario I.

Based on extensive discussions with management, we projected that the current three shareholders would most likely be able to take away about 15 percent of net sales in 1999 and 2000. After the company's implementation of defensive countermeasures, we estimated that the lost sales due to the most likely effects of competition from the selling shareholders would be 10 percent in 2001 and 5 percent thereafter.

The detailed calculation of projected net cash flow, based on the analytical premise of no protection from the most likely level of competition from the selling shareholders, is presented in Exhibit 15-8.

Exhibit 15-8 presents the indicated fair market value of the subject noncompete agreement after appropriate consideration of the fact that this noncompete agreement would itself be an amortizable intangible asset.

### Valuation Conclusion

Based upon the analysis presented herein, and in our opinion, the fair market value of the subject noncompete agreement, as of November 30, 1997, is (rounded) $2,100,000.

### BUSINESS ENTERPRISE VALUATION

#### Introduction

There are numerous methods and procedures for estimating the value of an ongoing business entity. All of these methods and procedures can be categorized into three distinct, generally accepted approaches for valuing businesses and business interests. The three generally accepted business valuation approaches are:

1. The asset-based approach.
2. The income approach.
3. The market approach.

In the instant case, we used the income approach (specifically, the discounted net cash flow method) and the market approach (specifically, the guideline publicly traded company method) to value NSSC.

EXHIBIT 15-8

North-South Supply Company, Inc., Noncompete Agreement, Fair Market Value, as of November 30,1997 ($ in 000s)

| SCENARIO I (business value without competition) | 1998 | 1999 | 2000 | 2001 | 2002 | Residual Value |
|---|---|---|---|---|---|---|
| Net sales growth rate | | 20% | 15% | 10% | 5% | 5% |
| Net sales | $22,500.0 | $27,000.0 | $31,050.0 | $34,155.0 | $35,862.8 | |
| Cost of goods sold | 16,650.0 | 19,980.0 | 22,977.0 | 25,274.7 | 26,538.4 | |
| Gross profit | 5,850.0 | 7,020.0 | 8,073.0 | 8,880.3 | 9,324.3 | |
| Total operating expenses | 2,520.0 | 3,000.0 | 3,450.0 | 3,795.0 | 3,984.8 | |
| Operating income | 3,330.0 | 4,020.0 | 4,623.0 | 5,085.3 | 5,339.6 | |
| Pretax Income | 3,330.0 | 4,020.0 | 4,623.0 | 5,085.3 | 5,339.6 | |
| Income taxes | 1,232.1 | 1,487.4 | 1,710.5 | 1,881.6 | 1,975.6 | |
| Net income | 2,097.9 | 2,532.6 | 2,912.5 | 3,203.7 | 3,363.9 | |
| Depreciation & amortization expense | 225.0 | 270.0 | 310.5 | 341.6 | 358.6 | |
| Capital expenditures | (225.0) | (270.0) | (310.5) | (341.6) | (358.6) | |
| Net working capital | 1,602.5 | (555.8) | (500.2) | (383.5) | (210.9) | |
| Net cash flow | $ 3,700.4 | $ 1,976.8 | $ 2,412.3 | $ 2,820.2 | $ 3,153.0 | $27,588.8 |
| Discount period | 0.5 | 1.5 | 2.5 | 3.5 | 4.5 | 5.0 |
| Present value discount factor | 0.9245 | 0.7902 | 0.6754 | 0.5772 | 0.4934 | 0.4561 |
| Discounted cash flow | $ 3,421.0 | $ 1,562.0 | $ 1,629.3 | $ 1,627.8 | $ 1,555.7 | $12,583.2 |
| Sum of discounted cash flow—Scenario I | $ 22,379 | | | | | |
| Sum of discounted cash flow—Scenario II | 20,604 | | | | | |
| Difference—noncompete agreement value indicator | $ 1,775 | | | | | |
| Income tax amortization effect factor | 1.17 | | | | | |
| Indicated fair market value (rounded) | $ 2,100 | | | | | |

| SCENARIO II (business value with the most likely level of competition) | 1998 | 1999 | 2000 | 2001 | 2002 | Residual Value |
|---|---|---|---|---|---|---|
| Lost sales due to most likely competition | | 15% | 15% | 10% | 5% | 5% |
| Resulting net sales | $22,500.0 | $22,950.0 | $26,392.5 | $30,739.5 | $34,069.6 | |
| Cost of goods sold | 16,650.0 | 15,930.0 | 19,530.4 | 22,747.2 | 25,211.5 | |
| Gross profit | 5,850.0 | 7,020.0 | 6,862.1 | 7,992.3 | 8,858.1 | |
| Total operating expenses | 2,520.0 | 3,000.0 | 2,932.5 | 3,415.5 | 3,785.5 | |
| Operating income | 3,330.0 | 4,020.0 | 3,929.6 | 4,576.8 | 5,072.6 | |
| Pretax Income | 3,330.0 | 4,020.0 | 3,929.6 | 4,576.8 | 5,072.6 | |
| Income taxes | 1,232.1 | 1,487.4 | 1,454.0 | 1,693.4 | 1,876.9 | |
| Net income | 2,097.9 | 2,532.6 | 2,475.6 | 2,883.4 | 3,195.7 | |
| Depreciation & amortization expense | 225.0 | 229.5 | 263.9 | 307.4 | 340.7 | |
| Capital expenditures | (225.0) | (229.5) | (263.9) | (307.4) | (340.7) | |
| Net working capital | 1,602.5 | (55.6) | (425.1) | (536.9) | (411.3) | |
| Net cash flow | $ 3,700.4 | $ 2,477.0 | $ 2,050.5 | $ 2,346.5 | $ 2,784.4 | $24,363.5 |
| Discount period | 0.5 | 1.5 | 2.5 | 3.5 | 4.5 | 5.0 |
| Present value discount factor | 0.9245 | 0.7902 | 0.6754 | 0.5772 | 0.4934 | 0.4561 |
| Discounted cash flow | $ 3,421.0 | $ 1,957.3 | $ 1,384.8 | $ 1,354.4 | $ 1,373.8 | $11,112.2 |
| Sum of discounted cash flow—Scenario II | $ 20,604 | | | | | |

Source: Company projections and Best Appraisal Company calculations.

Note: Numbers may not total due to rounding.

### Discounted Net Cash Flow Method

The discounted net cash flow method is based on the premise that the value of the business enterprise is the present value of the future economic income to be derived by the owners of the business. The discounted net cash flow method encompasses the following analyses: revenue analysis, expense analysis, investment analysis, capital structure analysis, and residual value analysis.

The revenue analysis includes a projection of prospective revenues from the sale of products or provision of services by the company.

The expense analysis includes consideration of the following aspects: fixed versus variable costs, product versus period costs, cash versus noncash costs, direct versus indirect costs, cost absorption principles, cost–efficiency relationships, cost–volume–profit relationships, and so on.

The investment analysis includes consideration of the following aspects: required minimum cash balances, days sales outstanding in accounts receivable, inventory turnover, plant utilization, capital expenditure budgets, and so on.

The capital structure analysis includes consideration of the following aspects: current capital structure, optimal capital structure, cost of various capital components, weighted average cost of capital (WACC), systematic and nonsystematic risk factors, marginal cost of capital, and so on.

The residual value analysis involves the estimation of the value of the prospective cash flow generated by the business after the conclusion of a discrete projection period. This residual value can be determined by various methods: price–earnings multiples, annuity in perpetuity method, Gordon growth model, and so on.

Based on the results of the above-mentioned analyses, a projection of net cash flow from business operations is made for a reasonable discrete projection period. The cash flow projection is discounted at an appropriate present value discount rate in order to determine the present value.

We concluded that a present value discount rate of 17 percent was appropriate in this business enterprise valuation. We also used this rate in the income approach valuation analyses of the individual NSSC intangible assets.

The residual value of the business enterprise is estimated at the end of the discrete projection period. This residual value is also discounted to determine its present value. The present value of the discrete net cash flow projection is summed to the present value of the residual value. This summation represents the indicated value of the subject business enterprise.

Exhibit 15-9 presents the discounted cash flow analysis that we used to estimate the business enterprise value of NSSC.

### Guideline Publicly Traded Company Method

The guideline publicly traded company method is based on the premise that the value of the business enterprise may be estimated based on what astute and rational capital market investors would pay to own the stock in the subject company. Using this method, the first step is to select a sample of companies that are comparative to the subject company, to the extent that the selected companies provide meaningful valuation guidance. However, in this case, the guideline companies are all companies that are publicly traded on organized capital market exchanges, such as the New York Stock Exchange, the American Stock Exchange, the over-the-counter market, and so forth. A key procedure of the guideline publicly traded company method is selecting the appropriate sample of guideline companies, based on reasonable comparability criteria.

Descriptions of the selected guideline companies are provided in the Guideline Company Descriptions section of this report. The fundamental pricing measures are presented in Exhibits 15-10 and 15-11. To mitigate the effect of the differences in financial leverage between the selected guideline publicly traded companies and NSSC, we have performed the valuation analyses on an invested capital basis.

## EXHIBIT 15-9

North-South Supply Company, Inc., Discounted Net Cash Flow Method, Fair Market Value, as of November 30, 1997

| Projection Period: | 1998 | 1999 | 2000 | 2001 | 2002 | Residual Value |
|---|---|---|---|---|---|---|
| Net sales growth rate [a] | | 20% | 15% | 10% | 5% | 5% |
| Net sales [a] | $22,500.0 | $27,000.0 | $31,050.0 | $34,155.0 | $25,862.8 | |
| Cost of goods sold | 16,650.0 | 19,980.0 | 22,977.0 | 25,274.7 | 26,538.4 | |
| Gross profit | 5,850.0 | 7,020.0 | 8,073.0 | 8,880.3 | 9,324.3 | |
| Total operating expenses | 2,520.0 | 3,000.0 | 3,450.0 | 3,795.0 | 3,984.8 | |
| Operating income | 3,330.0 | 4,020.0 | 4,623.0 | 5,085.3 | 5,339.6 | |
| Pretax income | 3,330.0 | 4,020.0 | 4,623.0 | 5,085.3 | 5,339.6 | |
| Income taxes | 1,232.1 | 1,487.4 | 1,710.5 | 1,881.6 | 1,975.6 | |
| Net income | 2,097.9 | 2,532.6 | 2,912.5 | 3,203.7 | 3,363.9 | |
| Depreciation & amortization expense | 225.0 | 270.0 | 310.5 | 341.6 | 358.6 | |
| Capital expenditures | (225.0) | (270.0) | (310.5) | (341.6) | (358.6) | |
| Additional net working capital requirements | 1,602.5 | (555.8) | (500.2) | (383.5) | (210.9) | |
| Net cash flow | 3,700.4 | $ 1,976.8 | $ 2,412.3 | $ 2,820.2 | $ 3,153.0 | $27,588.8 |
| Discount period | 0.5 | 1.5 | 2.5 | 3.5 | 4.5 | 5.0 |
| Present value discount factors | 0.9245 | 0.7902 | 0.6754 | 0.5772 | 0.4934 | 0.4561 |
| Discounted cash flow | $ 3,421.0 | $ 1,562.0 | $ 1,629.3 | $ 1,627.8 | $ 1,555.7 | $12,583.2 |
| Sum of discounted cash flow: | | | | | | |
|   Market value of invested capital [b] | $ 22,379 | | | | | |
| Long-term debt (i.e., note to shareholder) | 1,854 | | | | | |
| Indicated value of business equity | 20,525 | | | | | |
| Lack of marketability discount (25%) | 0.25 | | | | | |
| Indicated fair market value of business equity [c] | $ 15,394 | | | | | |

a. 1999/98 growth based on Company projection, growth thereafter Best Appraisal Company projections.

b. On a marketable, controlling ownership interest basis.

c. On a nonmarketable, controlling ownership interest basis.

Source: Based on Company supplied projections; expense ratios 2000 onward are same as 1999 projection.

Note: Numbers may not total due to rounding.

For each company in the sample of publicly traded companies, several capital market pricing multiples are calculated. These capital market pricing multiples may include the following: price–earnings multiple, price–dividends multiple, price–assets multiple, price–equity multiple, price–cash flow multiple, and so on. After the capital market pricing multiples are calculated for each company in the sample, the pricing multiples are analyzed in terms of means, medians, quartiles, standard deviations, and so on. From this analysis of the capital market–derived pricing multiples, the most appropriate pricing multiple is selected for each financial fundamental. The selected pricing multiples are then applied to the appropriate financial fundamentals of the subject business. The result of multiplying the selected pricing multiples by the subject company's financial fundamental data is the range of estimates of the fair market value of the subject business enterprise. The various indications of fair market value are synthesized—or weighted—in order to conclude a point estimate of the value of the subject business.

This preliminary point estimate may need to be adjusted for any lack of comparability of the subject company to the guideline publicly traded companies. These adjustments may include the following: lack of ownership control (or minority interest) discount, ownership control premium, lack of marketability discount, and so on. The adjusted point estimate, then, indicates the fair market value of the subject business enterprise.

Exhibit 15-10 summarizes the selection of the various capital market pricing multiples used in our valuation of NSSC.

### Guideline Company Search

In order to gain valuation guidance from the guideline publicly traded company method, the analyst identify a distinct group of publicly traded companies that are suitable for comparison to the subject company from an investment perspective. The first step in the search for guideline publicly traded companies is the determination of the appropriate Standard Industrial Classification (SIC) number. We identified the following SIC numbers as appropriate for NSSC:

No. 3661—Telephone and Telegraph Apparatus

No. 4812—Radiotelephone Communications

Using descriptions provided by *Standard & Poor's Corporations* (on CD-ROM), *Moody's Company Data* (on CD-ROM), *Disclosure Compact D/SEC,* and other CD-ROM and on-line sources, we selected 11 companies as being in the same or similar lines of business. A detailed review of the 1) SEC Forms 10-K and 10-Q and 2) trade pricing and volume information for the potential guideline companies resulted in the reduction of the sample size to three guideline companies. The reasons we rejected eight of the eleven potential guideline companies include the following: unrelated business, too diversified, no longer publicly traded, foreign, financial condition, market too inactive, and pending merger or acquisition. A brief description of the selected guideline publicly traded companies follows:

### Guideline Company Descriptions

- *Communications Systems, Inc.* Communications Systems, Inc., is a Minnesota corporation engaged in the manufacture and sale of modular connecting and telephone wiring devices. Additionally, the company provides contract manufacturing of electronic assemblies and products, including cable and harness and electromechanical assemblies, to original equipment manufacturers (OEMs). The company, headquartered in Hector, Minnesota, had sales of $54.8 million in 1996.

- *Nationwide Cellular Services, Inc.* Nationwide Cellular Services, a Delaware corporation headquartered in Valley Stream, New York, is engaged in the purchase and resale of cellular telephone service and the sale of cellular telephone equipment and accessories. The company had revenues of $141.8 million during fiscal year 1996.

- *Restor Industries, Inc.* Restor Industries, Inc., a Delaware corporation headquartered in Ocoee, Florida, provides electronics manufacturing, repair, and modification services to telecommunications and other technology companies. The company's principal businesses are circuit board manufacturing, repair, sales, and pay telephone refurbishment. As of fiscal year-end 1996, the company had assets of $12.2 million and total sales of $16.9 million.

## Lack of Marketability Discount

One of the primary differences between the shares of a closely held company and those of a company with an established public market is the ready marketability of the publicly traded shares. All other factors being equal, an investment is more valuable if it is easily marketable and, conversely, less valuable if it is not easily marketable. Simply stated, investors prefer liquidity to lack of liquidity. An investment in the shares of a closely held company is relatively illiquid compared to most other investments, and particularly compared to actively traded stocks.

EXHIBIT 15-10

North-South Supply Company, Inc., Guideline Publicly Traded Company Method, Valuation Summary, as of November 30, 1997

| Financial Fundamental | $000 | MVIC/Financial Fundamental | | | | Indicated MVIC $000 | Comments—Factors |
|---|---|---|---|---|---|---|---|
| | | High Pricing Multiple | Low Pricing Multiple | Median Pricing Multiple | Selected Pricing Multiple | | |
| Revenues | | | | | | | *Revenue growth most closely matches Communications Systems. |
| LTM [a] | 17,796 | 1.03 | 0.60 | 0.72 | 0.80 | 14,237 | *NSSC has some cellular resale business. |
| | | | | | | | *NSSC revenues are expected to continue growing rapidly. |
| 3-year average | 7,992 | 1.18 | 0.67 | 0.78 | 0.78 | 6,234 | *3-year average is not indicative of NSSC fundamental's current or future revenue level. |
| **Revenue indication** | | | | | | 14,237 | |
| EBIT | | | | | | | *NSSC has cellular resale business, not just parts manufacturer. |
| LTM | 2,268 | 407.3 | −5.7 | 8.0 | 10.0 | 22,680 | *3-year average is not indicative of NSSC fundamental's current or future revenue level. |
| 3-year average | 966 | 4,457.6 | −8.8 | 8.9 | 8.9 | 8,597 | |
| **EBIT indication** | | | | | | 22,680 | |
| EBDIT | | | | | | | *Restor Industries has relatively high level of depreciation as a percent of revenues. |
| LTM | 2,526 | 16.3 | 6.4 | 11.5 | 8.0 | 20,208 | *NSSC has lower depreciation as a percent of revenues. |
| 3-year average | 1,194 | 16.7 | 7.1 | 10.9 | 10.9 | 13,015 | *NSSC has cellular resale business, not just parts manufacturer. |
| **EBDIT indication** | | | | | | 20,208 | *3-year average is not indicative of NSSC fundamental's current or future revenue level. |
| TBVIC | | | | | | | *National Cellular Service closest in capital structure. |
| Latest quarter | 4,788 | 6.0 | 1.5 | 1.6 | 3.0 | 14,364 | *Communications Systems & Restor Industries closest in line of business. |
| **TBVIC indication** | | | | | | 14,364 | |

**Guideline Publicly Traded Company Method**

| | | ($000s) |
|---|---|---|
| Indicated market value of invested capital | | 17,782 |
| Less: outstanding long-term debt | | 1,854 |
| Residual value of equity on marketable, noncontrolling ownership basis | | 16,018 |
| Discount for lack of marketability | 25% | (4,005) |
| Residual value on nonmarketable, noncontrolling ownership basis | | 12,013 |
| Ownership control premium [b] | 35% | 4,205 |
| Indicated market value of equity on a marketable controlling ownership basis | | $16,218 |

[a] LTM Revenue figure is the average of the actual LTM revenues ($15,966, including Cellular) and the projected 1997 revenues ($19,596).

[b] Based on 1996 and 5-year average ownership control premiums for the following industries: Communications, Miscellaneous Manufacturing, Electrical Equipment, and All-Industry Average from *Mergerstat Review 1996* (Los Angeles: Houlihan Lokey Howard & Zukin, 1997).

*Note:* Numbers may not total due to rounding.

North-South Supply Company, Inc., Guideline Publicly Traded Companies, Market Value of Invested Capital

| Gudieline Company | Market/ Symbol | FYE | Lat. Qtr. TBV $000 | Lat. Qtr. BV IBD $000 | Lat. Qtr. TBVIC $000 | Lat. Qtr. MV IBD $000 | As of or for Period Ending | Bid/Close Price per Common Share 11/30/97 $ | Common Shares Outstg. [a] 000s | MV Common Equity $000 | MV Pref'd Equity $000 | MVIC $000 |
|---|---|---|---|---|---|---|---|---|---|---|---|---|
| Communications Systems, Inc. | NASDAQ/CSII | 12/31 | 38,373 | 295 | 38,668 | 0 | 9/97 | 13.250 | 4,438 | 58,807 | 0 | 58,807 |
| Nationwide Cellular Service | NASDAQ/NCEL | 12/31 | 11,177 | 6,511 | 17,688 | 0 | 9/97 | 14.250 | 7,403 | 105,497 | 0 | 105,497 |
| Restor Industries, Inc. | NASDAQ/REST | 12/31 | 845 | 5,556 | 6,400 | 0 | 9/97 | 2.125 | 4,724 | 10,039 | 0 | 10,039 |
| North-South Supply Company | NA | 12/31 | 489 | 309 | 798 | 0 | 11/93 | NA | 20 | NA | NA | NA |

Definitions, footnotes, and sources are found on the last page of this exhibit.

North-South Supply Company, Inc., Guideline Publicly Traded Companies, Revenues and Performance Ratios

| Gudieline Company | LTM Revenues $000 | Period Ending | Revenues 1996 $000 | Revenues 1995 $000 | Revenues 1994 $000 | 3-Yr. Avg. [b] Revenues $000 | Avg. Annual Compound Growth [c] % | Coeff. of Var. [d] % | MVIC $000 | MVIC/Revenues LTM | MVIC/Revenues 3-Year Avg. |
|---|---|---|---|---|---|---|---|---|---|---|---|
| Communications Systems, Inc. | 57,290 | 9/97 | 54,764 | 37,928 | 33,505 | 49,994 | 23.9 | 17.2 | 58,807 | 1.03 | 1.18 |
| Nationwide Cellular Service | 147,002 | 9/97 | 141,774 | 114,621 | 104,773 | 134,466 | 14.5 | 10.6 | 105,497 | 0.72 | 0.78 |
| Restor Industries, Inc. | 16,685 | 9/97 | 16,946 | 11,525 | 11,627 | 15,052 | 15.5 | 16.6 | 10,039 | 0.60 | 0.67 |
| MEAN | | | | | | | 18.0 | 14.8 | | 0.78 | 0.88 |
| MEDIAN | | | | | | | 15.5 | 16.6 | | 0.72 | 0.78 |
| STD. DEV. | | | | | | | 4.2 | 3.0 | | 0.18 | 0.22 |
| COEFF. VAR. (%) | | | | | | | 23.5 | 20.3 | | 22.93 | 24.86 |
| North-South Supply Company | 2,464 | 11/93 | 866 | 667 | 793 | 1,332 | 57.4 | 60.4 | NA | NA | NA |

| Gudieline Company | LTM Return on Revenues EBIT % | LTM Return on Revenues EBDIT % | LTM Return on Revenues DFNI % | LTM Return on Revenues DFCF % | 3-Year Avg. Return on Revenues EBIT % | 3-Year Avg. Return on Revenues EBDIT % | 3-Year Avg. Return on Revenues DFNI % | 3-Year Avg. Return on Revenues DFCF % |
|---|---|---|---|---|---|---|---|---|
| Communications Systems, Inc. | 12.9 | 16.1 | 10.5 | 13.7 | 13.2 | 16.5 | 10.6 | 13.9 |
| Nationwide Cellular Service | 0.2 | 6.3 | 0.1 | 6.1 | 0.0 | 4.7 | (0.0) | 4.6 |
| Restor Industries, Inc. | (10.6) | 3.7 | (10.9) | 3.5 | (7.6) | 6.1 | (7.9) | 5.8 |
| MEAN | 0.8 | 8.7 | (0.1) | 7.8 | 1.9 | 9.1 | 0.9 | 8.1 |
| MEDIAN | 0.2 | 6.3 | 0.1 | 6.1 | 0.0 | 6.1 | (0.0) | 5.8 |
| STD. DEV. | 9.6 | 5.3 | 8.7 | 4.3 | 8.6 | 5.3 | 7.6 | 4.1 |
| COEFF. VAR. (%) | 1,193.7 | 61.5 | (8,869.6) | 55.7 | 461.8 | 57.7 | 866.7 | 50.7 |
| North-South Supply Company | 15.3 | 17.1 | 9.7 | 11.4 | 12.1 | 14.9 | 7.6 | 10.5 |

Definitions, footnotes, and sources are found on the last page of this exhibit.

EXHIBIT 15-11 (continued)

## North-South Supply Company, Inc., Guideline Publicly Traded Companies, Earnings before Interest and Taxes

| Gudieline Company | LTM EBIT $000 | Period Ending | Earnings before Interest & Taxes (EBIT) | | | 3-Yr. Avg. [b] EBIT $000 | Avg. Annual Compound Growth [c] % | Coeff. of Var. [d] % | MVIC $000 | MVIC/EBIT | |
|---|---|---|---|---|---|---|---|---|---|---|---|
| | | | 1996 $000 | 1995 $000 | 1994 $000 | | | | | LTM | 3-Year Avg. |
| Communications Systems, Inc. | 7,375 | 9/97 | 6,967 | 5,407 | 4,078 | 6,583 | 26.7 | 12.9 | 58,807 | 8.0 | 8.9 |
| Nationwide Cellular Service | 259 | 9/97 | (176) | (12) | (6,293) | 24 | N/A | 757.9 | 105,497 | 407.3 | 4,457.6 |
| Restor Industries, Inc. | (1,774) | 9/97 | (1,951) | 289 | 906 | (1,145) | N/A | (88.8) | 10,039 | (5.7) | (8.8) |
| MEAN | | | | | | | 8.9 | 227.3 | | 136.5 | 1,485.9 |
| MEDIAN | | | | | | | N/A | 12.9 | | 8.0 | 8.9 |
| STD. DEV. | | | | | | | 12.6 | 377.5 | | 191.6 | 2,101.3 |
| COEFF. VAR. (%) | | | | | | | 141.4 | 166.0 | | 140.3 | 141.4 |
| North-South Supply Company | 378 | 11/93 | 90 | 14 | (152) | 161 | N/A | 97.3 | NA | NA | NA |

Definitions, footnotes, and sources are found on the last page of this exhibit.

EXHIBIT 15-11 (continued)

## North-South Supply Company, Inc., Guideline Publicly Traded Companies, Earnings before Depreciation, Interest, and Taxes

| Gudieline Company | LTM EBDIT $000 | Period Ending | Earnings before Depreciation, Interest & Taxes (EBDIT) | | | 3-Yr. Avg. [b] EBDIT $000 | Avg. Annual Compound Growth [c] % | Coeff. of Var. [d] % | MVIC $000 | MVIC/EBDIT | |
|---|---|---|---|---|---|---|---|---|---|---|---|
| | | | 1996 $000 | 1995 $000 | 1994 $000 | | | | | LTM | 3-Year Avg. |
| Communications Systems, Inc. | 9,213 | 9/97 | 8,650 | 6,893 | 5,427 | 8,252 | 23.6 | 12.0 | 58,807 | 6.4 | 7.1 |
| Nationwide Cellular Service | 9,200 | 9/97 | 5,963 | 3,748 | (4,043) | 6,304 | N/A | 35.5 | 105,497 | 11.5 | 16.7 |
| Restor Industries, Inc. | 616 | 9/97 | 533 | 1,625 | 1,915 | 925 | (36.5) | 53.7 | 10,039 | 16.3 | 10.9 |
| MEAN | | | | | | | (4.3) | 33.7 | | 11.4 | 11.6 |
| MEDIAN | | | | | | | (36.5) | 35.5 | | 11.5 | 10.9 |
| STD. DEV. | | | | | | | 24.7 | 17.1 | | 4.0 | 4.0 |
| COEFF. VAR. (%) | | | | | | | (574.6) | 50.6 | | 35.6 | 34.2 |
| North-South Supply Company | 421 | 11/93 | 121 | 54 | (106) | 199 | N/A | 80.2 | NA | NA | NA |

Definitions, footnotes, and sources are found on the last page of this exhibit.

EXHIBIT 15-11 (continued)

## North-South Supply Company, Inc., Guideline Publicly Traded Companies, Debt-Free Net Income

| Gudieline Company | LTM DFNI $000 | Period Ending | Debt-Free Net Income (DFNI) | | | 3-Yr. Avg. [b] DFNI $000 | Avg. Annual Compound Growth [c] % | Coeff. of Var. [d] % | MVIC $000 | MVIC/DFNI | |
|---|---|---|---|---|---|---|---|---|---|---|---|
| | | | 1996 $000 | 1995 $000 | 1994 $000 | | | | | LTM | 3-Year Avg. |
| Communications Systems, Inc. | 6,011 | 9/97 | 5,549 | 4,299 | 3,272 | 5,286 | 27.5 | 13.7 | 58,807 | 9.8 | 11.1 |
| Nationwide Cellular Service | 98 | 9/97 | (176) | (12) | (6,293) | (30) | N/A | (375.5) | 105,497 | 1,076.0 | (3,518.5) |
| Restor Industries, Inc. | (1,811) | 9/97 | (1,951) | 182 | 571 | (1,193) | N/A | (81.6) | 10,039 | (5.5) | (8.4) |
| MEAN | | | | | | | 9.2 | (147.8) | | 360.1 | (1,171.9) |
| MEDIAN | | | | | | | N/A | (81.6) | | 9.8 | (8.4) |
| STD. DEV. | | | | | | | 13.0 | 165.7 | | 506.2 | 1,659.3 |
| COEFF. VAR. (%) | | | | | | | 141.4 | (112.1) | | 140.6 | (141.6) |
| North-South Supply Company | 238 | 11/93 | 57 | 9 | (152) | 101 | N/A | 97.3 | NA | NA | NA |

Definitions, footnotes, and sources are found on the last page of this exhibit.

## North-South Supply Company, Inc., Guideline Publicly Traded Companies, Debt-Free Cash Flow

| Guideline Company | LTM DFCF $000 | Period Ending | Debt-Free Cash Flow (DFCF) | | | 3-Yr. Avg. [b] DFCF $000 | Avg. Annual Compound Growth [c] % | Coeff. of Var. [d] % | MVIC $000 | MVIC/DFCF | |
| | | | 1996 $000 | 1995 $000 | 1994 $000 | | | | | LTM | 3-Year Avg. |
|---|---|---|---|---|---|---|---|---|---|---|---|
| Communications Systems, Inc. | 7,849 | 9/97 | 7,232 | 5,785 | 4,621 | 6,955 | 23.6 | 12.4 | 58,807 | 7.5 | 8.5 |
| Nationwide Cellular Service | 9,039 | 9/97 | 5,963 | 3,748 | (4,043) | 6,250 | N/A | 34.7 | 105,497 | 11.7 | 16.9 |
| Restor Industries, Inc. | 579 | 9/97 | 533 | 1,518 | 1,579 | 877 | (33.0) | 51.7 | 10,039 | 17.3 | 11.4 |
| | | | | | | | | | | | |
| MEAN | | | | | | | (3.1) | 33.0 | | 12.2 | 12.3 |
| MEDIAN | | | | | | | (33.0) | 34.7 | | 11..7 | 11.4 |
| STD. DEV. | | | | | | | | 23.2 | 16.1 | | 4.0 | 3.5 |
| COEFF. VAR. (%) | | | | | | | (738.0) | 48.8 | | 33.1 | 28.4 |
| | | | | | | | | | | | |
| North-South Supply Company | 281 | 11/93 | 88 | 49 | (106) | 139 | N/A | 72.9 | NA | NA | NA |

Definitions, footnotes, and sources are found on the last page of this exhibit.

## North-South Supply Company, Inc., Guideline Publicly Traded Companies, Book Value of Invested Capital and Performance Ratios

| Guideline Company | MVIC $000s | MVIC/ Lat. Qtr. TBVIC Ratio | IBD/ TBVIC % | EBIT Return on TBVIC | | EBDIT Return on TBVIC | | DFNI Return on TBVIC | | DFCF Return on TBVIC | |
| | | | | LTM % | 3-Year Avg. % | LTM % | 3-Year Avg. % | LTM % | 3-Year Avg. % | LTM % | 3-Year Avg. % |
|---|---|---|---|---|---|---|---|---|---|---|---|
| Communications Systems, Inc. | 58,807 | 1.5 | 0.8 | 19.1 | 17.0 | 23.8 | 21.3 | 15.5 | 13.7 | 20.3 | 18.0 |
| Nationwide Cellular Service | 105,497 | 6.0 | 36.8 | 1.5 | 0.1 | 52.0 | 35.6 | 0.6 | (0.2) | 51.1 | 35.3 |
| Restor Industries, Inc. | 10.039 | 1.6 | 86.8 | (27.7) | (17.9) | 9.6 | 14.4 | (28.3) | (18.6) | 9.1 | 13.7 |
| | | | | | | | | | | | |
| MEAN | | 3.0 | 41.5 | (2.4) | (0.2) | 28.5 | 23.8 | (4.1) | (1.7) | 26.8 | 22.3 |
| MEDIAN | | 1.6 | 36.8 | 1.5 | 0.1 | 23.8 | 21.3 | 0.6 | (0.2) | 20.3 | 18.0 |
| STD. DEV. | | 2.1 | 35.3 | 19.3 | 14.3 | 17.6 | 8.8 | 18.2 | 13.2 | 17.8 | 9.4 |
| COEFF. VAR. (%) | | 69.0 | 85.1 | (805.6) | (5,788.4) | 61.8 | 37.1 | (447.6) | (772.2) | 66.3 | 41.9 |
| | | | | | | | | | | | |
| North-South Supply Company | NA | NA | 38.75 | 47.4 | 20.2 | 52.8 | 24.9 | 29.8 | 12.7 | 35.3 | 17.5 |

Definitions, footnotes, and sources are found on the last page of this exhibit.

In 1983, Lawrence H. Averill, Jr., Dean of the School of Law of the University of Arkansas at Little Rock, clearly articulated the rationale for a lack of marketability discount:

> The lack of marketability problem is inherent in the valuation of all business interests that are not actively traded on recognized markets. The poor marketability of nontraded business interests stems from several factors. First, most of these businesses are small, family-owned and -run operations. Such businesses run great risk of failure. The greater the risk, the lower the value. Second, these interests lack liquidity. There is no large pool of potential buyers for these interests when they come on the market. The longer it takes to sell an asset, the lower the value will be as compared to more actively tradable assets. Such a business interest must be sold at a substantial discount in order to attract buyers, as recognized by court decisions. The actual amount of the discount, of course, will vary from situation to situation.[4]

---

4. Lawrence H. Averill, Jr., *Estate Valuation Handbook* (New York: John Wiley & Sons, 1983), p. 177.

North-South Supply Company, Inc., Guideline Publicly Traded Companies, Definitions, Footnotes, and Sources

---

After identifying the appropriate Standard Industry Classification (SIC 3661, 4812), a preliminary list of potentially comparative companies was compiled using various on-line and CD-ROM information sources. The initial search yielded approximately 150 potential companies, which we reduced to 80 after a review of brief company descriptions. An examination of more detailed descriptions reduced the list to 11. The SEC Forms 10-K were examined for the 11 potential guideline companies and 8 companies were determined to be inappropriate for one or more of the following reasons: unrelated business; too diversified; too small a percentage of the business related; no longer publicly traded; financial condition; market too inactive; or other. The listed companies were selected as operating in the same or similar lines of business.

**Definitions:**

FYE = Fiscal year-end

LTM = Latest 12 months

MV = Market value

BV = Book value

IC = Invested capital

IBD = Interest-bearing debt

T = Tangible

MVIC = (Long-term debt) + (Short-term IBD) + (MV of preferred equity) + (MV of common equity)

TBVIC = (Stockholders' equity) − (Goodwill) + (Long-term debt) + (Short-term IBD)

NA = Not applicable

**Footnotes:**

a. Per most recently available data prior to the valuation date.

b. Includes latest 12 months if at least six months beyond latest fiscal year-end.

c. From earliest year on the exhibit to the latest 12-month period.

d. (Standard deviation/Mean) × 100.

---

*Sources:* Individual companies' Forms 10-K, Forms 10-Q, and annual reports; the *Wall Street Journal;* Best Appraisal Company calculations; CompuServe; and *Moody's Bond Guide.*

The market places a greater value differential on the liquidity factor alone in its pricing of common stocks than in its pricing of any other class of investment assets. For common stocks as a group, investors expect to realize the majority of their return in the form of capital gains at the time of sale of the stock and only a smaller part of their total return in the form of dividends while they hold the stock. Thus, the ability to sell the stock is crucial to the actual realization of the investor's return for buying and holding the stock.

*Empirical Research on Lack of Marketability Discounts.* While sophisticated participants in the capital market have always known that the pricing of common stocks is highly dependent on their liquidity, it is only since 1971 that a body of evidence has begun to be developed and disseminated to isolate and quantify the differential in security pricing that is due to the lack of marketability factors.

The current evidence providing empirical support for discounts for lack of marketability generally falls into two fields of study: studies of restricted stock transactions, and studies of private transactions in the common stock of companies that subsequently had initial public offerings. A discussion of the major studies in each of these two fields is presented below.

*Studies of Restricted Stock.* Studies of restricted stock specifically isolate the value of the marketability factor from all other factors. Restricted stock is stock of a publicly traded company that is subject to certain trading restrictions. A publicly traded company may sell securities that are not registered with the Securities and Exchange Commission (SEC) through private placements. However, these securities cannot be resold in the public capital market, except under SEC Rule 144, which requires a two-year holding period.[5] As a result of this trading restriction, such privately placed stock is restricted.

---

5. 55 Fed. Reg. 20894 (May 21, 1990).

Evidence of the price discount required by purchasers of restricted stock is found by comparing the price of a privately placed stock to the price of its unrestricted publicly traded counterpart. As literally hundreds of such arm's-length transactions have been studied, they provide a strong base of empirical evidence from which to quantify an appropriate discount for lack of marketability.

The studies of market prices of restricted stocks now cover a time span from the late 1960s through 1996. These comprehensive studies, covering literally hundreds of transactions, indicate quite consistently an average lack of marketability discount for the restricted stock of a publicly traded company of 35 percent as compared to its freely tradable counterpart stock.

However, this discount is based upon transactions in stock that will be freely tradable in a relatively short period of time. One would expect the appropriate discount for lack of marketability to be significantly higher for a noncontrolling ownership interest in a closely held company (which, in all likelihood, will never have a public market) than for the securities included in these restricted stock studies.

*Initial Public Offering Studies.* While studies of restricted stocks provide compelling evidence of the discounts for lack of marketability associated with stocks that are (temporarily) restricted from their public market, a second line of evidence is obtained through studies of initial public offerings (IPOs). The scope of these IPO studies includes transactions in the stock of companies that were private at the time of the transaction, but subsequently had a successful initial public offering.

The discount for lack of marketability is generally determined as the difference between a company's IPO stock price and the price at which the company's stock traded in private transactions prior to the IPO, when the company's stock did not trade on a public market, adjusted for factors such as changes in earnings levels and industry price–earnings multiples. The IPO studies add to the evidence presented by the restricted stock studies, and assist in determining lack of marketability discounts applicable to appraised values arrived at through methods based upon publicly traded companies.

There are two major studies of IPOs: 1) the Baird & Company (John Emory) study and 2) the Willamette Management Associates study. Similar to the restricted stock studies, the studies of IPOs now cover a significant time span from the late 1970s through 1996. Through these studies, nearly each and every IPO of the last 20 years has been examined for relevant evidence. Based upon the results of the Baird studies and the Willamette Management Associates studies, typical discounts for lack of marketability associated with private transactions in closely held stock compared to public market transactions in the same stock fall within a range of 25 to 50 percent.

*Summary and Conclusion of Empirical Research.* Based upon our review, we applied a 25 percent lack of marketability discount to the indicated results of the two valuation methods.

### Ownership Control Premium

Since the guideline publicly traded company method is indicative of a value on a noncontrolling ownership interest basis, we applied an ownership control premium of 35 percent to this indicator of value, to estimate the value of NSSC on a controlling ownership interest basis.

### Business Enterprise Valuation Conclusion

As mentioned, we applied the discounted net cash flow method and guideline publicly traded company method to arrive at a fair market value conclusion. The indicated values are presented below:

| Valuation Method | Indicated Value |
|---|---|
| Discounted net cash flow method | $15,394,000 |
| Guideline publicly traded company method | $16,218,000 |

Giving equal weight to the results of these two business valuation methods, we conclude the aggregate fair market value of the business equity of NSSC, as of November 30, 1997, to be $15,800,000.

## VALUATION SYNTHESIS AND CONCLUSION

Pursuant to your authorization, Best Appraisal Company has conducted valuation analyses in relation to the acquisition of the net assets of North-South Supply Company, Inc. (NSSC) by All Directions Supply, Inc.

NSSC, a division of World Wide Supply, Inc., is organized as an S corporation and was formed in October 1993. NSSC is a designer and manufacturer of pay telephone components and subassemblies that are marketed to the regional Bell and independent operating companies. In addition, NSSC is a reseller of cellular phone services, a distributor of imported Western Electric parts, and a contract manufacturer of various telephone components.

The objective of our analysis is to estimate 1) the fair market value of certain tangible and intangible assets of NSSC and 2) the fair market value of the NSSC owners' equity on a controlling ownership interest basis, as of November 30, 1997.

We understand that this appraisal report will be used for acquisition transaction structuring.

For purposes of this appraisal, we define the term *fair market value* as "the price that property will bring when it is offered for sale by one who is willing, but not obligated to sell it, and is bought by one who is willing or desires to purchase, but is not compelled to do so."

We appraised the subject assets under the premise of value in continued use, as part of a going-concern business enterprise.

Based upon our valuation analyses, and in our opinion, the fair market value of the tangible and intangible assets of NSSC, as of November 30, 1997, is presented below:

| NSSC Asset Category | Indicated Fair Market Value |
|---|---|
| Tangible personal property | $    544,000 |
| Patent license | 8,030,000 |
| Customer contracts | 1,410,000 |
| Cellular service customer list | 520,200 |
| Noncompete agreement | 2,100,000 |
| Total | $12,604,200 |

Based on our analysis, and in our opinion, the fair market value of the owners' equity of NSSC, on a controlling ownership interest basis, as of November 30, 1997, is $15,800,000.

Our appraisal was conducted in accordance with the *Uniform Standards of Professional Appraisal Practice* (USPAP), as promulgated by The Appraisal Foundation.

In accordance with the professional guidelines established by the American Society of Appraisers, we are independent of NSSC. We have no current or prospective financial interest in the assets subject to appraisal. Our fee for this appraisal was in no way influenced by the results of our valuation analysis.

During our appraisal, we were provided with audited and unaudited financial and operational data. The data were both historical and prospective in nature. We have relied upon the data as accurately reflecting the results of operations and financial position of NSSC.

The accompanying statement of contingent and limiting conditions, appraisal certification, and professional qualifications of the principal analysts are integral parts of the valuation opinion.

Sincerely,
Best Appraisal Company


Robert Best
Managing Director

## APPENDIX A—STATEMENT OF CONTINGENT AND LIMITING CONDITIONS

This appraisal is made subject to the following general contingent and limiting conditions:

1. We assume no responsibility for the legal description or matters including legal or title considerations. Title to the subject assets, properties, or business interests is assumed to be good and marketable unless otherwise stated.

2. The subject assets, properties, or business interests are appraised free and clear of any or all liens or encumbrances unless otherwise stated.

3. We assume responsible ownership and competent management with respect to the subject assets, properties, or business interests.

4. The information furnished by others is believed to be reliable. However, we issue no warranty or other form of assurance regarding its accuracy.

5. We assume no hidden or unapparent conditions regarding the subject assets, properties, or business interests.

6. We assume that there is full compliance with all applicable federal, state, and local regulations and laws unless the lack of compliance is stated, defined, and considered in the appraisal report.

7. We assume that all required licenses, certificates of occupancy, consents, or legislative or administrative authority from any local, state, or national government, or private entity or organization have been or can be obtained or reviewed for any use on which the opinion contained in this report is based.

8. Unless otherwise stated in this report, we did not observe, and we have no knowledge of, the existence of hazardous materials with regard to the subject assets, properties, or business interests. However, we are not qualified to detect such substances. We assume no responsibility for such conditions or for any expertise required to discover them.

9. Possession of this report does not carry with it the right of publication. It may not be used for any purpose by any person other than the client to whom it is addressed without our written consent, and, in any event, only with proper written qualifications and only in its entirety.

10. We, by reason of this opinion, are not required to furnish a complete valuation report, or to give testimony, or to be in attendance in court with reference to the assets, properties, or business interests in question unless arrangements have been previously made.

11. Neither all nor any part of the contents of this report shall be disseminated to the public through advertising, public relations, news, sales, or other media without our prior written consent and approval.

12. The analyses, opinions, and conclusions presented in this report apply to this engagement only and may not be used out of the context presented herein. This report is valid only for the effective date(s) specified herein and only for the purpose(s) specified herein.

## APPENDIX B—APPRAISAL CERTIFICATION

We hereby certify the following statements regarding this appraisal:

1. We have personally inspected the assets, properties, or business interests encompassed by this appraisal.

2. We have no present or prospective future interest in the assets, properties, or business interests that are the subject of this appraisal report.

3. We have no personal interest or bias with respect to the subject matter of this report or the parties involved.

4. Our compensation for making the appraisal is in no way contingent upon the value reported or upon any predetermined value.

5. To the best of our knowledge and belief, the statements of facts contained in this report, upon which the analyses, conclusions, and opinions expressed herein are based, are true and correct.

6. Our analyses, opinions, and conclusions were developed, and this report has been prepared, in conformity with the *Uniform Standards of Professional Appraisal Practice,* as promulgated by The Appraisal Foundation.

7. No persons other than the individuals whose qualifications are included herein have provided significant professional assistance regarding the analyses, opinions, and conclusions set forth in this report.

8. The reported analyses, opinions, and conclusions are limited only by the reported contingent and limiting conditions, and they represent our unbiased professional analyses, opinions, and conclusions.

9. The reported analyses, opinions, and conclusions were developed, and this report has been prepared, in conformity with the requirements of the Code of Professional Ethics and the Standards of Professional Appraisal Practice of the Appraisal Institute, of the American Society of Appraisers, and of the other professional organizations of which we are members.

10. Disclosure of the contents of this report is subject to the requirements of the Appraisal Institute, the American Society of Appraisers, and the other professional organizations of which we are members, related to review by their duly authorized representatives.

## APPENDIX C—QUALIFICATIONS OF THE PRINCIPAL ANALYSTS

### Robert Best, CPA, CFA, ASA

Robert Best is a managing director of Best Appraisal Company.

With regard to valuation consulting, Mr. Best routinely serves clients in the following appraisal disciplines: business valuation and security analysis, intangible asset and intellectual property appraisal, real estate and real property interest appraisal, and tangible personal property appraisal.

Mr. Best has performed the following types of valuation and economic analyses: event analysis, merger and acquisition appraisals, divestiture and spin-off appraisals, solvency analysis, fairness opinions, ESOP feasibility and formation analysis, post-acquisition purchase price allocation appraisals, business and stock valuations, real estate valuations and evaluations, tangible personal property appraisals, real estate feasibility and investment analyses, ad valorem assessment appeal appraisals, construction cost segregation appraisals, insurance appraisals, restructuring and workout appraisals, litigation support appraisals, and tangible and intangible asset transfer pricing analyses.

These valuation and economic analyses have been performed for the following purposes: transaction pricing and structuring (merger, acquisition, liquidation, and divestiture), taxation planning and compliance (federal income, gift, and estate tax, and state and local property tax), financing securitization and collateralization, employee corporate ownership, litigation support and dispute resolution, strategic information and planning, insolvency and troubled debt workout analysis (recapitalization, restructuring), and fiduciary advice and financial counseling.

Mr. Best has appraised the following types of business entities and securities: close corporations—entity value, close corporations—fractional interests, public corporations—restricted stock, portfolios of marketable and nonmarketable securities, complex capital structures (various classes of common equity, preferred equity, and warrants, grants, rights), general and limited partnership interests, joint ventures, proprietorships, professional service corporations, professional practices, license agreements, franchises, and intercompany transfer pricing agreements.

He has performed economic analyses, valuation analyses, and remaining useful life analyses, and/or has estimated the appropriate transfer price on the following types of intangible assets and intellectual properties: advertising campaigns and programs, appraisal plant, bank customers, broadcast licenses, building permits, cable franchise ordinances, certificates of need, computer databases, computer software, copyrights, core depositors, credit information files, customer and supplier contracts, customer lists, distribution rights, distribution systems, employment contracts, engineering drawings, film libraries, franchise contracts and rights, going-concern value, goodwill, leasehold interests, licenses, literary compositions, loan portfolios, management contracts, manuscripts, medical charts and records, mortgage servicing rights, musical compositions, noncompete covenants, patent applications, patents, patient files and records, permits, possessory interests, prizes and awards, procedural manuals, production backlogs, proprietary technology, solicitation rights, subscriber lists, technical libraries, trained and assembled workforces, trade names, trademarks, training manuals and documentation, unpatented technology, and use rights—air, water, and land.

Mr. Best has performed pre-acquisition and post-acquisition business and asset appraisals in the following industries: accounting and consulting, advertising, apparel, appraisal, automobile dealerships, automobile manufacturing, aviation, bottling, brokerage, cable television, cement, chemical, commercial banking, communications, computer services, construction and contracting, consumer finance, cosmetics, data processing, decontamination, distribution, education, entertainment, equipment leasing, fast food, food service, forest products, health care, hotel and hospitality, insurance, investment banking, leasing, manufacturing, medical and dental practice, mining and mineral extraction, money management, natural resources, petrochemical, pharmaceuticals, plastics, printing, public utilities, publishing, radio broadcasting, railroads, real estate development, recreational services, restaurant, retailing, shipping, steel, television broadcasting, textiles, thrift institutions, transportation and trucking, vocational training, and wholesaling.

He has prepared numerous financial advisory analyses and economic analyses for merger and acquisition purposes. These analyses include: identification of merger and acquisition targets, appraisal of synergistic and strategic benefits of targets, identification and assessment of divestiture and spin-off opportunities, economic analysis of alternative deal structures, negotiation and consummation of deals, assessment of the fairness of proposed transactions, analysis of initial public offering (IPO) alternative pricing strategies, and design and valuation of alternative equity and debt instruments within a multi-investor environment.

He has prepared valuation engineering, value enhancement, and owner wealth maximization analyses. Valuation engineering involves the development and implementation of tactics and strategies designed to maximize the value of assets, properties, and business interests. Mr. Best routinely performs valuation engineering analyses for owners of close corporations and for owners of income-producing real property. These valuation engineering analyses are performed for transaction pricing, intergenerational wealth transfer, and management information purposes.

Mr. Best conducts engineering depreciation, technological obsolescence and economic obsolescence studies for purposes of ad valorem property tax assessment appeal. These appraisals typically encompass the quantification of physical deterioration and functional, technological, and economic obsolescence of both real and personal property. These appraisals generally involve technology life cycle analyses and economic/product life cycle analyses.

Mr. Best has performed real estate appraisals and feasibility/development/investment analyses of the following types of properties: commercial office buildings, easements, facades, hospitals, hotels, industrial cooperatives, industrial and manufacturing facilities, industrial parks, land improvements and infrastructures, mines, nursing homes, quarries, railroads, regional shopping malls, residential apartment complexes, restaurants, retail stores, strip shopping malls, timber land, vacant rural land, vacant urban land, and warehouses. These appraisals have encompassed the following real estate interests: fee simple, leasehold interest, leasehold estate, possessory interests, life interests, reversionary interest, air rights, water rights, mineral rights, use rights and development rights. These appraisals have concluded the following standards of value: market value, fair value, insurable value, use value, collateral value, investment value, and ad valorem value.

He has appraised the following types of tangible personal property: manufacturing machinery and equipment, processing machinery and equipment, mining and extractive equipment, construction equipment, data processing and office automation equipment, communications and telecommunications equipment, broadcasting equipment, office furniture and fixtures, vehicles and transportation equipment, aircraft, and laboratory and scientific equipment.

Mr. Best has been accepted as an expert witness on over 100 occasions in various federal, state, and international courts and before various state boards of equalization and tribunals. These litigation support services have related to business, stock, and asset appraisal matters and to economic damages matters. As an appraiser and economist, he has been an expert witness in the following types of litigation: bankruptcy, breach of contract, condemnation, conservatorship, corporate dissolution, expropriation, federal income tax, gift and estate tax, infringement (value of intangible assets), marital dissolution, minority shareholder rights, property tax appeal, reasonableness of executive compensation, solvency and insolvency, stockholder suits, tortious damages, and reasonableness of royalty rates and/or transfer prices.

He has served as a court-appointed arbitrator with respect to minority squeeze-out merger shareholder rights actions.

Education
Master of Business Administration, Finance, Columbia University Graduate School of Business

Bachelor of Arts, Economics, Columbia University

Professional Affiliations
Certified Public Accountant (Ohio and Illinois)
Accredited Senior Appraiser (ASA)—American Society of Appraisers, in business valuation
Chartered Financial Analyst (CFA)—Association of Investment Management and Research

From 1987 through 1989, Mr. Best served as an examiner for the Board of Examiners—the examination and certification division—of the American Society of Appraisers, the national standards setting and certification organization in the appraisal industry.

Mr. Best is a member of the American Bankruptcy Institute, American Economic Association, American Institute of Certified Public Accountants, American Society of Appraisers, Business Valuation Association, The ESOP Association, Illinois Society of Certified Public Accountants, Institute of Chartered Financial Analysts, Institute of Property Taxation, Institute of Management Accountants, National Association of Business Economists, National Association of Real Estate Appraisers, Ohio Society of Certified Public Accountants, and Society of Manufacturing Engineers.

Mr. Best is a state-certified general real estate appraiser in the states of Illinois, Virginia, Utah, and Oregon. He is a state certified affiliate of the Appraisal Institute.

### Amelia Analyst, Ph.D., ASA

Amelia Analyst is a senior associate of Best Appraisal Company. She specializes in the valuation of business entities and fractional business interests, in the analysis and appraisal of debt and equity security instruments, and in the valuation and remaining life analysis of intangible assets and intellectual properties.

Dr. Analyst has particular experience in the identification, valuation, and remaining life analysis of certain types of intangible assets and intellectual properties, including: computer software, core depositors, credit card portfolios (including private label and affinity programs), customer and supplier contracts, customer lists, employment contracts, going-concern value, goodwill, licenses, loan portfolios, noncompete covenants, patents and patent applications, proprietary technology, subscriber lists, trained and assembled workforces, trademarks, and trade names.

These appraisals are performed for purposes of licensing; financing securitization and collateralization; depreciation and amortization; purchase price allocation; abandonment; intercompany transfer pricing; infringement, breach of contract, and other damages analyses; and other litigation support and dispute resolution purposes.

She has substantial experience in the appraisal of closely held business entities and business interests and in the appraisal of fractional and nonmarketable security interests in private corporations and in public corporations. These security interests include various types of stock options, warrants, grants, and rights; convertible securities; general and limited partnership interests; and securities with and without voting, participation, and other stockholder rights.

These appraisals are performed for purposes of mergers, acquisitions, liquidations, divestitures, refinancing, restructuring, gift and estate tax compliance, estate planning, charitable contribution, employee stock ownership plan (ESOP) formation and compliance, ESOP security transactions, ESOP (and other transaction) fairness and "adequate consideration" determination, fraudulent conveyance determination, ad valorem property taxation, solvency and insolvency analysis, bankruptcy and reorganization, and various types of litigation support and dispute resolution matters. She has also performed valuation analyses for dissenting shareholder interests and minority shareholder "appraisal rights" matters.

Dr. Analyst utilizes her engineering expertise in the appraisal of various categories of tangible personal property such as: production machinery and equipment, processing machinery and equipment, transportation and distribution equipment, office furniture and fixtures, computer hardware and office automation equipment, laboratory and technical equipment, telecommunications equipment, and various types of industrial and commercial property. This engineering background includes cost estimation from flow charts and construction cost analysis.

Dr. Analyst has a thorough knowledge of asset and property remaining life analysis techniques. She routinely performs the following types of analyses in order to quantify remaining useful lives of various types of assets and properties: statistical analysis of retirement and active data for survivor curve fitting, product life cycle concept, technology life cycle forecasting, and engineering depreciation and functional obsolescence analysis.

Education
Doctor of Philosophy, Engineering Valuation, Iowa State University

Master of Engineering, Industrial Engineering, Iowa State University

Bachelor of Engineering, Mechanical Engineering, Oregon State University

Professional Affiliations
Dr. Analyst is an accredited senior appraiser (ASA) of the American Society of Appraisers, certified in business valuation. She is a member of the American Institute of Industrial Engineers, the Society of Depreciation Professionals, and the Licensing Executives Society.

# Analysis of Specific Types of Intangible Assets

# CHAPTER 16

# Contract Intangible Assets

## DESCRIPTION OF CONTRACT INTANGIBLES

The class of intangible assets referred to as *contract intangibles* generally represents value attributable to that broad category of rights accruing to an individual or to a business entity as a result of a written, legally enforceable contractual arrangement. While common logic dictates that two parties generally would not enter into a contractual agreement unless it was viewed as economically advantageous by both parties, a change in general industry or economic conditions subsequent to the original consummation of a contract may exert a positive or negative impact on the current value of an existing contract, based on the contract terms initially established. Therefore, an explicit need exists regarding an analyst's ability to identify and analyze contractual arrangements at a specific point in time and to estimate the current value of beneficial interests conveyed by the subject contract.

Because contracts are established for a myriad of reasons and purposes, the scope of this chapter is necessarily limited to a discussion of the general framework under which the analysis and valuation of contract intangibles can be performed. For purposes of demonstration, however, an example is presented that addresses the valuation of a favorable supplier contract.

*Black's Law Dictionary* defines a contract as follows:

> An agreement between two or more persons which creates an obligation to do or not to do a particular thing. . . . Its essentials are competent parties, subject matter, a legal consideration, mutuality of agreement, and mutuality of obligation.[1]

The fact that most contracts contain liquidating damages clauses, and the significant amount of annual litigation in the judicial system based on breach of contract claims, provide compelling evidence with regard to the general recognition of the inherent value contained within many contract intangibles.

Based upon the definition provided above, a contract intangible can result from any number of the numerous and diverse binding agreements consummated daily between businesses and individuals. Generally, contract intangibles can be categorized based upon the source of the benefit giving rise to the existence of the related intangible value. Contract intangibles relating to the receipt of goods or services at an economically advantageous rate or to the granting of exclusive or protective rights to an entity are generally classified as *receiver-based*. Contract intangibles relating to the provision of goods or services at favorable rates (relative to the underlying cost of the goods or services provided) or to the securing of future economic benefit streams or provider rights for an entity are generally classified as *provider-based*.

Exhibit 16-1 presents a nonexhaustive illustrative listing of contract intangibles classified by category.

While not all contract intangibles are conveniently categorized as either receiver-based or provider-based, a careful review of the terms of a contractual relationship, and an analysis of existing industry and market conditions with respect to the basis of the subject contract, should enable the analyst to

---

1. Henry Campbell Black, *Black's Law Dictionary*, 6th ed. (St. Paul, MN: West Publishing Co., 1990), p. 322.

| Category | | Beneficial Character |
|---|---|---|
| **Receiver-Based** | **Provider-Based** | |
| Leasehold interests | | Below market rental rate |
| Distribution agreements | | Favorable distribution rights |
| Employment contracts | | Secure employment services |
| Noncompete agreements | | Protected market area/customer base |
| Financing agreements | | Favorable financing |
| Insurance contracts | | Favorable insurance rate |
| Supply contracts | | Below market cost/favorable terms |
| Service agreements | | Below market cost/favorable terms |
| Operating licenses | | Restricted control over market segment |
| Broadcast licenses | | Restricted control over market segment |
| Franchisee rights | | Rights to market segment/product line |
| Licensing rights | | Restricted use of intellectual property |
| | Franchise rights | Protection of territory or product line/fees |
| | License rights | Protection of intellectual property/royalties |
| | Subscription rights | Protection of subscriber base/fees |
| | Futures contracts | Maintenance of future revenue/favorable rates |
| | Service agreements | Maintenance of future revenue |
| | Debt agreements | Secure future economic returns |
| | Mortgage servicing rights | Maintenance of future revenue |
| | Provider contracts | Maintenance of future revenue/favorable rates |

determine the beneficial character, if any, provided by the contract. To the extent that the aforementioned review and analysis results in the conclusion that an existing contract conveys a diminutive economic benefit to its holder (or no economic benefit), the related contract may have little value.

## COMMON VALUATION METHODS

As discussed in Chapters 7 through 10, there are several methods and procedures that may be appropriate for appraising intangible assets. These methods fall into the three general approaches: the cost approach, the market approach, and the income approach.

While some intangible assets are readily appraised by all three approaches, certain approaches provide more credible results than others for particular categories of intangible assets. With regard to contract intangibles, the income approach is often considered to include the more widely accepted methods and procedures for achieving relevant value conclusions. The following discussion of common valuation methods within the cost, market, and income approaches addresses considerations regarding the valuation of contract intangibles based on each approach. However, the final valuation of the example favorable supplier contract is based upon the widely accepted income approach.

## Cost Approach

To estimate the value of a favorable supplier contract using the cost approach, an internal analysis should be performed of the total cost required to identify and evaluate the reliability of the supplier, and negotiate, draft, and consummate the subject contract. These costs include direct costs (e.g., the cost of dedicated employee-related time and outside counsel, and out-of-pocket expenses) and indirect costs (e.g., allocated overhead, including support staff and supplies). Unfortunately, few companies, if any, diligently monitor the contract process in place at their respective organizations, or maintain the necessary detailed records required to estimate the cost to replace a particular contract with one that would provide comparable benefits.

Possibly more significant than the difficulty associated with quantifying and supporting the costs incurred to establish a favorable supplier contract is the intuitive difficulty associated with the notion that a "favorable" contract can be replaced or negotiated at any point in time. The existence of a favorable supplier contract is generally the product of a unique set of interrelated market and economic conditions and company-specific factors at a certain point in time. This unique set of factors is typically not expected to occur with any degree of regularity.

For these reasons, the estimation of the value of a favorable supplier contract is typically not concluded through the application of the cost approach.

## Market Approach

To estimate the value of a favorable supplier contract using the market approach would require the identification and analysis of actual arm's-length transactions of comparative contract intangibles. Ignoring the fact that no organized exchange market exists for the purpose of transferring contract intangibles, contracts, by their very nature, are private legal agreements that are generally not transferable unless occurring as a part of a complete business transfer. Therefore, similar to the difficulties associated with using the cost approach to value contract intangibles, it is difficult to apply the market approach to estimate the value of contract intangibles due to insufficient support data (market-based transactional information, in this instance).

## Income Approach

An investor anticipates some measure of economic income (e.g., net cost savings) from favorable supplier contract intangibles over an expected period of time. The expected period of time for the enjoyment of economic income is based on the remaining term of the contract plus the expected contract renewal periods, if any. The economic income may be quantified in various measures such as net cash flow, debt-free net income, or net income.

To estimate the value of a favorable supplier contract using the income approach, the future net cost savings expected to be realized over the remaining term of the contract, including expected renewal periods, may be discounted to a present worth. The cost savings are discounted at the investor's (i.e., the purchaser established in the contract) required rate of return on the investment generating the cost savings. As most contract intangibles originate during the normal course of business operations, it is sometimes reasonable to assume that the underlying investment required by the purchaser to consummate the contract reflects risk elements comparable to those considered in developing the purchasing entity's weighted average cost of capital. Therefore, the weighted average cost of capital of the purchasing entity, developed on either a pretax or post-tax basis consistent with the development of the associated measure of economic income, is sometimes used to discount to a present value the anticipated cost savings expected from a favorable supplier contract.

## DATA SOURCES

Chapter 5 describes the types of data sources typically relied upon to value intangible assets. The following discussion addresses these data sources as they apply to the analysis of contract intangibles.

## Internal Data Sources

Internal financial reports, such as historical financial statements and budgets, are useful in performing almost all intangible asset valuation methods. Payroll records and project management or timekeeping reports are usually relevant to any cost approach valuation method.

A complete summary of all contracts in effect at the valuation date should be requested and reviewed. The summary should provide information regarding the purpose of the contract, pricing or other significant factors pertaining to the basis of the contract, the contracting parties, the effective date of the contract, the term of the contract, and renewal period options.

A review of the contract summary may be supplemented by interviews with key members of management. Although the contract summary may provide considerable information regarding the underlying contracts, interviews with relevant members of management generally provide the first clear indication of the existence of contract intangible value. The following list provides examples of key contract-related factors that are often only ascertainable through the interview process:

- The specific impact on the operations of the subject company of industry and economic market conditions existing at the time of the contract's origination and currently.
- Company-specific circumstances (e.g., phase in the business cycle or financial condition) regarding the contractor (e.g., supplier) at the time of the contract's origination and currently.
- The length of the business relationship with the contractor and the contractor's representative.
- The history of the contract negotiation and renewal process.
- Information regarding terms offered by the contractor to market competitors.
- Information regarding substitute goods or services offered by other contractors and the related contract terms offered.

## External Data Sources

As previously discussed, a contract generally represents a private agreement between parties. Therefore, it is commonly accepted that external data sources for the appraisal of contract intangibles are often nonexistent. Further, the specific terms of contracts typically are not made available to parties who are not bound by the related agreements.

While they will not provide actual contract agreements, trade publications may prove useful as data sources for the purpose of identifying contractors who provide comparative services, products, or rights granted by the subject contract. Advertisements within the journals may provide leads regarding the number and identity of key competitors who can often be contacted for the purpose of obtaining preliminary quote sheets and limited terms. Leasing agents often supply current market rental rates and quote sheets that can be used to determine whether a lease agreement reflects a below-market rental rate. Also, published catalogs often provide an initial indication regarding whether a supplier arrangement has been established at a favorable rate. Newsletters specializing in intangible asset licensing, as described in Chapter 5, can be a good source of market-derived, empirical royalty rates.

In most instances, however, interviews with management may provide some indication regarding the basis for the management opinion that a particular binding agreement represents a contract intangible of value. Often, the support for this opinion is represented by external documents and information in management's possession. This information should be requested and can generally be relied upon by the analyst.

## VALUATION EXAMPLE

Exhibits 16-2 and 16-3 present an example of the valuation of a hypothetical favorable supplier contract using the income approach. In the example, we consider the valuation of a supplier contract between Polyethylene Supply Company (PSC) and Plastic Products, Inc. (PPI).

The objective of the subject appraisal is to estimate the fair market value of a fee simple interest in the supplier contract as part of an asset accumulation valuation analysis performed in order to estimate the total business enterprise value of PPI as of September 30, 1997.

## Fact Set and Assumptions

For purposes of this example, let's assume that PPI is a $250 million annual revenue, regular C-type corporation. PPI has a 50-year operating history and manufactures and distributes a wide variety of polyethylene-based plastic containers, bags, and pipe, both domestically and internationally. Further, we assume that the PPI effective income tax rate is 40 percent, and that a rigorous analysis has concluded that the relevant weighted average cost of capital present value discount rate for the company is 14 percent.

As of the valuation date, PSC has been supplying an average of 25 percent of the PPI total raw material needs for the past 10 years, and has been a continuous supplier to PPI for approximately 25 years. PSC is financially sound and is among the top five suppliers in the industry.

We performed due diligence procedures relating to the asset accumulation valuation analysis, including a review of the contract summary prepared by management and extensive interviews with management. These procedures resulted in the identification of the favorable supplier contract with PSC. Exhibit 16-2 presents the key terms and considerations regarding the subject contract.

EXHIBIT 16-2

Illustrative Supplier Contract Valuation, Favorable Contract Summary and Key Considerations, as of September 30, 1997

| | |
|---|---|
| Contract renewal date (No.) | July 15, 1995 (3) |
| Purchaser | Plastic Products, Inc. (PPI) |
| Contractor/provider | Polyethylene Supply Company (PSC) |
| Product | Raw material—polyethylene beads |
| Annual contract rate | $0.48 per pound, first 15MM pounds; $0.45 per pound, next 9MM pounds; $0.43 per pound in excess of 24MM pounds |
| Annual contract quantity | Minimum of 2MM pounds per month/24MM pounds per year |
| | Maximum of 3MM pounds per month/36MM pounds per year |
| Average annual contract rate | $0.47 per pound currently assuming minimum requirement |
| | $0.45 per pound currently assuming maximum requirement |
| | Annual cost escalation at 2.5 percent per year |
| Effective date | October 1, 1995 |
| Expiration date | September 30, 2000 |
| Renewal options | Renewable every five years with 60-day notice at a negotiated rate based on existing market spot rates and estimated supply |

| | |
|---|---|
| Key event giving rise to favorable rate | Political and civil conflict in key producer countries resulting in restricted supply anticipated to last for approximately three years until production facilities are repaired and production resumes at normal levels |
| Existing market spot rate | $0.58 per pound |
| Expected market price movement | Annual price declines of 5.5 percent per year over the next three years as production capacity is restored |
| PPI expected requirements over remaining term | Maximum requirement level based on projected end product sales through 2000 |
| Probability of PSC ability to satisfy PPI requirements | 100% based on market position as a supplier and financial soundness |

## Income Approach—Discounted Cost Savings Method

Exhibit 16-3 presents our discounted cost savings method analysis relating to the favorable supplier contract between PPI and PSC. As presented in Exhibit 16-3, we have projected that the favorable cost rate that PPI currently enjoys will continue only until the contract expiration date on September 30, 2000. This is because the contract rate is subject to renegotiation at that date. At the time of the contract renegotiation and renewal, the contract rate is expected to approximate market rates, with minor price breaks based on volume purchases.

As presented in Exhibit 16-3, we have also projected that the spread between existing market rates and contracted rates for the raw material that PPI will acquire over the next three operating periods will narrow as the market supply of the material increases and price escalation incorporated in the contract takes effect. Further, we have incorporated into our analysis the economic impact on total cost savings that results from the fact that without the associated supporting assets—both tangible and intangible—the projected cost savings would not be achievable. This is because PPI would not have the productive capacity necessary to maximize the potential benefit of the PSC contract. This economic impact, referred to as a *capital charge,* represents the annual return required on all corporate assets used or used up in the production of the economic income associated with the subject favorable supplier contract. The capital charge is re-

Illustrative Supplier Contract Valuation, Income Approach—Present Value of Projected Cost Savings, as of September 30, 1997

| | 1998 | 1999 | 2000 |
|---|---|---|---|
| Estimated purchases from PSC (000 lbs) | 36,000 | 36,000 | 36,000 |
| Estimated market spot rate (per pound) | $ 0.58 | $ 0.55 | $ 0.52 |
| Estimated cost at market rate ($000) | 20,880 | 19,732 | 18,646 |
| Average contract rate (per pound) | $ 0.45 | $ 0.46 | $ 0.47 |
| Estimated cost at contract rate ($000) | 16,200 | 16,605 | 17,020 |
| Cost savings (market cost in excess of contract cost) | 4,680 | 3,127 | 1,626 |
| Less: allocated capital charge on supporting assets | (1,312) | (1,379) | (1,447) |
| Cost savings before income tax considerations | 3,368 | 1,748 | 179 |
| Estimated additional income taxes on cost savings | (1,347) | (699) | (71) |
| Net cost savings | 2,021 | 1,049 | 108 |
| Present value factor (assuming midyear convention) | 0.9366 | 0.8216 | 0.7207 |
| Discounted net cost savings | 1,892 | 862 | 77 |
| Indicated value of PSC supplier contract | 2,831 | | |
| Indicated fair market value of PSC supplier contract (rounded) | **$ 2,800** | | |

**Key Valuation Analysis Variables**

| | |
|---|---|
| Anticipated annual price change through 2000—market rate | −5.5% |
| Contract rate annual price escalation | 2.5% |
| PPI total revenue base—1997 ($000) | 250,000 |
| Portion of PPI revenue resulting from PSC contract ($000) | 25.0% |
| Estimated annual growth in PPI revenue | 5.0% |
| Estimate capital charge on supporting assets (% of related rev.) | 2.0% |
| Effective income tax rate | 40.0% |
| After-tax, weighted average cost of capital present value discount rate | 14.0% |

*Note:* Numbers may not total due to rounding.

flected in Exhibit 16-3 as a percentage of the estimated portion of the PPI annual revenue attributable to product sales resulting from raw material inputs relating to the PSC contract.

Based upon the analysis presented in Exhibit 16-3, the favorable supplier contract between PPI and PSC results in a present value economic benefit to PPI, or an estimated fair market value, of $2.8 million.

## Contract Intangibles Valuation Considerations

The example presented represents a somewhat simplistic summary of the many quantitative and qualitative considerations that occur during the valuation of contract intangibles. Further, the example is based on the premise that the subject favorable supplier contract has a determinable, and *certain,* remaining useful life of three years.

Because contracts can be so diverse and result from innumerable circumstances that are affected differently by changes in industry and market conditions, no cookbook approach to the valuation of contract intangibles is available. While this chapter has provided an example with regard to the valuation of a favorable supplier contract, a seemingly similar contract between different entities may require considerable adjustments to the method presented as a result of factors specific to each of the contracting parties.

The following list presents some key issues that should be considered in the valuation and economic analysis of contract intangibles:

- The number and different types of contracts maintained by an entity.
- An entity's history regarding the renewals and the premature termination of contracts by category.
- The average service life of contracts by category (see Part 3, Remaining Useful Life Analysis).
- An entity's history regarding breach of contract claims and related litigation.

## BIBLIOGRAPHY

### Articles

"Acquired Work Force Not Amortizable, but Contracts Were." *Journal of Taxation*, December 1991, pp. 348–349.

Cava, Anita. "Trade Secrets and Covenants Not to Compete: Beware of Winning the Battle but Losing the War." *Journal of Small Business Management*, October 1990, pp. 99–103.

Dennis-Escoffier, Shirley. "Is a Solution to the Intangibles Problem on the Horizon?" *Journal of Corporate Accounting and Finance*, Winter 1992-1993, pp. 247–250.

King, Jerry G., and Paul D. Torres. "The Purchase of a Going Concern: Planning for Intangibles." *National Public Accountant*, March 1991, pp. 32–35.

Mullen, Maggie. "How to Value Intangibles." *Accountancy*, November 1993, pp. 92–94.

Rabe, James G. "Methods to Identify and Value Intangible Assets—The Appraisal Perspective." Public Utilities Workshop Proceedings, August 1995, pp. 115–118.

Reilly, Robert F., and Manoj P. Dandekar. "Contract-Related Intangible Asset Appraisal for Gas Processing Plants." *Journal of Property Tax Management*, Winter 1997, pp. 52–57.

### Periodicals

*Licensing Economics Review*, monthly. Published by AUS Consultants, 155 Gaither Drive, Moorestown, New Jersey 08057, (609) 234-1199.

*The Licensing Journal*, ten issues per year. Published by Aspen Law & Business, 1185 Avenue of the Americas, New York, New York 10036 (212) 597-0200.

# CHAPTER 17

# Copyright Intangible Assets

## DESCRIPTION OF COPYRIGHT INTANGIBLES

Copyright intangibles have many similar valuation and economic characteristics to trademark intangibles and patent intangibles. All of these intangibles are intellectual properties that are specifically protected by either federal or state statutes. The statutes provide very specific economic protection to (and, thereby, very specific development motivation for) the creative and innovative owners of these intangible assets.

First, we describe the factors that are relevant to the identification and valuation of copyright intangibles. Second, we discuss common valuation methods. Third, we review common internal and external data sources that are useful in the analysis of copyrights. Last, we present two fairly simple examples, using two different analytical methods, regarding the valuation of copyright intangibles.

In this section, we attempt to answer several straightforward but important questions regarding the identification and valuation of copyright intangibles:

1. What is a copyright and what economic advantage does it provide?
2. What are the social benefits of copyright protection?
3. What types of works are subject to—and not subject to—copyright protection?
4. What are the various categories of copyrights?
5. What is the legal term of copyright protection?
6. What is the economic impact of copyright registration?
7. What are the common forms of transfer of the copyright intangible?

## Economic Benefits Associated with Copyright Intangibles

As with all intellectual properties, a copyright is a special set of legal rights and protections afforded to the owner of the copyright. *The Copyright Permission and Libel Handbook* answers the question, "What is a copyright?" as follows:

> *Copyright* is a bundle of exclusive rights that provides authors of original literary, musical, dramatic, and artistic works with the sole right to authorize (or prohibit) the following uses of their copyrighted works:
>
> - To reproduce all or part of the work.
> - To make new (derivative) versions.
> - To distribute copies by selling, renting, leasing, or lending them.
> - To perform (e.g., recite, dance, or act) the work publicly.
> - To display the work publicly, directly or by means of film, TV, slides, or other device or process.
>
> The first three rights are violated when anyone copies, excerpts, adapts, or publishes a copyrighted work without permission. In rare cases, an author may dedicate a work to the public domain, but unless the facts prove otherwise, you should assume that all original works published less than 75 years ago in the United States are protected by copyright.[1]

---

1. Lloyd J. Jassin and Steven C. Schechter, *The Copyright Permission and Libel Handbook: A Step-by-Step Guide for Writers, Editors, and Publishers* (New York: John Wiley & Sons, 1998), pp. 10–11.

It is interesting that the above definition uses the term *author*. As we will see, and as mentioned in the definition, copyrights cover a variety of creative and artistic works, many of which are not literary. Under copyright law, the term *author* includes artists, composers, photographers, computer software programmers, and other individuals of creative talent, in addition to writers. Because copyrights are sometimes granted to businesses, an *author* can be a corporation or other nonindividual business form.

Basically, copyrights provide legal protection regarding the original expression of ideas. Copyrights do not protect the ideas themselves. In other words, an idea cannot be copyrighted. It is the *expression* of the idea—the way the idea is presented—that is copyrighted. A copyright gives the owner the exclusive right to (and prohibits all other parties the right to) perform, reproduce, alter, distribute, or display the original work of expression. In other words, a copyright allows the owner to—and prevents another party's ability to—profit from the original work.

There are some legal and economic similarities between copyrights and trade secrets. These similarities are described as follows in the book *Patent, Copyright & Trademark:*

> Copyright and trade secret laws sometimes protect the same kinds of information and sometimes are mutually exclusive of each other. Here are the salient points of how trade secret and copyright legal protections can work together under the Copyright Act of 1976:
>
> - Trade secret and copyright protection are both available for unpublished works as long as the idea (or ideas) in the work are sufficiently innovative to qualify as a trade secret (any confidential information that provides a business with a competitive advantage), and the information is kept confidential.
> - Trade secret and copyright protection may both be available for works that are distributed on a limited and restricted basis under a copyright licensing arrangement requiring the licensee (user) to recognize and maintain the trade secret aspects of the work. This dual protection is especially pertinent for the computer software business.
> - Trade secret protection is generally not available for software if the source code is made available to the public on an unrestricted basis through such means as listing it in a computer magazine or on a medium of distribution (for instance, a floppy disk).
> - Works that are widely distributed without specific licensing agreements will generally lose their trade secret status but may be entitled to copyright protection.
> - The deposit of a physical copy of the work that is being registered with the U.S. Copyright Office operates to disclose any trade secrets in the work unless the deposit in some way masks the material that comprises the trade secret. For instance, it is impossible to deposit samples of source code with major portions blacked out so that the parts of the code being maintained as a trade secret are not disclosed. There are several other methods for simultaneously registering a computer program and maintaining trade secrets. One common way is to withhold the source code altogether and deposit object code—which is impossible to understand when read in the U.S. Copyright Office.[2]

---

2. Stephen Elias, *Patent, Copyright & Trademark*, 2d ed. (Berkeley, CA: Nolo Press, 1997), pp. 24, 26.

Generally, the author of the original work owns the copyright. Again, with regard to copyrights, the creative person in any discipline (e.g., the artist, composer, musician, etc.) is called the author. There are three exceptions to this rule regarding copyright ownership:

1. If the copyrighted material is created by an employee in the normal course of employment, the copyright is owned by the employer. Such copyrighted materials are called *work made for hire.*

2. If the copyrighted material is commissioned by a patron and the patron and the author sign a work made for hire agreement, then the copyright is owned by the patron. An example of this is the commission of a family or executive portrait.

3. If the author sells the copyright, then the copyright is owned by the buyer, regardless of whether the buyer is an individual, corporation, or other form of entity.

As an important aside, all of the material in an original work does not have to be new. Some people believe that the compilations of the work of other authors are not subject to copyright protection. This is not correct. In fact, the compilation of existing work may be considered an original expression subject to copyright.

*The Copyright Permission and Libel Handbook* defines a compilation as follows:

> A compilation is a copyrightable work that is the result of bringing together or arranging preexisting material (regardless of whether that material is protected by copyright) in an original—or nonobvious—way. Copyright protection is based on the original selection, coordination, or arrangement of the material, not the copyright status of the preexisting material itself.
>
> There are two types of compilations: (1) fact compilations, and (2) collective works. A *fact compilation* is created by arranging public domain information, such as names and addresses or other data, in some minimally creative way. Common examples of fact compilations are electronic databases, directories, almanacs, price lists, and catalogs. . . .
>
> A *collective work* is a special type of compilation created by arranging copyrightable elements in a single work. Common examples are poetry anthologies, encyclopedias, newspapers, and magazines.[3]

Copyrights allow monopolistic exploitation benefits to the copyright owners. There is a general social benefit to providing these individual economic benefits. This general social benefit is explained as follows in *The Copyright Handbook:*

> The Founding Fathers recognized that everyone would benefit if creative people were encouraged to create new intellectual and artistic works. When the United States Constitution was written in 1787, the framers took care to include a copyright clause (Article I, Section 8) stating that "The Congress shall have Power . . . To promote the Progress of Science and useful Arts, by securing for limited times to Authors . . . the exclusive Right to their . . . writings."
>
> The primary purpose of copyright, then, is not to enrich authors; rather, it is to promote the progress of science and the useful arts—that is, human knowledge. To pursue this goal, copyright encourages authors in their cre-

---

3. Jassin and Schechter, *The Copyright Permission and Libel Handbook,* pp. 14–15.

ative efforts by giving them a mini-monopoly over their works—termed a copyright. But this monopoly is limited when it appears to conflict with the overriding public interest in encouraging creation of new intellectual and artistic works generally.[4]

## Categories of Materials Subject to Copyright

While there is only one legal form of a copyright, there are several categories of types of work that are subject to copyright protection:

1. Artistic, including paintings, sculptures, and drawings.
2. Choreographic works, including ballet.
3. Dramatic works, including plays operas.
4. Literary works, including books, manuscripts, newspapers, magazines, poetry, and advertisements.
5. Musical works, including compositions, song lyrics, and advertising jingles; musical works include the compositions themselves and the recordings of the works.
6. Pictorial and photographic, including cartoons, pictures, maps, prints, drawings, and photographs.
7. Video and audiovisual works, including movies and motion pictures, music videos, and television programs.

It is noteworthy that these works do not have to be published, recorded, or performed in order to be subject to copyright protection. For example, an unpublished and never performed play may still be protected by copyright.

## Term of Copyright Protection

Estimating the term of copyright protection is somewhat confusing because the law related to this point changed in 1976. The current U.S. Copyright Act was enacted in 1976 and covers works created after December 31, 1977. The previous U.S. Copyright Act was enacted in 1909 and covers works created up to December 31, 1977.

With consideration to these statutory changes, *The Copyright Handbook* summarizes the term of copyright protection as follows:

> Few things in this world last as long as copyright protection. Indeed, an author's work is likely to be long forgotten before her copyright in it expires. The copyright in works created after 1977 by individuals usually lasts for the life of the author plus an additional 50 years. The copyright in works created by employees for their employers lasts for 75 years from the date of publication, or 100 years from the date of creation, whichever occurs first.
>
> The copyright in works *created and published* before 1978 lasts for 75 years from the date of publication if they were (or are) timely renewed. . . . As a result, it may be necessary to do some legwork to find out if certain pre-1978 published works are still under copyright. The copyright in works created *but not published* before 1978 lasts at least until December 31, 2002.[5]

---

4. Stephen Fishman, *The Copyright Handbook: How to Protect & Use Written Works*, 4th ed. (Berkeley, CA: Nolo Press, 1997), p. 2/2.
5. Ibid., p. 2/5.

## Copyright Registration

Many people believe that it is necessary for an author to register the created work in order for it to be subject to copyright protection. True for patents and trademarks, this is not true with regard to copyrights.

Attorney Stephen Elias explains the process of how a copyright is created, even without the formal process of registration, in the book *Patent, Copyright & Trademark*. However, as Elias explains below, there are some reasons why authors may wish to formally register their work with the U.S. Copyright Office:

> A creative work is protected by copyright the moment the work assumes a tangible form—which in copyright circles is referred to as "fixed in a tangible medium of expression." Contrary to popular belief, providing a copyright notice and/or registering the work with the U.S. Copyright Office are not necessary to obtain basic copyright protection. But there are some steps that can be taken to enhance the creator's chances for success if he or she turns to the courts to enforce a copyright:
>
> - *Place a copyright notice on a published work.* The copyright notice, or "copyright bug" as it is sometimes called, commonly appears in this form: "© (year of publication) (author or other basic copyright owner)." By placing this notice on a work that is published (distributed to the public without restriction), the author prevents others from copying the work without permission and claiming that they did not know that the work was covered by copyright. This can be important if the author is forced to file a lawsuit to enforce the copyright, since it is much easier to recover significant money damages from a deliberate (as opposed to innocent) copyright infringer.
> - *Register works with the U.S. Copyright Office.* Timely registration within three months of the work's publication date—or before the infringement actually begins—makes it much easier to sue and recover from an infringer. Specifically, timely registration creates a legal presumption that the copyright is valid, and allows the copyright owner to recover up to $100,000 (and possibly attorney fees) without proving any actual monetary harm.[6]

## Transferability of Copyrights

Copyright rights can be, and often are, sold or transferred, in whole or in part. In fact, the transfer of copyright rights is the most common way for authors to commercialize their copyrighted work. As described in *Patent, Copyright & Trademark*, the two most common types of copyright transfers are assignments and licenses:

> When all copyright rights are transferred unconditionally, it is generally termed an "assignment." When only some of the rights associated with the copyright are transferred, it is known as a "license." An exclusive license exists when the right being licensed can only be exercised by the licensee, and no one else. If the license allows others to exercise the same rights being transferred in the license, the license is said to be non-exclusive.[7]

*The Copyright Permission and Libel Handbook* recognizes licensing as the most common form of the transfer of copyright rights. The authors some-

---

6. Elias, *Patent, Copyright & Trademark,* 2d ed., pp. 67–68.
7. Ibid., p. 69.

times refer to a license as splitting the bundle of legal (and economic) rights associated with copyrights. These split copyrights are described as follows:

> Any of the exclusive rights that make up a copyright can be subdivided, or split, into smaller and smaller pieces and then transferred to one or more parties. Just think about the way books are marketed. In addition to book rights, there are audio rights, foreign translation rights, performance rights, film adaptation rights, and even future technology rights. Each exclusive right is jealously guarded and, as a rule, sold piecemeal to one or more persons to maximize the author's return. The ways in which the copyright pie can be sliced is [are] almost endless.
>
> A copyright owner may limit any (or all) of the rights granted to another by (1) time, (2) geography, (3) language, or (4) type of use. Rights can even be split by market segment or channels of distribution (e.g., hardcover vs. paperback rights). Copyrights are infinitely divisible. Bear in mind that rights are seldom sold, licensed, or transferred in their totality or nonspecifically.[8]

## COMMON VALUATION METHODS

To a greater or lesser extent, all three valuation approaches are applicable to the analysis of copyrights. The cost approach is less commonly used than the income and market approaches. Because the copyright grants monopolistic rights to the owner, the cost approach is not always applicable to copyright analysis. However, if properly performed, it does have application in certain instances.

## Cost Approach

Both creation cost and recreation cost methods are sometimes used with regard to copyright analysis. Since copyrights represent a creative or artistic type of intellectual property, the term creation cost is used more commonly than the term replacement cost. Likewise, the term recreation cost is used more commonly than the term reproduction cost. Nonetheless, there are conceptual and procedural similarities between creation cost and replacement cost and between recreation cost and reproduction cost.

In all cost approach analyses of copyrights (and in all cost approach analyses of intangibles, in general), it is important for the analyst to consider developer's profit and entrepreneurial incentive in the analysis. In the case of intellectual properties (as a specific subset of intangible assets), developer's profit and entrepreneurial incentive can represent the largest components of value, as estimated by the cost approach.

The cost approach does have certain limitations with regard to the analysis of copyrights. Because of these limitations, the cost approach is often considered to provide a floor (or minimum) estimate of value as opposed to a ceiling (or maximum) estimate of value.

The application limitation of the cost approach relates to the fact that the copyright grants the holder exclusive or monopolistic rights with regard to the subject work. The cost approach is based on the economic principle of substitution. This principle tells us that an investor will typically pay no more for a property than the cost to purchase or construct a substi-

---

8. Jassin and Schechter, *The Copyright Permission and Libel Handbook*, p. 15.

tute property. However, it is not legally possible to purchase or construct a substitute property with regard to copyrights. Copyrights are only granted with regard to unique and original work. Therefore, the hypothetical investor who attempts to purchase or construct a substitute property is, by definition, guilty of copyright infringement.

Therefore, the willing buyer in a copyright market value transaction cannot legally recreate the subject copyright. The willing seller in a copyright market value transaction will typically not sell for less than his or her cost (i.e., investment) in the subject copyright. For this reason, the cost approach analysis often provides a minimum indication of value with regard to copyright.

## Market Approach

Market approach methods are commonly used with regard to copyright valuation and economic analyses. There is a fairly active market with regard to the fee simple sales of copyrights. This is true with regard to all the types of copyrighted materials (e.g., literary, musical, artistic, etc.) discussed here.

Often, however, the transactional (particularly pricing) details regarding copyright sales are not publicly disclosed. More importantly, it is often difficult for analysts to develop units of comparison in order to extract market-derived pricing multiples from these transactional data. In other words, it is difficult to convert pricing data regarding the actual sale of a copyright into a meaningful "per picture," "per lyric," or "per word" pricing multiple.

There is a very active market with regard to the license of all types of copyrighted materials. Therefore, royalty rate or similar license analysis is the most common market approach method.

Analysts sometimes have the problem of developing units of comparison if the selected empirical license agreements call for fixed periodic dollar payments, for example, $100,000 per year. However, many copyright license agreements are on either a royalty rate formula or a per-use formula. With regard to the royalty rate formula, the license agreement typically compensates the author by a percentage of the total revenues generated through the use of the copyrighted materials. With regard to the per-use formula, the license agreement typically compensates the author as a dollar amount for each time the copyrighted material is performed, displayed, or otherwise used.

## Income Approach

Income approach methods are very commonly used with regard to the valuation and economic analysis of copyrights. The various income approach methods typically involve some form of:

1. Incremental analysis—the estimation of the difference between a) the amount of income that an economic unit (e.g., business enterprise) would generate with the use of the subject copyright and b) the amount of income the same economic unit would generate without the use of the subject copyright.
2. Profit split analysis—the estimation of the total income that an economic unit (e.g., business enterprise) would generate from the

use of the subject copyright where the total income estimate is allocated (in part) to the subject copyright and (in part) to all of the other tangible and intangible assets that contribute to the generation of the total income estimate.

3. Royalty income analysis—the estimation of the total amount of royalty income that the author of the work could generate through the licensing of the copyrighted material.

With regard to all of these income approach analyses, the copyright income is projected over an estimate of the remaining useful life of the income stream. Typically, the remaining useful life estimate is much shorter than the (very long) period associated with the legal life of the copyright. Most often, the remaining useful life is an expectation of the period of popular and commercial acceptance of the book, movie, song, play, poem, or other copyrighted work. The present value of the income projection over this expected remaining useful life is an indication of the value of the copyright.

In particular, income approach methods are commonly used with regard to infringement and similar damages analyses. The question with regard to copyright (or other intellectual property) infringement is: Should the economic income stream subject to analysis be:

1. The economic income that the copyright owner lost (i.e., lost profits) as a result of infringement?
2. The economic income that the infringing party earned (i.e., found profits) as a result of the infringement?

The question can be answered from either a legal perspective or an economic perspective. From a legal perspective, the answer is based on statutory authority and judicial precedent that may be jurisdiction-specific. Accordingly, competent legal counsel should be consulted in that regard. From an economic perspective, the argument is often made that the copyright owner is due both measures of income—that is, the lost profits of the copyright owner and the found profits of the infringing party.

## DATA SOURCES

When cost approach methods are used in copyright analysis, internal data sources are most relevant. When market approach methods are used, external data sources are most relevant. When income approach methods are used, both external and internal data sources are relevant.

## Internal Data Sources

Analysts attempt to obtain the following information either from the original author of the copyrighted material or from the current owner of the copyrighted material. The information may be obtained through interviews or through the analysis of historical or prospective documents:

- The remaining legal life of the copyright (including date of the original copyright).
- The expected economic life of the copyright right.
- Historical customer (i.e., subscriber, advertiser, listener, or viewer) attrition patterns.

- A description of overlapping value with any other intangible assets.
- A listing of all of the copyright rights currently in use.
- Appropriate rates of return on all assets employed to generate copyright-related income.
- Forecast of the economic trends in the subject industry.
- Analysis of any key people associated with the creation or exploitation of the copyrighted material.
- Any restrictions to copyright exploitation rights.
- Association of the appropriate revenue and expense stream to the specific copyright.
- Forecast of future revenue associated with the subject copyright.
- Extent of investment required to commercialize or otherwise exploit the copyright.
- Nature of the competitive environment in which the copyright will be exploited.
- Availability of any income tax benefits associated with the amortization of the copyright value.
- Description or history of the development of the copyrighted material.
- All historical and prospective financial information regarding the commercialization of the copyright.
- Any specific market and industry studies available.
- Historical or projected unit sales, if available.
- Estimate of the cost of capital for the subject industry or company.
- Life cycle and operating data on comparative copyrights.
- Sale or license transaction pricing data regarding comparative copyrights.
- Strategic, marketing, and business plans regarding the historical and the planned commercialization of the subject copyright.

## External Data Sources

*Attorneys and Agents Registered to Practice before United States Patent and Trademark Offices.* U.S. Patent and Trademark Office. Washington, DC: U.S. Government Printing Office, published irregularly.

*Forms and Agreements on Intellectual Property and International Licensing.* Leslie W. Melville. Deerfield, IL: Clark Boardman Callaghan, 1979, three looseleaf volumes, supplemented periodically.

*Intellectual Property Law Review.* W. Bryan Forney. Deerfield, IL: Clark Boardman Callaghan, 1997, updated annually, covers patent, trademark, and copyright practices.

*International Licensing Directory.* Woldingham, Surrey, U.K.: A4 Publications, Ltd., published annually. Lists more than 4,000 licensors and agents in over 60 countries for over 10,000 films, television series, characters, personalities, trademarks, logos, and other properties available from licensors.

*Investing, Licensing, and Trading Conditions Abroad.* New York: Economist Intelligence Unit, published semiannually. Key laws, rules, and licensing provisions are explained for each of 60 countries. Information is provided on political conditions, markets, price policies, foreign exchange practices, labor, and export-import.

*Licensing Executives Society Membership Directory.* Alexandria, VA: Licensing Executives Society, published annually. Membership directory.

### On-line Databases

Legal Resource Index. Information Access Co., updated monthly. Broad coverage of law literature appearing in legal, business, and other periodicals from 1980 to the present.

LEXIS. LEXIS-NEXIS. The various LEXIS databases provide full text and indexing for a wide variety of legal cases, statutes, orders, and opinions regarding copyright issues.

WILSONLINE: Index to Legal Periodicals. H.W. Wilson Co., updated weekly. Broad coverage of law journals from 1981 to the present.

### Trade and Professional Societies

American Intellectual Property Law Association, 2001 Jefferson Davis Highway, Suite 203, Arlington, VA 22202, phone (703) 415-0780, fax (703) 415-0786.

International Intellectual Property Association, 1255 23rd Street NW, Suite 850, Washington, DC 20037, phone (202) 785-1814, fax (202) 833-3636.

International Licensing Industry and Merchandisers' Association, 350 Fifth Avenue, Suite 6210, New York, NY 10118, phone (212) 244-1944, fax (212) 563-6552. Promotes the legal protection of licensed properties.

Licensing Executives Society, 1800 Diagonal Road, Suite 280, Alexandria, VA 22314, phone (703) 836-3106, fax (703) 836-3107. Concerned with the transfer of copyrights and technology.

### VALUATION EXAMPLE

This section presents two examples. Example I is an illustration of a cost approach analysis. In Example I, we estimate the value of the copyright associated with a video training film. Example II is an illustration of an income approach analysis. In Example II, we estimate one measure of damages associated with the infringement of a copyrighted musical composition.

## Example I—Cost Approach Analysis

Willamette Management Associates ("Willamette") is a preeminent valuation consulting, economic analysis, and financial advisory firm. The firm's analysts are brilliant practitioners of applied microeconomics. However, some of the firm's analysts have not developed their more mundane skills. With this fact in mind, and in order to keep the Willamette offices properly illuminated, firm management produced a video training film entitled "How to Change a Light Bulb."

This training video proved to be remarkably successful at all of the Willamette offices. Willamette Capital ("Capital") is the specialized investment banking firm affiliate of Willamette. The Capital analysts were so impressed with the "Light Bulb" training film that they requested Willamette management to transfer the copyright on this original video work to Capital.

The objective of this analysis is to estimate a fair transfer price for the subject copyright, as of December 31, 1998, between two related corporate entities.

**Fact Set and Assumptions.** The subject copyright relates to the original video "How to Change a Light Bulb" ("Light Bulb"). The video is a safety and training film of approximately 18 minutes in length. The video was physically produced by Universal Training Corporation, an independent producer of institutional training films. The video represents the culmination of a safety research project conducted by Willamette with the objective of reducing job-related injuries and resulting workers' compensation costs.

The findings of an extensive safety research project conducted by Willamette are embodied within the video. The research project related to an injury and illness prevention program that was developed to educate and train approximately 100 Willamette analysts. The video represents the only training film at the time of its development produced exclusively for the promotion of safety and prevention of job-related injuries at economic consulting firms.

**Approaches and Methods.** Based on the availability of information and the relevant facts and circumstances in the instant case, we have concluded that the cost approach is appropriate for estimating the fair market value of the subject copyright. We base this conclusion upon the following:

- The video was developed specifically for the purpose of training and educating Willamette analysts in safety awareness and injury prevention. Accordingly, the intellectual content of the video represents the culmination of knowledge and experience in safety awareness particularly relevant to Willamette operations.
- The costs, including direct, indirect, and opportunity-related, of creating the subject copyrighted video are readily determinable and traceable.
- The video represents the only known safety film produced specifically for economic consulting firms. Based upon this fact, transactions in comparative copyrights were not available for our analysis; therefore, application of the market approach was impractical.
- The video was not created for income producing purposes (i.e., resale). Therefore, it would be difficult to apply the income approach.

Exhibit 17-1 summarizes our cost approach analysis. As presented in Exhibit 17-1, our analysis considers the following factors with respect to estimating the fair market value of the subject copyright:

- An estimate of the direct compensation, overhead, and benefits-related cost of the intellectual content of the video.
- The accumulation of all direct costs incurred during the actual production of the video.

The cost of the intellectual content of the video is best described as the cost resulting from the requisite accumulation of safety-related knowledge and experiences that would facilitate the conceptual development of the video. If faced with the task of replacing the video, Willamette would have to call upon individuals with considerable experience regarding both the operations of economic consulting firms and job-related accidents and potential safety hazards.

EXHIBIT 17-1

Cost Approach Analysis, Copyright Related to "How to Change a Light Bulb," as of December 31, 1998

| | Direct Compensation | Overhead/ Benefits | | |
|---|---|---|---|---|
| **INDIRECT COSTS:** | | | | |
| *Estimate of Cost of Intellectual Content:* | | | | |
| Total annual cost of experience-appropriate individual [a] | $ 76,750 | $ 34,538 | | |
| Percentage of annual cost devoted to safety area [b] | 40% | 40% | | |
| Estimated annual cost of intellectual development time | $ 30,700 | $ 13,815 | | |
| Estimated required intellectual development period (years) [c] | 10 | 10 | | |
| Estimated total intellectual content cost | $207,000 | $138,150 | | |
| Percentage of intellectual development cost applicable to the video [d] | 25% | 25% | | |
| Estimated cost of intellectual content | $ 76,750 | $ 34,538 | | |
| Total indirect costs (rounded) | | | $111,300 | |
| **DIRECT COSTS:** | | | | |
| *Cost of Subject Video Production:* | | | | |
| Universal Training Corporation script, video production, and quick reference guide drafting cost [e] | | $ 24,200 | | |
| Willamette personnel direct labor costs [f] | | $ 14,300 | | |
| Additional direct expenses [g] | | $ 2,400 | | |
| Total direct costs | | | $ 40,900 | |
| Initial development cost of "How to Change a Light Bulb" | | | | $152,200 |
| Obsolescence factor [h] | | | | 25% |
| Indicated transfer price of "How to Change a Light Bulb" copyright (rounded) | | | | $114,000 |

a. Salary estimate and related overhead and benefits (45% of salary) for 10-year experience level in relevant training and development rates.

b. Safety-related time commitments are based upon interview, and discussion, with the safety and training manager.

c. Based on the historical analysis of the director of employee relations and development employment history.

d. Estimated based upon the historical technological advancement of economic consulting firms during the 10-year conceptual development period.

e. Cost estimate provided by the copyright author.

f. Cost estimate provided by the copyright author.

g. Cost estimate provided by the copyright author.

h. Projects a 10-year life for the video based on the estimated conceptual development period and discussions with the director of employee relations and development. Approximately 2.5 years of the video's estimated useful life had elapsed as of the valuation date.

As summarized in Exhibit 17-1, we estimated the following indirect costs relating to the intellectual content of the video:

- **Annual cost of experience-appropriate individual.** An experience-appropriate individual is a Willamette employee considered to have the necessary knowledge and experience regarding safety-related issues required for the development of the concepts and objectives that are contained in the video.

  An employee with at least a 10-year history would possess the requisite experience, and would command direct compensation approximating $77,000 per year. In order to reflect the true total cost of this individual's conceptual development time, we have also included an estimate for overhead and benefits-related (i.e., health insurance, pension, etc.) costs. The overhead and benefits-related component of the conceptual development cost approximates $35,000 on an annual basis, or roughly 45 percent of annual compensation. Included within the overhead component are the direct costs of support staff personnel (e.g., administrative assistants and secretaries) and their work-related benefits (e.g., medical, dental, pension, etc.).

- **Percentage of annual cost devoted to safety area.** The percentage of annual cost devoted to the safety area represents that portion of the experience-appropriate employee's time devoted to safety-related issues. Discussions with the Willamette Safety and Training Manager indicated that approximately 30 percent to 50 percent of her activities were related to the safety function.

- **Estimated annual cost of intellectual development time.** Projecting a 40 percent safety-related annual time commitment translates into a total annual cost of the safety function of approximately $45,000, represented by $31,000 in direct compensation and $14,000 in overhead and benefits-related cost.

- **Estimated required intellectual development period.** Based upon a review of the employment history of the director of employee relations and development, a reasonable estimate for the intellectual development period is 10 years.

    In other words, the safety concepts relayed by the video would provide relevant guidance and training to Willamette employees approximately 10 years before technological innovation within the firm would render then-existing safety concepts and practices obsolete.

- **Estimated total intellectual content cost.** Projecting a 10-year intellectual development period and a total annual cost of the safety function of approximately $45,000 results in an estimated total intellectual cost of approximately $450,000. This total cost is represented by approximately $310,000 in direct compensation and $140,000 in overhead and benefits-related costs.

- **Percentage of intellectual development cost applicable to the video.** As discussed above, an estimated 40 percent time commitment to the safety function is required of an experience-appropriate employee. With regard to the video, however, redundant activities and technological advancements during the 10-year intellectual development period would render some of the experiences and knowledge irrelevant. Therefore, a portion of the attendant safety function costs are necessarily excludable from the total cost of intellectual development.

    Based upon discussions with the director of employee relations and development, and the estimated 10-year intellectual development period, we projected that 25 percent of total work commitment dedicated to the safety function would relate to concepts and information appropriately included within the content of the video.

- **Estimate of cost of intellectual content.** Projecting a 10-year intellectual development period, a total intellectual content cost approximating $450,000, and a 25 percent safety function relevance factor, the estimated cost of the intellectual content of the video is approximately $111,000. This cost is represented by approximately $77,000 in direct compensation and $35,000 in overhead and benefits-related costs.

As presented in Exhibit 17-1, total indirect costs associated with the development of the intellectual content of the video are $111,000. No allowance was included for developer's profit or entrepreneurial incentive.

The cost of actual video production represents all direct costs incurred to bring the video to its more tangible, and functionally effective, form. The following direct production costs were incurred:

- **Universal Training Corporation fee.** Willamette contracted with Universal Training Corporation for the actual production of the video. Universal Training Corporation wrote the original script for the video, produced the video, and drafted the initial quick reference guide relating to the video for a total fee of $24,200.

- **Willamette direct labor costs.** A task force comprised of eight Willamette employees was established to oversee the activities of Universal Training. The task force was also responsible for reviewing and editing all materials produced by Universal Training Corporation. We estimated total direct labor charges and attendant overhead and benefits costs relating to the efforts of the task force at $14,300.

- **Additional direct expenses.** Incidental direct expenses in the form of miscellaneous support items such as administrative costs, duplication, reproduction and postage charges, back belts, shirts, and voice-overs were incurred during the production of the video. The total cost of these incidental direct expenses was $2,400.

As presented in Exhibit 17-1, the total direct costs associated with the development of the tangible components of the video were $40,900.

Based upon the nature of the film, the only relevant obsolescence factor in this particular instance is that of technological obsolescence. In our opinion, the video would remain relevant for an estimated 10-year period. It is our opinion that a straight-line decay rate is reasonable regarding the technological relevance of the content of the video.

**Valuation Reconciliation and Value Conclusion.** Based upon the procedures described above, and in our opinion, an appropriate transfer price between Willamette and Capital for the subject copyright, as of December 31, 1998, is $114,000.

## Example II—Income Approach Analysis

Billy-Joe Bob is a composer of country and western music and lyrics. Last year, Billy-Joe composed the words and music to "I Love My Horse," a soulful country and western ballad. Billy-Bob Joe is also a composer of country music. Unbeknownst to Billy-Joe, Billy-Bob misappropriated the words and music to "Horse." Billy-Bob represented the copyrighted work as his own and signed a license agreement with Country Music Corporation (CMC), a record production and distribution company. CMC will pay Billy-Bob a license fee equal to 50 percent of the net income associated with the sale of all recordings of "Horse." In the license agreement, net income is defined as:

|       | Revenue for sales of all recordings |
|-------|-------------------------------------|
| Less: | Cost of goods sold (including payments to the recording talent) |
| Less: | Selling, general and administrative expenses |
| Equals: | Net income |

After "Horse" is recorded and released, Billy-Joe learns of Billy-Bob's treachery. Billy-Joe initiates a copyright infringement action against Billy-Bob. A relevant question in this infringement action is: What is the amount of damages to Billy-Joe? At the request of Billy-Joe's legal counsel, the objective of our analysis is to estimate how much Billy-Bob has been unjustly enriched as a result of this copyright infringement.

**Fact Set and Assumptions.** The date of the copyright infringement is May 31, 1998.

CMC management has prepared a projection of the income it expects to earn from the recording and distribution of "Horse." For country songs like "Horse," it is CMC's experience that the average life of consumer popularity is five years. Also, according to CMC historical experience, consumer demand for such music approximates an exponential decay curve function. Therefore, starting with the May 31, 1998, infringement date, the percent surviving in the demand curve will be less than 10 percent (i.e., immaterial) after the year 2009. This decay curve for consumer demand is based upon a five-year average life and an exponential decay function.

Based upon our analysis, we have concluded that the appropriate present value discount rate is 16 percent.

**Approaches and Methods.** Based upon the information available to us (i.e., the CMC business plan) and upon the objective of the analysis (i.e., to estimate the unjust enrichment of Billy-Bob), the income approach is the most applicable type of analysis.

Exhibit 17-2 summarizes the CMC business plan with regard to its recording and distribution of "Horse." The exhibit projects total revenue generation, gross profit (i.e., total revenues less cost of goods sold), and net income (i.e., gross profit less selling, general, and administrative expense). Based upon the CMC projection of net income over the expected life cycle of the production and distribution of "Horse" recordings, we have estimated the projected license payments to the subject copyright author.

Based upon a present value discount rate of 16 percent, Exhibit 17-2 presents the present value of the expected license payments to the author of the "Horse" copyright.

**Valuation Reconciliation and Value Conclusion.** Based upon the income approach analysis summarized in Exhibit 17-2, Billy-Bob has been unjustly enriched in the amount of $110,000 (rounded) due to his infringement of Billy-Joe's copyright. This amount represents one measure of damages due to Billy-Joe associated with the copyright infringement of the country and western song, "I Love My Horse."

### BIBLIOGRAPHY

## Articles

Bertolotti, Nick. "Valuing Intellectual Property." *Managing Intellectual Property,* February 1995, pp. 28–32.

DeSouza, Glenn. "Royalty Methods for Intellectual Property." *Business Economics,* April 1997, pp. 46–52.

Durchslag, Stephen P. "Courts Split on Parody Standards." *The National Law Journal,* October 7, 1991, pp. 23, 31–32.

Elgison, Martin J. "Capitalizing on the Financial Value of Patents, Trademarks, Copyrights, and Other Intellectual Property." *Corporate Cashflow,* November 1992, pp. 30–32.

Gordon, Wendy J. "On Owning Information: Intellectual Property and the Restitutionary Impulse." *Virginia Law Review,* February, 1992, pp. 149–281.

Hardin, Russell. "Valuing Intellectual Property." *Chicago-Kent Law Review,* Vol. 68, No. 2, 1993, pp. 659–675.

Hughes, Justin. "The Philosophy of Intellectual Property." *The Georgetown Law Journal,* December 1988, pp. 287–366.

Rechtin, Michael D. "Intellectual Property: Ticking Time Bombs for the Unwary Buyer." *Mergers & Acquisitions,* January/February 1992, pp. 28–31.

Reilly, Robert F. "How Buyers Value Intellectual Properties." *Mergers & Acquisitions,* January/February 1996, pp. 40–44.

———. "Valuing Intangible Assets and Intellectual Property." *Management Advisor,* Spring 1988, pp. 26–34.

Silverman, Noel L. "Valuation of Intellectual Property in Connection with the Estates of Authors and Other Creative Persons." *Proceedings of the 11th Annual Institute on Estate Planning.* Miami: University of Miami Law Center, 1977.

Stewart, Thomas A. "Your Company's Most Valuable Asset: Intellectual Capital." *Fortune,* Oct. 3, 1994, pp. 68–74.

Stueber, Thomas J., and David R. Fairbairn. "Lawful Photocopying: Where Fair Use Becomes Unfair." *The Journal of Technical Valuation,* January 1993, pp. 18–23.

———. "Trying to Grasp the Intangible." *Fortune,* Oct. 2, 1995, pp. 157–161.

**EXHIBIT 17-2**

Copyright Infringement Damages Analysis, Value of Expected Copyright License Payments, as of May 31, 1998

| Projection Period | Part Year 1998 | 1999 | 2000 | 2001 | 2002 | 2003 | 2004 | 2005 | 2006 | 2007 | 2008 | 2009 |
|---|---|---|---|---|---|---|---|---|---|---|---|---|
| Consumer demand decay function (average remaining life = 5 years) | 0.9433 | 0.8052 | 0.6592 | 0.5397 | 0.4419 | 0.3618 | 0.2962 | 0.2425 | 0.1986 | 0.1626 | 0.1331 | 0.1090 |
| Total recording and distribution | $622,600 | $956,570 | $822,330 | $706,930 | $607,720 | $522,440 | $449,120 | $386,100 | $331,920 | $285,290 | $245,290 | $210,870 |
| Gross profit margin | 14.99% | 17.01% | 17.75% | 18.40% | 18.84% | 18.50% | 18.50% | 18.50% | 18.50% | 18.50% | 18.50% | 18.50% |
| Gross profit (revenues less cost of goods sold) in dollars | $ 93,320 | $162,690 | $145,960 | $130,080 | $114,470 | $ 96,650 | $ 83,090 | $ 71,430 | $ 61,400 | $ 52,790 | $ 45,380 | $ 39,010 |
| Selling, general and administrative expenses | 88,020 | 122,940 | 96,470 | 76,570 | 60,680 | 48,300 | 38,810 | 31,470 | 25,770 | 21,100 | 17,270 | 14,140 |
| Net income | 5,300 | 39,760 | 49,490 | 53,510 | 53,790 | 48,350 | 44,280 | 39,950 | 35,640 | 31,690 | 28,110 | 24,870 |
| License payment to copyright author [a] | 2,650 | 19,880 | 24,745 | 26,760 | 26,895 | 24,175 | 22,140 | 19,975 | 17,820 | 15,845 | 14,055 | 12,435 |
| Present value discount factors at 16% discount rate | 0.9576 | 0.8515 | 0.7340 | 0.6328 | 0.5455 | 0.4703 | 0.4054 | 0.3495 | 0.3013 | 0.2597 | 0.2239 | 0.1930 |
| Discounted copyright license payments | 2,538 | 16,927 | 18,164 | 16,930 | 14,671 | 11,369 | 8,975 | 6,981 | 5,369 | 4,115 | 3,147 | 2,400 |
| Total present value of copyright license payments | $111,586 | | | | | | | | | | | |
| Value of expected copyright license payments (rounded) | $110,000 | | | | | | | | | | | |

a. Equals 50% of net income.

*Note:* Numbers may not total due to rounding.

# Books

Battersby, Gregory J., and Charles W. Grimes. *An Insider's Guide to Royalty Rates: A Comprehensive Survey of Royalty Rates and Licensed Products.* Stamford, CT: Kent Press, 1996.

Bertolotti, Nick. *Valuing Intellectual Property.* New York: John Wiley & Sons, 1994, supplemented annually.

Eckstrom, Lawrence J. *Eckstrom's Licensing Law Library.* Deerfield, IL: Clark Boardman Callaghan, periodic supplementation.

Elias, Stephen. *Patent, Copyright, and Trademark: A Desk Reference to Intellectual Property Law.* Berkeley, CA: Nolo Press, 1996.

Epstein, Michael A. *Modern Intellectual Property.* New York: Aspen Law & Business, 1995.

Fishman, Stephen. *The Copyright Handbook—How to Protect & Use Written Works,* 4th ed. Berkeley, CA: Nolo Press, 1997.

Jassin, Lloyd J., and Steven C. Schechter, *The Copyright Permission and Libel Handbook.* New York: John Wiley & Sons, 1998.

Kohn, Al, and Bob Kohn. *Kohn on Music Licensing.* New York: Aspen Law & Business, 1998.

Lee, Lewis C., and J. Scott Davidson. *Managing Intellectual Property Rights.* New York: John Wiley & Sons, 1993.

Parr, Russell L. *Intellectual Property Infringement Damages.* New York: John Wiley & Sons, 1993.

———. *Investing in Intangible Assets: Finding and Profiting from Hidden Corporate Value.* New York: John Wiley & Sons, 1991.

Simensky, Melvin, and Lanning G. Bryer. *The New Role of Intellectual Property in Commercial Transactions.* New York: John Wiley & Sons, 1994.

Smith, Gordon, and Russell Parr. *Valuation of Intellectual Property and Intangible Assets.* New York: John Wiley & Sons, 1994, supplemented annually.

Weil, Ben H., and Barbara F. Polansky. *Modern Copyright Fundamentals.* Information Today, Inc., 1989.

# Periodicals

*Intellectual Property Newsletter,* monthly. Published by Monitor Press, Suffolk House, Church Field Road, Sudbury, Suffolk CO10 6YA, U.K., (44) (0) 1787 378607.

*Intellectual Property Strategist,* monthly. Published by Leader Publications, 345 Park Avenue South, New York, NY 10010, (212) 545-6170.

*Intellectual Property Today,* monthly. Published by The Law Works, 1935 Plum Grove Road, Suite 158, Palatine, IL 60067, (847) 705-7194.

*International New Product Newsletter,* monthly. Published by INPN, Inc., Box 1146, Marblehead, MA 01945, (508) 741-0224.

*IP Litigator,* bimonthly. Published by Aspen Law & Business, 1185 Avenue of the Americas, New York, NY 10036, (212) 597-0200.

*Licensing Economics Review,* monthly. Published by AUS Consultants, 155 Gaither Drive, Moorestown, NJ 08057, (609) 234-1199.

*The Licensing Journal,* ten issues per year. Published by Aspen Law & Business, 1185 Avenue of the Americas, New York, NY 10036, (212) 597-0200.

*Licensing Law and Business Report,* bimonthly. Published by Clark Boardman Callaghan, 125 Hudson Street, New York, NY 10014, (212) 929-7500.

*The Licensing Letter,* monthly. Published by EPM Communications Inc., 488 East 18th Street, Brooklyn, NY 11226, (212) 941-0099.

*Mealey's Litigation Report: Intellectual Property,* semimonthly. Published by Mealey Publications, Inc., P. O. Box 446, Wayne, PA 19087-0446, (215) 688-6566.

# CHAPTER 18

# Customer Intangible Assets

## DESCRIPTION OF CUSTOMER INTANGIBLES

This chapter explores several topics that are essential to the valuation and economic analysis of customer-related intangible assets. First, we consider the various types of customer intangibles that analysts frequently encounter. We consider how these customer intangibles are, in fact, bought and sold when they are involved in commercial transactions. We consider what is needed in order for there to exist a customer intangible. We consider these intangible asset requirements from two perspectives: data requirements and relationship requirements.

Second, we explore the nature of customer relationships, including an examination of the various types of customer relationships that may be subject to analysis. In particular, we examine how established customer relations can represent a much more important and valuable asset than the mere listing of current customers or potential customers.

Third, we discuss the significant differences between customer intangibles and goodwill. The differences are both conceptual and practical. The question of why continued customer patronage isn't just another description of goodwill has confused government administrators, judges, intangible asset market participants (i.e., buyers and sellers), and even intangible asset analysts.

Fourth, we describe the specific application of the generally accepted intangible asset valuation approaches to customer intangibles. In particular, we focus on which approaches and which methods have the greatest applicability to customer intangible analysis. As is always the case, methodological applicability relates in good measure to the quantity and quality of data. Accordingly, we list the most common (and most useful) internal data sources and external data sources with regard to customer intangible analysis.

Last, we present an illustrative example of the valuation of a customer intangible. The example may be slightly more complex and more complete than those presented in other chapters. There are two reasons for this. First, the analysis of customer intangibles is a necessarily complex set of procedures (compared to the analysis of some other types of intangibles). Second, the analysis of customer intangibles may be a more commonly encountered task for analysts (compared to assignments involving other types of intangibles). This is because the analysis of customer intangibles is an essential component to the valuation of most going-concern businesses and professional practices. This is true whether the business or professional practice valuation is performed for transaction pricing, transaction structuring, financing, taxation, litigation, or other purposes.

The most common types of customer intangibles are listed here and then described briefly.

1. Patients or clients.
2. Product customers.
3. Service customers.
4. Financial service customers.
5. Product and service customers.

The analysis of patient or client customer relationships may be one of the most important elements in the valuation of professional practices. In fact, when they are bought and sold, many professional practices are priced based upon per patient or per client multiples. The transactions are often structured so that the buyer is paying the seller for patient charts and records or accounting workpaper files. However, what the acquiring practitioner is really buying is the expected ongoing and continuing relationships with the seller's patients or clients. This type of customer relationship includes physician patients, dentist patients, veterinarian patients, accounting clients, legal clients, and so forth.

Product customers are, of course, principally buying a product. They may also be buying a service, but it is a service in relationship to a product. An example is the recurring customers of an automobile dealership. The customer is obviously buying an automobile. However, as long as the manufacturer continues to produce a commercially acceptable product, the dealer can expect to sell a new automobile to its repeat customers every three or four years. The dealer will attempt to maintain the customer relationship between major purchases by providing high-quality maintenance or other services. Also, product customers do not have to involve big ticket purchases. For example, the regular customers of a bottled water delivery service are product customers. Likewise, the regular office or factory customers of a commercial coffee delivery service are product customers.

Service customers, on the other hand, are principally purchasing an intangible service as compared to a tangible product. Customers of barber shops and beauty parlors are examples of service customers, as are customers of 10-minute automotive oil change shops. Utility customers (gas, electric, water, landline telephone, cellular telephone, etc.) are also examples of service customers. Service customers are distinguished from patients and clients because there is not the same type of professional relationship between the service provider and the service receiver. We all hope that our barber is professional, and we know he or she is licensed as a barber by the state (or other authority). However, service recipients generally maintain a different level of professional relationship with their internist, their dentist, their lawyer, or their CPA.

Financial service customers are a special type of service customer. They are customers of organizations such as banks, savings and loans, finance companies, leasing companies, securities brokerage companies, and insurance companies. This type of customer intangible is distinguished from the general service customers for two reasons. First, the service involves, directly or indirectly, the transfer of money. Money is a *good* that most customers pay a great deal of attention to. Second, there is a substantial amount of empirical data available regarding sale transactions of financial service customers.

Product and service customers receive a product as part of their commercial transactions. However, the service element of the transaction is often what drives customer loyalty. Various types of subscribers provide examples of product and service customers. Cable television subscribers and daily newspaper subscribers may be considered product and service customers. In fact, they are receiving a product. However, the customer's perception of the provider is more as a service provider than a product provider.

Finally, it may be important to distinguish between consumer customers and reseller customers in the analysis of customer intangibles. The distinction does not represent another type of customer intangible. However, the distinction is important in understanding how the customer relates to the product or service provider. Consumers, of course, consume or otherwise use the product or service directly. Resellers are exemplified by retail stores, distributors, and wholesalers. From a manufacturer's perspective, retailers, wholesalers, and distributors are the direct customers. However, the direct customer relationship may also be influenced by the preferences (or whims) of—and the other competitive pressures on—the ultimate consumers of the manufacturer's products.

Customer intangibles of all types are frequently bought and sold in the commercial marketplace. In terms of how intangible asset analysts view these transactions, there are three ways in which customer intangibles are sold:

1. Separately from any other assets—that is, only the customer relationships are sold.
2. With certain other assets—for example, the customer relationships are sold with a noncompetition agreement granted by the seller.
3. As part of the sale of a going-concern business or professional practice—that is, as one of a bundle of tangible and intangible assets.

It is noteworthy that customer intangible assets can and do transact in any of these three ways. From the perspective of collecting empirical data from which to derive pricing multiples, the first type of transaction is the cleanest and most useful to the analyst. However, if all components of the transactions are disclosed, the second type of transaction may also be useful to the analyst in the process of extracting pricing multiples from empirical data. The third type of transaction is less useful to the analyst in terms of extracting empirically derived pricing multiples. However, the third type of transaction is no less useful to the analyst in proving the existence and value of customer intangibles. When customer intangibles sell as part of a bundle of assets, they are no less real and no less valuable than the real estate or tangible personal property assets that are also sold as part of the bundle.

In order for a customer intangible to exist as an intangible asset (rather than merely as a listing of actual or potential customers), two elements must exist:

1. There must, in fact, be a relationship between the customer and the vendor.
2. There must be data and documentation regarding the relationship that would be useful to the buyer (or the user) of the intangible.

These two elements are discussed below.

In order for a customer intangible to rise to the level of an intangible asset, there should a personal relationship between the customer and the vendor. The term personal relationship does not mean to imply a family or friendship relationship. It does mean to imply that the customer knows who the vendor is and the vendor knows who the customer is. The customer has a way to contact the vendor (e.g., a name, address, and telephone number). Likewise, the vendor has a way to contact the customer (e.g., a name, address, and telephone number). Because of this, there can be some form of two-way communication between the customer and the vendor.

As additional evidence of a customer relationship, there should be an identifiable income stream generated from the customer to the vendor. Furthermore, there should be a rationale (that could be based upon historical performance) for the continued expectation or renewal of that income stream. Finally, there should be a rationale (that could also be based upon historical performance) for an expected life or duration to that income stream.

In order for a customer intangible to rise to the level of an intangible asset, there should also be documentation of the historical customer relationship. The documentation is typically more than a simple listing. It is often in the form of customer or patient records, credit files, and charts. These records and charts typically contain the following information:

1. Customer name.
2. Customer identification number.
3. Customer address.
4. Customer telephone number.
5. Date customer first became a customer.
6. Historical purchase pattern.
7. Historical payment and credit pattern.
8. Amount of last purchase.
9. Date of last purchase.
10. Current account balance or outstanding receivable.

With this type of historical relationship and this type of data, an analyst can perform a rigorous valuation or economic analysis regarding the customer intangible. Perhaps more importantly, with this type of historical relationship and this type of data, a buyer can make an informed pricing and purchase decision regarding the customer intangible.

Customer relationships themselves can be related to several stages in the relationship between the customer and the vendor. These stages relate to: 1) the degree of imminence of the customer purchase transaction, and 2) the degree of formality (or contractual rigor) of the customer purchase transaction. Several of these stages are listed and described here:

1. Open purchase orders or backlog.
2. Customer contracts.
3. Customer contract renewals.
4. At-will customers.

With regard to the open purchase orders, the customer has already somehow communicated the purchase decision to the vendor. The vendor is in the process of fulfilling the purchase order. From the vendor's perspective, this customer order represents unfilled backlog. As soon as the product or service is delivered, the unfilled backlog will be fulfilled and the order will convert into an account receivable.

With regard to customer contracts, the vendor has entered into a contractual arrangement to provide goods or services. The contract may call for a certain volume of goods or services (e.g., the customer will buy one thousand units of product). Or, the contract may run for a stated term or period (e.g., the customer will buy data processing services for the next three years).

Contract renewals, as the name implies, relate to a renewal of the original customer contract. The contract renewal could be the first renewal or the hundredth renewal. The point is that the customer has made the conscious decision, at least once, to renew the commercial relationship with the vendor. From the vendor's perspective, this implies an expectation of continued contract renewals and continued customer business.

At-will customers have no formal contractual relationship with the vendor. They may have established a pattern of repeat commercial relationships. However, there is no contract (or even current purchase order) that will ensure the continued relationship. From the vendor's perspective, the continued relationship with at-will customers is a function of the historical pattern of purchase activities. While the customer relationship is subject to change due to current competitive pressures, the expected remaining useful life of the relationship can be estimated based upon an analysis of historical trends.

It is not uncommon for a single customer to represent several types of customer relationships. Let's consider an example. Gasguzzler Motors Corporation (GM) is a large automobile manufacturer. They purchase automobile brake components from Low Bid Parts Manufacturer, Inc. (Low Bid). GM is the largest customer of Low Bid and Low Bid has a valuable customer relationship with GM.

In fact, Low Bid may have several customer relationships with GM. Low Bid has a one-year contract with GM to produce all of the brake components for the new model of the flagship GM luxury car, the Boat. GM produces about 100,000 Boats a year. Currently, GM has placed an order on the contract with Low Bid to ship 10,000 brake components.

Based upon the average historical production life of an automobile model of eight years, Low Bid expects that GM will renew its annual purchase contract with them several more times. Given the fact that Low Bid has produced brake components for several other GM automobile models over the last 20 years, Low Bid expects to sell component parts to GM for some automobile model for at least another dozen years.

In this example, the Low Bid customer intangible regarding GM has four components:

1. The open purchase order of 10,000 units.
2. The remaining term of the current annual contract regarding the Boat model.
3. The expected contract renewals to continue to supply brake components over the remaining life of the production of the Boat model line.
4. The customer relationship related to the expectation of awarding additional supply contracts related to the production of new (post-Boat) automobile models.

An analysis of the Low Bid customer intangible asset should include consideration of all four of these customer relationship components.

Given the complexity of such multifaceted customer relationships, how can the analyst distinguish between customer intangible value and intangible value in the nature of goodwill? Historically, goodwill has been defined as expected customer patronage or as the likelihood that customers will continue to do business with a certain vendor. How is the customer intangible, then, distinguished from goodwill?

Goodwill generally relates to undefined, unknown, and uncertain customer patronage. In the identification and analysis of goodwill, there is no consideration of:

1. Who the individual customers are.
2. How the vendor can contact the customers.
3. How the purchaser of the goodwill can contact the customers.
4. How the owner of the goodwill can motivate continued customer business.
5. How the owner of the goodwill can motivate increased customer business.
6. What the expected income stream from individual (or groups of) customers is.
7. What the relative profitability of individual (or groups of) customers is.
8. What the expected remaining life of the customer income stream is.

The concept of goodwill generally (and simplistically) considers that some customers will return to the vendor and generate some amount of income for some period of time in the future. Goodwill is discussed in Chapter 20.

On the other hand, the analysis of the customer intangible specifically encompasses the consideration of each of the factors listed above. The value of the customer intangible relates to the mathematical expectation that specific customers will transact with the vendor and generate an expected amount of income over an expected period of time.

As an illustrative example, let's consider the McDonald's Corporation fast service restaurant business. McDonald's may be the classic example of continued customer patronage. Each day, millions of customers walk through the doors of McDonald's. The McDonald's restaurant business appears to possess some amount of goodwill. However, the business may not possess the customer intangible asset. While McDonald's Corporation may know a great deal about their customers collectively, they may not know very much about their customers individually. This type of relationship stands in contrast to the customer intangible owned by the local cable television franchise, for example. The cable TV franchise operator knows the name, address, telephone number, spending habits, viewing habits, basic service versus premium service preferences, pay-for-TV purchases, and payment history of each of its subscribers. While McDonald's may possess an impressive amount of goodwill (in the nature of continued customer patronage), the cable TV franchise operator owns a customer intangible asset.

## COMMON VALUATION METHODS

As with most types of intangible assets, all three valuation approaches may be used in the analysis of customer intangibles, but some valuation approaches (and some valuation methods) are more commonly used than others. We first discuss cost approach methods, then market approach methods, then income approach methods. Coincidentally, cost approach methods are the least commonly used in the analysis of customer intangibles; market approach methods are used with regard to certain types of customer intangibles; and, income approach methods are most commonly used in the analysis of customer intangibles.

# Cost Approach

Although least commonly used in practice, cost approach methods are applicable to the analysis of customer intangibles when it is possible for the analyst to collect all of the costs associated with the development and maintenance of the subject customer relationships. However, this is usually not possible because most businesses simply do not keep track of all of the costs associated with the development and maintenance of customer relationships.

The relevant costs that would be considered in a cost approach analysis include the following:

**1.** Costs to obtain the subject customers. This includes all the historical costs associated with calling on, advertising to, soliciting, mailing to, and otherwise communicating with potential customers. In some industries, it may take 10 solicitations before a prospect becomes a customer; in that case, the cost of all 10 solicitations should be considered. In other industries, the vendor may have to solicit 100 prospects before one prospect becomes a customer; in that case, the cost of all 100 solicitations should be considered (because they represent a necessary cost to obtain one customer).

**2.** Costs to maintain the current customers over their age to date. This includes all the costs of calling on, advertising to, entertaining, and so on, the current customers after the time that they first became customers. It also includes the costs of promotion, discounting, dealing, or other concessions made to current customers to keep them as customers.

**3.** Costs to maintain customer files and records. This includes the bookkeeping and administrative costs associated with maintaining customer sales records, credit records, receivables and payment records, and so on, over the entire duration of each customer relationship.

**4.** Opportunity costs. This includes the cost of lost income during the time that was required to create (or recreate) the current customer relationships, as compared to the income that would be earned if, for example, an established customer intangible were purchased from a competitor. This is an often overlooked but very important component of the cost approach analysis of customer intangibles. For example, let's assume that it would take 18 months for a business to recreate its current customer relationships. During that recreation period, the subject company would generate little or no income from the subject customer intangible. However, if the subject business purchased established customer relationships from a competitor, it would earn $10 million of income during that 18-month period. Then, the opportunity cost of creating the subject customer relationships would be $10 million. The opportunity cost procedure is one way to quantify the entrepreneurial incentive component in the cost approach analysis.

If all of the described costs can be identified and quantified, then the cost approach can be used in the customer intangible analysis. Practically, most businesses do not record these types of costs in the normal course of their business operations. Because of the practical data constraints, the cost approach is not frequently used in the valuation and economic analysis of customer intangibles.

# Market Approach

Sales of discrete customer intangibles (separate from other tangible and intangible assets) do occur fairly frequently in certain industries. These transactions provide a basis for the application of the market approach. The practical restriction on the use of the market approach does not relate to a paucity of transactions involving the sale of customer intangibles, but from a paucity of reliable transactional data regarding these sales. More often than not, analysts can find information regarding the occurrence of customer intangible sales. However, more often than not, it is very difficult to find reliable and verifiable information regarding the price paid for the sales and the financial or operational statistics regarding the customer intangibles needed to derive pricing multiples.

The sale of customer intangibles occurs frequently with regard to professional practices. For example, such sales often occur when a professional practitioner (e.g., physician, dentist, lawyer, CPA) decides to retire. The retiring professional practitioner sells the customer intangible (e.g., client or patient files representing the ongoing customer relationship) to a professional down the street. For example, a competing dentist may not want to buy the equipment, supplies, or receivables of the retiring dentist but may want to buy the recurring dental patient relationships.

The sale of customer intangibles also occurs frequently in other service businesses. Again, these sales often relate to a decision by one service business to close up shop or to otherwise stop servicing a certain location or territory. Examples include the sale of bottled water distribution customers, bottled gas distribution customers, and so forth. In these cases, the buyer is typically a competing service provider.

In the financial services industry, there continue to be numerous sales of customer intangibles. The financial services industry includes such organizations as banks, savings institutions, leasing companies, finance companies, securities companies, and insurance companies. The types of customer intangibles that are frequently bought and sold include:

1. Credit card accounts and customer relationships.
2. Automobile loan accounts and customer relationships.
3. Mortgage servicing rights.
4. Leasing customers.
5. Insurance in force.

In most cases, the selling financial institution has decided to get out of a certain business line (e.g., the consumer credit card business) and the buying financial institution has decided to expand its operations in that business line.

When adequate, reliable transactional data are available, analysts may use a standard application of the market approach procedures. The only procedure specific to this intangible asset type is the selection of the appropriate units of comparison. The units of comparison, of course, are used to develop pricing multiples. Some units of comparison that may be particularly relevant to customer intangibles include: price per dollar of revenue multiples, price per customer (or client or patient) multiples, and percentage premium paid over the current customer account balance. An example of the last unit of comparison is the purchase of a credit card portfolio for 140 percent of the outstanding account balance. In that example, the 40 percent premium is attributable to the value of the expected ongoing customer relations with the subject credit card holders.

# Income Approach

The income approach is most commonly used with respect to the analysis of customer intangibles. Many income approach methods are applicable to the analysis of customer intangibles. However, all of these methods have a common objective: to estimate the present value of the future income expected to be generated from the customer relationship over the expected remaining useful life of that relationship.

Applicable income approach methods include both yield capitalization and direct capitalization. For either category of method, the analyst has to decide whether to value every customer relationship individually, or the entire portfolio of customer relationships collectively. If the analysis is performed correctly (i.e., if all valuation variables are consistent), the analyst will reach the same conclusion whether customers are valued individually or the customer portfolio is valued collectively. In other words, the total value of the customer intangible should equal the sum of the values of the individual customer relationships. Therefore, the decision as to individual valuation versus collective valuation is more a reporting presentation decision than an analytical decision.

When direct capitalization methods are used, the income generated by the customer intangible is capitalized over the average remaining life of the customer relationships. When yield capitalization methods are used, the income generated by the customer intangible may be presently valued over the average remaining life of the customer relationships or over the total decay curve that represents the annual attrition of the customer relationships. Depending upon the shape of the remaining useful life decay curve, these two analytical procedures will produce different valuation results. If adequate data are available to project the entire customer intangible remaining useful life decay curve, this procedure is preferred from a conceptual correctness perspective.

Another important issue with regard to the income approach is the selection of the appropriate discount rate or capitalization rate. The following questions should be considered:

1. Should the discount or capitalization rate be specific to the buyer, to the seller, or to the market in general?
2. Should the discount or capitalization rate be specific to the overall business enterprise in which the customer intangible will operate or to the customer intangible itself?

The answer to the first question depends upon the objective of the analysis. Is the analyst attempting to quantify a value to the buyer, a value to the seller, or a market value? The answer to the second question relates to both the purpose of the analysis and how the analyst believes that the subject customer intangible will actually transact (i.e., be sold as part of a business or be sold separately from other business assets).

## DATA SOURCES

With regard to the cost and income approaches, internal data sources typically provide the most meaningful data to the analyst. With regard to the market approach, external data sources typically provide the most meaningful data to the analyst. Ideally, the analyst has both reliable internal data and reliable external data available for consideration in the valuation or economic analysis. However, with regard to customer intangibles, that is not always the case.

## Internal Data Sources

The analyst rarely finds complete data with regard to the costs of developing and maintaining the customer intangible in the typical business historical accounting records because business organizations simply do not capture and record these costs in their accounting systems. Therefore, most of the data needed to perform a cost approach analysis is obtained through interviews. Typically, marketing and sales executives can provide information with regard to the process of developing and maintaining the subject customer relationships. Typically, interviews with financial and accounting executives are needed to quantify the costs associated with conducting the process delineated by the marketing and sales executives.

With regard to the application of any income approach method, the analyst ideally collects and analyzes internal data regarding:

1. The age (including start date) of each individual current customer relationship.
2. The life (including start and stop dates) of each individual terminated customer relationship.
3. The revenue generated by each customer relationship.
4. The cost of servicing (either goods or products) each customer.
5. The accounting profit generated by each customer relationship.
6. The nature and value of other assets that are also used or used up in the production of customer revenue.
7. The relationship of capital expenditures to customer revenue.
8. The relationship of net working capital to customer revenue.
9. The cost of capital associated with the subject intangible.
10. Any planned changes in the operation of the subject intangible that will affect the historical cost–volume–profit relationships.

Of course, the analyst collects and analyzes as much historical data as possible and, because all income approach analyses are intrinsically prospective, the analyst collects and analyzes as much prospective data as possible. This includes whatever plans, budgets, forecasts, and projections are available that include the "as of" date of the analysis.

## External Data Sources

The analyst searches external data sources principally to obtain information regarding actual sales (or listings) of customer intangibles. This empirical pricing information is then used in the market approach analysis. There are relatively few consistent and organized data sources regarding sale transactions of customer intangibles. However, publications in certain industries periodically report on transactions involving intangibles in that industry. Some of these sources are listed here.

> *ABA Banking Journal.* American Bankers Association. New York: Simmons Boardman Publishing Corp., monthly. Covers commercial lending and retail banking news and events.

*America's Community Bankers.* Washington: America's Community Bankers, monthly. Covers operations, management, and developments of community savings and loan banks.

*Banking Information Source* (on-line), UMI: A Bell & Howell Co. Provides indexing and abstracting of periodical and other literature from 1982 to date, with weekly updates. It covers the financial services industry, including banks, savings institutions, investment houses, credit unions, insurance companies, and real estate organizations.

*Broadcasting & Cable* (formerly *Broadcasting*). Washington: Cahners Publishing Co., weekly. Provides coverage of the cable industry's corporate and industry news.

*Commercial Lending Newsletter.* Philadelphia: Robert Morris Associates, monthly. Focuses on the latest commercial lending trends and industry news.

*Communications Daily: The Authoritative News Service of Electronic Communications.* Washington: Warren Publishing, Inc., daily. Covers telecommunications, including the telephone industry, broadcasting, cable TV, satellites, data communications, and electronic publishing. Features corporate and industry news.

*Insurance Advocate.* Boulder, CO: Roberts Publishing Corp., weekly. News and features on all aspects of insurance business for industry professionals.

*Investment Dealers' Digest.* New York: Investment Dealers' Digest, weekly. Includes articles on brokerage firms and industry-related issues.

*Wireless and Cable Voice Services: Forecasts and Competitive Impacts,* 1995. Austin, TX: Technology Futures, Inc., sponsored by the Telecommunication Technology Forecasting Group. Includes forecast data for prices, demand, and competitive factors. Similar publications are available for other telecommunications industry sectors.

*Wireless Week.* New York: Chilton Co., weekly. Covers news of cellular telephones, mobile radios, communications, satellites, microwave transmission, and the wireless industry in general.

## VALUATION EXAMPLE

Let's consider the valuation of a pharmacy prescription drug file customer intangible. Live Long and Prosper (LLP) is a local pharmacy chain. LLP offers the full range of retail health care products. They also offer prescription pharmacy services. For various reasons, the management of LLP has made the strategic decision to stop offering prescription pharmacy services. In the future, they intend to focus all their business activities on nonprescription health care and general merchandise products.

LLP management believes that its prescription drug files and associated customer relationships represent a valuable intangible asset. There are several competing pharmacy chains in town. LLP management believes that any one of these competitors would be interested in buying the customer intangible from LLP. The valuation date in this example is December 31, 1997.

The assignment is to estimate the market value of the prescription drug files and customer relationships so that LLP management can conduct informed sale negotiations with several potential pharmacy chain buyers.

After careful consideration of the purpose and objective of the analysis and the quantity and quality of available data, we have decided to use the income approach to intangible asset valuation. In particular, we will use the yield capitalization method, and we will use net cash flow as the appropriate measure of economic income. Accordingly, this example will illustrate an application of the discounted net cash flow valuation method.

## Fact Set and Assumptions

Prescription drug files represent an expectancy of continued business due to the unique nature of this intangible asset. Unlike the purchase of over-the-counter pharmaceutical products, a direct and personal relationship is established between a pharmacy and the prescription drug customer.

First, the pharmacy maintains fairly detailed records regarding each customer. These records include: name, address, telephone number, physician's name, physician's telephone number, historical purchases of current prescriptions, historical purchases of other prescriptions, number of remaining permissible refills on current prescriptions, and so on.

Second, prescription customers exhibit a tendency to return to the same pharmacy. One reason for this is customer expediency. The pharmacist retains the actual prescription. In order for prescription customers to change pharmacies, they have to return to the original pharmacy to physically retrieve the prescription document. Since this process is inconvenient, customers generally return to the original pharmacy, at least during the term of the prescription refills. Another reason is that pharmacists usually check for harmful drug interactions for customers who have multiple prescriptions. Accordingly, it is in the customers' best health interests to conduct all their prescription drug business at the same pharmacy (i.e., so that the multiple prescription records are all at the same pharmacy).

Accordingly, the prescription drug file list represents a predictable stream of future business from the current prescription customers. This future business translates into future economic income that can be directly associated with the prescription drug files and associated customer list.

However, as with all customer relationships, prescription drug customer relationships have a finite life. Prescription drug customers move, they become dissatisfied with the current pharmacist, they become cured (i.e., no longer in need of medication) and, eventually, they die. A rigorous analysis of historical placements and retirements of customer accounts (and quantification of the associated customer turnover rates) allows us to predict the average expected remaining life of the acquired prescription drug customer relationships with a high degree of certainty.

As will be described algebraically in the next section, there are five principal steps in our valuation model of the subject customer intangible. Each step encompasses several key input variables.

**1.** Actual customer revenues. We use the total account revenues for the subject customer account over a 12-month period. The annual revenue return eliminates seasonality and cyclicality factors. The three-year average revenue for each customer was calculated using revenue from 1995, 1996, and 1997. We did not, however, annualize customer revenues for the first year of the customer relationship.

2. Customer revenue growth rate. This is the expected average growth rate (or shrinkage rate) in the subject customer account balance over its expected remaining life. The growth rate percentage is determined by analyzing historical account revenues, by interviews with the management of the subject pharmacy chain, and by consideration of published regional and national historical and projected data, specifically, the Consumer Price Index Prescription Drugs historical trend factors. The growth rates applied are as follows:

| 1998–2002 | 8% |
| 2003 and thereafter | 5% |

3. Cost of sales. This expense is equal to 65 percent of sales. We determined the cost of sales through discussions with management and an analysis of historical income statements.

4. General and administrative expense. The expense is equal to 6 percent of sales. The expense includes salary and benefits, computer charges, and other administrative expenses. General and administrative expenses were determined through discussions with management and an analysis of historical income statements.

5. Return on associated fixed assets and net working capital. The valuation model charges a return on associated fixed asset investments and working capital as an expense against the cash flow generation of the customer account. This model incorporates the fair market value of the tangible and intangible assets as of December 31, 1997. A change in value, either an increase or decrease, of any of the subject assets results in a different return and a different fair market value for the prescription drug file customer intangible.

6. Present value interest factor. The present value interest factor is a function of the present value discount rate. In this example, the present value discount rate is the subject industry weighted average cost of capital. To determine the weighted average cost of capital, we analyzed the retail pharmacy industry actual capital structure and cost of capital components (including all forms of permanent debt and equity financing). The discount rate selected is unique to the subject industry and represents a weighted average, risk-adjusted rate of return to all stakeholders (i.e., debt holders and equity holders). We used a 14 percent present value discount rate in our analysis of the subject customer intangible.

## Approaches and Methods

The market value of the subject customer intangible was estimated by calculating the present value of the after-tax net cash flow attributed to each individual customer over that customer's expected remaining life. While this concept is easy to describe in theory, it is complex to implement in practice.

Several key input variables are encompassed in our valuation model for the subject customer intangible. The quantitative relationships that define our prescription drug file customer relationships valuation model are described algebraically as follows:

***Step One***

This year's actual prescription drug file customer revenues
× <u>Growth (shrinkage) rate in revenues</u>
= Next year's expected customer revenues

***Step Two***

Expected customer revenues
− Cost of sales
− General and administrative expenses
− <u>Amortization expense related to the intangible customer value</u>
= Net income before tax from customer
× <u>1 − Effective income tax rate for subject customer</u>
= Net income after tax from customer

***Step Three***

Net income after tax from customer
+ Amortization expense related to the intangible customer value
− <u>Capital charge related to a return on associated fixed assets and working capital</u>
= Net cash flow from customer

***Step Four***

Net cash flow from customer
× <u>Present value interest factor</u>
= Present value of net cash flow from customer

***Step Five***

<u>Sum of present value of net cash flow for each year in expected remaining life of customer account</u>
= Market value of prescription drug file customer relationships

This section presents the quantitative mechanics associated with the useful life analysis of the subject prescription drug file customer relationships.

The theory of survivor curves was developed at Iowa State University in the early 1900s. Survivor curves are used to predict the mortality or decay of a group of similar data points as the data points age. Survivor curve theory is similar to the mortality table theory used by actuaries to estimate the human life span. This topic is discussed in Chapter 11.

A lifing study is the process of predicting the behavior of a group of data points by fitting a test group of the data points to various survivor curves. Thus, by selecting the survivor curve that best describes the decay of the test group in the past, the future behavior of each data point in the group can be estimated.

Exhibit 18-1 is a graphical presentation of a typical survivor curve. The $x$ axis represents the age of the data and the $y$ axis represents the percent of the original data points that are still surviving at a given age. For example, at age zero, 100 percent of the group is surviving. As time passes, members of the group retire. Therefore, the percent (of the group) surviving decreases. This creates the downward sloping characteristic of the survivor curve. A survivor curve can be any mathematical function of age that can accurately (and logically) depict the test group's mortality.

The age at which 50 percent of the original group still survives is defined as the group's average life. That is, a new group member who starts or has started at any given time would have an expected life of the average life of the group. In reality, group members are live (active) across a wide range of possible time units. However, the expected live time (i.e., the mean live time) is the average life for the group.

A Typical Survivor Curve

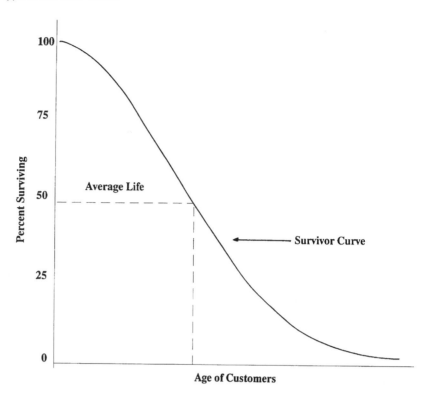

There are three basic types of survivor curves: left modal, symmetric, and right modal. A left modal survivor curve depicts a group that retires at a faster rate before the average life is reached and at a slower rate after the average life is reached. In other words, if the left modal survivor curve accurately predicts a group's past behavior, it could be interpreted as "The group's older members are more loyal than its younger members and tend to have a longer relative probable life."

A symmetrical survivor curve predicts that a group will retire at a similar age at any given relative age on either side of the group's average life.

A right modal survivor curve is the opposite of the left modal survivor curve. Customers that have reached the group's average life tend to decay faster than a customer that has yet to reach average life.

An example of a left modal survivor tendency is the survival of an integrated computer chip. An average computer chip usually malfunctions early or, after it reaches a certain age, will function properly forever!

Tangible personal and real estate improvements generally display right modal survivor tendencies. For example, new machinery seldom breaks down in the first few years of operation. However, after a certain age, wear and tear quickly retire the machinery.

Exhibit 18-2 illustrates the curve structure of left modal, symmetrical, and right modal survivors plotted on the same graph.

The ultimate purpose of a remaining useful life analysis is to assign a specific remaining useful life to each data point (i.e., customer) within the group. Remaining life is defined as the amount of time before a data point

The Three Basic Survivor Curves

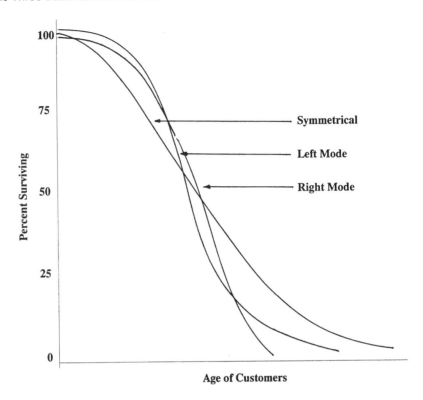

(i.e., the customer) will retire (and no further economic benefit can be derived from it). An example of how remaining useful life could be interpreted is to state that "Savings account customer number 123456 will remain a depositor for two and a half more years," where two and a half years is the remaining life of customer 123456.

The key to estimating remaining useful life is to calculate the probable life for each customer within the group. Probable life is the age at which a customer would retire, given that it has already reached its current age. By subtracting the current age of a customer from its probable life, the remaining life can be obtained. That is, remaining life *equals* probable life *minus* current age.

The mathematical definition of the probable life of a given customer is the area under the survivor curve (i.e., using calculus, the integral) to the right of the current age of the customer. Every survivor curve has a corresponding probable life curve. For any customer that is *x* age units old, this relationship can be summarized in the form:

$$Probable\ life = \int_{\chi}^{\infty} Survivor\ curve$$

Exhibit 18-3 illustrates the relationship between percent surviving and probable life. The probable life of a customer at age *x* is within the shaded area.

By solving for probable life in the equation given for all possible ages, a probable life curve can be constructed. A typical survivor curve and its corresponding probable life curve are illustrated in Exhibit 18-4.

EXHIBIT 18-3

The Probable Life Integral

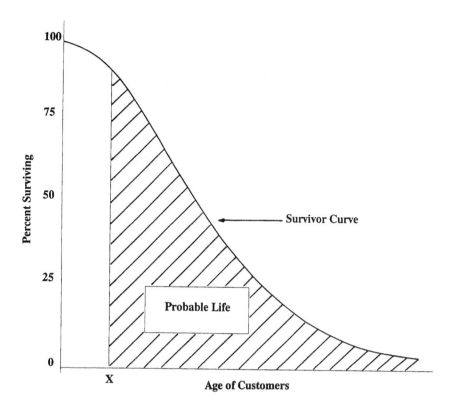

EXHIBIT 18-4

A Typical Probable Life Curve

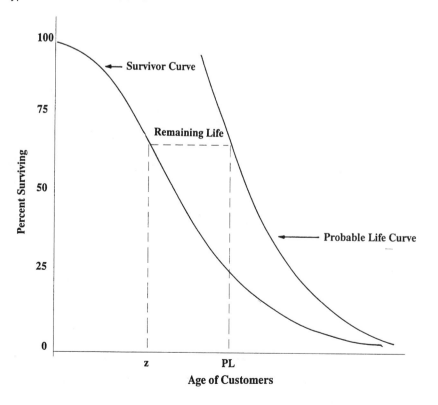

To determine the probable life of a data point that is $z$ age units old using Exhibit 18-4, first locate $z$ age units on the $x$ axis and find the corresponding point on the survivor curve. Then, draw a ray parallel to the $x$ axis to the point of intersection with the probable life curve. The probable life is obtained by moving down the $y$ axis to the age units on the $x$ axis. Exhibit 18-4 illustrates the probable life (point PL) of a data point that is $z$ age units old.

The remaining life of the data point can be calculated by using the formula presented earlier.

There are several sets or series of survivor curve mathematical functions that are generally used in probable life analyses. The survivor curve mathematical functions include: 1) Iowa State University modified Pearson-type frequency functions, 2) Weibull distribution functions, 3) Gompertz-Makeham distribution functions, 4) H-curves (a single parametic series of curves derived by truncating a normal probability distribution), and 5) polynomial (least squares regression fitting) functions. All these mathematical functions may be considered when selecting the best-fitting survivor curve relative to a specific set of data.

In summary, by selecting a survivor curve that accurately depicts the past decay performance of a group of data, the future decay can be predicted from which the remaining life of each data point within the group can be calculated.

The procedure used to select an appropriate survivor curve is typically called curve fitting. The basic concept is to find the survivor curve that best depicts (fits) the test group's prior decay. The following steps are involved in selecting a best fit survivor curve:

**1.** Selection of a retired data sample population: A statistically valid random selection of the most recent retired data points is generated. The key information needed for the retired data sample is the start date and the retirement date of each retired data point. This information is usually obtained from a computer database, client files, or discussions with the client.

**2.** Selection of a live (active) data sample population: A statistically valid random selection of all live data points of the valuation data is generated. The key information needed for the live data sample is the start date and the valuation units. A valuation unit represents a quantifiable economic benefit that is obtained from the live data point. For example, in a lifing study of a customer list, the valuation units might be annual gross profit received from each customer's purchases. Again, this information is usually gathered from a computer database, client files, or through discussions with the client.

**3.** Creation of the survivor table: A survivor table is created by using the random samples of retired and live data points described above. A survivor table shows the percent surviving of the sample group at a given age. Exhibit 18-5 presents a typical survivor table. The percent surviving at a given age $x$ is:

$$\begin{matrix} Percent\ surviving \\ at\ age\ x \end{matrix} = \begin{bmatrix} Percent\ surviving \\ at\ age\ (x-1) \end{bmatrix} \times \begin{bmatrix} 1 - Retirement\ rate \\ at\ age\ (x) \end{bmatrix}$$

The retirement rate at any age is the ratio of data points that retired during the age divided by the data points exposed to retirement at the beginning of the age interval. The number of data points exposed to retirement is simply the number of live data points at the beginning of the age interval.

PART 5   Analysis of Specific Types of Intangible Assets

For example, assume that:

At age interval 5, percent surviving = 78.448%

At age interval 5, retirement rate = 4.268%

Percent surviving at age interval 6 is: (78.448%) × (1 − 4.268%) = 75.099%

**4.** Plotting of the survivor table: By selecting the pairs of coordinates (x, y), where x is the age (the first column in Exhibit 18-5) and y is the percent surviving (the last column in Exhibit 18-5), an actual data curve is plotted. This is illustrated by the P markings on Exhibit 18-6.

**5.** Selection of best fit curve: All predetermined survivor curves are plotted on the same graph as the actual (survivor table) data described above. These curves are called the ideal curves. The difference between the actual percent surviving (the survivor table) and the ideal percent surviving is the fitting error at the age being examined. By summing all the squares of the fitting errors for a curve, a ranking factor describing the fit of the curve can be ascertained. The errors are squared both to remove the canceling effect of negative fitting errors and to put more emphasis on large errors. As a formula, the curve fitting procedure described above is:

$$Ranking\ factor = \sum_{i=1}^{n} \begin{bmatrix} Survivor\ table\ (age\ i) \\ (minus) \\ Survivor\ curve\ (age\ i) \end{bmatrix}^2$$

where n is the number of entries in the survivor table selected for the fitting. The method described above is called a stub period fitting and is illustrated in Exhibit 18-6.

**EXHIBIT 18-5**

Example for Deriving Percent Surviving Table

| Periodic Age Interval | Exposed to Retirement Beginning of Interval | Retired During Interval | Retirement Rate (%) | Percent Surviving Beginning of Interval |
|---|---|---|---|---|
| 1 | 305 | 27 | 8.852 | 100.000 |
| 2 | 244 | 12 | 4.918 | 91.143 |
| 3 | 207 | 12 | 5.797 | 86.665 |
| 4 | 179 | 7 | 3.910 | 81.641 |
| 5 | 164 | 7 | 4.268 | 78.448 |
| 6 | 149 | 5 | 3.355 | 75.099 |
| 7 | 135 | 5 | 3.703 | 72.579 |
| 8 | 122 | 3 | 2.459 | 69.891 |
| 9 | 114 | 3 | 2.631 | 68.172 |
| 10 | 106 | 1 | 0.943 | 66.378 |
| 11 | 95 | 0 | 0.000 | 65.752 |
| 12 | 91 | 10 | 10.989 | 65.752 |
| 13 | 76 | 1 | 1.315 | 58.526 |
| 14 | 72 | 2 | 2.777 | 57.756 |
| 15 | 68 | 0 | 0.000 | 56.152 |
| 16 | 62 | 1 | 1.612 | 56.152 |
| 17 | 54 | 2 | 3.703 | 55.246 |
| 18 | 7 | 1 | 14.285 | 53.200 |
| 19 | 6 | 0 | 0.000 | 45.600 |
| 20 | 6 | 2 | 33.333 | 45.600 |

**EXHIBIT 18-6**

Stub Period Curve Fitting

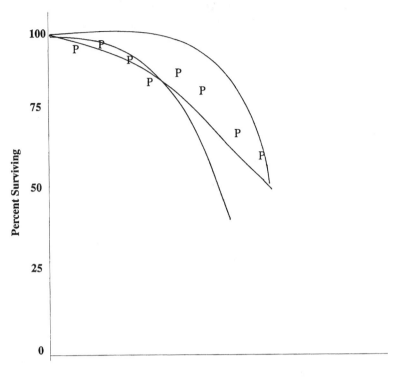

**Age of Customers**

All potential survivor curves are fitted over a logical range of average lives and a ranking factor is assigned to each fitting.

The best fit curve is the survivor curve at the specified average life that has the smallest ranking factor. This is referred to as minimizing the sum of the squared errors.

As each curve is fitted, a correlation coefficient is determined. The correlation coefficient is a ranking from –1 to +1 that describes how well the curve fits the survivor table. A correlation coefficient of +1 suggests that the survivor curve at the average life being fitted accurately predicts the subject intangible's past decay pattern. A correlation coefficient of –1 suggests that the survivor being fitted is not a good estimator of the subject intangible's past decay pattern.

Once a best fit curve has been selected, the remaining useful life for all live customers is calculated using the procedure described above.

The expected remaining life represents the remaining number of years that the business will enjoy the economic benefit from the customer—for example, that the pharmacy will enjoy the economic benefit from the prescription drug file customer relationship. The expected remaining useful life is the basis for a proper valuation of the subject customer intangible.

Based upon our regression analysis, the best fitting curve is an Iowa-type Left 0.0 curve with an average new customer total life of five years. This curve is presented in Exhibit 18-7. The curve is presented as the decay pattern in the surviving prescription drug file customer accounts.

EXHIBIT 18-7

Iowa-Type Survivor Curve Type L 0.0, Five-Year Average, New Customer Life

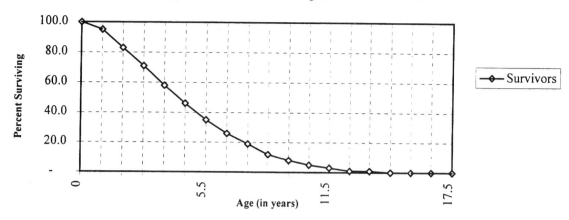

Exhibit 18-8 presents the detailed prescription drug file customer account decay tables. Exhibit 18-9 summarizes the projections used in our discounted net cash flow valuation analysis. The summary valuation analysis is presented in Exhibit 18-10.

## Valuation Reconciliation and Value Conclusion

Based upon the analyses described herein, the market value of the prescription drug file customer intangible, as of December 31, 1997, is (rounded): $16,400,000.

## BIBLIOGRAPHY

Ben-Amos, Omri. "Alex Brown Client List May Be an Asset for Bankers Trust N.Y. Corp." *The American Banker*, April 8, 1997, p. 22.

————. "J.P. Morgan, above the Fray, Relies on Client List." *The American Banker*, August 13, 1997, p. 20.

Boose, Mary Ann, and Virginia S. Ittenbach. "Depreciation of Customer-Based Intangibles: Good News for Taxpayers." *CPCU Journal*, December 1993, pp. 232–242.

Ellentuck, Albert B. "The High Court's Ruling on Customer Lists." *Nation's Business*, September 1993, p. 71.

Flashner, Martin J. "Acquired Customer List Is Classified as Goodwill." *CPA Journal*, February 1992, p. 56.

Goldberg, Michael J. "The Cost of Customer Lists." *Small Business Reports*, July 1993, p. 66.

Klim, Michael S. "It's Time to Cultivate Your Client List." *Trusts & Estates*, January 1996, p. 4.

Mastracchio, Nicholas J. Jr., and Cornelia M. Cahill. "Merging? Tax Rules Can Make a Deal Even Sweeter." *ABA Banking Journal*, March 1995, pp. 69–72.

Mather, Audrey. "The Value of Customer Relationships." *Journal of Bank Cost & Management Accounting*, Vol. 8, No. 2, 1995, pp. 32–39.

McKenna, Jon. "Mississippi Lawyer Says Client List Growing in IRS Taxability Investigation." *The Bond Buyer*, August 26, 1997, p. 30.

Moore, Mary G. "Bank Annuities Sales: Who Owns Customer Lists?" *Financial Services Week*, May 18, 1992, p. 21.

EXHIBIT 18-8

Live Long and Prosper Prescription Drug Files, Customer Survival Table, As of December 31, 1997

**Customer Type: Customer relationships**
**Curve Type: Iowa-type L 0.0**
**Valuation Date: 12/31/97**
**Average Life/New Customer: 5.0 Years**
**Average Remaining Customer Life: 4.2 Years**

| Age of Customer | As of Valuation Date | 1998 | 1999 | 2000 | 2001 | 2002 | 2003 | 2004 | 2005 | 2006 | 2007 | 2008 | 2009 | 2010 | 2011 | 2012 | 2013 | 2014 | 2015 |
|---|---|---|---|---|---|---|---|---|---|---|---|---|---|---|---|---|---|---|---|
| 00-01 | 40,962 | 39,217 | 34,664 | 29,422 | 24,251 | 19,366 | 14,934 | 11,080 | 7,874 | 5,331 | 3,416 | 2,055 | 1,147 | 586 | 269 | 107 | 35 | 9 | 1 |
| 01-02 | 27,073 | 25,397 | 21,718 | 17,901 | 14,295 | 11,024 | 8,179 | 5,812 | 3,935 | 2,522 | 1,517 | 847 | 433 | 198 | 79 | 26 | 6 | 1 | 0 |
| 02-03 | 22,732 | 21,025 | 17,486 | 13,964 | 10,768 | 7,989 | 5,678 | 3,844 | 2,463 | 1,481 | 827 | 423 | 194 | 77 | 25 | 6 | 1 | 0 | 0 |
| 03-04 | 19,342 | 17,652 | 14,245 | 10,985 | 8,150 | 5,792 | 3,921 | 2,513 | 1,511 | 844 | 431 | 198 | 79 | 26 | 6 | 1 | 0 | 0 | 0 |
| 04-05 | 3,525 | 3,170 | 2,474 | 1,836 | 1,305 | 883 | 566 | 340 | 190 | 97 | 45 | 18 | 6 | 1 | 0 | 0 | 0 | 0 | 0 |
| 05-06 | 163 | 144 | 109 | 77 | 52 | 33 | 20 | 11 | 6 | 3 | 1 | 0 | 0 | 0 | 0 | 0 | 0 | 0 | 0 |
| 06-07 | 7 | 6 | 4 | 3 | 2 | 1 | 1 | 0 | 0 | 0 | 0 | 0 | 0 | 0 | 0 | 0 | 0 | 0 | 0 |
| 07-08 | 0 | 0 | 0 | 0 | 0 | 0 | 0 | 0 | 0 | 0 | 0 | 0 | 0 | 0 | 0 | 0 | 0 | 0 | 0 |
| 08-09 | 0 | 0 | 0 | 0 | 0 | 0 | 0 | 0 | 0 | 0 | 0 | 0 | 0 | 0 | 0 | 0 | 0 | 0 | 0 |
| 09-10 | 0 | 0 | 0 | 0 | 0 | 0 | 0 | 0 | 0 | 0 | 0 | 0 | 0 | 0 | 0 | 0 | 0 | 0 | 0 |
| Totals | 113,804 | 106,611 | 90,700 | 74,188 | 58,823 | 45,088 | 33,299 | 23,600 | 15,979 | 10,278 | 6,237 | 3,541 | 1,859 | 888 | 379 | 140 | 42 | 10 | 1 |

**EXHIBIT 18-9**

Live Long and Prosper Prescription Drug Files, Valuation Variables,
as of December 31, 1997

| Valuation Variables | 1998 | 1999 | 2000 | 2001 | 2002 | 2003 |
|---|---|---|---|---|---|---|
| Revenue growth rate | 20.00 | 6.00 | 6.00 | 6.00 | 2.00 | 2.00 |
| Cost of sales percent | 65.00 | 65.00 | 65.00 | 65.00 | 65.00 | 65.00 |
| General & administrative expense | 16.00 | 16.00 | 16.00 | 16.00 | 16.00 | 16.00 |
| Capital charge percent | 4.00 | 4.00 | 4.00 | 4.00 | 4.00 | 4.00 |
| Income tax rate | 50.00 | 50.00 | 50.00 | 50.00 | 50.00 | 50.00 |
| Present value discount rate | 14.00 | 14.00 | 14.00 | 14.00 | 14.00 | 14.00 |

Rabe, James G., and Robert F. Reilly. "Looking beneath the Surface: Valuing Health Care Intangible Assets." *National Public Accountant,* March 1996, pp. 14–17+.

Reilly, Robert F. "How to Determine the Value and Useful Life of Core Deposit Intangibles." *The Journal of Bank Taxation,* Winter 1991, pp. 10–18.

Siconolfi, Michael. "Illicit Trade in Client Lists Worries Brokers." *Wall Street Journal,* May 30, 1991, pp. C1, C3.

Wyner, Gordon A. "Customer Valuation: Linking Behavior and Economics." *Marketing Research: A Magazine of Management & Applications,* Summer 1996, pp. 36–38.

**E X H I B I T  18-10**

Live Long and Prosper Prescription Drug Files, Customer Relationships Valuation Analysis, as of December 31, 1997

| Valuation Variables | 1998 | 1999 | 2000 | 2001 | 2002 | 2003 | 2004 | 2005 | 2006 |
|---|---|---|---|---|---|---|---|---|---|
| Surviving customers | 106,611 | 90,700 | 74,188 | 58,823 | 45,088 | 33,299 | 23,600 | 15,979 | 10,278 |
| Total revenue | $60,604,210 | $62,114,510 | $53,784,720 | $45,092,047 | $36,484,463 | $27,613,480 | $20,016,840 | %13,834,305 | $9,068,888 |
| Operating expense | 39,392,738 | 40,374,432 | 34,960,068 | 29,309,832 | 23,174,901 | 17,948,997 | 13,010,758 | 8,992,299 | 5,894,778 |
| General & administrative expense | 9,696,673 | 9,938,321 | 8,605,554 | 7,214,728 | 5,837,514 | 4,418,213 | 3,202,647 | 2,213,489 | 1,451,021 |
| Amortization expense [1] | 1,093,333 | 1,093,333 | 1,093,333 | 1,093,333 | 1,093,333 | 1,093,333 | 1,093,333 | 1,093,333 | 1,093,333 |
| Total expense | 50,182,744 | 51,406,086 | 44,658,955 | 37,617,893 | 30,645,748 | 23,460,543 | 17,306,738 | 12,299,121 | 8,439,132 |
| Pretax income | 10,421,466 | 10,708,424 | 9,125,765 | 7,474,154 | 5,838,715 | 4,153,297 | 2,709,812 | 1,535,184 | 629,756 |
| Income tax expense | 5,210,733 | 5,354,212 | 4,562,883 | 3,737,077 | 2,919,357 | 2,076,648 | 1,354,906 | 767,592 | 314,878 |
| Amortization expense [1] | 1,093,333 | 1,093,333 | 1,093,333 | 1,093,333 | 1,093,333 | 1,093,333 | 1,093,333 | 1,093,333 | 1,093,333 |
| Capital charge [2] | 2,424,168 | 2,484,580 | 2,151,389 | 1,803,682 | 1,459,379 | 1,104,554 | 800,362 | 553,372 | 362,756 |
| Net cash flow | 3,879,898 | 3,962,965 | 3,504,826 | 3,026,728 | 2,553,312 | 2,065,428 | 1,647,577 | 1,307,533 | 1,045,456 |
| Present value interest factor | 0.9440 | 0.8346 | 0.7321 | 0.6422 | 0.5634 | 0.4942 | 0.4335 | 0.3803 | 0.3336 |
| Discounted net cash flow | $3,662,670 | $3,307,673 | $2,566,044 | $1,943,865 | $1,438,442 | $1,020,689 | $714,207 | $497,202 | $348,718 |

| Valuation Variables: | 2007 | 2008 | 2009 | 2010 | 2011 | 2012 | 2013 | 2014 | 2015 |
|---|---|---|---|---|---|---|---|---|---|
| Surviving customers | 6,237 | 3,541 | 1,859 | 888 | 379 | 140 | 42 | 10 | 1 |
| Total revenue | $5,599,401 | $3,227,148 | $1,717,889 | $829,414 | $357,661 | $134,870 | $41,227 | $10,126 | $1,042 |
| Operating expense | 3,639,611 | 2,097,647 | 1,116,629 | 539,118 | 232,479 | 87,607 | 26,798 | 6,582 | 677 |
| General & administrative expense | 895,905 | 516,344 | 274,863 | 132,706 | 57,225 | 21,565 | 6,596 | 1,620 | 167 |
| Amortization expense [1] | 1,093,333 | 1,093,333 | 1,093,333 | 1,093,333 | 1,093,333 | 1,093,333 | | | — |
| Total expense | 5,628,849 | 3,707,324 | 2,484,825 | 1,765,157 | 1,383,037 | 1,202,505 | 33,394 | 8,202 | 844 |
| Pretax income | (29,448) | (480,176) | (766,936) | (935,743) | (1,025,376) | (1,067,725) | 7,833 | 1,924 | 198 |
| Income tax expense | (14,724) | (240,088) | (383,468) | (467,872) | (512,688) | (533,863) | 3,917 | 962 | 99 |
| Amortization expense [1] | 1,093,333 | 1,093,333 | 1,093,333 | 1,093,333 | 1,093,333 | 1,093,333 | | | — |
| Capital charge [2] | 223,976 | 129,086 | 68,716 | 33,177 | 14,306 | 5,391 | 1,649 | 405 | 42 |
| Net cash flow | 854,633 | 724,159 | 641,150 | 592,285 | 566,339 | 554,079 | 2,267 | 557 | 57 |
| Present value interest factor | 0.2926 | 0.2567 | 0.2251 | 0.1975 | 0.1732 | 0.1520 | 0.1333 | 0.1169 | 0.1026 |
| Discounted net cash flow | $250,060 | $185,863 | $144,349 | $116,972 | $98,111 | $84,200 | $302 | $65 | $6 |
| Indicated total market value (rounded) | $16,400,000 | | | | | | | | |

1. Per Internal Revenue Code Section 197, the amortization period for the intangible customer value is 15 years.

2. Capital charge related to a return on associated fixed assets and net working capital.

*Note:* Numbers may not total due to rounding.

# CHAPTER 19

# Data Processing
# Intangible Assets

## DESCRIPTION OF DATA PROCESSING INTANGIBLES

The class of intangible assets referred to as data processing intangibles has traditionally consisted of computer software and electronic databases. With the advent of new technology, additional types of data processing assets are being legally recognized, such as mask works, computer screen displays, and multimedia works. Intellectual property protection may be afforded these assets in the form of copyrights, patents, trademarks, or trade secrets.

## Computer Software

Computer software is sometimes defined as the programs that tell the computer what to do. The broadest definition of computer software is that software includes everything that is not hardware. In Revenue Procedure 69-21,[1] the Internal Revenue Service defines computer software as:

> All programs or routines used to cause a computer to perform a desired task or set of tasks, and the documentation required to describe and maintain those programs. Computer programs of all classes, for example, operating systems, executive systems, monitors, compilers, and translator assembly routines, and utility programs, as well as application programs are included. "Computer software" does not include procedures which are external to computer operations, such as instructions to transcription operators and external control procedures.

Computer software can be classified into functional groups as summarized in the following table:

| Functional Group | Representative Types of Software | Examples |
|---|---|---|
| System Software | Operating Systems | Windows 95, UNIX |
| | Languages | COBOL, C++ |
| | Utilities | anti-virus, backup programs |
| Business Operation Applications | Accounting | payroll, general ledger |
| | Manufacturing Control | bill of materials, inventory control |
| | Engineering | computer-aided design |
| Office Automation | Word Processing | WordPerfect |
| | Spreadsheet | Microsoft Excel |
| | Groupware | Lotus Notes |
| Educational and Recreational | Reference | encyclopedia, atlas |
| | Tutorials | foreign language, math |
| | Games | card or board games, simulators |

With respect to the intangible asset owner or user, software falls into two general categories. The first category consists of software intended for sale or license, or product software. The second category consists of software intended for internal use, or operational software. Operational software may include both internally developed software and software purchased or licensed from another party.

---

1. Rev. Proc. 69-21, 1969-2 C.B. 303.

## Electronic Databases

Electronic databases are organized collections of related data stored in an electronic format (e.g., computer disks). These databases are accessed, maintained, and manipulated using computer software. Most electronic databases are created as a normal part of the operations and recordkeeping of a business. They include customer information, inventory records, open order files, and so forth.

However, there are many specialized proprietary databases that have broad commercialization potential. Examples of this type of database are mailing lists, credit information, financial studies or compilations, and scientific data. These databases are sometimes bought and sold in their entirety, including the associated proprietary rights. More often, the database is used to generate income either directly, through the sale or license of the data to customers, or indirectly, through the internal use of the data to perform a service for customers.

## Tangible or Intangible Assets

Generally speaking, computer software and electronic databases are considered intangible assets, though they may exist on tangible media such as diskettes, magnetic tape, or hard-copy program listings. In most cases, the *intrinsic value* of these assets is attributable to the programs or data, not to the physical medium on which they are stored or copied.

Taxpayers have claimed investment tax credit (ITC) for purchased computer software and electronic databases as tangible property. However, in *Ronnen v. Commissioner,*[2] the U.S. Tax Court found that computer software is intangible and, therefore, ineligible for the investment tax credit. Litigants in subsequent cases have introduced the *master media* argument, in which the tapes or disks containing the software or data are likened to master recordings or master negatives in the music or film industry. Under certain circumstances, these masters may be viewed as tangible productive assets because they are used in the manufacture of prints or copies for sale or license. More recently, the U.S. Tax Court ruled that computer software qualified for the investment tax credit, because Congress intended for the ITC to encourage expansion and modernization of productive facilities. Therefore, the Tax Court concluded that Congress meant for the term *tangible personal property* to be broadly construed.

The following representative cases discuss the tangible and intangible qualities of software or electronic databases:

- *Computing & Software, Inc. v. Commissioner,* 64 T.C. 223 (May 15, 1975).
- *Comshare, Inc. v. United States,* KTC 1992-152 (E.D. Mich. 1992).
- *Comshare, Inc. v. United States,* KTC 1994-281 (6th Cir. 1994).
- *Kansas City Southern Industries v. Commissioner,* 98 T.C. 242 (Mar. 5, 1992).
- *Norwest Corporation and Subsidiaries v. Commissioner,* 108 T.C. 18 (Apr. 30, 1997).

---

2. *Ronnen v. Commissioner,* 90 T.C. 74 (Jan. 21, 1988).

- *Ronnen v. Commissioner,* 90 T.C. 74 (Jan. 21, 1988).
- *Sierra Club, Inc. v. Commissioner,* T.C. Memo 1993-199.
- *Sprint Corporation and Subsidiaries, f.k.a. United Telecommunications, Inc. v. Commissioner,* 108 T.C. 19 (Apr. 30, 1997).
- *Texas Instruments Inc. v. Commissioner,* 551 F.2d 599 (5th Cir. 1977).

In November 1996, the Internal Revenue Service issued proposed regulation 1.861-18 regarding the classification of computer software transactions for tax purposes. A transaction relating to computer programs is treated as one of the following: a transfer of a copyright right, a transfer of a copyrighted article, the provision of services, or the provision of know-how. Transfers of copyright rights are further classified either as a sale or exchange, or as a license generating royalty income. Similarly, transfers of copyrighted articles are further classified either as a sale or an exchange, or as a lease generating rental income.

Unfortunately, the proposed regulations do not address the treatment of computer software as either tangible or intangible property.

## Intellectual Property Protection Related to Data Processing Intangibles

Software and electronic databases, when they are original works of authorship and have been fixed in a tangible medium, are entitled to copyright protection. Computer screen displays can be protected as part of the software. Multimedia works, which combine two or more media (print, audiovisual, audio, or machine-readable), are also recognized under copyright law. Copyrights are discussed in Chapter 17.

Mask works are protected under the Semiconductor Chip Protection Act of 1984, administered by the Copyright Office. A mask work is most simply described as firmware, or software stored permanently on a ROM (read-only memory) chip as a series of stencils of integrated circuitry.

Computer programs can be patented, though most do not meet the requirements for patentable technology. Computer programs can also contain trade secrets, which are protected under state laws. Patents and trade secrets are mentioned in Chapter 24.

Data processing intangibles that are available for sale or license to customers may have associated trademarks or service marks. A relatively new area of dispute related to both trademarks and data processing in general is the use of domain names, or electronic addresses, used on the Internet. Domain names have been issued for years without any checking against registered trademarks. This practice has resulted in claims of trademark rights violations against domain name holders. Trademarks and service marks are discussed further in Chapter 23.

### COMMON VALUATION METHODS

There are several methods and procedures that may be appropriate to the valuation of data processing intangible assets, such as computer software. These methods fall into the three general categories of methods, or approaches, discussed in Part 2 of this text: the cost approach, the market approach, and the income approach.

The following discussion of common valuation methods addresses the valuation of computer software. However, similar methods may be used to value other data processing intangibles.

Any valuation of data processing intangibles must include an adjustment for obsolescence, if any. This adjustment may be either made discretely or embedded in the valuation analysis. The issue of obsolescence, as it applies to data processing intangibles, is examined in more detail following the discussion of the three approaches.

## Cost Approach

There are two common types of cost that may be estimated within the cost approach. The first is *reproduction cost,* or the cost to construct an exact replica of the subject intangible asset. The second is *replacement cost,* or the cost to recreate the functionality or utility of the subject intangible asset, but in a form or appearance that may differ from the actual asset subject to appraisal. The replacement asset may be created using different tools and methods than were used to create the subject asset.

*Replacement cost new* typically establishes the maximum amount that a prudent investor would pay for a fungible intangible asset. However, specially developed computer software may be unique, and may not qualify as a fungible intangible asset. In many cases, an intangible asset is less useful than its ideal replacement. The value of the subject intangible asset should then be adjusted to reflect the loss in economic value due to functional, technological, and economic obsolescence.

The two primary cost approach methods used to estimate the value of computer software are the trended historical cost method and the software engineering model method. While they are generally applicable to the valuation of purchased software, these methods are particularly suited to the valuation of internally developed software.

### Trended Historical Cost Method

The most straightforward cost method is the trended historical cost method. In this method, actual historical asset development (or acquisition) costs are identified and quantified and then *trended* to the valuation date by an appropriate inflation-based index factor. Care should be taken to include all costs associated with the development (or acquisition) of the software and only those costs. For example, an allocation of overhead costs and the cost of fringe benefits should be included in addition to employee payroll costs (and payroll taxes). However, if data processing personnel are involved in tasks unrelated to software development (e.g., computer center operations), then only those costs associated with their time spent on software development tasks should be included.

Often, historical software development costs are not readily available. In this case, development costs are sometimes estimated using actual, or estimated, development time (hours, person-months). The development cost estimate is computed by multiplying the development time by an associated cost figure, using either specific costs per person or a weighted average cost. Typically, an analysis of payroll taxes, fringe benefits, overhead costs, and any other relevant costs is performed so that these costs may be added as a percentage of salaries or wages. The development costs should be estimated in current dollars as of the valuation date.

In addition, if the trended historical cost method is used, it is important that the historical costs include 1) the software developer's profit on the development project and 2) an allowance for entrepreneurial incentive to motivate the development project, in addition to 3) direct development costs such as salaries and wages and 4) indirect development costs such as overhead and employment taxes and benefits.

The trended historical cost method estimates the reproduction cost of the intangible asset. In many cases (due to technological advances in programming languages or programming tools, for example) the replacement cost for software may be lower than the reproduction cost. For older computer software, or for software that was developed or modified over an extended period of time, it is recommended that a replacement cost analysis be performed. This typically involves the use of a software engineering model.

## Software Engineering Model Method

Analysts often employ software engineering models in order to estimate the reproduction cost or the replacement cost of software systems. The models were not necessarily created for valuation purposes, but rather to assist software developers in estimating the effort, time, and human resources needed to complete a software project. The primary input to these models is some measure of program, or system, size or functionality. Historically, the measure or metric has been lines of code (i.e., source program instructions). The definition of lines of code and the associated counting conventions vary among the models.

Another metric, function points, has more recently been incorporated into software engineering models. The number of function points in a program is calculated with an algorithm that uses a weighted count of the number of inputs, outputs, inquiries, data files, and interfaces.

Other inputs to the models include attributes such as programming language, experience and quality of the project team, tools used, programming practices, complexity, type of application, time constraints, level of documentation, and required reliability. The analyst may use different assumptions with respect to these attributes for a replacement cost analysis than would be used for a reproduction cost analysis. For example, if the subject software was written in Assembler, the programming language used in a reproduction cost analysis would be Assembler. However, the language assumed in a replacement cost analysis may be COBOL, a higher-level (and more efficient) language.

Two of the most commonly used line-of-code cost estimation models are the Constructive Cost Model (COCOMO) and the Software Lifecycle Management (SLIM) model. The most commonly used model that uses function points as its size metric is Checkpoint.

All three models are considered *empirical* cost estimation models. That is, the development time and development cost of the subject software is estimated by reference to a large database of actual software development projects, the actual development times of which were carefully monitored. The cost estimation models calculate an estimate of effort to develop a software system in terms of person-months. To estimate the cost to develop that system, the number of months should be multiplied by a cost per person-month.

For valuation purposes, the cost per person-month is a fully loaded cost per person-month that includes both the average base salary of the project team and other factors. The other factors include, but are not limited to, employee perquisites, payroll taxes (FUTA, SUTA, FICA, and worker's compensation), fringe benefits (life, health, disability, and dental insurance; pension plans; and continuing education), and an allocation for overhead (including secretarial support, office space, computer use, supplies, marketing, management, and supervisory time).

*COCOMO.* The Constructive Cost Model (COCOMO) was developed by Barry W. Boehm and is described in the authoritative textbook entitled *Software Engineering Economics.*[3] This cost estimation method projects the amount of effort required to develop the software, taking into consideration the size of the programs, the program characteristics, and the environment in which they are to be developed.

An updated model, COCOMO II, has been developed by Barry Boehm and his associates at the Center for Software Engineering (CSE), University of Southern California. The model has recently undergone calibration (i.e., numbers were assigned to the effort multipliers and other constants were finalized) and was completed in early 1997. The *COCOMO II Model Definition Manual* is available from the CSE via their Web site.[4]

*SLIM.* A computerized cost estimation model is marketed by Quantitative Software Management, Inc. (QSM). This model, called SLIM (Software Lifecycle Management), was developed by Lawrence H. Putnam, a former Special Assistant to the Commanding General of the Army Computer Systems Command and the founder of QSM.

Much of the basic theory of the SLIM model is presented in a three-part article by Lawrence H. Putnam and Ann Fitzsimmons.[5] The SLIM model is described in detail in a book written by Lawrence H. Putnam and Ware Myers, entitled *Measures for Excellence: Reliable Software on Time, within Budget.*[6]

*Checkpoint & KnowledgePLAN.* Software Productivity Research, Inc. (SPR), has created a software product called Checkpoint, an estimation, measurement, and assessment tool. The company was founded by Capers Jones, the author of several books including *Programming Productivity*[7] and *Applied Software Measurement.*[8]

Checkpoint also supports the use of feature points, a metric developed by SPR that is an expansion of function points. A companion product, Function Point Workbench, is also available from SPR. It expedites the function point counting process and maintains a company's function point database.

Software Productivity Research has recently developed another software estimation tool, SPR KnowledgePLAN. It has a knowledge base of nearly 7,000 actual software projects.

---

3. Barry W. Boehm, *Software Engineering Economics* (Englewood Cliffs, NJ: Prentice Hall, Inc., 1981).
4. Center for Software Engineering, http://sunset.usc.edu.
5. Lawrence H. Putnam and Ann Fitzsimmons, "Estimating Software Costs," *Datamation,* September, October, and November 1979, pp. 190–98, 171–78, and 137–40.
6. Lawrence H. Putnam and Ware Myers, *Measures for Excellence: Reliable Software on Time, within Budget* (Englewood Cliffs, NJ: Prentice Hall, Inc., 1992).
7. Capers Jones, *Programming Productivity* (New York: McGraw-Hill, 1986).
8. Capers Jones, *Applied Software Measurement* (New York: McGraw-Hill, 1991).

*Other Models.* Other software engineering cost estimation models include CA-Estimacs from Computer Associates International, Inc.; Price S from PRICE Systems, a Lockheed Martin Company; and BYL (Before You Leap) from The Remarkable Software Company Limited.

## Income Approach

In the income approach, the value of an intangible asset is estimated as the present value of the future economic income attributable to the ownership of the intangible asset over its expected remaining useful life. The economic income may result from prospective revenues, cost savings, or royalty or license income associated with the intangible asset.

The two most common income approach methods used in the valuation of data processing intangibles are the discounted cash flow method and the relief from royalty method. The discounted cash flow method is one application of the yield capitalization method. The relief from royalty method may also be considered a market approach method because a market-derived royalty rate is used in the analysis.

### Discounted Cash Flow Method

The discounted cash flow method is typically used in the valuation of data processing intangibles when there is an identifiable income stream associated with the intangible asset. Therefore, this method is usually used in the valuation of product software or databases that generate income through their sale or license. The future cash flow related to software, for example, may be calculated by projecting revenues, expenses (excluding depreciation and amortization), and capital investments over its estimated remaining economic life. A capital charge is normally included in the analysis when additional assets (e.g., existing computer equipment) are used or used up to produce the projected revenues. These future cash flows are discounted to a present value using an appropriate present value discount rate or direct capitalization rate.

The remaining economic life of the data processing intangible is a key variable in a discounted cash flow analysis. Purchased software may have a life of 3, 5, or 15 years for income tax depreciation and amortization purposes. The income tax life of software depends primarily upon whether it was purchased before or after August 11, 1993, and whether it was purchased as part of the acquisition of a substantial portion of a business. However, the economic life of computer software is an entirely different issue. In estimating the remaining economic life of software, the analyst should consider a number of factors, including:

- The age of the software and maintenance or enhancement practices.
- The market for the software (customers, competitors).
- The functional characteristics of the software (how well it satisfies users' needs and complies with industry standards, regulatory reporting, etc.).
- The technological characteristics of the software (speed and efficiency, programming language, associated hardware and operating systems).
- The historical economic lives of similar software.

### Relief from Royalty Method

The relief from royalty method is used to estimate the cost savings that accrue to the owner of an intangible asset who would otherwise have to pay royalties (or license fees) on revenues earned through use of the asset. The royalty rate used in the analysis is based on an analysis of empirical, market-derived royalty rates for comparable or guideline intangible assets. For this reason, this method may also be classified as a market approach method. In the case of product software, revenues are projected over the expected remaining economic life of the software. The market-derived royalty rate is then applied to estimate the royalty savings. The net after-tax royalty savings are calculated for each year in the remaining economic life of the software and then discounted to a present value, as in the discounted cash flow method.

## Market Approach

The market approach estimates the value of an intangible asset by reference to actual market transactions involving comparable or guideline intangible assets. This approach is seldom used in the valuation of internally developed custom software for several reasons. First, information about sales of this type of software is not readily available. Second, these sales are typically part of an acquisition of an entire business. Third, by definition, custom software is usually unlike other software observable in the marketplace.

However, it is sometimes possible to use market approach methods in the valuation of computer software. The two market approach methods that are most often used to value software are the *market transaction method* and a hybrid method that we'll call the *market replacement cost method.*

### Market Transaction Method

When arm's-length market transaction data are available for comparable or guideline software, the implied value is typically expressed as a dollars per line of code (or dollars per function point) figure. This unit value is then applied to the subject software lines of code (or function points) to estimate the value of the subject software. As with any method that relies on comparable or guideline assets, adjustments must be made for material differences between the comparable or guideline assets and the subject asset.

Because of the lack of information typically available for software transactions, this method is frequently used only as a reasonableness check for the estimates of value indicated by the other methods. It is often difficult to determine the comparability of the software in order to conclude what adjustments, if any, need to be made, and it is not always clear what line-of-code counting conventions were used.

### Market Replacement Cost Method

This hybrid cost and market approach method contemplates the replacement cost of the software in the open market. If commercial, off-the-shelf software packages can be found that provide meaningful guidelines to the subject software, the cost to purchase or license these packages may be used to estimate the replacement cost of the subject software. However, if the proprietary rights associated with the subject software have any economic value (i.e., the subject software is, or could be, sold or licensed to others), this method may understate the value of the software.

In a variation of this method, the analyst may approach software developers and request hypothetical proposals to develop software comparable to the subject software. The proposed estimates may assume the development of a completely custom system or the modification of an existing package. If objective arm's-length estimates can be obtained, they may be good indications of the market replacement cost of the software. Again, proprietary rights may be an issue.

## Obsolescence

As previously discussed, when an intangible asset is less useful than its ideal replacement, its value should be adjusted to reflect the loss in economic value due to functional, technological, and economic obsolescence. A fourth form of obsolescence, physical deterioration, is not generally applicable to data processing intangibles because they typically do not experience physical wear and tear. However, the possibility of physical deterioration should be considered.

Functional obsolescence is the loss in value of an asset because the subject asset does not have the functionality of—or is less useful than—a replacement asset. In the case of software, functional obsolescence is often immaterial when the software is continually maintained and enhanced. However, a perfect example of functional obsolescence is the inability of some software to accommodate the year 2000.

The Year 2000 problem has resulted from the common data processing practice of storing only two digits for the year in date fields on computer files. Software developers who did not have the foresight to anticipate this problem are now scrambling to make their software Year-2000 compliant before the proverbial stroke of midnight. If they don't make it, 65-year-old people may suddenly be listed as 35 years old, and no creditor's invoices will be past due. In fact, users of many systems will have problems before the new millennium, as budgets, ship dates, and so on creep past 1999. Systems that are not Year-2000 compliant may have increasing functional obsolescence as January 1, 2000, approaches, if this functional obsolescence is not cured.

Technological obsolescence is often considered a specific form of functional obsolescence. It is the loss in value of an asset due to technological improvements that make its replacement more efficient or effective. In the valuation of software, technological obsolescence usually exists 1) when the software is written in an inefficient or outdated language, 2) when the software runs on a platform (hardware, operating system, etc.) that is becoming obsolete (and the software is not portable), or 3) if the outmoded methods or practices of the developers result in a less than optimal use of resources.

Economic obsolescence is a reduction in the value of a subject asset due to events that are typically outside the control of the owner of the asset, such as legal or regulatory changes or restrictions, social or economic changes, or market conditions (e.g., new competitors). Economic obsolescence may be an important issue in the valuation of product software. Economic obsolescence is generally not evident with regard to internally developed operational software that is being used by a financially successful company.

In valuing computer software, all forms of obsolescence should be considered. Again, functional obsolescence may not be evident in software that is properly maintained, but the analyst should determine the extent of any functional obsolescence. When a reproduction cost method, such as the trended historical cost method, is used to value software, technological obsolescence can be significant due to increasing productivity and technological advances over time. The use of a replacement cost method typically eliminates the productivity-related technological obsolescence, but other adjustments for technological obsolescence may be necessary. Economic obsolescence usually has more relevance with respect to product software. However, this form of obsolescence should be examined in the valuation of operational software as well. Discrete adjustments for obsolescence are generally not necessary when the value of software is estimated using the income approach, because the revenue and expense projections implicitly take obsolescence into account.

Though the value of tangible assets is often estimated using depreciation schedules, properly maintained software does not become obsolete in any predictable, continuous way. Software value tends to vary over time by a relatively small amount (due to increasing productivity or technological advances on the one hand and increasing labor costs and software enhancements on the other hand) until the usually unpredictable point in time that its replacement is contemplated. Software value also tends to vary over time for any number of reasons. Therefore, any attempt to estimate obsolescence for properly maintained software by depreciating it over some finite period of time is arbitrary and simplistic.

## Special Considerations in Software Valuation

A number of issues that are specific to computer software should be considered in a software valuation, particularly when software engineering models are used in the analysis.

### Ownership

As with any asset, the ownership of the asset is a critical consideration. In the case of the appraisal of an automotive fleet, for example, ownership is quite straightforward. A vehicle is either leased or owned. It is extremely unlikely for the engine to be leased while the body is owned. Furthermore, a leased car should not be valued, as an owned vehicle may, by reference to published used car prices, though the lease may have some value.

The ownership of software is often more difficult to determine than the ownership of tangible assets. Source codes for software packages are frequently sold or, more likely, licensed to companies that then modify the programs for their own internal use. Depending on their standards and methods, it may be fairly simple—or nearly impossible—to separate the internally developed additions and modifications from the original purchased, or licensed, code.

The distinction may not be critical in a historical cost method, where both the purchase price or license fee and the cost to modify the software are included in the analysis. However, care should be taken in the application of software engineering models not to include the purchased or licensed lines of code. The most economic replacement cost, in this case, would probably assume the purchase or license of the packaged software—not the actual development of the programs—and the rights of ownership differ between internally developed and licensed software. Proprietary rights may also be an issue when using the market replacement cost method.

## Obsolete and Duplicate Code

A particular concern when using software metrics, such as lines of code or function points, is obsolete or duplicate code. It is not uncommon for source code libraries to contain obsolete programs or duplicate copies (or multiple versions) of the same program. Similarly, some programs are developed by cloning other programs. Therefore, the effort to develop the second program may be significantly less than the effort to develop the original program, though they may be close to the same size. Also, sections of code that would ideally be stored in shared subroutine libraries or copybooks (e.g., date validation routines, credit card check-digit calculations, file definitions) are sometimes written once but copied into the source code of multiple programs. This could result in those lines being counted several times, though the effort to develop them was expended only once.

The analyst should make every effort to quantify and eliminate duplicate or obsolete code from the analysis. This typically includes an examination of the software developer's standards, methods, and practices.

## Software Life Cycle

The definition of software typically used in the valuation of software, as part of a going-concern business enterprise, reflects the software's function in satisfying its users' needs. Thus, software is the culmination of an entire range of life cycle activities, including feasibility studies, planning and requirements, product design and architecture (including file structures and layouts), coding, integration, testing, documentation, and implementation, all of which permit delivery of computer processing services to the end-users.

Software cost estimation models often break down the development effort over the software life cycle by development phase or activity (e.g., feasibility study, design, coding, testing, maintenance). The models in their generic form usually assume a certain level of documentation, testing, and so forth. Many models allow the user to modify these levels and to include or exclude certain phases of the life cycle.

The analyst should use a cost estimation model in such a way that it reflects the characteristics of the subject software (or its ideal replacement). If the model does not allow for modification of the life cycle or activities, then an adjustment may need to be made to the resulting effort estimation. For example, if the model assumes an average level of documentation and there is no user documentation for the subject software, then an estimate of the average user documentation effort (usually, a percentage of total effort) should be subtracted from the total effort estimated by the model.

## Software Metric Counting Conventions

As discussed previously, line of code definitions and counting conventions vary among the software engineering models. Most exclude comment and blank lines, including only executable source instructions. Typically, declarative statements such as data definition lines (while not, perhaps, strictly speaking, executable) are usually included as well as any job control language (JCL), procedures, batch files, and so on, required to run the programs. The lines of code for the subject software should be counted in a manner consistent with the conventions used to gather the empirical data for the model being used.

Allan J. Albrecht of IBM Corporation introduced the function point metric in 1979. Another fairly well-known variation (particularly in the

United Kingdom) of Albrecht's function point is the Mk II (Mark II) function point, developed by Charles R. Symons.[9] The counting of function points has been standardized to a large extent by the International Function Point Users' Group (IFPUG). IFPUG is a nonprofit, membership-governed organization that publishes the *Function Point Counting Practices Manual*. As of this writing, the most recent release of this manual, release 4.0, was published in January 1994. IFPUG may be reached at Blendonview Office Park, 5008-28 Pine Creek Drive, Westerville, OH 43081-4899, telephone (614) 895-7130, fax (614) 895-3466.

### DATA SOURCES

Chapter 5 describes the types of data sources typically used in the valuation of intangible assets. The following discussion addresses these data sources as they apply to the valuation of data processing intangibles.

## Internal Data Sources

Internal financial reports such as historical financial statements and budgets are needed for almost all the methods described in this chapter. Payroll records and project management or timekeeping reports are relevant to any cost approach valuation method.

Internal documentation related to the data processing intangible should be reviewed by the analyst. This documentation may include system or user documentation as well as marketing materials. Reports showing lines of code or function points for software—or records or data items for databases—should be used whenever possible. In the case of software, examination of sample source code and a demonstration of the software are advisable.

Client interviews are useful to any valuation assignment. With respect to data processing intangibles, these interviews can inform the analyst on a variety of topics including:

- Prior market transactions or offers for data processing intangible assets of the subject company or similar assets of other companies.
- Competitors and comparable software or databases available in the marketplace.
- Software development history, environment, methods, and practices.
- Characteristics of the software (e.g., functionality, complexity, reliability, etc.).
- Obsolescence and remaining useful life of the intangible assets.

## External Data Sources

Trade publications are useful data sources in the valuation of data processing intangibles. Advertisements for and reviews of software packages and databases can be helpful in locating comparable assets. Published soft-

---

9. Charles R. Symons, *Software Sizing and Estimating: Mk II FPA (Function Point Analysis)* (New York: John Wiley & Sons, 1991).

ware catalogs list off-the-shelf software packages that may be used in a replacement cost analysis of operational software. Newsletters specializing in intangible asset licensing, as described in Chapter 5, can be a good source of royalty rates.

Salary surveys published in computer publications and available from personnel consulting or placement companies may be used in the calculation of the estimated cost per person-month for the cost approach methods, or to check the reasonableness of the actual compensation of development personnel at the subject company. Many of these are available on the Internet.

Press releases and articles available from a variety of new sources may provide information about market transactions for the sale or license of data processing intangibles. Court cases may provide valuable guidance to the analyst with respect to analytical methods, royalty rates, costs per line of code, and economic lives appropriate to the valuation of data processing intangibles.

Software engineering textbooks provide a great deal of information pertaining to the time and cost required to develop software. Another excellent source of articles related to software engineering is the *IEEE Transactions on Software Engineering*, published by the Institute of Electrical and Electronics Engineers, Inc.[10]

It is not surprising that a wealth of information related to data processing intangibles can be found on the Internet. Software developers and software engineering companies are more likely to have Web sites than perhaps any other industry group. Of course, the level of reliability of information from Internet sources should be taken into consideration by the analyst.

## VALUATION EXAMPLE

Exhibits 19-1 through 19-3 present an example of the valuation of product software using one method from each of the three valuation approaches.

### Cost Approach—Software Engineering Model Method (COCOMO 1981)

For the sake of simplicity, let us apply the 1981 COCOMO model and assume the following set of facts with respect to the software:

1. The line-of-code counts are as shown below.
2. System 3 has been abandoned with little likelihood of being revived.
3. The other systems are continually maintained and are running on a state-of-the-art hardware and operating system platform.
4. The calculated Effort Adjustment Factor (EAF), based on the ranking of the 15 attributes defined by the model, is 0.43.
5. One system has been classified as organic and the other four as semidetached.

---

10. *IEEE Transactions on Software Engineering* is published monthly in both print and electronic formats by the Institute of Electrical and Electronics Engineers, Inc., 345 East 47th Street, New York, NY 10017-2394, (212) 705-7900.

EXHIBIT 19-1

Software Valuation, Software Engineering Model Method, COCOMO 1981, as of December 31, 1996

| Subsystem | Total Lines of Code | Less Nonexecutable Lines | Executable Source Instructions | Delivered Source Instructions | Effort to Develop (PM) | |
|---|---|---|---|---|---|---|
| | | | | | Organic Systems | Semidetached Systems |
| System 1 | 51,000 | 5,000 | 46,000 | 46,000 | | 94 |
| System 2 | 66,000 | 7,000 | 59,000 | 59,000 | | 124 |
| System 3 | 12,000 | 1,000 | 11,000 | | | |
| System 4 | 18,000 | 2,000 | 16,000 | 16,000 | 25 | |
| System 5 | 47,000 | 5,000 | 42,000 | 42,000 | | 85 |
| Totals | 194,000 | 20,000 | 174,000 | 163,000 | 25 | 303 |
| | | | | | Total PM to develop | 328 |
| | | | | | Times cost per PM | 8,750 |
| | | | | | Indicated value of software | $2,870,000 |
| | | | | | Indicated value of software (rounded) | $2,900,000 |

PM = person-month.

6. An average annual salary of $60,000 was assumed, with an estimate of employment benefits and overhead at 75 percent of salary.

7. The valuation date is December 31,1996.

8. The software development effort equations defined by the model are:

Organic: $\qquad$ $PM = 3.2 \, (KDSI)^{1.05} \times EAF$

Semidetached: $\qquad$ $PM = 3.0 \, (KDSI)^{1.12} \times EAF$

where:

PM $\quad$ = $\quad$ Person-months

KDSI = Thousands of delivered source instructions

EAF $\quad$ = $\quad$ Effort adjustment factor

Exhibit 19-1 presents the calculations for this method.

EXHIBIT 19-2

Software Valuation, Relief from Royalty Method, as of December 31, 1996.

| | Year 1 | Year 2 | Year 3 | Year 4 | Year 5 | Year 6 |
|---|---|---|---|---|---|---|
| Software-related sales | $9,500,000 | $10,450,000 | $11,495,000 | $12,644,500 | $13,908,950 | $15,299,845 |
| Royalty savings | 760,000 | 836,000 | 919,600 | 1,011,560 | 1,112,716 | 1,223,988 |
| Income taxes | 266,000 | 292,600 | 321,860 | 354,046 | 389,451 | 428,396 |
| Net royalty savings | $ 494,000 | $ 543,400 | $ 597,740 | $ 657,514 | $ 723,265 | $ 795,592 |
| Periods discounted | 0.5 | 1.5 | 2.5 | 3.5 | 4.5 | 5.5 |
| Present value interest factor | 0.9206 | 0.7801 | 0.6611 | 0.5603 | 0.4748 | 0.4024 |
| Present value of net royalty savings | $ 454,776 | $ 423,906 | $ 395,166 | $ 368,405 | $ 343,406 | $ 320,146 |
| Indicated value of software | $2,305,806 | | | | | |
| Indicated value of software (rounded) | $2,300,000 | | | | | |

EXHIBIT 19-3

Software Valuation, Market Transaction Method, as of December 31, 1996

| | Lines of Code | Transaction Price | Price per Line of Code |
|---|---|---|---|
| Comparable transaction 1 | 225,000 | $3,300,000 | $ 14.67 |
| Comparable transaction 2 | 150,000 | $1,700,000 | $ 11.33 |
| | Low End of Indicated Value Range | High End of Indicated Value Range | Average Indicated Value |
| Subject software lines of code | 198,000 | 198,000 | 198,000 |
| Times dollars per line of code | $ 11.33 | $ 14.67 | $ 13.00 |
| Indicated value of software | $2,243,340 | $2,904,660 | $2,574,000 |
| Indicated value of software (rounded) | | | $2,600,000 |

## Relief from Royalty Method

Let us assume the following additional facts related to the same software for our relief from royalty method example:

| Economic Variable | Projection |
|---|---|
| Next year projected revenues attributable to the sale or license of software | $9,500,000 |
| Revenue growth rate | 10% |
| Market-derived royalty rate | 8% |
| Effective income tax rate | 35% |
| Present value discount rate | 18% |
| Expected remaining economic life of the software (until replacement) | 6 years |

Exhibit 19-2 presents an illustration of this method.

## Market Transaction Method

Let us assume that we are able to find arm's-length market transactions for comparable software where all proprietary rights were conveyed in the transactions. Let us further assume that no material adjustments are necessary and that the line-of-code counts represent total lines of code, including comments, and so on. Our equivalent lines of code is 198,000 (i.e., 210,000 – 12,000 for System 3). Exhibit 19-3 presents an illustration of this method.

## Valuation Reconciliation and Conclusion

Based upon the analyses described herein, the market value of the subject computer software, as of December 31, 1996, is (rounded) $2,600,000.

### BIBLIOGRAPHY

## Articles

"Computer Software Was Tangible Personal Property." *Tax Week*, May 16, 1997, p. 3.

Christensen, Barbara. "Computer Software—Is It Tangible or Intangible?" *Small Business Taxation*, January/February 1990, pp. 174–76.

Davidson, Stephen J., and Nicole A. Engisch. "'Trademark Misuse' in Domain Name Disputes." *The Computer Lawyer*, August 1996, pp. 13–19.

Levenson, Alan; Alan Shapiro; Edward Maguire; and Martin McClintock. "Proposed Software Regulations." *The Tax Advisor*, March 1997, pp. 145–49.

Millon, Tom. "Computer Software Valuation: Don't Be Led Astray by a Quick Approach." *National Public Accountant*, September 1992, pp. 14–17.

———. "Software Development: Cost vs. Value (Determining Fair Market Value of Internally Developed Computer Software)." *Practical Accountant*, October 1992, p. 48.

Putnam, Lawrence H., and Ann Fitzsimmons. "Estimating Software Costs." *Datamation*, September, October, and November 1979, pp. 190–98, 171–78, and 137–40, respectively.

Reilly, Robert F. "The Valuation of Computer Software." *ASA Valuation*, March 1991, pp. 34–54.

Shapiro, Alan. "Lost in Cyberspace: Transfer Pricing Aspects of Proposed 861 Computer Software Regulations." *Tax Management Transfer Pricing*, December 11, 1996, pp. 495–97.

## Books

Boehm, Barry W. *Software Engineering Economics*. Englewood Cliffs, NJ: Prentice Hall, Inc., 1981.

Jones, Capers. *Applied Software Management*. New York: McGraw-Hill, 1991.

———. *Patterns of Software System Failure and Success*. Florence, KY: International Thomson Publishing, 1996.

———. *Programming Productivity*. New York: McGraw-Hill, 1986.

Putnam, Lawrence H., and Ware Myers. *Measures for Excellence: Reliable Software on Time, within Budget*. Englewood Cliffs, NJ: P T R Prentice Hall, Inc., 1992.

Simensky, Melvin, and Lanning G. Bryer, eds. *The New Role of Intellectual Property in Commercial Transactions*. New York: John Wiley & Sons, Inc., 1994.

Smith, Gordon V., and Russell L. Parr. *Valuation of Intellectual Property and Intangible Assets*. New York: John Wiley & Sons, Inc., 1989.

Symons, Charles R. *Software Sizing and Estimating: Mk II FPA (Function Point Analysis)*. Chichester, UK: John Wiley & Sons Ltd., 1991.

## Other

Kleinrock's Tax Library, Kleinrock Publishing, Inc., a division of United Communications Group.

# CHAPTER 20

# Goodwill Intangible Assets

## DESCRIPTION OF GOODWILL INTANGIBLES

This chapter discusses and illustrates the commonly used methods with regard to the identification, valuation, and economic analysis of goodwill-related intangible assets. In such a discussion, the first topic must necessarily be a definition of goodwill. In 1928, the British philosopher and mathematician Bertrand Russell (actually, the third Earl Russell) wrote a book entitled *Sceptical Essays*. One of the essays in the book is called "The Recrudescence of Puritanism." The following quote is from that essay: "It is obvious that 'obscenity' is not a term capable of exact legal definition; in the practice of the Courts, it means 'anything that shocks the magistrate.'" Some fifty years later, no less of an articulate jurist than U.S. Supreme Court Justice William J. Brennan still struggled to define obscenity. Justice Brennan's famous "definition" regarding obscenity is often quoted: "I can't define it, but I know it when I see it." There is nothing necessarily obscene about goodwill except, perhaps, its ability to escape definition. However, regarding goodwill, many analysts believe that they know it when they see it.

While there is no universally accepted definition of goodwill, this chapter presents the common types of goodwill intangibles and the common components of goodwill intangibles. Common valuation methods are then discussed. Some analysts believe that only income approach methods are appropriate to value goodwill. In response to that belief, we discuss cost approach, market approach, and income approach valuation methods. Data and other research sources are presented next. The data sources relate principally to sources of empirical transaction data regarding the sale of goodwill intangibles. Last, we present an example of the analysis and valuation of goodwill.

There are many interpretations (and misinterpretations) of goodwill. All of these interpretations can generally be grouped into two categories: accounting interpretations and economics interpretations. From the analyst's perspective, the economics interpretations may be more conceptually rigorous and more practically useful. However, analysts should be familiar with both categories of interpretations. Both sets of interpretations generally agree on the components of (or factors that create) goodwill and the types of goodwill (or situations in which goodwill arises).

## Components of Goodwill

There are three principal components of goodwill. The components may be considered the factors that cause goodwill or the reasons why goodwill exists in certain circumstances.

The first component of goodwill is the existence of assets in place and ready to use. This component is sometimes referred to as the going-concern value element of goodwill. The fact that all elements of a business enterprise are physically and functionally assembled creates value. These elements include capital (e.g., equipment), labor (e.g., employees), and coordination (e.g., management). Some of the created value enhances the value of these elements. For example, the value of the equipment will likely be greater when appraised on an assembled, going-concern basis (as compared to on a piece-meal, liquidation basis). Some of the value attaches to discrete intangible assets. For example, a trained and assembled workforce intangible asset may be created. Finally, some of the value may inure to the goodwill intangible.

The second component of goodwill is the existence of excess economic income. This component is discussed at length in the methodology section of this chapter. Briefly, excess income is that level of income generated by a business that is greater than the amount that would be considered a fair rate of return on all of the other tangible and intangible assets that are used in the business. The excess economic income component relates directly to the concept of goodwill as the value of a business (or other economic unit) that cannot be assigned to any of the other tangible assets or identified intangible assets of the business.

The third component of goodwill is the expectation of future events that are not directly related to the current operation of the business. For example, goodwill may be created by investors' expectations of future capital expenditures, future mergers and acquisitions, future products or services, and future customers or clients. The expectation component relates directly to the concept of goodwill as the current value of future assets not yet in existence as of the valuation date. Investors (and owners) assign a goodwill value to a business if they expect net present value of the income associated with the future events to be positive. Of course, the net present values of the assets currently in existence (e.g., capital assets, product lines, customers, etc.) are assigned to those respective tangible and intangible assets.

## Types of Goodwill Intangibles

There are three categories of circumstances in which the goodwill intangible comes into existence. These sets of circumstances may affect the identification and the ownership of goodwill. However, they should not affect the valuation of goodwill.

The first type of goodwill is institutional. This is the goodwill that relates to an industrial or commercial business enterprise. This goodwill results from the collective operations of—and the collective assemblage of assets of—the subject business enterprise.

The second type of goodwill is professional practice goodwill. As the name implies, this type of goodwill relates to medical, dental, legal, accounting, and other professional practices. This type of goodwill is distinguished because it has two components: the practitioner component and the business component. The practitioner component relates to the goodwill created by the reputation and skills of the individual human practitioners—that is, the actual physicians, dentists, lawyers, CPAs, and other professionals. The business component relates to the goodwill created by the location, reputation, longevity, assembled assets, and operating procedures of the institutional practice. An important issue of this type of goodwill is: Who owns each of the two components? This issue can become very controversial in marital dissolution or shareholder dispute litigation matters.

The third type of goodwill is celebrity goodwill. As the name implies, this is the goodwill associated with being a famous individual. There are three categories of celebrities that enjoy such goodwill: sports celebrities, entertainment celebrities, and achievement celebrities. These various categories of celebrity goodwill are distinguished by the factors that created the goodwill. For example, the sports celebrity goodwill is created by physical prowess. That prowess (and the associated goodwill) may wane with the age of the athlete. Entertainment goodwill relates to singers, musicians, actors, television talk show hosts, radio disk jockeys, and so on.

This type of goodwill also relates to skill and ability. But for many entertainers, professional skill and ability may increase (and not decrease) with age. The component of achievement celebrities includes prominent corporate executives' goodwill, politicians, clergy, or organizational leaders. The goodwill of an achievement celebrity often relates to the career or other professional accomplishments of that individual. Unlike other types of goodwill, it is quite difficult to transfer celebrity goodwill.

## Accountant's Interpretation of Goodwill

Under generally accepted accounting principles (GAAP), the goodwill that a business enterprise develops is rarely recorded on the financial statements of the business. Most commonly, purchased goodwill is recorded by a corporate acquiror after a business is acquired. Even then, goodwill is recorded on the books and records of the acquired business only if the acquisition qualifies under the purchase accounting rules (as compared to the pooling of interest accounting rules).

There are a few other isolated instances when a company's goodwill is recorded on the company's financial statements, such as under the pushdown accounting rules related to corporate reorganization. But the instances in which a company's developed goodwill (as opposed to its purchased goodwill) is recorded for accounting purposes are extremely rare.

Accordingly, accountants use a fairly broad definition of goodwill. To the accountant, intangible value in the nature of goodwill often represents the total value of the business enterprise (represented by the actual purchase price for the business in an acquisitive transaction) less the fair market value of the business enterprise tangible real property and tangible personal property. That is, the value of goodwill is the total value (i.e., the acquisition purchase price) of the business less the value of the business's tangible assets.

So, by the accountant's broad definition, goodwill generally includes all of the intangible value of a business enterprise. This is usually the case even if the intangible value comes from identifiable intangible personal property assets or identifiable intangible real property assets. Therefore, the accountant's broad definition captures the total intangible value of a subject business enterprise.

## Economist's Interpretation of Goodwill

The economist's interpretation of goodwill is somewhat less global than the accountant's interpretation. Also, the economist's interpretation of goodwill may be more useful to analysts who are interested in the identification and valuation of the specific intangible asset goodwill, as opposed to the total intangible value of a subject business enterprise.

Economists define the intangible asset goodwill as the capitalization of all of the economic income from a business enterprise that cannot be associated with any other asset (tangible or intangible) of the business. For purposes of this definition of the goodwill intangible, economic income can be defined several different ways: It can mean net cash flow, before or after business debt service; net income, before or after taxes; net operating income; and so forth. The important consideration is that in the economic income capitalization process, the capitalization rate (whether yield or direct) used should be consistent with the definition of economic income used.

So, the economist would first quantify all of the economic income (as defined) of a subject business enterprise. Second, he or she would allocate or assign some portion of the business's total economic income to each of the assets (tangible and intangible) that contribute to the production of that income—that is, to the net working capital assets, to the tangible personal property, to the real estate, and to the specifically identified intangible assets and intellectual properties (e.g., to patents, trademarks, copyrights, contracts, licenses, etc.). Third, that portion of the business's total economic income that cannot be reasonably allocated to any other asset—that is, the residual economic income—is quantified and assigned to the goodwill intangible. Fourth, the capitalization of this residual economic income represents the intangible value in the nature of goodwill.

## THE ANALYSIS OF GOODWILL

In most valuation and economic analyses, the goodwill intangible may include concepts from both the accountant's definition and the economist's definition. Analysts may sometimes identify and value goodwill globally as the total intangible value of a business enterprise (akin to the accountant's interpretation). In this regard, goodwill is valued using a general residual method. In other words, goodwill is valued as the unidentified residual after the values of the total identified tangible assets are subtracted from the total value of the subject business.

More commonly, analysts value the goodwill intangible on a more discrete basis. By this discrete definition, the goodwill intangible is the remaining unidentified intangible value of a business enterprise after the appropriate values have been assigned to all of the other identified tangible and intangible assets. In this regard, the goodwill intangible is valued using a very specific residual method. In other words, intangible value in the nature of goodwill is that value that is not assigned to: working capital assets (e.g., receivables and inventory), tangible personal property (e.g., machinery and equipment), real estate (e.g., land and buildings), intangible personal property (e.g., trademarks and patents), and intangible real property (e.g., leases and easements).

This discrete definition and analysis of goodwill is often more applicable to the many reasons for which goodwill is subject to analysis.

## REASONS TO ANALYZE THE GOODWILL INTANGIBLE

There are many circumstances that require the analysis of intangible value in the nature of goodwill. Some of the more common reasons to analyze this intangible asset are described briefly here.

**1. Damage Analyses.** When a business or professional practice has suffered a tortious action (e.g., breach of contract, infringement, business interference, etc.), one measure of the damages suffered is the reduction in the value of the company's goodwill due to the action. This analysis may encompass the comparative valuation of the company's goodwill before and after the tortious action. This method is also useful for quantifying the economic effects of a prolonged labor strike, a natural disaster, or a similar phenomenon.

**2. Business or Professional Practice Merger.** When two businesses or professional practices merge, the equity of the merged enterprise has to be allocated to the merger partners. One way to allocate equity in the merged enterprise is in proportion to the relative value of the assets contributed, including the contributed goodwill intangible.

**3. Business or Professional Practice Separation.** When a business or professional practice splits up, the assets of the consolidated business have to be allocated to the new separate businesses. One way to allocate the assets to the separating partners is in proportion to the relative value of the assets controlled by or developed by each partner, including the goodwill intangible of each partner.

**4. Solvency Test.** The solvency of a business is a particularly important issue with regard to lender's fraudulent conveyance concerns during a financing or a financial restructuring. One of the specific tests to determine if a business is solvent is: Does the value of the company's assets exceed the value of the company's liabilities (after the financing)? One of the assets that should be considered in a solvency analysis is the company's goodwill intangible.

**5. Insolvency Test.** The degree of insolvency of a business has very important income tax consequences if debt is forgiven (in whole or in part) during a refinancing or financial restructuring. One of the specific tests to determine if a business is insolvent is: Is the value of the company's assets less than the value of the company's liabilities (after the debt forgiveness)? The federal income tax regulations specifically indicate that one of the assets that should be considered in an insolvency analysis is the company's goodwill intangible.

**6. Transfer Price.** When intangible assets are transferred between controlled corporations (e.g., between a corporate parent and subsidiary), an arm's-length transfer price should be estimated for the transfer of the subject assets. This is true both from a financial accounting perspective and (perhaps more importantly) from an income tax perspective. Such transfers may have state (as compared to federal) income tax ramifications if both of the controlled corporations are domestic. Such transfers will have federal income tax consequences if one of the controlled corporations is international. This transfer pricing analysis may apply if one of the intangible assets transferred is the company's goodwill intangible. Transfer pricing is discussed in Chapter 25.

**7. Bankruptcy and Reorganization.** Parties in interest to a bankruptcy estate often have to decide if the subject business enterprise is worth more as a going-concern business (pursuant to a plan of reorganization) or as a mass disposition of assets (pursuant to a plan of liquidation). An analysis of the company's intangible value in the nature of goodwill (if any) may be useful in assessing whether the business is worth reorganizing or not. A particularly thoughtful discussion of the analysis of professional practice goodwill for bankruptcy purposes is presented in the fairly recent decision of the United States Court of Appeals for the Seventh Circuit, *In the Matter of Douglas R. Prince and Jane Prince.*[1] In that decision, a significant portion of the value of a bankrupt orthodontics practice was related to the goodwill intangible.

**8. Conversion of a C Corporation to an S Corporation.** One important factor in the analysis of the costs and benefits of converting from C

---

1. *In the Matter of Douglas R. Prince and Jane Prince,* 85 F.3d 314, 1996 U.S. App LEXIS 13151.

corporation to S corporation (federal income tax) status is the quantification of any built-in gains tax (BIG tax) associated with the assets of the subject business. The federal income tax regulations related to the BIG tax are clear that the subject company's goodwill is one asset that should be considered in the analysis.

**9. Business Enterprise Valuation.** The identification and quantification of the goodwill intangibles are important parts of any business valuation that uses an asset-based valuation approach. Such business enterprise valuations are routinely performed for taxation (e.g., gift tax, estate tax, charitable contribution, abandonment, loss, etc.) as well as for transaction, financing, litigation, and other purposes.

**10. Deprivation Analysis.** The valuation of the intangible asset goodwill is often a critical assessment in the damage analysis associated with a business that has been subject to a condemnation, expropriation, or eminent domain action. Analysts sometimes only consider the value of the real estate and tangible personal property that was subject to the taking. However, even if the subject business is relocated to a new location, the business may have suffered a loss of all or part of its goodwill intangible.

**11. Ownership Allocation Litigation.** Several forms of litigation involve the allocation of direct or indirect ownership interests in business entities. Two common examples of such litigation include marital dissolution cases (typically allocating indirect ownership interests in the business interests to the marital estate) and minority shareholder squeeze-out merger cases (typically allocating direct ownership interests to the minority stockholders). In such litigation, the identification and quantification of the goodwill of the subject business or professional practice is often a vigorously debated topic.

**12. Ad Valorem Property Taxation.** State and local ad valorem property taxation typically only applies to real estate and to tangible personal property. However, the existence of economic obsolescence (a particular form of external obsolescence) may have a direct effect on the value of the taxpayer's tangible assets. Accordingly, an assessment of the existence of economic obsolescence may be an important step in an appraisal performed for property tax purposes. While there are several common methods for quantifying economic obsolescence, most methods incorporate some analysis of the goodwill of the business that operates the subject tangible assets. Generally, if the subject business enjoys positive goodwill value, then the tangible assets will not experience economic obsolescence. However, if the subject business experiences negative goodwill, then the tangible assets are likely to be subject to economic obsolescence.

This discussion of the reasons to analyze the goodwill intangible is not intended to be exhaustive. There are other reasons to analyze the goodwill intangible, including for purposes of the allocation of a lump-sum purchase price for an acquired business.

## COMMON VALUATION METHODS

As with all intangible assets, cost approach, market approach, and income approach methods are all applicable to the valuation and economic analysis of goodwill intangibles. Cost approach methods are least commonly used. Market approach methods are fairly commonly used. Income approach methods are most commonly used.

## Cost Approach

Using the cost approach, the analyst estimates the amount of current cost required to recreate the elements of the subject goodwill intangible. The most common cost approach method is typically called the component build-up method. The first step to the component build-up method is to list all of the individual components of the subject goodwill. The second step is to estimate the amount of cost required to recreate each component. This method is based upon the concept of goodwill as the value of assets in place and ready to use.

A common application of the build-up method is the analysis of foregone economic income (i.e., the opportunity cost) during the time period required to recreate all of the going-concern elements of the business enterprise associated with the subject goodwill. For example, let's assume that it would take two elapsed years to recreate all of the assets (both tangible and intangible) of the subject business enterprise. This would include the purchase and installation of all equipment, the construction or purchase of all real estate, the selection of suppliers, the creation of a distribution system, the training of all employees, the building of a level of consumer recognition and confidence, and the recreation of a level of customer relationships (commensurate with the actual level of business of the subject enterprise). Let's also assume that the subject business will earn $10,000,000 per year in income (however defined) during the two-year recreation period. The present value of the $20,000,000 in opportunity cost during the recreation period is one indication of the value of the subject goodwill intangible.

## Market Approach

There are two common market approach methods. The first method estimates the value of goodwill as the residual from the purchase price of the actual sale of the subject business enterprise. The second method estimates the value of goodwill based upon an analysis of actual guideline sales transactions. Goodwill intangibles are rarely sold totally separately from other assets, so guideline sale transactions usually involve the sale of going-concern businesses or professional practices. In these transactional data, the allocation of the sale price between goodwill and all other assets is reported. This means that even this second market approach method relies upon a residual from sale price procedure to estimate the value of goodwill.

To use the residual from purchase price method, obviously there has to be a sale of the business enterprise related to the subject goodwill. First, the analyst should confirm that the subject sale was an arm's-length sale. Second, the analyst should confirm that the purchase price represents a cash equivalency price. If there are noncash components or deferred payments (e.g., an earn-out provision) related to the purchase price, then the analyst should convert the entire amount of consideration to a cash equivalency value. Third, the analyst should estimate the value of all the identified tangible and intangible assets of the subject business. Fourth, the analyst should subtract the total value of all the identified tangible and intangible assets from the purchase price. The residual represents the value of the goodwill intangible.

To use the analysis of guideline sales transactions method, the analyst should identify and select actual sales of businesses that are sufficiently comparative to the subject business enterprise. For certain industries (such as professional practices), these guideline sale transactional data are fairly accessible because they are reported in publications and periodicals. With regard to these empirical transactions, goodwill is typically expressed as a percent of the total transaction price or a percent of the total annual revenue earned by the subject business. These market-derived pricing multiples are then applied to the subject business enterprise in order to conclude a value for the subject goodwill. Of course, it is noteworthy that the market-derived pricing multiples are themselves estimated based upon an allocation of the sale price for each business or professional practice included in that data source.

## Income Approach

The three most common income approach methods are:

1. Residual from business enterprise value method.
2. Capitalized excess economic income method.
3. Present value of future economic events method.

Each of these methods is based upon the concept of goodwill representing the expectation of some future economic benefit.

### Residual from Business Enterprise Value Method

The residual from business enterprise value method values goodwill as follows: overall business enterprise value less the value of financial assets, less the value of tangible assets, and less the value of identified intangible assets, equals the intangible value in the nature of goodwill.

There are several generally accepted methods for valuing going-concern business entities. Analysts synthesize one or more of these methods to conclude the value of going-concern business entities. Of course, the objective of using more than one method is to develop mutually supporting evidence as to the valuation conclusion. Several of the more common business valuation methods are:

1. Asset accumulation method (an asset-based approach method).
2. Discounted cash flow method (an income approach method).
3. Guideline merged and acquired company method (a market approach method).
4. Guideline publicly traded company method (a market approach method).

The use of any of these valuation methods and their respective procedures and analyses depends upon the analyst's judgment and upon the quantity and quality of available financial and operational data. While any of these valuation methods may be used in the residual from business enterprise value method, the discounted cash flow method is one of the more common methods for the purpose of goodwill valuation.

The discounted cash flow method is based on the premise that the value of the business enterprise is the present value of the future economic income to be derived by the stakeholders of the business. The discounted cash flow method requires the following valuation analyses: revenue analysis, expense analysis, investment analysis, capital structure analysis, and residual value analysis.

The revenue analysis involves a projection of prospective revenues from the sale of products or provision of services from the subject company. This analysis includes consideration of the following market factors: sales volume, average selling price or contract rate, market dynamics, competitive pressures, price elasticities of demand, regulatory changes, technological changes, and so forth.

The expense analysis involves consideration of the following factors: fixed versus variable costs, product versus period costs, cash versus noncash costs, direct versus indirect costs, cost absorption principles, cost–efficiency relationships, cost–volume–profit relationships, and so on.

The investment analysis involves consideration of the following factors: required minimum cash balances, days sales outstanding in accounts receivable, inventory turnover, plant utilization, capital expenditure budgets, and so forth.

The capital structure analysis involves consideration of the following factors: current capital structure, optimal capital structure, cost of various capital components, weighted average cost of capital, systematic and nonsystematic risk factors, marginal cost of capital, and so on.

The residual value analysis involves the estimate of the value of the prospective cash flow generated by the subject business after the conclusion of a discrete projection period. The residual value can be estimated by various methods, including: the capital market pricing multiple, capitalization method, the annuity in perpetuity method, and the Gordon dividend capitalization model, among other methods.

Based on the results of the listed analyses, a projection of cash flow from business operations is made for a reasonable discrete projection period. The cash flow projection is discounted at an appropriate present value discount rate in order to determine the present value.

The residual value of the subject business enterprises is estimated at the end of the discrete projection period. The residual value is also discounted in order to determine a present value. The present value of the discrete cash flow projection is summed with the present value of the company's residual value. The summation represents the value of the business enterprise.

The estimated value of the subject business enterprises minus the estimated value of the identifiable tangible and intangible assets (including net working capital) indicates the intangible value in the nature of goodwill.

## Capitalized Excess Economic Income Method

The capitalized excess economic income method for the valuation of goodwill involves the quantification and capitalization of any excess economic income (as defined) earned by the subject company. There are several acceptable versions of the capitalized excess economic income method. The following paragraphs describe one of the common versions of this method.

First, this method requires the estimation of an amount of normal economic income that investors would expect, given the risk of the subject business. This often involves an assessment of industry average rates of return on investment. Typically, an industry average rate of return on net identified assets is multiplied by the value of the subject company's net tangible assets in order to quantify the fair economic return for the subject company. The value of the net identified assets of the company includes all of the company's financial assets, tangible assets, and identified intangible assets and intellectual properties (net of current liabilities).

Second, the difference between the actual economic earnings of the subject company and the fair economic return of the subject company net identified assets is computed. If the actual economic earnings of the company exceed the fair or expected economic income, then excess economic earnings exist with regard to the subject company.

Third, the amount of excess economic income is capitalized as an annuity in perpetuity, using an appropriate direct capitalization rate. Of course, the derivation of the appropriate direct capitalization rate should be consistent with the measurement of economic income used. The result of the capitalization process is the economic value of the intangible value in the nature of goodwill for the subject company. This method is illustrated in the Valuation Example section of this chapter.[2]

## Present Value of Future Economic Events Method

The first step in this method is to list all of the future economic events associated with the subject business enterprise that are not already encompassed in the value of the identified tangible and intangible assets. This may include expected future capital expenditures, mergers, acquisitions, product lines, or customers. Obviously, creating a comprehensive list of all expected future economic events is an extremely difficult task.

For purposes of illustrating a practical application of this method, let's limit the discussion to analyzing the present value of the expected future customers of the subject business. As part of either of the residual methods to the valuation of goodwill, it is common for analysts to quantify and capitalize the prospective economic income associated with the company's identified current customer list, over the expected remaining life of those identified customer relationships. Basically, the value of the company's current customer list is the present value of the economic income to be earned from future product or service sales to current (identified) customers.

Using the present value of future economic events method, goodwill is estimated as the present value of the future economic income to be earned from the prospective sales of goods and services to future (unidentified) customers. These future customers are unidentified new customers who presumably will take the place of the company's identified current customers, as those identified current customers retire or turn over.

This valuation method requires a projection of the net economic income-generating capacity of the company, beginning with the expiration of the company's current income sources (i.e., identified current customers) and continuing (essentially) into perpetuity. The present value of the prospective economic income stream (which should provide for a fair return *of* and *on* all the tangible and intangible assets employed to service

---

2. The capitalized economic income method is discussed in detail in Shannon P. Pratt, Robert F. Reilly, and Robert P. Schweihs, *Valuing a Business: The Analysis and Appraisal of Closely Held Companies*, 3rd ed. (New York: McGraw-Hill, 1996) and Pratt, Reilly, and Schweihs, *Valuing Small Businesses and Professional Practices*, 3rd ed. (New York: McGraw-Hill, 1998).

the unidentified future customers) is an indication of the value of the company's goodwill. Using this method, the value of the company's goodwill is the present value of the economic income to be earned from future sales to future (unidentified) customers.

This valuation method is one of the most intellectually appealing and conceptually correct methods to value a company's goodwill. Consistent with the way economists perceive goodwill, this method quantifies and assigns all of the value of a business enterprise that cannot be associated with any of its current identified assets. In other words, goodwill is quantified as the present value of all prospective economic income that cannot be associated with the current sources of economic income (i.e., the company's currently identified tangible and intangible assets).

However, due to the uncertainties of such long-term projections of economic income generation from unidentified sources (i.e., from potential future customers whom we currently don't serve and whom we currently don't even know), it is often difficult to use this method in the practical valuation of the goodwill intangible.

## DATA SOURCES

Data sources can either be internal to the subject business enterprise or external to the subject business enterprise. Internal data sources relate to documentation regarding historical and prospective results of operations. External data sources relate to empirical pricing data with regard to business and professional practice sale transactions involving goodwill.

## Internal Data Sources

Analysts are interested in various data sources regarding the business enterprise that encompasses the subject goodwill. These internal data sources fall into the following categories:

1. Existence of identified tangible and intangible assets, including detailed listing of net working capital accounts, real estate, tangible personal property, and discrete intangible assets and intellectual properties.
2. Valuation of identified tangible and intangible assets, including recent appraisals of any asset categories.
3. Historical results of operations, including historical income statements, balance sheets, cash flow statements, and capital statements.
4. Prospective results of operations, including current budgets, plans, forecasts, and projections prepared for any purpose.

Information from any of these internal data sources can be used in all of the goodwill intangible valuation methods described here.

## External Data Sources

For certain industries (principally professional practices), there are publications, periodicals, and other data sources that report on the goodwill components of actual business sale transactions. These data sources are listed below.

*Goodwill Registry.* Plymouth Meeting, PA: The Health Care Group. Annual. The *Goodwill Registry* provides goodwill valuation data based upon comparative sales transactions. Data are submitted on transactions in medical practices from appraisers, brokers, and other professionals. The book is divided by medical specialty. The 1997 edition contains over 3,000 reports from transactions during the years 1988 to 1997.

*Bank Mergers & Acquisitions: The Authoritative Newsletter Providing In-Depth Analysis of the Restructuring of American Banking.* Charlottesville, VA: SNL Securities. Monthly. Includes information on transactions assisted by the Federal Deposit Insurance Corporation (FDIC) for commercial banks or by the Resolution Trust Corporation (RTC) for savings and loan institutions.

*Media Mergers and Acquisitions.* Carmel, CA: Paul Kagan Associates, Inc. Monthly. Newsletter on media merger activity. Covers broadcasting, motion pictures, advertising, and publishing.

*Valuation and Performance Monitor.* New York: Vert Independent Capital Research, Inc. Monthly. Shows detailed equity valuation and financial performance data for 86 industries, including leverage and risk profiles. A general analysis of important merger and acquisition transactions is covered.

*Valuation Survey of Architecture, Engineering, Planning & Environmental Consulting Firms.* Natick, MA: Zweig White & Associates. Annual. Reliable comparative data on actual values of privately held firms.

## Financial Ratios

*Almanac of Business and Industrial Financial Ratios.* Leo Troy. Englewood, NJ: Prentice Hall. Annual. Contains financial ratios derived from federal tax returns. Ratios for each of about 200 industries are arranged according to company asset size.

*RMA Annual Statement Studies.* Philadelphia: Robert Morris Associates. Annual. Median and quartile financial ratios are given for over 400 kinds of manufacturing, wholesale, retail, construction, and consumer finance establishments. Data are sorted by both asset size and sales volume.

*Industry Norms and Key Business Ratios, Desk Top Edition.* New York: Dun and Bradstreet Corp. Business Information Services. Annual. Five volumes. Covers over 800 kinds of businesses, arranged by SIC code. More detailed editions covering longer periods of time are also available.

## Directories, Periodicals, and Newsletters

*Dental Practice and Finance.* Medical Economics Publishing Co., Inc. Bimonthly. Controlled circulation. Covers practice management and financial topics.

*Law Office Economics and Management.* Clark Boardman Callaghan. Quarterly.

*Medical Economics.* Medical Economics Co., Inc. Semimonthly. Covers the financial, economic, insurance, administrative, and other nonclinical aspects of private medical practice.

*Public Accounting Report.* Strafford Publications, Inc. Semimonthly. Newsletter. Presents news and trends affecting the accounting profession.

### Trade and Professional Societies

*American Bar Association.* 750 N. Lake Shore Dr., Chicago, IL 60611. Phone: (800) 621-6159 or (312) 988-5000. Fax: (312) 988-6281.

*American Institute of Architects.* 1735 New York Ave., NW, Washington, DC 20006. Phone: (202) 626-7300. Fax: (202) 626-7421.

*American Institute of Certified Public Accountants.* 1211 Ave. of the Americas, New York, NY 10036-8775. Phone: (800) 862-4272 or (212) 596-6200. Fax: (212) 596-6213.

*American Medical Association.* 515 N. State St., Chicago, IL 60610. Phone: (312) 464-5000. Fax: (312) 464-4184.

*Institute of Certified Professional Business Consultants.* 330 S. Wells St., Suite 1422, Chicago, IL 60606-7101. Phone: (800) 447-1684 or (312) 360-0384. Fax: (312) 360-0388.

### VALUATION EXAMPLE

This valuation example presents an application of the capitalized excess economic income method of goodwill analysis.

## Fact Set and Assumptions

Exhibit 20-1 presents the historical financial statements for the business enterprise that encompasses the goodwill intangible that is the subject of this analysis. This illustrative company is named Lotsa Goodwill, Inc. (hereinafter "Lotsa"). Exhibit 20-1 presents a balance sheet, income statement, and cash flow statement for Lotsa.

The objective of this analysis is to estimate the value of the goodwill intangible of Lotsa, as of December 31, 1998.

Exhibit 20-2 presents the value of the net identified assets of Lotsa, including the net tangible assets plus the discrete intangible assets.

## Approaches and Methods

Exhibit 20-3 presents a common method for estimating the overall rate of return and the overall direct capitalization rate. The method that is used to estimate both rates with respect to the company overall is the company's weighted averaged cost of capital.

Exhibit 20-4 presents the estimation of the Lotsa excess economic income.

Lotsa Goodwill, Inc., Summary Balance Sheet (Historical Cost Basis), as of December 31, 1998

| ASSETS | | LIABILITIES AND OWNER'S EQUITY | |
|---|---|---|---|
| Current assets | $1,000,000 | Current liabilities | $1,000,000 |
| (cash, receivables, and inventory) | | (payables and accruals) | |
| Tangible assets | 2,000,000 | Long-term debt | 1,000,000 |
| (real estate and equipment—net of | | Owners' equity | 1,000,000 |
| accumulated depreciation) | | | |
| | | TOTAL LIABILITIES AND | |
| TOTAL ASSETS | $3,000,000 | OWNERS' EQUITY | $3,000,000 |

Lotsa Goodwill, Inc., Summary Income Statement for the Twelve Months Ended December 31, 1998

| | |
|---|---|
| Net revenues | $5,000,000 |
| Operating expenses | |
| Cash expenses | 3,700,000 |
| Depreciation expense | 200,000 |
| Interest expense | 100,000 |
| Total expenses | 4,000,000 |
| Profit before taxes | 1,000,000 |
| Income taxes | 400,000 |
| Profit after taxes | $ 600,000 |

Lotsa Goodwill, Inc., Summary Results of Operations for the Twelve Months Ended December 31, 1998

| | | | |
|---|---|---|---|
| *Net cash flow (to invested capital):* | | | |
| | Profit after taxes | | $600,000 |
| Plus: | Tax-affected interest expense ($100,000 interest expense less $40,000 income tax expense) | | 60,000 |
| Equals: | Profit after taxes—debt-free | | $660,000 |
| Plus: | Depreciation expense | | 200,000 |
| Less: | Capital expenditures (during 1997) | | 200,000 |
| Less: | Increase in net working capital (from 12/31/96 to 12/31/97) | | 100,000 |
| Equals: | Net cash flow (debt-free) | | $560,000 |
| | | | |
| *Operating cash flow (to invested capital):* | | | |
| | Profit after taxes | | $600,000 |
| Plus: | Tax-affected interest expense | | 60,000 |
| Equals: | Profit after taxes (debt-free) | | 660,000 |
| Plus: | Depreciation expense | | 200,000 |
| Equals: | Operating cash flow (debt-free) | | $860,000 |

EXHIBIT 20-2

Lotsa Goodwill, Inc., Application of Capitalized Excess Economic Income Method, Value of Net Identified Assets

| Value of Net Tangible Assets and Identified Discrete Intangible Assets | Value as of 12/31/98 |
|---|---|
| Current assets | $1,000,000 |
| Minus: Current liabilities | 1,000,000 |
| Equals: Net working capital | 0 |
| Plus: Tangible assets (based on contemporaneous market value appraisals of real estate and equipment) | 2,500,000 |
| Plus: Identified individual intangible assets (based on contemporaneous market value appraisals of individually identified intangible assets, such as computer software, patents, trademarks, or copyrights) | 500,000 |
| Equals: Fair market value of net tangible assets and of identified discrete intangible assets | $3,000,000 |

## Valuation Reconciliation and Value Conclusion

Exhibit 20-5 illustrates the procedure for capitalizing the excess economic income measure into an estimate of intangible value in the nature of goodwill. Based upon this analysis, the indicated value of the Lotsa goodwill intangible, as of December 31, 1998, is $733,000.

Exhibit 20-6 illustrates the Lotsa business value indication based on the indicated value of the Lotsa goodwill intangible. As presented in Exhibit 20-6, the indicated value of the Lotsa total owners' equity, as of December 31, 1998, is $2,733,000.

## BIBLIOGRAPHY

Bloomberg, Lawrence N. *The Investment Value of Goodwill.* Baltimore: Johns Hopkins University, Studies in the Social Sciences, 1983.

Blumberg, Grace Ganz. "Identifying and Valuing Goodwill at Divorce." *Law and Contemporary Problems,* Spring 1993, pp. 217–72.

Cenker, William, and Robert Bloom. "Valuation of an Accounting Practice and Goodwill." *Journal of Accounting Education,* Fall 1990, pp. 311–19.

Chauvin, Keith W. and Mark Hirschey. "Goodwill, Profitability, and Market Value of the Firm." *Journal of Accounting & Public Policy,* Summer 1994, pp. 159–180.

Cohen, Robert Stephan, and Arthur J. Ciampi. "Goodwill, Though Intangible, Can Be Assigned Value: Methodologies Considered." *New York Law Journal,* March 3, 1997, p. S2.

Cosman, Madeleine Pelner, Thomas Russell Lang, and Marin C. Goodheart. "Comparing Medical and Business Goodwill Components." *Fair$hare: The Matrimonial Law Monthly,* January 1990, pp. 3–7.

Crouch, Holmes F. *Selling Your Business: Goodwill & Intangibles—Paths to Maximum Gain,* 2d ed. Saratoga, CA: Allyear Tax Guides, 1997.

Dandekar, Manoj P., and Robert F. Reilly. "The Valuation of Goodwill." Willamette Management Associates *Insights,* Spring 1993, pp. 7–12.

Elliott, Robert K. and Don M. Pallais. "First: Know Your Market." *Journal of Accountancy,* July 1997, pp. 56–63.

Evans, Frank C. "Business Valuation: Applications for Equitable Distribution in Divorce." *CPA Management Consultant,* Summer 1996, pp. 7–8.

Fenton, Edmund D. Jr., Lucinda VanAlst, and Patricia Isaacs. "The Determination and Valuation of Goodwill: Using a Proven, Acceptable Method to Withstand IRS Challenge." *Tax Adviser,* September 1991, pp. 602–612.

Fishman, Jay E., and William J. Morrison. "Goodwill Valuation in an Insurance Business." *Fair$hare: The Matrimonial Law Monthly,* May 1997, pp. 8–9.

Gallinger, George W. "Valuation of Community Goodwill in Divorce Proceedings Involving Closely-Held Businesses." *ASA Valuation,* January 1992, pp. 34–41.

Lotsa Goodwill, Inc., Application of Capitalized Excess Economic Income Method, Overall Required Rate of Return and Overall Direct Capitalization Rate

## Weighted Average Cost of Capital

Based upon book value of capital components from December 31, 1998, balance sheet:

| Type of Capital Component in Capital Structure | Before-Tax Cost of Capital Component | After-Tax Cost of Capital Component | Weighting in Capital Structure | Weighted Cost of Capital Component |
|---|---|---|---|---|
| Long-term debt | 10% | 6% | 50% | 3% |
| Owners' equity | 24% | 24% | 50% | 12% |
| Total | | | 100% | 15% |
| After-tax weighted average cost of capital (rounded) | | | | 15% |

Notes:
a. Let's assume that the blended interest rate on the Lotsa long-term debt is 10%. Let's also assume that the required risk-adjusted rate of return on the owners' equity of Lotsa is 24%.
b. The effective income tax rate for Lotsa is 40%; the cost of debt capital (i.e., the interest rate) is affected by this income tax rate, where the cost of equity capital is already "paid" from after-tax dollars.

## Required Fair Rate of Return on Assets

If the after-tax weighted average cost of capital is 15%, then this means that the subject business must "pay" (on an after-tax basis) a blended rate of 15% on its total sources of capital—that is, long-term debt and owners' equity.

If the after-tax weighted average cost of capital is 15%, then this means that the subject business must "earn" (on an after-tax basis) a blended rate of 15% on its net working capital, on its tangible assets, and on its intangible assets.

Of course, intangible assets (including intangible value in the nature of goodwill) generally have greater risk than tangible assets. And, tangible assets (including real estate and equipment) generally have greater risk than net working capital assets (including cash, receivables, and inventory). Accordingly, a business would typically expect that intangible assets would have an asset-specific cost of capital that is higher than tangible assets, and that fixed tangible assets would have an asset-specific cost of capital that is higher than net working capital assets. Likewise, a business would typically expect to earn a higher rate of return on intangible assets than on tangible assets, and a higher rate of return on fixed tangible assets than on net working capital.

However, since we are valuing all of the operating assets of Lotsa collectively—that is, as one going-concern business enterprise—we apply the overall required rate of return to all of the net assets of the business. This overall required rate of return on net assets has to equal the company's overall weighted average cost of capital—or 15% in this example.

## Direct Capitalization Rate

A direct capitalization rate can be mathematically derived as follows:

$$c = k - g$$

where:

$c$ = direct capitalization rate
$k$ = present value discount rate
$g$ = expected long-term growth rate

One procedure for estimating a company's present value discount rate is to calculate its weighted average cost of capital.

Since we have just calculated the Lotsa weighted average cost of capital to be 15%, we use that indication as the appropriate present value discount rate. For purposes of simplicity, we assume a 0% expected long-term growth rate. Therefore, we use 15% as the direct capitalization rate for the estimated measure of excess earnings.

This direct capitalization rate (i.e., the present value discount rate *minus* the expected long-term growth rate) is only appropriate when the same required rate of return is being applied to all of the company's net asset values. A different direct capitalization rate would be appropriate when an asset-specific rate of return is applied to the company's net asset values.

Gitlin, Gunnar. "Business Valuation in Divorce—What Is Double-Dipping and How Is It Quantified?" *American Journal of Family Law,* Summer 1997, pp. 109–118.

"'Goodwill' Value of Partnership Is Not Deemed a Marital Asset." *New York Law Journal,* July 15, 1997, p. 25.

Jimmerson, James J. "Celebrity Goodwill: Is It Real or Is It a Mirage?" *American Journal of Family Law,* Summer 1997, pp. 145–151.

Lotsa Goodwill, Inc., Application of Capitalized Excess Economic Income Method, Estimation of Excess Economic Income

| | | |
|---|---|---|
| Net cash flow (after-tax) | | $560,000 |
| Fair market value of net tangible assets and of identified discrete intangible assets | $3,000,000 | |
| Times: Overall required rate of return on net assets | 15% | |
| Required level of economic income | | $450,000 |
| (to provide a fair return on the fair market value of net tangible assets and on identified discrete intangible assets) | | |
| Excess economic income (i.e., net cash flow less required level of economic income) | | $110,000 |

Lotsa Goodwill, Inc., Application of Capitalized Excess Economic Income Method, Capitalization of Excess Economic Income

| | |
|---|---|
| Excess economic income—after a fair return on the fair market value of net tangible assets and identified discrete intangible assets | 110,000 |
| Divided by: direct capitalization rate (based upon applying an overall required rate of return on all net identified assets) | 15% |
| Equals: Estimate of intangible value in the nature of goodwill | $733,333 |
| Value of goodwill intangible (rounded) | $733,000 |

Lotsa Goodwill, Inc. Capitalized Excess Economic Income Method, Indicated Value of Business Enterprise

| ASSETS | | LIABILITIES & OWNERS' EQUITY | |
|---|---|---|---|
| Current assets | $100,000 | Current liabilities | $1,000,000 |
| Tangible assets at fair market value | 2,500,000 | Long-term debt | 1,000,000 |
| Identified individual intangible assets at fair market value | 500,000 | | |
| Intangible value in the nature of goodwill | 733,000 | Owners' equity | 2,733,000 |
| | | TOTAL LIABILITIES & | |
| TOTAL ASSETS | $4,733,000 | OWNERS' EQUITY | $4,733,000 |

The indicated value of the Lotsa owners' equity is $2,733,000. This residual is calculated as follows:

| | | |
|---|---|---|
| | Value of total assets | $4,733,000 |
| Less: | Value of total liabilities | 2,000,000 |
| Equals: | Value of owners' equity | $2,733,000 |

Jurinski, James John, and Linda B. Samuels. "The Professional Service Corporation: Is It Even a Better Alternative Than a Flow-Through Entity?" *Practical Tax Lawyer,* Summer 1997, pp. 23–37.

Knights, Rob. "Nervous about Practice Goodwill Values?" *Charter,* September 1996, p. 40.

McMahon, Martin J. "Valuation of Goodwill in Medical or Dental Practice for Purposes of Divorce Court's Property Distribution." *American Law Reports,* 78 ALR4th 853, supplemented September 1995, pp. 853–957.

Osborne, Kent. "Is the Goodwill of a Business Subject to Ad Valorem Taxation?" *The Journal of Technical Valuation,* December 1991, pp. 11–15.

Oswald, Lynda J. "Goodwill and Going-Concern Value: Emerging Factors in the Just Compensation Equation." *Boston College Law Review,* March 1991, pp. 283–376.

Paulsen, Jon. "Goodwill and Going Concern Value Revisited." *Mergers & Acquisitions,* Winter 1980, pp. 10–13.

Pride, James. "Dentists of Distinction." *Dental Economics,* September 1997, pp. 35–38+.

Rabe, James G., and Robert F. Reilly. "Looking beneath the Surface: Valuing Health Care Intangible Assets." *National Public Accountant,* March 1996, pp. 14–17+.

Reibelt, Graham. "Valuing Goodwill." *Charter,* March 1996, p. 46–47+.

Schwab, Carl E., and Kent W. Goates. "Valuation of Goodwill and Going Concern Important in Matters Involving Insolvency and Change of Ownership." *Tax Adviser,* July 1992, p. 451–452.

Scott, Robert B. Jr. "Determining the Value of a Small Business for Divorce Proceedings." *National Public Accountant,* November 1995, pp. 25–27.

Shenkman, Martin M. "When Should Professional Goodwill Be Valued?" *The Matrimonial Strategist,* March 1997, pp. 1–2.

Udinsky, Jerald H. "Goodwill Depreciation: A New Method for Valuing Professional Practices in a Marital Dissolution." *Community Property Journal,* Fall 1982, pp. 307–22.

Vincent, Linda. "Equity Valuation Implications of Purchase versus Pooling Accounting." *The Journal of Financial Statement Analysis,* Summer 1997, pp. 5–19.

Vinso, Joseph D. "Valuing Professional Goodwill: The Slivka Case Revisited." *ASA Valuation,* June 1988, pp. 66–75.

# Human Capital Intangible Assets

## DESCRIPTION OF HUMAN CAPITAL INTANGIBLES

The class of intangible assets referred to as human capital intangible assets generally includes a company's assembled workforce and contracts with employees (or former employees), such as employment contracts, personality or other entertainment industry contracts, sports player contracts, covenants not to compete, and noncompete agreements.

This chapter focuses on the typical valuation methods used to estimate the value of a company's trained and assembled workforce and noncompetition agreements.

## Trained and Assembled Workforce

A trained and assembled workforce is a highly valuable intangible asset for many companies. In addition, several court cases confirm that an assembled workforce can be properly identified as having a separate, measurable value. In *Ithaca Industries, Inc. v. C.I.R.,*[1] the appellate court held that an in-place workforce was an intangible asset with an ascertainable value. Additionally, taxpayers have been successful in several court cases in requiring that the value of identified appraised intangible assets (such as an assembled workforce) be subtracted from the unit value in states where intangible assets are not taxable for ad valorem purposes. In a case involving Burlington Northern Railroad, the Federal District Court allowed a 10 percent deduction from the value of the unit for the intangible asset value.[2] Intangible assets identified and appraised in that case included an assembled workforce, computer software, and coal (freight delivery) contracts.

## Covenants Not to Compete and Noncompete Agreements

A covenant not to compete is an agreement between a buyer and a seller of a business in which the seller is restricted from competing in the same industry for a specific period of time, often within a defined geographic area. When a business is sold, the buyer often obtains a noncompete agreement from the seller, whether the seller is an individual selling the family business or a corporation divesting a subsidiary. The agreement may be included as one of the terms of the overall asset or stock sale agreement (a covenant not to compete) or it can be created and bargained for as a separate asset sold to the buyer (a noncompete agreement).

### COMMON VALUATION METHODS

Several methods and procedures may be considered in the valuation of assembled workforces and noncompetition agreements. These methods fall into the three general categories of approaches, as discussed in Part 2 of this text: the cost approach, the market approach, and the income approach.

---

1. *Ithaca Industries, Inc. v. C.I.R,* 17 F.3d 684 (4th Cir. 1994).
2. *Burlington Northern R.R. Co. v. Bair,* 815 F.Supp. 1223 (S.D. Iowa, 1993), *aff'd* 60 F.3d 410 (8th Cir. 1995).

# Cost Approach

Estimating the fair market value of a human capital intangible asset using the cost approach typically involves estimating either the reproduction cost or replacement cost of the intangible asset. The reproduction cost equals the cost to construct an exact replica of the subject intangible asset, while the replacement cost is defined as the cost to recreate a property with an equivalent utility of the subject intangible asset.

However, while the replacement intangible asset performs the same task as the subject intangible asset, to the extent that an intangible asset is less useful than the ideal replacement asset, the value of the subject intangible asset must be adjusted for any differences in value due to physical deterioration, functional obsolescence, technological obsolescence, and economic obsolescence.

One method sometimes used to estimate the reproduction cost of an intangible asset is to restate actual historical development costs in current dollars. This provides an estimate of the costs that would need to be incurred to reproduce the property.

A method that is used to estimate the replacement cost is a direct estimate of the current costs necessary to create a similar asset.

## Trained and Assembled Workforce

The replacement cost method is frequently used to estimate the value of an assembled workforce. Costs to replace an assembled workforce include the costs to recruit, hire, and train a replacement workforce.

In applying the replacement cost method to estimate the value of an assembled workforce, some examples of recruiting and hiring costs to consider include the following:

- Salaries and benefits of company employees who are involved in recruiting replacement employees.
- Salaries and benefits of company employees who are involved in interviewing replacement employees.
- Overhead costs (e.g., office space, utilities, and clerical support) related to employees who are involved in recruiting and hiring the replacement employees.
- Headhunter recruitment fees.
- Direct recruitment and hiring expenditures (advertisements, travel and lodging expenses for job candidates, relocation costs, signing bonuses, and so on).

In applying the replacement cost method to estimate the value of an assembled workforce, some examples of the training costs to consider include the following:

- Salaries and benefits of company employees who are involved in training replacement employees.
- Overhead costs (e.g., office space, utilities, and clerical support) related to employees who are involved in training the replacement workforce.
- Salary and benefits paid to employees as they are being trained, until they become productive.

- Direct training expenditures (for example, fees paid for replacement employees to attend formal external training courses).

Typically, in the replacement cost method, the estimated costs to recruit, hire, and train are expressed as a percentage of total compensation for employees. In some instances, if employees of a company are separated by grades (where the grades represent different levels of responsibility within the company), it may be appropriate to separate the estimated costs to recruit, hire, and train by employee grade. Another possible classification to differentiate various groups of employees for this method is the number of years employed by the company.

The estimated costs to recruit, hire, and train are then multiplied by the historical total compensation for the different employee levels to result in a value of the assembled workforce.

### Covenants Not to Compete and Noncompete Agreements

The cost approach is rarely useful in estimating the value of noncompetition agreements. The approach that is most typically used to value noncompetition agreements is the income approach, as discussed in the next section.

## Income Approach

The income approach is based on the premise that the company will receive specified rewards or returns from human capital in future periods.

### Trained and Assembled Workforce

The income approach is less commonly used than the cost approach to estimate the value of assembled workforces because it may be difficult to estimate the economic income that will be generated by each specific employee of a company.

### Covenants Not to Compete and Noncompete Agreements

The income approach is most commonly used in estimating the value of noncompete agreements. A reasonable value can be placed on a noncompete agreement through the following steps:

1. Estimate the value of the subject business *with* the covenant in place, based on the company's projected cash flow generation over the term of the covenant, discounted to the net present value.
2. Estimate the value of the subject business *without* the covenant in place, based on the company's projected cash flow generation over the term of the covenant, discounted to the net present value.
3. Determine the difference between the two business values.

The difference between the two values is the fair market value of the noncompetition agreement.

## Market Approach

In the market approach, transactions involving similar intangible assets are used as reference points to estimate the value of the subject intangible asset.

## Trained and Assembled Workforce

The market approach is less commonly used in the valuation of assembled workforces, because transactions specifically involving the sale, lease, or other transfer of company workforces are not common.

## Covenants Not to Compete and Noncompete Agreements

Similarly, the market approach is not normally used in the valuation of noncompetition agreements, since transactions involving the sale of existing noncompetition agreements do not frequently occur.

## SPECIAL CONSIDERATIONS IN THE VALUATION OF HUMAN CAPITAL INTANGIBLES

### Trained and Assembled Workforce

Several issues may need to be considered and incorporated in the valuation of an assembled workforce. When using the replacement cost method, the analyst should consider whether some of the current workforce would not be rehired if the company's employee base was being replaced. Several companies in various industries have announced workforce reductions over the past few years. If the company has an excess workforce, excess employees are not normally included in the assembled workforce calculation.

In addition, if management is considering the termination of a product line, it may be appropriate to exclude employees who work exclusively on that product, if the employees would be terminated upon elimination of the product line.

In some situations, a company may be forced to operate with an excess labor force in order to be in compliance with union contracts. In the example of a railroad company that could operate just as successfully with 15 percent fewer employees, it is important that the analyst consider and, if appropriate, adjust for the excess labor force in the estimate of the value of the assembled workforce. In this example, the excess labor force is clearly not an intangible asset of the company, since it decreases the company's profitability and does not improve operations.

### Covenants Not to Compete and Noncompete Agreements

When valuing a noncompetition agreement, it is important to consider the following issues, established in Revenue Ruling 77-403:

1. Whether, in the absence of the covenant, the covenantor would desire to compete with the covenantee.
2. The ability of the covenantor to effectively compete with the covenantee in the activity in question.
3. The feasibility, in view of the activity and market in question, of effective competition by the covenantor within the time and area specified in the covenant.[3]

---

3. Rev. Rul. 77-403, 1977-2 C.B. 302.

## DATA SOURCES

Chapter 5 describes the types of data sources typically used in the valuation of intangible assets. The following discussion addresses these data sources as they apply to the valuation of human capital intangible assets.

## Internal Data Sources

Internal financial reports such as historical financial statements are needed in order to apply both the replacement cost method and the income approach described in this chapter. Additionally, payroll records are especially relevant to the replacement cost method. In determining compensation in the replacement cost method, it is important to calculate the *total* compensation for each employee, including base compensation, retirement plan contributions, health care benefits, additional perks such as company automobiles, and so on.

Management interviews are useful to completing the cost approach for appraising an assembled workforce and the income approach for appraising noncompetition agreements.

In an appraisal of an assembled workforce, interviews, especially with key management in various departments and with human resource personnel, can inform the analyst on a variety of topics including:

- The existence of different employee classifications within the company, such as different employee grades.
- Prior studies completed by management of the cost of recruiting, hiring, and training employees of various grades or tenure.
- Management estimates of the cost to recruit, hire, and train employees of various grades or tenure.
- The existence of excess workforce.

In an appraisal of a noncompetition agreement, interviews with key management personnel (for example, the chief executive officer, the chief marketing officer, and the chief financial officer) can inform the analyst on a variety of topics including:

- If the seller were to compete, how would it be done?
- If the seller were to compete, what would be the most likely competition scenario?
- What is the likely effect of the potential competition on the company's net sales, net earnings, and net cash flow over the term of the covenant?

## External Data Sources

Salary surveys available from trade associations may be used in estimating compensation in the cost approach method or to check the reasonableness of the actual compensation of personnel at the subject company. In addition, studies regarding the average cost to recruit, hire, and train employees with various experience may be available from trade associations.

Court cases may also provide valuable guidance to the analyst with respect to analytical procedures appropriate to the valuation of human capital intangible assets.

## VALUATION EXAMPLE

## Trained and Assembled Workforce

Exhibits 21-1 through 21-3 present an example of the valuation of an assembled workforce, as of December 31, 1998, using the replacement cost method, which is the method most commonly used to value this type of intangible asset.

In this example, the value of the company workforce is based on the cost to recruit, hire, and train new employees of comparable experience and expertise to the subject workforce. We estimated the cost as a percent of total compensation for various grades of employees and by employee tenure. In the example, as the employee grade increases, the compensation and level of responsibility within the company increases.

Exhibit 21-1 presents the estimated historical cost to recruit and hire employees by employee grade and years of experience with the company. In addition, the exhibit presents the estimated historical cost to train employees by employee grade and tenure. The cost estimates were based on in-depth discussions with appropriate company management, and on an analysis of historical company recruiting, hiring, and training cost surveys.

Exhibit 21-2 presents the number of employees by employee grade, separated by tenure. In addition, Exhibit 21-2 presents total compensation data and average compensation for employees by grade and tenure.

Exhibit 21-3 presents the assembled workforce value, based on the cost to recruit, hire, and train and on historical compensation data presented in Exhibits 21-1 and 21-2, respectively.

**EXHIBIT 21-1**

Historical Cost Data Expressed as a Percent of Total Annual Compensation by Employee Grade and Tenure, as of December 31, 1998

| Employee Grade | Employee Years of Tenure with Company | Estimated Historical Cost to Recruit & Hire | Estimated Historical Cost to Train |
|---|---|---|---|
| 1 | Less than 1 Year | 5% | 10% |
| 1 | 1–3 Years | 10% | 15% |
| 1 | 4–6 Years | 15% | 20% |
| 1 | 7–9 Years | 20% | 25% |
| 1 | 10 Years or More | 20% | 25% |
| 2 | Less than 1 Year | 15% | 20% |
| 2 | 1–3 Years | 20% | 25% |
| 2 | 4–6 Years | 25% | 30% |
| 2 | 7–9 Years | 30% | 35% |
| 2 | 10 Years or More | 30% | 35% |
| 3 | Less than 1 Year | 20% | 25% |
| 3 | 1–3 Years | 25% | 30% |
| 3 | 4–6 Years | 30% | 35% |
| 3 | 7–9 Years | 35% | 40% |
| 3 | 10 Years or More | 35% | 40% |
| 4 | Less than 1 Year | 30% | 35% |
| 4 | 1–3 Years | 35% | 40% |
| 4 | 4–6 Years | 40% | 45% |
| 4 | 7–9 Years | 45% | 50% |
| 4 | 10 Years or More | 45% | 50% |

Historical Compensation Data and Number of Employees by Employee Grade and Tenure, as of December 31, 1998

| Employee Grade | Employee Years of Tenure with Company | Current Number of Employees | Total Compensation | Average Total Compensation |
|---|---|---|---|---|
| 1 | Less than 1 Year | 30 | $ 511,350 | $17,045 |
| 1 | 1–3 Years | 44 | 806,960 | 18,340 |
| 1 | 4–6 Years | 68 | 1,400,528 | 20,596 |
| 1 | 7–9 Years | 50 | 1,127,650 | 22,553 |
| 1 | 10 Years or More | 30 | 740,730 | 24,691 |
| Total | | 222 | 4,587,218 | |
| 2 | Less than 1 Year | 70 | $ 1,543,920 | 22,056 |
| 2 | 1–3 Years | 94 | 2,230,808 | 23,732 |
| 2 | 4–6 Years | 104 | 2,771,704 | 26,651 |
| 2 | 7–9 Years | 24 | 700,392 | 29,183 |
| 2 | 10 Years or More | 50 | 1,597,500 | 31,950 |
| Total | | 342 | 8,844,324 | |
| 3 | Less than 1 Year | 44 | $ 1,663,420 | 37,805 |
| 3 | 1–3 Years | 68 | 2,766,104 | 40,678 |
| 3 | 4–6 Years | 50 | 2,284,050 | 45,681 |
| 3 | 7–9 Years | 24 | 1,200,504 | 50,021 |
| 3 | 10 Years or More | 28 | 1,533,364 | 54,763 |
| Total | | 214 | 9,447,442 | |
| 4 | Less than 1 Year | 22 | $ 1,145,232 | 52,056 |
| 4 | 1–3 Years | 30 | 1,680,360 | 56,012 |
| 4 | 4–6 Years | 42 | 2,767,884 | 65,902 |
| 4 | 7–9 Years | 18 | 1,239,786 | 68,877 |
| 4 | 10 Years or More | 20 | 1,508,140 | 75,407 |
| Total | | 132 | 8,341,402 | |
| Overall Total | | 910 | $31,220,386 | |

*Note:* Numbers may not total due to rounding.

## Valuation Reconciliation and Conclusion

Based on these estimated costs, the total cost to recruit, hire, and train the company's workforce, or the indicated fair market value of the workforce based on the replacement cost method of the cost approach, as of December 31, 1998, is (rounded) $18.9 million.

## Covenants Not to Compete and Noncompete Agreements

Exhibits 21-4 and 21-5 present a simple example of the valuation of a noncompetition agreement, as of December 31, 1998, using the income approach, the approach most commonly used to value this type of intangible asset.

In this example, the value of the noncompetition agreement is equal to the difference between the value of the business with the noncompetition agreement in place and the value of the business without the noncompetition agreement in place.

EXHIBIT 21-3

Estimated Replacement Cost of Assembled Workforce, as of December 31, 1998

| Employee Grade | Total Compensation | As a Percent of Annual Compensation | | Indicated Total Cost | Assembled Workforce Value |
| | | Estimated Historical Cost to Recruit & Hire | Estimated Historical Cost to Train | | |
|---|---|---|---|---|---|
| 1 | $ 511,350 | 5% | 10% | 15% | $ 76,703 |
| 1 | 806,960 | 10% | 15% | 25% | 201,740 |
| 1 | 1,400,528 | 15% | 20% | 35% | 490,185 |
| 1 | 1,127,650 | 20% | 25% | 45% | 507,443 |
| 1 | 740,730 | 20% | 25% | 45% | 333,329 |
| Total | $ 4,587,218 | | | | $ 1,609,398 |
| 2 | $ 1,543,920 | 15% | 20% | 35% | $ 540,372 |
| 2 | 2,230,808 | 20% | 25% | 45% | 1,003,864 |
| 2 | 2,771,704 | 25% | 30% | 55% | 1,524,437 |
| 2 | 700,392 | 30% | 35% | 65% | 455,255 |
| 2 | 1,597,500 | 30% | 35% | 65% | 1,038,375 |
| Total | $ 8,844,324 | | | | $ 4,562,303 |
| 3 | $ 1,663,420 | 20% | 25% | 45% | $ 748,539 |
| 3 | 2,766,104 | 25% | 30% | 55% | 1,521,357 |
| 3 | 2,284,050 | 30% | 35% | 65% | 1,484,633 |
| 3 | 1, 200,504 | 35% | 40% | 75% | 900,378 |
| 3 | 1,533,364 | 35% | 40% | 75% | 1,150,023 |
| Total | $ 9,447,442 | | | | $ 5,804,930 |
| 4 | $ 1,145,232 | 30% | 35% | 65% | $ 744,401 |
| 4 | 1,680,360 | 35% | 40% | 75% | 1,260,270 |
| 4 | 2,767,884 | 40% | 45% | 85% | 2,352,701 |
| 4 | 1,239,786 | 45% | 50% | 95% | 1,777,797 |
| 4 | 1,508,140 | 45% | 50% | 95% | 1,432,733 |
| Total | $ 8,341,402 | | | | $ 6,967,902 |
| Overall Total | $31,220,386 | | | | $18,900,000 |

Note: Numbers may not total due to rounding.

The example is based on the following hypothetical facts:

| Economic Variable | Projection |
|---|---|
| Projected short-term growth rate | 7.0% |
| Projected long-term growth rate | 4.0% |
| Projected loss in revenue | 30.0% |
| Effective income tax rate | 40.0% |
| Present value discount rate | 20.0% |

Exhibit 21-4 presents the enterprise value of the business assuming the noncompetition agreement is in place.

Exhibit 21-5 presents the enterprise value of the business assuming the noncompetition agreement is not in place.

According to the information presented in these exhibits, the value of the noncompetition agreement based on the income approach is the difference between the two indicated values, or $1.202 million.

Loss of Income Method, Scenario I Projections with Noncompetition Agreement in Place, as of December 31, 1998 (in $000s)

| Projection Variable | Year 1 Value | Year 2 | Year 3 | Year 4 | Residua |
|---|---|---|---|---|---|
| Revenue | 12,000 | 12,840 | 13,739 | 14,701 | |
| Gross margin | 5,040 | 5,521 | 6,045 | 6,395 | |
| Operating expenses | (4,200) | (4,622) | (5,028) | (5,322) | |
| EBIT | 840 | 899 | 1,017 | 1,073 | |
| Income tax expense | (336) | (360) | (407) | (429) | |
| Debt-free net income | 504 | 539 | 610 | 644 | |
| Depreciation expense | 160 | 168 | 176 | 184 | |
| Capital expenditures | (168) | (176) | (184) | (192) | |
| Additional net working capital investments | (128) | (112) | (92) | (64) | |
| Net cash flow | 368 | 419 | 510 | 572 | 3,717 |
| Present value discount factor | 0.9129 | 0.7607 | 0.6339 | 0.5283 | 0.5283 |
| Discounted net cash flow | 336 | 319 | 323 | 302 | 1,964 |
| Sum of discounted net cash flow | | | | | 3,244 |

EBIT = Earnings before interest and taxes.

*Note:* Numbers may not total due to rounding.

Loss of Income Method, Scenario II Projections without Noncompetition Agreement in Place, as of December 31, 1998 (in $000s)

| Projection Variable | Year 1 Value | Year 2 | Year 3 | Year 4 | Residua |
|---|---|---|---|---|---|
| Revenue with noncompetition agreement | 12,000 | 12,840 | 13,739 | 14,701 | |
| Most likely revenue decrement | (3,600) | (3,852) | (4,122) | (4,410) | |
| Revenue without noncompetition agreement in place | 8,400 | 8,988 | 9,617 | 10,290 | |
| Gross margin | 3,528 | 3,865 | 4,232 | 4,476 | |
| Operating expenses | (2,940) | (3,236) | (3,520) | (3,725) | |
| EBIT | 588 | 629 | 712 | 751 | |
| Income tax expense | (235) | (252) | (285) | (300) | |
| Debt-free net income | 353 | 377 | 427 | 451 | |
| Depreciation expense | 160 | 175 | 180 | 190 | |
| Capital expenditures | (190) | (196) | (189) | (192) | |
| Additional net working capital investments | (130) | (120) | (95) | (75) | |
| Net cash flow | 193 | 237 | 323 | 374 | 2,429 |
| Present value discount factor | 0.9129 | 0.7607 | 0.6339 | 0.5283 | 0.5283 |
| Discounted net cash flow | 176 | 180 | 205 | 198 | 1,283 |
| Sum of discounted net cash flow | | | | | 2,042 |

EBIT = Earnings before interest and taxes.

*Note:* Numbers may not total due to rounding.

# Valuation Reconciliation and Conclusion

Based on the analyses described herein, the market value of the subject noncompetition agreement, as of December 31, 1998, is (rounded) $1,200,000.

## BIBLIOGRAPHY

### Articles

Cava, Anita. "Trade Secrets and Covenants Not to Compete: Beware of Winning the Battle but Losing the War." *Journal of Small Business Management,* October 1990, pp. 99–103.

Cramer, Tyler W., and Jerry Gonick. "Covenants Not to Compete: An Objective Approach to Valuation." *The Journal of Real Estate Taxation,* Winter 1986, pp. 168–176.

Dal Santo, Jacquelyn. "Valuation Concern in the Appraisal of Covenants Not to Compete." *The Appraisal Journal,* January 1991, pp. 111–114.

Finkel, Sidney R. "Conflicts Continue in the Valuation of Non-Competition Agreements." *Valuation Strategies,* January/February 1998, pp. 29–33.

Flamholtz, Eric G., and Russell Coff. "Valuing Human Resources in Buying Service Companies." *Mergers and Acquisitions,* January/February 1989, pp. 40–44.

Johnson, Arlene A. "The Business Case for Work-Family Programs." *Journal of Accountancy,* August 1995, pp. 53–57.

Millon, Thomas J. "The Valuation and Amortization of Non-Compete Agreements." *CPA Litigation Service Counselor,* May 1991, pp. 1–3.

Rabe, James G. "Methods to Identify and Value Intangible Assets—The Appraisal Perspective." *Proceedings of the 1995 Public Utilities Workshop—Appraisal: Communications, Energy and Transportation Properties for Ad Valorem Taxation,* August 1995, pp. 115–118.

Reilly, Robert F. "Appraising and Amortizing Noncompete Covenants." *CPA Journal,* July 1990, pp. 28–38.

———. "Maximizing Amortization Deductions for Noncompete Covenants." *The Practical Accountant,* December 1991, pp. 40–44.

———. "The Valuation and Amortization of Noncompete Covenants." *The Appraisal Journal,* April 1990, pp. 211–220.

Russell, Lee C. "How to Value Covenants Not to Compete." *Journal of Accountancy,* September 1990, pp. 85–92.

Schlessinger, Michael R. "A Covenant Not to Compete Still Can Provide Tax Savings to a Buyer." *Taxation for Accountants,* February 1990, pp. 96–99.

### Books

Parr, Russell L. *Investing in Intangible Assets: Finding and Profiting from Hidden Corporate Value.* New York: John Wiley & Sons, 1991.

Pratt, Shannon, Robert F. Reilly, and Robert P. Schweihs. *Valuing a Business: The Analysis and Appraisal of Closely Held Companies,* 3d ed. Burr Ridge, IL: McGraw-Hill, 1996.

Smith, Gordon, and Russell Parr. *Valuation of Intellectual Property and Intangible Assets.* New York: John Wiley & Sons, 1994, supplemented annually.

# CHAPTER 22

# Location Intangible Assets

## DESCRIPTION OF LOCATION INTANGIBLES

Location-related intangible assets derive both their existence and their value either directly from real estate or indirectly from real property rights. Ultimately, whether the value is derived directly or indirectly, location intangible assets relate to the right to use or the forbearance of the use of real estate. Therefore, all location intangibles relate to one or more of a subset of the bundle of rights associated with real estate ownership. Of course, the location intangible can only relate to a subset of the bundle of real estate ownership rights, because the total set of the bundle of rights would represent a fee simple ownership interest in the subject real estate. At that point, the property subject to appraisal would be the tangible asset real estate and not the intangible asset partial bundle of real property rights.

The right to use real estate could include the right to enter and occupy real estate, transgress (cross over) it, build on it, develop it, drill on it, mine it, fly over it, tunnel under it, extract the water from it, operate the water on it, and so on. These rights all relate to real property interests. Another important location intangible is the right to sublease or sublicense any of the other use rights.

The individual components in the real estate bundle of rights can be sold or otherwise permanently transferred. Such rights are transferred through deeds, deed restrictions, or contracts. Also, the individual components in the real estate bundle of rights can be transferred for a limited period of time. Such rights are transferred by lease, license, or similar contract with a stated, limited term.

The forbearance of the use of real estate includes the promise not to enter, occupy, build on, develop, drill, mine, cross, tunnel under, fly over, extract or otherwise use the water, and so on, on a parcel of real estate. Other forbearance agreements include the promise not to change the current use of real estate, not to change the current (or natural condition) of real estate, and not to transfer any or all of the bundle of ownership rights related to a parcel of real estate. These promises are typically documented in—and conveyed by means of—a deed restriction, an easement, or a contract.

Often, the forbearance of the use of (or the rights to use) real estate is granted in perpetuity. One example is the real estate owner who transfers an easement to the city promising never to build a commercial structure or a residential structure higher than two stories on the parcel that is immediately adjacent to the city park. However, the forbearance could be granted for a specific finite term. An example is a property owner who grants a deed restriction and agrees not to change the naturally forested condition of the property for a 20-year period. Finally, the forbearance could be granted conditional upon an event occurring (or not occurring). An example is a property owner who grants an agreement to the local municipality that he will not operate a bar or other establishment selling liquor as long as a public school operates across the street from the subject property.

A significant number of real property rights qualify as location intangibles. For the most part, all of the individual location intangibles may be grouped into the following categories:

1. Easements—including scenic easements, development easements, height restrictions, and so forth.
2. Permits—including construction, development and building permits, occupancy permits, density permits.

3. Leases—including both lessee and lessor estates, such as favorable (i.e., below market rental rate) leasehold interests for lessees and profitable leased fee estates for lessors.

4. Zoning waivers and variance—including the right to build a certain type of improvement, the right to deviate from setback, height, or land-to-building square foot ratio restrictions, the right to operate a certain type of commercial establishment, and so forth.

5. Use rights—including air, water, subterranean and subface, drilling, mining, and other rights.

At this point, it is meaningful to reiterate some of the differences between intangible assets and intangible influences. For many inexperienced analysts (and for many property owners), this distinction is more confusing with regard to location intangibles than with regard to other types of intangible assets. Intangible assets may enhance the value of the tangible assets (or the other intangible assets) with which they are associated. However, intangible assets have a value of and to themselves. That value derives from legal rights (including the right to use, or not to use, tangible property). However, that value does not derive from the tangible property itself. The discrete intangible asset can be transferred separately from any particular tangible asset. While an intangible asset may need to use (or use up) tangible assets in order to realize its value, it does not need to use (or use up) a particular, specifically identified tangible asset.

On the other hand, intangible influences only enhance the value of tangible or intangible assets. While they have value (in terms of utility or functionality), they do not rise to the level of an asset. They derive all of their value from their association with a particular, specifically identified tangible or intangible asset. They cannot be transferred separately from a particular, specifically identified tangible or intangible asset.

There are numerous examples of intangible influences with regard to real estate and real property interests. These influences enhance the value of the associated real estate. However, these intangible influences are not themselves intangible assets. Some examples of location-related intangible influences include the following:

1. View—such as the desirable view of a skyline, the mountains, a beach or other shoreline, or other desirable view.

2. Proximity—the closeness of a parcel of real estate to the central business district, an airport, the shore, a train station, and so forth.

3. Address prestige—the affinity of an owner, operator, or tenant to a well-known and prestigious address, such as the World Trade Center, the Sears Tower, Water Tower Place, Trump Tower, and so forth.

4. Convenient access—such as access to major arteries, to interstate highway exchanges, to docks or other waterway shipping, and so on.

5. Commercial appeal—a location that benefits from a great deal of foot traffic, such as locations near train stations, in airports, or near amusement or similar entertainment locations.

6. Development appeal—such as a parcel that is the "perfect location" for a hotel (e.g., near an airport), restaurant (e.g., in a downtown office complex), gasoline service station (at an interstate highway oasis), and so on.

7. Assemblage and plottage potential—Assemblage is the act of putting together separate typically adjacent parcels to create a single parcel of greater value than the cumulative value of the individual parcels; plottage is the incremental value that is created through the process of assemblage. For example, a developer may buy three out of the four parcels in a square city block for $1 million each. If the entire assembled city block parcel is worth $10 million, then the remaining fourth parcel has the potential to experience assemblage and create plottage value.

All of the examples given represent desirable conditions or circumstances to the owner or buyer or tenant of the subject real estate. However, each of these desirable conditions represents intangible influences and not intangible assets. The intangible influences may add significantly to the value of the associated real estate and there are generally accepted procedures to quantify the incremental value associated with the intangible influences. However, since they do not relate to discrete intangible assets, a discussion of these procedures is beyond the scope of this book.

## COMMON VALUATION METHODS

As with all intangible assets, location intangibles can be analyzed by reference to all three valuation approaches—cost, market, and income. Also, as with all intangible assets, some valuation approaches (and some valuation methods within each approach) are more commonly used in practice than are others. Ideally, the analyst will be able to use two or all three approaches in the valuation or economic analysis of the subject location intangible. More than conceptual applicability, data constraints typically limit the application of numerous valuation methods with regard to the analysis of location intangibles.

## Cost Approach

The cost approach is the least commonly used approach to the valuation of location intangibles. The cost approach is most applicable to the valuation of fungible assets, both tangible and intangible. The value of a location intangible is less related to the cost of creating or developing the associated real property rights than it is to the income that can be generated through the use (or forbearance of use) of those rights. Nonetheless, the cost approach may be used in the valuation and economic analysis of location intangibles, if all components of the cost approach are considered and analyzed.

Regardless of the measure of cost considered, there are four components to a cost approach analysis. Sometimes, one or more of these components has no effect on the value estimate—that is, the economic impact of an individual component may be zero dollar value increment. Nonetheless, the analyst should consider each of the following four components in each cost analysis.

**1.** Direct costs—These typically include material, labor, and overhead (sometimes called hard costs) related to the tangible elements of real estate and personal property. With regard to location intangibles, this cost component could include the application fees directly associated with obtaining a permit, an easement, a variance, a lease, and so on.

**2.** Indirect costs—These typically include architectural, engineering, consulting, and other administrative costs (sometimes called soft costs) related to the tangible elements of real estate and personal property. With regard to location intangibles, this cost component could include lawyers' fees, travel and entertainment expenses, and consulting fees related to obtaining the subject bundle of real property interests.

**3.** Developer's profit—A developer (other than an owner or operator of the subject property) will expect to earn a profit associated with the property development process. This is sometimes expressed as a fair rate of return in the direct costs and the indirect costs related to the development project. With regard to location intangibles, this cost component could include the value of the owner or operator's time during the process of obtaining the permit, lease, or other intangible, or it may be represented by an agent's fee for representing the owner/operator during the period of obtaining the permit, lease, or other intangible.

**4.** Entrepreneurial incentive—This is the amount of income required to motivate the property owner to develop this particular tangible or intangible asset development project, compared to an alternative development project. Alternatively, it is the amount of income required to motivate the property-owning entrepreneur to accept the risk of project development. It is measured sometimes as a dollar amount and sometimes as a percentage return on all other project costs. With regard to location intangibles, this cost component could include the difference between the entrepreneurial incentives associated with developing a real estate project *with* versus *without* the subject permit, lease, or other intangible.

Of the four cost components, the most significant component with regard to a location intangible will likely be the analysis of entrepreneurial profit.

## Market Approach

The market approach is often used with regard to the valuation and economic analysis of location intangibles. As with most intangibles, there are two commonly used market approach methods. Both methods rely upon the collection and analysis of market-derived empirical data with respect to transactions involving intangible assets that are comparative to the subject.

The first market approach method involves the analysis of sales of comparative intangible assets. Using this method, the analyst first develops a thorough understanding of the risk and expected return characteristics regarding the subject location intangible. The analyst then selects reasonable comparability criteria to be used in the search and selection of comparative sale transactions. Third, the analyst performs comprehensive market research in order to obtain data regarding the sale or listing of comparative intangibles. Fourth, as needed, the analyst verifies the transactional data.

Next, the analyst categorizes the sale and listing data either as comparable transactions or as guideline transactions. Comparable transactions relate to sales of easements, permits, leases, variances, rights, and so on, that are physically similar to the subject location intangible. With regard to comparable transactions, relatively fewer individual adjustments may need to be made in order to adjust the comparables to the subject for analytical purposes. Guideline transactions relate to sales of easements, permits, leases, variances, rights, and so on, that may not be physically similar to the subject location intangible, but that are comparative to the subject from a risk and expected return perspective. While guideline transactions provide meaningful market-derived pricing guidance to the analyst, they may require relatively more aggregate adjustments in order to adjust the guidelines to the subject for analytical purposes.

Next, from the adjusted transactional data (either comparable or guideline), empirically derived pricing multiples are determined. The pricing multiples should represent a reasonable unit of comparison for application to the subject intangible. Such reasonable units of comparison may include price per square foot, per acre, per floor, per dollar of direct and indirect construction cost, per ton of ore extraction, and so forth. The selected empirically derived pricing multiples are applied to the fundamental unit of comparison of the subject location intangible in order to indicate an estimate of value for the subject intangible.

The second market approach method involves the analysis of leases, licenses, or other rentals of comparative intangible assets. Essentially, this method incorporates many of the same procedures as the analysis of the sales of location intangibles. Obviously, instead of researching and verifying transactional data regarding the sale or listing of comparative intangibles, the analyst assembles and sorts transactional data regarding term rental agreements with respect to comparative intangibles.

Of course, the units of comparison will be slightly different using this method. Instead of applying price per square foot multiples to the subject fundamentals, the analyst will apply rental multipliers per square foot to the subject fundamentals. The rental multipliers could be gross rental income, net rental income, rental net operating income, or some other multiplier. The units of comparison could include such variables as per square foot, per lineal foot, per acre, per floor, per use, per barrel extracted, per ton extracted, and so on.

Finally, and unlike the analysis of sales transactional data, the use of comparative rental transactions requires the capitalization of the rental income (gross, net, net operating, etc.) implied by the fundamental characteristics of the subject intangible. In other words, the market-derived rental income per square foot times the subject square footage yields the rental income associated with the subject location intangible. The rental income still has to be converted into a value, and that value estimate is the result of the subject rental income capitalized by a direct capitalization rate that is appropriate for that particular measure of rental income.

Depending upon the type of location intangible, both market approach methods are routinely used. If properly applied, either market approach method should conclude a reasonable estimate of value.

## Income Approach

Several income approach methods are available for the valuation and economic analysis of location intangibles. The three most commonly applied income approach methods are:

1. The capitalization of incremental income.
2. The capitalization of the loss of income.
3. The capitalization of total income less appropriate capital charges.

As a first example, let's consider the valuation of a zoning variance. The current zoning regulations contain a height density requirement. The height density regulation is that no building can be constructed that is higher than 10 stories tall. The real estate owner applied for and received a height density zoning variance. The variance allows the construction of a building not higher than 14 stories tall. There is sufficient demand for this type of rental space in the marketplace so as to absorb the additional four floors of rental space.

Each of the four additional floors will contain 25,000 square feet of gross rental space. The market dictates that the rental rate will be $20 per gross rentable square foot and the market-derived gross rental income pricing multiple is eight times. The cost to construct the top four floors of the new building is $120 per square foot of gross rental space. The construction cost includes all four components of cost discussed earlier in this chapter.

The value of the height density zoning variance location intangible may be estimated as follows:

| | |
|---|---|
| Total incremental gross rental space (four additional floors times 25,000 square feet per floor) | 100,000 square feet |
| × Rental rate per square foot | $ 20 |
| = Total incremental gross rental income | $ 2,000,000 |
| × Gross rental income pricing multiple | 8 |
| = Value of incremental income associated with four additional floors | $16,000,000 |
| − Cost of construction of four additional floors (100,000 square feet times $120 cost per square foot) | $12,000,000 |
| = Value of height density zoning variance | $ 4,000,000 |

In this example, $4 million of value was created due to the subject location intangible.

Second, let's consider the valuation of a scenic easement. Grantor Corporation owns 10 acres of natural, scenic real estate. Grantor Corporation decides to improve five of the acres by building a corporate headquarters complex. Grantor Corporation decides to leave the other five acres vacant and unimproved. Being a good corporate citizen, Grantor Corporation grants a scenic easement to the local municipality, permanently restricting any development on the five-acre natural parcel. What is the value of the scenic easement location intangible?

Ground rents for vacant natural parcels comparable to the subject are currently $1.00 per square foot, based on our analysis of recent arm's-length ground leases. Also based on recent sales transactions, the current market conditions indicate a ground rental income pricing multiplier of 10 times. Of course, an acre includes 43,560 square feet.

The value of the scenic easement location intangible may be estimated as follows:

| Size of parcel subject to scenic easement | 217,800 square feet |
|---|---|
| × Ground rental income per square foot lost to grantor due to easement | $ 1.00 |
| = Total ground rental income lost to grantor | $ 217,800 |
| × Ground rental income pricing multiple | 10 |
| = Capitalized lost income value of scenic income | $ 2,178,000 |

In this example, the value of the scenic easement location intangible is $2,178,000.

Third, let's consider the valuation of mining rights. Black Lung Corporation has the right to mine coal from a certain parcel for the next 10 years. There are enough coal reserves under the parcel so that the mine can continue to operate profitably, and at its current level of extraction, for the next 10 years. What is the value of these subsurface mining rights?

Black Lung Corporation generates $6 million per year of net cash flow from its mining operation at the subject location. After we analyzed expected coal prices and extraction production costs, we concluded that Black Lung Corporation will continue to generate about $6 million per year of net cash flow for each of the next 10 years.

In addition to using the subject mining rights, Black Lung Corporation uses various other tangible and intangible assets in the production of this annual amount of net cash flow. For example, the company uses net working capital, machinery and equipment, trucks and automobiles, a trained and assembled workforce, a trademark and trade name, and proprietary mining procedures in its mining operation at this location. We estimated that a fair rate of return on all these tangible and intangible assets (other than the value of the location intangible, of course) would require a capital charge of $4 million per year.

We also concluded that the weighted average cost of capital for the subject mining operation is 15 percent. This is the cost of capital (present value discount rate) that is consistent both with the measurement of economic income as net cash flow and with the average fair rate of return we used to estimate the appropriate capital charge on all other assets associated with the subject mining operations.

The value of the subsurface mining rights location intangible may be estimated as follows:

| Annual net cash flow associated with the subject mining operations | $ 6,000,000 |
|---|---|
| − A capital charge, equal to a fair rate of return on all associated assets other than the subject location intangible | 4,000,000 |
| = Economic income associated with the subject location intangible | $ 2,000,000 |
| × Present value of an annuity factor based on a 15% present value discount rate, a ten-year time horizon, and the year-end compounding convention | 5.0188 |
| = Capitalized residual income value of the subsurface mining rights | $10,037,600 |

In this example, the value of the subsurface mining rights location intangible is estimated to be $10,037,600.

## DATA SOURCES

Transactions involving location intangibles are obviously real estate–related transactions. As with the sale or other transfer of fee simple interests in real estate, a fair amount of empirical data is available for use in the valuation or economic analysis of location intangibles. First, we consider internal data sources available to the analyst. Second, we consider external data sources.

## Internal Data Sources

There is a wide diversity of participants in the market for location intangibles. This group of participants includes developers, real estate management companies, real estate investment holding companies, and the owner-operators of residential, commercial, industrial, and mixed use real estate.

In many cases, the analyst will find that the subject client is an excellent source of data for use in the location intangible analysis. This is particularly true if the client has participated in a number of sale or lease transactions involving location intangibles. The data regarding other transactions may be reviewed for possible consideration as comparative transactions. The other parties to the transactions may be contacted to see if they have participated in other transactions. Then, those transactions can be analyzed for possible consideration as comparative data sources.

The subject client records may be a valuable source of information to use in the analysis of the subject location intangible. These records (or interviews with appropriate client personnel) could indicate how the client did use or will use the subject intangible. In particular, the analyst may be interested in reviewing any plans, budgets, projections, or forecasts related to the actual or possible use of the subject intangible either in a real estate development activity or in any income-producing commercial activity.

The analyst may compare the actual or expected results of operations related to the subject intangible to other properties or business enterprises owned by the subject client. The objective of this comparison is to quantify any meaningful differences in either financial or operational results that may be associated with the subject location intangible.

The analyst may also compare the actual or expected results of operations related to the subject intangible to comparative industry data. These data would relate to comparative properties or business enterprises. Data elements such as rental rates, occupancy levels, net operating income percentages, sales per square foot of retail space, and other elements, are all meaningful points of comparison in order to identify a comparative economic advantage associated with the subject location intangible. Several sources for these type of comparative industry data are listed in the next section.

It is noteworthy that clients and even direct client competitors are often relatively forthcoming with regard to transactional and other data related to location intangibles, as compared to other types of intangibles. Regarding other types of intangibles, industry participants (and even the subject client) consider transactional and related data to be confidential and proprietary. However, transactions involving location tangibles (i.e., actual real estate) are typically recorded and often publicly available in the local property recorder's office. Therefore, industry participants seem to be somewhat less concerned about sharing data regarding location intangibles.

# External Data Sources

There are both formal and informal external data sources regarding location intangibles. The formal data sources include periodic print sources, CD-ROM services, and on-line services. These services are marketed principally to the real estate appraisal community and typically include such information as transactional pricing data (listings and consummated transactions involving sales and leases of location intangibles) and income, expense, and capitalization rate data (regarding the sales and leases of location intangibles).

One source of information is *BOMA Experience Exchange Report: Operating a Cost Effective Office Building: Your Guide to Income and Expense Data*, published by Building Owners and Managers Association International, 1201 New York Avenue, NW, Suite 300, Washington, DC 20005, telephone (202) 408-2662. This is the industry's standard reference for office building financial and operations information.

Information brokers are another source of transactional data. On a fee basis, the brokers can provide customized data reports to meet your needs. Two such brokers are listed below.

- First Realty Advisors, Inc., 1901 West 47th Place, Westwood, KS 66205-1834, phone (913) 236-4750, fax (913) 236-4307.
- RealQuest Technologies, 444 South Flower Street, Suite 4525, Los Angeles, CA 90071, phone (213) 448-9001, fax (213) 627-9155.

Data can also be obtained from newsletters that provide an information exchange section in their publication. The Appraisal Institute offers this service to the readers of the *Appraiser News in Brief*. On a monthly basis, each newsletter contains a special section in which readers can advertise for assistance in identifying specific data. Advertisements for data are written with the assumption that an experienced appraiser will reply to the ad either to exchange or to sell the requested data. The Appraisal Institute is located at 875 N. Michigan Avenue, Suite 2400, Chicago, IL 60611-1980, phone (312) 335-4100, fax (312) 335-4400.

## VALUATION EXAMPLE

Let's consider a damages analysis with respect to a location intangible. Hotel Developer Corporation (HDC) was granted the exclusive permit to build a hotel on the grounds of the newly built airport in Central City. The old airport was relatively close to downtown Central City. The new airport is quite distant from downtown Central City. Therefore, there will be little competition from downtown hotels. There will be several off-airport hotels, of course. But HDC was awarded the right to develop and construct the only hotel actually located on the airport property (and within walking distance of the main airport terminal).

Just before HDC was about to begin the construction project, there was a mayoral election in Central City. A new mayor was elected who revoked the building permit to HDC. The exclusive permit was then granted to the mayor's brother-in-law. HDC Corporation claims that it was damaged as a result of the loss of the building permit. The question is: How much was HDC damaged due to the loss of this location intangible?

For purposes of simplicity, the example only values the subject building permit. We do not consider any other damages suffered by HDC (e.g., lost opportunity costs, architectural and design fees incurred, etc.).

## Fact Set and Assumptions

Before being granted the permit, HDC went through an extensive application process. HDC hired attorneys and public relations specialists to assist them in this process and paid these advisors $250,000 to help them obtain the coveted permit. In addition, HDC personnel spent a great deal of time assembling their corporate credentials during the application process. Based on actual salaries and related overhead expenses, HDC incurred $50,000 of costs related to that effort.

The hotel was planned to cost $100 million to build (including all hard costs, soft costs, and developer's profit). Based on the HDC actual experience in other cities and published hotel industry data, HDC would expect to earn a 10 percent entrepreneurial incentive on the development and construction of an off-airport hotel. Also, based on HDC actual experience and hotel industry data, HDC would expect to earn an 18 percent entrepreneurial incentive in the development and construction of an on-airport hotel.

HDC does not necessarily intend to operate the hotel after it is built. HDC is considering two options with regard to the ownership of the hotel. First, it can continue to own the improvements; of course, the land is owned by the airport. Under this option, HDC will lease the hotel to a hotel operator. HDC will be the landlord and collect rental income from the lessee (i.e., the hotel operator). Second, it can sell the improvements to a hotel operator. HDC believes that many of the major hotel chains would be interested in buying (and then operating) the planned hotel.

Regarding the first option, HDC estimates that it can lease the hotel to any of the major hotel chains and earn $12.5 million per year of net operating income from the lease. The net operating income estimate is a measure of income after providing for all operating expenses, an allowance for repairs and replacement of improvements, a provision for collection loss, and a management fee to the lessor.

We have researched equity and mortgage markets in order to estimate current costs of capital related to hotel property financings. Based upon our analysis, the appropriate net operating income direct capitalization rate for the subject hotel is 10 percent.

Regarding the second option, HDC believes that it can quickly and easily sell the hotel to a major hotel chain. We have researched recent sales of on-airport hotel properties. We have collected data regarding the recent sales of eight comparable properties. After making standard adjustments for size, timing of sale, location, and so forth, we have concluded that the subject hotel would sell for $160 per square foot once it is completed. The subject hotel is planned to be a 780,000 square foot structure.

## Approaches and Methods

We analyze the damages related to the revocation of the subject location intangible using all three valuation approaches.

First, we consider the cost approach. We quantify the costs related to obtaining the subject building permit. We also consider the incremental entrepreneurial incentive that could be earned by the owner of the subject permit.

Second, we consider the income approach. We value the entire development project using the direct capitalization of income method. We subtract from the indicated value the total cost of constructing the tangible assets (i.e., the hotel building and improvements). The residual is the amount of the value of the development project that is associated with the subject permit.

Third, we consider the market approach. We value the expected sales price of the entire development project, once it is completed. We subtract from that expected sale price the cost of constructing the tangible assets (i.e., the hotel building and improvements). The residual value represents the value of the subject permit.

The cost approach analysis is summarized in Exhibit 22-1.

The income approach analysis is summarized in Exhibit 22-2.

The market approach analysis is summarized in Exhibit 22-3.

## Valuation Reconciliation and Conclusion

The valuation synthesis and conclusion is summarized in Exhibit 22-4.

Based upon the above analyses, we conclude that Hotel Developer Corporation was damaged in the amount of $7,300,000 due to the revocation of the subject building permit.

### BIBLIOGRAPHY

Asabere, Paul K., and Forrest E. Huffman. "The Value Discounts Associated with Historic Facade Easements." *Appraisal Journal*, April 1994, pp. 270–277.

Burke, Kenneth J. "Water Rights Valuation and Appraisal." *ASA Valuation*, June 1992, pp. 18–41.

**E X H I B I T  22-1**

Hotel Development Corporation, Value of Subject Building Permit, Cost Approach Analysis, as of the Date of Revocation

| | |
|---|---|
| **Direct costs, indirect costs, and developer's profit associated with obtaining the subject permit:** | |
| Legal fees and public relations fees | $ 250,000 |
| Cost of HDC personnel devoted to permit application process | 50,000 |
| Subtotal | $ 300,000 |
| **Lost entrepreneurial incentive associated with permit revocation:** | |
| Total cost of designing and building subject hotel (include all hard costs, soft costs, and developer's profit) | $100,000,000 |
| × Incremental entrepreneurial incentive associated with constructing an on-airport hotel (i.e., the difference between 18% on-airport percentage and 10% off-airport percentage) | 8% |
| = Lost entrepreneurial incentive related to subject permit | $8,000,000 |
| **Total indicated value of subject building permit** | **$8,300,000** |

EXHIBIT 22-2

Hotel Development Corporation Value of Subject Building Permit, Income Approach Analysis, as of the Date of Revocation

| Market value of hotel property, based on direct capitalization of net operating income (NOI): | |
|---|---|
| Projected annual NOI | $ 12,500,000 |
| ÷ Direct capitalization rate (overall NOI rate) | 10% |
| = Indicated market value of hotel property | $125,000,000 |
| **Cost of constructing hotel building and improvements:** | |
| Total hard costs, soft costs, and developer's profit | 100,000,000 |
| Entreprenurial incentive (18% times $100,000,000) | 18,000,000 |
| Indicated cost approach value of hotel buildings and improvements | 118,000,000 |
| **Residual, indicated value of subject building permit** | $ 7,000,000 |

Colby, Bonnie G. "Alternative Approaches to Valuing Water Rights." *Appraisal Journal,* April 1989, pp. 180–196.

Coughlin, Thomas A. "Handling Easement Valuation Disputes before the IRS and in the Courts." *The Practical Real Estate Lawyer,* January 1987, pp. 81–91.

Dushoff, Jay, and Denise J. Henslee. "Valuation of Power Life Easements." *Institute on Planning, Zoning, and Eminent Domain,* Southwestern Legal Foundation, 1989, pp. 10.1–10.32.

Fischer, Ward H., and William R. Fischer. "Title and Valuation of Water Rights." *Proceedings of the 30th Rocky Mountain Mineral Law Institute,* Sun Valley, 1984. pp. 16-1–16-36.

Green, Gordon G. "Easement-to-Fee-Simple Value Ratios for Electric Transmission Line Easements." *Appraisal Journal,* July 1992, pp. 399–412.

Huffaker, John B. "Post-Death Offer Supported Valuation of Leasehold, Despite Later Sale for Less." *Journal of Taxation,* September 1996, p. 152.

———. "Residential Zoning Did Not Control the Valuation of Decedent's Realty." *Journal of Taxation,* April 1996 , p. 212.

Jones, Robert N., and Stephen D. Roach. "Valuation of Long-Term Leases." *The Appraisal Journal,* October 1989, pp. 451–459.

Kellough, W.R. "An Overview of Easements." *Valuation,* January 1993, pp. 68–74.

Mastroieni, Maureen. "How to Allocate a Leasehold Interest between Land and Improvements." *Real Estate Review,* Fall 1986, pp. 60–63.

EXHIBIT 22-3

Hotel Development Corporation, Value of Subject Building Permit, Market Approach Analysis, as of Date of Revocation

| Market value of hotel property based on the market approach, direct sales comparison method: | |
|---|---|
| Size of subject hotel building and improvements | $ 780,000 |
| × Market price per square foot | 160 |
| = Indicated market value of hotel property | $124,800,000 |
| **Cost of constructing hotel building and improvements:** | |
| Total hard costs, soft costs, and developer's profit | 100,000,000 |
| Entreprenurial incentive (18% times $100,000,000) | 18,000,000 |
| Indicated cost approach value of hotel building and improvements | 118,000,000 |
| **Residual, indicated value of subject building permit** | $ 6,800,000 |

Hotel Development Corporation, Value of Subject Building Permit, Valuation Synthesis and Conclusion, as of Date of Revocation

| Valuation Approach | Indicated Value | Weight Assigned | Weighted Value |
|---|---|---|---|
| Cost | $8,300,000 | 30% | $2,490,000 |
| Income | 7,000,000 | 35% | 2,450,000 |
| Market | 6,800,000 | 35% | 2,380,000 |
| Weighted average value indication | | | $7,320,000 |
| Value of subject building permit (rounded) | | | $7,300,000 |

McBurney, Christian M. "15-Year Amortization May Hold Opportunities for Realty-Related Intangibles." *The Journal of Taxation,* August 1994, pp. 94–99.

Reilly, Robert F. "Allocation of Value in Location-Dependent Businesses." *Journal of Property Tax Management,* Spring 1993, pp. 1–17.

————. "Location-Dependent Businesses: Allocating Value between Intangible Assets and Real Estate." *Real Estate Accounting & Taxation* (Parts I and II), Fall 1992 and Winter 1993, pp. 81–87 and 57–63.

Reilly, Robert F., and Daniel Lynn. "The Valuation of Leasehold Interests." *Real Estate Accounting & Taxation,* Winter 1991, pp. 24–33.

Rhodes, Richard M. "Air Rights, Subsurface Easements, and Other Fractional Interests." *Appraisal Journal,* April 1974, pp. 261–272.

Roddewig, Richard J. "Preservation Easement Law: An Overview of Recent Developments." *The Urban Lawyer,* Winter 1986, pp. 229–246.

Sandfort, James D., and Carl W. Gilmore. "Valuation of Leases as Property in Divorce Proceedings." *American Journal of Family Law,* Vol. 9, 1995, pp. 191–199.

Shearlock, Peter. "Valuing Route Rights." *Airfinance Journal,* July 1993, pp. 4–8.

Sirmans, C.F., and Norman G. Miller. "Research on Leases." *Real Estate Finance,* Spring 1997, pp. 78–83.

Summers, Lyle C. "An Economic Framework for Valuing Transient Water Rights in the Arid West." *Appraisal Journal,* January 1981, pp. 9–14.

Tenenbaum, Wayne A. "Property Values and Long-Term Leases: How Different Courts View Actual vs. Market Rent." *Journal of Multistate Taxation,* January/February 1996, pp. 270–278.

Thompson, Charles K. "Busterback Ranch: Valuing Water Rights in a Scenic Easement Area." *Appraisal Journal,* April 1987, pp. 169–179.

Williams, Lawrence E., and Daniel J. McNichol. "Valuation of Air Space." *Appraisal Journal,* April 1973, pp. 234–253.

# CHAPTER 23

# Marketing Intangible Assets

## DESCRIPTION OF MARKETING INTANGIBLES

The class of intangible assets referred to as *marketing intangible assets* generally consists of trademarks, brands, company logos, marketing strategy and promotion concepts, design of labels or packages, trade dress, trademark registrations, shelf space, and other similar intangible assets.

The focus of this chapter is on the valuation and analysis of one specific marketing intangible: trademarks. However, the valuation methods discussed in this chapter also generally apply to other marketing intangible assets.

The importance of marketing intangible assets, such as trademarks, to management of both publicly traded companies and closely held companies is increasing. For example, in September 1997, Sara Lee Corp. announced a major restructuring in which the company will sell a substantial portion of its manufacturing assets to focus exclusively on the development of its remaining assets, the most significant of which are various brand names. According to a company spokesperson, "the operating model for today's exemplary companies no longer needs to include significant manufacturing assets." The company's stock increased by 14 percent on the news. It is clear that the valuation of marketing intangible assets, such as trademarks, is an important issue, given the focus of Wall Street and company management on these intangible assets.

For the purpose of this chapter, we use a fairly broad definition of the term *trademarks*. The statutory source of federal trademark law is the Lanham Act of 1947, which is Title 15 of the United States Code. The Lanham Act provides for the registration of trademarks, which are broadly defined to include any *device* used to identify the origin of goods. The Lanham Act also provides for the registration of three other types of marks: 1) service marks—that is, marks used in the sale or advertising of services; 2) collective marks—that is, marks used to identify the goods or services of members of a group; and 3) certification marks—that is, marks used to certify the geographic origin or other characteristics of goods and services.

Technically, trade names and commercial names cannot be registered under the Lanham Act. However, for purposes of this chapter, we include trade names, commercial names, and similar descriptive marks and names in the definition of trademarks.

There are numerous attributes or factors to consider in the assessment of trademarks. These attributes or factors may be either quantitative or qualitative in nature. It is common for an analyst to perform an overall assessment of the quality and nature of the trademark before conducting the actual valuation analysis. Of course, the assessment may be either implicit or explicit. The assessment will assist the analyst in understanding the use and function of the subject trademark and in identifying the factors (and, ultimately, the methods and procedures) that are important in the analysis of the subject trademark.

Exhibit 23-1 presents a nonexhaustive list of the attributes that are often considered important in the valuation-related assessment of commercial trademarks. The general influences on trademark value are also indicated in the table.

Attributes That Affect the Valuation of Trademarks and Trade Names

| Item | Attribute | Positive Influence on Value | Negative Influence on Value |
|---|---|---|---|
| 1 | Age—absolute | Long-established trademark | Newly created trademark |
| 2 | Age—relative | Older than competing trademarks | Newer than competing trademarks |
| 3 | Use—consistency | Name used consistently on related products and services | Name used inconsistently on unrelated products and services |
| 4 | Use—specificity | Name is general and can be used on a broad range of products and services | Name is specific and can only be used on a narrow range of products and services |
| 5 | Use—geography | Name has wide appeal, e.g., can be used internationally | Name has narrow appeal, e.g., can only be used locally |
| 6 | Potential for expansion | Unrestricted ability to use name on new or different products and services | Restricted ability to use name on new or different products and services |
| 7 | Potential for exploitation | Unrestricted ability to license name into new industries and uses | Restricted ability to license name into new industries and uses |
| 8 | Associations | Name associated with positive person, event, location | Name associated with negative person, event, location |
| 9 | Connotations | Name has positive connotations and reputation among consumers | Name has negative connotations and reputation among consumers |
| 10 | Timeliness | Name is perceived as modern | Name is perceived as old-fashioned |
| 11 | Quality | Name is perceived as respectable | Name is perceived as less respectable |
| 12 | Profitability—absolute | Profit margins or investment returns on products and services higher than industry average | Profit margins or investment returns on products and services lower than industry average |
| 13 | Profitability—relative | Profit margins or investment returns on products and services higher than competing names | Profit margins or investment returns on products and services lower than competing names |
| 14 | Expense of promoting | Low cost of advertising, promotion, deals, or other marketing of name | High cost of advertising, promotion, deals, or other marketing of name |
| 15 | Means of promoting | Numerous means available to promote name | Few means available to promote name |
| 16 | Market share—absolute | Products and services have high market share | Products and services have low market share |
| 17 | Market share—relative | Products and services have higher market share than competing names | Products and services have lower market share than competing names |
| 18 | Market potential—absolute | Products and services are in an expanding market | Products and services are in a contracting market |
| 19 | Market potential—relative | Market for products and services expanding faster than competing names | Market for products and services expanding slower than competing names |
| 20 | Name recognition | Name has high recognition, e.g., high aided or unaided recall among consumers | Name has low recognition, e.g., low aided or unaided recall among consumers |

Clearly, not all of the attributes or factors apply to every trademark. It is noteworthy that the attributes do not have an equal influence on the economic value of a trademark. Some of the attributes are more important in some industries than in others, and some are more important for certain products and services than others. Also, note that there is a substantial range (both qualitative and quantitative) of positive to negative influences for each individual attribute.

## COMMON VALUATION METHODS

There are several methods that may be appropriate for appraising marketing intangible assets such as trademarks. The methods fall into the three general approaches, as discussed in Part II of this text: the cost approach, the income approach, and the market approach.

Although the following discussion of common valuation methods addresses the valuation of trademarks, similar methods may be used to value other marketing intangible assets.

## Cost Approach

The cost approach is generally the least applicable approach in the appraisal of marketing intangible assets. In many instances, the cost approach will understate the value of a trademark. However, one example of a cost approach method that is sometimes used to estimate the value of marketing intangible assets is the *trended historical cost method.* In this method, actual historical asset development or acquisition costs are identified and then trended to the valuation date by an appropriate inflation-based index factor. When using this method, it is important to include only costs associated specifically with the development or acquisition of the subject trademarks. These costs typically include, for example, advertising and promotion expenditures, legal costs, and registration fees.

Generally, historical advertising and promotion expenditures by trademark are available in various historical reports prepared by companies. Other costs related to trademark development may need to be gathered through the review of detailed income statement line items, in conjunction with management interviews. The historical expenditures need to be trended in order to reflect current dollars as of the valuation date.

## Income Approach

In the income approach, the value of a marketing intangible asset is estimated as the present value of the future economic income attributable to the ownership of the asset over its expected remaining useful life. One example of an income approach method that may be used to estimate the value of a trademark is the *profit split method.*

Estimating the value of a trademark using the profit split method requires reference to the amount of economic income the subject branded product generates. In the projection of the economic income related to the trademark, it is important to consider all applicable capital charges associated with assets, other than the subject trademark, that are used or used up in the production of income associated with the trademark. The economic income less capital charges is then hypothetically split between the licensee and licensor to estimate the amount of income the subject trademark provides to the licensor for use of the name. This method assumes an independent third party owns the trademark and licenses it, for a percent, or split, of the associated profit, to the business that uses the trademark.

The quantification of the operating profit split percentages is based on risk and return investment characteristics, including an analysis of the product, its markets and industry, its financial profitability and price relative to the other products in the industry, its degree of consumer recognition, its life cycle, the range of trademark protection, its brand extension potential, and so on.

The next step is to apply the derived split to the estimated economic income that will be generated by the use of the trademark.

The estimated economic income is then capitalized, as an annuity in perpetuity, at an appropriate capitalization rate. The capitalization rate is equal to the difference between the appropriate present value discount rate and the expected long-term growth rate in operating profit income. The capitalization results in the estimated economic value of the subject trademark.

## Market Approach

The market approach estimates the value of an intangible asset by reference to actual market transactions involving either comparable or guideline intangible assets. The most common market approach method used in the valuation of marketing intangible assets is the *capitalized royalty income method*. The capitalized royalty income method can also be considered an income approach method, because the estimated royalty income is capitalized to result in an indicated value.

In the capitalized royalty method, the subject trademark is valued by reference to the amount of royalty income it could generate if it was licensed, in an arm's-length transaction, to a third party. In using this method, a sample of guideline, arm's-length royalty or license agreements are analyzed. The license agreements selected should represent transactions that reflect similar risk and return investment characteristics that make them comparable to the subject trademark. The risk and return investment characteristics may include industry conditions, the ability to generate an expected level of economic earnings for the owner or licensee, the age of the trademark, the degree of consumer recognition, geographical coverage of the trademark, remaining number of years of legal protection of the trademark, the life cycle of the trademark, and so forth. Based on an assessment of the risk and return investment factors of the subject trademark as compared to the guideline transactions, a fair royalty rate is estimated for the subject trademark.

The benchmark royalty rate is then multiplied by the net revenues (or similar measure of gross receipts) expected to be generated by the subject trademark. The product is an estimate of the royalty income that could be generated hypothetically by licensing the subject trademark.

Next, the estimated royalty income is capitalized, as an annuity over the expected life of the trademark, at an appropriate capitalization rate. The capitalization rate is the difference between the appropriate present value discount rate and the expected long-term growth rate in royalty income. The result of the capitalization is the fair market value of the trademark based on the capitalized royalty income method.

## Remaining Useful Life

The valuation methods presented above typically assume that the subject trademark has a remaining useful life in perpetuity. However, the remaining useful life of a brand may only be five or ten years. Therefore, it is important that the analyst consider the remaining useful life as part of the valuation or economic analysis of a trademark. Chapters 11 and 12 present the various methods used to estimate the remaining useful life of an intangible asset such as a trademark.

Under the cost approach to valuation, a remaining useful life analysis may be performed in order to estimate the amount of obsolescence, if any, that should be deducted from the measures of reproduction, replacement, creation, or recreation cost of the subject trademark.

Under the income approach to valuation, a remaining useful life analysis may be performed in order to estimate the prospective period for the economic income projection subject to capitalization (whether the direct capitalization or the yield capitalization method is used).

Under the market approach to valuation, a remaining useful life analysis may be performed in order to select, reject, or adjust either the guideline trademark sale or license transaction data, so that the adjusted transactional data are more comparative to the subject trademark.

## DATA SOURCES

Chapter 5 describes the types of data sources typically used in the valuation of intangible assets. The following discussion addresses these data sources as they apply to the valuation of marketing intangible assets.

### Internal Data Sources

Internal financial reports such as historical financial statements and budgets are needed for all of the methods used to value marketing intangible assets. For the valuation of a trademark using the cost approach methods, historical advertising and promotion expenditure data should be available from the company's historical income statements. Additionally, for the income and market approach methods, historical revenue generated by the subject trademark should also be presented either in the company's income statements or, more typically, in various additional financial statement reports prepared for top management of the company.

In addition to gathering various internal financial data to value marketing intangible assets, it is important that the analyst interview relevant top management personnel. With respect to marketing intangible assets, these interviews can provide insight regarding the following topics:

- Trademarks or brands of competitors in the marketplace.
- Transactions involving similar marketing intangible assets of other companies, or offers for marketing intangible assets of the subject company.
- Historical development efforts by the company regarding the subject marketing intangible asset.
- General characteristics of the marketing intangible asset—for example, the relative strengths and weaknesses of the subject trademark compared to similar trademarks in the market. In many instances, management has historically retained consultants to perform surveys and compile the survey results regarding the relative strengths and weaknesses of the subject trademark.

### External Data Sources

Typically, the most useful external data sources for the valuation and economic analysis of marketing intangible assets are books and newsletters specializing in intangible asset licensing. Examples of these sources include *An Insider's Guide to Royalty Rates* by Battersby and Grimes and *Licensing Economics Review* (see the Bibliography at the end of the chapter for information on these publications). These sources provide historical data regarding royalty rates for various types of licensed products. Royalty rates used in comparable or guideline transactions are useful in estimating the value of a subject trademark, after considering adjustments to reflect any key differences between the subject trademark and those involved in the comparable or guideline transactions. In addition, press releases and articles available from a variety of news sources provide information about market transactions for the sale or license of marketing intangible assets.

## VALUATION EXAMPLE

Exhibits 23-2 through 23-4 present examples of the valuation of a trademark using one method from each of the three valuation approaches. In these examples, we consider the valuation of the hypothetical trade name "Money-Maker" and the associated trademark. The objective of the valuation assignment is to estimate the fair market value of a fee simple ownership interest in the trademark and trade name MoneyMaker, as of January 31, 1998.

As part of the examples, we assume that the trade name MoneyMaker is used on a product that is projected to generate $10 million of net revenues next year. The assumed appropriate effective income tax rate is 40 percent, and the appropriate market-derived direct capitalization rate (corresponding to after-tax net income) is 20 percent.

## Cost Approach—Trended Historical Cost Method

The first method we considered was the trended historical cost method. The product MoneyMaker was introduced in fiscal 1995, and for this method we calculated historical advertising and promotion expenses for MoneyMaker for fiscal years 1995 through 1997. Next, we trended the expenses to the January 31, 1998, valuation date based on the appropriate inflation factor for each year.

Based on the historical advertising and promotion expenses for the product, the indicated value of the trademark is $1.7 million, as presented in Exhibit 23-2.

## Income Approach—Profit Split Method

The second method we used to value MoneyMaker was the profit split method. A simplified example of this method is presented in Exhibit 23-3.

---

**EXHIBIT 23-2**

Illustrative Trademark Valuation, Cost Approach—Trended Historical Cost Method, as of January 31, 1998 (in 000s)

| | |
|---|---:|
| Advertising and promotion expense for MoneyMaker, fiscal 1995 (year product was introduced, trended to current dollar value) | $1,000 |
| Advertising and promotion expense for MoneyMaker, fiscal 1996 (trended to current dollar value) | 400 |
| Advertising and promotion expense for MoneyMaker, fiscal 1997 (trended to current dollar value) | 300 |
| Trademark value indication | 1,700 |
| Indicated fair market value (rounded) | $1,700 |

EXHIBIT 23-3

Illustrative Trademark Valuation, Income Approach—Profit Split Method, as of January 31, 1998 (in 000s)

| Analysis Variables | Projected Next Period | |
|---|---|---|
| Projected MoneyMaker net revenues | $10,000 | |
| Operating expense (30% of revenues) | 3,000 | |
| Selling and general & administrative (50% of revenues) | 5,000 | |
| Income before taxes | 2,000 | |
| Less: income tax expense | 800 | |
| After-tax income | 1,200 | |
| Less: capital charge | 400 | |
| Projected economic income | 800 | |
| Market-derived profit split percentage between licensor and licensee | Licensor 50% | Licensee 50% |
| Projected economic income after profit split | 400 | |
| Divided by: market-derived direct capitalization rate | 20% | |
| Trademark value indication | 2,000 | |
| Indicated fair market value (rounded) | $ 2,000 | |

Based upon our analysis of the historical results of operations of the MoneyMaker product line, we projected operating expenses at 30 percent of net revenues and selling, general, and administrative expenses at 50 percent of net revenues. We also analyzed the other (nontrademark) assets that are used or used up in the production of income from the MoneyMaker product line. We concluded that the appropriate capital charge (or periodic return) associated with these other assets is $400,000 for the next year.

Our analysis of market-derived guideline trademark license agreements indicates that arm's-length licensors and licensees in the same industry as MoneyMaker have agreed—either implicitly or explicitly—to a royalty arrangement equating to a profit split of approximately 50 percent. Based upon this market-derived profit split, the indicated value of the MoneyMaker trademark is $2 million.

## Market Approach—Capitalized Royalty Income Method

Based upon our research and analysis, we concluded that comparable trademarks in the same industry as MoneyMaker have been licensed. An analysis of the comparable license agreements indicates that the market-derived royalty rate appropriate for the license of the MoneyMaker name would range from 6 percent to 6.5 percent of net revenues.

A simplified example of one market approach method—the capitalized royalty income method—is presented in Exhibit 23-4. Based upon the market-derived royalty rate range, the indicated values range from $1.8 million to $1.95 million, with a fair market value estimate of $1.9 million.

## Valuation Reconciliation and Conclusion

Based upon the analyses described herein, the market value of the Money-Maker trademark, as of January 31, 1998, is (rounded) $1,900,000.

**EXHIBIT 23-4**

Illustrative Trademark Valuation Market Approach—Capitalized Royalty Income Method, as of January 31, 1998 (in 000s)

| Analysis Variables | Projected Next Period | |
|---|---|---|
| Projected MoneyMaker net revenues | $10,000 | $10,000 |
| Market-derived range of royalty rates | 6.0% | 6.5% |
| Projected annual royalties | 600 | 650 |
| Less: income tax expense | 240 | 260 |
| Projected after-tax royalties | 360 | 390 |
| Divided by: market-derived direct capitalization rate | 20% | 20% |
| Trademark value indication | 1,800 | 1,950 |
| Indicated fair market value (rounded) | $ 1,900 | |

It is noteworthy that each of these three methods assumes, essentially, a perpetual remaining useful life for the subject trademark. This assumption may be appropriate if the analyst has concluded that the subject trademark can remain economically viable indefinitely (given reasonable periodic maintenance expenditures for advertising and promotion).

Of course, the three valuation methods are presented as representative methods. In any particular valuation, the quantity and quality of available data—and the facts and circumstances of the valuation—influence the selection of the appropriate valuation method or methods.

## BIBLIOGRAPHY

# Articles

Anson, Weston. "Trademark/Brand Licensing and Valuations." *Journal of Business*, October 1990, pp. 213–220.

Bertolotti, Nick. "Valuing Intellectual Property." *Managing Intellectual Property*, February 1995, pp. 28–32.

Biel, Alexander L. "How Brand Image Drives Brand Equity." *Journal of Advertising Research*, November 1992, pp. RC6–RC12.

Blackett, Tom. "Brand and Trademark Valuation—What's Happening Now?" *Marketing, Intelligence & Planning*, November 1993, pp. 28–30.

DeSouza, Glenn. "Royalty Methods for Intellectual Property." *Business Economics*, April 1997, pp. 46–52.

Elgison, Martin J. "Capitalizing on the Financial Value of Patents, Trademarks, Copyrights, and Other Intellectual Property." *Corporate Cashflow*, November 1992, pp. 30–32.

Gordon, Wendy J. "On Owning Information: Intellectual Property and the Restitutionary Impulse." *Virginia Law Review*, February 1992, pp. 149–281.

Hardin, Russell. "Valuing Intellectual Property." *Chicago-Kent Law Review*, Vol. 68, No. 2, 1993, pp. 659–675.

Hughes, Justin. "The Philosophy of Intellectual Property." *The Georgetown Law Journal*, December 1988, pp. 287–366.

Keller, Kevin Lane. "Conceptualizing, Measuring, and Managing Customer-Based Brand Equity." *Journal of Marketing*, January 1993, pp. 1–22.

King, Alfred M., and James Cook. "Brand Names: The Invisible Assets." *Management Accounting*, November 1990, pp. 41–45.

Martin, Michael J. "Valuing the Glamour in Brand Name Acquisitions." *Mergers & Acquisitions*, January-February 1991, pp. 31–37.

Mullen, Maggie. "What is a Brand Name or Trademark Really Worth—How Can That Value Be Measured?" *Journal of Business*, October 1990, pp. 203–212.

Murphy, John. "Assessing the Value of Brands." *Long Range Planning*, June 1990. pp. 23–29.

————. "A Brand New Look to Valuations." *World Accounting Report*, August-September 1992, pp. ii–iii.

Ourusoff, Alexandra, Michael Ozanian, Paul B. Brown, and Jason Starr. "What's in a Name—What the World's Top Brands Are Worth." *Financial World*, September 1992, pp. 32–49.

————. "Who Says Brands Are Dead." *Financial World*, September 1993, pp. 40–50.

Parr, Russell L. "The Double-Barreled Benefits of Acquiring a Brand Name." *Mergers & Acquisitions*, March-April 1993, pp. 36–38.

Rechtin, Michael D. "Intellectual Property: Ticking Time Bombs for the Unwary Buyer." *Mergers & Acquisitions*, January-February 1992, pp. 28–31.

Reilly, Robert F. "How Buyers Value Intellectual Properties." *Mergers & Acquisitions*, January-February 1996, pp. 40–44.

Smith, Gordon V. "Trademark Valuations Run Amuck." *Business Valuation Review*, December 1992, pp. 179–82.

Wilkins, Mira. "The Neglected Intangible Asset: The Influence of the Trade Mark on the Rise of the Modern Corporation." *Business History*, January 1992, pp. 66–95.

## Books

Aaker, David A., and Alexander L. Biel. *Brand Equity & Advertising.* Hillsdale, NJ: Lawrence Erlbaum Associates, 1993.

Battersby, Gregory J., and Charles W. Grimes. *An Insider's Guide to Royalty Rates: A Comprehensive Survey of Royalty Rates and Licensed Products.* Stamford, CT: Kent Press, 1996.

Bertolotti, Nick. *Valuing Intellectual Property.* New York: John Wiley & Sons, 1994, supplemented annually.

Elias, Stephen. *Patent, Copyright, and Trademark: A Desk Reference to Intellectual Property Law.* Berkeley, CA: Nolo Press, 1996.

Epstein, Michael A. *Modern Intellectual Property.* New York: Aspen Law & Business, 1995.

Lee, Lewis C., and J. Scott Davidson. *Managing Intellectual Property Rights.* New York: John Wiley & Sons, 1993.

Marconi, Joe. *Beyond Branding: How Savvy Marketers Build Brand Equity to Create Products and Open New Markets.* Chicago: Probus Publishing Company (McGraw-Hill), 1993.

Martin, David N. *Romancing the Brand: The Power of Advertising and How to Use It.* New York: American Management Association, 1989.

Parr, Russell L. *Intellectual Property Infringement Damages.* New York: John Wiley & Sons, 1993.

————. *Investing in Intangible Assets: Finding and Profiting from Hidden Corporate Value.* New York: John Wiley & Sons, 1991.

Simensky, Melvin, and Lanning G. Bryer. *The New Role of Intellectual Property in Commercial Transactions.* New York: John Wiley & Sons, 1994.

Smith, Gordon, and Russell Parr. *Valuation of Intellectual Property and Intangible Assets.* New York: John Wiley & Sons, 1994, supplemented annually.

————. *Intellectual Property: Licensing and Joint Venture Profit Strategies,* 2nd ed. New York: John Wiley & Sons, 1998.

## Periodicals

*Intellectual Property Strategist,* monthly. Published by Leader Publications, 345 Park Avenue South, New York, NY 10010, (212) 545-6170.

*IP Litigator,* bimonthly. Published by Aspen Law & Business, 1185 Avenue of the Americas, New York, NY 10036, (212) 597-0200.

*Licensing Economics Review,* monthly. Published by AUS Consultants, 155 Gaither Drive, Moorestown, NJ 08057, (609) 234-1199.

*The Licensing Journal,* ten issues per year. Published by Aspen Law & Business, 1185 Avenue of the Americas, New York, NY 10036, (212) 597-0200.

*Licensing Law and Business Report,* bimonthly. Published by Clark Boardman Callaghan, 125 Hudson Street, New York, NY 10014, (212) 929-7500.

*The Licensing Letter,* monthly. Published by EPM Communications Inc., 488 East 18th Street, Brooklyn, NY 11226, (212) 941-0099.

*Mealey's Litigation Report: Intellectual Property,* semimonthly. Published by Mealey Publications, Inc., P. O. Box 446, Wayne, PA 19087-0446, (215) 688-6566.

# Technology Intangible Assets

## DESCRIPTION OF TECHNOLOGY INTANGIBLES

The class of intangible assets referred to as *technology intangibles* generally represents value attributable to proprietary knowledge and processes that have been developed or purchased by a company and are recognized as actually providing, or having the potential to provide, significant competitive advantages or product differentiation. Often, and inappropriately, only participants in the high-tech industries are recognized as controlling technology intangibles of any significant value. However, as suggested above, any proprietary technology that confers to its owner competitive or product differentiation advantages relative to its competitors is generally recognized as a valuable technology intangible. This statement applies to companies across all industries.

Historically, investments in technological know-how have not gone unnoticed by investors, with the market as a whole often responding quite favorably to corporate announcements of planned increases in research and development expenditures. Further, historical analysis of companies with positive excess stock returns and above-average rates of return on investment suggests that these companies historically have maintained higher than average levels of investment in research and development.

Within our definition of technology intangibles we generally include the following intellectual properties:

- Patents.
- Patentable inventions.
- Mask works.
- Trade secrets.
- Know-how.
- Confidential information.
- Copyrights of such technical material as computer software, databases, and instruction manuals.

Copyright-related intangibles and data processing intangibles are addressed in Chapters 17 and 19, respectively. Therefore, the technology intangibles that are the focus of this chapter include patents and patentable inventions, trade secrets, know-how, and confidential information.

There are many areas in the operation of a company where technology intangibles may exist. Therefore, an analyst should be prepared to both identify a technology intangible and arrive at a reasonable indication of the intangible's value. The purposes of technology intangible appraisals are numerous, and include:

1. The identification of licensing opportunities and estimation of related royalty rates.
2. Purchase price allocations in business enterprise acquisitions.
3. Value allocations in ad valorem property tax assessment disputes.
4. Collateral valuations in debtor-in-possession financing arrangements in bankruptcy matters.

Numerous attributes economically impact the value of technology intangibles. Industry, product, and service considerations provide a wide range of positive to negative influences, which should be qualitatively and quantitatively assessed by the analyst. Exhibit 24-1 presents a nonexhaustive listing of the attributes that should be considered when valuing technology intangibles, including their general influences on value.

## COMMON VALUATION METHODS

As discussed in Part 2 of this text, there are several methods and procedures that may be appropriate for appraising intangible assets. The methods fall into three general approaches: the market approach, the cost approach, and the income approach.

While some intangible assets are readily appraised by all three approaches, certain approaches provide more credible results than others for particular categories of intangible assets. With regard to technology intangibles, all three approaches to value are generally employed. However, the indications of value resulting from each approach are often assigned different weights in arriving at a conclusion of value, based on the quantity and quality of data supporting each approach.

The following discussion of common valuation methods within the market, cost, and income approaches addresses considerations regarding the valuation of technology intangibles based on each approach.

## Market Approach

When valuing technology intangibles, analysts generally attempt to apply the market (sometimes called the sales comparison) approach methods first. This is based on the widely held belief that the market (i.e., the economic environment where arm's-length transactions between unrelated parties occur) is typically the best indicator of the value of a technology. Analysts research the market for both sales transactions and license (i.e., rental) transactions that may be useful in analyzing the subject technology.

A very general and systematic process often employed during the application of market approach methods includes the following steps:

1. Research the appropriate exchange market to obtain information on sale transactions, listings, and offers to purchase or license *guideline* (i.e., generally similar) or *comparable* (i.e., essentially identical) technologies that are similar to the subject in terms of characteristics such as technology type, technology use, industry in which the technology functions, date of sale, and so forth.

2. Verify the information by confirming that the data are factually accurate and that the technology sale or license exchange transactions reflect arm's-length market considerations. (If the guideline transaction was not at arm's-length market conditions, then adjustments to the transactional data may be necessary.)

3. Select relevant units of comparison (e.g., income multipliers or dollars per unit—units such as "per patent") and develop a comparative analysis for each unit of comparison.

4. Compare guideline technology sale or license transactions with the subject using the elements of comparison and adjust the sale or license price of each guideline transaction appropriately to the subject property, or eliminate the sale or license transaction as a guideline for future consideration.

Attributes That Influence the Value of Technology Intangible Assets

| Attribute | Influence on Value | |
| --- | --- | --- |
| | **Positive** | **Negative** |
| Age—absolute | Newly created, state-of-the-art technology | Long-established, dated technology |
| Age—relative | Newer than competing technology | Older than competing technology |
| Use—consistency | Technology proven or used consistently on products and services | Technology unproven or used inconsistently on products and services |
| Use—specificity | Technology can be used on a broad range of products and services | Technology can be used only on a narrow range of products and services |
| Use—industry | Technology can be used in a wide range of industries | Technology can be used only in a narrow range of industries |
| Potential for expansion | Unrestricted ability to use technology on new or different products and services | Restricted ability to use technology on new or different products and services |
| Potential for exploitation | Unrestricted ability to license technology into new industries and uses | Restricted ability to license technology into new industries and uses |
| Proven use | Technology has proven application | Technology does not have proven application |
| Proven exploitation | Technology has been commercially licensed | Technology has not been commercially licensed |
| Profitability—absolute | Profit margins or investment returns on products and services higher than industry average | Profit margins or investment returns on products and services lower than industry average |
| Profitability—relative | Profit margins or investment returns on products and services higher than competing names | Profit margins or investment returns on products and services lower than competing names |
| Expense of continued development | Low cost to maintain the technology as state-of-the-art | High cost to maintain the technology as state-of-the-art |
| Expense of commercialization | Low cost of bringing technology to commercial exploitation | High cost of bringing technology to commercial exploitation |
| Means of commercialization | Numerous means available to commercialize technology | Few means available to commercialize technology |
| Market share—absolute | Products and services using technology have high market share | Products and services using technology have low market share |
| Market share—relative | Products and services using technology have higher market share than competing names | Products and services using technology have lower market share than competing names |
| Market potential—absolute | Products and services using technology are in an expanding market | Products and services using technology are in a contracting market |
| Market potential—relative | Market for products and services using technology expanding faster than competing names | Market for products and services using technology expanding slower than competing names |
| Competition | Little or no competition for technology | Considerable established competition for technology |
| Perceived demand | Perceived currently unfilled need for the technology | Little or no perceived need for the technology |

5. Reconcile the various value indications produced from the analysis of the guideline technology transactions into a single value indication or a range of values. In an imprecise market, subject to varying economics, a range of values may sometimes be a better conclusion for the subject technology than a single value estimate.

At least ten basic elements of comparison have been identified as requiring careful consideration when selecting and analyzing guideline technology sale or license transactions:

1. The legal rights of technology ownership conveyed in the guideline transaction.
2. The existence of any special financing terms or arrangements (e.g., between the buyer and the seller).

3. The existence, or absence, of arm's-length sale conditions.
4. The economic conditions existing in the appropriate secondary market at the time of the guideline technology sale or license transaction.
5. The industry in which the technology will be used.
6. The geographic or territorial characteristics of the guideline sale or license transactions compared to the subject technology.
7. The term or duration characteristics of the guideline sale or license transactions compared to the subject technology.
8. The use or exploitation characteristics of the guideline sale or license transactions compared to the subject technology.
9. The economic characteristics of the guideline sale or license transactions compared to the subject technology (i.e., who is responsible for continued development, commercialization, or legal protection of the technology).
10. The inclusion of other (nontechnology) assets in the guideline sale or license transactions. (This may include the sale of a bundle or a portfolio of assets that could include marketing assistance, trademarks, product development, or other contractual rights).

The reconciliation step represents the last phase of any market approach valuation analysis in which two or more value indications have been derived from guideline market data. In the reconciliation step, the analyst reviews the data and analyses that resulted in each value indication, weighting each indication based on the quantity and reliability of underlying data and the relevance of the analysis, given the fact set specific to the subject technology intangible.

## Cost Approach

The most common types, or measures, of cost that are used for technology valuation purposes are *reproduction cost* and *replacement cost.*

Reproduction cost is the total cost, at current prices, to create an exact duplicate technology. The duplicate would be created using the same scientific research, design, and development methods used to create the original technology.

The replacement cost is the total cost to create, at current prices, a technology having equal utility to the technology subject to appraisal. However, the replacement technology would be created with contemporary scientific research, design, and development methods. Accordingly, the replacement technology may have greater utility (in terms of, for example, commercial potential and technological accomplishment) than the subject property.

Replacement cost new typically establishes the maximum amount that a prudent investor would pay for a fungible, or replaceable, technology. It is noteworthy that some proprietary technologies are so unique that they are not replaceable. In these instances, replacement cost new may not establish the maximum amount that a buyer would pay for the subject intangible, because the buyer simply could not recreate the subject unique technology even if the buyer expended the dollar amount of the replacement cost new.

To the extent that a technology is less than an ideal replacement for itself, the value of the subject technology should be adjusted accordingly. As with the application of the cost approach to any intangible asset, the subject technology replacement cost new should be adjusted for losses in economic value due to:

- Functional obsolescence.
- Technological obsolescence.
- Economic obsolescence (which is often called external obsolescence).

## Income Approach

An investor (i.e., owner) anticipates economic returns, or income, from technology intangibles during their economic lives. There are numerous measures of economic income that may be relevant to the various income approach methods, including:

- Gross or net revenues.
- Gross income (or gross profit).
- Net operating income.
- Net income before tax.
- Net income after tax.
- Operating cash flow.
- Net cash flow.
- Several others (including incremental income).

Several categories of income approach methods are listed below:

1. Methods that quantify incremental levels of economic income (i.e., the technology owner will enjoy a greater level of economic income by owning [as compared to not owning] the technology).
2. Methods that quantify decremental levels of economic costs (i.e., the technology owner will suffer a lower level of economic costs, such as otherwise required investments or operating expenses, by owning [as compared to not owning] the technology).
3. Methods that estimate a relief from a hypothetical royalty or rental payment (i.e., the amount of a royalty or rental payment that the technology owner would be willing to pay to a third party in order to obtain the use of—and the rights to—the subject technology).
4. Methods that quantify the difference in the value of an overall business enterprise, or similar economic unit, as the result of owning the subject technology (and using it in the business enterprise), as compared to not owning the subject technology (and not using it in the business enterprise).
5. Methods that estimate the value of the subject technology as a residual from the value of an overall business enterprise (or of a similar economic unit), or as a residual from the value of an overall estimation of the total intangible value of a business enterprise (or of a similar economic unit).

## DATA SOURCES

Chapter 5 describes the types of data sources typically used in the valuation of intangible assets. The following discussion addresses these data sources as they apply to the valuation of technology intangibles.

### Internal Data Sources

Internal financial reports such as historical financial statements and budgets are useful in performing almost all intangible asset valuation methods. Payroll records and project management or timekeeping reports are particularly relevant to any cost approach valuation method.

A complete summary of all purchased or licensed technology and internally developed technology (including patented and patentable technology), trade secrets, know-how, and confidential information in use at the valuation date should be requested and reviewed. The summary should provide information regarding the purpose of the technology, the acquisition date or development period of the technology, the acquisition cost or estimated development cost of the technology, the expected economic life of the technology, cost advantages or other benefits conferred by the technology, the market potential for the technology, existing competing technologies, and recent sales or licensing information regarding competing or comparative technologies.

A review of the technology summary may be supplemented by interviews with key members of management. Although the technology summary may provide considerable information regarding the underlying technology, interviews with relevant members of management generally provide the first clear indication of the existence of technology intangible value. The following list provides examples of key technology-related factors that are often only ascertainable through the interview process:

- Expectations regarding market potential and commercialization of the technology.
- The number of identifiable competitors developing comparative technology, and their respective stages of development or market share.
- Identifiable market barriers with regard to market entry and the cost to develop the technology.
- Acquisitions of companies owning similar technologies or licensing similar technologies.
- Expected impact of regulatory policy or other external factors on the commercial viability of the technology.

### External Data Sources

The following sources provide useful data regarding actual sales or licenses of technology:

- *Intellectual Property Strategist,* monthly. New York: Leader Publications.
- *Licensing Economics Review,* monthly. Moorestown, NJ: AUS Consultants.

- *The Licensing Letter,* monthly. Brooklyn, NY: EPM Communications Inc.
- *Royalty Rates for Technology.* Yardley, PA: Intellectual Property Research Associates, 1997.

While they do not provide actual licensing or transaction agreements, trade publications may prove to be useful data sources for the purpose of identifying companies that offer technology comparative to that of the subject company. In addition, numerous newsletters specializing in intangible asset licensing, as listed in the Bibliography at the end of this chapter, can be good sources of market-derived, empirical royalty rates. The professional societies listed in Chapter 17 are another source of data for technology intangibles.

In many instances, interviews with management may provide relevant information regarding comparable technology currently in use in the marketplace or recently developed by competitors. Often, support for management assertions is represented by external documents and information in management's possession. This information should be requested and reviewed before it is relied upon by the analyst.

### VALUATION EXAMPLE

Exhibits 24-2 through 24-5 present an example of the valuation of the hypothetical technology intangible Cutting Edge, and the associated technical documentation. Cutting Edge is an advanced cutting process that uses a stream of high-pressure water to cut through solid materials such as steel and concrete.

### Fact Set and Assumptions

The objective of the appraisal is to estimate the fair market value of a fee simple ownership interest in the Cutting Edge technology as of December 31, 1997. The technology intangible Cutting Edge is used on a product that is projected to generate $30 million in net revenues next year. As general valuation variables, assume that the appropriate effective income tax rate is 40 percent and the appropriate market-derived direct capitalization rate (corresponding to after-tax net income) is 20 percent.

### Market Approach—Relief from Royalty Method

Exhibit 24-2 presents our relief from royalty analysis relating to the Cutting Edge technology. Based upon our research and analysis, we concluded that comparable technologies in the same industry as Cutting Edge have been licensed. An analysis of the license agreements indicates that the market-derived royalty rate appropriate for the license of the Cutting Edge technology ranges from 5 to 6 percent of net revenues. Since Cutting Edge owns its technology, it will not have to pay these royalty payments for the use of the technology.

As presented in Exhibit 24-2, the indicated value of the Cutting Edge technology, based on the relief from royalty method of the market approach, as of December 31, 1997, is $5,000,000.

EXHIBIT 24-2

Illustrative Technology Valuation, Market Approach—Relief from Royalty Method, as of December 31, 1997 (000s)

| Valuation Analysis Variables | | Projected Next Period |
|---|---|---|
| Projected Cutting Edge net revenues | $30,000 | $30,000 |
| Market-derived range of royalty rates | 5% | 6% |
| Projected annual relief from royalty payments | 1,500 | 1,800 |
| Less: Projected income tax expense | 600 | 720 |
| After-tax relief from royalty payments | 900 | 1,080 |
| Divided by: Direct capitalization rate | 20% | 20% |
| Indicated value of Cutting Edge technology | 4,500 | 5,400 |
| Indicated fair market value (rounded) | $ 5,000 | |

# Cost Approach—
# Research and Development
# Cost Savings Method

Exhibit 24-3 presents our research and development cost savings analysis relating to the Cutting Edge technology. Our analysis of the industry indicates that the Cutting Edge product line (as a result of its proven technology) enjoys substantial research and development expense cost savings (measured as a percent of net revenues) compared to the industry average. Accordingly, we performed a research and development cost savings method valuation analysis. A comparative analysis of research and development expenditures for the Cutting Edge technology, in relation to similar expenditures of Cutting Edge competitors, results in an estimated cost savings for Cutting Edge of 6 percent.

As presented in Exhibit 24-3, the indicated value of the Cutting Edge technology, based on the research and development cost savings method of the cost approach, as of December 31, 1997, is $5,400,000.

EXHIBIT 24-3

Illustrative Technology Valuation, Cost Approach—Research and Development Cost Savings Method, Comparative Cost Savings Analysis, as of December 31, 1997 (000s)

| | |
|---|---|
| Average R&D expense of Cutting Edge competitors | 8% of net revenues |
| Average R&D expense of Cutting Edge | 2% of net revenues |
| Estimated R&D cost advantage of Cutting Edge | 6% of net revenues |

| Valuation Analysis Variables | Projected Next Period |
|---|---|
| Projected Cutting Edge net revenues | $30,000 |
| Times: Research and development cost advantage | 6% |
| Equals: Incremental income before income taxes | 1,800 |
| Less: Projected income tax expense | 720 |
| Equals: Incremental income after income taxes | 1,080 |
| Divided by: Direct capitalization rate | 20% |
| Indicated value of Cutting Edge technology | 5,400 |
| Indicated fair market value (rounded) | 5,400 |

## Income Approach—Profit Split Method

Exhibit 24-4 presents our profit split analysis relating to the Cutting Edge technology. We projected operating expenses at 45 percent of net revenues and selling, general, and administrative expenses at 35 percent of net revenues. We also analyzed the other (nontechnology) assets that are consumed in the production of income from the Cutting Edge product line. We concluded that the appropriate capital charge associated with (or periodic return on) these other assets is $1.5 million for next year.

Our analysis of guideline license agreements indicates that arm's-length licensors and licensees in the same industry as Cutting Edge have agreed—either implicitly or explicitly—to a royalty arrangement equating to a profit split of approximately 50 percent.

As presented in Exhibit 24-4, the indicated value of the Cutting Edge technology, based on the profit split method of the income approach, as of December 31, 1997, is $5,300,000.

## Valuation Reconciliation and Conclusion

In synthesizing the results of these three valuation methods, and based on both the quantity and quality of data underlying each analysis and the relevance of each method based on factors specific to Cutting Edge, we decided to assign slightly more weight to the first valuation method.

Based on the analyses summarized in Exhibit 24-5, the market value of the Cutting Edge technology, as of December 31, 1997, is (rounded) $5,200,000.

### BIBLIOGRAPHY

## Articles

Bertolotti, Nick. "Valuing Intellectual Property." *Managing Intellectual Property,* February 1995, pp. 28–32.

**EXHIBIT 24-4**

Illustrative Technology Valuation, Income Approach—Profit Split Method, As of December 31, 1997 (000s)

| Valuation Analysis Variables | | Projected Next Period | |
|---|---|---|---|
| Projected Cutting Edge net revenues | | $30,000 | |
| Operating expense (45% of revenues) | | (13,500) | |
| Selling, general & administrative expense (35% of revenues) | | (10,500) | |
| Income before income taxes | | 6,000 | |
| Less: Projected income tax expense | | 2,400 | |
| After-tax income | | 3,600 | |
| Less: Capital charge | | 1,500 | |
| Projected economic income | | 2,100 | |
| | | | |
| Market-derived "profit split" percentage between technology licensor | | Licensor | Licensee |
| and technology licensee | | 50% | 50% |
| Projected economic income after profit split | | 1,050 | 1,050 |
| Divided by: Direct capitalization rate | | 20% | |
| Indicated value of Cutting Edge technology | | 5,250 | |
| Indicated frair market value (rounded) | | $5,300 | |

**EXHIBIT 24-5**

Illustrative Technology Valuation, Valuation Synthesis and Conclusion,
as of December 31, 1997 (000s)

| Valuation Approach | Valuation Method | Indicated Value |
|---|---|---|
| Market | Relief from royalty method | 5,000 |
| Cost | Research and development cost savings method | 5,400 |
| Income | Profit split method | 5,300 |
| | Fair market value conclusion (rounded) | $5,200 |

DeSouza, Glenn. "Royalty Methods for Intellectual Property." *Business Economics*, April 1997, pp. 46–52.

Doukas, John, and Lorne Switzer. "The Stock Market's Valuation of R&D Spending and Market Concentration." *Journal of Economics & Business*, May 1992, pp. 95–114.

Elgison, Martin J. "Capitalizing on the Financial Value of Patents, Trademarks, Copyrights, and Other Intellectual Property." *Corporate Cashflow*, November 1992, pp. 30–32.

Fearing, Jennifer, Atanu Saha, and Roy Weinstein. "Beyond Georgia-Pacific: A New Approach to the Calculation of Reasonable Royalties." *Micronomics, Inc.* (http://www.micronomics.com/pubs/9701jlf.html), February 1997.

Gordon, Wendy J. "On Owning Information: Intellectual Property and the Restitutionary Impulse." *Virginia Law Review*, February 1992, pp. 149–281.

Hardin, Russell. "Valuing Intellectual Property." *Chicago-Kent Law Review*, Vol. 68, No. 2, 1993, pp. 659–675.

Hughes, Justin. "The Philosophy of Intellectual Property." *The Georgetown Law Journal*, December 1988, pp. 287–366.

Kitchen, Mable W. "Taking Full Advantage of Research Expenditures." *Ohio CPA Journal*, August 1995, pp. 53–54.

Laverde, Lorin, and Eric Knapp. "Evaluating Intangible Assets in the Sale of Technology-Based Companies." *The Corporate Growth Report*, October 1990, pp. 23–25.

Neil, D. J. "The Valuation of Intellectual Property." *International Journal of Technology Management*, 1988, Vol. 3, No. 1-2, pp. 31–42.

Oosterhuis, Paul W. "International R&D and Technology Transfer Arrangements." *Taxes*, December 1995, pp. 905–922.

Paulsen, Jon. "Valuation of Patent Infringement Damages." *Valuation*, March 1994, pp. 18–23.

Pinches, George E., V.K. Narayanan, and Kathryn M. Kelm. "How the Market Values the Different Stages of R&D—Initiation, Progress, and Commercialization." *BankAmerica Journal of Applied Corporate Finance*, Spring 1996, pp. 60–69.

Rechtin, Michael D. "Intellectual Property: Ticking Time Bombs for the Unwary Buyer." *Mergers & Acquisitions*, January-February 1992, pp. 28–31.

Reilly, Robert F. "How Buyers Value Intellectual Properties." *Mergers & Acquisitions*, January-February 1996, pp. 40–44.

———. "Putting the Right Price on Proprietary Technology." *ABI Journal*, December-January 1997, pp. 30–31, 42.

———. "The Valuation of Proprietary Technology." *Multimedia and Technology Licensing Law Report*, January 1996, pp. 3–6.

Robbins, Billy A. "Three Methods Can Set Value for Tech Licenses." *The National Law Journal*, January 26, 1998, p. C26.

Rotman, David. "Do You Know How Much Your Technology Is Worth?" *Chemical Week*, April 10, 1996, p. 50.

Schweihs, Robert P. "The Valuation of Proprietary Technology." *Journal of Property Tax Management*, Fall 1996, pp. 34–44.

Sougiannis, Theodore. "The Accounting Based Valuation of Corporate R&D." *The Accounting Review*, June 1993, pp. 44–68.

Wagner, Michael J., and Bruce McFarlane. "Court Expands Lost Profits Damages from Patent Infringement." *CPA Expert,* Summer 1996, pp. 1–3.

## Books

Bertolotti, Nick. *Valuing Intellectual Property.* New York: John Wiley & Sons, 1994, supplemented annually.

Elias, Stephen. *Patent, Copyright, and Trademark: A Desk Reference to Intellectual Property Law.* Berkeley, CA: Nolo Press, 1996.

Epstein, Michael A. *Modern Intellectual Property.* New York: Aspen Law & Business, 1995.

Lee, Lewis C., and J. Scott Davidson. *Managing Intellectual Property Rights.* New York: John Wiley & Sons, 1993.

Parr, Russell L. *Intellectual Property Infringement Damages.* New York: John Wiley & Sons, 1993.

———. *Investing in Intangible Assets: Finding and Profiting from Hidden Corporate Value.* New York: John Wiley & Sons, 1991.

Parr, Russell L., and Patrick H. Sullivan. *Technology Licensing: Corporate Strategies for Maximizing Value.* New York: John Wiley & Sons, 1996.

*Royalty Rates for Technology.* Yardley, PA: Intellectual Property Research Associates, 1997.

Simensky, Melvin, and Lanning G. Bryer, eds. *The New Role of Intellectual Property in Commercial Transactions.* New York: John Wiley & Sons, Inc., 1994.

Smith, Gordon V., and Russell L. Parr. *Valuation of Intellectual Property and Intangible Assets.* New York: John Wiley & Sons, 1994, supplemented annually.

———. *Intellectual Property: Licensing and Joint Venture Profit Strategies,* 2nd ed. New York: John Wiley & Sons, 1998.

## Periodicals

*Intellectual Property Strategist,* monthly. Published by Leader Publications, 345 Park Avenue South, New York, NY 10010, (212) 545-6170.

*IP Litigator,* bimonthly. Published by Aspen Law & Business, 1185 Avenue of the Americas, New York, NY 10036, (212) 597-0200.

*Journal of Proprietary Rights,* monthly. Published by Aspen Law & Business, 1185 Avenue of the Americas, New York, NY 10036, (212) 597-0200.

*Licensing Economics Review,* monthly. Published by AUS Consultants, 155 Gaither Drive, Moorestown, NJ 08057, (609) 234-1199.

*The Licensing Journal,* ten issues per year. Published by Aspen Law & Business, 1185 Avenue of the Americas, New York, NY 10036, (212) 597-0200.

*Licensing Law and Business Report,* bimonthly. Published by Clark Boardman Callaghan, 125 Hudson Street, New York, NY 10014, (212) 929-7500.

*The Licensing Letter,* monthly. Published by EPM Communications Inc., 488 East 18th Street, Brooklyn, NY 11226, (212) 941-0099.

*Mealey's Litigation Report: Intellectual Property,* semimonthly. Published by Mealey Publications, Inc., P. O. Box 446, Wayne, PA 19087-0446, (215) 688-6566.

*Mealey's Litigation Report: Patents,* semimonthly. Published by Mealey Publications, Inc., P. O. Box 446, Wayne, PA 19087-0446, (215) 688-6566.

*Multimedia and Technology Licensing Law Report,* monthly. Published by West Publishing, P.O. Box 64833, St. Paul, MN 55164-0833, (800) 328-4880.

# Special Topics

# CHAPTER 25

# Intercompany Transfer Pricing and Royalty Rate Analysis

# INTRODUCTION

Most business managers are at least somewhat familiar with the concept of commercial goodwill. The common understanding is that goodwill reflects the favorable reputation created by a business over time, which serves to attract new customers, thereby generating an economic benefit for the enterprise.

From an analyst's perspective, however, corporate goodwill has a more distinct meaning, especially when made with reference to a company that has recently acquired another entity. Except in a *pooling of interests* transaction, goodwill is an asset recorded on the balance sheet that measures the portion of the purchase price paid by the buyer for the target company in excess of the net value of the target's identifiable tangible and intangible assets, as of the acquisition date.

Even within the more astute business community, however, relatively few people are aware of the diverse array of separately identifiable intangible assets discussed in this book. For those who recognize the contribution of these types of properties to the value of a business, the concept of corporate goodwill takes on a whole new meaning. The intangible assets comprising a business enterprise's portfolio can be proactively developed, maintained, and nurtured in order to enhance the overall value of the business.

Recently, multinational corporations have more actively managed their portfolios of corporate intangible assets by transferring or licensing them to their foreign subsidiaries (or to foreign corporations under their control). The transferred or licensed intangible assets are then used in the generation of business income in various locations.

Under one common structure for this program, the U.S. corporation transfers a separately identifiable intangible asset, such as a manufacturing patent or proprietary technology, to a 100 percent owned foreign subsidiary. In carrying out its normal business operations, the foreign subsidiary uses the technology and pays a license fee or royalty payment to the U.S. corporation in the form of an intercompany transfer price.

There are a number of operational, strategic, and legal motivations for implementing this type of intangible asset transfer program. Corporate trademarks and trade names are one of the more common types of intangible assets subject to an asset transfer program. In the retail industry, for example, because of the practical necessity for the transferor to protect, manage, and control the use of trademarks and trade names, the transferee is only allowed to use, but not own, the asset. However, corporations in just about every line of business—wholesale, distribution, manufacturing, service, and so on—clearly have an advantage if they protect, manage, and optimize the deployment of their intangible assets.

In determining which intangible assets to include in an asset transfer program, the corporate taxpayer considers a number of factors, including the following:

- Which intangible assets have legal existence?
- Which intangible assets have economic substance?
- Which intangible assets can be legally transferred to a foreign subsidiary?
- For which intangible assets is there a practical business reason to be transferred to a foreign subsidiary?

- Which intangible assets are actually used, or consumed, in normal business operations in another country?

- Which intangible assets can be associated with a determinable royalty rate or other type of transfer price, in order to effectively quantify the value of the asset transfer program?

- Which intangible assets have a reasonably long-term and determinable remaining useful life?

- Which intangible assets will not have to be sold, abandoned, or otherwise transferred back out of the foreign domicile in the foreseeable future?

As with just about every strategic planning technique, numerous pros and cons are associated with the implementation of an intercompany intangible asset transfer program. In terms of the plusses, the corporation may enjoy increased control over its intangible assets. By implementing a legal and organizational structure to effect the transfer or to investigate licensing, the corporation may be acting to maximize the value of its intangible assets and intellectual properties. In terms of the disadvantages, legal and organizational structures cost money, both at implementation and on an ongoing basis. Periodic legal and valuation consulting fees are associated with both the start-up and the implementation of the program.

One potential benefit not mentioned above is the possible reduction in the worldwide federal income taxes paid by the consolidated corporation. When the opportunity for tax reduction exists, however, the national taxing authorities are on the alert, which itself represents another possible negative aspect of the program.

Such intangible asset transfers and intercompany transactions have certainly drawn scrutiny from the Internal Revenue Service, especially when the transfer program is perceived to have been set up to arbitrarily shift income from a U.S. corporation to a foreign subsidiary. Over time, the Treasury Department has contended that the U.S. federal income tax code was not effectively protecting the U.S. taxing jurisdiction from such arbitrary shifting of income. Various methods have been promulgated and refined to assess whether or not related or controlled parties receive fair value, or a fair and reasonable price including a reasonable profit, in consideration for the use of the intangible property.

In the following section we discuss the nature of intercompany transfer pricing as it relates to intangible assets.

## THE NATURE OF INTERCOMPANY TRANSFER PRICING

In a nonbarter market economy, prices reflect the monetary terms at which property, or the right to use property, is bought and sold. Under this type of economic system, a market determined price represents, to some extent, one outcome of a tacit negotiating process between the transaction's two primary participants: the buyer and the seller.

For transactions involving a buyer and a seller possessing no overlapping interests, both parties presumably negotiate terms that are more directly favorable to their own self-interests. For example, a prospective buyer seeks a lower price, more favorable financing arrangements, discounted companion or add-on products or services, and so on. When negotiations between buyer and seller lead to the consummation of a transaction, economic theory suggests that each party is "better (or, at least, no worse) off" by virtue of having agreed to transact at the market price.[1] Market prices emanating from arm's-length transactions simultaneously reflect the underlying value of the property to each transactor. The arm's-length price is a proxy both for the property's utility to the buyer and for the seller's cost to bring the property to market.

The presence of competing economic self-interests between buyers and sellers defines the arm's-length setting. The arm's-length standard uses the behavior of independent or uncontrolled parties and the outcomes of their transactions as benchmarks to compare to the behavior and outcomes of transactions that are not exposed to the same market forces.

This standard underlies the spirit of fair market value, as well as certain portions of the U.S. Internal Revenue Code. Section 482 of the Internal Revenue Code (hereinafter, Section 482) authorizes the Department of the Treasury to allocate income, expenses, and other items related to corporate reporting of taxable income among related taxpayers so that their respective incomes reflect the outcome occurring when an uncontrolled taxpayer deals at arm's length with a separate uncontrolled taxpayer.

For an example, we use the case of a consolidated U.S. business enterprise engaged exclusively in arm's-length transactions. All of its economic activity—the sale of goods and services, the procurement of materials and resources, and the acquisition and disposition of business assets—occurs in a number of arm's-length situations. The consolidated enterprise's economic activity is measured at prices that reflect contemporaneous market conditions. Since market prices reflect the collective influences of market participants, the income earned by the consolidated enterprise, denominated at market prices, is satisfactory from the government taxing authorities' point of view.

In contrast, two parties under common economic control may bilaterally transact without confronting these same market forces. Negotiating in a vacuum, two commonly controlled entities can transfer property at any "price" of their own choosing. This "internal" transfer price may vary from the arm's-length outcome, or the market price, that two unrelated parties would agree to under identical circumstances. In effect, two commonly controlled parties have the opportunity to concertedly maximize the interests of the combined group, as opposed to individually and competitively maximizing their separate individual interests.

The distinction between the internal transfer prices established between controlled parties and market prices observed within arm's-length transactions is the focus of this chapter.

For a business enterprise exclusively engaged in arm's-length transactions, operating income is measured at market prices. Since market prices directly impact the enterprise's taxable income as reported to the government, income tax liability is satisfactory. For commonly controlled enterprises, however, the federal tax liability is only satisfactory if the internal transfer prices have no impact on the computation of the combined national income tax liability, as compared to the size of the federal tax liability that would have occurred under arm's-length conditions.

---

1. For the untold number of unconsummated transactions, the parties presumably cannot agree to a price that is both sufficiently high enough to induce the seller to deliver the property while simultaneously being low enough to induce the buyer to accept the property.

Consider the example of a hypothetical U.S. corporation, Ace Window Frames, Inc. ("Ace"). Ace manufactures aluminum casement window units from a single East Coast facility. Over the years, Ace has developed a proprietary technology that allows it to employ a unique aluminum extrusion process that produces a superior, stronger product. As a result of this internally developed technology, Ace is able to sell its standard configuration window units to third-party distributors for a unit price of $200. The direct cost associated with the production of each standard window unit is $50.

Ace decides to expand its operations by setting up a separate, wholly owned manufacturing subsidiary on the West Coast ("Ace West"). The Ace marketing department decides that the unit prices of windows manufactured by Ace West will be identical to the prices charged for the same windows manufactured on the East Coast. Production costs in each location are expected to be identical.

For internal accounting purposes, Ace implements a royalty charge of $10 per window, which is recognized as royalty revenue by Ace and royalty expense by Ace West. This price is internally instituted to reflect the consideration paid by Ace West to Ace in return for use of the proprietary technology provided by Ace to its West Coast subsidiary.

On a consolidated basis, the existence and magnitude of this internal royalty charge has absolutely no impact on the Ace consolidated taxable income. Every dollar of royalty expense incurred by Ace West is matched by a dollar of earned revenue by Ace. Accordingly, the mere existence of this related party transaction is of no concern to the Internal Revenue Service. In this case, the internal transfer price does not affect the consolidated arm's-length taxable income earned and reported by Ace. From a domestic perspective, however, the internal royalty rate does shift income from the West Coast to the East Coast.[2]

If the same transaction takes place between two controlled parties located in different countries, however, the Internal Revenue Service would be much more likely to examine the terms of the arrangement. To the extent that related parties are located in separate national tax jurisdictions with different effective tax rates, the opportunity exists for the consolidated entity to actually influence its overall tax liability by adjusting its internal transfer pricing policy.

Continuing with the example, let us assume that Ace could, alternatively, expand its operations by engaging a foreign manufacturer. One way to implement this strategy would entail Ace starting up or acquiring its own manufacturing concern. Ace could then transfer its proprietary technology to the new foreign subsidiary ("Ace International") in return for a stream of royalties based upon production levels. Ace and Ace International, as two related parties bilaterally isolated from the marketplace, can establish any royalty rate charges they choose.

If Ace and Ace International agree to an intercompany royalty charge that is less than what two uncontrolled parties would agree to as part of an otherwise identical arm's-length setting, then income is being shifted from the United States toward the foreign jurisdiction in which Ace International does business. In this case, Ace is receiving less royalty income from

---

2. The implications of interstate intangible asset transfers are discussed in the section, "Transfer Pricing for Domestic Taxation Purposes."

Ace International than it would have received had Ace licensed the same intangible asset to a third party. Therefore, Ace is giving up royalty income. On the other side of the transaction, however, Ace International benefits from the controlled party licensing arrangement because the foreign subsidiary recognizes less royalty expense than it would in an uncontrolled transaction.

Accordingly, when the royalty rate used in the controlled party transaction is less than the royalty rate that arm's-length participants would agree to, the relative income of the foreign entity using the transferred intangible asset increases. In fact, the relative income increases by an amount equal to the amount by which the domestic licensor is foregoing royalty income by virtue of discounting the royalty rate below the market rate. In this case, the consolidated company is basically shifting income from the United States toward the foreign jurisdiction.

The net impact of the internal royalty rate program on the Ace consolidated pretax income is zero. However, if the program successfully shifts income out of a relatively high marginal tax rate nation into a jurisdiction with a lower marginal tax rate, the consolidated corporate income tax liability is reduced.

As the pace of international commerce accelerates and as more corporations set up foreign operations, the revenues (expenses) of a subsidiary located in a particular national taxing jurisdiction will represent the mirror image of the expenses (revenues) of its related or controlled corporation involved on the other side of an international transaction. If the two corporations are unrelated to each other, there is every reason to believe that the impact of the international transaction on each party's income reflects the return required by each party as compensation for engaging in the transaction. Indeed, no one could reasonably argue that the international aspects of the uncontrolled transaction represent any unusual circumstances with regard to the proper reporting of each party's taxable income to its respective taxing authority.

Using any hypothetical U.S. company as our point of reference, when that company exchanges goods or services across national borders with an unrelated foreign company, the international nature of the transaction does not normally give rise to suspicion regarding the transfer price. However, when exchanges of goods or services across national borders take place between subsidiaries of a consolidated group of companies, potential disputes may arise between taxpayers and national taxing jurisdictions.

In order to attract outside capital, some foreign governments legislate a favorable tax environment for multinational companies. For U.S. companies with multinational business interests, some portion of their economic activity, as reflected in the generation of sales revenue or the incidence of expenses, may be attributable to activities carried out outside the United States. In this type of situation, questions may arise about the proper apportionment of income between the two nations. In such a situation, a U.S. corporation with operations in a tax-favored nation would be inclined to shift income into the country with the lower tax rate.

The analysis of intercompany transfer pricing and royalty rates is relevant to certain economic transactions involving separate but related companies. The transactions typically involve the transfer of a valuable economic good, service, or resource, such as the assignment of tangible assets (i.e., inventory), supporting services, or identifiable intangible assets.

As part of an intercompany transfer, an explicit or implicit price is used to value the goods, services, or resources exchanged in the transaction. Since the transfer price is agreed upon by two related parties, the influence of market forces may be less prevalent than what unrelated parties would experience. Therefore, the actual intercompany transfer price may differ from what would be established by two independent parties engaged in an arm's-length exchange.

As a result of the intercompany transaction, the revenues or expenses and, therefore, the taxable income of each related party, are impacted by the magnitude of the transfer price. To the extent that the related parties have some discretion in establishing their internal transfer price, the price may be set so as to minimize the combined companies' global tax liability, by shifting taxable income between companies according to differences in national tax rates.

Since the enactment of the War Revenue Act of 1917, the Commissioner of the Internal Revenue Service has been authorized by the Congress to scrutinize the tax returns of multinational U.S. companies to ensure that taxable income is equitably reported. The Treasury Department was concerned that these corporations could establish internal transfer prices for the purpose of shifting taxable income from the United States into another taxing authority.

Section 482 authorizes the Secretary of the Treasury to allocate income, deductions, and other tax items among related taxpayers to prevent the evasion of taxes or to clearly reflect income. The Tax Reform Act of 1986 amended Section 482 by providing that the income from a transfer or license of intangible property must be commensurate with the income attributable to the intangible asset.

In July 1994, the Internal Revenue Service issued final regulations on the intercompany pricing of both tangible and intangible property under Section 482. The Service also revised the temporary Section 6662 regulations, which include penalty provisions for valuation misstatements.

The following section briefly outlines the key features of the final Section 482 regulations.

## KEY FEATURES OF THE FINAL 482 REGULATIONS

### Reporting Taxable Income

The final 1994 transfer pricing regulations elaborate on the issue that may arise when a company transacts with an affiliate at terms that are not at arm's length. The issue is whether or not the company is required to report the true taxable income rather than the results of the actual transaction.

The 1994 regulations provide that, "if necessary to reflect an arm's-length result, a controlled taxpayer may report . . . the results of its controlled transactions based upon prices different from those actually charged."[3]

---

3. Regs. Section 1.482-1(a)(3).

The previous regulations had imposed various preconditions to the revised reporting of transactions by taxpayers. Taxpayers wishing to depart from its form and report true taxable income on their returns were required to enter into a formal written agreement with an affiliate to make compensating adjustments on their books and in their records.

The 1994 regulations, however, removed the compensating adjustment mechanism with an obligation of contemporaneous reporting. Taxpayers wishing to use Section 482 must affirmatively report the results on a timely filed tax return and may not do so on an amended return.

## The Arm's-Length Standard

The arm's-length standard was somewhat altered by the 1994 final regulations. The construction of true taxable income remains the fundamental remedy of Section 482. According to the final regulations, true taxable income is a condition that exists when a controlled taxpayer reports financial results that are consistent with the results that an uncontrolled taxpayer would have attained under comparable circumstances.

This formulation contains two core components: *consistency* with uncontrolled results and *comparable circumstances*. Consistency tests a controlled taxpayer's financial results against the arm's-length results of a comparable uncontrolled taxpayer. The arm's-length results are established by using methods that are determined under the *best method rule.*

## The Best Method Rule

Although similar in scope and purpose to its predecessor in the pre-1994 regulations, the formulation of the best method rule was changed somewhat by the final regulations. Rather than being the most accurate measure, the best method under the final regulations is the method that provides the most reliable measure of an arm's-length result, determined by taking into account the same factors that were identified in the previous temporary regulations.

The series of factors to be considered in searching for the most reliable result under the arm's-length standard of transfer pricing thereby remain: 1) the particular facts and circumstances of the transaction; 2) the completeness and accuracy of available data; and 3) the degree of comparability between controlled and uncontrolled transactions.

## The Arm's-Length Range

Consistency with an arm's-length result is determined by creating an arm's-length range based on comparable information. The arm's-length range is established by a group of comparables in the case such that all the information of both the controlled transaction and the uncontrolled comparables is sufficiently complete, and any material differences that have an ascertainable effect on the prices or profits of the comparables can be adequately reconciled by adjustments.

If the data on the comparables are not sufficiently complete, all comparables with a similar level of comparability and reliability are then considered, with their reliability enhanced using appropriate statistical techniques.

# Determining Comparable Circumstances

The most useful portions of the regulations, carried over in large part from the previous regulations, are the factors to determine comparability. Under the 1994 regulations, all factors that could affect a financial result are to be taken into account. The previous regulations listed specific factors that were required to be considered in determining comparability. The 1994 regulations clarify that this is not necessarily a complete listing.

## Comparability Factors

The factors to be considered in determining comparability include:

1. *Functional analysis.* A functional analysis of the economically significant activities of the controlled and uncontrolled taxpayers includes research and development, manufacturing, marketing, distribution, and managerial functions. In order for the two transactions (i.e., the controlled and the uncontrolled) to be comparable, the entities should perform similar economic functions with respect to the transactions.

2. *Contractual terms.* To be considered comparable, an uncontrolled transaction should have similar significant contractual terms that could affect the prices that would be earned.

3. *Risk analysis.* The risks borne by each party in the controlled and uncontrolled transactions must be analyzed, including market risks, research and development, financial risks, product liability risks, and general business risks. The economic substance of transactions will be reviewed by the Service to determine risks borne. Taxpayers should be certain not to mismatch the allocation of risks and potential rewards for bearing those risks.

4. *Economic conditions.* The economic conditions surrounding the transactions should be similar and should consider factors such as: 1) alternatives realistically available to the buyer and seller (e.g., make versus buy); 2) the similarity of the geographic markets; 3) the relative size of each market and the extent of economic development; and 4) the level of the market, market share for items transferred, location-specific costs, and competition in the market.

The final 1994 regulations also address the three special circumstances from the previous regulations, that may affect comparability: 1) market share strategies, 2) differences in geographic markets, and 3) extraordinary or tax-motivated transactions.

## Multiple-Year Data

The 1994 regulations provide that the results of a controlled transaction ordinarily will be compared with the results of uncontrolled comparables occurring in the taxable year under review. It is appropriate to consider earlier or later years' data to examine circumstances—such as the assumption of risk and market share strategies—that are perceived as involving longer time periods.

The regulations continue to make available the use of multiple-year averages to establish a range. However, if the taxpayer's results for a particular year fall outside of the multiple-year range, a new provision states that the requisite adjustment should ordinarily be based on the range of the uncontrolled comparable results for the single-year and not the multiple-year average. This requirement appears to be unfavorable to taxpayers and undermines the more economically relevant use of the multiple year averages.

The principles and mechanics of the final Section 482 regulations set the stage for elaborate routines of investigation, analysis, comparison, and documentation. The final regulations also require careful analysis of the facts and circumstances surrounding each intercompany transaction (including comparable transactions) and impose a substantial factual burden of proof on taxpayers (including detailed documentation of their intercompany transfer pricing policies and analyses in support of their prices as arm's length).

As a result, multinational taxpayers will have to devote significant resources to comply with these regulations. Taxpayers need to rely on their advisors increasingly to assist in choosing and documenting the method or methods that best determine the most appropriate intercompany price, given the economic and business circumstances of a controlled transaction.

The following section discusses a number of possible purposes that may necessitate an intercompany transfer pricing analysis and the companion role that the intangible asset analysts may play in that process.

## TWO MAJOR TYPES OF INTERCOMPANY TRANSFERS

There are two primary types of intercompany asset transfers between a first party and a second party which, in turn, create the intercompany transfer price or royalty rate relationships subject to analysis: 1) import or export of tangible assets (that is, inventory), the cost of which or revenues received therefrom are affected by the transfer price; and 2) outbound or inbound conveyance of intangible assets in return for royalty income or royalty expenses.[4]

To offer an illustrative example of an intercompany transfer of tangible assets, assume that Nifty Shirts, a U.S. company, sells golf shirts manufactured by its foreign subsidiary located in Mexico. Nifty Shirts, which sells the golf shirts to various retail outlets in the United States, pays its Mexican subsidiary a price for each manufactured shirt. The amount charged by the foreign subsidiary to Nifty Shirts represents Nifty Shirts' cost of goods sold, which is deductible for U.S. federal income tax purposes. Nifty Shirt's requirement under the Section 482 regulations is to establish a transfer price that will reflect its cost of goods sold as if Nifty Shirts had been dealing with an uncontrolled third party.

Acting to minimize its U.S. federal income tax liability, Nifty Shirts may attempt to establish a high, but supportable, transfer price for each shirt manufactured by the Mexican manufacturing subsidiary. That relatively high transfer price would, everything else equal, lower Nifty Shirts' U.S. federal income tax liability. The corresponding side of the Nifty Shirts'

---

4. Intercompany transfer of services is another category not discussed herein.

efforts to establish a high but supportable transfer price is that the Mexican subsidiary recognizes higher sales revenues, which by itself increases its profits as reported to Mexico's national taxing authority.

Holding all other factors constant, the profitability of the consolidated group (Nifty Shirts and its foreign manufacturing subsidiary) is not affected by the transfer price established by the two related parties. The transfer price decision only affects the allocation of total taxable income between the two entities. In situations where the tax rates in the two different tax jurisdictions differ, Nifty Shirts could lower its global tax liabilities by allocating more income or less expense to the jurisdiction with the lower marginal tax rate.

The following is an example of the second category of intercompany transfers, an outbound transfer of intangible assets.

A U.S. parent company (USPAR) agrees to transfer its internally developed technology protected by U.S. patent to one of its foreign subsidiaries (FORSUB). FORSUB will use the patent to manufacture certain products for sale in the country in which FORSUB is located. FORSUB agrees to compensate USPAR by making periodic royalty payments based upon a fixed royalty rate, as applied to sales revenues from the goods manufactured using the transferred patent.

The result of this transaction is that USPAR receives royalty income, which is subject to federal income taxes. Acting to minimize its U.S. federal income tax liability, USPAR may attempt to establish a low, but supportable, royalty rate. That relatively low royalty rate would, everything else being equal, lower the USPAR royalty income and its U.S. federal income tax liability. The corresponding side of the USPAR efforts to establish a low but supportable royalty rate is that FORSUB incurs lower royalty expenses, which by itself increases FORSUB's profitability.

Holding all other factors constant, the profitability of the consolidated group (USPAR and FORSUB) is not affected by the royalty rate charged by USPAR to FORSUB. The royalty rate decision only affects the allocation of total income between the two entities. In situations where the tax rates in the two tax jurisdictions differ, USPAR could lower its global tax liabilities by allocating more income or less expense to the jurisdiction with the lower marginal tax rate.

The Internal Revenue Service, in examining the USPAR consolidated federal income tax return, has the authority to ensure that USPAR is clearly and accurately reflecting economic income attributable to its transactions with FORSUB and to prevent the avoidance of U.S. income taxes with respect to those transactions. The Service would consider whether any controlled transaction meets the arm's-length standard, which is the case if the results are consistent with the results that would have been realized if uncontrolled taxpayers had engaged in a comparable transaction under similar circumstances. In other words, the inquiry turns on what transfer price or royalty rate would have resulted had ownership control not been present in the relationship.

Under all methods promulgated in the regulations, the arm's-length result is derived from an analysis of data pertaining to comparable uncontrolled transactions. Although the comparable transactions need not be identical, there should be sufficient similarity so as to provide a reasonable benchmark.

## INTANGIBLE ASSET PRICING METHODS

Intercompany royalty rate analysis opportunities arise in connection with the transfer of intangible assets between related parties. These transfers may result from the outright sale, licensing, or contribution of intangible personal property. Under these circumstances, the currently acceptable transfer pricing methods are applied.

Section 482 defines an intangible asset as any commercially transferable interest in any item included in the following six classes that has substantial economic value independent of the services of any individual:

1. Patents, innovations, formulas, processes, designs, patterns, or know-how.

2. Copyrights and literary, musical, or artistic compositions.

3. Trademarks, trade names, or brand names.

4. Franchises, licenses, or contracts.

5. Methods, programs, systems, procedures, campaigns, surveys, studies, forecasts, estimates, customer lists, or technical data.

6. Other similar items.

This list of intangible assets subject to the transfer pricing regulations is very broad. Of particular interest is the clause that introduces this list of intangibles—that is, "any commercially transferable interest." Historically, analysts involved in transfer pricing studies conceptualized intangible assets from an economic perspective (that is, any item that contributes to the profitability of an enterprise) and not from a legal perspective (that is, whether the item constituted property that was commercially transferable). This wording appears to limit the number and type of intangible assets that would be subject to transfer pricing analysis.

For transfer pricing purposes, it is important to identify any and all nonroutine, valuable intangible assets. These assets are typically developed in the United States and then transferred to low-tax-rate jurisdictions. The Treasury Department developed the commensurate with income standard to ensure that domestic corporations refrain from shielding the income generated by these assets from U.S. taxes.

Section 482 specifies four methods to determine an arm's-length transfer price in connection with a transfer of intangible property. In general, the estimated transfer price must be commensurate with the income attributable to the subject intangible asset(s). The four methods presented in the final regulations are:

1. The comparable uncontrolled transaction method (CUT).
2. The comparable profits method (CPM).
3. Profit split methods.
4. Other methods.

## The Comparable Uncontrolled Transaction Method

The comparable uncontrolled transaction (CUT) method requires that the controlled party consideration be equal to the consideration that would be paid in a comparable uncontrolled transaction. Despite the fact that the final 482 regulations still suggest that the results of the CUT method are considered the most accurate measure of value, there are several ever-present considerations, including access to relevant data and the existence of an active market, that impede its routine application.

The standards of comparability within the CUT method relate to the nature of the intangible property and the circumstances under which the transaction takes place.

## Comparable Intangible Property

In order to be considered comparable intangible property, an intangible asset or intellectual property should be in the same one of the six classes of assets already listed. Additionally, the subject asset should be involved in the same type of products, processes, or know-how. The subject and comparable assets should also be employed in the same general industry and market, and they should have substantially the same profit potential.

The profit potential of an intangible asset is measured as the net present value of the economic benefits associated with the use or transfer of the property. The present value of the benefits should consider any required capital outlays, start-up expenses, incremental risk factors, and so forth. Although the data may be relatively ascertainable with regard to the subject intangible asset, comparable data to measure the profit potential of the third-party transaction data are likely to be unavailable to the analyst.

## Comparable Circumstances

Besides involving a comparable property, the third-party uncontrolled transfer should also have occurred under comparable circumstances. This assessment requires consideration of the following factors:

1. Terms of the transfer (restrictions on the use of the asset, exclusive versus nonexclusive rights of use, etc.).
2. Stage of development (such as any necessary government approvals, licenses, etc.).
3. Rights to receive and use periodic updates or improvements.
4. Uniqueness of the property and the expected time period during which it will remain unique.
5. Duration of the intangible asset transfer contract or agreement, with consideration of any cancellation or renegotiation rights.
6. Economic and product process liability risks to be assumed by the transferor versus the transferee.
7. Collateral transactions or other ongoing business relationships between the transferor and the transferee.
8. Companion functions to be performed by each party to the asset transfer agreement.

Several of the factors may prove to be difficult to analyze when conducting a transfer pricing analysis. For example, the stage of development of the intangible asset is an issue that the Internal Revenue Service may emphasize, because transfer pricing professionals often use comparable license agreements that were executed early in the technological life of the comparable asset—that is, prior to the time at which the property was usable to manufacture a commercially viable product. In related party transactions, the transferred intangible property has typically been employed in the manufacture of a commercially viable product for some time in advance of the transfer to the controlled entity.

Beyond these two difficult hurdlesófinding comparable transactions involving similar enough intangible assets transferred under similar enough circumstances—the transfer pricing analyst also faces a more daunting reality, that royalty rates involved in the publicly disclosed uncontrolled party transactions are rarely divulged within SEC documents. As such, even though the CUT method theoretically represents the most reliable indication of value and royalty rates, there are overwhelming limitations to its use by outside analysts.

The CUT method is illustrated in the following hypothetical example. Major Motors, Inc., a U.S. corporation, licenses its proprietary technology to its German subsidiary, Major MotorWerks, AG, which employs the technology to manufacture a product sold for $30,000. If Major Motors, Inc., had alternatively manufactured and sold the product itself, a $10,000 per unit sales price would be sufficient to provide the U.S. company with a reasonable rate of return on its investment. An uncontrolled comparable transaction involves a royalty of $5,000 per unit.

The conclusion reached in this case is that Major Motors, Inc., would not accept a royalty rate of less than $20,000 per unit. Therefore, the uncontrolled $5,000 per unit transaction is not a CUT, since this royalty rate would not adequately compensate the U.S. company for the development of its technology.

## The Comparable Profits Method

The comparable profits method actually applies to the transfers of both tangible assets (e.g., inventory) and intangible assets. Under the best method rule, the comparable profits method results are preferred, or will provide the most reliable indication of an arm's-length transfer price, unless the tested party uses valuable nonroutine, intangible assets that are acquired from uncontrolled taxpayers or developed internally. Accordingly, in applying the CPM, the tested party usually does not employ these super intangible assets. The tested party is usually the party to the controlled transaction that does not employ valuable, nonroutine intangible assets or intellectual properties.

The overall purpose of the CPM is to measure the total return on the business activities of the tested party. Accordingly, Section 482 only requires that the controlled and uncontrolled transactions be broadly similar. Substantial product diversity and substantial functional diversity between the subject company and the comparable companies are acceptable.

The first step in applying the comparable profits method is to determine which of the two controlled parties is the *tested party*. The tested party is more often the participant that does not use valuable, nonroutine intangible assets. Conceptually, it may be relatively easy to identify the tested party. However, the transfer pricing analyst would be well advised to consider whether the CPM could be applied to other members of the controlled group. This strategy could be useful to estimate the downside risk of the outside scrutinizer selecting a different tested party.

The analyst should identify and compile financial data of companies engaged in the appropriate industry segment. The financial data includes the operating profit and the related assets and liabilities for both the tested party and the comparables. In selecting the exact comparables, the analyst should avoid assembling too diverse a group of companies. The more similar the exact comparables are to the tested party, the better.

Selecting the proper industry segment or product grouping can also be a significant problem in applying the CPM. Assuming a proper classification is possible, the analyst should gather profitability and balance sheet data, which usually are not presented on an industry-by-industry basis. Even allowing for the functional and product diversity permitted under this method, the greater the similarity between the comparables and the subject, the more reliable is the evidence gathered as a measure of the arm's-length transfer price.

The latter point was strongly emphasized in the *Westreco* decision,[5] in which one of the expert witnesses used companies reporting the same SIC (Standard Industry Classification) as Westreco and applied the data to what amounted to be a CPM analysis. The U.S. Tax Court essentially rejected that analysis, in part because of the diversity of companies within the group of comparable companies listed under that SIC code and their basic lack of similarity to Westreco, the subject company.

However, again assuming that comparable company data can be developed, adjustments are typically made to the profit level indicators of the family of comparable companies to improve their own consistency as well as to provide greater similarity between the guideline companies as a group and the tested party. The regulations require such adjustments to reflect differences in accounting classifications, functions performed, and risks assumed that are material and that have a definite and ascertainable impact on profitability.

After completing the selection of comparables and adjustments of the data, the transfer pricing analyst is prepared to analyze and compute various profit level indicators. The profit level indicators are intended to show the profits actually earned by the comparable companies engaged in business activity similar to that of the tested party. The profit level indicators are then applied to the relevant fundamental data of the tested party to compute constructive operating profits (COP).

To control for any vagaries of the marketplace, data covering several periods may be considered. The number of years selected should be sufficient to measure the returns that accrue to uncontrolled taxpayers with risk characteristics similar to those of the tested party. As a practical matter, database constraints may limit this type of data to three to five years.

If the preceding analyses have been conducted and all of the required adjustments have been applied, then the arm's-length transfer price range includes all the constructive cost operating profits derived from the comparable company group. However, if the adjustments were not made, then the appropriate range consists of the interquartile range, which includes the observations between the 25th and 75th percentile values of the COP derived from the profit level indicators of the comparable parties.

The Section 482 regulations list several profit level indicators that the Internal Revenue Service will accept as providing a reliable basis for comparing operating profits of similar controlled and uncontrolled taxpayers. These profit level indicators include the rate of return on capital employed and financial ratios.

---

5. *Westreco, Inc. v. Commissioner*, 64 T.C.M. 849 (1992).

It is noteworthy that operating profit is defined as gross profit less operating expenses, where operating expenses include all expenses not included in cost of sales except interest expense, foreign and domestic income taxes, interest and dividend income, income from business activities not being tested by this method, and extraordinary gains or losses.

The rate of return on capital employed (ROCE) is defined as operating profit divided by operating assets. The regulations suggest that ROCE is appropriate when the tested party has substantial fixed assets or working capital that play a significant role in generating an economic return. Therefore, this profit level indicator can be applied to a manufacturing concern.

Because many financial ratios do not directly relate operating profit to the level of investment and risk in a trade or business, their use requires more stringent comparability than is present when a ROCE is used. Financial ratios include operating profit as a percentage of sales, as well as gross profit—operating expenses.

After the exact comparables are selected, profit level indicators are computed using the financial data of the guideline companies. The profit level indicators are applied to the data of the tested party, thereby generating the COP interval. To control for any vagaries of the marketplace, data covering several periods are considered.

Consider the case of a U.S. drug company that transfers its manufacturing technology to its wholly owned French subsidiary. The French subsidiary sells its manufactured product back to the same U.S. parent for sale in the United States. The French subsidiary is selected as the tested party, and its financial data are presented below:

| | |
|---|---|
| Assets | $35 |
| Sales of product (to U.S. parent) | $40 |
| Cost of goods sold | $28 |
| Operating expenses | $ 5 |

The COP interval is computed as between $4 and $6.

This data supports the conclusion that the arm's-length royalty rate should be set at 5 percent of sales revenue. Such a rate would increase the French subsidiary expenses by $2 per unit, thereby reducing the operating profit to $5, which is the midpoint of the COP interval.


## Profit Split Methods

At least three profit split methods may be used to estimate the appropriate transfer price or royalty rate for intangible assets and intellectual properties: the residual allocation rule, the capital employed allocation rule, and the comparable profit split rule.

A profit split method may be applied if the following conditions are met:

- Each controlled taxpayer owns a valuable, nonroutine intangible asset that it either acquired from uncontrolled taxpayers or developed itself.

- Such intangible assets contribute significantly to earning the combined profit.

- There are significant transactions between the controlled tax-payers, and the activities of each party contribute significantly to the combined profit or loss.
- The controlled taxpayer elects to apply the profit split method and complies with the procedural requirements contained in the regulations.

Profit split methods rely either wholly or in part on internal data rather than on data derived from unrelated party transactions. Consequently, it is generally accepted that methods that rely upon comparable transactions generally provide a more reliable and accurate measure of the arm's-length royalty rate. This is one reason that the regulations allow taxpayers to apply a profit split methodology: if, and only if, each controlled party owns valuable nonroutine internally developed intangible assets.

### Residual Allocation Rule

The application of the residual allocation rule version of the profit split method is a two-step process. First, the taxpayer should assign market returns to the various related parties' routine functions. For example, if one of the related parties is a distributor, a market return for this function is estimated by reference to the returns earned by uncontrolled taxpayers engaged in similar distribution activities. A functional analysis may be required to identify the contribution made by each of the related taxpayers through their routine activities.

In the second step, since a profit split method can only be used in cases where each taxpayer owns valuable nonroutine intangible assets, there will be residual profits left to be allocated after assigning each related party a return to its routine economic activities. The residual profit should typically be divided among the related parties based upon the relative value of the contributions of the valuable nonroutine intangible assets to their relevant business activities. The method used to value each of the parties' contributions should be adapted to the particular circumstances of the intercompany transactions.

For example, in cases where technology development expenditures are relatively constant over time, the relative value of actual expenditures in recent years may be used to estimate the relative value of the technology-related intangible asset contributions. Alternatively, in cases where these expenditures vary over time or where the facts and circumstances indicate that comparison of such expenditures does not satisfactorily approximate the relative values of the controlled taxpayer's contributions, other methods of approximating the relative values may be appropriate.

### Capital Employed Allocation Rule

Under this profit split method, the combined profit or loss from the relevant business activities of the two (or more) controlled parties is allocated to each party according to the ratio of the taxpayers' average capital employed in the business activity. This rule applies only if each taxpayer involved in the controlled transaction assumes approximately equal levels of risk with respect to its investment in the business activity.

Section 482 requires that risk be measured on the basis of the probability of success or failure rather than on the basis of absolute measures of the maximum potential gain or loss. It suggests that approximately equal levels of risk exist when the activities of all parties involved in the transaction are so interdependent that the degree of risk or failure of any one participant is inexorably linked to the success or failure of all the other participants. As a practical matter, this argument can usually be made with reference to all intercompany relationships.

The capital employed allocation rule requires that the operating assets of each controlled party be adjusted for the value of the intangible assets employed as part of the controlled transaction. The capital attributable to the subject intangible assets is measured by one or more valuation methods representing an example of either a cost, market, or income approach method.

The method selected becomes important because the regulations also require that the method used to estimate capital attributable to intangible assets and intellectual properties be used consistently from year to year. Furthermore, if fair market value is the standard selected to value either the tangible or intangible assets of the controlled parties, then all assets should be valued on this basis.

### Comparable Profit Split Rule

This allocation rule under the profit split method looks to the division of the combined profits earned by unrelated taxpayers in transactions that are comparable with respect to functions performed and risks assumed by each party, products brought to market, and intangible assets developed and owned. As with most comparable transaction methods, the profit split observed within the comparable transaction is applied to the combined profit earned in the related party transaction in order to calculate the arm's-length pricing policy.

In order to apply this particular method properly, a thorough functional analysis is required (as is the case with all methods involving comparisons) to determine the degree of comparability between the related and unrelated parties. Beyond this qualitative analysis, business segment financial data should also be available. Accordingly, the method is rarely applicable due to both the difficulty of identifying decent comparable transactions and the lack of detailed financial data.

The comparable profit split method may not be applied if the combined return on capital earned by the uncontrolled taxpayer varies significantly from that of the subject taxpayer.

## Other Methods

Since the CPM cannot be applied when both parties have valuable nonroutine intangible assets, it is likely that taxpayers in such situations may have to resort to some other method when no appropriate comparable companies can be found. To be permitted to employ another method, a taxpayer should disclose the use of such a method by attaching a disclosure statement to its income tax return. It is worth noting that the taxpayer should also prepare contemporaneous supporting documentation regarding the specific analysis adopted, the rationale for using the method (that is, why it satisfies the best method rule), and all supporting data.

## TRANSFER PRICING FOR DOMESTIC TAXATION PURPOSES

In recent years, many multistate corporations have formed subsidiaries in the state of Delaware and then transferred legal title to various corporate intangible assets and intellectual properties to the Delaware subsidiary. The structure for these types of interstate intangible asset programs is identical to those set up across national boundaries that were described earlier.

A common tactic is to form a holding company subsidiary, typically chartered in the state of Delaware, which has no state corporate income tax. The legal title to the intangible asset is transferred to the Delaware holding company (DHC). The DHC subsequently licenses the use of the intangible assets to related parties operating their businesses in other states.

The related parties make royalty payments to the DHC, which represent deductible expenses for the operating companies for state income tax purposes. However, no income tax liability is realized by the DHC on the licensing or leasing revenues from these intangible assets. The overall result of the transaction is to reduce the aggregate state income tax obligation of the combined entities.

In order to validate this interstate transfer pricing strategy, the DHC should have form and substance as well as a legitimate business purpose. One very obvious result of forming an active DHC is that it allows the business to manage its valuable intangible assets more effectively.

The following traditional approaches are used to value the intangible assets at the point of their transfer to the DHC: cost approach methods, income approach methods, and market approach methods. For subsequent interstate intangible asset transfer pricing purposes, it is also reasonable to consider the adoption of international transfer pricing methods, as described earlier.

## TRANSFER PRICING–RELATED VALUATION MISSTATEMENT PENALTIES

Over the years, the statutory pronouncements have codified certain valuation-related penalties, and safe harbor exceptions to the penalties, with regard to international intercompany transfer pricing. These pronouncements encompass not only quantifying an incorrect transfer price for goods and services, but also selecting the wrong transfer pricing method and failing to document the method actually used and the related transfer price calculations.

We next focus upon the current transfer pricing method and calculation documentation requirements to avoid intercompany transfer pricing–related valuation penalties.

The transfer pricing rules under Section 482 allow the Internal Revenue Service to adjust transfer prices, if necessary, in order to prevent the evasion of taxes or to clearly reflect the income of any of the related parties. If the adjustment is large enough, under Section 6662, the taxpayer may have either a *substantial valuation misstatement* or a *gross valuation misstatement*.

A substantial valuation misstatement subjects the taxpayer to an accuracy-related penalty of 20 percent of the underpayment of tax due to the misstatement. A gross valuation misstatement subjects the taxpayer to an accuracy-related penalty of 40 percent of the underpayment of tax due to the misstatement.

## The Revenue Reconciliation Act of 1993

The Revenue Reconciliation Act of 1993 increased the possibility of incurring an accuracy-related penalty under the valuation misstatement provisions because the definition of a substantial valuation misstatement was expanded to include an intercompany transfer price adjustment that exceeds 10 percent of the taxpayer's gross receipts. In addition, the amount of the transfer price adjustment that may cause a substantial valuation misstatement was lowered to $5 million from $10 million.

The Revenue Reconciliation Act of 1993 also lowered the threshold transfer price adjustment that causes a gross valuation misstatement. A gross valuation misstatement now includes transfer price adjustments exceeding the lesser of $20 million or 20 percent of the taxpayer's gross receipts. (Prior to 1994 only the $20 million threshold existed.)

## Transfer Pricing Penalty Safe Harbor Provisions

Prior to the 1993 Act, taxpayers could reduce the accuracy-related penalties to the extent they could show reasonable cause for the transfer price and could show that they acted in good faith with respect to the setting of the transfer price. The 1993 Act replaced this subjective test for avoiding misstatement penalties with two objective safe harbor tests.

The first safe harbor provision excludes transfer price adjustments attributable to prices determined in accordance with one of the specified Section 482 methods. Exclusion is permitted if 1) the use of such an accepted and specified transfer price method is reasonable, 2) the taxpayer has contemporaneous documentation supporting the use of the specified method, and 3) the taxpayer provides such documentation to the Secretary of the Treasury within 30 days of a request for such documentation.

The second safe harbor applies to those taxpayers who do not use one of the specified pricing methods listed in the Section 482 regulations. The transfer price adjustment is excluded if the taxpayer establishes that none of those methods would likely result in a price clearly reflecting income and the method selected would do so. The taxpayer also must have contemporaneous documentation supporting the pricing method used and be able to provide that documentation to the Treasury within 30 days of notice.

## THE PURPOSES AND ROLES OF INTANGIBLE ASSET EXPERTS

The critical element in evaluating, developing, and presenting transfer pricing issues, from the standpoint of the taxpayer or tax administrator, is the development and interpretation of the facts relevant to the matter at hand. The importance of the development of pricing positions has been highlighted by the Section 482 penalty provisions under Section 6662 and the reasonable cause exception thereto in Section 6662(e).

There are typically three steps that need to be followed in developing and presenting transfer pricing positions:

1. Identify the pertinent facts and circumstances.
2. Evaluate the facts and circumstances to determine the appropriate pricing methodology and result.
3. Present the position.

These steps are critical regardless of the purpose of the evaluation: development of a tax return position, identification of positions by the Internal Revenue Service in an examination, response to an examination by the Service, formulation of a transfer pricing mechanism in an Advance Pricing Agreement context, or presentation of the position in a court of law.

## POTENTIAL PURPOSES OF TRANSFER PRICING ANALYSIS

The potential range of purposes that may necessitate an intercompany transfer pricing study is quite broad and includes the following:

1. An evaluation of existing or new intercompany pricing policies.
2. Documentation required by the 1994 final regulations.
3. Assessment of exposure in the event of Internal Revenue Service (or foreign taxing authority) examination.
4. IRS examination positions.
5. An Advance Pricing Agreement submission.
6. Due diligence for a reasonable documentation opinion for Section 6662(e) purposes.
7. State tax planning matters.
8. Other purposes unique to particular situations.

## TYPES OF EXPERTS

The development and presentation of an intercompany transfer pricing position often requires the use of experts for the purpose of developing certain data, evaluating proper pricing methods, and determining the result of specific issues.

### Financial Analysis Experts

A frequent issue in transfer pricing cases is the appropriate financial accounting treatment of the respective elements of a multinational taxpayer's business. This is often critical to an appropriate determination of the situation, especially when the selected pricing method involves the use of financial margin analyses, such as the comparable profits method. In order to properly apply this method, the financial data of the entities or the product lines in question must be accurately determined. In these cases it may prove useful to engage the services of a financial analysis expert to prepare and present this type of product line segmentation.

A financial analysis expert can assist the taxpayer in making a redetermination of the pertinent financial information on a profit-center basis. This redetermination may include the partitioning of the taxpayer's sales revenue into major product categories. Net profits for each category can then be estimated by tracing all of the direct costs to each type of product revenue and by allocating the common costs (such as the fixed costs of production or research, engineering, selling, advertising, and general and administrative expenses) to each profit center using an appropriate allocation method.

Financial analysis expertise can thereby be used effectively to present financial data in a manner appropriate for the pricing issues that develop in taxation disputes or with respect to intercompany transactions occurring in later periods.

The need for financial analysis expertise can also arise in a variety of circumstances, including questions regarding comparability, application of foreign accounting principles, and various other related matters.

## Economists

Perhaps the most frequently used experts in transfer pricing controversies are economists. Economists have been prominently used since at least the *E.I. DuPont de Nemours & Co. v. United States* case, in which the profits earned by a high-profit, low economic risk Swiss distribution subsidiary of a U.S. parent were at issue.[6] There were no comparable transactions in that case, and the taxpayer and government struggled through their expert witnesses to define the parameters of what arm's-length pricing would be in the situation. Since the DuPont case, economists have been present in most transfer pricing cases and have been used to evaluate pricing issues involving the various methods promulgated by the Section 482 regulations.

## The Role of Consultants and Experts in Transfer Pricing Analysis

Taxpayers can also draw upon the expertise of consultants and experts to assess their exposure to potential Internal Revenue Service transfer pricing adjustments before the fact and to develop a defense of existing pricing practices once the Service has begun a transfer pricing examination. Consultants and experts can also develop planning strategies that minimize tax burdens and audit-associated risks. Among their virtues, both defense and planning have the salutary effect of reducing the likelihood of double taxation. Equally important, a well-conceived and economically defensible transfer pricing policy significantly reduces the likelihood of valuation misstatement penalties.

### Exposure Analysis and Defense
Exposure analysis is similar to the compliance analysis that Internal Revenue Service economists conduct in evaluating taxpayer intercompany pricing practices. In fact, exposure analysis essentially duplicates this analysis before the fact, to determine whether a given transfer pricing policy is likely to be challenged. Consultants' and experts' efforts to defend a multinational company's status quo transfer pricing policies have been,

---

6. *E.I. DuPont de Nemours & Co. v. United States*, 608 F.2d 445 (Cl. Ct. 1979).

and under the current regulations will continue to be, directed toward identifying a sample of comparable uncontrolled transactions or companies and demonstrating that the tested party's results are reasonable.

A consultant or expert can also generally challenge the controversial or questionable assumptions and methodologies used by the Internal Revenue Service economist in developing pricing adjustments, thereby casting doubt on proposed reallocations of income on conceptual grounds.

Consultants and experts employed a variation of the arm's-length range as part of their exposure and defense analyses long before the range was incorporated into the regulations. The Internal Revenue Service basis for a pricing adjustment is clearly undermined in the defense scenario if the consultant or expert can construct a range of profits earned by reasonably comparable uncontrolled companies, and demonstrate either that the controlled company's reported profits fall within this range (for either exposure analysis or defense purposes); or that the controlled company's profits after the Internal Revenue Service adjustments fall outside this range (for defense only).

### Planning and Compliance

Planning analysis, another potential service offered by consultants and experts, seeks to balance multinational companies' objectives of minimizing global tax burdens, while conforming to the arm's-length standard. The planning mode allows more flexibility and creativity than the defensive mode. Whereas an analyst should take into account the actual facts and circumstances characterizing a case as given for the purposes of defending a transfer pricing policy after the fact, the analyst may recommend restructuring intercompany dealings so as to create the facts and circumstances necessary to justify a desired pricing structure for planning purposes.

An entity can restructure for income tax purposes in a variety of ways to justify corresponding changes in pricing policies, although the restructuring must be substantive, not simply a matter of form. For example, the ways in which related parties share risks is an important determinant of how combined income should be allocated among members of the controlled group. At the same time, it is fairly easy to shift risks (in a real sense) within the controlled group. Similarly, ownership of intangible assets plays a very significant role in determining how global profits should be apportioned within a controlled group. This feature, too, can be modified in a variety of real ways to justify desired modifications in arm's-length pricing policies.

### Allocation of Economic Risk

The 1994 final regulations to Section 482 enumerate different types of risk in some detail and expressly impose a number of requirements on the allocation of risk. Enumerated risks include the following:

1. Market risks from fluctuations in cost, demand, pricing, and inventory levels.
2. Research and development risks associated with the success or failure of research activities.
3. Financial risks associated with fluctuations in foreign currency exchange rates and interest rates.

4. Credit and collection risks.
5. Product liability risks.
6. General business risks related to ownership of property, plant, and equipment.

Some of these risks relate more to manufacturing operations, while others are related to the distribution function. Under the final regulations, an entity is deemed to bear a given risk only if: 1) it has a reasonable opportunity to realize an economic benefit that is commensurate with the risk(s) assumed, and that would induce a similarly situated uncontrolled taxpayer to bear the risk that the controlled taxpayer assumed; 2) it has the financial capacity to fund the losses that may result from assuming the indicated risk; and 3) it is engaged in the active conduct of a trade or business to which the risk relates and carries out substantial managerial and operational control thereover.

## Ownership of Intangible Assets

Ownership of intangible assets (both manufacturing and marketing intangibles) and, hence, the arm's-length allocation of combined income, can likewise be varied within a controlled group. In this regard, multinational companies have several options. One entity can develop the intangible asset (i.e., incur all the associated development expenses and risks), retain sole ownership rights thereto, and sell products embodying the intangible assets to controlled entities. In this event, all income associated with the intangible asset should accrue to the developer. Although the product embodies intangible assets, the developer has not transferred any rights to the intangibles simply by selling the product itself.

Alternatively, a sole developer may permit another group member to use its intangible assets in specified ways via licenses, while retaining sole ownership. For example, suppose the intangible at issue is a cost-reducing technology used in the production of a product with an established market. The developer is a U.S. entity (the parent), and the licensee is a foreign subsidiary that both manufactures the product and sells it directly to third parties. In this event, the licensee should pay an arm's-length royalty in return for its rights to use the parent's technology, and intangible income will be divided between licenser and related licensee via this payment, in accordance with arm's-length practices.

Finally, two or more members of a controlled group may enter into a qualified cost-sharing agreement, whereby the costs and risks are shared on some economic basis. The intangible assets ultimately developed are jointly owned, and the earned intangible income is allocated among cost-sharing participants. Per the cost-sharing provisions in the 1994 final regulations, costs are shared in proportion to reasonably anticipated benefits, as variously measured by anticipated units of production, sales, gross or net profit, or some other defensible measure.

## SUMMARY

For years, multinational companies have been conscious of the income taxation consequences of transferring tangible assets, intangible assets, or services between controlled related parties. Many multistate corporations have formed active corporate subsidiaries in the state of Delaware to hold, manage, and license their valuable intangible asset and intellectual properties.

In both cases, some taxing authority will scrutinize the pricing terms embedded within the related party transactions, because these terms ultimately impact the income taxes due to the authority.

Several intangible asset pricing methods were described, including the comparable uncontrolled transaction method, the comparable profits method, and profit split methods.

This chapter presented a number of issues pertaining to (for the most part, international) intercompany transfer pricing. The reader should appreciate that this is a complex issue, and that taxpayers are well advised to seek appropriate professional advice with regard to the legal, valuation, and taxation issues at stake.

## BIBLIOGRAPHY

Boatman, Kara. "OECD Transfer Pricing Guidelines Updates: Challenges for Taxpayers and Tax Authorities." *International Tax Journal*, Summer 1997, pp. 1–5.

Brewer, Thomas L., and Rebecca J. Klemm. "An Asset-Based Approach to the Profit Split Method of International Transfer Pricing." *The International Tax Journal*, Winter 1993, pp. 34–48.

Brooks, Robin C. "The Valuation of Trademarks and Trade Names for Transfer Pricing Purposes." *Willamette Management Associates Insights*, 1993 Transfer Pricing Issue, pp. 3–6.

Casinelli, Elio J., Kevin M. Hennessey, and Richard F. Yates. "Final Intercompany Transaction Regs. Focus on Broad Concepts Rather Than Mechanics." *The Journal of Taxation*, December 1995, pp. 325–332.

Copeland, Tom, Tim Koller, and Jack Murrin. "How to Value a Multinational Business." *Planning Revue*, May-June 1990, pp. 16–27.

Cornwell-Kelly, Malachy. "Customs Offer Planning Opportunities." *International Tax Revue*, May 1995, pp. 25–27.

Dal Santo, Jackie. "IRS Issues Final Transfer Pricing Regulations." *Willamette Management Associates Insights*, Winter 1995, pp. 16–17.

_____. "Transfer Pricing Issues Related to Service-Type Intangible Assets." *Willamette Management Associates Insights*, 1993 Transfer Pricing Issue, pp. 1–2.

Granwell, Alan Winston, and Kenneth Klein. "'Objective' Tests of Transfer Pricing Prop. Regs. Require Subjective Determinations." *The Journal of Taxation*, May 1992, pp. 308–315.

Kuga, Mark W. "Current Temporary and Proposed Regulations and IRS Positions Related to Intercompany Transfer Pricing." *Willamette Management Associates Insights*, 1993 Transfer Pricing Issue, pp. 17–19.

_____. "Transfer Pricing Analyses: Their Purposes and the Role of Financial Accounting and Economic Consultants and Experts." *Willamette Management Associates Insights*, Winter 1995, pp. 1–3.

Levey, Marc M., and Gregg A. Grauer. "Recognizing 'Parent-Survival Premium' in Transfer Pricing." *The Journal of International Taxation*, December 1994, pp. 541–545.

Levey, Marc M., Jonathan E. Lubick, and Robert T. Bossart. "Defining 'Quality' Data in a Transfer Pricing Analysis." *The Journal of International Taxation*, January 1996, pp. 4–11.

Levey, Marc M., and Russ O'Haver. "Transfer Pricing Guidance Offered by Sundstrand." *The Journal of International Taxation*, July-August 1991, pp. 69–77.

Levey, Marc M., Russ O'Haver, and James P. Clancy. "Application of 482 Prop. Regs. to Transfer of Intangibles Is Likely to Create Problems." *The Journal of Taxation*. November 1992, pp. 308–315.

_____. "New 482 Regs. Still Favor the Comparable Profits Method." *The Journal of International Taxation*, May 1993, pp. 202–210.

Levey, Marc M., Stanley C. Ruchelman, and William R. Seto. "Transfer Pricing of Intangibles after the Section 482 White Paper." *The Journal of Taxation*, July 1989, pp. 38–44.

Levey, Marc M., and Casey J. Schoen. "Better Comparable Analysis Persuades Tax Court in Westreco." *The Journal of International Taxation*, January 1993, pp. 39–42.

Lowell, Cym H. "Relationship of Section 482 to International Corporate Tax Planning." *The Journal of Corporate Taxation*, Spring 1996, 36–56.

Millon, Thomas J., and Robert F. Reilly. "Transfer Issues Related to Tangible Property." *Willamette Management Associates Insights*, 1993 Transfer Pricing Issue, pp. 13–16.

_____. "Valuation of Tangible and Intangible Assets as Part of a Transfer Pricing Analysis." *ASA Valuation*, June 1997, pp. 46–54.

Moore, Sharon K. "Transfer Pricing–Related Valuation Misstatement Penalties and Safe Harbor Provisions." *Willamette Management Associates Insights*, Winter 1995, pp. 10–11.

Reilly, Robert F. "Foreign Sales Corporation Transfer Pricing Methods." *Willamette Management Associates Insights*, Winter 1995, pp. 12–15.

_____. "Intercompany Transfer Pricing Issues with Regard to Technology-Related Intangible Assets." *Willamette Management Associates Insights*, 1993 Transfer Pricing Issue, pp. 7–12.

_____. "IRS Issues Temporary Regulations Regarding Section 6662 Valuation Misstatement Penalties." *Willamette Management Associates Insights*, Spring 1994, pp. 1–2.

_____. "What Appraisers Need to Know about Interstate Intangible Asset Transfer Programs." *ASA Valuation*, June 1992, pp. 42–51.

Rollinson, Barbara L., and Rom P. Watson. "The New Intercompany Pricing Regulations (Section 482)." *National Tax Journal*, September 1992, pp. 225–232.

Schweihs, Robert P. "Section 482 Transfer Pricing Valuation Penalties." *Willamette Management Associates Insights*, 1993 Transfer Pricing Issue, p. 18.

_____. "Westreco Section 482 Decision Based on Selection and Analysis of 'Comparable Companies.' *Willamette Management Associates Insights*, Spring 1993, pp. 4–6.

Shanda, Lawrence P. "Incorporating Intangible Assets into the Transfer Formula." *Taxes*, February 1991, pp. 100–105.

_____. "Royalties and Super-royalties." *Taxes*, September 1989, pp. 576–582.

Sherman, Richard, and Jennifer L. McBride. "International Transfer Pricing: Application and Analysis." *The Ohio CPA Journal*, August, 1995, pp. 29–35.

Sherwood, Stanley G., Michael Godbee, and Siv D. Janger. "The Price of Flexibility: The New Section 482 Regulations." *Tax Planning International Review*, March 1993, pp. 3–15.

Smith, Gordon V., and Russell L. Parr. "Valuation Issues in Transfer Pricing." In *Valuation of Intellectual Property and Intangible Assets*, 2d ed., 1996 Cumulative Supplement. New York: John Wiley & Sons, 1996.

Tang, Roger Y.W. "Transfer Pricing in the 1990s." *Management Accounting*, February 1992, pp. 22–26.

# Case Studies

## INTRODUCTION

In this chapter, we present a number of intangible asset valuation and economic analysis case studies. These case studies demonstrate analyses performed for a variety of purposes: transfer pricing, charitable contribution, licensing of patented technology, and copyright infringement litigation. In some of the illustrative case studies, the conclusion of the analysis is not a value estimate, but a royalty rate or transfer price.

The case studies are intended to present examples, within a limited context, of how these analyses performed. The cases are presented as excerpts from a narrative report (or an opinion letter) with accompanying exhibits. The cases present representative analyses and should not be construed to indicate that the analytical methods illustrated are the only—or even the best—applicable methods.

## CASE 1: SALE TRANSACTION TRANSFER PRICE—NICE NAME DEPARTMENT STORES, INC.

### Case Description

The objective of this economic analysis is to estimate the fair arm's-length transfer price for the Nice Name trademark and trade name (hereinafter the "Nice Name trademark") between Nice Name Department Stores, Inc., and Nice Name Canada Limited (an affiliate of Nice Name Department Stores, Inc.).

The purpose of the economic analysis is to provide an independent opinion to assist Nice Name Department Stores, Inc., management in their selection of an arm's-length transfer price regarding the Nice Name trademark currently controlled by Nice Name Canada Limited, for both internal accounting and federal income tax reporting purposes.

It is understood that the Nice Name Canada Limited business enterprise, without the Nice Name trademark intangible asset, will be sold to a third party.

It is also understood that the use of the Nice Name trademark and trade name will be restricted in the Canadian marketplace for a period of 10 years as a result of certain contractual covenants-not-to-compete. Accordingly, the economic analysis will be based on the fair arm's-length transfer price of the Nice Name trademark and trade name under the conditions of these restrictive covenants.

The analysis was conducted as of August 23, 1998.

### Valuation Theory and Methodology

We used three methods to estimate the market value (i.e., the expected arm's-length sale transaction transfer price) of the Nice Name trademark and trade name:

1. The capitalized advertising cost savings method.
2. The profit split method.
3. The relief from royalty method.

The results of our intangible asset valuation analysis are summarized in Exhibit 26-1. The values estimated using each of the three methods were given equal weight in arriving at our overall valuation conclusion.

EXHIBIT 26-1

Nice Name Department Stores, Inc., Nice Name Canada Limited Trademark and Trade Name, Valuation Synthesis and Conclusion, as of August 23, 1998

| Valuation Approach | Valuation Methods | In Canadian $ |
|---|---|---|
| Cost | Capitalized advertising cost savings method [a] | 2,500,000 |
| Income | Profit split method [b] | 3,500,000 |
| Market | Relief from royalty method [c] | 3,000,000 |
| | Indicated value—based on equal weighting of value estimates | 3,000,000 |
| | Valuation synthesis and conclusion (rounded) | 3,000,000 |

a. As provided on Exhibit 26-2.

b. As provided on Exhibit 26-4.

c. As provided on Exhibit 26-5.

## Economic Variables and Analyses

All three analyses estimate the value of the subject trademark and trade name by capitalizing some economic benefit (advertising cost savings, profit split, or royalty payment), calculated as a function of sales, 10 years in the future—at the expiration of the noncompetition period. Future sales are estimated using the latest 12 months sales' as of August 23, 1998, ($1,247,154,912) as a base and applying a 4 percent estimated long-term sales growth rate. The economic benefit in the first year following the expiration of the noncompetition period is calculated using this sales estimate. The present value of the future economic benefit is then calculated using a present value discount rate of 25 percent. The present value of the future economic benefit is then capitalized using a direct capitalization rate of 21 percent (i.e., the 25 percent discount rate less the 4 percent expected growth rate).

EXHIBIT 26-2

Nice Name Department Stores, Inc., Nice Name Canada Limited Trademark and Trade Name, Capitalized Advertising Cost Savings Valuation Method, as of August 23, 1998

| Valuation Variables | In Canadian $ |
|---|---|
| Present value of future advertising cost savings [a] | 614,872 |
| Intangible asset direct capitalization factor [b] | 4.054× |
| Capitalized advertising cost savings | 2,492,739 |
| Indicated value (rounded) | 2,500,000 |

a. Based on 4.0% compounded annual expected growth rate in sales over the projected 10-year noncompetition period. Beginning sales based on latest 12 months calculation as of August 23, 1998. Based on the 0.33% advertising cost savings percentage, as estimated in Exhibit 26-3.

b. Based on a 21% direct capitalization rate over a 10-year period.

Nice Name Department Stores, Inc., Nice Name Canada Limited Trademark and Trade Name, Capitalized Advertising Cost Savings Method, U.S. Retail Stores Advertising Analysis, Annual Advertising Expense as a Percent of Total Sales as of August 23, 1998

| Comparatitive Company Name | Current Fiscal Year | 1998 U.S. $000s | 1997 U.S. $000s | 1996 U.S. $000s |
|---|---|---|---|---|
| SALES | | | | |
| Retail Store A | Jan-98 | 2,155.223 | 2,139.055 | 2,442.897 |
| Retail Store B | Jan-98 | 1,916.555 | 1,880.511 | 1,830.955 |
| Retail Store C | Jan-98 | 166.278 | 170.345 | 233.889 |
| Retail Store D | Jan-98 | 2,748.634 | 2,414.124 | 2,127.684 |
| Retail Store E | Jan-97 | 225.903 | 217.236 | NA |
| Retail Store F | Aug-97 | 1,428.440 | 1,297.431 | 1,158.704 |
| Retail Store G | Jan-98 | 380.702 | 347.903 | 316.494 |
| Retail Store H | Jan-98 | 840.113 | 1,023.567 | 1,160.914 |
| Retail Store I | Jan-98 | 711.019 | 656.910 | 622.941 |
| Retail Store J | Jan-98 | 731.926 | 1,203.223 | 1,362.243 |
| Retail Store K | Feb-98 | 1,852.929 | 1,738.746 | 1,682.854 |
| Retail Store L | Jan-98 | 2,017.283 | 1,862.580 | 1,718.369 |
| ADVERTISING EXPENSE | | | | |
| Retail Store A | Jan-98 | NA | 86.753 | 97.070 |
| Retail Store B | Jan-98 | NA | 62.005 | 60.000 |
| Retail Store C | Jan-98 | NA | 5.464 | 9.977 |
| Retail Store D | Jan-98 | NA | 28.562 | 29.270 |
| Retail Store E | Jan-97 | 4.737 | 4.654 | NA |
| Retail Store F | Aug-97 | 35.804 | 33.511 | 28.151 |
| Retail Store G | Jan-98 | 7.276 | 6.821 | 6.389 |
| Retail Store H | Jan-98 | NA | 18.287 | 19.183 |
| Retail Store I | Jan-98 | 14.539 | 13.726 | 13.507 |
| Retail Store J | Jan-98 | NA | 30.871 | 32.022 |
| Retail Store K | Feb-98 | NA | 19.765 | 20.953 |
| Retail Store L | Jan-98 | NA | 42.008 | 34.974 |
| ADVERTISING/SALES | | | | |
| Retail Store A | | NA | 4.06% | 3.97% |
| Retail Store B | | NA | 3.30% | 3.28% |
| Retail Store C | | NA | 3.21% | 4.27% |
| Retail Store D | | NA | 1.18% | 1.38% |
| Retail Store E | | 2.10% | 2.14% | NA |
| Retail Store F | | 2.51% | 2.58% | 2.43% |
| Retail Store G | | 1.91% | 1.96% | 2.02% |
| Retail Store H | | NA | 1.79% | 1.65% |
| Retail Store I | | 2.04% | 2.09% | 2.17% |
| Retail Store J | | NA | 2.57% | 2.35% |
| Retail Store K | | NA | 1.14% | 1.25% |
| Retail Store L | | NA | 2.26% | 2.04% |

| | 1998 | 1997 | 1996 | Weighted Average |
|---|---|---|---|---|
| Nice Name Canada advertising percentage | 1.87% | 1.99% | 1.97% | 1.93% |
| U.S. retailer mean advertising cost percentage 2.14% | 2.36% | 2.44% | 2.26% | |
| Nice Name Canada advertising cost savings | 0.27% | 0.37% | 0.47% | 0.33% |
| Selected advertising cost savings percentage | | | | 0.33% |

Exhibits 26-2 and 26-3 present the capitalized advertising cost savings valuation analysis. The analysis in Exhibit 26-3 illustrates that Nice Name Canada enjoys an advertising savings of 0.33 percent of sales as compared to guideline publicly traded U.S. retail store chains. This advertising cost savings percentage is used in Exhibit 26-2 to calculate the present value of future advertising cost savings in the first year following the expiration of the noncompetition period. The indicated value of the subject trademark and trade name, using a direct capitalization rate of 21 percent for a 10-year period, is $2,500,000.

Exhibit 26-4 presents the profit split valuation method analysis. An after-tax operating margin of 1.18 percent and a profit split percentage of 33.33 percent were used to calculate the present value of the expected future profit split in the first year following the expiration of the noncompetition period. The indicated value of the subject trademark, using a direct capitalization rate of 21 percent, is $3,500,000.

**EXHIBIT 26-4**

Nice Name Department Stores, Inc. Nice Name Canada Limited Trademark and Trade Name, Profit Split Valuation Method as of August 23, 1998

| Valuation Variable | 1998 Canadian $ | 1997 Canadian $ | 1996 Canadian $ | Weighted Average Canadian $ |
|---|---|---|---|---|
| Nice Name Canada Limited sales | 1,249,818,420 | 1,224,833,495 | 1,231,199,620 | 1,238,386,978 |
| Nice Name Canada Limited EBT [a] | 16,049,383 | 36,565,374 | 35,058,761 | 26,056,276 |
| Pretax operating profit margin | 1.28% | 2.99% | 2.85% | 2.11% |
| Estimated income tax rate | 44.0% | 44.0% | 44.0% | 44.0% |
| Nice Name Canada after-tax operating profit margin | 0.72% | 1.67% | 1.59% | 1.18% |
| | | | | Canadian $ |
| Present value of future profit split [b] | | | | 726,850 |
| Market-derived intangible asset direct capitalization rate | | | | 21% |
| Present value of profit split attributable to subject trademark and trade name | | | | 3,461,192 |
| Indicated value (rounded) | | | | 3,500,000 |

a. EBT = Earnings before taxes and nonrecurring items.

b. Based on 4.0% compounded expected annual growth in sales over the projected 10-year noncompetition period. Beginning sales based on latest 12 months calculation as of August 23, 1998.

Note: Numbers may not total due to rounding.

Exhibit 26-5 presents the relief from royalty valuation method analysis. A market-derived royalty rate of 0.34 percent for Nice Name Canada is used to calculate the present value of future royalty payments in the first year following the expiration of the noncompetition period. The indicated value of the subject trademark, using a direct capitalization rate of 21 percent, is $3,000,000.

Exhibits 26-6 and 26-7 present the historical income statements and balance sheets, respectively, of Nice Name Canada.

## Sources of Information

In gathering information and data for our valuation and economic analysis, we considered the following:

EXHIBIT 26-5

Nice Name Department Stores, Inc., Nice Name Canada Limited Trademark and Trade Name, Relief from Royalty Valuation Method, as of August 23, 1998

| Valuation Variable | 1998 Canadian $ | 1997 Canadian $ | 1996 Canadian $ | Average Canadian $ |
|---|---|---|---|---|
| Nice Name Canada Limited sales | 1,249,818,420 | 1,224,833,495 | 1,231,199,620 | 1,238,386,978 |
| Market-derived trademark license royalty rate | 1.00% | 1.00% | 1.00% | 1.00% |
| Nice Name Canada Limited profit adjustment | 31.50% | 31.50% | 31.50% | 31.50% |
| Profit-adjusted trademark license royalty rate | 0.6850% | 0.6850% | 0.6850% | 0.6850% |
| Trade name risk adjustment | 50.00% | 50.00% | 50.00% | 50.00% |
| Estimated Nice Name Canada Limited trademark royalty rate | 0.3425% | 0.3425% | 0.3425% | 0.3425% |
| Total estimated trademark license royalty payments | 4,280,600 | 4,195,027 | 4,216,831 | 4,241,447 |

|  | Canadian $ |
|---|---|
| Present value of expected future trademark license royalty payments [a] | 631,524 |
| Market-derived intangible asset direct capitalization rate | 21.0% |
| Capitalized relief from future trademark license royalty payments | 3,007,256 |
| Indicated value (rounded) | 3,000,000 |

| Comparative Publicly Traded Canadian Retailer Operating Profit Margin Analysis | 1998 | 1997 | 1996 | 1995 |
|---|---|---|---|---|
| Canadian Store A | 8.69% | 8.78% | 9.06% | 10.04% |
| Canadian Store B | 3.46% | 3.13% | 1.90% | 0.41% |
| Canadian Store C | 2.78% | 2.58% | 1.40% | 1.81% |
| Canadian Store D | 28.76% | 34.78% | NM | NM |
| Average | 10.92% | 12.32% | 4.12% | 4.08% |
| Nice Name Canada Limited operating profit margins | 4.77% | 6.26% | 6.17% | 4.35% |

| Operating Profit Margins Analysis |  |
|---|---|
| Four-year average of comparative publicly traded Canadian retailer chains | 7.86% |
| Four-year average of Nice Name Canada Limited | 5.38% |
| Percentage difference in operating profit margins | 31.50% |

a. Based on 4.0% compounded expected annual growth in sales over the projected 10-year noncompetition period. Beginning sales based on latest 12 months calculation as of August 23, 1998.

Note: Numbers may not total due to rounding.

1. The nature of the business and history of the subject business enterprise.
2. The Canadian and U.S. economic outlook in general.
3. The operating results of Nice Name Canada Limited since fiscal 1991.
4. The historical operating results of Canadian general merchandise retail operations.
5. The historical operating results of U.S. general merchandise retail operations.
6. Historical rates of return in the U.S. equity capital markets.
7. Empirical, arm's-length royalty rates for the license of trademarks of comparative retail operations.
8. Comparative arm's-length profit split license transactions.

Nice Name Department Stores, Inc., Nice Name Canada Limited Trademark and Trade Name, Nice Name Canada Limited Income Statements

| | For the year ended: | | | | | For the year ended: | | | | |
|---|---|---|---|---|---|---|---|---|---|---|
| | 1/31/98 Canadian $ | 1/31/97 Canadian $ | 1/31/96 Canadian $ | 1/31/95 Canadian $ | 1/31/94 Canadian $ | 1/31/98 % | 1/31/97 % | 1/31/96 % | 1/31/95 % | 1/31/94 % |
| Sales | 1,249,818,420 | 1,224,833,495 | 1,231,199,620 | 1,217,363,137 | 1,282,614,345 | 99.0 | 99.2 | 98.9 | 99.1 | 98.8 |
| Other revenue | 11,350,328 | 9,739,213 | 9,758,991 | 10,043,397 | 10,463,201 | 0.9 | 0.8 | 0.8 | 0.8 | 0.8 |
| Gain on disposal of property | 1,221,260 | 184,917 | 863,693 | 104,730 | 4,483,636 | 0.1 | 0.0 | 0.1 | 0.0 | 0.3 |
| Interest income | 161,473 | 314,874 | 2,531,810 | 632,452 | 971,223 | 0.0 | 0.0 | 0.2 | 0.1 | 0.1 |
| Total revenues | 1,262,551,481 | 1,235,072,499 | 1,244,354,114 | 1,228,143,716 | 1,298,532,405 | 100.0 | 100.0 | 100.0 | 100.0 | 100.0 |
| Cost of goods sold and operating expense | 1,202,340,482 | 1,157,785,550 | 1,167,622,885 | 1,174,778,992 | 1,223,158,164 | 95.2 | 93.7 | 93.8 | 95.7 | 94.2 |
| Depreciation and amortization expense | 25,560,022 | 23,291,948 | 22,729,659 | 20,829,091 | 20,789,213 | 2.0 | 1.9 | 1.8 | 1.7 | 1.6 |
| Interest expense | 18,601,594 | 17,429,627 | 18,942,809 | 20,344,604 | 22,037,284 | 1.5 | 1.4 | 1.5 | 1.7 | 1.7 |
| Total expenses | 1,246,502,098 | 1,198,507,125 | 1,209,295,353 | 1,215,952,687 | 1,265,984,661 | 98.7 | 97.0 | 97.2 | 99.0 | 97.5 |
| Income before nonrecurring items and taxes | 16,049,383 | 36,565,374 | 35,058,761 | 12,191,029 | 32,547,744 | 1.3 | 3.0 | 2.8 | 1.0 | 2.5 |
| Nonrecurring items | | | | | | | | | | |
| Loss on settlement of lease obligations | — | — | 22,750,104 | — | — | — | — | 1.8 | — | — |
| Provision for loss on note receivable | — | — | — | 7,450,000 | — | — | — | — | 0.6 | — |
| Loss on sale of investment | — | — | — | — | 37,539,000 | — | — | — | — | 2.9 |
| Restructuring charge | — | 50,294,000 | — | 5,000,000 | — | | | | | |
| Total nonrecurring items | — | 50,294,000 | 22,750,104 | 12,450,000 | 37,539,000 | — | 4.1 | 1.8 | 1.0 | 2.9 |
| Income (loss) before income taxes | 16,049,383 | (13,728,626) | 12,308,657 | (258,971) | (4,991,256) | 1.3 | (1.1) | 1.0 | (0.0) | (0.4) |
| Provision for income taxes | 7,285,000 | (4,898,000) | 5,832,000 | 3,845,000 | 1,683,952 | 0.6 | (0.4) | 0.5 | 0.3 | 0.1 |
| Net income (loss) for the fiscal year | 8,764,383 | (8,830,626) | 6,476,657 | (4,103,971) | (6,675,208) | 0.7 | (0.7) | 0.5 | (0.3) | (0.5) |

Note: Numbers may not total due to rounding.

EXHIBIT 26-7

Nice Name Department Stores, Inc., Nice Name Canada Limited Trademark and Trade Name, Nice Name Canada Limited Balance Sheets

| | 1/31/95 Canadian $ | 1/31/94 Canadian $ | 1/31/93 Canadian $ | 1/31/92 Canadian $ | 1/31/91 Canadian $ | As of: 1/31/95 % | 1/31/94 % | 1/31/93 % | 1/31/92 % | 1/31/91 % |
|---|---|---|---|---|---|---|---|---|---|---|
| ASSETS | | | | | | | | | | |
| Current assets | | | | | | | | | | |
| Cash | 3,786,799 | 3,943,032 | 4,159,173 | 4,739,543 | 4,078,683 | 0.6 | 0.7 | 0.7 | 0.9 | 0.8 |
| Short-term investment | — | 9,958,400 | 29,904,950 | — | — | — | 1.7 | 5.3 | — | — |
| Accounts receivable | 14,508,296 | 11,801,487 | 12,308,171 | 10,164,889 | 26,255,918 | 2.3 | 2.1 | 2.2 | 1.9 | 4.9 |
| Due from subsidiary companies | 7,271 | 7,271 | 7,271 | 7,271 | 7,271 | 0.0 | 0.0 | 0.0 | 0.0 | 0.0 |
| Due from parent and affiliated companies | — | — | — | 1,363,892 | 366,513 | — | — | — | 0.3 | 0.1 |
| Merchandise inventories | 324,722,125 | 303,660,760 | 309,935,274 | 306,039,657 | 291,451,381 | 50.6 | 52.8 | 55.3 | 57.3 | 54.5 |
| Operating supplies and prepaid expenses | 1,213,244 | 2,203,680 | 3,197,421 | 3,327,060 | 4,644,483 | 0.2 | 0.4 | 0.6 | 0.6 | 0.9 |
| Income taxes recoverable | 5,801,765 | — | — | 6,982,228 | 5,962,911 | 0.9 | — | — | 1.3 | 1.1 |
| Deferred income taxes | 5,000,000 | 8,200,000 | — | — | — | 0.8 | 1.4 | — | — | — |
| Property held for resale | 7,637,967 | — | — | — | — | 1.2 | — | — | — | — |
| Total current assets | 362,677,467 | 339,774,630 | 359,512,260 | 332,624,540 | 332,767,160 | 56.5 | 59.0 | 61.1 | 62.3 | 62.3 |
| Investment in shares of subsidiary | 10,001 | 10,001 | 10,001 | 10,001 | 10,001 | 0.0 | 0.0 | 0.0 | 0.0 | 0.0 |
| Property | | | | | | | | | | |
| Property owned | 205,258,427 | 148,496,166 | 113,910,166 | 101,627,662 | 93,663,675 | 32.0 | 25.8 | 20.3 | 19.0 | 17.5 |
| Capital leases | 58,888,453 | 67,237,636 | 75,903,100 | 85,153,282 | 85,355,682 | 9.2 | 11.7 | 13.5 | 15.9 | 16.0 |
| Total property | 264,146,880 | 215,733,801 | 189,813,266 | 186,780,944 | 179,019,357 | 41.1 | 37.5 | 33.8 | 35.0 | 33.5 |
| Note receivable | — | — | — | — | 7,450,000 | — | — | — | — | 1.4 |
| Deferred income taxes | 11,519,377 | 18,179,377 | 8,791,377 | 8,688,377 | 8,978,377 | 1.8 | 3.2 | 1.6 | 1.6 | 1.7 |
| Other assets a goodwill | 3,783,266 | 1,812,461 | 2,833,312 | 5,882,035 | 6,213,536 | 0.6 | 0.3 | 0.5 | 1.1 | 1.2 |
| TOTAL ASSETS | 642,136,991 | 575,510,271 | 560,960,216 | 533,985,897 | 534,438,431 | 100.0 | 100.0 | 100.0 | 100.0 | 100.0 |

Note: Numbers may not total due to rounding.

EXHIBIT 26-7 (continued)

|  | 1/31/95 Canadian $ | 1/31/94 Canadian $ | 1/31/93 Canadian $ | 1/31/92 Canadian $ | 1/31/91 Canadian $ | 1/31/95 % | 1/31/94 % | 1/31/93 % | 1/31/92 % | 1/31/91 % |
|---|---|---|---|---|---|---|---|---|---|---|
| **As of:** | | | | | | | | **As of:** | | |
| **LIABILITIES AND SHAREHOLDERS' EQUITY** | | | | | | | | | | |
| **Current liabilities** | | | | | | | | | | |
| Bank indebtedness | 25,903,584 | 13,725,457 | 7,877,869 | 5,301,691 | 6,614,378 | 4.0 | 2.4 | 1.4 | 1.0 | 1.2 |
| Promissory notes payable | 55,282,440 | — | — | 9,199,339 | 14,837,100 | 8.6 | — | — | 1.7 | 2.8 |
| Accounts payable—trade | 135,114,810 | 102,760,977 | 110,838,173 | 105,076,345 | 101,324,280 | 21.0 | 17.9 | 19.8 | 19.7 | 19.0 |
| Accrued payrolls and other | 51,248,750 | 55,334,435 | 47,901,584 | 38,287,061 | 30,621,656 | 8.0 | 9.6 | 8.5 | 7.2 | 5.7 |
| Income taxes payable | — | 7,575,501 | 6,101,432 | — | — | — | 1.3 | 1.1 | — | — |
| Advance from parent company | 18,415,871 | 15,385,857 | 13,954,366 | — | — | 2.9 | 2.7 | 2.5 | — | — |
| Obligations under capital leases | 8,559,326 | 9,840,934 | 10,091,495 | 10,240,285 | 9,815,689 | 1.3 | 1.7 | 1.8 | 1.9 | 1.8 |
| Total current liabilities | 294,524,781 | 204,623,161 | 196,764,919 | 168,104,721 | 163,213,103 | 45.9 | 35.6 | 35.1 | 31.5 | 30.5 |
| **Long-term debt** | | | | | | | | | | |
| Obligations under capital leases | 68,253,713 | 76,813,039 | 86,282,784 | 95,913,958 | 96,952,778 | 10.6 | 13.3 | 15.4 | 18.0 | 18.1 |
| Debentures payable | 34,650,000 | 49,850,000 | 50,000,000 | 50,000,000 | 50,000,000 | 5.4 | 8.7 | 8.9 | 9.4 | 9.4 |
| Total long-term debt | 102,903,713 | 126,663,039 | 136,282,784 | 145,913,958 | 146,952,778 | 16.0 | 22.0 | 24.3 | 27.3 | 27.5 |
| Other liabilities and deferred income | 21,256,691 | 29,536,648 | 4,394,464 | 2,925,826 | 3,127,187 | 3.3 | 5.1 | 0.8 | 0.5 | 0.6 |
| Total liabilities | 124,160,404 | 156,199,687 | 140,677,248 | 148,839,784 | 150,079,965 | 19.3 | 27.1 | 25.1 | 27.9 | 28.1 |
| **Shareholders' equity** | | | | | | | | | | |
| Capital stock | 250,000 | 250,000 | 250,000 | 250,000 | 250,000 | 0.0 | 0.0 | 0.0 | 0.0 | 0.0 |
| Contributed surplus | 8,590,873 | 8,590,873 | 8,590,873 | 8,590,873 | 8,590,873 | 1.3 | 1.5 | 1.5 | 1.6 | 1.6 |
| Retained earnings | 214,610,933 | 205,846,550 | 214,677,176 | 208,200,519 | 212,304,490 | 33.4 | 35.8 | 38.3 | 39.0 | 39.7 |
| Total shareholders' equity | 223,451,806 | 214,687,423 | 223,518,049 | 217,041,392 | 221,145,363 | 34.8 | 37.3 | 39.8 | 40.6 | 41.4 |
| **TOTAL LIABILITIES & SHAREHOLDERS' EQUITY** | 642,136,991 | 575,510,271 | 560,960,216 | 533,985,897 | 534,438,431 | 100.0 | 100.0 | 100.0 | 100.0 | 100.0 |

Note: Numbers may not total due to rounding.

During the course of our analysis, we conducted interviews with Mr. Hy Value, Divisional Vice President for Nice Name Department Stores, Inc., and Mr. Lou Price, Assistant Director of Taxes for Nice Name Department Stores, Inc.

We researched and analyzed relevant Canadian and U.S. general economic and retailing industry data.

## Valuation Synthesis and Conclusion

Based on our valuation analysis as described above, and in our opinion, the market value (i.e., fair arm's-length transfer price) of the Nice Name trademark and trade name currently controlled by Nice Name Canada Limited (an affiliate of Nice Name Department Stores, Inc.), as of August 23, 1998, is (rounded) Canadian $3,000,000.

### CASE 2: CHARITABLE CONTRIBUTION—BENEVOLENT SOFTWARE CORPORATION

## Case Description

The objective of the appraisal is to estimate the market value of the "Manage Everything for Doctors" software (hereinafter the "subject software" or "MED software"), developed by Benevolent Software Corporation (BSC). The valuation date is December 29, 1996, the date of the Gift Assignment Agreement (hereinafter the "Agreement"). According to the Agreement, BSC contributed all of its rights, title, and interest in the subject software to the College of Medicine, Excellent University, as a charitable gift. The gift includes all source and object code and manuals, diskettes, and all other related documentation and materials (including existing and future enhancements) necessary for the College to fully understand, implement, and utilize the software.

The purpose of the appraisal is to provide an independent valuation opinion regarding the subject software to assist BSC in recording its charitable contribution for federal income tax purposes.

## Description of the Computer Software Subject to Analysis

The MED software is a client-server system capable of managing the administrative and clinical aspects of medical practices. It can support practices ranging from a single doctor to large multiclinic practices with many doctors and very large patient databases.

The subject software is written using the C++ programming language and Microsoft Access®, a relational database management system. It runs under Windows 3.x, Windows NT, and Windows 95. It uses standard Windows user interfaces and includes on-line user manuals and context-sensitive help.

The development of the MED software began in late 1992 and continued through 1996.

## Computer Software Valuation Methods

Because of the unique features of the MED software and the lack of information regarding the sale of similar applications software, we did not use the market approach in the valuation of the subject software.

The MED software was donated prior to its release for license to customers. Beta tests were being performed at several installations, but no revenue had been realized. Any analysis based on projected income for the MED software would be highly speculative. Therefore, we did not use the income approach in the valuation of the subject software.

We performed two cost approach methods. The first cost approach method is the *constructive cost model* (COCOMO). The second cost approach method is the *software lifecycle management model* (SLIM).

We reached an overall valuation conclusion regarding the subject software based upon a synthesis of the results of the two cost approach methods.

## The Constructive Cost Model (COCOMO)

This software cost estimation method estimates the amount of effort required to recreate the software, taking into consideration the size of the programs, the characteristics of the programs, and the environment in which they are developed. The COCOMO model defines an effort equation that estimates the number of person-months necessary to develop a software product as a function of the number of delivered source instructions, or executable lines of code, in the system. Once the number of person-months of development effort is estimated, then the cost to develop the software can be estimated.

## The Software Lifecycle Management Model (SLIM)

This software cost estimation method uses a computerized model developed by Quantitative Software Management (QSM) from a database of over 3,000 actual software projects. The SLIM model allows the user to estimate the development costs associated with a particular software project based upon various parameters including: time, effort, cost limits, staffing, and reliability limits. The system development costs are calculated based upon the estimation of the number of person-months necessary to complete the software product.

## Lines of Code

BSC management provided us with the number of executable lines of code for each of the MED software subsystems. Comment lines were excluded and shared code was counted only once. The subject software contained approximately 498,000 lines of executable code.

## Cost per Person–Time

The cost per person–time (where time is measured in hours, months, or years) is a fully loaded cost which includes the average base salary of the software development team and other factors. The other factors include, but are not limited to, perquisites, payroll taxes (e.g., FUTA, SUTA, FICA, and workers' compensation), fringe benefits (e.g., life, health, disability, and dental insurance; pension plans; and continuing education), an allocation of overhead (including secretarial support, office space, computer use, supplies, marketing, management and supervisory time), and so forth.

We conducted interviews with BSC management and gathered information regarding the number of employees on the applications development staff, their job titles, and the average salary by job title. We also collected data regarding the factors for overhead and fringe benefits, including payroll taxes.

The development staff members are very experienced in both the applications (medical and insurance) and the technical (hardware, operating system, and programming language) areas, and are judged by BSC management to be highly capable. Most of the BSC staff members have bachelor's degree, and many staff members have earned advanced degrees.

Based on our analysis of the average salary structure for the applications development staff at BSC, and other personnel-related expenses incurred by BSC, we estimated a fully loaded cost per month of $10,500 to be appropriate in this case.

## COCOMO Valuation Variables

We used the Intermediate COCOMO model, as described in the authoritative textbook, entitled *Software Engineering Economics*, by Barry W. Boehm.[1]

Dr. Boehm describes three development modes in his model: organic, semidetached, and embedded. The software development effort equations in the intermediate COCOMO model are:

| | |
|---|---|
| Organic | $PM = 3.2 (KDSI)^{1.05} \times EAF$ |
| Semidetached | $PM = 3.0 (KDSI)^{1.12} \times EAF$ |
| Embedded | $PM = 2.8 (KDSI)^{1.20} \times EAF$ |

where:

| | | |
|---|---|---|
| PM | = | Person-months |
| KDSI | = | Thousands of delivered source instructions |
| EAF | = | Effort adjustment factor |

Based upon our research and analysis, we concluded that the development mode for all the software systems, including the subject software, was semidetached.

For our analysis, we used the number of actual executable lines of code (or delivered source instructions) per each subject subsystem as provided by BSC. We used a fully burdened cost of development time of $10,500 per month.

Also, based on our discussions with BSC management, we estimated the effort adjustment factor (EAF) for the subject software. The EAF is the product of the effort multipliers associated with 15 cost drivers defined in the model. Exhibit 26-8 presents our analysis and estimation of the EAF for the MED software.

The subject software was fully functional and ready to be released as of December 29, 1996. It was a recently developed, state-of-the-art system. We concluded that there is no material amount of functional, technical, or economic obsolescence associated with this software. Accordingly, we did not apply any separate obsolescence allowance to the software development cost estimate concluded by the COCOMO model.

## COCOMO Analysis and Conclusion

A summary of the COCOMO analysis is presented in Exhibit 26-9. Using this software development cost estimation method, the cost to develop the MED software, as of December 29, 1996, is $6,700,000.

---

1. Barry W. Boehm, *Software Engineering Economics* (Englewood Cliffs, NJ: Prentice Hall, Inc., 1981).

**EXHIBIT 26-8**

Benevolent Software Corporation, MED Software, COCOMO—Effort Adjustment Factor Estimation, as of December 29, 1996

|  |  | Range | Rating | Value |
|---|---|---|---|---|
| **Project Attributes** | | | | |
| RELY | Required software reliability | 0.75-1.40 | Nominal | 1.00 |
| DATA | Database size | 0.94-1.16 | Very High | 1.16 |
| CPLX | Product complexity | 0.70-1.65 | Varied | 1.13 |
| **Computer Attributes** | | | | |
| TIME | Execution time constraint | 1.00-1.66 | Nominal | 1.00 |
| STOR | Main storage constraint | 1.00-1.56 | High | 1.06 |
| VIRT | Virtual machine volatility | 0.87-1.30 | Low | 0.87 |
| TURN | Computer turnaround time | 0.87-1.15 | Low | 0.87 |
| **Personnel Attributes** | | | | |
| ACAP | Analyst capability | 0.71-1.46 | Very High | 0.71 |
| AEXP | Applications experience | 0.82-1.29 | Very High | 0.82 |
| PCAP | Programmer capability | 0.70-1.42 | Very High | 0.70 |
| VEXP | Virtual machine experience | 0.90-1.21 | High | 0.90 |
| LEXP | Programming language experience | 0.95-1.14 | High | 0.95 |
| **Project Attributes** | | | | |
| MODP | Use of modern programming practices | 0.82-1.24 | Very High | 0.82 |
| TOOL | Use of software tools | 0.83-1.24 | Very High | 0.83 |
| SCED | Required development schedule | 1.00-1.23 | Nominal | 1.00 |
|  | Resultant effort adjustment factor | | | <u>0.25</u> |

**EXHIBIT 26-9**

Benevolent Software Corporation, MED Software, COCOMO Cost Estimation Method Market Value Indication, as of December 29, 1996

| Subject System [1] | Delivered Source Instructions (DSI) [1] | Effort Adjustment Factor (EAF) [2] | a | b | Person-Months (PM) [3] | Market Value Estimate [4] |
|---|---|---|---|---|---|---|
| Carrier Database Manager | 7,500 | 0.25 | 3.00 | 1.12 | 7.2 | 75,218 |
| Clinical Transactions Manager | 35,000 | 0.25 | 3.00 | 1.12 | 40.2 | 422,286 |
| Employer Database Manager | 7,500 | 0.25 | 3.00 | 1.12 | 7.2 | 75,218 |
| Fee Schedule Manager | 35,000 | 0.25 | 3.00 | 1.12 | 40.2 | 422,286 |
| Financial Transactions Manager | 37,000 | 0.25 | 3.00 | 1.12 | 42.8 | 449,404 |
| Help Subsystem | 15,000 | 0.25 | 3.00 | 1.12 | 15.6 | 163,483 |
| Insurance Claims Manager | 15,000 | 0.25 | 3.00 | 1.12 | 15.6 | 163,483 |
| Kernel | 253,900 | 0.25 | 3.00 | 1.12 | 370.1 | 3,885,731 |
| Patient Manager | 41,000 | 0.25 | 3.00 | 1.12 | 48.0 | 504,160 |
| Practice Configuration | 11,000 | 0.25 | 3.00 | 1.12 | 11.0 | 115,508 |
| Records Manager | 15,000 | 0.25 | 3.00 | 1.12 | 15.6 | 163,483 |
| Referrals Manager | 5,000 | 0.25 | 3.00 | 1.12 | 4.5 | 47,764 |
| Reports Manager | 10,000 | 0.25 | 3.00 | 1.12 | 9.9 | 103,813 |
| Staff/Provider Manager | <u>10,000</u> | 0.25 | 3.00 | 1.12 | 9.9 | <u>103,813</u> |
|  | 497,900 | | | | | $6,695,648 |
| Market value indication (rounded) | | | | | | <u>$6,700,000</u> |

1. Company-provided data.
2. Exhibit 26-8.
3. Intermediate COCOMO effort equation: $PM = a(DSI)^b \times EAF$
4. Based on $10,500 per person-month.

## SLIM Model Valuation Variables

For our analysis, we used the same number of actual executable lines of code per each subject subsystem as we used for the COCOMO model. We again used a fully-burdened cost of development time of $10,500 per month.

For our analysis as of December 29, 1996, we used SLIM version 3.2. This version of the SLIM model uses the current QSM database as of that date. The Productivity Index defaults assigned by SLIM take current historical information into consideration. We used the QSM defaults for the phase parameters, and no constraints were imposed.

SLIM bases the phase parameters on recent history, and we would expect staff scheduling to become more efficient, if anything, over time. In actual project development, it is rare for there to be no staffing or time constraints, and the imposition of such typical constraints could significantly increase the effort and the cost.

As discussed previously, in our opinion, the subject software was fully functional and ready to be released as of December 29, 1996. It was a recently developed, state-of-the-art system. We concluded that there is no material functional, technological, or economic obsolescence associated with the subject software. Accordingly, we did not apply any separate obsolescence allowance to the software development cost estimate concluded by the SLIM model.

## SLIM Model Analysis and Conclusion

A summary of the SLIM analysis is presented in Exhibit 26-10, and sample outputs from the SLIM model are presented in Exhibit 26-11. Using this software development cost estimation method, the cost to develop the MED software, as of December 29, 1996, is $5,500,000.

**EXHIBIT 26-10**

Benevolent Software Corporation, MED Software, SLIM Cost Estimation Method Market—Value Indication, as of December 29, 1996

| Subject System [1] | Delivered Source Instructions (DSI) [1] | Market Value Estimate [2] |
|---|---|---|
| Carrier Database Manager | 7,500 | 105,000 |
| Clinical Transactions Manager | 35,000 | 526,000 |
| Employer Database Manager | 7,500 | 105,000 |
| Fee Schedule Manager | 35,000 | 526,000 |
| Financial Transactions Manager | 37,000 | 560,000 |
| Help Subsystem | 15,000 | 153,000 |
| Insurance Claims Manager | 15,000 | 153,000 |
| Kernel | 253,900 | 2,158,000 |
| Patient Manager | 41,000 | 636,000 |
| Practice Configuration | 11,000 | 129,000 |
| Records Manager | 15,000 | 153,000 |
| Referrals Manager | 5,000 | 83,000 |
| Reports Manager | 10,000 | 122,000 |
| Staff/Provider Manager | 10,000 | 122,000 |
| | 497,900 | $5,531,000 |
| Market value indication (rounded) | | $5,500,000 |

1. Company-provided data.
2. Based on system development cost of $10,500 per person-month.

EXHIBIT 26-11

Sample Outputs from SLIM Model

## Current Solution Summary

**Assumptions**
PI (User specified) 18.4
Size (ESLOC) 35000

MBI 4.1

**Tuning Factors**
Feas Time 46 % of MB
FD Time 71 % of MB
Feas/FD Overlap 33 % of Feas
MB/Maint Gap 0 % of MB

Feas Effort 14 % of MB
FD Effort 32 % of MB
FD/MB Overlap 40 % of FD
Total Defects 100 %

### Current Solution and Probability

| | Solution | | Constraints | | |
| Parameters | Expected 50% Value | Actual Probability | Desired Value | Desired Probability | Weight |
|---|---|---|---|---|---|
| Time (Months) | 12.65 | 100 % | 20.00 | 90 % | 16 |
| Effort (PM) | 50.12 | 100 % | 100.00 | 90 % | 16 |
| Uninf Cost ($ 1000) | 526 | 90 % | 750 | 90 % | 16 |
| Min Peak Staff (People) | 6.48 | 95 % | 3.00 | 90 % | 16 |
| Max Peak Staff (People) | 6.48 | 100 % | 20.00 | 90 % | 16 |
| FOC MTTD (Days) | 2.78 | 81 % | 2.00 | 90 % | 16 |
| End Date | 1/17/97 | 100 % | 8/28/97 | 90 % | 16 |

### Current Solution Uncertainty

| | | +- 1 Standard Deviation | |
| Parameters | Expected 50% Value | Value | % of Mean |
|---|---|---|---|
| Time (Months) | 12.65 | 1.23 | 9.76 |
| Effort (PM) | 50.12 | 16.01 | 31.95 |
| Uninf Cost ($ 1000) | 526 | 175 | 33.24 |
| Peak Staff (People) | 6.48 | 2.07 | 31.95 |
| FOC MTTD (Days) | 2.78 | 0.89 | 31.95 |
| Total Defects | 146 | 47 | 31.95 |

### Current Solution by Phase

| | Expected 50 % Value | | | |
| Parameters | Feas | FD | MB | Maint |
|---|---|---|---|---|
| Time (Months) | 2.58 | 3.99 | 5.60 | 2.91 |
| Effort (PM) | 3.64 | 8.50 | 26.77 | 11.22 |
| Uninf Cost ($ 1000) | 38 | 89 | 281 | 118 |
| Peak Staff (People) | 2.13 | 3.22 | 6.48 | 5.33 |
| MTTD (Days) | n/a | n/a | 2.78 | 93.13 |
| Start Date | 12/29/95 | 2/21/96 | 5/3/96 | 10/21/96 |

Fee Scheduled Manager
$ 10500 / PM burdened labor rate
0 % of Main Build time coding offset

EXHIBIT 26-11 (continued)

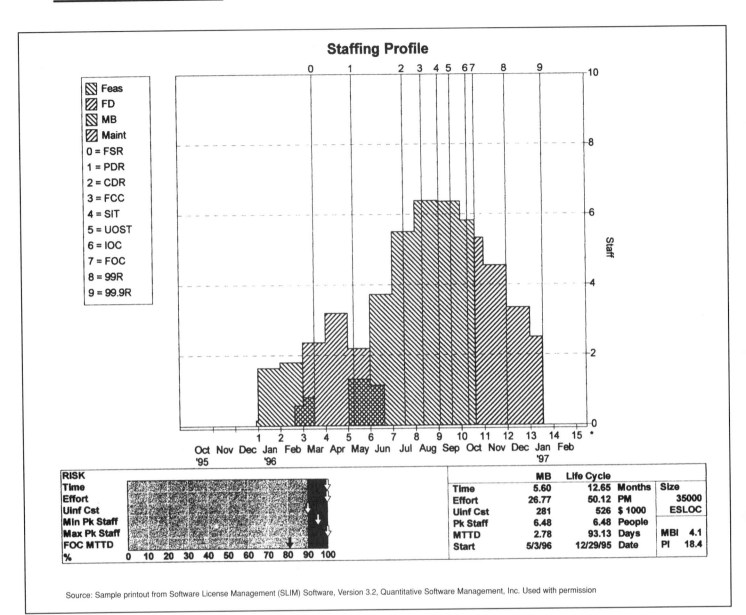

Source: Sample printout from Software License Management (SLIM) Software, Version 3.2, Quantitative Software Management, Inc. Used with permission

## Valuation Synthesis and Conclusion

We relied upon the two software cost estimation methods summarized above to obtain indications of the market value of the subject software. The market value indications of the two cost estimation valuation methods, as of December 29, 1996, are as follows:

| Cost Estimation Method | Value Indication |
|---|---|
| Constructive cost model (COCOMO) | $6,700,000 |
| Software lifecycle management model (SLIM) | $5,500,000 |

Based upon the appraisal procedures described above, and in our opinion, the market value of the subject MED software, as of December 29, 1996, is (rounded) $6,000,000.

## CASE 3: LICENSE TO USE PATENTED AND PROPRIETARY TECHNOLOGY—WAY COOL REFRIGERATION, INC.

## Case Description

We performed an appraisal of the Option and Technical Assistance Agreement (hereinafter the "Agreement") between Clever Research ("Clever") and Way Cool Refrigeration, Inc. ("Way Cool"). The Agreement provides Way Cool with the license to use certain patented and proprietary refrigeration technology developed by Clever (1) with regard to certain products, (2) within limited geographic areas, and (3) for a stated contractual period of time. The Agreement was executed by Clever and Way Cool on December 9, 1991, and December 27, 1991, respectively.

The analysis will assist Parent Company ("Parent") in its estimation of the fair market value of the Agreement and in its estimation of an appropriate fair market value royalty rate applicable to the Agreement, as of December 31, 1997.

As of December 31, 1997, the Agreement has a 12-year remaining useful life contractual term. Accordingly, the 12-year contractual period is the appropriate remaining useful life over which to estimate the value of the license to use the subject patented and proprietary technology.

Based upon our highest and best use analysis with regard to the Agreement, the subject intangible asset was appraised under the premise of value in continued use, as part of a going-concern business enterprise.

## Valuation and Royalty Rate Analysis Methodology

Based upon our consideration of the relevant facts and circumstances, we have concluded that an appropriate methodology for the valuation of the subject Agreement technology license intangible is to value the underlying patented and proprietary technology to Way Cool over the life of the Agreement.

### Fair Market Value of the Agreement

There are numerous methods available for estimating the fair market value of license agreements related to patented and proprietary technologies. Our analysis was conducted using the following valuation approaches and methods: (1) the income approach and yield capitalization method (and specifically discounted cash flow analysis), and (2) the market approach and relief from royalty method. These valuation analyses are presented in Exhibits 26-12 and 26-15.

In both valuation analyses, sales projections were provided by the owner of the subject intangible; the effective income tax rate was estimated to be 39 percent; and the appropriate present value discount rate was estimated to be 24 percent.

In the discounted cash flow analysis, the projected operating costs were estimated as a percentage of sales; this is true for all operating costs except freight expense, which was estimated on a cost per unit basis (adjusted for inflation).

Based upon the income approach and the discounted cash flow analysis presented in Exhibit 26-12, the indicated value of the subject patented and proprietary technology, as of December 31, 1997, is

**E X H I B I T  26-12**

Way Cool Refrigeration, Inc., Clever Research, Patented and Proprietary Technology Valuation, Discounted Cash Flow Analysis, as of December 31, 1997 ($ in 000s)

| Valuation Variables | 1998 | 1999 | 2000 | 2001 | 2002 | 2003 | 2004 | 2005 | 2006 | 2007 | 2008 | 2009 |
|---|---|---|---|---|---|---|---|---|---|---|---|---|
| *Projected Sale Units* | | | | | | | | | | | | |
| All Electric Freezer / Fan 2Cft | 1,000 | 20,000 | 30,000 | 35,000 | 35,000 | 35,000 | 33,000 | 31,000 | 29,000 | 27,000 | 25,000 | 23,000 |
| Tri-Fuel Refrigerator / Natural 2Cft | — | 2,000 | 20,000 | 30,000 | 40,000 | 40,000 | 38,000 | 36,000 | 34,000 | 32,000 | 30,000 | 28,000 |
| Tri-Fuel Freezer / Natural 2Cft | — | — | 5,000 | 10,000 | 15,000 | 15,000 | 13,000 | 11,000 | 9,000 | 7,000 | 5,000 | 3,000 |
| Tri-Fuel Refrigerator-Freezer / Natural 4Cft | — | — | 5,000 | 15,000 | 20,000 | 20,000 | 18,000 | 16,000 | 14,000 | 12,000 | 10,000 | 8,000 |
| All Electric Refrigerator-Freezer / Natural 4Cft | — | — | 20,000 | 30,000 | 40,000 | 40,000 | 38,000 | 36,000 | 34,000 | 32,000 | 30,000 | 28,000 |
| Projected Total Units Sold | 1,000 | 22,000 | 80,000 | 120,000 | 150,000 | 150,000 | 140,000 | 130,000 | 120,000 | 110,000 | 100,000 | 90,000 |
| *Projected Net Unit Price ($)* | | | | | | | | | | | | |
| All Electric Freezer / Fan 2Cft | 142.83 | 147.11 | 151.53 | 156.07 | 160.76 | 165.58 | 170.55 | 175.66 | 180.93 | 186.36 | 191.95 | 197.71 |
| Tri-Fuel Refrigerator / Natural 2Cft | 147.75 | 152.18 | 156.75 | 161.45 | 166.29 | 171.28 | 176.42 | 181.71 | 187.17 | 192.78 | 198.56 | 204.52 |
| Tri-Fuel Freezer / Natural 2Cft | 152.68 | 157.26 | 161.98 | 166.84 | 171.84 | 177.00 | 182.31 | 187.78 | 193.41 | 199.21 | 205.19 | 211.34 |
| Tri-Fuel Refrigerator-Freezer / Natural 4Cft | 300.43 | 309.44 | 318.73 | 328.29 | 338.14 | 348.28 | 358.73 | 369.49 | 380.58 | 391.99 | 403.75 | 415.87 |
| All Electric Refrigerator-Freezer / Natural 4Cft | 147.75 | 152.18 | 156.75 | 161.45 | 166.29 | 171.28 | 176.42 | 181.71 | 187.17 | 192.78 | 198.56 | 204.52 |
| *Income Statement Analysis ($000s)* | | | | | | | | | | | | |
| Total projected net sales | 143 | 3,247 | 13,219 | 21,742 | 28,270 | 29,118 | 27,863 | 26,506 | 25,043 | 23,468 | 21,776 | 19,961 |
| Standard costs | 76 | 1,721 | 7,006 | 11,523 | 14,983 | 15,433 | 14,767 | 14,048 | 13,273 | 12,438 | 11,541 | 10,580 |
| Freight | 3 | 68 | 255 | 393 | 506 | 522 | 502 | 480 | 456 | 431 | 403 | 374 |
| Other variable costs | 16 | 357 | 1,454 | 2,392 | 3,110 | 3,203 | 3,065 | 2,916 | 2,755 | 2,581 | 2,395 | 2,196 |
| Total operating costs | 95 | 2,146 | 8,715 | 14,308 | 18,599 | 19,158 | 18,333 | 17,444 | 16,484 | 15,450 | 14,339 | 13,150 |
| Operating income | 48 | 1,101 | 4,504 | 7,434 | 9,671 | 9,960 | 9,529 | 9,063 | 8,559 | 8,018 | 7,437 | 6,811 |
| Income tax expense (@39%) | 18 | 429 | 1,757 | 2,899 | 3,772 | 3,885 | 3,716 | 3,535 | 3,338 | 3,127 | 2,900 | 2,656 |
| After-tax income 30 | 672 | 2,747 | 4,535 | 5,899 | 6,075 | 5,813 | 5,529 | 5,221 | 4,891 | 4,537 | 4,154 | |
| Plus: depreciation expense | 4 | 97 | 397 | 652 | 848 | 874 | 836 | 795 | 751 | 704 | 653 | 599 |
| Less: capital charge on associated tangible and intangible assets | (27) | (617) | (2,512) | (4,131) | (4,241) | (4,368) | (4,179) | (3,976) | (3,756) | (3,520) | (3,266) | (2,994) |
| Less: capital expenditures | — | — | — | — | (1,000) | (874) | (836) | (795) | (1,500) | (704) | (653) | (599) |
| Equals: net cash flow | 7 | 152 | 633 | 1,056 | 1,507 | 1,707 | 1,633 | 1,553 | 716 | 1,371 | 1,271 | 1,160 |
| Discounting period—using midyear convention | 0.5 | 1.5 | 2.5 | 3.5 | 4.5 | 5.5 | 6.5 | 7.5 | 8.5 | 9.5 | 10.5 | 11.5 |
| Present value interest factor (@24%) | 0.8980 | 0.7242 | 0.5840 | 0.4710 | 0.3798 | 0.3063 | 0.2470 | 0.1992 | 0.1607 | 0.1296 | 0.1045 | 0.0843 |
| Discounted net cash flow | 6 | 110 | 370 | 497 | 572 | 523 | 403 | 309 | 115 | 178 | 133 | 98 |
| Sum of discounted net cash flow | 3,314 | | | | | | | | | | | |
| Patented and proprietary technology value (rounded) | $3,300 | | | | | | | | | | | |

Source: Income statement-related projections provided by the management of Way Cool Refrigeration, Inc.
Note: Numbers may not total due to rounding.

patented and proprietary technology, as of December 31, 1997, is $3,300,000.

In the royalty income stream analysis, royalty income was estimated using the royalty rate estimate derived from the return on investment analysis documented in Exhibits 26-13 and 26-14. The royalty rate derived from this return on investment analysis is 8.5 percent. The royalty rate estimation analysis is presented in Exhibit 26-15.

Based upon the royalty rate analysis summarized in Exhibits 26-13 and 26-14 and the market approach and relief from royalty method presented in Exhibit 26-15, the indicated value of the subject patented and proprietary technology, as of December 31, 1997, is $3,300,000.

## Valuation Synthesis and Conclusion

We concluded that, based upon the quantity and quality of available data, each valuation method provides a valid indication of value. Therefore, we have assigned equal weight to the indications of value provided by the two valuation methods.

Based upon these analyses, and in our opinion, the value of the license to use the Clever Research patented and proprietary technology to Way Cool Refrigeration, Inc., based upon the 12-year contractual term of the subject Agreement, is $3,300,000.

**EXHIBIT 26-13**

Way Cool Refrigeration, Inc., Clever Research, Patented and Proprietary Technology, Royalty Rate Analysis, Profit Split Analysis, as of December 31, 1997 ($ in 000s)

| Royalty Rate Analysis Variable | Total | Median |
|---|---|---|
| Projected total units sold | 1,213,000 | 115,000 |
| Total projected net sales | $240,358 | $ 22,622 |
| Standard costs | 127,390 | 11,990 |
| Freight expense | 4,392 | 417 |
| Other variable costs | 26,439 | 2,488 |
| Total operating costs | $158,221 | $ 14,895 |
| Operating income | $ 82,137 | $ 7,727 |
| Average level of profits available for profit split | | $ 7,727 |
| Market-derived profit split percentage [a] | | 25% |
| Amount of profit attributable to subject patented and proprietary technology | | $ 1,932 |
| Amount of profit attributable to subject patented and proprietary technology | | $ 1,932 |
| Projected net sales | | 22,622 |
| Indicated royalty/license rate for the subject patented and proprietary technology | | 8.5% |
| Indicated royalty/license rate (rounded) | | 8.5% |

Source: Exhibit 26-12.

a. Based upon our analysis of arm's-length technology license agreements, the typical profit split percentages average between 25% and 50%. We selected the appropriate profit split to be at the low end of the market derived range of empirical data due to 1) the speculative nature of the subject patented and proprietary technology and 2) the lack of subject-specific historical operating and financial history.

Note: Numbers may not total due to rounding.

**EXHIBIT 26-14**

Way Cool Refrigeration, Inc., Clever Research, Patented and Proprietary Technology, Royalty Rate Analysis, Return on Investment Analysis, as of December 31, 1997 ($ in 000s)

| Royalty Rate Analysis Variables Asset Category [c] | Indicated Fair Market Value [a] | Percent of Total Asset Value | Market-Derived Required Rate of Return [b] | Weighted Rate of Return | Required Amount of Return on Asset Investment | Percent of Total Return on Asset Investment | Asset Category Yield Allocation |
|---|---|---|---|---|---|---|---|
| Net working capital | 3,057 | 22.9% | 24.0% | 5.5% | 734 | 22.9% | 1,769 |
| Machinery & equipment | 3,000 | 22.5% | 24.0% | 5.4% | 720 | 22.5% | 1,736 |
| Jigs & fixtures | 2,000 | 15.0% | 24.0% | 3.6% | 480 | 15.0% | 1,157 |
| Other tangible & intangible assets | 2,000 | 15.0% | 24.0% | 3.6% | 480 | 15.0% | 1,157 |
| Patented and proprietary technology | 3,300 | 24.7% | 24.0% | 5.9% | 792 | 24.7% | 1,909 |
| Total | $13,357 | 100.0% | 24.0% | 24.0% | $3,206 | 100.0% | $ 7,727 |
| Total median level of operating income | | | | | | | 7,727 |
| Asset category yield related to patented and proprietary technology | | | | | | | $ 1,909 |
| Median level of total projected net sales | | | | | | | 22,622 |
| Patented and proprietary technology yield, calculated as a return on investment percentage | | | | | | | 8.4% |
| Indicated royalty rate for the patented and proprietary technology (rounded) | | | | | | | 8.5% |

Source: Exhibit 26-12.

a. Based on the industry average balance sheet information as contained in *RMA Annual Statement Studies, 1997* (Philadelphia: Robert Morris Associates, 1997).

b. The risk-adjusted cost of capital is based on information provided in Ibbotson Associates, *Stocks, Bonds, Bills & Inflation,* 1997 Yearbook (Chicago: Ibbotson Associates, 1998).

c. Allocation of the median level of Clever Research operating income as provided in Exhibit 26-13. The allocation of the median level of operating income is based on the pro rata share of the required amount of return on asset investment for each asset category.

Note: Numbers may not total due to rounding.

# EXHIBIT 26-15

Way Cool Refrigeration, Inc., Clever Research, Patented and Proprietary Technology Valuation, Royalty Income Stream Analysis, as of December 31, 1997 ($ in 000s)

| Valuation Variables | 1998 | 1999 | 2000 | 2001 | 2002 | 2003 | 2004 | 2005 | 2006 | 2007 | 2008 | 2009 |
|---|---|---|---|---|---|---|---|---|---|---|---|---|
| **Projected Sale Units** | | | | | | | | | | | | |
| All Electric Freezer / Fan 2Cft | 1,000 | 20,000 | 30,000 | 35,000 | 35,000 | 35,000 | 33,000 | 31,000 | 29,000 | 27,000 | 25,000 | 23,000 |
| Tri-Fuel Refrigerator / Natural 2Cft | — | 2,000 | 20,000 | 30,000 | 40,000 | 40,000 | 38,000 | 36,000 | 34,000 | 32,000 | 30,000 | 28,000 |
| Tri-Fuel Freezer / Natural 2Cft | — | — | 5,000 | 10,000 | 15,000 | 15,000 | 13,000 | 11,000 | 9,000 | 7,000 | 5,000 | 3,000 |
| Tri-Fuel Refrigerator-Freezer / Natural 4Cft | — | — | 5,000 | 15,000 | 20,000 | 20,000 | 18,000 | 16,000 | 14,000 | 12,000 | 10,000 | 8,000 |
| All Electric Refrigerator-Freezer / Natural 4Cft | — | — | 20,000 | 30,000 | 40,000 | 40,000 | 38,000 | 36,000 | 34,000 | 32,000 | 30,000 | 28,000 |
| Projected total units sold | 1,000 | 22,000 | 80,000 | 120,000 | 150,000 | 150,000 | 140,000 | 130,000 | 120,000 | 110,000 | 100,000 | 90,000 |
| **Projected Net Unit Price ($)** | | | | | | | | | | | | |
| All Electric Freezer / Fan 2Cft | 142.83 | 147.11 | 151.53 | 156.07 | 160.76 | 165.58 | 170.55 | 175.66 | 180.93 | 186.36 | 191.95 | 197.71 |
| Tri-Fuel Refrigerator / Natural 2Cft | 147.75 | 152.18 | 156.75 | 161.45 | 166.29 | 171.28 | 176.42 | 181.71 | 187.17 | 192.78 | 198.56 | 204.52 |
| Tri-Fuel Freezer / Natural 2Cft | 152.68 | 157.26 | 161.98 | 166.84 | 171.84 | 177.00 | 182.31 | 187.78 | 193.41 | 199.21 | 205.19 | 211.34 |
| Tri-Fuel Refrigerator-Freezer / Natural 4Cft | 300.43 | 309.44 | 318.73 | 328.29 | 338.14 | 348.28 | 358.73 | 369.49 | 380.58 | 391.99 | 403.75 | 415.87 |
| All Electric Refrigerator-Freezer / Natural 4Cft | 147.75 | 152.18 | 156.75 | 161.45 | 166.29 | 171.28 | 176.42 | 181.71 | 187.17 | 192.78 | 198.56 | 204.52 |
| **Income Statement Analysis ($000s)** | | | | | | | | | | | | |
| Total projected net sales | 143 | 3,247 | 13,219 | 21,742 | 28,270 | 29,118 | 27,863 | 26,506 | 25,043 | 23,468 | 21,776 | 19,961 |
| Royalty income (@8.5%) [a] | 12 | 276 | 1,124 | 1,848 | 2,403 | 2,475 | 2,368 | 2,253 | 2,129 | 1,995 | 1,851 | 1,697 |
| Effective income tax (@39%) | 5 | 108 | 438 | 721 | 937 | 965 | 923 | 879 | 830 | 778 | 722 | 662 |
| Net royalty income | 7 | 168 | 686 | 1,127 | 1,466 | 1,510 | 1,445 | 1,374 | 1,299 | 1,217 | 1,129 | 1,035 |
| Discounting period—using midyear convention | 0.5 | 1.5 | 2.5 | 3.5 | 4.5 | 5.5 | 6.5 | 7.5 | 8.5 | 9.5 | 10.5 | 11.5 |
| Present value interest factor (@24%) | 0.8980 | 0.7242 | 0.5840 | 0.4710 | 0.3798 | 0.3063 | 0.2470 | 0.1992 | 0.1607 | 0.1296 | 0.1045 | 0.0843 |
| Discounted net cash flow | 6 | 122 | 401 | 531 | 557 | 462 | 357 | 274 | 209 | 158 | 118 | 87 |
| Sum of discounted net cash flow | 3,282 | | | | | | | | | | | |
| Patented and proprietary technology value (rounded) | $3,300 | | | | | | | | | | | |

a. Based on rate derived from return on investment analysis.

Source: Exhibit 26-12.

Note: Numbers may not total due to rounding.

Based on our analysis, and in our opinion, the fair market value of the Option and Technical Assistance Agreement technology license intangible asset owned by Way Cool Refrigeration, Inc., as of December 30, 1997, is (rounded) $3,300,000.

## Fair Market Royalty Rate

We estimated the fair market value royalty rate using a profit split analysis and a return on investment analysis. These analyses are presented in Exhibits 26-13 and 26-14.

The profit split analysis uses median sales and operating cost figures from Exhibit 26-13 and a profit split percentage of 25 percent to calculate the profit attributable to the patent or technology. This profit amount divided by the median net sales amount yields the indicated royalty rate for the patent or technology.

The return on investment analysis estimates the fair market value of the asset categories based on industry percentages. Using a 24 percent required rate of return, the required return is calculated for each asset category. The median operating income from Exhibit 26-13 is then allocated to the asset categories based on the pro rata share of the required amount of return for each asset class. The average yield for the patent or technology class is divided by the median net sales amount to calculate the indicated royalty rate for the patent or technology.

Based on our analysis, and in our opinion, the fair market value royalty rate applicable to the Option and Technical Assistance Agreement owned by Way Cool Refrigeration, Inc., as of December 30, 1997, is (rounded) 8.5 percent.

## CASE 4: COPYRIGHT INFRINGEMENT LITIGATION— THICK METROPOLITAN DIRECTORY COMPANY, INC.
### Case Description

Thick Metropolitan Directory Company, Inc. (TMD) owns a copyright for its publication known as the *Greater Metropolis Industrial Buying Guide (GMI)*. The *GMI* copyright is registered with the U.S. Copyright Office.

There is ongoing litigation between Thick Directory Publishing Company ("Thick" or the "Company") and CopyCat Publishing Corporation (hereinafter "CopyCat"), alleging the infringement upon the copyrights held by TMD.

The objective of the economic analysis is to estimate a fair arm's-length royalty rate that would be appropriate for the license of the *GMI* copyright as of September 30, 1998.

The purpose of the economic analysis is to provide an independent opinion to assist legal counsel in its representation of Thick Directory Publishing Company with respect to its copyright infringement litigation with CopyCat.

## Description of the Intellectual Property Subject to Analysis

For over 35 years, Thick Directory Publishing Company has specialized in providing industrial and commercial buyers with up-to-date product and service information. Thick is an acknowledged leader in this field.

TMD is a wholly owned subsidiary of Thick Directory Publishing Co., Inc. TMD publishes the *Thick Metropolitan Industrial Buying Guides.* The guides are comprehensive metropolitan directories of industrial and commercial manufacturers and suppliers of products and services. TMD currently publishes 19 metropolitan guides.

Historically, the *Greater Metropolis Industrial Guide (GMI)* is the second oldest of the 19 guides published by TMD. The *GMI* is published annually covers Metropolis and the surrounding suburbs.

By virtue of the superior consumer reputation, name recognition, and product loyalty associated with it, the TMD copyrighted material known as *GMI* confers a competitive advantage to its owner. These intangible attributes indicate that the subject copyright has economic value would and command a significant royalty rate for its license or use.

## Financial Statement Analysis

Exhibits 26-16 through 26-19 present a summary of the financial statements for the TMD for fiscal years ended September 30, 1993 to 1998, and a summary of the profit and loss statements for *GMI* for fiscal years ended September 30, 1993 to 1998.

### TMD Balance Sheets

Exhibit 26-16 presents the comparative and common-size balance sheets for TMD for fiscal years ended in 1993 through 1998.

Assets have been steadily increasing from 1993 through 1997, with a small decline in 1998. Because of the nature of the business, the asset mix is more than 95 percent current assets—with fixed and other assets making up less than 5 percent. This has remained constant during the fiscal years 1993 through 1998.

TMD has no long-term debt, and the majority of its liabilities is current intercompany accounts payable.

Finally, TMD retained earnings has been an increasingly negative number for the last six fiscal years.

### TMD Income Statements

Exhibit 26-17 presents the comparative historical statements of the TMD results of operations for fiscal years ending September 30, 1993 through 1998. Exhibit 26-17 also presents the common-size statements of results of operations for the same time period.

Total revenue has increased to $27.9 million in fiscal 1998, an increase of 9 percent over fiscal 1997 results. The annual compound growth rate in net sales during the fiscal period 1993 through 1998 is approximately 11.8 percent.

Cost of sales has steadily increased from fiscal 1993, primarily because of the continuous launching of new regional industrial buying guides.

The launching of new buying guides has meant pretax losses for TMD for the fiscal period 1993 through 1998. The fiscal 1998 net loss is considerably smaller than the loss recorded in the previous two years. Fiscal 1998 net loss is ($1.1 million) versus ($1.9 million) in 1997.

Exhibit 26-18 presents the TMD ratio analysis for the period of September 30, 1993 through September 30, 1998.

**E X H I B I T  26-16**

Thick Metropolitan Directory Company, Inc., Historical and Common-Size Balance Sheets, as of September 30, 1998

| | As of September 30: | | | | | | As of September 30: | | | | | |
| --- | --- | --- | --- | --- | --- | --- | --- | --- | --- | --- | --- | --- |
| | 1998 $000 | 1997 $000 | 1996 $000 | 1995 $000 | 1994 $000 | 1993 $000 | 1998 % | 1997 % | 1996 % | 1995 % | 1994 % | 1993 % |
| **ASSETS** | | | | | | | | | | | | |
| Current assets: | | | | | | | | | | | | |
| Cash & cash equivalents | 733 | 603 | 94 | 517 | 172 | 689 | 4.3 | 3.4 | 0.6 | 3.7 | 1.5 | 6.6 |
| Accounts receivable | 10,145 | 10,422 | 9,865 | 9,432 | 7,502 | 6,181 | 59.4 | 59.6 | 60.7 | 66.8 | 63.2 | 59.4 |
| Inventories | 493 | 428 | 385 | — | — | — | 2.9 | 2.4 | 2.4 | — | — | — |
| Postage funds | 610 | 547 | 359 | 129 | 132 | 98 | 3.6 | 3.1 | 2.2 | 0.9 | 1.1 | 0.9 |
| Advances to salesmen | 4,804 | 5,006 | 4,951 | 3,736 | 3,828 | 3,201 | 28.1 | 28.6 | 30.5 | 26.4 | 32.3 | 30.8 |
| Advances to officers & employees | (0) | 24 | — | 8 | — | 2 | (0.0) | 0.1 | — | — | — | 0.0 |
| Prepaid taxes | — | — | — | — | 16 | — | — | — | — | — | 0.1 | — |
| Total current assets | 16,784 | 17,029 | 15,655 | 13,814 | 11,658 | 10,170 | 98.2 | 97.4 | 96.3 | 97.8 | 98.1 | 97.8 |
| Total fixed assets, net | 146 | 210 | 273 | 266 | 206 | 159 | 0.9 | 1.2 | 1.7 | 1.9 | 1.7 | 1.5 |
| Other assets: | | | | | | | | | | | | |
| Deposits | 77 | 110 | 9 | 1 | 1 | 6 | 0.4 | 0.6 | 0.1 | 0.0 | 0.0 | 0.1 |
| Deferred expenses | 72 | 135 | 321 | 43 | 4 | 59 | 0.4 | 0.8 | 2.0 | 0.3 | 0.0 | 0.6 |
| Notes receivable | 10 | — | — | — | — | 5 | 0.1 | — | — | — | — | 0.0 |
| Other noncurrent assets | — | — | — | — | — | — | — | — | — | — | — | — |
| Total other assets | 159 | 245 | 330 | 44 | 5 | 70 | 0.9 | 1.4 | 2.0 | 0.3 | 0.0 | 0.7 |
| **TOTAL ASSETS** | 17,089 | 17,484 | 16,258 | 14,124 | 11,869 | 10,399 | 100.0 | 100.0 | 100.0 | 100.0 | 99.9 | 100.0 |
| **LIABILITIES & STOCKHOLDERS' EQUITY** | | | | | | | | | | | | |
| Current liabilities: | | | | | | | | | | | | |
| Trade accounts payable | 1,386 | 1,651 | 1,154 | 832 | 707 | 686 | 8.1 | 9.4 | 7.1 | 5.9 | 6.0 | 6.6 |
| Income taxes payable | 8 | 4 | (2) | (5) | — | (4) | 0.0 | 0.0 | (0.0) | (0.0) | (0.0) | (0.0) |
| Bonuses payable | (11) | — | — | — | — | — | (0.1) | — | — | — | — | — |
| Intercompany accounts payable | 22,176 | 21,224 | 18,714 | 15,295 | 12,642 | 9,746 | 129.8 | 121.4 | 115.1 | 108.3 | 106.5 | 93.7 |
| Unearned income | 278 | 260 | 210 | 267 | 237 | 152 | 1.6 | 1.5 | 1.3 | 1.9 | 2.0 | 1.5 |
| Total current liabilities | 23,836 | 23,139 | 20,076 | 16,389 | 13,585 | 10,580 | 139.5 | 132.3 | 123.5 | 116.0 | 114.5 | 101.7 |
| Stockholders' equity: | | | | | | | | | | | | |
| Common stock | 1 | 1 | 1 | 1 | 1 | 1 | 0.0 | 0.0 | 0.0 | 0.0 | 0.0 | 0.0 |
| Paid-in capital | — | — | — | — | — | — | — | — | — | — | — | — |
| Retained earnings | (6,749) | (5,657) | (3,819) | (2,266) | (1,717) | (182) | (39.5) | (32.4) | (23.5) | (16.0) | (14.5) | (1.7) |
| Total stockholders' equity | (6,748) | (5,656) | (3,818) | (2,265) | (1,716) | (181) | (39.5) | (32.3) | (23.5) | (16.0) | (14.5) | (1.7) |
| **TOTAL LIABILITIES & STOCKHOLDERS' EQUITY** | 17,089 | 17,484 | 16,258 | 14,124 | 11,869 | 10,399 | 100.0 | 100.0 | 100.0 | 100.0 | 100.0 | 100.0 |

Source: Company internally prepared financial statements as presented.
Note: Numbers may not total due to rounding.

Thick Metropolitan Directory Company, Inc., Historical and Common-Size Income Statements, as of September 30, 1998

| | Fiscal Years Ending September 30: | | | | | | Fiscal Years Ending September 30: | | | | | |
| | 1998 $000 | 1997 $000 | 1996 $000 | 1995 $000 | 1994 $000 | 1993 $000 | 1998 % | 1997 % | 1996 % | 1995 % | 1994 % | 1993 % |
|---|---|---|---|---|---|---|---|---|---|---|---|---|
| Revenues: | | | | | | | | | | | | |
| Gross advertising revenue | 27,852 | 25,494 | 21,119 | 21,829 | 18,510 | 15,969 | 100.6 | 100.5 | 100.4 | 100.3 | 100.2 | 100.6 |
| Gross subscription revenue | 63 | 59 | 55 | 56 | 43 | 40 | 0.2 | 0.2 | 0.3 | 0.3 | 0.2 | 0.3 |
| Total revenues | 27,915 | 25,553 | 21,174 | 21,885 | 18,554 | 16,009 | 100.8 | 100.8 | 100.6 | 100.5 | 100.5 | 100.8 |
| Less: discounts and allowances | (234) | (191) | (134) | (112) | (87) | (128) | (0.8) | (0.8) | (0.6) | (0.5) | (0.5) | (0.8) |
| Total income | 27,681 | 25,361 | 21,041 | 21,773 | 18,467 | 15,882 | 100.0 | 100.0 | 100.0 | 100.0 | 100.0 | 100.0 |
| Cost of sales: | | | | | | | | | | | | |
| Composition costs | 482 | 411 | 347 | 259 | 358 | 307 | 1.7 | 1.6 | 1.6 | 1.2 | 1.9 | 1.9 |
| Printing & binding | 2,154 | 2,180 | 2,113 | 1,927 | 2,072 | 1,873 | 7.8 | 8.6 | 10.0 | 8.9 | 11.2 | 11.8 |
| Paper consumption | 1,410 | 1,368 | 1,074 | 1,038 | 963 | 834 | 5.1 | 5.4 | 5.1 | 4.8 | 5.2 | 5.3 |
| Distribution costs | 705 | 636 | 467 | 421 | 395 | 375 | 2.5 | 2.5 | 2.2 | 1.9 | 2.1 | 2.4 |
| Total cost of goods sold | 4,750 | 4,595 | 4,002 | 3,645 | 3,787 | 3,389 | 17.2 | 18.1 | 19.0 | 16.7 | 20.5 | 21.3 |
| Gross profit | 22,931 | 20,767 | 17,039 | 18,128 | 14,679 | 12,492 | 82.8 | 81.9 | 81.0 | 83.3 | 79.5 | 78.7 |
| Operating expenses: | | | | | | | | | | | | |
| Contractors' commissions | 8,406 | 8,341 | 5,912 | 6,681 | 5,763 | 4,437 | 30.4 | 32.9 | 28.1 | 30.7 | 31.2 | 27.9 |
| Revenue adjustments | 3,440 | 2,752 | 1,213 | 1,049 | — | — | 12.4 | 10.9 | 5.8 | 4.8 | — | — |
| Advertising & promotion | 1,607 | 1,786 | 1,788 | 1,602 | 1,575 | 1,798 | 5.8 | 7.0 | 8.5 | 7.4 | 8.5 | 11.3 |
| Marketing costs | 6,264 | 5,904 | 5,854 | 5,268 | 5,730 | 4,665 | 22.6 | 23.3 | 27.8 | 24.2 | 31.0 | 29.4 |
| Editorial & production | 1,795 | 1,894 | 2,011 | 2,013 | 1,281 | 1,014 | 6.4 | 7.4 | 9.5 | 9.2 | 6.9 | 6.3 |
| Circulation costs | 2,336 | 2,217 | 2,100 | 1,720 | 1,824 | 1,971 | 8.4 | 8.7 | 9.9 | 7.9 | 9.8 | 12.3 |
| Total operating expenses | 23,848 | 22,894 | 18,877 | 18,332 | 16,173 | 13,885 | 86.0 | 90.2 | 89.6 | 84.1 | 87.5 | 87.3 |
| Net publishing income | (917) | (2,128) | (1,838) | (204) | (1,494) | (1,393) | (3.2) | (8.3) | (8.6) | (0.8) | (8.0) | (8.6) |
| General & admin. expenses | 882 | 925 | 745 | 618 | 849 | 722 | 3.2 | 3.6 | 3.5 | 2.8 | 4.6 | 4.5 |
| Pretax income | (1,799) | (3,052) | (2,583) | (822) | (2,343) | (2,115) | (6.3) | (11.9) | (12.1) | (3.7) | (12.6) | (13.1) |
| Federal & state taxes (credit) | (707) | (1,214) | (1,030) | (273) | (808) | (719) | (2.6) | (4.8) | (4.9) | (1.3) | (4.4) | (4.5) |
| Net income | (1,092) | (1,838) | (1,552) | (549) | (1,535) | (1,396) | (3.8) | (7.1) | (7.2) | (2.4) | (8.2) | (8.6) |

Source: Company internally prepared financial statements as presented.
Note: Numbers may not total due to rounding.

Thick Metropolitan Directory Company, Inc., Ratio Analysis, as of September 30, 1998

| | Fiscal Years Ending September 30: | | | | | |
| | 1998 | 1997 | 1996 | 1995 | 1994 | 1993 |
|---|---|---|---|---|---|---|
| **LIQUIDITY** | | | | | | |
| Current ratio | 0.70 | 0.74 | 0.78 | 0.84 | 0.86 | 0.96 |
| Quick ratio | 0.46 | 0.48 | 0.50 | 0.61 | 0.56 | 0.65 |
| Working capital | (7,052) | (6,111) | (4,421) | (2,575) | (1,927) | (410) |
| **ACTIVITY** | | | | | | |
| Turnover: | | | | | | |
| Inventory | 10.3 | 11.3 | 20.8 | NM | NM | NM |
| Receivables | 2.7 | 2.5 | 2.2 | 2.6 | 2.7 | NM |
| Total assets | 1.6 | 1.5 | 1.4 | 1.7 | 1.7 | NM |
| Average collection period (days) | 134 | 144 | 165 | 140 | 133 | NM |
| Days to sell inventory | 35 | 32 | 17 | NM | NM | NM |
| Operating cycle (days) | 169 | 176 | 182 | NM | NM | NM |
| **PERFORMANCE** | | | | | | |
| Sales/net property, plant & equipment | 190.1 | 120.7 | 77.0 | 81.8 | 89.7 | 99.9 |
| Sales/stockholder equity | (4.1) | (4.5) | (5.5) | (9.6) | (10.8) | (87.8) |
| **PROFITABILITY (%)** | | | | | | |
| Operating margin before depreciation | 5.1 | 0.4 | 1.2 | 7.0 | 1.8 | 3.6 |
| Operating margin after depreciation | (3.3) | (8.4) | (8.7) | (0.9) | (8.1) | (8.8) |
| Pretax profit margin | (6.5) | (12.0) | (12.3) | (3.8) | (12.7) | (13.3) |
| Net profit margin | (3.9) | (7.2) | (7.4) | (2.5) | (8.3) | (8.8) |
| Return on: | | | | | | |
| Assets | (6.4) | (10.5) | (9.5) | (3.9) | (12.9) | (13.4) |
| Equity | 16.2 | 32.5 | 40.7 | 24.2 | 89.5 | 771.8 |
| Investment | 16.2 | 32.5 | 40.7 | 24.2 | 89.5 | 771.8 |
| Average assets | (6.3) | (10.9) | (10.2) | (4.2) | (13.8) | NM |
| Average equity | 17.6 | 38.8 | 51.0 | 27.6 | 161.9 | NM |
| Average investment | 17.6 | 38.8 | 51.0 | 27.6 | 161.9 | NM |
| **LEVERAGE** | | | | | | |
| Interest coverage before tax | NM | NM | NM | NM | NM | NM |
| Interest coverage after tax | NM | NM | NM | NM | NM | NM |
| Long-term debt/common equity (%) | NM | NM | NM | NM | NM | NM |
| Long-term debt/shareholders' equity (%) | NM | NM | NM | NM | NM | NM |
| Total debt/invested capital (%) | — | — | — | — | — | — |
| Total debt/total assets (%) | — | — | — | — | — | — |
| Total assets/common equity | (2.5) | (3.1) | (4.3) | (6.2) | (6.9) | (57.5) |

Source: Exhibits 26-16 and 26-17 and analyst's calculations.

## GMI Income Statements

Exhibit 26-19 presents the income statements for *GMI* for the fiscal periods ended September 30, 1993 through 1998. The *GMI* net revenue has remained fairly constant for the fiscal period 1993 through 1998. The annual compound growth in revenue from fiscal 1993 to 1998 was less than 1 percent, while revenue growth from fiscal 1997 to 1998 was flat. The guide has been in publication since fiscal 1979, and its revenue base has remained fairly constant in the last six years.

Correspondingly, cost of sales and operating expenses have also remained fairly consistent. Cost of sales has been approximately 12 percent of revenue for most of the last six years. Operating expenses have aver-

**E X H I B I T   26-19**

Greater Metropolis Industrial Buying Guide, Historical and Common-Size Income Statements, as of September 30, 1998

| | Fiscal Years Ending September 30: | | | | | | Fiscal Years Ending September 30: | | | | | |
|---|---|---|---|---|---|---|---|---|---|---|---|---|
| | 1998 | 1997 | 1996 | 1995 | 1994 | 1993 | 1998 | 1997 | 1996 | 1995 | 1994 | 1993 |
| | $000 | $000 | $000 | $000 | $000 | $000 | % | % | % | % | % | % |
| Revenues: | | | | | | | | | | | | |
| Gross advertising revenue | 3,002 | 2,995 | 3,141 | 3,435 | 3,377 | 2,947 | 100.9 | 100.6 | 100.3 | 100.3 | 100.3 | 100.7 |
| Gross subscription revenue | 5 | 5 | 6 | 6 | 4 | 4 | 0.2 | 0.2 | 0.2 | 0.2 | 0.1 | 0.1 |
| Total revenues | 3,007 | 3,000 | 3,247 | 3,441 | 3,381 | 2,951 | 101.1 | 100.8 | 100.5 | 100.5 | 100.5 | 100.8 |
| Less: discounts and allowances | (33) | (24) | (17) | (18) | (15) | (24) | (1.1) | (0.8) | (0.5) | (0.5) | (0.5) | (0.8) |
| Total income | 2,974 | 2,976 | 3,230 | 3,423 | 3,366 | 2,927 | 100.0 | 100.0 | 100.0 | 100.0 | 100.0 | 100.0 |
| Cost of sales: | | | | | | | | | | | | |
| Composition costs | 30 | 31 | 32 | 23 | 33 | 30 | 1.0 | 1.1 | 1.0 | 0.7 | 1.0 | 1.0 |
| Printing & binding | 180 | 171 | 232 | 211 | 245 | 207 | 6.1 | 5.8 | 7.2 | 6.2 | 7.3 | 7.1 |
| Paper consumption | 113 | 119 | 114 | 100 | 108 | 91 | 3.8 | 4.0 | 3.5 | 2.9 | 3.2 | 3.1 |
| Distribution costs | 40 | 39 | 36 | 36 | 31 | 32 | 1.3 | 1.3 | 1.1 | 1.0 | 0.9 | 1.1 |
| Total cost of goods sold | 363 | 360 | 414 | 370 | 417 | 360 | 12.2 | 12.1 | 12.8 | 10.8 | 12.4 | 12.3 |
| Gross profit | 2,611 | 2,616 | 2,816 | 3,053 | 2,948 | 2,567 | 87.8 | 87.9 | 87.2 | 89.2 | 87.6 | 87.7 |
| Operating expenses: | | | | | | | | | | | | |
| Contractors' commissions | 766 | 742 | 832 | 930 | 907 | 797 | 25.8 | 24.9 | 25.8 | 27.2 | 27.0 | 27.2 |
| Revenue adjustments | 374 | 345 | 62 | 188 | — | — | 12.6 | 11.6 | 1.9 | 5.5 | — | — |
| Advertising & promotion | 88 | 107 | 102 | 214 | 214 | 288 | 3.0 | 3.6 | 3.2 | 6.2 | 6.4 | 9.8 |
| Marketing costs | 219 | 202 | 203 | 517 | 507 | 551 | 7.4 | 6.8 | 6.3 | 15.1 | 15.1 | 18.8 |
| Editorial & production | 124 | 140 | 135 | 154 | 106 | 95 | 4.1 | 4.7 | 4.1 | 4.5 | 3.1 | 3.2 |
| Circulation costs | 131 | 121 | 113 | 110 | 106 | 161 | 4.4 | 4.0 | 3.5 | 3.2 | 3.1 | 5.4 |
| Total operating expenses | 1,702 | 1,657 | 1,447 | 2,113 | 1,840 | 1,892 | 57.1 | 55.6 | 44.7 | 61.7 | 54.6 | 64.6 |
| Net publishing income | 909 | 959 | 1,369 | 940 | 1,109 | 675 | 30.7 | 32.3 | 42.4 | 27.5 | 33.0 | 23.1 |
| General & admin. expenses | 93 | 121 | 117 | 102 | 146 | 141 | 3.1 | 4.0 | 3.6 | 3.0 | 4.3 | 4.8 |
| Pretax income | 816 | 838 | 1,253 | 839 | 963 | 534 | 27.6 | 28.3 | 38.8 | 24.6 | 28.7 | 18.3 |
| Federal & state taxes | 321 | 333 | 499 | 271 | 332 | 181 | 10.8 | 11.2 | 15.5 | 7.9 | 9.9 | 6.2 |
| Net income | 495 | 505 | 752 | 567 | 631 | 353 | 16.8 | 17.1 | 23.4 | 16.6 | 18.8 | 12.1 |

Source: Company internally prepared financial statements as presented.
Note: Numbers may not total due to rounding.

of revenue for most of the last six years. Operating expenses have averaged approximately 56 percent for the last six years.

*GMI* has been profitable for each of the last six years, with net income averaging approximately 17.5 percent of net revenue.

## Analysis of the Publishing Industry

Shipments of the U.S. book publishing industry (SIC 2731) totaled $17.1 billion in 1997, an increase in constant dollars of 2.9 percent from 1996. With the economy on an upswing, U.S. consumers responded positively to publishers' offerings.

Professional books—a category that includes technical, scientific, medical, law, business, and reference materials addressed primarily to individuals in the professions and trades—constitute the second largest book market, accounting for 18 percent of book sales in 1996. Sales in this category increased 1.8 percent over year earlier levels in 1996, for a compound average annual growth rate of 6.4 percent in the five years through 1996. Professional book sales increased in 1997 by 7.6 percent.

## Royalty Rate Analysis

Inasmuch as the primary objective of this economic analysis is to estimate a fair, arm's-length royalty rate that would be appropriate to the license of the *GMI* copyright, the first step in the analysis is the estimation of a fair level of economic income—or a fair economic return—attributable to the *GMI* copyright.

There are several individual procedures to estimate the fair economic income attributable to copyrights. The individual procedures may generally be grouped into several valuation and economic analysis methods, including the following:

> Income approach methods:
> > Profit split method
> > Excess earnings method
> Cost approach methods:
> > Replacement cost method
> > Reproduction cost method
> Market approach methods:
> > Comparative sale transaction method
> > Comparative license transaction method

As part of our consideration of the market transaction analyses, we researched different sources of information regarding the contemporaneous arm's-length licensing of copyrights. We also researched studies and other database compilations regarding empirical royalty rates associated with copyright license agreements.

In this section of the report, we discuss the income approach, cost approach, and market approach methods of royalty rate analyses.

### Income Approach Methods

There are two income approach methods that we relied upon in the analysis: 1) the profit split method and 2) the excess earnings method. These two analytical methods are described below.

*Profit Split Method.* The profit split method requires reference to the amount of operating profit that the subject copyright generates. The profit split method is based on the allocation (or split) of an operating profit margin that a hypothetical licensee would be willing to pay to a hypothetical licensor for the use of the subject copyright.

Through the payment of a license fee royalty rate (typically expressed as a percentage of revenues), the licensee of the intangible asset is willing to pay a split of its profits to the licensor of the intangible asset because the use of the copyright generates operating profits. The estimation of the appropriate profit split percentage includes an analysis of the following factors related to the subject copyrights: 1) the product, 2) the markets, 3) the financial profitability relative to other providers in the industry, and 4) the degree of consumer recognition.

The estimated operating profit split percentage is compared to the projected annual revenue in order to estimate the appropriate royalty rate for the subject copyright. The actual royalty payments based on the royalty rate would then be a necessary cost of goods sold to the licensee in order to maintain that level of operating profit.

In the profit split method, the first step is to estimate the average projected net sales. From the *GMI* historical financial statements, we estimate the average projected net sales to be $2.97 million per year.

The projected average pretax profit margin is 27 percent. Accordingly, we calculate the average projected pretax profit.

Next, we estimate the share or split of the adjusted pretax profit that the licensee would be willing to pay to the licensor for the use of the subject copyright. We analyzed arm's-length copyright license agreements with regard to profit split percentages. We concluded that the typical range of such a split is between 25 percent and 50 percent. In the subject analysis, we used a 25 percent, a 33 percent, and a 50 percent profit split between the licensor and the licensee in order to estimate a reasonable range of appropriate royalty rates.

The pretax income profit split attributable to the subject copyright is then compared to the average projected revenue, and the resulting ratio is expressed as a royalty rate percent.

Exhibit 26-20 summarizes the calculation of the estimated range of *GMI* copyright royalty rates, using the profit split method.

Based on our analysis, the appropriate range of fair, arm's-length royalty rates for the *GMI* copyright, as of September 30, 1993, using the profit split method, is 6.8 percent to 13.5 percent of net revenue.

*Excess Earnings Method.* The excess earnings method is based on the amount of excess economic income that will be generated by the subject business enterprise as the result of its use of the subject copyright.

Using this method, we first estimated a fair rate of return for: 1) all identified net tangible and intangible assets (i.e., net property, plant and equipment, and other intangible assets used or used up in the production of the subject business enterprise income); and 2) all the net working capital assets (i.e., cash plus receivables plus inventory less payables less accrued liabilities) used in the subject business.

We applied this fair rate of return against the total value of the associated net tangible assets and net working capital assets in order to conclude a fair return on the business stakeholders' investment—that is, the level of economic income required to satisfy the stakeholders.

Thick Metropolitan Directory Company, Inc., Greater Metropolis Industrial Buying Guide, Royalty Rate Analysis, Profit Split Method, as of September 30, 1998 ($ in 000s)

| | | Low Split | Median Split | High Split |
|---|---|---|---|---|
| Projected 1999 net sales | | $2,970 | $2,970 | $2,970 |
| Projected pretax income (profit margin of 27%) | | 802 | 802 | 802 |
| Profit split percentage | | 25.0% | 33.0% | 50.0% |
| Profit attributable to the subject copyright | | 200 | 265 | 401 |
| **Indicated royalty rate for the subject copyright** | | **6.8%** | **8.9%** | **13.5%** |
| Projected pretax profit attributable to copyright | | $ 200 | $ 265 | $ 401 |
| Less: income taxes (at 40%) | | 80 | 106 | 160 |
| Projected after-tax profit attributable to copyright | | 120 | 159 | 241 |
| Capitalized at: | | | | |
|   Present value discount rate | 17.0% | | | |
|   Less: expected long-term growth | 4.0% | | | |
|   Direct capitalization rate | | 13.0% | 13.0% | 13.0% |
| Capitalized profit split attributable to subject copyright | | 925 | 1,221 | 1,851 |
| Indicated fair market value of subject copyright (rounded) | | $ 900 | $1,200 | $1,800 |

Sources: For the estimation of the profit split percentages, G. V. Smith and R. L. Parr, *Valuation of Intellectual Property and Intangible Assets*, 2d ed. (New York: John Wiley & Sons, 1996); G. DeSouza, "Royalty Methods for Intellectual Property," *Business Economics*, April 1997; R. Caves, et al., "The Imperfect Market for Technology Licenses," *Oxford Bulletin of Economics and Statistics*, 1983.

Note: Numbers may not total due to rounding.

Next, we quantified the economic income projected to be earned by the company that is using the subject copyright. The economic income can be defined many different ways. For purposes of the analysis, we defined economic income as pretax income. Next, we compared the projected level of economic income to the required level of economic income.

If the projected level of economic income is greater than the required level of economic income, then excess economic income exists. Part of the excess economic income is attributable to the economic value of the subject copyright.

Finally, we compared the amount of excess economic income attributable to the subject copyright to the projected net sales in order to estimate a fair, arm's-length royalty rate for the subject copyright.

*Required Rate of Return.* The required rates of return on the various tangible and intangible assets of a business vary with the level of business risk—specifically with market risk, financial risk, managerial risk, and other uncertainties.

Generally, the rates of return on net working capital assets are lower than the rates of return on most of the other assets of the business. These rates of return are sometimes related to the effective cost of borrowing funds by the company. On the other end of the spectrum, intangible assets (due to their comparatively risky nature) are typically associated with a higher rate of return than net working capital assets and tangible assets. These rates of return on intangible assets are sometimes related to the cost of equity capital for the subject business enterprise.

Thick Metropolitan Directory Company, Inc., Greater Metropolis Industrial Buying Guide, Royalty Rate Analysis, Estimation of Present Value Discount Rate, as of September 30, 1998

| COST OF DEBT CAPITAL | |
|---|---|
| **Corporate Bond Yields [a]:** | |
| Bond Rating Group | 29-Sep-98 |
| A | 7.15% |
| Baa | 7.43% |
| Estimated subject company cost of debt capital | 7.50% |
| **Effective Income Tax Rate:** | |
| State income tax rate | 7.00% |
| Federal income tax rate | 34.00% |
| Effective income tax rate | 38.62% |
| Estimated subject company effective income tax rate (rounded) | 40.00% |
| AFTER-TAX COST OF DEBT CAPITAL | 4.50% |

| COST OF EQUITY CAPITAL | | |
|---|---|---|
| **Historical Equity Returns (1926-1997) [b]:** | | |
| | Total Long-Term Return | Equity Risk Premium |
| Long-term government bonds | 5.20% | -- |
| All common stocks | 12.40% | 7.20% |
| Small common stocks | 17.60% | 5.20% |
| **Equity Risk Premiums:** | | |
| Risk-free rate of return [a] | | 6.03% |
| Common stock risk premium | 7.20% | |
| Small stock risk premium | 5.20% | |
| Total system equity risk premium | | 12.40% |
| Company-specific risk premium [c] | | 5.00% |

| WEIGHTED AVERAGE COST OF CAPITAL | | | |
|---|---|---|---|
| | | | Industry |
| | Percent | Percent of | Average |
| Debt Ratio | of LTD | Net Worth | Debt Ratio |
| Industry group: | | | |
| RMA SIC # 2741 | 21.40 | 37.10 | 36.58% |
| | | | |
| Debt ratio selected for analysis (rounded) | | | 35.00% |

**Estimation of Beta:**

| Guideline Publicly Traded Companies | Beta |
|---|---|
| Range of industry data from CD-ROM [d] | 0.30-1.89 |
| Median industry beta | 0.98 |
| Mean industry beta | 1.01 |
| Estimate of subject company beta | 1.00 |

After-Tax Cost of Equity Capital Formula (CAPM Model)

$I_e = (R_f + Beta (R_m - R_f) + R_s + a) =$  18.23%

| where: | $I_e$ | = Pretax cost of equity capital | |
|---|---|---|---|
| | $R_f$ | = Risk-free rate | 6.03% |
| | $R_m$ | = Market equity risk premium | 7.20% |
| | $R_s$ | = Small stock risk premium | 5.20% |
| | Beta | = Market volatility factor | 1.00 |
| | a | = Alpha factor | 5.00% |

Weighted Average Cost of Capital (WACC)

$WACC = (DR*D) + ((1 - DR)*I_e)$  13.42%

| where: | $I_e$ | = Cost of equity capital | 18.23% |
|---|---|---|---|
| | DR | = Debt ratio | 35.00% |
| | D | = After-tax cost of debt capital | 4.50% |

| AFTER-TAX COST OF EQUITY CAPITAL | 18.23% |
|---|---|

| Present Value Discount Rate (Rounded) | 17.00% |
|---|---|

a. U.S. government long-term bonds, from *Federal Reserve Bulletin*, December 1998, Table I.35.
b. *Stocks, Bonds, Bills and Inflation, 1997 Yearbook* (Chicago: Ibbotson Associates, 1997).
c. Based upon our analysis of the company-specific nonsystematic risk factors.
d. CD-Rom Compustat, data for selected guideline publicly traded companies.

In the instant case, the required rate of return is based on our analysis of the capital structure of a typical willing buyer within the publishing industry.

The capital structure components are presented on the right-hand (or equity) side of the balance sheet, including: 1) various types of long-term debt, 2) preferred stock, and 3) common equity. Any net increase in assets must be financed by an increase in current liabilities, or by one or more of the capital structure components. Capital is a factor of production. And like any other factor of production, it has a cost. The cost of each capital structure component is defined as the component cost of that particular type of capital. For example, if the company can borrow money at 8 percent, then the pretax component cost of debt is 8 percent.

For consistency purposes, we have identified the component capital structure costs by the following symbols throughout this discussion:

$k^d$ = after-tax component cost of debt capital

$k^e$ = component cost of equity capital

$WACC$ = weighted average cost of capital

The after-tax component cost of debt capital is the company's current cost of debt (1 – the marginal income tax rate). The yield on 10-year, medium quality corporate bonds is approximately 7.43 percent as of September 30, 1998. Based on a 40 percent effective income tax rate, the after-tax cost of debt ($k^d$) for TMD is 4.50 percent.

For a company with one class of common stock outstanding (such as TMD), the cost of equity capital, $k^e$, is the expected (or required) rate of return on the company's common stock. The company is expected to earn the rate of $k^e$ on the equity portion of its investments in order to keep the price of its stock from falling. There are several generally accepted procedures for estimating the cost of equity capital. We used the capital asset pricing model (CAPM) in our analysis.

We used CAPM to estimate the cost of equity capital of TMD as of September 30, 1998. In our application of the capital asset pricing model to estimate $k^e$, we performed the following procedures:

Step 1.   Estimate the risk-free rate of return, $R^f$—that is the long-term U.S. Treasury bond rate as of the analysis date.

Step 2.   Estimate the beta coefficient ($B$) of the subject company common stock and use this as an index of the subject stock systematic risk.

Step 3.   Estimate the market equity risk premium. This is indicated as ($R^m - R^f$) in the CAPM equation.

Step 4.   Estimate a small company stock equity risk premium and estimate a company-specific nonsystematic equity risk premium, often called *alpha* or *A*.

Step 5.   Calculate the required cost of equity capital as follows:

$$K_e = R_f + B ( R_m - R_f) + A$$

In the capital asset pricing model, systematic (or market-related) risk is the only type of risk that is considered relevant in the pricing of securities and the estimation of expected returns. Systematic risk is measured by the beta *(B)* coefficient. Beta provides a measure of the tendency of a security's return to move with the overall market's return (e.g., the return on the S&P 500). For example, a stock with beta of 1.0 tends to rise and fall by the same percentage as the market (i.e., S&P 500 index). Thus, "$B = 1.0$" indicates an average level of systematic risk.

Stocks with betas greater than 1.0 tend, on average, to rise and fall by a greater percentage than the market. Likewise, stocks with betas less than 1.0 have a low level of systematic risk and, therefore, are less sensitive to changes in the market.

In the case of TMD, the current yield to maturity on the 20-year U.S. Treasury bond was 6.03 percent as of September 30, 1998. This is according to the Federal Reserve Statistics as of December 1998. Thus, 6.03 percent is the appropriate risk-free rate of return ($R_f$).

We reviewed the beta coefficients of guideline publicly traded companies; these guideline companies were all corporations engaged in the same industry as TMD. Based upon our analysis of the industry average beta coefficient, we applied an average beta coefficient of 1.0 in our estimation of the cost of equity capital for TMD.

To estimate the capital market equity risk premium ($R_m - R_f$), we used the average historical spread between small stocks and long-term government bonds. We obtained these data from the Ibbotson Associates book, *Stocks, Bonds, Bills and Inflation, 1997 Yearbook.*[2] The capital market equity risk premium was 12.4 percent. We also applied a company-specific equity risk premium, called *alpha* or *A*. We estimated the company-specific equity risk premium to be 5.0 percent.

The calculation of the TMD present value discount rate is presented in Exhibit 26-21.

*Excess Economic Income.* As discussed above, we first calculated a fair return on the net tangible assets and on the net working capital assets associated with TMD. The present value discount rate is our basis for estimating a fair rate of return on the various asset categories.

For our analysis, we projected the appropriate yield rate for the GMI intangible assets to be equal to the present value discount rate of 17 percent.

Since net property and equipment is generally less risky than intangible assets, we concluded that a rate of return of 10 percent is a fair rate of return on net tangible assets.

For the *GMI* net working capital assets, we used a debt-related interest rate of 7.5 percent as a fair rate of return. We extracted this fair rate of return from an analysis of guideline publicly traded companies that we concluded to be of comparable risk to TMD.

As we estimated the present value discount rate on an after-tax basis, we adjusted the rate in order to estimate the appropriate before-tax rate of return for the net tangible assets and the intangible assets of *GMI*.

Exhibit 26-22 presents the analysis and calculation of the excess economic income associated with the *GMI* intangible assets. We concluded that there are other intangible assets separate from the subject copyright, associated with TMD and the *GMI* business operations. Accordingly, we concluded three possible excess economic income allocation percentages—that is, 25 percent, 33 percent, and 50 percent—in order to estimate the amount of excess economic income attributable to the subject *GMI* copyright.

The excess economic income that is attributable to the *GMI* copyright is then compared to the projected net sales in order to estimate the appropriate royalty rate related to a license for the subject copyright.

Based on our analysis, the range of fair, arm's-length royalty rates for the subject *GMI* copyright, as of September 30, 1998, using the excess earnings method is 6.6 percent to 13.1 percent of net revenues.

---

2. *Stocks, Bonds, Bills and Inflation, 1997 Yearbook* (Chicago: Ibbotson Associates, 1998).

EXHIBIT 26-22

Thick Metropolitan Directory Company, Inc., Greater Metropolis Industrial Buying Guide, Royalty Rate Analysis, Excess Earnings Method—Net Asset Basis, as of September 30, 1998 ($ in 000s)

| Projected 1999 net sales | | $2,970 | |
| Projected 1999 pretax income (profit margin of 27%) | | 802 | |

| The *GMI* net asset structure: | Indicated Fair Market Value | Required Pretax Rate of Return | Required Return on Investment in GMI Net Assets |
|---|---|---|---|
| Less: return on fixed and other assets [a] | 30 | 10.0% | 3 |
| Less: return on net working capital [b] | 300 | 7.5% | 23 |
| Total economic return to the *GMI* net asset structure | 330 | | 26 |

| | | Excess Economic Income Allocation | | |
|---|---|---|---|---|
| Excess economic income after return to the *GMI* net capital structure | | 777 | 777 | 777 |
| Percentage of excess economic income attributable to the subject copyright [c] | | 25.0% | 33.0% | 50.0% |
| Excess economic income attributable to the subject copyright | | $ 194 | $ 256 | $ 388 |
| **Indicated royalty rate for the license of the subject copyright** | | **6.6%** | **8.6%** | **13.1%** |
| Projected pretax excess economic income attributable to the subject copyright | | $ 194 | $ 256 | $ 388 |
| Less: income taxes (estimated at 40%) | | 78 | 102 | 155 |
| Projected after-tax excess economic income attributable to the subject copyright | | 116 | 154 | 233 |
| Capitalized at: | | | | |
| Present value discount rate | 17.0% | | | |
| Less: expected long-term growth rate | 4.0% | | | |
| Direct capitalization rate [d] | 13.0% | 13.0% | 13.0% | 13.0% |
| Capitalized excess economic income | | 896 | 1,183 | 1,792 |
| Indicated fair market value of the subject copyright | | $ 900 | $1,200 | $1,800 |

a. Applicable return to the fair market value of the net fixed assets and the other asset categories that are used or used up in the production of income associated with the subject copyright.

b. Industry average rate of return derived from ratio from *RMA Annual Statement Studies* for SIC Code 2741 industry group data for 1997.

c. The percentage of excess economic income attributable to the subject copyright; the remaining excess economic income is attributed to other intangible assets associated with the *GMI* business operations.

d. Based upon our financial analysis of the *GMI* business operations, we have concluded that the amount of depreciation expense included in the projected pretax income is adequate to provide for prospective capital expenditures; we have also concluded that prospective net working capital increments will be negligible; accordingly, the projected level of economic income will be adequate to support the 4 percent expected long-term growth rate encompassed in the estimation of the direct capitalization rate.

Note: Numbers may not total due to rounding.

## Cost Approach—Recreation Cost Method

We performed a recreation cost valuation method as part of our damages analysis.

The recreation cost method is an analytical procedure that uses the concept of replacement cost as an indicator of value. The premise of the recreation cost method is that a prudent investor would typically pay no more for an intangible asset than the amount for which he or she could replace the intangible asset with a new one.

In the analysis, we delineated the tasks that would be required in order to recreate (or replace) the subject *GMI* guide. The tasks fall under six major categories. The six categories are:

1. Selecting the appropriate geographic region.
2. Building a headings file.
3. Building an editorial file.
4. Building an advertiser base.
5. Building a controlled circulation list.
6. Incurring entrepreneurial incentive.

The detailed list of all the individual tasks required under each major category of recreation tasks is presented in Exhibit 26-23.

Based upon comprehensive interviews with TMD management, we delineated the individual tasks involved in replacing the *GMI* guide and estimated the current costs to recreate each individual task. The costs include both direct costs (i.e., salaries and benefits) and indirect costs (i.e., departmental overhead). The total of the costs is one indication of the value of the subject *GMI* copyrighted materials.

When estimating the costs to recreate the *GMI*, Thick management was not always able to provide historical costs. Accordingly, Thick management used current dollar costs to estimate the recreation costs of certain copyright development costs in some instances.

The economic value that is attributable to the *GMI* copyright using this cost approach method is then converted to an appropriate copyright license royalty income stream. The royalty income stream is then compared to the projected annual revenues for the year 1999 in order to estimate the appropriate arm's-length royalty rate for the license of the subject copyright.

Based on our analysis, an indication of a fair, arm's-length royalty rate for the licensing of the subject *GMI* copyright as of September 30, 1998 using the recreation cost method is 12.0 percent to 13.7 percent of net revenue.

### Market Approach—Guideline License Royalty Rate Analysis

We performed an analysis of actual arm's-length market transactions (e.g., license agreements, annual minimum royalty payment agreements, etc.) related to the license of copyrights that are reasonable guidelines with respect to the subject copyright.

This analysis is appropriate when there are adequate transactional data in order 1) to extract units of comparison and 2) to support adjustments for any elements of dissimilarity between the subject copyright and the guideline copyrights. However, the reliability of this analysis is somewhat reduced when the guideline copyrights are not adequately comparative (i.e., when there are substantial differences in either 1) the contractual terms of the licenses or 2) the economic conditions during which they were negotiated).

Market transactional evidence may be used in order to estimate an appropriate range of royalty rates by reference to transfers and licenses of comparative copyrights under comparative contractual terms and economic conditions.

Copyrights can be bought, sold, or licensed under various contractual terms and economic conditions. When licensed, the principal economic parameters in the license agreement contracts are royalty rate, term, mini-

EXHIBIT 26-23

Thick Metropolitan Directory Company, Inc., Greater Metropolis Industrial Buying Guide, Royalty Rate Analysis, Recreation Cost Method, as of September 30, 1998

| Individual Tasks Involved in Recreating the Greater Metropolis Industrial Guide | | | Total Recreation Cost |
|---|---|---|---|
| **I. Selecting the appropriate geographic region** | | | |
| A. Research trading areas | | | |
| B. Determination of final geographic boundaries | | | |
| **Cost of selecting the appropriate geographic region** | | | $ 80,200 |
| **II. Building the headings list** | | | |
| A. Define the guide's focus | | | |
| B. Research & review heading universe | | | |
| C. Determination of headings file | | | |
| **Cost of building the headings list** | | | 245,500 |
| **III. Building the editorial file** | | | |
| A. Estimation of the size of the final editorial file | | | |
| B. Research & review universe of companies for selection | | | |
| C. Verification of company information | | | |
| D. Editorial review of company information | | | |
| E. Finalize file for publication | *Number of Listings* | *Recreation Cost per Listing* | |
| **Cost of building the editorial file** | 19,800 × | $11.50 = | 227,700 |
| **IV. Building an advertiser base** | | | |
| A. Hire sales management and retain sales contractors | | | |
| B. Develop sales and marketing materials and rate structure | | | |
| C. Manage sales campaign | | | |
| **Cost of building an advertiser base** | | | 1,225,600 |
| **V. Building a controlled circulation list** | | | |
| A. Estimation of the size of the final circulation file | | | |
| B. Research and review universe of potential subscribers | | | |
| C. Contact potential subscribers and receive & review direct requests from qualified subscribers | | | |
| D. Determination of final controlled circulation list | *Number of Listings* | *Recreation Cost per Listing* | |
| **Cost of building a controlled circulation list** | 35,935 × | $3.14 = | 112,800 |
| **VI. Entrepreneurial incentive** | | | |
| Losses incurred during the start-up phase of the publication | | | 0 |
| (Start-up phase = approximately 3-years to the publication break-even point) | | | |
| Total cost to recreate the *Greater Metropolis Industrial Guide* | | | 1,891,800 |
| **Estimated value of the *Greater Metropolis Industrial Guide* (rounded)** | | | **$1,900,000** |

| | Analysis Based on 15-Year License Term | Analysis Based on 10-Year License Term |
|---|---|---|
| Total cost to recreate the *Greater Metropolis Industrial Guide* (rounded) | $1,900,000 | $1,900,000 |
| Fair rate of return on recreation cost method estimated value [a] | 17% | 17% |
| Estimated license period in which to recover the cost of the subject copyright (in years) [b] | 15 | 10 |
| Annual royalty payment required to (1) recover cost of the subject copyright and (2) provide a fair rate of return on the value of the subject copyright (rounded) | 357,000 | 408,000 |
| Divided by: projected 1999 net sales | 2,970,000 | 2,970,000 |
| **Equals: indicated royalty rate attributable to the subject copyright** | **12.0%** | **13.7%** |

a. For the fair rate of return on the value of the subject copyright, we used the present value discount rate (WACC) that is estimated to be 17% per Exhibit 26-21.

b. Represents the typical range of terms for copyright license agreements, based on our analysis of comparative arm's-length license agreements.

mum payments, industry or use restrictions, product restrictions, and geographical restrictions, in addition to the intrinsic uniqueness of the copyrighted material being licensed.

We researched empirical copyright licensing activity through a comprehensive literature search (including research of published periodicals and other journals and of several electronic databases). The confidential nature of most license agreements did not permit us to obtain detailed data regarding all economic parameters of all of the license contracts. However, the actual transactional data that we did extract provided us with empirical evidence from which to conclude a reasonable range of market-derived copyright license agreement royalty rates.

Exhibit 26-22 summarizes our findings with regard to the publishing industry royalty rate analysis and to the subject copyright license royalty rate analysis. As already indicated, the economic parameter details of some of these guideline copyright license agreements are not always available.

However, within the limited information available, we can generalize that the relevant market-derived range of copyright license royalty rates is from between 7 percent to 14 percent of net revenues.

Exhibit 26-24 presents the tabulation of empirical arm's-length copyright license agreement information.

Based on our analysis, a conservative indication of the range of fair, arm's-length royalty rates for the *GMI* copyright, as of September 30, 1998, based on this market-derived empirical evidence, is 7 percent to 14 percent of net revenue.

**EXHIBIT 26-24**

Thick Metropolitan Directory Company, Inc., Greater Metropolis Industrial Buying Guide, Royalty Rate Analysis, Arm's-Length Copyright License Royalty Rate Evidence, as of September 30, 1998 ($ in 000s)

| Product Category Subject to Copyright License | Range | Arm's Length Royalty Rates Average for 1997 | Average for 1998 |
|---|---|---|---|
| Accessories | 7–14% | 10.5% | 10.7% |
| Apparel | 7–12% | 10.5% | 10.8% |
| Domestics | 7–10% | 8.0% | 8.2% |
| Electronic (nongame) | 7–10% | 9.5% | 9.7% |
| Food & beverage | 4–6% | 5.0% | 5.1% |
| Footwear | 6–11% | 8.0% | 8.1% |
| Furniture | 6–10% | 8.0% | 8.2% |
| Gifts & novelties | 6–12% | 8.5% | 8.6% |
| Health/beauty | 6–10% | 7.0% | 7.1% |
| Housewares | 6–10% | 8.0% | 8.2% |
| Infant products | 6–10% | 8.0% | 8.7% |
| Music/video | 8–20% | 10.5% | 10.7% |
| **Publishing** | **8–12%** | **10.5%** | **10.7%** |
| Sporting goods | 6–10% | 8.0% | 8.2% |
| Stationery | 8–12% | 8.5% | 8.7% |
| Toys & games | 8–12% | 10.0% | 10.2% |

## Economic Analysis Synthesis and Conclusion

We have performed an economic analysis regarding the *GMI* copyright owned by TMD, as of September 30, 1998.

The indicated range of arm's-length royalty rates for the subject *GMI* copyright using the profit split method is 6.8 percent to 13.5 percent of net revenue.

The indicated range of arm's-length royalty rates for the subject *GMI* copyright using the excess earnings method is 6.6 percent to 13.1 percent of net revenue.

The indicated range of arm's-length royalty rates for the subject *GMI* copyright using the recreation cost method is 12.0 percent to 13.7 percent of net revenues.

The indicated range of arm's-length royalty rates for the subject *GMI* copyright using the empirical, market-derived transactional evidence is 7 percent to 14 percent of net revenues.

Based on the results of the summarized economic analyses, and in our opinion, a fair, arm's-length royalty rate for the license of the copyrighted materials known as *GMI*, as of September 30, 1998, is 10 percent of net revenue.

# Index

Albrecht, Allan J., 374
Alico, John, 15n
American Institute of Certified Public
Accountants (AICPA), 251
American Society of Appraisers (ASA), 40, 53,
67, 251, 267, 302
Business Valuation Committee, 41
Business Valuation Standards, 41
Amortization deductions, 44
*Applied Software Measurement*, 369
Appraisal Foundation, The, 40, 53-54, 251, 260,
302 (*see also Uniform Standards of
Professional Appraisal Practice* (USPAP))
*The Appraisal of Real Estate*, xxv, 15, 16, 17, 18n,
121
Appraisal
objective of, 57-58
purpose of, 58, 68
reasons for, 29-38
ad valorem property tax, 34
allocation of purchase price, 32
bankruptcy and reorganization, 33
business dissolution, 35
business formation, 35
corporate planning, 35
establishing royalty rates for licensing, 33-34
financing, 33
income tax, 34
litigation support, 34-35
preacquisition assessment, 32
purchase of intangibles, 33
transfer pricing, 34
reports, 93-94, 116, 259-267
*See also* valuation
*Appraising Machinery and Equipment*, 15, 16
Averill, Lawrence H. Jr., 299

Bean, Carol Anne, 22n
Black, Henry Campbell, 19n, 312n
*Black's Law Dictionary*, 18, 19, 312
Bodie, Zvi, 189
Boehm, Barry W., 369, 486
Bonbright, James C., xxv, 28
Brealey, Richard A., 188

Bryer, Lanning, 22n
*Burlington Northern R.R. Co. v. Bair*, 400n
*Business Periodicals Index*, 81
*Business Valuation Review*, 87
*Business Wire*, 81
BYL (Before You Leap), 370

CA-Estimacs. *See* data processing intangibles,
cost approach to value, software cost
engineering models
Capitalization rate. *See* income approach, direct
capitalization rate
Capitalized advertising cost savings method.
*See* income approach
Capitalized excess economic income method.
*See* income approach
Capitalized royalty income. *See* market approach
Cash equivalency value, 109, 148, 155-156
Charitable contribution, 484-490
Checkpoint. *See* data processing intangibles,
cost approach to value, software cost
engineering models
*Ciba-Geigy Corp. v. Commissioner*, 280, 282n
*COCOMO II Model Definition Manual. See* data
processing intangibles, cost approach to
value, software cost engineering models
Comparative business valuation method. *See*
income approach
Comparative income differential method. *See*
market approach
Comparative transaction method. *See* market
approach, guideline publicly traded
company method
Computer Associates International, Inc., 370
*Computing & Software, Inc. v. Commissioner*, 365
*Comshare, Inc. v. United States*, 365
Constructive Cost Model (COCOMO). *See* data
processing intangibles, cost approach to
value, software cost engineering models
Contingent and limiting conditions, 92-93
Contract intangibles, 283, 285-286, 311-319
cost approach to value, 313-314
data sources, 315-316
description of, 312-313

Iowa curves. *See* remaining useful life analysis, survivor curve analysis
Iowa State University, 352, 356
*Ithaca Industries, Inc. v. C.I.R.,* 400

Jassin, Lloyd J., 321n, 323n, 326n
Jones, Capers, 369

Kane, Alex, 189
*Kansas City Southern Industries v. Commissioner,* 365
Keynes, John Meynard, xxv

Lanham Act, 22-23, 425
*Legal Resource Index,* 81
Legal rights, bundle of, 66-67
    development rights, 67
    exploitation rights, 67
    fee simple interest, 66
    licensee (or franchisee) interest, 66
    licenser (or franchiser) interest, 66
    life estate, 66
    life interest, 66
    reversionary interest, 67
    sub-licensee (or sub-franchisee) interest, 66
    term estate, 66
    term interest, 66
    use rights, 67
*Licensing Economics Review,* 81, 157, 429, 441
*Licensing Journal,* 81
*Licensing Law and Business Report,* 81
*Licensing Letter, The,* 441
Life, types of, 207
    economic life, 207
    physical life, 207
    service life, 207
Lifing. *See* remaining useful life analysis
Location intangibles, 410-423
    cost approach to value, 413-414, 421
    data sources, 418-419
    description of, 411-413
    easements, 416-417
    income approach to value, 415-417, 421, 422
    market approach to value, 414-415, 421, 422
    mining rights, 417
    valuation example, 419-423
    zoning variance, 416
*Los Angeles Times,* 81

Malthus, Thomas, xxv
*Managing Intellectual Property,* 81
Marcus, Alan J., 189
Market approach, 101-113, 146-158, 254-255
    capitalized royalty income method, 428, 431-432
    comparative income differential method, 153, 255
    comparative transaction method. *See* guideline publicly traded company method
    comparative transactions
        selection of, 104-107, 147-148
        verification of, 107-110
    comparable vs. guideline transactions, 105-107

guideline publicly traded company method, 293-300, 371, 378, 436-438
industry valuation formulas. *See* rules of thumb
market replacement cost method, 154, 371-372
market transaction method. *See* guideline publicly traded company method
pricing multiples, 111-112, 149-152
relief from royalty method, 152-153, 255
    with technology, 441-442, 495
    with trademarks, 479-480
    remaining life and, 210-212
    residual from purchase price, 387
    royalty rate analysis, 511
rules of thumb, 154
sales transaction method, 152, 255
units of comparison, 110
Market replacement cost method. *See* market approach
Marketability, lack of, 155, 295, 299
    public offering studies, 301
        Baird & Company studies, 301
        Willamette Management Associates studies, 301
    restricted stock studies, 300-301
Marketing intangibles, 424-433
    cost approach to value, 427
    data sources, 429-430
    description of, 425-426
    income approach to value, 427-428
    market approach to value, 428
    trade names, 23, 195, 197-200, 425, 476-484
    trademarks, 22-23, 195, 197-200, 425-432, 476-484
    valuation example, 430-432
Marshall, Alfred, xxv
*Marshall Valuation Service,* 279
Marston, Anson, 218, 224
Masks and masters, 24-25, 366
*Matter of Douglas R. Prince and Jane Prince, In the,* 385
*Measures for Excellence: Reliable Software on Time, within Budget,* 367
Midyear discounting convention, 187-188
Mill, John Stuart, xxv
Myers, Stewart C., 188
Myers, Ware, 369

National Association of Certified Valuation Analysts (NACVA), 251
Net cash flow, definition of, 290
*The New Role of Intellectual Property in Commercial Transactions,* 22-25
Noncompete agreements, 288, 290-92, 400, 402-403, 406-409 (see also human capital intangibles)
*Norwest Corporation and Subsidiaries v. Commissioner,* 365

Obsolescence, 131-134
    expectancy life factor, 210
    percent good factor, 210
    types of,
        economic obsolescence, 100, 128, 133-134
        external obsolescence, 100, 128